Heat packs, neck
Standard terry cover
Neck terry cover
Fluorimethane
Cold spray
Ice bags
Ice bags, Cramer
Kwik-heat pack
Cramer Atomic Rub Down
Flexi-wrap (small, large)
Flexi-wrap handles
Lotion, 1 gal

First Aid
Cotton rolls (nose plugs)
Tongue depressors
Pocket masks
Cotton tip applicators
Cotton tip applicators (sterile)
Sani Cloths
Latex gloves (med., large)
Cotton balls
Skin-preps
Save-A-Tooth
Penlights
Biohazard bags
Safety goggles

Taping Accessories
Heel and lace pads
Tape Adherent Spray
Tape remover

Sharps
Stainless steel prep blades
Scalpel blades, #10, #11 (sterile)
Scissors bandage
Scissors, small

Tweezers
Tweezers (sterile)
Suture sets
Nail clippers (large, small)
Tape cutters
Stethoscopes
Shark refill blades

Inhalants
Afrin

Antiseptics
Triadine
Peroxide
Rubbing alcohol
Betasept, small bottles
Betasept, 1 gal jug
Antimicrobial skin cleaner
Super Quin 9
Zorbicide Spray

Skin Treatments
Polysporin
Bacitracin
1% Tolnaftate Powder
Lamisil
1% Hydrocortisone
Second skin
Collodion
2% Miconazole
10% Hydrocortisone
Baby powder
Tincture of benzoin

Eye Treatment
Dacriose Irrigation
Saline
Eye wash

ReNu contact cleaning agent
Penlights

Teeth Treatment
Blue mouth guards, 25/box
Clear mouth guards, 25/box

Oral Medications
Acetaminophen bottle
Acetaminophen, 2 pk
Cepastat
Chlorpheniramine, 4 mg
Diphenhydramine, 25 mg
Ibuprofen bottle
Ibuprofen, 2 pk
Imodium AD
Pepto-Bismol tabs
Q-fed pkg
Sudodrin, 2 pk
Titralac
Robitussin DM

Crutches
Large
Medium
Small
Large aluminum

Water
Bottle carriers
Water bottles
Coolers (3, 7, 10 gal)
Chest

Other
Stools
Spray bottles
Bucket
Cloth towels

IMPORTANT

HERE IS YOUR REGISTRATION CODE TO ACCESS MCGRAW-HILL PREMIUM CONTENT AND MCGRAW-HILL ONLINE RESOURCES

For key premium online resources you need THIS CODE to gain access. Once the code is entered, you will be able to use the web resources for the length of your course.

Access is provided only if you have purchased a new book.

If the registration code is missing from this book, the registration screen on our website, and within your WebCT or Blackboard course will tell you how to obtain your new code. Your registration code can be used only once to establish access. It is not transferable.

To gain access to these online resources

1. **USE** your web browser to go to: **www.mhhe.com/esims**

2. **CLICK** on "First Time User"

3. **ENTER** the Registration Code printed on the tear-off bookmark on the right

4. After you have entered your registration code, click on "Register"

5. **FOLLOW** the instructions to setup your personal UserID and Password

6. **WRITE** your UserID and Password down for future reference. Keep it in a safe place.

If your course is using WebCT or Blackboard, you'll be able to use this code to access the McGraw-Hill content within your instructor's online course.

To gain access to the McGraw-Hill content in your instructor's WebCT or Blackboard course simply log into the course with the user ID and Password provided by your instructor. Enter the registration code exactly as it appears to the right when prompted by the system. You will only need to use this code the first time you click on McGraw-Hill content.

These instructions are specifically for student access. Instructors are not required to register via the above instructions.

The McGraw-Hill Companies

Mc Graw Hill Higher Education

Thank you, and welcome to your McGraw-Hill Online Resources.

ISBN 13: 978-0-07-304257-2
ISBN 10: 0-07-304257-9

AKKK-JWG4-FXFW-KC7V-BMGW

REGISTRATION CODE
REGISTRATION CODE

The McGraw-Hill Companies

Mc Graw Hill Higher Education

Athletic Training:
An Introduction to Professional Practice

William E. Prentice, Ph.D., A.T.C., P.T.
Professor, Coordinator of Sports Medicine Program
Department of Exercise and Sport Science
The University of North Carolina
Chapel Hill, North Carolina

Boston   Burr Ridge, IL   Dubuque, IA   Madison, WI   New York   San Francisco   St. Louis
Bangkok   Bogotá   Caracas   Kuala Lumpur   Lisbon   London   Madrid   Mexico City
Milan   Montreal   New Delhi   Santiago   Seoul   Singapore   Sydney   Taipei   Toronto

Higher Education

ATHLETIC TRAINING: AN INTRODUCTION TO PROFESSIONAL PRACTICE
Published by McGraw-Hill, a business unit of The McGraw-Hill Companies, Inc., 1221 Avenue
of the Americas, New York, NY, 10020. Copyright © 2006 by The McGraw-Hill Companies,
Inc. All rights reserved. No part of this publication may be reproduced or distributed in any form
or by any means, or stored in a database or retrieval system, without the prior written consent of
The McGraw-Hill Companies, Inc., including, but not limited to, in any network or other
electronic storage or transmission, or broadcast for distance learning.
Some ancillaries, including electronic and print components, may not be available to customers outside
the United States.

This book is printed on acid-free paper.

2 3 4 5 6 7 8 9 0 VNH/VNH 0 9 8 7

ISBN-13: 978-0-07-319561-2
ISBN-10: 0-07-319561-8

Editor in Chief: *Emily Barrosse*
Publisher: *William Glass*
Executive Editor: *Nicholas Barrett*
Executive Marketing Manager: *Pamela S. Cooper*
Director of Development: *Kathleen Engelberg*
Senior Developmental Editor: *Michelle A. Turenne*
Developmental Editor, E-Content: *Julia D. Ersery*
Editorial and Marketing Coordinator: *Nancy Null*
Managing Editor: *Jean Dal Porto*
Senior Project Manager: *Jill Moline-Eccher*
Production Service: *Jan Nickels*
Manuscript Editor (freelance): *Jan Nickels*
Art Director: *Jeanne Schreiber*
Designer: *Preston Thomas*
Cover Designer: *Yvo Riezebos*
Art Editor: *Emma C. Ghiselli*
Manager, Photo Research: *Brian J. Pecko*
Cover Credit: © *AP/Wide World Photos*
Senior Media Project Manager: *Ron Nelms*
Associate Production Supervisor: *Jason I. Huls*
Media Producer: *Lance Gerhart*
Composition: *10/12 Meridien by Cenveo*
Printing: *PMS Black, 45 # Pub Matte, Von Hoffman Corporation*

Credits: The credits section for this book begins on page C-1 and is considered an extension of the
copyright page.

Library of Congress Control Number: 2005926151

The Internet addresses listed in the text were accurate at the time of publication. The inclusion of a
website does not indicate an endorsement by the authors of McGraw-Hill, and McGraw-Hill does not
guarantee the accuracy of the information presented at these sites.

www.mhhe.com

Brief Contents

Detailed Contents

Preface

This first edition of *Athletic Training: An Introduction to Professional Practice* was created from the foundations established in *Arnheim's Principles of Athletic Training: A Competency-Based Approach,* currently in its twelfth edition. For four decades, *Arnheim's Principles of Athletic Training* has been considered by many as the leading text in this field. Over the years, it has served as the primary text for professional athletic trainers and other individuals interested in sports medicine.

In 1998, the Education Council, established by the National Athletic Trainers' Association, took responsibility for identifying knowledge and skills that need to be included in educational programs that prepare students to enter the athletic training profession. The Education Council developed a list of educational competencies and clinical proficiencies categorized according to twelve domains that comprise the role of the athletic trainer. This move toward a competency-based approach has to some extent changed the way that coursework in entry-level athletic training educational programs is organized. Many accredited curriculums now offer a course that essentially serves as an introduction to the profession for students who are ultimately interested in becoming athletic trainers. Some instructors in these introductory courses have asked that I provide a shorter, less comprehensive text that would essentially include only those chapters that would effectively introduce the athletic training student to professional practice. *Athletic Training: An Introduction to Professional Practice* is offered as an alternative to the much more comprehensive *Arnheim's Principles of Athletic Training* to better meet the needs of those instructors who wish to use a shorter textbook for the introductory course, while still providing a resource for those eventually seeking professional certification.

WHAT IS INCLUDED IN THIS FIRST EDITION?

An extensive survey of entry level athletic training education program directors was conducted by McGraw-Hill to determine exactly what material needed to be included in an introductory text. This first edition includes serious consideration and incorporation of suggestions made by program directors, athletic training educators, and other respected authorities in the field. Consequently, this first edition reflects only the basic dynamic trends in the profession of athletic training.

The chapters in this text have been divided into three sections:

Part I: Professional Development and Responsibilities

The first chapter details the specific roles and responsibilities of the professional athletic trainer, understanding how the athletic trainer fits into the sports medicine team, and the athletic trainer's place in the field of health care. Chapter 2 addresses how the athletic trainer functions as an administrator of an athletic health care program. Chapter 3 discusses ways to minimize the chances of litigation and also to make certain that both the athlete and the athletic trainer are protected by appropriate insurance coverage.

Part II: Preventing Injury and Minimizing Risk

This section discusses a variety of different factors that the athletic trainer needs to have some knowledge about, which can either individually or collectively prevent or minimize risk of injury. Chapters are included on training and conditioning techniques to get the athlete fit, nutritional and environmental considerations, selecting and fitting protective sports equipment, bandaging and taping techniques, and the mechanisms and characteristics of sports trauma.

Part III: Injury Management

This third section concentrates on basic skills necessary for the athletic trainer to manage the injured athlete, including a chapter on how to incorporate universal precautions and concerns with bloodborne pathogens.

PEDAGOGICAL AIDS

Numerous pedagogical devices are included in this text:

- *Chapter objectives*   Goals begin each chapter to reinforce important key concepts to be learned.
- *Margin information*   Key concepts, selected definitions, helpful training tips, and illustrations are placed in the margins throughout the text for added emphasis and ease of reading and studying.
- *Focus boxes*   Important information has been highlighted and boxed to make key information easier to find and to enhance the text's flexibility and appearance.
- *Critical Thinking Exercises*   Individual case studies are included that encourage the student to apply the content presented to the clinical setting.
- *Color throughout text*   A second color is used throughout the text to accentuate and clarify illustrations and textual material.
- *Chapter summaries*   Each chapter's salient points are summarized to reinforce key content.
- *Review questions and class activities*   Located at the end of each chapter, review questions and class activities are provided to enhance the learning process.
- *References*   Extensive referencing provides the most current information available.
- *Annotated bibliography*   For students and instructors who want to learn more about the information presented in each chapter.
- *Glossary*   An extensive list of key terms and their definitions is presented to reinforce information in one convenient location.
- *End pages*   Front and back end pages inside the covers of the text provide helpful lists of suggested supplies for the athletic training room and the athletic trainer's kit, along with charts for metric and Celsius conversions.

INSTRUCTOR'S RESOURCE MATERIALS

Course Integrator Guide

This guide was prepared by Terri Jo Rucinski, M.A., ATC, P.T., from the University of North Carolina. It includes all the useful features found in an Instructor's Manual, including learning objectives, brief chapter overviews, key terminology, discussion questions, class activities, worksheets and the accompanying answer keys, media resources, and Web links.

Test Bank

Each chapter of the test bank contains true-false, multiple choice, and completion test questions. The worksheets in each chapter also include a separate test bank of matching, short answer, listing, essay, and personal or injury assessment questions that can be used as self-testing tools for students or as additional sources for examination questions.

Computerized Test Bank CD-ROM

The test bank is available on the Instructor's CD-ROM as Word files and with EZ Test computerized testing software. EZ Test provides a powerful, easy-to-use test maker to create printed quizzes and exams. EZ Test runs on both Windows and Macintosh systems. For secure online testing, exams created in EZ Test can be exported to WebCT,

Blackboard, PageOut, and (beginning fall 2005) EZ Test Online. The EZ Test CD is packaged with a Quick Start Guide; once the program is installed, users have access to the complete User's Manual, including multiple Flash tutorials. Additional help is available at www.mhhe.com/eztest.

PowerPoint Presentation

Developed by Jason Scibek, M.A., ATC, of Eastern Michigan University, a comprehensive and extensively illustrated PowerPoint presentation accompanies this text for use in classroom discussion. The PowerPoint presentation may also be converted to outlines and given to students as a handout. You can easily download the PowerPoint presentation from the Online Learning Center at www.mhhe.com/prentice1e. Adopters of the text can obtain the login and password to access this presentation by contacting their local McGraw-Hill sales representative.

INTERNET RESOURCES

Course Management Systems

www.mhhe.com/support
Now instructors can combine their McGraw-Hill Online Learning Center with today's most popular course-management systems and/or McGraw-Hill's PageOut. The McGraw-Hill Online Learning Center has also been converted into a cartridge that can be used in most course management systems. Our Instructor Advantage program offers customers toll-free telephone support, and unlimited e-mail support. Instructors who use 500 or more copies of a McGraw-Hill textbook can enroll in our Instructor Advantage Plus program, which provides on-campus, hands-on training from a platform specialist. We have also built an interactive support site accessible to anyone with an Internet connection. Located at www.mhhe.com/support, you can ask questions of the prebuilt database, or e-mail a McGraw-Hill specialist. Consult your McGraw-Hill sales representative to learn what other course management systems are easily used with McGraw-Hill online materials.

Online Learning Center

www.mhhe.com/prentice1e
This website offers resources to students and instructors. It includes downloadable ancillaries, Web links, student quizzes, additional information on topics of interest, and more. Resources for the instructor include:
- Downloadable PowerPoint presentations
- Lecture outlines
- Discussion questions
- Concept summaries

Resources for the student include:
- Flashcards
- Online chapter reviews
- Interactive quizzes
- PowerWeb

eSims

www.mhhe.com/esims
eSims is an online assessment tool that provides students with computerized simulation tests with instant feedback that emulate the actual Athletic Training certification exam, and is available with each new purchase of *Athletic Training: An Introduction to Professional Practice*. (It is available for purchase online too!) Check out eSims at the address above.

ACKNOWLEDGMENTS

I would like to thank my editor, Nick Barrett, my developmental editor, Michelle Turenne, and the many survey respondents for their help in making this first edition become a reality.

Gerald W. Bell
University of Illinois

Matthew J. Comeau
Arkansas State University

Carl R. Cramer
Barry University

Paul R. Geisler
Georgia Southern University

Melody "Dee" Higgins
Clarke College

Scott McGonagle
University of Miami

Renee Polubinsky
Western Illinois University

Lee Ann Price
Eastern Illinois University

Brian Ragan
University of Illinois

Charles Redmond
Springfield College

As always I want to thank my wife Tena, and our sons, Brian and Zach, for helping me stay grounded and focused in every project that I choose to pursue.

William E. Prentice

Applications at a Glance

The Athletic Trainer and the Sports Medicine Team

Chapter 1

When you finish this chapter you should be able to

- Recognize the historical foundations of athletic training.
- Identify the various professional organizations dedicated to athletic training and sports medicine.
- Differentiate the roles and responsibilities of the athletic trainer, the team physician, and the coach.
- Explain the function of support personnel in sports medicine.
- Identify various employment settings for the athletic trainer.
- Discuss certification and licensure for the athletic trainer.
- Clarify the role of the physical therapist in sports medicine.

A n athletic trainer is concerned with the well-being of the athlete and generally assumes the responsibility for overseeing the total health care for the athlete. Participation in sports places the athlete in a situation in which injury is likely to occur. Fortunately, most of the injuries are not serious and lend themselves to rapid rehabilitation, but the athletic trainer must be capable of dealing with any type of trauma or catastrophic injury.

Although millions of individuals participate in organized and recreational sports, there is a relatively low incidence of fatalities and catastrophic injuries among them. A major problem, however, lies with the millions of sports participants who incur injuries or illnesses that could have been prevented and who later, as a consequence, develop more serious chronic conditions. Athletes in organized sports have every right to expect that their health and safety will be kept as the highest of priorities. The field of athletic training, as a specialization, provides a major link between the sports program and the medical community for the implementation of injury prevention, emergency care, and rehabilitative procedures (Figure 1-1).[66]

HISTORICAL PERSPECTIVES
Early History

The drive to compete was important in many early societies. Sports developed over a period of time as a means of competing in a relatively peaceful and nonharmful way. Early civilizations show little evidence of highly organized sports. Some evidence indicates that in Greek and Roman civilizations there were coaches, trainers (people who helped the athlete reach top physical condition), and physicians to assist the athlete in reaching optimum performance.[51] Many of the roles that emerged during this early period are the same in modern sports.

For many centuries after the fall of the Roman Empire there was a complete lack of interest in sports activities. Not until the beginning of the Renaissance did these activities slowly gain popularity. Athletic training as we know it came into existence during the late nineteenth century with the firm establishment of intercollegiate and interscholastic athletes in the United States. The first athletic trainers of this era were hangers-on who "rubbed down" the athlete. Because they possessed no technical

The certified athletic trainer is a highly educated and skilled professional specializing in athletic health care for the physically active.

The history of athletic training draws on the disciplines of exercise, medicine, physical therapy, physical education, and sports.

Figure 1-1

The field of athletic training provides a major link between the sports program and the medical community.

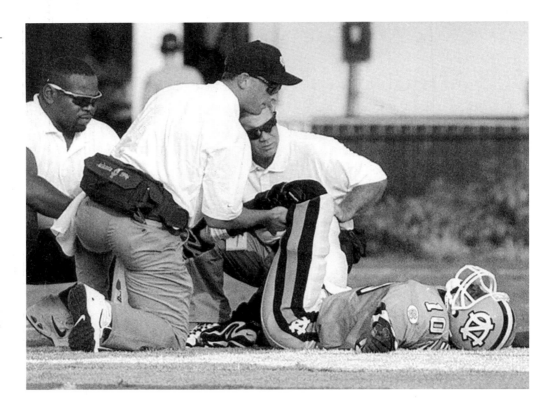

knowledge, their athletic training techniques usually consisted of a rub, the application of some type of counterirritant, and occasionally the prescription of various home remedies and poultices. Many of those earlier athletic trainers were persons of questionable background and experience. As a result, it has taken many years for the athletic trainer to attain the status of a well-qualified allied health care professional.[61]

Evolution of the Contemporary Athletic Trainer

The terms *training* and *athletic training, trainer,* and *athletic trainer* are often used interchangeably and are frequently confused with one another. Historically, training implies the act of coaching or teaching. In comparison, athletic training has traditionally been known as the field that is concerned with the athlete's health and safety. A trainer refers to someone who trains dogs or horses or functions in coaching or teaching areas. The *certified athletic trainer* is one who is a specialist in athletic training. Athletic training has evolved over the years to play a major role in the health care of the physically active in general and the athlete in particular. This evolution occurred rapidly after World War I with the appearance of the athletic trainer in intercollegiate athletics. During this period, the major influence in developing the athletic trainer as a specialist in preventing and managing athletic injuries came from the work of Dr. S. E. Bilik, a physician who wrote the first major text on athletic training and the care of athletic injuries, called *The Trainer's Bible,* in 1917.[8]

In the early 1920s the Cramer family in Gardner, Kansas, started a chemical company and began producing a liniment to treat ankle sprains. Over the years, the Cramers realized that there was a market for products to treat injured athletes. In an effort to enhance communication and facilitate an exchange of ideas among coaches, athletic trainers, and athletes, Cramer began publication of the *First Aider* in 1932. The members of this family were instrumental in the early development of the athletic training profession and have always played a prominent role in the education of student athletic trainers.[61]

During the late 1930s an effort was made, primarily by several college and university athletic trainers, to establish a national organization named the National Athletic

A Certified Athletic Trainer provides health care to physically active individuals

Trainers' Association (NATA). After struggling for existence from 1938 to 1944, the association essentially disappeared during the difficult years of World War II.

Between 1947 and 1950 university athletic trainers once again began to organize themselves into separate regional conferences, which would later become district organizations within NATA. In 1950 some 101 athletic trainers from the various conferences met in Kansas City, Missouri, and officially formed the National Athletic Trainers' Association. The primary purpose for its formation was to establish professional standards for the athletic trainer.[61] Since NATA was formed in 1950 many individuals have made contributions to the development of the profession.

After 1950 the growth of the athletic training profession has been remarkable. In 1974 when NATA membership numbers were first tracked there were 4,500 members. Today those numbers have grown to more than 30,000 members. Originally, the traditional settings where athletic trainers worked were in colleges and secondary schools, dealing almost exclusively with the athletic population. Today the contemporary certified athletic trainer can be found not only in schools, but also on the sidelines of professional sports, in hospitals and clinics, in industrial settings, in the military, working as physician extenders, in medical equipment sales and support, and even in NASA and NASCAR, as the profession that began with college sports has expanded its scope to deal with all people involved in physical activity. As the athletic training profession has grown and evolved over the last fifty years, many positive milestones have occurred that have collectively shaped the future direction of the profession, including, among many, recognition of athletic trainers as health care providers; increased diversity of practice settings; the passage of practice acts that regulate athletic trainers in most states; third party reimbursement for athletic training services; and ongoing reevaluation, revision, and reform of athletic training educational programs.

SPORTS MEDICINE AND ATHLETIC TRAINING
The Field of Sports Medicine

The term *sports medicine* refers generically to a broad field of medical practice related to physical activity and sport. The field of sports medicine encompasses under its umbrella a number of more specialized aspects of dealing with the physically active or athletic populations that may be classified as relating either to performance enhancement or to injury care and management (Figure 1-2). Those areas of specialization that are primarily concerned with performance enhancement include exercise physiology, biomechanics, sport psychology, sports nutrition, and strength and conditioning. Areas of specialization that focus more on injury care and management specific to the athlete are the practice of medicine, athletic training, sports physical therapy, sports massage therapy, sports dentistry, osteopathic medicine, orthotists/prosthetists, and chiropractic. The

Figure 1-2

Areas of specialization under the sports medicine "umbrella."

Sports Medicine

Performance Enhancement	Injury Care & Management
Exercise Physiology	Practice of Medicine
Biomechanics	Athletic Training
Sport Psychology	Sports Physical Therapy
Sports Nutrition	Sports Massage Therapy
Strength & Conditioning	Sports Dentistry
	Osteopathic Medicine
	Orthotists/Prosthetists
	Chiropractic

American College of Sports Medicine (ACSM) has defined sports medicine as multidisciplinary, including the physiological, biomechanical, psychological, and pathological phenomena associated with exercise and sports.[2] The clinical application of the work of these disciplines is performed to improve and maintain an individual's functional capacities for physical labor, exercise, and sports. It also includes the prevention and treatment of diseases and injuries related to exercise and sports.

Growth of Professional Sports Medicine Organizations

The twentieth century brought with it the development of a number of professional organizations dedicated to athletic training and sports medicine. Professional organizations have many goals: (1) to upgrade the field by devising and maintaining a set of professional standards, including a code of ethics; (2) to bring together professionally competent individuals to exchange ideas, stimulate research, and promote critical thinking; and (3) to give individuals an opportunity to work as a group with a singleness of purpose, thereby making it possible for them to achieve objectives that, separately, they could not accomplish. The organizations in the following list are presented in chronological order according to their year of establishment. Addresses, phone numbers, and/or websites for these and other related sports medicine organizations are in *Focus Box:* "Addresses of professional sports medicine organizations."

Several of these professional organizations also disseminate information to the general public about safe participation in sport activities in the form of guidelines or position statements. *Focus Box:* "Guidelines and position statements" lists the guidelines and position statements that are published by several different organizations.

Many professional organizations that are dedicated to achieving health and safety in sports have developed in the twentieth century.

1-1

Critical Thinking Exercise

A student athletic trainer has been given a class assignment to put together a list of various sports medicine organizations and to define the missions of those organizations.

? Where can the student find the most information about these organizations?

Focus

Addresses of professional sports medicine organizations

American Academy of Family Physicians, 8880 Ward Parkway, Kansas City, MO 64114. http://home.aafp.org/

American Academy of Ophthalmology Eye Safety and Sports Ophthalmology Committee, 655 Beach St., Box 7424, San Francisco, CA 94120-7424. (415) 561-8500.

American Academy of Orthopaedic Surgeons (AAOS), 6300 N. River Rd., Rosemont, IL 60018-4262. http://www.aaos.org/

American Academy of Pediatrics, Sports Committee, 141 NW Point Boulevard, Elk Grove Village, IL 60007-1098. http://www.aap.org/

American Academy of Physical Medicine and Rehabilitation (AAPMR), Special Interest Group on Sports Medicine, One IBM Plaza, Suite 2500, Chicago, IL 60611-3604. (312) 464-9700.

American Academy of Podiatric Sports Medicine (AAPSM), 1729 Glastonberry Rd., Potomac, MD 20854. http://www.aapsm.org/

American Association of Industrial Sports Medicine, 116 Foxboro Dr., Rochester Hills, MI 48309. (810) 375-9377. www.aaism.org

American Chiropractic Association Council on Sports Injuries and Physical Fitness, ACA Sports Council, 2444 Solomons Island Rd., #218 Annapolis, MD 21401. (410) 266-8285.

American College of Sports Medicine, 401 W. Michigan St., Indianapolis, IN 46202-3233. http://www.acsm.org/

American Massage Therapy Association, 820 Davis St., Evanston, IL 60201. http://www.amtamassage.org/

American Medical Athletic Association (AMAA), 4405 East West Highway, Suite 405, Bethesda, MD 20814. amaasportsmed@aol.com

Continued

Focus

Addresses of professional sports medicine organizations—continued

American Medical Soccer Association (AMSA), 350 Cheshire Dr., Birmingham, AL 35242-3100. (205) 991-6054. www.amsa.org

American Medical Society for Sports Medicine (AMSSM), 7611 Elmwood Ave., Suite 203, Middleton, WI 53562. (608) 831-4484. www.amssm.org

American Medical Tennis Association, 2301 Waleska Rd., Canton, GA 30114. http://www.mdtennis.org/

American Optometric Association (AOA) Sports Vision Section (SVS), 243 N. Lindbergh Blvd., St. Louis, MO 63141-7881. http://www.aoanet.org/

American Orthopaedic Society for Sports Medicine, 6300 N. River Road, Suite 200, Rosemont, IL 60018. http://www.sportsmed.org/

American Osteopathic Academy of Sports Medicine, 7611 Elmwood Ave., Suite 201, Middleton, WI 53562. (608) 831-4400. www.aoasm.org

American Osteopathic Orthopedic Society for Sports Medicine (AOOSSM), RD 3, Clarion, PA 16214. www.aoosm.org

American Physical Therapy Association, 1111 N. Fairfax St., Alexandria, VA 22314. http://apta.edoc.com/

American Physical Therapy Association (APTA), Sports Physical Therapy Section, 505 King St., Suite 115, La Crosse, WI 54601. http://www.apta.org/

American Running Association, 4405 East West Hwy., Suite 405, Bethesda, MD 20814. http://www.americanrunning.org

American Society of Biomechanics (ASB), c/o Joan E. Bechtold, PhD, Secretary/Treasurer, Biomechanics Laboratory, Hennepin County Medical Center, 701 Park Ave., S/860C, Minneapolis, MN 55415. http://www.asb-biomech.org bechto1@attglobal.net

American Sports Medicine Association, 660 W. Duarte Rd, Suite 1, Arcadia, CA 91007. (818) 445-1978.

Association of Volleyball Physicians, 1229 N. North Branch, Suite 122, Chicago, IL 60622. (708) 210-3112.

Canadian Academy of Sport Medicine, Unit 14, 1010 Polytek Street, Suite 100, Ottawa, ON K1J 9H9. (877) 585-2394. http://www.casm-acms.org

Canadian Athletic Therapists Association (CATA), 1600 James Naismith Dr., Suite 507, Gloucester, ON K1B 5N4. (403) 240-7228. jburke@rtm.cdnsport.ca

Canadian Sport Massage Therapists Association (CSMTA), P.O. Box 1330, Unity, SK S0K 4L0. (306) 228-2808.

College Athletic Trainers' Society, Thorp Reed & Armstrong, LLPOne Oxford Centre, 301 Grant Street, 14th Floor, Pittsburgh, PA 15219-1425.

College of Chiropractic Sports Sciences (Canada), c/o Canadian Chiropractic Association, 1396 Eglington Ave. W., Toronto, ON M6C 2E4. (416) 781-5656.

Cooper Institute For Aerobics Research, 12330 Preston Rd., Dallas, TX 75230. (972) 341-3200. www.cooperinst.org

Gatorade Sport Science Institute, 617 W. Main St., Barrington, IL 60010. http://www.gssiweb.com

Institute for Preventative Sports Medicine, P.O. Box 7032, Ann Arbor, MI 48107. (734) 434-3390. www.ipsm.org

International Academy of Sports Vision (IASV), 200 S. Progress Ave., Harrisburg, PA 17109. (717) 652-8080.

International Powerlifting Federation Medical Committee, Box 4160, Opelika, AL 36803. (334) 749-6222.

The International Society for Sport Psychiatry, 316 N. Milwaukee St., Suite 318, Milwaukee, WI 53202. (414) 271-2900.

Joint Commission on Sports Medicine and Science, 90 South Cascade, Suite 1190, Colorado Springs, CO 80903. (719) 475-8609.

Continued

Focus

Addresses of professional sports medicine organizations—continued

National Academy of Sports Medicine (NASM), 26632 Agoura Road, Calabascas, CA 91302. (866) 292-6276. www.nasm.org

National Collegiate Athletic Association (NCAA) Injury Surveillance System (ISS), 6201 College Blvd., Overland Park, KS 66211. (913) 339-1906.

National Athletic Trainers' Association, 2952 Stemmons Freeway, Dallas, TX 75247. http://www.nata.org/

National Collegiate Athletic Association, Competitive Safeguards and Medical Aspects of Sports Committee, 6201 College Boulevard, Overland Park, KS 66211-2422. http://www.ncaa.org/

The National Council for Sports Medicine Education (NCSME), P.O. Box 3, Saratoga Springs, NY 12866. (518) 786-1529.

The National Federation of State High School Athletic Associations, 11724 Plaza Circle, P.O. Box 20626, Kansas City, MO 64195. http://nfshsa.org/

National Strength and Conditioning Association, P.O. Box 38909, Colorado Springs, CO 80937-8909. http://www.nsca-lift.org/

North American Society for Pediatric Exercise Medicine (NASPEM), Box 5076, 1607 N. Market St., Champaign, IL 61825-5076. (217) 351-5076.

North American Society for the Psychology of Sport and Physical Activity (NASPSPA), Dept. of Exercise and Sport Science, 254 HHP, UNC Greensboro, Greensboro, NC 27412. (910) 334-3255.

Sports Medicine Council of British Columbia (SMCBC), #3 - 6501 Sprott St., Burnaby, BC V5B 3B8. (604) 473-4850.

United States Rowing Association (USRA) Sports Medicine Society, 201 S. Capitol Ave., Suite 400, Indianapolis, IN 46225-1068. (317) 237-5656.

U.S. Olympic Committee Sports Medicine Society, 1 Olympic Plaza, Colorado Springs, CO 80909-5760. (719) 578-4546.

U.S. Weightlifting Federation Sports Medicine Committee, Box 4160, 2000 Waverly Parkway, Opelika, AL 36803-4160. (334) 749-6222.

Wilderness Medical Society, Box 2463, Indianapolis, IN 46206. (317) 631-1745.

Focus

Guidelines and position statements

National Athletic Trainers' Association (NATA)

Position Statements
- Emergency planning in athletics
- Exertional heat illnesses
- Fluid replacement for athletes
- Head down contact and spearing in tackle football

- Lightning safety for athletics and recreation
  - Endorsed by the *American Academy of Pediatrics*
- Management of sport-related concussion

Consensus Statements
- Appropriate medical care for secondary school-age athletes
- Prehospital care of the spine-injured athlete

- Inter-association task force on exertional heat illnesses

Continued

Focus

Guidelines and position statements—continued

National Athletic Trainers' Association (NATA)—continued

Official Statements

- Commotio cordis
- Drug and performance enhancement supplement use in athletics
- Full-time, on-site athletic trainer coverage for secondary school athletic programs

- Use of qualified athletic trainers in secondary schools
- Automated external defibrillators
- Community-acquired MRSA infections
- Youth football and heat-related illnesses

Cooperative and Support Statements

- *American Academy of Family Physicians'* support of athletic trainers for high school athletes
- *American Medical Association's* support of athletic trainers in secondary schools
- Appropriate medical care for secondary school-age athletes (Manuscript)
- Endorsement of NATA Lightning Position Statement by the *American Academy of Pediatrics*

- Recommendations and guidelines for appropriate medical coverage of inter-collegiate athletics
  - NCAA support of Recommendations and guidelines for appropriate medical coverage of intercollegiate athletics

National Collegiate Athletic Association (NCAA) guidelines

- Sports Medicine Administration
- Medical Evaluations, Immunizations and Records
- Dispensing Prescription Medication
- Lightning Safety
- Institutional Alcohol, Tobacco and Other Drug Education Programs
- Emergency Care and Coverage
- Medical Disqualification of the Student-Athlete
- Skin Infections in Wrestling
- Prevention of Heat Illness
- Weight Loss—Dehydration
- Assessment of Body Composition
- Nutrition and Athletic Performance
- Menstrual-Cycle Dysfunction
- Blood-Borne Pathogens and Intercollegiate Athletics
- Nontherapeutic Drugs
- Nutritional Ergogenic Aids
- The Use of Local Anesthetics in College Athletics

- The Use of Injectable Corticosteroids in Sports Injuries
- Cold Stress
- "Burners" (Bracial Plexus Injuries)
- Concussion and Second-Impact Syndrome
- Participation by the Impaired Student-Athlete
- Participation by the Pregnant Student-Athlete
- The Student-Athlete with Sickle Cell Trait
- Protective Equipment
- Eye Safety in Sports
- Use of Trampoline and Minitramp
- Mouth Guards
- Use of the Head as a Weapon in Football and Other Contact Sports
- Guidelines for Helmet Fitting and Removal in Athletics
- Transparent Eye Shield Exception Procedure for Football

American Academy of Pediatrics (AAP)

- Intensive Training and Sports Specialization in Young Athletes
- Medical Concerns in the Female Athlete
- Human Immunodeficiency Virus and Other Blood-Borne Viral Pathogens in the Athletic Setting

- Promotion of Healthy Weight-Control Practices in Young Athletes
- Adolescents and Anabolic Steroids: A Subject Review
- Protective Eyewear for Young Athletes
- Medical Conditions and Sports Participation

Continued

Focus

Guidelines and position statements—continued

American Academy of Pediatrics (AAP)—continued

- Amenorrhea in Adolescent Athletes
- Medical Conditions Affecting Sports Participation
- Strength Training, Weight and Power Lifting, and Body Building by Children and Adolescents
- Triathlon Participation by Children and Adolescents
- Cardiac Dysrhythmias and Sports
- Athletic Participation by Children and Adolescents Who Have Systemic Hypertension
- Risks in Distance Running for Children
- Knee Brace Use by Athletes
- Risk of Injury from Baseball and Softball in Children 5 to 14 Years of Age
- Injuries in Youth Soccer: A Subject
- Organized Athletics for Preadolescent Children
- Guidelines for Emergency Medical Care in School
- Climatic Heat Stress and the Exercising Child and Adolescent
- Mitral Valve Prolapse and Athletic Participation in Children and Adolescents
- Participation in Boxing by Children, Adolescents, and Young Adults
- Sports with High Risk of Eye Injury

American College of Sports Medicine (ACSM)

- Nutrition and Athletic Performance
- Exercise and Type 2 Diabetes
- The Recommended Quantity and Quality of Exercise for Developing and Maintaining Cardiorespiratory and Muscular Fitness, and Flexibility in Healthy Adults
- Exercise and Physical Activity for Older Adults
- Recommendations for Cardiovascular Screening, Staffing, and Emergency Policies at Health/Fitness Facilities
- Diabetes Mellitus and Exercise
- The Female Athlete Triad
- Heat & Cold Illnesses During Distance Running
- Exercise and Fluid Replacement
- The Use of Blood Doping as an Ergogenic Aid
- Weight Loss in Wrestlers
- Osteoporosis and Exercise
- Exercise for Patients with Coronary Artery Disease
- Physical Activity, Physical Fitness, and Hypertension
- The Use of Anabolic-Androgenic Steroids in Sports
- Proper and Improper Weight-Loss Programs
- The Use of Alcohol in Sports
- Exercise & Hypertension
- Automated External Defibrillators in Health/Fitness Facilities
- Progression Models in Resistance Training for Healthy Adults
- Appropriate Intervention Strategies for Weight Loss and Prevention of Weight Regain for Adults

International Federation of Sports Medicine

Among the first major organizations was the Federation Internationale de Medecine Sportive (FIMS). It was created in 1928 at the Olympic Winter Games in St. Moritz, Switzerland, by Olympic medical doctors with the principal purpose of promoting the study and development of sports medicine throughout the world. FIMS is made up of the national sports medicine associations of more than 100 countries. This organization is multidisciplinary and includes many disciplines that are concerned with the physically active individual. To some degree the ACSM has patterned itself after this organization.

American Academy of Family Physicians

The American Academy of Family Physicians (AAFP) was founded in 1947 to promote and maintain high quality standards for family doctors who are providing continuing comprehensive health care to the public. AAFP is a medical association of more than 93,000 members. Many team physicians are members of this organization. It publishes the *American Family Physician*.

National Athletic Trainers' Association

Before the formation of the National Athletic Trainers' Association, Inc. in 1950, athletic trainers occupied a somewhat insecure place in the athletic program. Since that time, as a result of the raising of professional standards and the establishment of a code of ethics, there has been considerable professional advancement. The stated mission of NATA is:

> To enhance the quality of health care provided by certified athletic trainers and to advance the profession of athletic training.

The association accepts as members only those athletic trainers who are properly qualified and who are prepared to subscribe to a code of ethics and to uphold the standards of the association. NATA currently has more than 30,000 members. It publishes a quarterly journal, *The Journal of Athletic Training,* and holds an annual convention at which members have an opportunity to keep abreast of new developments and to exchange ideas through clinical programs. The organization is constantly working to improve both the quality and the status of athletic training.

American College of Sports Medicine

As discussed previously, the ACSM is interested in the study of all aspects of sports. Established in 1954, ACSM's membership of 18,000 is composed of medical doctors, doctors of philosophy, physical educators, athletic trainers, coaches, exercise physiologists, biomechanists, and others interested in sports. The organization holds national and regional conferences and meetings devoted to exploring the many aspects of sports medicine, and it publishes a quarterly magazine, *Medicine and Science in Sports and Exercise.* This journal includes articles in French, Italian, German, and English and provides complete translations in English of all articles. It reports recent developments in the field of sports medicine on a worldwide basis.

American Orthopaedic Society for Sports Medicine

The American Orthopaedic Society for Sports Medicine (AOSSM) was created in 1972 to encourage and support scientific research in orthopedic sports medicine; the organization works to develop methods for safer, more productive, and more enjoyable fitness programs and sports participation. Through programs developed by the AOSSM, members receive specialized training in sports medicine, surgical procedures, injury prevention, and rehabilitation. AOSSM's 1,200 members are orthopedic surgeons and allied health professionals committed to excellence in sports medicine. Its official bimonthly publication is the *American Journal of Sports Medicine.*

National Strength and Conditioning Association

The National Strength and Conditioning Association (NSCA) was formed in 1978 to facilitate a professional exchange of ideas in strength development as it relates to the improvement of athletic performance and fitness and to enhance, enlighten, and advance the field of strength and conditioning.

NSCA has a membership of more than 14,500 professionals, including strength and conditioning coaches, personal trainers, exercise physiologists, athletic trainers, researchers, educators, sport coaches, physical therapists, business owners, exercise instructors, fitness directors, and students training to enter the field. In addition, the NSCA Certification Commission offers two of the finest and the only nationally accredited certification programs: the Certified Strength and Conditioning Specialist (CSCS) and the NSCA Certified Personal Trainer (NSCA-CPT). NSCA publishes both the *Journal of Strength and Conditioning Research* and *Strength and Conditioning.*

American Academy of Pediatrics, Sports Committee

The American Academy of Pediatrics, Sports Committee, was organized in 1979. Its primary goal is to educate all physicians, especially pediatricians, about the special needs of children who participate in sports. Between 1979 and 1983, this committee developed guidelines that were incorporated into a report, *Sports Medicine: Health Care for Young Athletes,* edited by Nathan J. Smith, M.D.

American Physical Therapy Association, Sports Physical Therapy Section

In 1981, the Sports Physical Therapy Section of the American Physical Therapy Association (APTA) was officially established. The mission of the Sports Physical Therapy Section is "to provide a forum to establish collegial relations between physical therapists, physical therapist assistants, and physical therapy students interested in sports physical therapy." The Section and its 9,000 members promote the prevention, recognition, treatment, and rehabilitation of injuries in an athletic and physically active population; provide educational opportunities through sponsorship of continuing education programs and publications; promote the role of the sports physical therapist to other health professionals; and support research to further establish the scientific basis for sports physical therapy. The Section's official journal is the *Journal of Orthopaedic and Sports Physical Therapy.*

NCAA Committee on Competitive Safeguards and Medical Aspects of Sports

The National Collegiate Athletic Association (NCAA) Committee on Competitive Safeguards and Medical Aspects of Sports collects and develops pertinent information about desirable training methods, prevention and treatment of sports injuries, utilization of sound safety measures at the college level, drug education, and drug testing; disseminates information and adopts recommended policies and guidelines designed to further the objectives just listed; and supervises drug-education and drug-testing programs.

National Academy of Sports Medicine

The National Academy of Sports Medicine (NASM) was founded in 1987 by physicians, physical therapists, and fitness professionals and focuses on the development, refinement, and implementation of educational programs for fitness, performance, and sports medicine professionals. According to its mission statement "NASM is dedicated to transforming lives and revolutionizing the health and fitness industry through its unwavering commitment to deliver innovative education, solutions and tools that produce remarkable results." In addition to offering a fitness certification (Certified Personal Trainer) and performance certification (Performance Enhancement Specialist), NASM offers advanced credentials and more than twenty continuing education courses in a variety of disciplines. NATA currently has an agreement whereby NASM offers its Performance Enhancement Specialist and Integrated Flexibility Specialist certifications to NATA members. NASM serves more than 100,000 members and partners in eighty countries.

Other Health-Related Organizations

Many other health-related professions such as dentists, podiatrists, and chiropractors have, over the years, become interested in the health and safety aspects of sports. Besides national organizations that are interested in athletic health and safety, there are state and local associations that are extensions of the larger bodies. National, state, and local sports organizations have all provided extensive support to the reduction of illness and injury risk to the athlete.

Other Sports Medicine Journals

Athletic training must be considered a specialization under the broad field of sports medicine.

Other journals that provide an excellent service to the field of athletic training and sports medicine are *The International Journal of Sports Medicine,* which is published in English by Thieme-Stratton, Inc., New York; *The Journal of Sports Medicine and Physical Fitness,* published by Edizioni Minerva Medica SPA, ADIS Press Ltd., Auckland 10, New Zealand; the *Journal of Sport Rehabilitation and Athletic Therapy Today,* both published by Human Kinetics Publishers, Inc., Champaign, Illinois; the *Physician and Sportsmedicine,* published by McGraw-Hill, Inc., New York; *Physical Therapy* and *Clinical Management,* both published by the American Physical Therapy Association, Fairfax, Virginia; *Physi-*

Focus

Sports medicine-related journals

Acta Orthopaedica Scandinavica
Adapted Physical Activity Quarterly
Advances in Orthopaedic Surgery
American Journal of Medicine and Sport
American Journal of Orthodontics and Dento-facial Orthopedics
American Journal of Sports Medicine
Archives of Orthopaedic and Trauma Surgery
Archives of Physical Medicine and Rehabilitation
Arthroscopy
Arthroskopie
Athletic Therapy Today
Baillière's Clinical Orthopaedics
Bone
British Journal of Sport Medicine
Canadian Journal of Applied Physiology
Clinical Exercise Physiology
Clinical Journal of Sports Medicine
Clinical Orthopaedics and Related Research
Clinics in Sports Medicine
Complications in Orthopedics
Current Opinion in Orthopedics
Current Orthopaedics
Exercise Immunology Review
European Journal of Orthopaedic Surgery and Traumatology
European Spine Journal
Foot and Ankle
Foot and Ankle Clinics
Hand Clinics
Hand Surgery
International Journal of Sports Medicine
International Journal of Sport Nutrition
International Orthopaedics
Internet Journal of Orthopedic Surgery and related subjects
Journal of Aging and Physical Activity
Journal of the American Academy of Orthopaedic Surgeons
Journal of Athletic Training
Journal of Applied Biomechanics
Journal of Arthroplasty
Journal of Back and Musculoskeletal Rehabilitation
The Journal of Bone and Joint Surgery

Journal of Hand Surgery (American)
Journal of Hand Surgery (British and European Volume)
Journal of Musculoskeletal Research
Journal of Orthopaedic Science
Journal of Orthopaedic Trauma
Journal of Orthopedic and Sports Physical Therapy
Journal of Pediatric Orthopaedics
Journal of Science and Medicine in Sport
Journal of Spinal Disorders
Journal of Sport Rehabilitation
Journal of Sports Chiropractic and Rehabilitation
Journal of Sports Medicine and Physical Fitness
Journal of Strength and Conditioning Research
The Knee
Medicine and Science in Sport and Exercise
Medscape Orthopedics and Sports Medicine
Neuro-Orthopedics
Operative Techniques in Orthopaedics
Operative Techniques in Sports Medicine
Orthopaedic Physical Therapy Clinics
Orthopedic Clinics
Orthopedics
Orthopedics Today
Orthopedic Surgery
Pediatric Exercise Science
Physical Therapy
Physical Therapy in Sport
Physical Medicine and Rehabilitation Clinics
Physician and Sports Medicine
Scandinavian Journal of Medicine and Science in Sports
Seminars in Musculoskeletal Radiology
Skeletal Radiology
Spine
Sports Medicine
Sports Medicine and Arthroscopy Review
Sports Medicine: Health Care for the Young Athlete
Strength and Conditioning
Techniques in Orthopaedics
Training and Conditioning

cal Medicine and Rehabilitation Clinics and *Clinics in Sports Medicine*, both published by W. B. Saunders, Philadelphia; and *Training and Conditioning*, published by MAG, Inc., Ithaca, New York.

There is a significant number of other journals that relate in some way to sports medicine. They are listed in *Focus Box:* "Sports medicine-related journals."

THE SPORTS MEDICINE TEAM

The primary individuals on the sports medicine team consist of the coach, the athletic trainer, and the team physician.

The provision of health care to the athlete requires a group effort to be most effective.[66] The sports medicine team involves a number of individuals, each of whom must perform specific functions relative to caring for the injured athlete.[11] Those people having the closest relationship with the injured athlete are the athletic trainer, the team physician, and the coach.

THE ATHLETIC TRAINER

Of all the professionals charged with injury prevention and health care provision for the athlete, perhaps none is more intimately involved than the athletic trainer.[66] The athletic trainer is the one individual who deals with the athlete throughout the period of rehabilitation, from the time of the initial injury until the athlete's complete, unrestricted return to practice or competition.[66] The athletic trainer is most directly responsible for all phases of health care in an athletic environment, including preventing injuries from occurring, providing initial first aid and injury management, evaluating injuries, and designing and supervising a timely and effective program of rehabilitation that can facilitate the safe and expeditious return of the athlete to activity.

The athletic trainer must be knowledgeable and competent in a variety of specialties encompassed under the umbrella of "sports medicine" if he or she is to be effective in preventing and treating injuries to the athlete.[19] The specific roles and responsibilities of the athletic trainer differ and to a certain extent are defined by the situation in which he or she works.[58]

Roles and Responsibilities of the Athletic Trainer

Board of Certification*

Six performance domains of the athletic trainer:
- Prevention of athletic injuries
- Clinical evaluation and diagnosis
- Immediate care
- Treatment, rehabilitation, and reconditioning
- Organization and administration
- Professional responsibility

Performance Domains In 2004 the Board of Certification (BOC) completed the latest role delineation study,** which defined the profession of athletic training.[10] This study was designed to examine the primary tasks performed by the entry-level athletic trainer and the knowledge and skills required to perform each task. The panel determined that the roles of the practicing athletic trainer could be divided into six major areas, or performance domains: (1) prevention of athletic injuries; (2) clinical evaluation and diagnosis; (3) immediate care of injuries; (4) treatment, rehabilitation, and reconditioning of athletic injuries; (5) organization and administration; and (6) professional responsibilities.

Education Council competencies and clinical proficiencies In 1997, the leadership of NATA established the Education Council to dictate the course of educational preparation for the student athletic trainer.[71] The focus of this Education Council has shifted to competency-based education at the entry level, and thus the Council has significantly expanded and reorganized the educational competencies and clinical proficiencies identified in the NATA's document, the 1999 Athletic Training Educational Competencies.[60] Whereas BOC defined the minimum knowledge base that an entry-level athletic trainer should possess to be able to work in the profession, the Education Council was charged with determining the competencies that should be taught in accredited educational programs.

1-2

Critical Thinking Exercise

An athletic training student must develop a sound knowledge base in and demonstrate competent performance skills in six major domains: prevention of athletic injuries; clinical evaluation and diagnosis; immediate care of injuries; treatment, rehabilitation, and reconditioning of athletic injuries; health care administration; and professional development and responsibility.

? How can athletic training students best prepare themselves to be competent professional athletic trainers?

The twelve domains established by the Education Council include (1) risk management, (2) pathology of injuries and illnesses, (3) orthopedic assessment and evaluation, (4) acute care of injury and illnesses, (5) pharmacology, (6) therapeutic modalities, (7) therapeutic exercise, (8) general medical conditions and disabilities, (9) nutritional aspects of injuries and illnesses, (10) psychosocial intervention and referral, (11) health care administration, and (12) professional development and responsibilities.

*The Board of Certification (BOC) has been responsible for the certification of athletic trainers since 1969. Upon its inception, the BOC was The Certification Committee for NATA, the profession's membership association. However, in 1989, the BOC became an independent nonprofit corporation. Formerly known as the NATABOC, the BOC officially changed its name in 2004.
**The 2004 Role Delineation study goes into effect in 2006.

Focus

Domains and competencies

Six performance domains established by the BOC*

- Prevention
- Clinical evaluation and diagnosis
- Immediate care
- Treatment, rehabilitation, and reconditioning

- Organization and administration
- Professional responsibility

Education competencies content areas established by the Education Council**

- Risk management
- Pathology of injuries and illnesses
- Orthopedic assessment and evaluation
- Acute care of injury and illnesses
- Pharmacology
- Therapeutic modalities
- Therapeutic exercise

- Medical conditions and disabilities
- Nutritional aspects of injuries and illnesses
- Psychosocial intervention and referral
- Health care administration
- Professional development and responsibilities

*Based on the 2004 Role Delineation Study[10]
**Based on the *Athletic training educational competencies*, ed 4. These will take effect in Fall 2006.

These competencies are required for both curriculum development and the education of students enrolled in entry-level athletic training education programs. As can be seen in *Focus Box:* "Domains and competencies," it is obvious that a great deal of overlap exists between the six performance domains identified by the BOC and the twelve competency domains established by the Education Council.[49]

Risk Management

Participation in competitive sports places the athlete in situations in which injuries are possible at any time. One major responsibility of the athletic trainer is to make the competitive environment as safe as possible to minimize the risk of injury. If injury can be prevented initially, there will be no need for first aid and subsequent rehabilitation.

The athletic trainer can minimize the risk of injury by (1) ensuring appropriate training and conditioning of the athlete; (2) monitoring environmental conditions to ensure safe participation; (3) selecting, properly fitting, and maintaining protective equipment; (4) making certain that the athlete is eating properly; and (5) making sure the athlete is using medications appropriately while discouraging substance abuse.

Developing training and conditioning programs   Perhaps the most important aspect of injury prevention is making certain that the athlete is fit and thus able to handle the physiological and psychological demands of athletic competition. The athletic trainer works with the coaches to develop and implement an effective training and conditioning program for the athlete (see Chapter 4). It is essential that the athlete maintain a consistently high level of fitness during the preseason, the competitive season, and the off-season. This consistent level of fitness is critical not only for enhancing performance parameters but also for preventing injury and reinjury. An athletic trainer must be knowledgeable in the area of applied physiology of exercise, particularly with regard to strength training, flexibility, improvement of cardiorespiratory fitness, maintenance of body composition, weight control, and nutrition. Many colleges and most professional teams employ full-time strength coaches to oversee this aspect of the total program. The athletic trainer, however, must be acutely aware of any aspect of the program that may have a negative impact on an athlete or group of athletes and must offer constructive

1-3

Critical Thinking Exercise

All American High School is considering hiring an athletic trainer instead of using an emergency medical technician. However, the administrators do not completely understand why an athletic trainer may be more beneficial for their athletes. A group of area athletic trainers will be holding a meeting to discuss the potential change.

? What reasons should the athletic trainers use to persuade the administrators to hire an athletic trainer?

suggestions for alternatives when appropriate. At the high-school level, the athletic trainer may be totally responsible for designing, implementing, and overseeing the fitness and conditioning program for the athletes.

Ensuring a safe playing environment   To the best of his or her ability, the athletic trainer must ensure a safe environment for competition. This task may include duties not typically thought to belong to the athletic trainer, such as collecting trash, picking up rocks, or removing objects (e.g., hurdles, gymnastics equipment) from the perimeter of the practice area, all of which might pose potential danger to the athlete. The athletic trainer should call these potential safety hazards to the attention of an administrator. The interaction between the athletic trainer and a concerned and cooperative administrator can greatly enhance the effectiveness of the sports medicine team.

The athletic trainer should also be familiar with potential dangers associated with practicing or competing under inclement weather conditions, such as high heat and humidity, extreme cold, or electrical storms. Practice should be restricted, altered, or canceled if weather conditions threaten the health and safety of the athlete. If the team physician is not present, the athletic trainer must have the authority to curtail practice if the environmental conditions become severe (see Chapter 6).

Selecting, fitting, and maintaining protective equipment   The athletic trainer works with coaches and equipment personnel to select protective equipment and is responsible for maintaining its condition and safety (see Chapter 7). Because liability lawsuits have become the rule rather than the exception, the athletic trainer must make certain that high-quality equipment is purchased and that it is constantly being worn, maintained, and reconditioned according to specific guidelines recommended by the manufacturers.

Protective equipment and devices can consume a significant portion of the athletic budget. The person responsible for purchasing protective equipment is usually inundated with marketing literature on a variety of braces, supports, pads, and other types of protective equipment. Decisions on purchasing specific pieces or brands should be based on research data that clearly document effectiveness in reducing or preventing injury (Figure 1-3).

Equipment is expensive, and schools are certainly subject to budgeting restrictions. However, purchasing decisions about protective equipment should always be made in the best interest of the athlete. Most colleges and professional teams hire full-time equipment managers to oversee this area of responsibility, but the athletic trainer must be knowledgeable about and aware of the equipment being worn by each athlete.

The design, building, and fitting of specific protective orthopedic devices are also responsibilities of the athletic trainer. Once the physician has indicated the problem and how it may be corrected, the athletic trainer should be able to construct an orthopedic device to correct it.

Explaining the importance of nutrition   Good nutrition can have a substantial impact on health and well-being. Poor nutritional habits can certainly have a negative effect on an athlete's ability to perform at the highest level possible. Yet for all

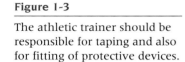

Figure 1-3

The athletic trainer should be responsible for taping and also for fitting of protective devices.

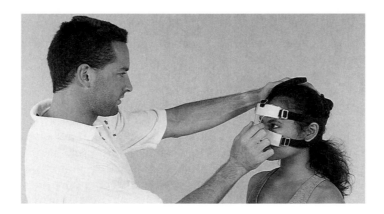

the attention that athletes, coaches, and athletic trainers direct at practicing sound nutritional habits, good nutritional decisions are still subjected to a tremendous amount of misunderstanding, misinformation, and occasionally, quackery. An athletic trainer is often asked for advice about matters related to diet, weight loss, and weight gain, and is occasionally asked about disordered eating. The athletic trainer does not need to be an expert on nutrition but must possess some understanding of the basic principles of nutrition.[79] (See Chapter 5.)

Using medications appropriately   The athlete, like anyone else, may benefit greatly from using medications prescribed for various medical conditions by qualified physicians. Under normal circumstances an athlete would be expected to respond to medication just like anyone else would. However, because of the nature of physical activity, the athlete's situation is unique; intense physical activity requires that special consideration be given to the effects of certain types of medication.

For the athletic trainer who is overseeing the health care of the athlete, some knowledge of the potential effects of certain types of drugs on performance is essential. Occasionally, the athletic trainer must make decisions regarding the appropriate use of medications based on knowledge of the indications for use and of the possible side effects in athletes who are involved in training and conditioning as well as in injury rehabilitation programs. The athletic trainer must be cognizant of the potential effects and side effects of over-the-counter and prescription medications on the athlete during rehabilitation as well as during competition.

In addition, the athletic trainer should also be aware of the problems of substance abuse, both in ergogenic aids that may be used in an effort to enhance performance and in the abuse of so-called recreational or street drugs. The athletic trainer may be involved in drug testing of the athlete and should thus be responsible for educating the athlete in drug use and substance abuse.

Clinical Evaluation and Diagnosis

Frequently, the athletic trainer is the first person to see an athlete who has sustained an injury. The athletic trainer must be skilled in recognizing the nature and extent of an injury through competency in injury evaluation. Once the injury has been evaluated, the athletic trainer must be able to provide the appropriate first aid and then refer the athlete to appropriate medical personnel.

Conducting physical examinations   The athletic trainer, in cooperation with the team physician, should obtain a medical history and conduct physical examinations of the athletes before participation as a means of screening for existing or potential problems (see Chapter 2). The medical history should be reviewed closely, and clarification should be sought for any point of concern.

The preparticipation examination should include measurement of height, weight, blood pressure, and body composition. The physician examination should concentrate on cardiovascular, respiratory, abdominal, genital, dermatological, and ear, nose, and throat systems and may include blood work and urinalysis. A brief orthopedic evaluation would include range of motion, muscle strength, and functional tests to assess joint stability. When the athletic trainer knows at the beginning of a season that an athlete has a physical problem that may predispose that athlete to an injury during the course of the season, he or she may immediately implement corrective measures that may significantly reduce the possibility of additional injury.

The athletic trainer must be able to efficiently and accurately evaluate an injury. Information obtained in this initial evaluation may be critical later on when swelling, pain, and guarding mask some of the functional signs of the injury.

It is essential that the athletic trainer be alert and observe, as much as possible, everything that goes on in practice. Invaluable information regarding the nature of an injury can be obtained by seeing the mechanism of the injury.

The subsequent off-the-field examination should include (1) obtaining a brief medical history of exactly what happened, according to the athlete, (2) observation, (3) palpation, (4) special tests that might include range of motion, muscle strength, joint stability, or a brief neurological examination. Information obtained in this initial examination should be documented by the athletic trainer and given to the physician once the athlete is referred. The team physician is ultimately responsible for providing an accurate diagnosis of an injury. The initial evaluation often provides the basis for this diagnosis.

Understanding the pathology of injury and illness The athletic trainer must be able to recognize the various types of musculoskeletal and nervous system injuries that can occur in the physically active population. Based on this knowledge of different injuries, the athletic trainer must possess some understanding of both the sequence and time frames for the various phases of healing, realizing that certain physiological events must occur during each of the phases. Anything done during training and conditioning or during a rehabilitation program that interferes with this healing process will likely delay a return to full activity. The healing process must have an opportunity to accomplish what it is supposed to. At best the athletic trainer can only try to create an environment that is conducive to the healing process. Little can be done to speed up the process physiologically, but many things may be done both during training and conditioning and during rehabilitation to impede healing.

Referring to medical care After the initial management of an injury, the athletic trainer should routinely refer the athlete to a physician for further evaluation and accurate diagnosis. If an athlete requires treatment from medical personnel other than the team physician, such as a dentist or ophthalmologist, the athletic trainer should arrange appointments as necessary. Referrals should be made after consultation with the team physician.

Referring to support services If needed, the athletic trainer must be familiar with and should have access to a variety of personal, school, and community health service agencies, including community-based psychological and social support services available to the athlete. With assistance and direction from these agencies, the athletic trainer together with the athlete should be able to formulate a plan for appropriate intervention following injury.

Immediate Care of Injury and Illness

The athletic trainer is often responsible for the initial on-the-field injury assessment following acute injury. Once this initial assessment is done, the athletic trainer then must assume responsibility for administering appropriate first aid to the injured athlete and for making correct decisions in the management of acute injury (see Chapter 10). Although the team physician is frequently present at games or competitions, in most cases he or she cannot be at every practice session, where injuries are more likely to occur. Thus the athletic trainer must possess sound skills not only in the initial recognition and evaluation of potentially serious or life-threatening injuries but also in emergency care.

The athletic trainer should be certified in cardiopulmonary resuscitation by the American Red Cross, the American Heart Association, or the National Safety Council. Athletic trainers should also be certified in first aid by the American Red Cross or the National Safety Council. Many athletic trainers have gone beyond these essential basic certifications and have completed emergency medical technician (EMT) requirements.

Emergency care procedures should be established by the athletic trainer in cooperation with local rescue squads and the community hospitals that can provide emergency treatment. Emergency care is expedited and the injured athlete's frustration and concern are lessened if arrangements regarding transportation, logistics, billing procedures, and appropriate contacts are made before an injury occurs.

Treatment, Rehabilitation, and Reconditioning

An athletic trainer must work closely with and under the supervision of the team physician with respect to designing rehabilitation and reconditioning protocols that

---

1-4

Critical Thinking Exercise

A basketball player suffers a grade 2 ankle sprain during midseason of the competitive schedule. After a three-week course of rehabilitation, most of the pain and swelling have been eliminated. The athlete is anxious to get back into practice and competitive games as soon as possible, and subsequent injuries to other players have put pressure on the coach to force the athlete's return. Unfortunately the athlete is still unable to perform functional tasks (cutting and jumping) essential in basketball.

? Who is responsible for making the decision regarding when the athlete can fully return to practice and game situations?

make use of appropriate therapeutic exercise, rehabilitative equipment, manual therapy techniques, or therapeutic modalities. The athletic trainer should then assume the responsibility of overseeing the rehabilitative process, ultimately returning the athlete to full activity.

Designing rehabilitation programs   Once the team physician has evaluated and diagnosed an injury, the rehabilitation process begins immediately. In most cases, the athletic trainer will design and supervise an injury rehabilitation program, modifying that program based on the healing process. It is critical for an athletic trainer to have a sound background in anatomy. Without this background, an athletic trainer cannot evaluate an injury. And if the athletic trainer cannot evaluate an injury, there is no point in the athletic trainer knowing anything about rehabilitation because he or she will not know at what phase the injury is in the healing process. The athletic trainer must also understand how to incorporate therapeutic modalities and appropriate therapeutic exercise techniques if the rehabilitation program is to be successful.

Supervising rehabilitation programs   The athletic trainer is charged with the responsibility of designing, implementing, and supervising the rehabilitation program for the athlete from the time of initial injury until the athlete returns to full activity. It is essential that the athletic trainer has a solid foundation in the various techniques of therapeutic exercise and an understanding of how those techniques can be most effectively incorporated into the rehabilitation program. The athletic trainer must establish both short-term and long-terms goals for the rehabilitation process and then be able to alter and modify the program to most effectively meet those goals.

Incorporating therapeutic modalities   Athletic trainers use a wide variety of therapeutic modalities in the treatment and rehabilitation of sport-related injuries. Modality use may involve a relatively simple technique such as using an ice pack as a first-aid treatment for an acute injury or may involve more complex techniques such as the stimulation of nerve and muscle tissue by electrical currents. Certainly, therapeutic modalities are useful tools in injury rehabilitation, and when used appropriately, these modalities can greatly enhance the athlete's chances for a safe and rapid return to athletic competition. It is essential for the athletic trainer to possess knowledge about the scientific basis and the physiologic effects of the various modalities on a specific injury. Modalities, though important, are by no means the single most critical factor in injury treatment. Therapeutic exercise that forces the injured anatomic structure to perform its normal function is the key to successful rehabilitation. However, therapeutic modalities play an important role in reducing pain and are extremely useful as an adjunct to therapeutic exercise.

Offering psychosocial intervention   The psychological aspect of how the individual athlete deals with an injury is a critical yet often neglected aspect of the rehabilitation process. Injury and illness produce a wide range of emotional reactions. Therefore the athletic trainer needs to develop an understanding of the psyche of each athlete. Athletes vary in terms of pain threshold, cooperation and compliance, competitiveness, denial of disability, depression, intrinsic and extrinsic motivation, anger, fear, guilt, and the ability to adjust to injury. Principles of sport psychology may be used to improve total athletic performance through visualization, self-hypnosis, and relaxation techniques. The athletic trainer plays a critical role in social support for the injured athlete.[6]

Organization and Administration

The athletic trainer is responsible for the organization and administration of the training room facility, including the maintenance of health and injury records for each athlete, requisition and inventory of necessary supplies and equipment, the supervision of assistant or student trainers, and the establishment of policies and procedures for day-to-day operation of the athletic training program (see Chapter 2).[82]

Record keeping   Accurate and detailed record keeping—including medical histories, preparticipation examinations, injury reports, treatment records, and rehabilitation programs—are critical for the athletic trainer, particularly in light of the number of lawsuits directed toward malpractice in health care. Although record keeping may be difficult and time consuming for the athletic trainer who treats and deals with a large number of patients each day, it is an area that simply cannot be neglected.

Ordering equipment and supplies   Although tremendous variations in operating budgets exist, depending on the level and the institution, decisions regarding how available money may best be spent are always critical. The athletic trainer must keep on hand a wide range of supplies to enable him or her to handle whatever situation may arise. At institutions in which severe budgetary restrictions exist, prioritization based on experience and past needs must become the mode of operation. A creative athletic trainer can make do with very little equipment, which should include at least a taping and treatment table, an ice machine, and a few free weights. Like in other professions, the more tools available for use, the more effective the practitioner can be, as long as there is an understanding of how those tools are used most effectively.

Supervising personnel   In an athletic training environment, the quality and efficiency of the assistants and athletic training students in carrying out their specific responsibilities is absolutely essential.[17] The person who supervises these assistants has a responsibility to design a reasonable work schedule that is consistent with other commitments and responsibilities they have outside the training room. It is the responsibility of the head athletic trainer to provide an environment in which assistants and athletic training students can continually learn and develop professionally.[3] The supervision of athletic training students necessitates constant visual and auditory interaction and the ability to physically intervene on behalf of the athlete or student.

Establishing policies for the operation of an athletic training program   Although the athletic trainer must be able to easily adjust and adapt to a given situation, it is essential that specific policies, procedures, rules, and regulations be established to ensure smooth and consistent day-to-day operation of the athletic training program. A plan should be established for emergency management of injury. Appropriate channels for referral after injury and emergency treatment should be used consistently.

Policies and procedures must be established and implemented that reduce the likelihood of exposure to infectious agents by following universal precautions, which can prevent the transmission of infectious diseases (see Chapter 2).

Professional Responsibilities

The athletic trainer should assume personal responsibility for continuously expanding his or her own knowledge base and expertise within the chosen field. This professional development may be accomplished by attending continuing education programs offered at state, district, and national meetings. Athletic trainers must also routinely review professional journals and consult current textbooks to stay abreast of the most up-to-date techniques. The athletic trainer should also make an effort to be involved professionally with national, regional, or state organizations that are committed to enhancing continued growth and development of the profession.

The athletic trainer as an educator   The athletic trainer must take time to help educate athletic training students. The continued success of any profession lies in its ability to educate its students. Education should not simply be a responsibility, it should be a priority.

To be an effective educator, the athletic trainer needs an understanding of the basic principles of learning and methods of classroom instruction. The athletic trainer should seek and develop competence in presenting information to students through the use of a variety of instructional techniques.[33] The athletic training educator should also make an effort to stay informed about the availability of relevant audiovisual aids, multimedia, newsletters, journals, workshops, and seminars that can enhance the breadth of the students' educational experience.[81] The athletic trainer must also be able to evaluate student knowledge and competencies through the development and construction of appropriate tests.[3] The athletic training educator should also assume

1-5

Critical Thinking E x e r c i s e

A young athletic trainer has taken his first job at All-American High School. The school administrators are extremely concerned about the number of athletes who get hurt playing various sports. They have charged the athletic trainer with the task of developing an athletic training program that can effectively help prevent the occurrence of injury to athletes in all sports at that school.

? What actions can the athletic trainer take to reduce the number of injuries and to minimize the risk of injury in the competitive athletes at that high school?

some responsibility for helping the students secure a professional position following graduation. Guiding the athletic training student in constructing an appropriate resume will help in this effort.

Students of athletic training must be given a sound academic background in a curriculum that stresses the competencies that are outlined in this chapter and presented in detail throughout this text. They must be able to translate the theoretical base presented in the classroom into practical application in a clinical setting if they are to be effective in treating patients.[17] The athletic training educator accomplishes this application by organizing appropriate laboratory and/or clinical experiences to evaluate the students' clinical competencies.[18] Certainly the clinical instructor can have a significant impact on the development of the athletic training student.[42]

Promoting the Profession   The athletic trainer must also educate the general public, in addition to a large segment of the various allied medical health care professions, as to exactly what athletic trainers are and the scope of their roles and responsibilities. This education is perhaps best accomplished by organizing workshops and clinics in athletic training, holding professional seminars, meeting with local and community organizations, publishing research in scholarly journals, and most important, doing a good and professional job of providing health care to the injured athlete.

The athletic trainer as a counselor   The athletic trainer should take responsibility for informing parents and coaches about the nature of a specific injury and how it may affect the ability of the athlete to compete. The athletic trainer should be concerned primarily with counseling and advising the athlete not only with regard to prevention, rehabilitation, and treatment of specific injuries but also on any matter that might be of help to the athlete.[49,50] Perhaps one of the most rewarding aspects of working as an athletic trainer can be found in the relationships that the trainer develops with individual athletes.

During the period of time that athletes are competing, the athletic trainer has the opportunity to get to know them very well on a personal basis because he or she spends a considerable amount of time with them. Athletes often develop a degree of respect and trust in the athletic trainer's judgment that carries over from their athletic life into their personal life. It is not uncommon for an athletic trainer to be asked questions about a number of personal matters, at which point he or she crosses a bridge from athletic trainer to friend and confidant. This considerable responsibility is perhaps best handled by first listening to the problems, presenting several options, and then letting the athlete make his or her own decision. Certainly, the role of counselor and advisor cannot be taken lightly.[69,70]

The athletic trainer as a researcher   As the athletic training profession continues to gain credibility as an allied health care profession, it is essential that athletic trainers work to enhance their visibility and credibility by engaging in research and scholarly publication.[75] Certainly not everyone who works as an athletic trainer, in every employment setting, would be expected to engage in research as part of their job responsibilities. Most often, the research that is published in professional journals is conducted by individuals who are program directors, faculty members, or doctoral students employed in colleges and universities.[72] These individuals along with graduate students seeking masters degrees at most NATA-approved graduate athletic training education programs, are required to conduct research either as part of their job description or as a requirement for attaining their degree. It is likely that as the numbers of educators, academicians, and graduate students continue to increase there will be more and more scholarly papers being submitted for publication in professional journals.[76] Regardless of whether an individual possesses the inclination or the ability to conduct research, each certified athletic trainer must at the very least take responsibility for developing some comprehension of basic research design and statistical analysis and thus be able to interpret and evaluate new research. The athletic training profession cannot continue to move forward unless its members generate its own specific body of knowledge.[64]

Personal Qualities of the Athletic Trainer

An athletic trainer's personal qualities:
- Stamina and ability to adapt
- Empathy
- Sense of humor
- Ability to communicate
- Intellectual curiosity
- Ethics

There is probably no field of endeavor that can provide more work excitement, variety of tasks, and personal satisfaction than athletic training. A person contemplating going into this field must love sports and must enjoy the world of competition, in which there is a level of intensity seldom matched in any other area.

An athletic trainer's personal qualities, not the facilities and equipment, determine his or her success. Personal qualities are the many characteristics that identify individuals in regard to their actions and reactions as members of society. Personality is a complex mix of the many characteristics that together give an image of the individual to those with whom he or she associates. The personal qualities of athletic trainers are important, because they in turn work with many complicated and diverse personalities. Although no attempt has been made to establish a rank order, the qualities discussed in the following paragraphs are essential for a good athletic trainer.

Stamina and Ability to Adapt

As a member of a helping profession, the athletic trainer is subject to burnout.

Athletic training is not the field for a person who likes an 8-to-5 job. Long, arduous hours of often strenuous work will sap the strength of anyone not in the best of physical and emotional health. Athletic training requires abundant energy, vitality, and physical and emotional stability.[70] Every day brings new challenges and problems that must be solved. The athletic trainer must be able to adapt to new situations with ease.[20] A problem that can happen in any helping profession and does on occasion occur among athletic trainers is burnout. This problem can be avoided if addressed early.

A problem with burnout   The term *burnout* is commonly used to describe feelings of exhaustion and disinterest toward work.[27] Clinically, burnout is most often associated with the helping professions; however, it is seen in athletes and other types of individuals engaged in physically or emotionally demanding endeavors.[14] Most persons who have been associated with sports have known athletes, coaches, or athletic trainers who just drop out.[15] Such workers have become dissatisfied with and disinterested in the profession to which they have dedicated a major part of their lives. Signs of burnout include excessive anger, blaming others, guilt, being tired and exhausted all day, sleep problems, high absenteeism, family problems, and self-preoccupation.[27] Athletic trainers who have high levels of perceived stress tend to experience higher emotional exhaustion and depersonalization and lower levels of personal accomplishment.[34] Persons experiencing burnout may cope by consuming drugs or alcohol.

The very nature of athletic training is one of caring about and serving the athlete. When the emotional demands of work overcome the professional's resources to cope, burnout may occur. Too many athletes to care for, the expectations of coaches to return an injured athlete to action, difficulties in caring for chronic conditions, and personality conflicts involving athletes, coaches, physicians, or administrators can leave the athletic trainer physically and emotionally drained at the end of the day. Sources of emotional drain include little reward for one's efforts, role conflicts, lack of autonomy, and a feeling of powerlessness to deal with the problems at hand. Commonly, the professional athletic trainer is in a constant state of high emotional arousal and anxiety during the working day.

Individuals entering the field of athletic training must realize that it is extremely demanding. Even though the field is often difficult, they must learn that they cannot be "all things to all people." They must learn to say no when their health is at stake, and they must make leisure time for themselves beyond their work.[16] Perhaps most important, athletic trainers must make time to spend with their family, friends, and loved ones.

Empathy

Empathy refers to the capacity to enter into the feeling or spirit of another person.[77] Athletic training is a field that requires both the ability to sense when an athlete is in distress and the desire to alleviate that stress.

Sense of Humor

Many athletes rate having a sense of humor as the most important attribute that an athletic trainer can have. Humor and wit help release tension and provide a relaxed atmosphere. The athletic trainer who is too serious or too clinical will have problems adapting to the often lighthearted setting of the sports world.

Communication

Athletic training requires a constant flow of both oral and written communication. As an educator, psychologist, counselor, therapist, and administrator, the athletic trainer must be a good communicator.

Intellectual Curiosity

The athletic trainer must always be a student. The field of athletic training is so diverse and ever changing that it requires constant study. The athletic trainer must have an active intellectual curiosity. Through reading professional journals and books, communicating with the team physician, and attending professional meetings, the athletic trainer stays abreast of the field.

Ethical Practice

The athletic trainer must act at all times with the highest standards of conduct and integrity.[29,75] To ensure this behavior, NATA has developed a code of ethics, which was approved at the NATA annual symposium in 1993,[55] and subsequently has been expanded. The five basic ethics principles are as follows:
1. Members shall respect the rights, welfare, and dignity of all individuals.
2. Members shall comply with the laws and regulations governing the practice of athletic training.
3. Members shall accept the responsibility for the exercise of sound judgment.
4. Members shall maintain and promote high standards in the provision of services.
5. Members shall not engage in conduct that constitutes a conflict of interest or that adversely reflects on the profession.

Members who act in a manner that is unethical or unbecoming to the profession can ultimately lose their certification.

Professional Memberships

It is essential that an athletic trainer become a member of and be active in professional organizations. Such organizations are continuously upgrading and refining the profession. They provide an ongoing source of information about changes occurring in the profession and include NATA, district associations within NATA, various state athletic training organizations, and ACSM. Some athletic trainers are also physical therapists. Increasingly, physical therapists are becoming interested in working with physically active individuals. Physical therapists and athletic trainers often have a good working relationship.

As a professional, the athletic trainer must be a member of and be active in professional organizations.

The Athletic Trainer and the Athlete

The major concern of the athletic trainer should always be the athlete. If it were not for athletes, the physician, the coach, and the athletic trainer would have nothing to do in sports. It is essential to realize that decisions made by the physician, coach, and athletic trainer ultimately affect the athlete. Athletes are often caught in the middle between coaches telling them to do one thing and medical staff telling them to do something else. Thus the injured athlete must always be informed and made aware of the why, how, and when that collectively dictate the course of an injury rehabilitation program.

The athletic trainer should make it a priority to educate the student-athlete about injury prevention and management. Athletes should learn about techniques of training and conditioning that may reduce the likelihood of injury. They should be well informed about their injuries and taught how to listen to what their bodies are telling them to prevent reinjury.

The Athletic Trainer and the Athlete's Parents

In the secondary school setting, the athletic trainer, must also take the time to explain to and inform the parents about injury management and prevention.[28] With an athlete of secondary school age, the parents' decisions regarding health are must be of primary consideration.

In certain situations, particularly at the high school and junior high levels, many parents will insist that their child be seen by their family physician rather than by the individual who may be designated as the team physician. It is also likely that the choice of a physician that the athlete can see will be dictated by the parents' insurance plan (IC, HMO, PPO). This creates a situation in which the athletic trainer must work and communicate with many different "team physicians." The opinion of the family physician must be respected even if the individual has little or no experience with injuries related to sports.

The coach, athletic trainer, and team physician should make certain that the athlete and his or her family are familiar with the Health Insurance Portability and Accountability Act (HIPAA), which regulates how individuals who have health information about an athlete can share that information with others and not be in violation of the privacy rule.[36,37] HIPAA was created to protect a patient's privacy and limit the number of people who could gain access to the athlete's medical records. HIPAA regulations will be discussed in more detail in Chapter 2.

RESPONSIBILITIES OF THE TEAM PHYSICIAN

In most situations, the athletic trainer works primarily under the supervision of the team physician, who is ultimately responsible for directing the total health care of the athlete (Figure 1-4). In cooperation with the team physician, the athletic trainer must make decisions that ultimately have a direct effect on the athlete who has sustained an injury.

From the viewpoint of the athletic trainer, there are a number of roles and responsibilities that the team physician should assume with regard to injury prevention and the health care of the athlete.[45,68] (See *Focus Box:* "Duties of the team physician.")

Figure 1-4

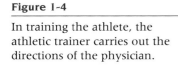

In training the athlete, the athletic trainer carries out the directions of the physician.

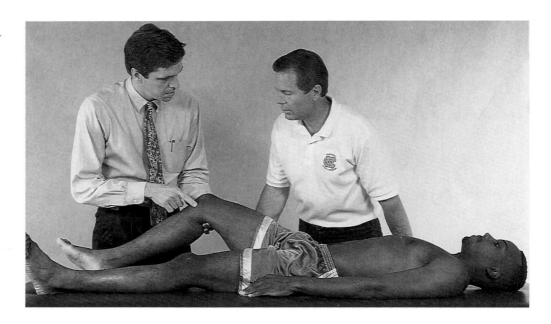

The Physician and the Athletic Trainer

The physician should be a supervisor and an advisor to the athletic trainer. However, the athletic trainer must be given flexibility to function independently in the decision-making process and must often act without the advice or direction of the physician. Therefore it is critical that the team physician and the athletic trainer share philosophical opinions regarding injury management and rehabilitation programs; this cohesion will help minimize any discrepancies or inconsistencies that may exist. Most athletic trainers would prefer to work with rather than for a team physician.

Compiling Medical Histories

The team physician should be responsible for compiling medical histories and conducting physical examinations for each athlete, both of which can provide critical information that may reduce the possibility of injury. Preparticipation screening done by both the athletic trainer and the physician are important in establishing baseline information to be used for comparison should injury occur during the season.

Diagnosing Injury

The team physician should assume responsibility for diagnosing an injury and should be keenly aware of the program of rehabilitation as designed by the athletic trainer after the diagnosis. Athletic trainers should be capable of doing an accurate initial evaluation after acute injury. Input from that evaluation may be essential to the physician, who may not see the patient for several hours or perhaps days after the injury. However, the physician has been trained specifically to diagnose injuries and to make recommendations to the athletic trainer for treatment based on that diagnosis. The athletic trainer, with a sound background in injury rehabilitation, designs and supervises an effective rehabilitation scheme. The closely related yet distinct roles of the physician and the athletic trainer require both cooperation and close communication if they are to be optimized.

Team physicians must have absolute authority in determining the health status of an athlete who wishes to participate in the sports program.

Deciding on Disqualification and Return to Play

The physician determines when a recommendation should be made that an athlete be disqualified from competition on medical grounds and must have the final say as to

---

≋ *Focus*

Duties of the team physician

- Seeing that a complete medical history of each athlete is compiled and is readily available
- Determining through a physical examination the athlete's health status
- Diagnosing and treating injuries and other illnesses
- Directing and advising the athletic trainer about health matters
- Acting, when necessary, as an instructor to the athletic trainer, assistant athletic trainer, and student athletic trainers about special therapeutic methods, therapeutic problems, and related procedures
- If possible, attending all games, athletic contests, scrimmages, and practices
- Deciding when, on medical grounds, athletes should be disqualified from participation and when they may be permitted to reenter competition
- Serving as an advisor to the athletic trainer and the coach and, when necessary, as a counselor to the athlete
- Working closely with the school administrator, school dentist, athletic trainer, coach, and health services personnel to promote and maintain consistently high standards of care for the athlete

when an injured athlete may return to activity.[35] Any decision to allow an athlete to resume activity should be based on recommendations from the athletic trainer. An athletic trainer often has an advantage in that he or she knows the injured athlete well, including how the athlete responds to injury, how the athlete moves, and how hard to push to return the athlete safely to activity. The physician's judgment must be based not only on medical knowledge but also on knowledge of the psychophysiological demands of a particular sport.[74]

Attending Practices and Games

A team physician should make an effort to attend as many practices, scrimmages, and competitions as possible. This attendance obviously becomes difficult at an institution that has twenty or more athletic teams. Thus the physician must be readily available should the athletic trainer (who generally is at most practices and games) require consultation or advice.

If the team physician cannot attend all practice sessions and competitive events or games, it is sometimes possible to establish a plan of rotation involving a number of physicians. In this plan, any one physician needs to be present at only one or two activities a year. The rotation plan has proved practical in situations in which the school district is unable to afford a full-time physician or has so limited a budget that it must ask for volunteer medical coverage. In some instances, the attending physician is paid a per-game stipend.

Commitment to Sports and the Athlete

Most important, the team physician must have a strong love of sports and must be generally interested in and concerned about the young people who compete. Colleges and universities typically employ someone to act as a full-time team physician. High schools most often rely on a local physician who volunteers his or her time. To serve as a team physician for the purpose of enhancing social standing in the community can be a frustrating and potentially dangerous situation for everyone involved in the athletic program.

When a physician is asked to serve as a team physician, arrangements must be made with the employing educational institution about specific required responsibilities. Policies must be established regarding emergency care, legal liability, facilities, personnel relationships, and duties.[23] It is essential that the team physician at all times promotes and maintains consistently high-quality care for the athlete in all phases of the sports medicine program.

Academic Program Medical Director

Accredited athletic training education programs must have a physician medical director who is responsible for the coordination and guidance of the medial aspects of the program. The medical director—who may or may not be the team physician—should provide input to the program's educational content and provide classroom, laboratory, and/or clinical instruction.

RESPONSIBILITIES OF THE COACH

It is critical for the coach to understand the specific roles and responsibilities of each individual who could potentially be involved in the sports medicine team. This becomes even more critical if there is no athletic trainer to oversee the health care and the coach is forced to assume this responsibility. Individual states differ significantly in the laws that govern what nonmedical personnel can and cannot do when providing health care. **It is the responsibility of coaches to clearly understand the limits of their ability to function as health care provider in the state where they are employed.**

The coach is directly responsible for preventing injuries by seeing that athletes have undergone a preventive injury conditioning program. The coach must ensure that sports equipment, especially protective equipment, is of the highest quality and is

All head and assistant coaches should be certified in CPR and first aid.

Figure 1-5

The coach is directly responsible for preventing injuries in his or her sport.

properly fitted. The coach must also make sure that protective equipment is properly maintained.[66] A coach must be keenly aware of what produces injuries in his or her particular sport and what measures must be taken to avoid them (Figure 1-5). When necessary, a coach should be able to apply proper first aid. This knowledge is especially important in serious head and spinal injuries. **All coaches (both head and assistants) should be certified in cardiopulmonary resuscitation** (CPR) by either the American Red Cross, the American Heart Association, or the National Safety Council. **Coaches should also be certified in first aid** by the American Red Cross or the National Safety Council.[64] For the coach, obtaining these certifications is important so that he or she is able to provide correct and appropriate health care for the injured athlete. But it is also true that not having these certifications can potentially have some negative legal implications for the coach and his or her employer.

It is essential that a coach have a thorough understanding of the skill techniques and environmental factors that may adversely affect the athlete. Poor biomechanics in skill areas such as throwing and running can lead to overuse injuries of the arms and legs, whereas overexposure to heat and humidity may cause death. Just because a coach is experienced in coaching does not mean that he or she knows proper skill techniques. Coaches must engage in a continual process of education to further their knowledge in their particular sport. When a sports program or specific sport is without an athletic trainer, the coach very often takes over this role.

Coaches work closely with athletic trainers; therefore both must develop an awareness of and an insight into each other's problems so that they can function effectively. The athletic trainer must develop patience and must earn the respect of the coaches so that his or her judgment in all medical matters is fully accepted. In turn, the athletic trainer must avoid questioning the abilities of the coaches in their particular fields and must restrict opinions to athletic training matters. To avoid frustration and hard feelings, the coach must coach, and the athletic trainer must conduct athletic training matters. In terms of the health and well-being of the athlete, the physician and the athletic trainer have the last word. This position must be backed at all times by the athletic director.

This is not to say, however, that the coach should not be involved with the decision-making process. For example, during the time the athlete is rehabilitating an injury, there may be drills or technical instruction sessions that the athlete can participate in that will not exacerbate the existing problem. Thus the coach, the athletic trainer, and the team physician should be able to negotiate what the athlete can and cannot do safely in the course of a practice.

Any personal relationship takes some time to grow and develop. The relationship between the coach and the athletic trainer is no different. The athletic trainer must demonstrate to the coach his or her capability to correctly manage an injury and guide the course of a rehabilitation program. It will take some time for the coach to develop trust and confidence in the athletic trainer. The coach must understand that what the athletic trainer wants for the athlete is exactly the same as what the coach wants—to get an athlete healthy and back to practice as quickly and safely as possible.

REFERRING THE ATHLETE TO OTHER MEDICAL AND NONMEDICAL SUPPORT SERVICES AND PERSONNEL

In certain situations, an athlete may require treatment from or consultation with a variety of both medical and nonmedical services or personnel other than the athletic trainer or team physician. After the athletic trainer consults with the team physician about a particular matter, either the athletic trainer or the team physician can arrange for appointments as necessary. When referring an athlete for evaluation or consultation, the athletic trainer must be aware of the community-based services available and the insurance or managed care plan coverage available for that athlete.

A number of support health services and personnel may be used by a sports program. These services and personnel may include school health services; nurses; physicians including orthopedists, neurologists, internists, family medicine specialists, ophthalmologists, pediatricians, psychiatrists, dermatologists, gynecologists, and osteopaths; dentists; podiatrists; physician's assistants; physical therapists; strength and conditioning specialists; biomechanists; exercise physiologists; nutritionists; sports psychologists; massage therapists; social workers; emergency medical specialists; sports chiropractors; orthotists/prosthetists; equipment personnel; or referees.

School Health Services

Colleges and universities maintain school health services that range from a department operating with one or two nurses and a physician available on a part-time basis to an elaborate setup comprised of a full complement of nursing services with a staff of full-time medical specialists and complete laboratory and hospital facilities. At the secondary-school level, health services are usually organized so that one or two nurses conduct the program under the direction of the school physician, who may serve a number of schools in a given area or district. This organization poses a problem, because it is often difficult to have qualified medical help at hand when it is needed. Local policy determines the procedure for referral for medical care. If such policies are lacking, the athletic trainer should see to it that an effective method is established for handling all athletes requiring medical care or opinion. The ultimate source of health care is the physician. The effectiveness of athletic health care service can be evaluated only to the extent to which it meets the following criteria:

1. Availability at every scheduled practice or contest of a person qualified and delegated to render emergency care to an injured or ill participant
2. Planned access to a physician by phone or nearby presence for prompt medical evaluation of the health care problems that warrant this attention
3. Planned access to a medical facility, including plans for communication and transportation

The Nurse

As a rule, the nurse is not usually responsible for the recognition and management of sports injuries. However, in certain institutions that lack an athletic trainer, the nurse

Support personnel concerned with the athlete's health and safety:
- Nurse
- School health services
- Physicians
- Dentist
- Podiatrist
- Physician's assistant
- Biomechanist
- Strength and conditioning coach
- Sport psychologist
- Physical therapist
- Exercise physiologist
- Nutritionist
- Massage Therapist
- Social worker
- Emergency Medical Specialist
- Sports Chiropractors
- Orthotist/Prosthetist
- Equipment Personnel
- Referees

Focus

Specializations for physicians

Orthopedist The orthopedist is responsible for treating injuries and disorders of the musculoskeletal system. Many colleges and universities have a team orthopedist on their staff.

Neurologist A neurologist specializes in treating disorders of and injuries to the nervous system. There are common situations in athletics in which consultation with a neurologist would be warranted, such as for head injury or peripheral nerve injury.

Internist An internist is a physician who specializes in the practice of internal medicine. An internist treats diseases of the internal organs by using measures other than surgery.

Family Medicine Physician A physician who specializes in family medicine supervises or provides medical care to all members of a family. Many team physicians in colleges and universities and particularly at the high-school level are engaged in family practice.

Ophthalmologist Physicians who manage and treat injuries to the eye are ophthalmologists. An optometrist evaluates and fits patients with glasses or contact lenses.

Pediatrician A pediatrician cares for or treats injuries and illnesses that occur in young children and adolescents.

Psychiatrist Psychiatry is a medical practice that deals with the diagnosis, treatment, and prevention of mental illness.

Dermatologist A dermatologist should be consulted for problems and lesions occurring on the skin.

Gynecologist A gynecologist is consulted in cases where health issues in the female athlete are of primary concern.

Osteopath An osteopath is a trained medical doctor who uses manual therapy and manipulation of joints extensively in their practice.

may assume the majority of the responsibility in providing health care for the athlete. The nurse works under the direction of the physician and in liaison with the athletic trainer and the school health services.

Physicians

A number of physicians with a variety of specializations can aid the sports medicine team in treating the athlete (see *Focus Box:* "Specializations for physicians").

Dentist

The role of team dentist is somewhat analogous to that of team physician. He or she serves as a dental consultant for the team and should be available for first aid and emergency care. Good communication between the dentist and the athletic trainer should ensure a good dental program. There are three areas of responsibility for the team dentist:

1. Organizing and performing the preseason dental examination
2. Being available to provide emergency care when needed
3. Conducting the fitting of mouth protectors

Podiatrist

Podiatry, the specialized field dealing with the study and care of the foot, has become an integral part of sports health care. Many podiatrists are trained in surgical procedures, foot biomechanics, and the fitting and construction of orthotic devices for the shoe. Like the team dentist, a podiatrist should be available on a consulting basis.

Physician's Assistant

Physician's assistants (PAs) are trained to assume some of the responsibilities for patient care traditionally done by a physician. They assist the physician by conducting preliminary patient evaluations, arranging for various hospital-based diagnostic tests, and dispensing appropriate medications. A number of athletic trainers have also become PAs in recent years.

Physical Therapist

Some athletic trainers use physical therapists to supervise the rehabilitation programs for injured athletes while the athletic trainer concentrates primarily on getting a player ready to practice or compete. In many sports medicine clinics, athletic trainers and physical therapists work in teams, jointly contributing to the supervision of a rehabilitation program. A number of athletic trainers are also physical therapists. A physical therapist can be certified as a Sports Certified Specialist (SCS). The physical therapist is prepared to treat a variety of different patient populations with different types of injuries, while the athletic trainer is focused primarily on treating and working with the physically active population.

Strength and Conditioning Specialist

Many colleges and universities and some high schools employ full-time strength coaches to advise athletes on training and conditioning programs. Athletic trainers should routinely consult with these individuals and advise them about injuries to a particular athlete and exercises that should be avoided or modified relative to a specific injury. A strength coach can be certified by the National Strength and Conditioning Association as a CSCS.

Biomechanist

An individual who possesses some expertise in the analysis of human motion can also be a great aid to the athletic trainer. The biomechanist uses sophisticated video and computer-enhanced digital analysis equipment to study movement. By advising the athlete, coach, and athletic trainer on matters such as faulty gait patterns or improper throwing mechanics, the biomechanist can reduce the likelihood of injury to the athlete.

Exercise Physiologist

The exercise physiologist can significantly influence the athletic training program by giving input to the trainer regarding training and conditioning techniques, body composition analysis, and nutritional considerations.

Nutritionist

Increasingly, individuals in the field of nutrition are becoming interested in athletics. Some large athletic training programs engage a nutritionist as a consultant who plans eating programs that are geared to the needs of a particular sport. He or she also assists individual athletes who need special nutritional counseling.

Sports Psychologist

The sports psychologist can advise the athletic trainer on matters related to the psychological aspects of the rehabilitation process. The way the athlete feels about the injury and how it affects his or her social, emotional, intellectual, and physical dimensions can have a substantial effect on the course of a treatment program and how quickly the athlete may return to competition. The sports psychologist uses different intervention strategies to help the athlete cope with injury. Sport psychologists can seek certification through the Association for the Advancement of Sport Psychology.

Massage Therapist

A qualified sports massage therapist should have training and experience in all areas of sports massage. The American Massage Therapy Association National Sports Massage

Team (NSMT) consists of massage therapists who have passed rigorous written and practical examinations in event sports massage. Team members are qualified to apply their specialized knowledge and skills in the precompetition and post-competition stages of athletic events. Members of the AMTA NSMT are trained to perform the highest level of sports massage therapy techniques while working cooperatively with other health care professionals.

Social Worker

Occasionally, athletes or their families may need a referral for social support services within the community. Social workers can offer counseling and support for a variety of personal or family difficulties, such as substance abuse, family planning, and other social concerns.

Emergency Medical Specialist (EMS)

These individuals are indispensable in providing transport to the injured athlete to a medical care facility.

Sports Chiropractors

Chiropractors make use of spinal extremity manipulation techniques to treat most musculoskeletal conditions.

Orthotist/Prosthetist

These individuals custom fit, design and construct braces, orthotics and support devices based on physician prescriptions.

Equipment Personnel

Sports equipment personnel are becoming specialists in the purchase and proper fitting of protective equipment. They work closely with the coach and the athletic trainer.

Referees

Referees must be highly knowledgeable regarding rules and regulations, especially those that relate to the health and welfare of the athlete. They work cooperatively with the coach and the athletic trainer. They must be capable of checking the playing facility for dangerous situations and equipment that may predispose the athlete to injury. They must routinely check athletes to ensure that they are wearing adequate protective pads.

EMPLOYMENT SETTINGS FOR THE ATHLETIC TRAINER

Opportunities for employment as an athletic trainer have changed dramatically during recent years.[4] Since the 1950s the traditional employment setting for the athletic trainer has been in an athletic training room at the college, university, or professional level. During the 1980s—primarily because of intensive public relations efforts by NATA—the majority of jobs available were at the high-school level.[12] Today the largest percentage of certified athletic trainers are employed in sports medicine clinics or hospitals.

The employment opportunities for athletic trainers continue to become more diverse, expanding to corporate/industrial settings and the military; even NASA and NASCAR employ certified athletic trainers.[39] Other athletic trainers work as physician extenders, and still others are employed in medical supply/equipment sales.

Athletic trainers work in a number of different settings:
- Secondary schools
- School districts
- Colleges and universities
- Professional sports
- Sports medicine clinics
- Corporate/Industrial settings
- The military
- Physician extenders
- Medical supply/equipment sales
- College/university educator
- Researcher
- Administrator

Secondary Schools

It would be ideal to have certified athletic trainers serve every secondary school in the United States.[45] Many of the physical problems that occur later from improperly managed sports injuries could be avoided initially if proper care from an athletic trainer had been provided. Many times a coach does all his or her own athletic training, although in some cases, a coach is assigned additional athletic training responsibilities

and is assisted by a student athletic trainer.[7] If a secondary school hires an athletic trainer, it is very often in a faculty-trainer capacity. This individual is usually employed as a teacher in one of the school's classroom disciplines and performs athletic training duties on a part-time or extracurricular basis.[65] Thus, student athletic trainers who hope to find a position in a secondary-school setting should be encouraged to seek teacher certification.[20] In this instance compensation usually is on the basis of released time from teaching, a stipend as a coach, or both.[38] Salaries for the secondary-school athletic trainer are continuing to improve.[5]

Another means of obtaining high-school or community-college athletic training coverage is using a certified graduate student from a nearby college or university. The graduate student receives a graduate assistantship with a stipend paid by the secondary school or community college. In this situation both the graduate student and the school benefit.[26] However, this practice may prevent a school from employing a certified athletic trainer on a full-time basis.

In 1995, the NATA adopted the official statement on hiring athletic trainers in secondary schools that appears in the *Focus Box:* "Secondary school official statement."

Based on a proposal from the American Academy of Pediatrics, in 1998 the American Medical Association adopted a policy calling for certified athletic trainers to be employed in all high-school athletic programs. Although this policy was simply a recommendation and not a requirement, it was a very positive statement supporting the efficacy of athletic trainers in the secondary schools.

Following the adoption of this policy, NATA provided a second official statement on certified athletic trainers in high schools which appears in the *Focus Box:* "Official statement on certified athletic trainers in high schools."

School Districts

Some school districts have found it effective to employ a centrally placed certified athletic trainer. In this case the athletic trainer, who may be full- or part-time, is a nonteacher who serves a number of schools. The advantage is savings; the disadvantage is that one individual cannot provide the level of service usually required by a typical school.

Colleges or Universities

At the college or university level, the athletic training positions vary considerably from institution to institution. In smaller institutions, the athletic trainer may be a half-time teacher in physical education and half-time athletic trainer. In some cases, if the athletic trainer is a physical therapist rather than a teacher, he or she may spend part of the time in the school health center and part of the time in athletic training. Increasingly at the college level, athletic training services are being offered to members of the general student body who participate in intramural and club sports. In most colleges

**Focus**

> **Official statement on certified athletic trainers in high schools**
>
> The National Athletic Trainers' Association (NATA) is confident the best way to protect the public is to allow only Board of Certification certified athletic trainers and state licensed athletic trainers to practice as athletic trainers. NATA is not alone in these beliefs. The American Medical Association has stated that certified athletic trainers should be used as part of a high school's medical team. The American Academy of Family Physicians agrees and states on its website, "The AAFP encourages high schools to have, whenever possible, a BOC certified or registered/licensed athletic trainer as an integral part of the high school athletic program."
>
> In states with athletic training regulation, allowing other individuals to continue practicing as athletic trainers without a valid state license or BOC certification places the public at risk. Athletic trainers have unique education and skills that allow them to properly assess and treat acute and traumatic injuries in high school athletics. In coordination with the team physician, they routinely make decisions regarding the return-to-play status of student-athletes. Other allied health professionals are not qualified to perform these tasks. Finally, most situations encountered by athletic trainers should not be left to a coach or layperson who does not have the necessary education and medical and emergency care training.

and universities, the athletic trainer is full-time, does not teach, works in the department of athletics, and is paid by the institution.

In February 1998, the NATA created the Task Force to Establish Appropriate Medical Coverage for Intercollegiate Athletics (AMCIA) to establish recommendations for the extent of appropriate medical coverage to provide the best possible health care for all intercollegiate student-athletes. Essentially the AMCIA task force made recommendations for the number of athletic trainers who should be employed at a college or university based on a mathematical model created by a number of variables existing at that particular institution. These guidelines were revised and updated in 2003. (For directions to determine the recommended number of athletic trainers, consult *Recommendations and Guidelines for Appropriate Medical Coverage for Intercollegiate Athletics*.)[56]

In August 2003, the NCAA Committee on Competitive Safeguards and Medical Aspects of Sports (CSMAS) recommended that NCAA institutions "examine the adequateness of their sports medicine coverage."[46] In particular, whether the increased time demands placed on certified athletic trainers reduces their ability to effectively provide high quality care to all student-athletes. After reviewing the *Recommendations and Guidelines*, the CSMAS "encouraged NCAA institutions to reference the NATA AMCIA in their assessment of the adequateness of their sports medicine coverage . . . and share the responsibility to protect student athlete health and safety through appropriate medical coverage of its sports and supporting activities."

Professional Teams

The athletic trainer for professional sports teams usually performs specific team athletic training duties for six months out of the year; the other six months are spent in off-season conditioning and individual rehabilitation. The athletic trainer working with a professional team is involved with only one sport and is paid according to contract, much like a player. Playoff and championship money may add substantially to the yearly income.

Sports Medicine Clinics

For years, sports medicine clinics have been considered a nontraditional setting for employment as an athletic trainer. Today, more athletic trainers are employed in

1-6

Critical Thinking Exercise

An athletic trainer has taken a job working in a sports medicine clinic that has four physical therapists and two physical therapy assistants. This clinic has never employed an athletic trainer before, and there is some uncertainty among the physical therapists as to exactly what role the athletic trainer will play in the function of the clinic.

? How does the role of the athletic trainer working in the clinic differ from the responsibilities of the athletic trainer working in a university setting?

sports medicine clinics than in any other employment setting. The role of the athletic trainer varies from one clinic to the next. Most clinical athletic trainers see patients with sports-related injuries during the morning hours in the clinic. In the afternoons, athletic trainers' services are contracted out to local high schools or small colleges for game or practice coverage. For the most part, private clinics have well-equipped facilities in which to work, and salaries for their trainers are generally somewhat higher than in the more traditional settings. In many sports medicine clinics, the athletic trainer may be responsible for formulating a plan to market or promote athletic training services offered by that clinic throughout the local community.[31]

Corporate/Industrial Settings

It is becoming relatively common for corporations or industries to employ athletic trainers to oversee fitness and injury rehabilitation programs for their employees.[1] The athletic trainer working in an industrial setting must have a sound understanding of the principles and concepts of workplace ergonomics, including inspecting, measuring, and observing dimensions of the work space, as well as specific tasks that are performed at the workstation.[24] Once a problem has been identified, the athletic trainer must be able to implement proper adjustments to workplace ergonomics to reduce or minimize possible risks for injury. In addition to these responsibilities, athletic trainers may be assigned to conduct wellness programs and provide education and individual counseling. It is likely that many job opportunities will exist for the athletic trainer in corporate/industrial settings in the next few years.

The Military

The United States military, particularly the Navy, the Marines, and the Army, have demonstrated increased emphasis on injury prevention and health care for the troops.[51] Treatment centers are being developed which closely resemble and, to a great extent, function as athletic training rooms. The centers are staffed by sports medicine physicians, orthopedists, athletic trainers, physical therapists, and support staff. Injured personnel are seen as soon as possible by an athletic trainer, who evaluates an injury, makes decisions on appropriate referral, and begins an immediate rehabilitation program. There are currently over 100 athletic trainers in the military either as active duty or reserve personnel.[51] Occasionally there are some contract positions available. It is likely that the role of the athletic trainer in the military will increase substantially over the next several years.

Physician Extender

While virtually all athletic trainers work under the supervision of a physician, those employed as a physician extender actually work in the physician's office where patients of all ages and backgrounds are being treated. The educational preparation for athletic trainers allows them to function in a variety of domains, including injury prevention, evaluation, management and rehabilitation, health education, nutrition, training and conditioning, organizing preparticipation physicals, and maintaining essential documentation.[52] When working directly in the presence of a physician, the athletic trainer can bill the patient for services provided and expect that they will be reimbursed for their services by third-party payers. While the contact with only the physically active population may not be as great as in other employment settings, the physician extender can expect regular hours, little weekend or evening responsibilities, opportunity for growth, and in general, better pay. All of these factors collectively make physician extender positions attractive for the athletic trainer. Potentially there could be many new jobs created as physicians become more and more aware of the value that an athletic trainer, functioning as a physician extender, can provide to their medical practice.[25]

Treating the Physically Active

In these various employment settings, athletic trainers no longer treat only athletes but instead a physically active population. Physically active individuals may include not only what we have traditionally referred to as athletes in their late teens or twenties, but also both adolescents and older adults who engage in physical activities either recreationally or competitively. *Physically active* individuals engage in athletic, recreational or occupational activities that require physical skills and utilize strength, power, endurance, speed, flexibility, range of motion, or agility. *Physical activity* consists of athletic, recreational or occupational activities that require physical skills and utilize strength, power, endurance, speed, flexibility, range of motion, or agility.

The Adolescent Athlete

Children have always been physically active. But in today's society, playtime or physical activity for many adolescents is focused on organized competition. Certainly many relevant sociological issues arise in answer to questions such as, how old should children be when they begin to compete, or when should a child begin training and conditioning? Skeletally immature adolescent athletes present a particular challenge to the athletic trainer involved in some aspect of their health care. Young athletes cannot be dealt with either physically or emotionally in the same manner as adult athletes. Thus the athletic trainer must be aware of patterns of growth and development and all the special considerations that this process brings with it.

The Aging Athlete

Aging involves a lifelong series of changes in physiological and performance capabilities. These capabilities increase as a function of the growth process throughout adolescence, peak sometime between the ages of eighteen and forty years, then steadily decline with increasing age. However, this decline may be due as much to the sociological constraints of aging as to biological effects. In most cases, after age thirty-five, qualities such as muscular endurance, coordination, and strength tend to decrease. Recovery from vigorous exercise requires a longer amount of time. Regular physical activity, however, tends to delay and in some cases prevent the appearance of certain degenerative processes.

It is possible for individuals to maintain a relatively high level of physiological functioning if they maintain an active lifestyle. Consistent participation in vigorous physical activity can result in improvement of many physiological parameters regardless of age. The effects of exercise on the aging process and the long-term health benefits of exercise have been convincingly documented.

Generally, exercise is considered a safe activity for most individuals. ACSM has recommended that individuals under age forty who are apparently healthy with no significant risks can generally begin an exercise program without further medical evaluation, as long as the exercise program progresses gradually and moderately and no unusual signs or symptoms develop.[1] Individuals who are over age forty or who are at high risk should have a complete medical examination and undergo an exercise test before beginning an exercise program.

RECOGNITION AND ACCREDITATION OF THE ATHLETIC TRAINER AS AN ALLIED HEALTH PROFESSIONAL

In June 1990 the American Medical Association (AMA) officially recognized athletic training as an allied health profession. The primary purpose of this recognition was to have the profession of athletic training recognized in the same context as other allied health professions and to be held to similar professional and educational expectations, as well as to allow for accreditation of educational programs.[45] Once overseen by NATA's Professional Education Committee, overseeing athletic training education programs became the responsibility of the AMA. The AMA's Committee on Allied Health Education and Accreditation (CAHEA) was charged with the responsibility of developing the requirements (Essentials and Guidelines) for the structure and function of academic programs to prepare entry-level athletic trainers. The Joint Review Committee on Athletic Training (JRC-AT) was originally charged with the responsibility of evaluating athletic training educational programs seeking accreditation and making recommendations to CAHEA as to whether those educational programs met the necessary

1-7

Critical Thinking Exercise

A second-semester college sophomore has decided that she is interested in becoming a certified athletic trainer. She happens to be in an institution that offers an advanced master's degree in athletic training yet does not offer an entry-level CAAHEP-approved curriculum.

? How can this student most effectively achieve her goal of becoming a certified athletic trainer?

criteria to become an accredited program in athletic training education. The JRC-AT is made up of representatives from the NATA, the American Academy of Pediatrics, the American Orthopedic Society for Sports Medicine, and the American Academy of Family Physicians. As of 1993, all entry-level athletic training education programs became subject to the CAHEA accreditation process.[18]

In June 1994, CAHEA was dissolved and was replaced immediately by the Commission on Accreditation of Allied Health Education Programs (CAAHEP). The CAAHEP is recognized as an accreditation agency for allied health education programs by the Council for Higher Education Accreditation (CHEA). Entry level bachelors and masters athletic training education programs that were at one time approved by NATA, and subsequently accredited by CAHEA, are now accredited by CAAHEP (through 2005).

In 2003, JRC-AT leadership decided that the profession of athletic training had matured and outgrown the structure and constraints of CAAHEP and that the profession would be better served if the JRC-AT became an independent accrediting agency like those in the other allied health professions. This change meant that instead of the JRC-AT making accreditation recommendations to CAAHEP, the JRC-AT would accredit athletic training education programs. The JRC-AT has begun the transition away from CAAHEP and will seek affiliation with the CHEA once it becomes independent. CHEA is a private, nonprofit national organization that coordinates accreditation activity in the United States. Formed in 1996, its mission is to promote academic quality through formal recognition of higher education accreditation bodies and to work to advance self-regulation through accreditation. Recognition by CHEA affirms that standards and processes of accrediting organizations are consistent with the quality, improvement, and accountability expectations that CHEA has established. Through recognition by CHEA, the JRC-AT will be in the same context/level as is CAAHEP and other national accreditors. CAAHEP accreditation will be discontinued in 2006, at which time the JRC-AT will change its name to the Committee for Accreditation of Athletic Training Education (CAATE). CAATE accreditation will begin at that point and the recognition process from CHEA will commence in 2007.

The JRC-AT also joined the Association of Specialized Professional Accreditors (ASPA), a membership organization. ASPA's members are specialized and professional accreditors. ASPA-member accreditors set national educational standards for entry into more than forty specialized disciplines or defined professions and work with higher education and government officials to enhance education and accreditation.

The effects of CHEA accreditation are not limited to just educational aspects. In the future, this recognition may potentially affect regulatory legislation, the practice of athletic training in nontraditional settings, and insurance considerations. This recognition will continue to be a positive step in the development of the athletic training profession.

Accredited Athletic Training Education Programs

As of February 2005, approximately 300 institutions across the United States offered entry-level athletic training education programs that have been accredited by CAAHEP, while more than 50 others were in the process of seeking CAAHEP accreditation. In addition, thirteen graduate programs in athletic training are accredited by the NATA Graduate Review Committee. The NATA-accredited Advanced Graduate Athletic Training Education Programs are designed to enhance the academic and clinical preparation of individuals who are already certified athletic trainers or those who have completed the requirements for certification.

Specialty Certifications

NATA is in the process of developing specialty certifications to further enhance the professional development of certified athletic trainers by expanding their scope of practice. Entry-level athletic training education programs provide a general educational foundation, whereas specialty certifications build on this foundation. Specialty certifications in athletic training will be voluntary areas of post-graduate study, and certification in areas more advanced than entry level and will ultimately enhance the marketability of certified athletic trainers. Seven specialty certification areas have been proposed: business practice, medical care management, occupational health, wellness, pediatric/adolescent health, adult/geriatric health, and special health populations. Once a specialty certification has been developed and approved, candidates will have to complete experiential requirements and pass a standardized examination.

Other Health Care Organization Accrediting Agencies

Although CAAHEP is the accrediting organization for athletic training, there are other organizations that accredit various health care agencies and organizations.

Joint Commission on Accreditation of Healthcare Organizations

The Joint Commission on Accreditation of Healthcare Organizations (JCAHO) is the nation's largest standards-setting and accrediting body in health care. JCAHO accredits more than 18,000 health care organizations and programs in the United States. Its mission is to improve the quality of care provided to the public through the provision of health care accreditation and related services that support performance improvement in health care organizations.

Commission on Accreditation of Rehabilitation Facilities (CARF)

The Commission on Accreditation of Rehabilitation Facilities (CARF) is an accrediting organization that promotes quality rehabilitation services by establishing standards of quality for organizations to use as guidelines in developing and offering their programs or services to consumers. CARF uses the standards to determine how well an organization is serving its consumers and how it can improve. CARF standards are developed with input from consumers, rehabilitation professionals, state and national organizations, and funders. Every year the standards are reviewed and new ones are developed to keep pace with changing conditions and current consumer needs.

REQUIREMENTS FOR CERTIFICATION AS AN ATHLETIC TRAINER

An athletic trainer who is certified by NATA is a highly qualified paramedical professional educated and experienced in dealing with the injuries that occur with participation in sports. Candidates for certification are required to have an extensive background of both formal academic preparation and supervised practical experience in a clinical setting, according to CAAHEP guidelines.[30] The guidelines listed in *Focus Box:* "Board of Certification requirements for certification as an athletic trainer" have been established by the Board of Certification (BOC).[56] The Board of Certification changed its official name in 2004. Previously the Board of Certification was referred to as the National Athletic Trainers Association Board of Certification. As of 2004 the only way that a candidate can become certified is by completing an entry-level athletic training education program that has been accredited by CAAHEP.

The Certification Examination

Once the requirements have been fulfilled, applicants are eligible to sit for the certification examination.[32] The certification examination has been developed by the BOC in conjunction with an independent examination development and administration company and is currently administered five times each year at various locations throughout the United States.[47,59] The examination consists of three sections: a written portion, a practical portion, and a simulation portion. In 2006 all sections of the certification examination will transition to a computer-based exam (CBE). The examination tests for knowledge and skill in six major domains: (1) prevention of athletic injuries; (2) clinical evaluation and diagnosis; (3) immediate care of injuries; (4) treatment, rehabilitation, and reconditioning of athletic injuries; (5) organization and administration; and (6) professional responsibility. Successful performance on the certification examination leads to BOC certification as an athletic trainer with the credential of **ATC.** (For the latest information on certification requirements, contact the BOC website at www. bocact.org.) BOC certification is a prerequisite for licensure in most states.

ATC
Certified Athletic Trainer

Focus

Board of Certification requirements for certification as an athletic trainer

Purpose of Certification

The Board of Certification (BOC) was incorporated in 1989 to provide a certification program for entry-level athletic trainers and recertification standards for certified athletic trainers. The purpose of this entry-level certification program is to establish standards for entry into the profession of athletic training. Additionally, the BOC has established the continuing education requirements that a certified athletic trainer must satisfy to maintain current status as a BOC-certified athletic trainer.

The Process

Annually, the Board of Certification reviews the requirements for certification eligibility and standards for continuing education. Additionally, the Board reviews and revises the certification examination in accordance with the test specifications of the BOC Role Delineation Study that is reviewed and revised every five years. The Board of Certification uses a criterion-referenced passing point for the anchor form of the examination. Each new examination version is equated to the anchor version to ensure that candidates are not rewarded or penalized for taking different versions of the examination.

Procedures for Certification

Requirements for Candidacy for the BOC Certification Examination

1. Candidates must successfully complete an entry-level athletic training program accredited by CAAHEP.*
2. Proof of graduation (an official transcript) at the baccalaureate level from an accredited college or university located in the United States of America. Graduates of foreign universities may petition for a substitution of this degree requirement. Such a request will be evaluated at the candidate's expense by an independent consultant selected by the BOC.

   Students who have begun their last semester or quarter of college are permitted to apply to take the certification examination prior to graduation provided all academic and clinical requirements of the section used for candidacy have been satisfied. A candidate will be permitted to take the examination on the date closest to his or her date of graduation.
3. Endorsement of the examination application by the CAAHEP* Accredited Program Director.
4. Proof of current certification in CPR (Note: CPR certification must be current at the time of initial application and at any subsequent exam retake registration).

*Beginning in 2006 programs will be accredited by CAATE.

Continuing Education Requirements

To ensure the ongoing professional growth and involvement by the certified athletic trainer, BOC has established requirements for continuing education.[9,60]

The purposes of the requirements are to encourage certified athletic trainers to continue to obtain current professional development information, to explore new knowledge in specific content areas, to master new athletic training-related skills and techniques, to expand approaches to effective athletic training, to further develop professional judgment, and to conduct professional practice in an ethical and appropriate manner.

To maintain certification, all certified athletic trainers must document a minimum of eighty continuing education units (CEUs) attained during each three-year recertification term. CEUs may be awarded for attending symposiums, seminars, workshops,

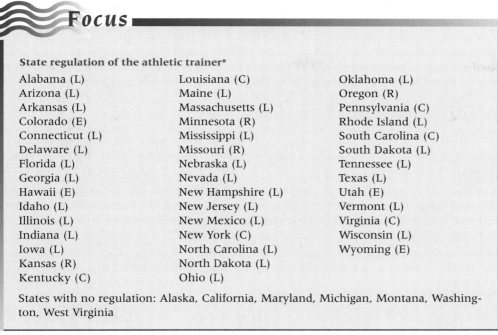

Focus

State regulation of the athletic trainer*

Alabama (L)	Louisiana (C)	Oklahoma (L)
Arizona (L)	Maine (L)	Oregon (R)
Arkansas (L)	Massachusetts (L)	Pennsylvania (C)
Colorado (E)	Minnesota (R)	Rhode Island (L)
Connecticut (L)	Mississippi (L)	South Carolina (C)
Delaware (L)	Missouri (R)	South Dakota (L)
Florida (L)	Nebraska (L)	Tennessee (L)
Georgia (L)	Nevada (L)	Texas (L)
Hawaii (E)	New Hampshire (L)	Utah (E)
Idaho (L)	New Jersey (L)	Vermont (L)
Illinois (L)	New Mexico (L)	Virginia (C)
Indiana (L)	New York (C)	Wisconsin (L)
Iowa (L)	North Carolina (L)	Wyoming (E)
Kansas (R)	North Dakota (L)	
Kentucky (C)	Ohio (L)	

States with no regulation: Alaska, California, Maryland, Michigan, Montana, Washington, West Virginia

*As of January 2005

E = Exempt from existing licensure standards; C = certification; R = registration; L = licensure. For additional information about individual state regulating boards, contact http://www.nata.org/ on the Web.

or conferences; serving as a speaker, panelist, or certification exam model; participating in the United States Olympic Committee (USOC) program; authoring a research article in a professional journal; authoring or editing a textbook; completing a Journal of Athletic Training quiz; completing postgraduate course work; and obtaining CPR, first aid, or EMT certification. All certified athletic trainers must also demonstrate proof of CPR certification at least once during the three-year term.

STATE REGULATION OF THE ATHLETIC TRAINER

During the early 1970s, the leadership of NATA realized the necessity of obtaining some type of official recognition by other medical allied health organizations of the athletic trainer as a health care professional. Laws and statutes specifically governing the practice of athletic training were nonexistent in most states.

Based on this perceived need, the athletic trainers in many states organized their efforts to secure recognition by seeking some type of regulation of the athletic trainer by state licensing agencies. To date, this ongoing effort has resulted in forty-three of the fifty states enacting some type of regulatory statutes governing the practice of athletic training.[54]

Rules and regulations governing the practice of athletic training vary tremendously from state to state. Regulation may be in the form of certification, registration, licensure, or exemption (see *Focus Box:* "State regulation of the athletic trainer").

For the most part, legislation regulating the practice of athletic training has been positive and to some extent protects the athletic trainer from litigation. However, in some instances, regulation has restricted the limits of practice for the athletic trainer. The leadership of NATA has strongly encouraged athletic trainers in all states to seek licensure.

Licensure

Licensing limits the practice of athletic training to those who have met minimal requirements established by a state licensing board. Through this licensing board the

Forms of state regulation:
■ Certification
■ Registration
■ Licensing
■ Exemption

1-8

Critical Thinking Exercise

A certified athletic trainer moves to a different state to take a new job. She discovers that in that state the ATC must be licensed to practice athletic training. Since she was registered as an athletic trainer in the other state, she wonders if she must go through the process of getting a license in her new state.

state limits the number of individuals who can perform functions related to athletic training as dictated by the practice act. Requirements for licensure vary from state to state, but most require a specific educational and training background, evidence of good moral character, letters of recommendation from current practitioners, and minimal acceptable performance on a licensing examination. Licensure is the most restrictive of all the forms of regulation. Individuals who are providing health care services to an athlete cannot call themselves athletic trainers in that particular state unless they have met the requirements for licensure.[13]

Certification

State certification as an athletic trainer differs from certification as an athletic trainer by BOC. An individual who has passed the BOC exam does not automatically obtain a state certification. Although certification does not restrict the use of the title of athletic trainer to those certified by the state, it can restrict the performance of athletic training functions to only those individuals who are state certified. State certification indicates that a person possesses the basic knowledge and skills required in the profession and has passed a certification examination. Many states that offer certification use the BOC exam as a criterion for granting state certification.[13]

Registration

Registration means that before an individual can practice athletic training, he or she must register in that state. Registration means that the individual has paid a fee for being placed on an existing list of practitioners. The state may or may not have a mechanism for assessing competency. However, registration does prevent individuals who are not registered with the state from calling themselves athletic trainers.[13]

Exemption

Exemption means that a state recognizes that athletic trainers perform functions similar to those of other licensed professions (e.g., physical therapy) yet still allows them to practice athletic training despite the fact that they do not comply with the practice acts of other regulated professions. Exemption is most often used in those states in which there are not enough practitioners to warrant the formation of a state regulatory board.[13]

THE PHYSICAL THERAPIST AND THE ATHLETIC TRAINER

As the certified athletic trainer continues to gain recognition among health care professionals, interest on the part of many individuals with backgrounds in other health-related professions likewise continues to increase. In particular, it is not unusual to find a physical therapist interested in sports and athletics who is working toward certification as an athletic trainer.[44] Conversely, the certified athletic trainer who is interested in working with patients outside the athletic population is often looking toward licensure as a physical therapist.

Historically, the relationship between athletic trainers and physical therapists has been less than cooperative. Many reasons underlie this lack of cooperation, but the main reason over the years has been failure to clarify the roles of each group in injury rehabilitation.

Athletic trainers have been trained to deal specifically with those injuries that occur in sports, whereas physical therapists have a much broader expertise in injury rehabilitation across many different patient populations. The physical therapist who has not been exposed to the athletic training environment is as inefficient in that setting as is the athletic trainer working with stroke patients in a rehabilitation setting.

The academic curricula required for the athletic trainer and for the physical therapist are similar, particularly in the basic sciences and in the clinical methods courses. The physical therapy curriculum provides a significantly broader background in treating patients of all ages who have a wide variety of physical problems. However, the physical therapist functioning in an athletic training environment must receive additional clinical instruction beyond that which is typically offered in a physical therapy curriculum. Otherwise the period of adjustment and orientation to a nontraditional physical therapy setting is often difficult.

The individual who achieves both certification as an athletic trainer and licensure as a physical therapist is extremely well qualified to function in various sports medicine settings, including both private clinics and colleges and universities. Today, the person who holds a dual credential is in high demand in the job market.

Certification as a Sports Physical Therapist

In the late 1970s the sports physical therapy section of the American Physical Therapy Association (APTA) began identifying competencies specific to the practice of physical therapy in a sports medicine setting. In 1985 the Professional Examination Service was contracted by APTA to develop a specialty examination based on specifically identified competencies.[44]

Candidates for the examination must fulfill the minimal criteria as outlined in the document *Minimal Criteria for Therapist to Sit for the Initial Certification Examination*. These criteria include the completion of a required number of hours of clinical practice in patient care, education, and administration. In addition, written evidence of competency in these areas and research must be submitted.

FUTURE DIRECTIONS FOR THE ATHLETIC TRAINER

The athletic training profession has made remarkable gains during the past decade. Today, certified athletic trainers possess a strong, highly structured academic background in addition to a substantial amount of closely supervised clinical experience in their chosen area of expertise. The athletic trainer continues to gain credibility and recognition as a health care professional trained to deal with injuries that occur in the physically active population. Certainly recognition as an allied health profession by the American Medical Association in 1990 was a major milestone for the profession. In the future, this recognition may potentially affect regulatory legislation, the practice of athletic training in nontraditional settings, and third-party reimbursement. Without question this recognition will continue to be a positive step in the development of the athletic training profession.

Future directions for athletic training will be determined by the efforts of NATA and its membership and will likely include the following:

- Ongoing reevaluation, revision, and reform of athletic training education programs will continue to be a priority.
- The JRC-AT (CAATE in 2006) will become the accrediting agency for entry-level athletic training education programs, and recognition of the JRC-AT by the Council for Higher Education Accreditation will further enhance the credibility of athletic training as an allied health profession.
- Third-party reimbursement for athletic training services provided will gradually become the rule rather than the exception as more and more third-party payers understand what athletic trainers do.
- Eventually every state will regulate the practice of athletic training, and there will be a move to standardize the state practice acts making them more consistent from state to state.
- Athletic trainers will seek and achieve specialty certifications to better assist athletic trainers in expanding their breadth and scope of practice. Initially many will become recognized as Performance Enhancement Specialists for the physically active.
- More and more secondary schools will employ certified athletic trainers.
- While the largest percentage of athletic trainers currently work in clinical settings, there will be an increase in the number of clinics owned and staffed by athletic trainers.

- There will be an increase in the recognition of the athletic trainer as a physician extender who can be incorporated into the daily operations of a physician's office.
- There is great potential for expansion of athletic trainers in the military.
- The potential exists for increasing job opportunities for certified athletic trainers in industrial and corporate settings.
- There will be opportunities for athletic trainers to work with children and teenagers as sport performance specialists.
- There will be increased opportunities for athletic trainers working in fitness and wellness settings.
- As the general population continues to age there will be an increase in opportunities for athletic trainers to work with the elderly physically active population.
- Athletic trainers must continue to enhance their visibility through research efforts and scholarly publication.[28,29,53] Certified athletic trainers must strive to develop some comprehension of basic research design and statistical analysis to be able to interpret new research.[63]
- Athletic trainers should continue to make themselves available for local and community meetings to discuss the health care of the athlete.
- The certified athletic trainer will become recognized internationally as a health care provider and will be found in Canada, South America, Europe, Asia, and Australia.
- Most important, athletic trainers must continue to focus on injury prevention and to provide appropriate, high-quality health care to physically active individuals who are injured while participating in a sport.

SUMMARY

- Athletic training is a specialization within sports medicine, with its major concern being the health and safety of athletes. The primary athletic training team consists of the coach, the athletic trainer, and the team physician. The coach must ensure that both the equipment that is worn and the environment are the safest possible, that all injuries and illnesses are properly cared for, that skills are properly taught, and that conditioning is at the highest level.
- The athletic trainer must be a highly educated, well-trained professional. The athletic trainer must be certified and, if possible, have a state license to practice. The successful athletic trainer loves sports and the competitive environment. He or she must have an abundance of vitality and emotional stability, empathy for people who are in physical or emotional pain, a sense of humor, the ability to communicate, and a desire to learn. All the athletic trainer's actions must follow the highest standards of conduct.
- The team physician can be in varied specializations. Team physicians, depending on their time commitment to a specific sports program, can perform a variety of responsibilities, including conducting the preparticipation health examination; diagnosing and treating illnesses and injuries; advising and teaching the athletic training staff; attending games, scrimmages, and practices; and counseling the athlete about health matters.

Websites

National Athletic Trainers' Association: http://www.nata.org/
This site describes the athletic training profession, how to become involved in athletic training, and the role of an athletic trainer.

American Sports Medicine Institute: http://www.asmi.org/
The American Sports Medicine Institute's mission is to improve through research and education the understanding, prevention, and treatment of sports-related injuries. In addition to stating this mission, the site provides access to current research and journal articles.

American Academy of Orthopaedic Surgeons:
http://www. aaos.org/
This site provides some information for the general public as well as information to its members. The public information is in the form of patient education brochures; the site also includes a description of the organization and a definition of orthopedics.

The American Orthopaedic Society for Sports Medicine:
http://www.sportmed.org/
This site is dedicated to educating health care professionals and the general public about sports medicine. The site provides access to the American Journal of Sports Medicine *and a wide variety of links to related sites.*

Athletic Trainer.com: http://athletictrainer.com/
This website is specifically designed to give information to athletic trainers, including students, and those interested in athletic training. It provides access to interesting journal articles and links to several informative websites.

NCAA: http://www.ncaa.org/
This site gives general information about the NCAA and the publications that the NCAA circulates. This site may be useful for those working in the collegiate setting.

NATA Education Council: http://www.cewl.com
This site contains information pertaining to the academic preparation of the athletic trainer.

Board of Certification: http://www.bocatc.org
This site provides up-to-date information on requirements for certification as well as a listing of certification test dates and sites.

National Organization for Competency Assurance:
http://www.noca.org
This site explains the function of NOCA in getting quality standards for credentialing organizations.

National Commission for Certifying Agencies:
http://www.nccaa.org
This site details the function of the NCCA in serving as a national accreditation body for private certification organizations.

Solutions to *Critical Thinking* EXERCISES

1-1 The student should be able to find all necessary information by simply going to the Internet and contacting these organizations via the World Wide Web.

1-2 Athletic training students must be like sponges, willing to soak up whatever knowledge they can attain to make themselves more efficient in performing their chosen profession. That knowledge may come from attending classes, reading books or journals, attending lectures and conferences, and actively learning the tricks of the trade during the hours spent in the training room and on the field. Students must be able to apply theoretical knowledge to a practical setting if they are to be competent clinicians.

1-3 Although emergency medical technicians are qualified to handle emergency situations, an athletic trainer is able to provide comprehensive health care to the All American High School athletes. An athletic trainer is responsible for the prevention of athletic injuries; the recognition, evaluation, and assessment of injuries; and the treatment and rehabilitation of athletic injuries.

1-4 Ultimately the team physician is responsible for making that decision. However, that decision must be made based on collective input from the athletic trainer, the coach, and the athlete. Remember that everyone on the sports medicine team has the same ultimate goal—to return the athlete to full competitive levels as quickly and safely as possible.

1-5 To help prevent injury, the athletic trainer should (1) arrange for physical examinations and preparticipation screenings to identify conditions that predispose an athlete to injury; (2) ensure appropriate training and conditioning of the athletes; (3) monitor environmental conditions to ensure safe participation; (4) select and maintain properly fitting protective equipment; and (5) educate parents, coaches, and athletes about the risks inherent to sport participation.

1-6 To some extent, the role of the clinical athletic trainer is dictated by that state's regulation of the practice of athletic training. Certainly the clinical and academic preparation of athletic trainers should enable them to effectively evaluate an injured patient and guide that patient through a rehabilitative program. The athletic trainer should treat only those individuals who have sustained injury related to physical activity and not patients with neurological or orthopedic conditions. The athletic trainer may work part-time in the clinic and then cover one or several high schools around the area. The athletic trainer and physical therapist should work as a team to maximize the effectiveness of patient care.

1-7 As of 2004, everyone must graduate from a CAAHEP-accredited program to become a certified athletic trainer. Therefore she must transfer to an institution that offers an entry-level CAAHEP-approved program in which she must complete course work and directly supervised clinical experience.

1-8 The laws regarding regulation of the certified athletic trainer vary from state to state. It is likely that she will have to apply for a license through the athletic training licensing board in her new state to get a new license to practice in that state. It is not likely that there is reciprocity between the two states.

REVIEW QUESTIONS AND CLASS ACTIVITIES

1. How do modern athletic training and sports medicine compare with early Greek and Roman approaches to the care of the athlete?
2. What professional organizations are important to the field of athletic training?

3. Why is athletic training considered a team endeavor? Contrast the coach's, athletic trainer's, and team physician's roles in athletic training.

4. What qualifications should the athletic trainer have in terms of education, certification, and personality?

5. What are the various employment opportunities available to the athletic trainer?

6. Explain the criteria for becoming certified as an athletic trainer.

7. Discuss the methods by which different states regulate the practice of athletic training.

REFERENCES

1. Albensi RJ: The impact of health problems affecting worker productivity in a manufacturing setting. *Athletic Therapy Today* 8(3):13, 2003.

2. American College of Sports Medicine: 1987 annual meeting, Las Vegas, Nev, May 27–30, 1987.

3. Anderson M, Larson G, Luebe J: Student and supervisor perceptions of the quality of supervision in athletic training education, *J Ath Train* 32(4):328, 1997.

4. Arnold B, Gansneder B, VanLunen B: Importance of selected athletic trainer employment characteristics in collegiate, sports medicine clinic, and high school settings, *J Ath Train* 33(3):254, 1998.

5. Arnold B, VanLunen B, Gansneder B: 1994 athletic trainer employment and salary characteristics, *J Ath Train* 31(3):215, 1996.

6. Barefield S, McCallister S: Social supports in the athletic training room: athletes' expectations of staff and student athletic trainers, *J Ath Train* 32(4):333, 1997.

7. Berry J: High school athletic therapy. Part 2, *Athletic Therapy Today* 3(1):47, 1998.

8. Bilik SE: *The trainer's bible,* New York, 1956, Reed (originally published 1917).

9. Board of Certification, Continuing Education Office: *Continuing education file 2003–2005,* Dallas, 2003, BOC.

10. Board of Certification: *Role delineation study,* 5th edition, Raleigh, NC, 2004, Castle Worldwide.

11. Brukner P, Khan, K: Sports medicine: the team approach. In Brukner P, editor: *Clinical sports medicine,* ed 2, Sydney, 2002, McGraw-Hill.

12. Buxton B, Okasaki E, Ho K: Legislative funding of athletic training positions in public secondary schools, *J Ath Train* 30(2):115, 1995.

13. Campbell D, Konin J: Regulation of athletic training. In Konin J: *Clinical athletic training,* Thorofare, NJ, 1997, Slack.

14. Campbell D, Miller M, Robinson W: The prevalence of burnout among athletic trainers, *Ath Train* 20(2):110, 1985.

15. Capel S: Attrition of athletic trainers, *Ath Train* 25(1):34, 1990.

16. Capel S: Psychological and organizational factors related to burnout in athletic trainers, *Ath Train* 21(4):322, 1986.

17. Coker CA: Consistency of learning styles of undergraduate athletic training students in the traditional classroom versus the clinical setting *J Ath Train* 35(4):441, 2000.

18. Committee on Allied Health Education and Accreditation: *Essentials and guidelines for an accredited educational program for athletic trainers,* Chicago, 1992, American Medical Association.

19. Cramer C: A preferred sequence of competencies for athletic training education programs, *Ath Train* 25(2):123, 1990.

20. Cuppett M, Latin R: A survey of physical activity levels of certified athletic trainers, *J Ath Train* 37(3):281, 2002.

21. Curtis N, Helion J, Domsohn M: Student athletic trainer perceptions of clinical supervisor behaviors: a critical incident study, *J Ath Train* 33(3):249, 1998.

22. Curtis N: Teacher certification among athletic training students, *J Ath Train* 30(4):349, 1995.

23. Editorial: The ethics of selecting a team physician. "Show me the money" shouldn't be part of the process, *Sports Med Digest* 23(4):37, 2001.

24. Fícca M: Injury prevention in the occupational setting, *Athletic Therapy Today* 8(3):6, 2003.

25. Finkam S: The athletic trainer or athletic therapist as physician extender, *Athletic Therapy Today* 7(3):50, 2002.

26. Fuller D: Critical thinking in undergraduate athletic training education, *J Ath Train* 32(3):242, 1997.

27. Geick J: Athletic training burnout: a case study, *Ath Train* 21(1):43, 1986.

28. Gould TE: Secondary-school administrators' knowledge and perceptions of athletic training, *Athletic Therapy Today* 8(1):57, 2003.

29. Graber G: Ethics 101, *Athletic Therapy Today* 8(2):6, 2003.

30. Grace P: Milestones in athletic trainer certification, *J Ath Train* 34(3):285, 1999.

31. Gray R: The role of the clinical athletic trainer. In Konin J: *Clinical athletic training,* Thoroughfare, NJ, 1997, Slack.

32. Harrelson G, Gallaspy J, Knight H: Predictors of success on the NATABOC certification examination, *J Ath Train* 32(4):323, 1997.

33. Harrelson GL, Leaver-Dunn D, Wright KE: An assessment of learning styles among undergraduate athletic training students, *J Ath Train* 33(1):50, 1998.

34. Hendrix AE, Acevedo EO, Hebert E: An examination of stress and burnout in certified athletic trainers at division 1-A universities, *J Ath Train* 35(2):139, 2000.

35. Herring SA, Bergfeld J, Boyd J, et al: Sideline preparedness for the team physician: a consensus statement. *Med Sci Sports Exer* 33(5):846, 2001.

36. Hunt V: Meeting clarifies HIPAA regulation, *NATA News,* February: 10, 2003.

37. Jones D: HIPAA: friend or foe to athletic trainers? *Athletic Therapy Today* 8(2):17, 2003.

38. Kahanov L, Andrews L: A survey of athletic training employers' hiring criteria, *J Ath Train* 36(4):408, 2001.

39. Kirkland MK: A case study of athletic training at the Kennedy Space Center, *Athletic Therapy Today* 8(3):9, 2003.

40. Knight KL, Ingersoll CD: Developing scholarship in athletic training, *J Ath Train* 33(3):271, 1998.

41. Knight K: Research in athletic training: a frill or a necessity, *Ath Train* 23(3):212, 1988.

42. Laurent T, Weidner T: Clinical instructors and student athletic trainers' perceptions of helpful clinical instructor characteristics, *J Ath Train* 36(1):58–61, 2001.

43. Lyznicki JM, Riggs JA, Champion HC: Certified athletic trainers in secondary school: report of the Council on Scientific Affairs, American Medical Association, *J Ath Train* 34(3):272, 1999.

44. Malone T: Sports physical therapy specialization, *J Orthop Sports Phys Ther* 7(5):273, 1986.

45. Mathies A, Denegar C, Arnhold R: Changes in athletic training education as a result of changing from NATA-PEC to CAAHEP, *J Ath Train* 30(2):129, 1995.

46. Mitten M: Support for certified athletic trainers in intercollegiate athletics. Memorandum from National Collegiate Athletic Association, August 14, 1993.

47. McLean JL: Does the National Athletic Trainers' Association need a certification examination? *J Ath Train* 34(3):292, 1999.

48. Mellion MB, Walsh WM: The team physician. In Mellion MB, editor: *Sports medicine secrets,* Philadelphia, 1999, Hanley-Balfus.

49. Misasi S, Davis C, Morin G: Academic preparation of athletic trainers as counselors, *J Ath Train* 31(1):39, 1996.

50. Moulton M, Molstad S, Turner A: The role of counseling collegiate athletes, *J Ath Train* 32(2):148, 1997.

51. A closer look at the military setting, *NATA News* 12:30, 2003.

52. National Athletic Trainers' Association: *2001 Standards and Guidelines,* Dallas, 2001, National Athletic Trainers' Association.

53. What is the physician extender?, *NATA News* 1:12, 2004.

54. National Athletic Trainers' Association Governmental Affairs Committee: www.nata.org/members1/committees/gac/statereg boards.htm.

55. National Athletic Trainers' Association: NATA code of ethics, NATA, Dallas, 1995.

56. National Athletic Trainers' Association: *Recommendations and Guidelines for Appropriate Medical Coverage for Intercollegiate Athletics,* Dallas, 2001, National Athletic Trainers' Association.

57. National Athletic Trainers' Association Board of Certification: *Certification Update,* Winter: 5–6, 2000.

58. National Athletic Trainers' Association Board of Certification: *Role delineation study of the entry level athletic trainer certification examination,* Philadelphia, 2004, Davis.

59. National Athletic Trainers' Association Board of Certification: *Study guide for the NATABOC entry level athletic trainer certification examination,* Philadelphia, 1995, Davis.

60. National Athletic Trainers' Association Education Council: Athletic Training Educational Competencies ed 3, Dallas, 2003, National Athletic Trainers' Association.

61. O'Shea M: *A history of the National Athletic Trainers' Association,* Greenville, NC, 1980, National Athletic Trainers' Association.

62. Osternig L: Research in athletic training: the missing ingredient, *Ath Train* 23(3):323, 1988.

63. Pitney WA: Continuing education in athletic training: an alternative approach based on adult learning theory, *J Ath Train* 33(1):72, 1998.

64. Pitney W, Parker J: Qualitative inquiry in athletic training: principles, possibilities, and promises. *J Ath Train* 36(2):, 2001.

65. Prentice W, Mischler B: A national survey of employment opportunities for athletic trainers in the public schools, *Ath Train* 21(3):215, 1986.

66. Prentice W: The athletic trainer. In Mueller F, Ryan A, editors: *Prevention of athletic injuries: the role of the sports medicine team,* Philadelphia, 1991, Davis.

67. Ransone J, Dunn-Bennett L: Assessment of first-aid knowledge and decision making of high school athletic coaches, *J Ath Train* 34(3):267, 1999.

68. Rich BS: All physicians are not created equal: understanding the educational background of the sports medicine physician, *J Ath Train* 28(2):177, 1993.

69. Rock J, Jones M: A preliminary investigation into the use of counseling skills in support of rehabilitation from sport injury, *J Sport Rehabil* 11(4):284, 2002.

70. Shelley GA: Practical counseling skills for athletic therapists, *Athletic Therapy Today* 8(2):57, 2003.

71. Starkey C: Reforming athletic training education, *J Ath Train* 32(2):113, 1997.

72. Starkey C, Ingersoll C: Scholarly productivity of athletic training faculty members, *J Ath Train* 36(2):156, 2001.

73. Staurowsky E, Scriber K: An analysis of selected factors that affect the work lives of athletic trainers employed in accredited educational programs, *J Ath Train* 33(3):244, 1998.

74. Team physician consensus statement. *Med Sci Sports Exer* 32(4):877, 2002.

75. Turocy P: Survey research in athletic training: the scientific method of development and implementation, *J Ath Train* 37(4S):s174, 2002.

76. Turocy P: Overview of athletic training education research publications, *J Ath Train* 37(4S):s162, 2002.

77. Udermann BE: The effect of spirituality on health and healing: a critical review for athletic trainer, *J Ath Train* 35(2):194, 2000.

78. Velasquez BJ: Sexual harassment in the athletic training room: implications for athletic trainers, *Athletic Therapy Today* 8(2):20, 2003.

79. Vinci DM: Nutrition communication and counseling skills, *Athletic Therapy Today* 6(4):34, 2001.

80. Whitehill W, Norton P, Wright K: Navigating the library maze: introductory research and the athletic trainer, *J Ath Train* 31(1):50, 1996.

81. Wiksten D, Spanjer J, LaMaster K: Effective use of multimedia technology in athletic training education, *J Ath Train* 37(4S):s213, 2002.

82. Winterstein A: Organizational commitment among intercollegiate head athletic trainers: examining our work environment, *J Ath Train* 33(1):54, 1998.

ANNOTATED BIBLIOGRAPHY

Bilik SE: *The trainer's bible,* ed 9, New York, 1956, Reed.

   A classic book, first published in 1917, by a major pioneer in athletic training and sports medicine.

Cartwright L, Pittney W: *Athletic training for student assistants,* Champaign, IL, 1999, Human Kinetics.

   A practical guide for student athletic training assistants, including their roles and responsibilities within the sports medicine team.

Hannum S: *Professional behaviors in athletic training,* Slack, Thorofare, NJ, 2000.

   Focuses on essentials of effective career development. Addresses many of skills students will require to build their image as health care professionals, such as communication, critical thinking, networking, interpersonal skills, and recognition of cultural differences.

Mueller F, Ryan A: *Prevention of athletic injuries: the role of the sports medicine team,* Philadelphia, 1991, F.A. Davis.

   Provides an in-depth discussion of the various members of the sports medicine team.

National Athletic Trainers' Association Board of Certification: *Role delineation study,* ed 5, Philadelphia, 2004, F.A. Davis.

   Contains a complete discussion of the 2003 role delineation study that redefined the responsibilities of the athletic trainer.

National Athletic Trainers' Association: *Code of ethics 1993,* National Athletic Trainers' Association, Dallas, 1993, National Athletic Trainers' Association.

   Contains a revision of the previous code of ethics; includes ethical principles, membership standards, and certification standards.

National Athletic Trainers Association: *Far Beyond a Shoe Box: Fifty Years of the National Athletic Trainers' Association,* Dallas, 1999, National Athletic Trainers Association.

   An interesting text about the history of NATA that should be read by any student interested in athletic training as a career.

Van Ost L, Manfre K: *Athletic training student guide to success,* Slack, Thorofare, NJ, 2000.

   This text emphasizes the roles and responsibilities of the student athletic trainer necessary to make them successful as health care professionals.

Chapter 2

Health Care Administration in Athletic Training

When you finish this chapter you should be able to

- Establish a strategic plan for the athletic training program.
- Plan a functional, well-designed athletic training facility.
- Identify policies and procedures that should be enforced in the athletic training room.
- Explain budgetary concerns for ordering supplies and equipment.
- Explain the importance of the preparticipation physical examination.
- Construct the necessary records that must be maintained by the athletic trainer.
- Describe current systems for gathering data on injuries.

Operating an effective athletic training program requires careful organization and administration regardless of whether the setting is a high school, college, university, professional facility, or a clinical or industrial facility. Besides being a clinical practitioner, the athletic trainer must be an administrator who performs both managerial and supervisory duties. This chapter looks at the administrative tasks required of the athletic trainer for successful operation of the program, including facility design, policies and procedures, budget considerations, personnel management, administration of physical examinations, record keeping, and collecting injury data.

ESTABLISHING A SYSTEM FOR ATHLETIC TRAINING HEALTH CARE
Developing a Strategic Plan

Perhaps the first step in establishing an athletic training program is to determine why there is a need for such a program and what the function of this program should be within the total scope of the athletic program.[35] These two basic questions in the strategic planning process must be answered by administrators, athletic directors, or school boards who, in most cases, will ultimately be responsible for funding and supporting the athletic training program. The depth of the commitment from these decision makers toward providing quality health care will to a large extent determine the size of the staff, the size of the facility, and the scope of operation of the athletic training program. A clearly written mission statement will help focus the direction of the program and should be an outcome of the strategic planning process.[20]

Strategic planning for an athletic training program should involve many individuals including administrators, student-athletes, coaches, physicians, staff athletic trainers, parents, and community-based health leaders. Including many individuals in the planning process will help to secure allies who are committed to seeing the program succeed.[35]

Strategic planning should be an ongoing process that takes a critical look at the strengths and weaknesses of the program and then takes immediate action to correct deficiencies. The *WOTS UP* analysis—which looks at Weaknesses, Opportunities, Threats, and Strengths underlying planning[38]—is a useful and effective technique in strategic planning for existing athletic training programs.

WOTS UP Analysis
- Weaknesses
- Opportunities
- Threats
- Strengths

Developing a Policies and Procedures Manual

Once the strategic planning process is complete and some consensus has been reached by those involved in the process, the next step is to create a detailed policies and procedures manual for use by everyone who is involved with providing some aspect of health care for the athlete, including the athletic training staff and student trainers, team physicians, other allied health personnel, coaches, and administrators. *Policies* are clear and accurate written statements that identify the basic rules and principles (the what and why) used to control and expedite decision making. Policies are essential for operating the athletic training room. *Procedures* describe the process by which something is done (the how). The manual should include much of the information presented in the following section titled "Athletic Training Program Operations." In addition, if the institution's budget permits, an abbreviated version of this manual, outlining the rules for using the athletic training room, should be prepared and distributed to the athletes and their parents. *Focus Box:* "Policies and procedures manual" includes recommendations for topics to be included.

ATHLETIC TRAINING PROGRAM OPERATIONS

It is imperative that every athletic training program develop policies and procedures that carefully delineate the daily routine of the program.

> Every athletic training program must develop policies and procedures that carefully delineate the daily routine of the program.

The Scope of the Athletic Training Program

A major consideration in any athletic training program is to determine who is to be served by the athletic training staff. The individual athlete, the institution, and the community are considered.

The Athlete

The athletic trainer must decide the extent to which the athlete will be served. For example, will prevention and care activities be extended to athletes for the entire year, including summer and other vacations, or only during the competitive season? Also, the athletic trainer must decide what care will be rendered. Will it extend to all systemic illnesses or to just musculoskeletal problems?

The Institution

A policy must be established as to who, other than the athletes, will be served by the athletic training program. Often, legal concerns and the school liability insurance dictate who, beyond the athlete, is to be served. A policy should make it clear whether students other than athletes, athletes from other schools, faculty, and staff are to receive care. If so, how are they to be referred and medically directed? Also, it must be decided whether the athletic training program will act as a clinical setting for student athletic trainers.

The Community

A decision must be made as to which, if any, outside group(s) or people in the community will be served by the athletic training staff. Again, legality and the institution's insurance program must be taken into consideration when making this decision. If a policy is not delineated in this matter, outside people may abuse the services of the athletic training facility and staff.

Clinical and Corporate/Industrial Setting Considerations

The athletic trainer working in the clinical or corporate/industrial setting will likely be working with patients other than high school or college athletes. The scope of practice within an individual clinic may include pediatric, work hardening, orthopedic, or even the occasional neurological patient. Athletic trainers in the clinical setting should be assigned to work only with patient populations that may generally be classified as physically active. Clinical administrators should not require athletic trainers to treat other patient populations, because athletic trainers have no formal education or training geared toward those patients' problems.

Athletic trainers in the corporate/industrial setting, in addition to overseeing preventive and rehabilitation programs, are often asked to take on responsibility for employee fitness programs. Therefore a more advanced understanding of the principles of training and conditioning will be necessary (see Chapter 4).

Providing Coverage

Facility Personnel Coverage

A major concern of any athletic department is whether proper personnel coverage is provided for the athletic training facility and specific sports. If a school has a full-time athletic training staff, an athletic training facility could, for example, operate from 7 A.M. to 10 P.M. Mornings are commonly reserved for treatments and exercise rehabilitation; early afternoons are for treatment, exercise rehabilitation, and preparation for practice or a contest; and late afternoons and early evenings are spent in injury management. High schools with limited available supervision may be able to provide athletic training facility coverage only in the afternoons and during vacation periods.

Sports Coverage

Ideally, all sports should have a certified, or at least a student, athletic trainer in attendance at all practices and contests, both at home and away. Many colleges and universities have sufficient personnel to provide coverage to a variety of sports simultaneously. At the secondary-school level, however, only one or occasionally two athletic trainers may be available to cover every sport that the high school offers. Thus it is impossible for the athletic trainer to be in several places at one time. The athletic trainer in this difficult situation must make some decisions about where the greatest need for coverage is, based on the potential risk of a particular sport and the number of athletes involved.

Hygiene and Sanitation

Good hygiene and sanitation are essential for an athletic training program.

The practice of good hygiene and sanitation is of the utmost importance in an athletic training program. The prevention of infectious diseases is a direct responsibility of the athletic trainer, whose duty it is to see that all athletes are surrounded by the most hygienic environment possible and that each individual is practicing sound health habits. Chapter 14 discusses the management of bloodborne pathogens. The athletic trainer must be aware of and adhere to guidelines for the operation of an athletic care facility as dictated by the Occupational Safety and Health Administration (OSHA).

The Athletic Training Facility

The athletic training room should be used only for the prevention and care of sports injuries. Too often the athletic training facility becomes a meeting or club room for the coaches and athletes. Unless definite rules are established and practiced, room cleanliness and sanitation become an impossible chore. Unsanitary practices or conditions must not be tolerated. The following are some important athletic training room policies:

1. No cleated shoes are allowed. Dirt and debris tend to cling to cleated shoes; therefore cleated shoes should be removed before athletes enter the athletic training facility.
2. Game equipment is kept outside. Because game equipment such as balls and bats add to the sanitation problem, they should be kept out of the athletic training room. Coaches and athletes must be continually reminded that the athletic training room is not a storage room for sports equipment.
3. Shoes must be kept off treatment tables. Because of the tendency of shoes to contaminate treatment tables, they must be removed before any care is given to the athlete.
4. Athletes should shower before receiving treatment. The athlete should make it a habit to shower before being treated if the treatment is not an emergency. This procedure helps keep tables and therapeutic modalities sanitary.
5. Roughhousing and profanity should not be allowed. Athletes must be continually reminded that the athletic training facility is for injury care and prevention. Horseplay and foul language lower the basic purpose of the athletic training room.
6. No food or smokeless tobacco should be allowed.

General cleanliness of the athletic training room cannot be stressed enough. Through the athletic trainer's example, the athlete may develop an appreciation for cleanliness and in turn develop wholesome personal health habits. Cleaning responsibilities in most schools are divided between the athletic training staff and the maintenance crew. Care of permanent building structures and trash disposal are usually the responsibilities of maintenance, whereas the upkeep of specialized equipment falls within the province of the training staff.

The division of routine cleaning responsibilities may be organized as follows:

1. Maintenance crew
   a. Sweep floors daily.
   b. Clean and disinfect sinks and built-in tubs daily.
   c. Mop and disinfect hydrotherapy area twice a week.
   d. Refill paper towel and drinking cup dispensers as needed.
   e. Empty wastebaskets and dispose of trash daily.
2. Athletic training staff
   a. Clean and disinfect treatment tables daily.
   b. Clean and disinfect hydrotherapy modalities daily.
   c. Clean and polish other therapeutic modalities weekly.

The Gymnasium

Maintaining a clean environment in sports is a continual battle in the athletic training setting. Practices such as passing a common towel to wipe off perspiration, using common water dispensers, or failing to change dirty clothing for clean are prevalent violations of sanitation in sports. The following is a suggested cleanliness checklist that may be used by the athletic trainer:

1. Facilities cleanliness
   a. Are the gymnasium floors swept daily?
   b. Are drinking fountains, showers, sinks, urinals, and toilets cleaned and disinfected daily?
   c. Are lockers aired and sanitized frequently?
   d. Are mats cleaned routinely (wrestling mats and wall mats cleaned daily)?

2. Equipment and clothing issuance
   a. Are equipment and clothing fitted to the athlete to avoid skin irritations?
   b. Is swapping of equipment and clothes prevented?
   c. Is clothing laundered and changed frequently?
   d. Is wet clothing allowed to dry thoroughly before the athlete wears it again?
   e. Is individual attention given to proper shoe fit and upkeep?
   f. Is protective clothing provided during inclement weather or when the athlete is waiting on the sidelines?
   g. Are clean, dry towels provided each day for each individual athlete?

The Athlete

To promote good health among the athletes, the athletic trainer should encourage sound health habits. The following checklist may be a useful guide for coaches, athletic trainers, and athletes:

1. Are the athletes medically cleared to participate?
2. Is each athlete insured?
3. Does the athlete promptly report injuries, illnesses, and skin disorders to the coach or the athletic trainer?
4. Are good daily living habits of resting, sleeping, and proper nutrition practiced?
5. Do the athletes shower after practice?
6. Do they dry thoroughly and cool off before departing from the gymnasium?
7. Do they avoid drinking from a common water dispenser?
8. Do they avoid using a common towel?
9. Do they avoid exchanging gym clothes with teammates?
10. Do they practice good foot hygiene?
11. Do they avoid contact with teammates who have a contagious disease or infection?

Emergency Telephones

The accessibility of an emergency telephone adjacent to all major activity areas is also essential. It should be possible to use this telephone to call outside for emergency aid and to contact the athletic training facilities when additional assistance is required. Two-way radios or, preferably, cellular or digital telephones provide the greatest flexibility in the communication system and should be bought if the budget permits.

Budgetary Concerns

A major problem often facing athletic trainers is a budget of sufficient size.

One of the major problems faced by athletic trainers is to obtain a budget of sufficient size to permit them to perform a creditable job of athletic training. Most high schools provide only limited budgetary provisions for athletic training except for the purchase of tape, ankle wraps, and an athletic training kit that contains a minimum amount of supplies.[6] Many fail to provide a room and any of the special facilities that are needed to establish an effective athletic training program. Some school boards and administrators fail to recognize that the functions performed in the athletic training facility are an essential component of the athletic program and that even if no specialist is used, the facilities are nonetheless necessary.[6] Colleges and universities are not usually faced with this problem to the extent that high schools are. By and large, athletic training at the college level is recognized as an important aspect of the athletic program.

Budgetary needs vary considerably within programs; some require only a few thousand dollars, whereas others spend hundreds of thousands of dollars. The amount spent on building and equipping a training facility, of course, is entirely a matter of local option. In purchasing equipment, immediate needs and the availability of personnel to operate specialized equipment should be kept in mind.

The budget process should be a continuous process involving prioritizing, planning, documenting and evaluating the goals of the athletic training program, and formulating a plan for how available resources can be utilized and expended during the next budget period.[34]

Budget records should be kept on file so that they are available for use in projecting the following year's budgetary needs. The records present a picture of the distribution of current funds and serve to substantiate future budgetary requests.

Supplies

The supplies that the athletic trainer uses to carry out daily tasks may be classified as either expendable or nonexpendable. Some athletic trainers spend much of their budget on expendable supplies that cannot be reused. Supplies that are expendable are used for injury prevention, first aid, and management. Examples of expendable supplies are adhesive tape, adhesive bandages, and hydrogen peroxide. Nonexpendable supplies are those that can be reused. Examples are compression wraps, scissors, and neoprene sleeves. An annual inventory must be conducted at the end of the year or before the ordering of supplies. Accurate records must be kept to justify future requests.

Supplies may be expendable or nonexpendable.

Equipment

The term *equipment* refers to items that may be used by the athletic training room for a number of years. Equipment may be further divided into capital and nonconsumable capital equipment. Nonconsumable capital equipment is not usually removed from the athletic training facility. Examples of nonconsumable capital equipment are ice machines, treatment tables, isokinetic machines, and electrical therapeutic modalities. Capital equipment includes things like crutches, coolers, and training kits.

Equipment may be nonconsumable capital or capital.

Purchasing Systems

Purchasing of supplies and equipment must be done through either direct buy or competitive bid. For expensive purchases, an institutional purchasing agent is sent out to competing vendors who quote a price on specified supplies or equipment. Orders are generally placed with the lowest bidder. Smaller purchases or emergency purchases may be made directly from a single vendor.[33]

Purchasing may be done through direct buy or competitive bid.

An alternative to purchasing expensive equipment is to lease it. Many manufacturers and distributors are now willing to lease equipment on a monthly or yearly basis. Over the long run, purchasing equipment will be less costly. In the short term, however, if a large capital expenditure is not possible, a leasing agreement should be considered.[34]

Additional Budget Considerations

In addition to supplies and equipment, the athletic trainer must also consider other costs that may be included in the operation of an athletic training program; these include telephone and postage, utilities, contracts with physicians or clinics for services, professional liability insurance, memberships in professional organizations, the purchase of professional journals or textbooks, travel and expenses for attending professional meetings, and clothing to be worn in the training room.[34,35]

Developing a Risk Management Plan

The athletic trainer, working in conjunction with the appropriate administrative personnel, must be responsible for developing a risk management plan that covers security issues, fire safety, electrical and equipment safety, and developing emergency action plans.[39]

Security Issues

The athletic trainer must decide who will have access to the athletic training room facility. In addition to the staff athletic trainers, the team physician must have keys to access the athletic training room. Student athletic trainers may also be given keys as necessary at the collegiate level; at the high school level, however, student athletic trainers should only be in the athletic training room when directly supervised. At the collegiate level, coaches do not need to have access to the athletic training room; but

2-1

Critical Thinking E x e r c i s e

The principal at All-American High School has received a mandate from the school board to develop a risk management plan for the athletic program. The principal asks the athletic trainer to chair a committee to develop this plan.

? What considerations are important for inclusion in this risk management plan?

Focus

Safety when using electrical equipment

- The entire electrical system of the building or athletic training room should be designed or evaluated by a qualified electrician.
- Problems with the electrical system may exist in older buildings or in situations in which rooms have been modified to accommodate therapeutic devices (e.g., putting a whirlpool in a locker room in which the concrete floor is always wet or damp).
- It should not be assumed that all three-pronged wall outlets are automatically grounded. The ground must be checked. Ground fault interrupters (GFI) should be installed, particularly in those areas in which water may be present (e.g., whirlpools).
- The athletic trainer should become very familiar with the equipment being used and with any potential problems that may exist or develop. Any defective equipment should be immediately removed from the clinic. The plug should not be jerked out of the wall by pulling on the cable.
- Extension cords or multiple adapters should never be used.
- Equipment should be reevaluated on a yearly basis and should conform to National Electrical Code guidelines. A clinic or training room that is not in compliance with this code has no legal protection in a lawsuit.
- Common sense should always be exercised when using electrotherapeutic devices. A situation that appears to be potentially dangerous may in fact result in injury or death.

at the high school level, coaches might need to have a key to get into the facility at times when the athletic trainer may not be available. Access to areas of the building other than the athletic training room should be strictly limited.

Fire Safety

The athletic trainer should establish and have clearly posted a plan for evacuating the athletic training facility should a fire occur. Smoke detectors and fire alarm systems must be periodically tested and inspected to make certain that they are functioning normally.

Electrical and Equipment Safety

Electrical safety in the athletic training setting should be of maximal concern to the athletic trainer. Unnecessary accidents can be avoided by taking some basic precautions and acquiring some understanding of the power distribution system and electrical grounds. *Focus Box:* "Safety when using electrical equipment" lists considerations for electrical safety.

Emergency Action Plan

In cooperation with existing community-based emergency health care delivery systems, the athletic trainer should develop a systematic plan for accessing the emergency medical system and subsequent transportation of injured athletes to an emergency care facility.[5] Meetings should be scheduled periodically with EMTs or paramedics who work in the community to make certain that they understand the role of the athletic trainer as a provider of emergency health care. It is important to communicate the special considerations for dealing with athletic equipment issues before an emergency arises. Chapter 10 discusses the emergency action plan in detail.

Accessing Community-Based Health Services

In addition to the community-based emergency medical services personnel, the athletic trainer should become familiar with existing local and regional community health services and agencies that may be accessed should a need arise to refer an athlete for

Focus

Models of supervision for the head athletic trainer*

Clinical supervision—Involves direct observation of the assistant trainers in the performance of their written job responsibilities, followed by an analysis of strengths and weaknesses and a collaborative effort to correct weaknesses.

Developmental supervision—A mentoring approach in which the head athletic trainer works in a collaborative manner with the assistants, helping them to develop professionally while meeting the needs of the day-to-day athletic training program.

Inspection production supervision—An authoritative management style in which the head athletic trainer demands that lines of authority be strictly maintained to accomplish the stated goals of the athletic training program.

*These models should not be confused with models of clinical supervision established by the Education Council for Students.

psychological or sociological services. Referrals should be made with input and assistance from the team physician. The family of an athlete requiring referral for psychological or sociological counseling must be informed of the existing problems, particularly when the athlete is a minor.

Human Resource and Personnel Issues

The importance of putting together the sports medicine team was discussed in Chapter 1. Any team is only as good as the group of individuals who make up that team. Recruiting, hiring, and retaining the most qualified personnel is essential if the athletic training program is to be effective.

- Specific policies dealing with recruitment, hiring and firing, performance evaluations, and promotions are mandated by federal law.[12] The policies for recruitment and hiring clearly mandate that all qualified applicants should receive equal consideration regardless of their race, gender, religion, or nationality. Athletic trainers who are in a position to hire new staff must strictly adhere to these mandates.
- Once an individual has been hired, it is important for everyone on the sports medicine team to clearly understand what the roles and responsibilities are within that team. Individual job descriptions and job specifications that describe qualifications, accountability, a code of conduct, and the scope of that position should be written. A well-defined organizational chart should be created to show the chain of command.[35]
- The head athletic trainer must serve as a supervisor for the staff assistants, graduate students, and undergraduate student athletic trainers.[22] The supervisor should strive to improve job performance and enhance professional development of those being supervised. *Focus Box:* "Models of supervision for the head athletic trainer" defines supervisory models.[35]
- Performance evaluations should be routinely done at regularly scheduled intervals to analyze the quality of the work being performed. Evaluations should focus first on the positive aspects of job performance and then on any weaknesses.[22]

Each of these policies relative to personnel issues should be included in the policies and procedures manual.

DESIGNING AN ATHLETIC TRAINING FACILITY

Maximizing the use of facilities and effectively using equipment and supplies are essential to the function of any athletic program.[27] The athletic training facility must be specially designed to meet the many requirements of the athletic training program (Figure 2-1).[26,37] The size and the layout of the athletic training facility will depend on

2-2

Critical Thinking Exercise

State University has an opening for an assistant athletic trainer in its Department of Athletics. The athletic director has asked the head athletic trainer to be in charge of the recruitment and hiring process for the new position.

? What factors must be considered in hiring a new employee?

The athletic training facility is a multipurpose area used for first aid, therapy and rehabilitation, injury prevention, medical procedures such as the physical examination, and athletic training administration.

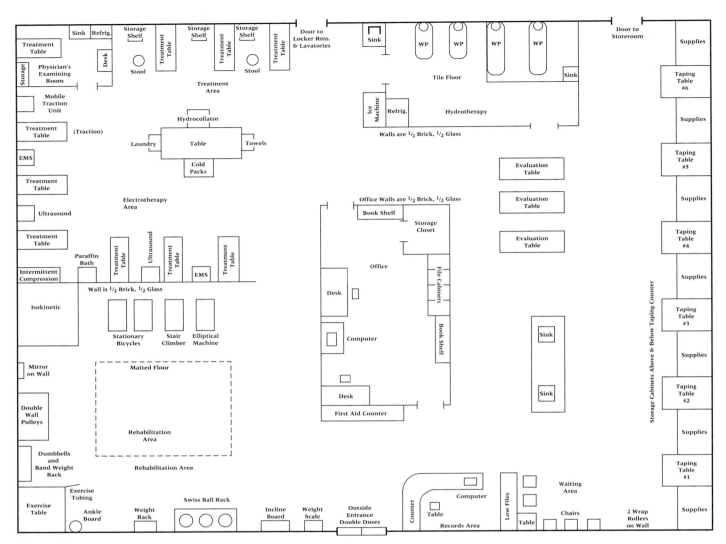

Figure 2-1A

The ideal athletic training room facility should be well designed to maximize its use. **A,** Larger athletic training facility found at a college or university.

Continued

the scope of the athletic training program, including the size and number of teams and athletes and what sports are offered.[29] The clinical setting has a much broader patient population than a school or university program, and thus the requirements for equipment and supplies will be somewhat different.[26] To accommodate the various functions of an athletic training program, the athletic training room must serve as a health care center for athletes.[11,13]

Size

The size of the athletic training room can range anywhere from a large storage closet in some high schools or middle schools to 15,000-square-foot sports medicine complexes in some universities. Certainly the size of the facility can have a major impact on how the athletic training program is managed. But the most important consideration is to organize the athletic training program in a manner that most efficiently takes advantage of the space available. When designing a new athletic training facility, the athletic trainer should work closely with design architects to communicate the specific needs of the institution and the number of athletes who will be served.

Location

The athletic training facility should have an outside entrance from the athletic field or court. This arrangement makes it unnecessary to bring injured athletes in through the

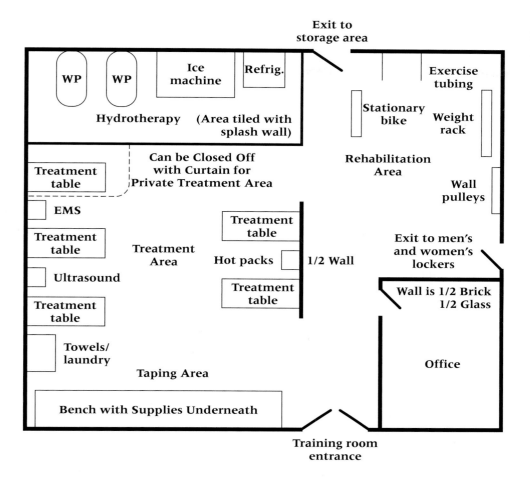

Figure 2-1B—continued

B, Small athletic training facility found at a high school.

building and possibly through several doors; it also permits access when the rest of the building is not in use. A double door at each entrance is preferable to allow easy passage of a wheelchair or a stretcher. A ramp at the outside entrance is safer and far more functional than are stairs.

The athletic training room should be near the locker rooms if possible so that showers are readily available to athletes coming in for treatment following practice. Toilet facilities should be located adjacent to the athletic training room and should be readily accessible through a door in the training room.

Because the athletic training facility is where emergency treatment is given, its light, heat, and water sources should be independent from those for the rest of the building.

Illumination

The athletic training facility should be well lighted throughout. Lighting should be planned with the advice of a technical lighting engineer. Obviously, certain areas need to be better lit than others. For example, the wound care and taping areas need better lighting than is necessary in the rehabilitation area. Ceilings and walls act as reflective surfaces to help provide an equable distribution and balance of light. Natural lighting through windows or skylights can certainly be helpful.

Special Service Areas

Apart from the storage and office space, a portion of the athletic training room should be divided into special sections, preferably by half walls or partial glass walls. Space, however, may not permit a separate area for each service section, and an overlapping of functions may be required.

2-3

Critical Thinking Exercise

The members of the school board at All-American High School voted to allocate $25,000 to renovate a 25' × 40' storage space and to purchase new equipment for an athletic training room. The athletic trainer has been asked to provide the school principal with a wish list of what should be included in this facility. The physical renovation will cost approximately $17,000.

? How may this space be best used, and what type of equipment should be purchased to maximize the effectiveness of this new facility?

Treatment Area

The treatment area should include four to six treatment tables, preferably of adjustable height, that can be used during the application of ice packs or hydrocollator packs or for manual therapy techniques such as massage, mobilization, or proprioceptive neuromuscular facilitation (PNF). Three or four adjustable stools on rollers should also be readily available. The hydrocollator unit and ice bags should be easily accessible to this area.

Electrotherapy Area

The electrotherapy area is used for treatment by ultrasound, diathermy, or electrical stimulating units. Equipment should include at least two treatment tables, several wooden chairs, one or two dispensing tables for holding supplies, shelves, and a storage cabinet for supplies and equipment. The area should contain a sufficient number of grounded outlets, preferably in the walls and several feet above the floor. It is advisable to place rubber mats or runners on each side of the treatment tables as a precautionary measure. This area must be under supervision at all times, and the storage cabinet should be kept locked when not in use.

Hydrotherapy Area

In the hydrotherapy area, the floor should slope toward a centrally located drain to prevent standing water. Equipment should include two or three whirlpool baths (one permitting complete immersion of the body), several lavatories, and storage shelves. Because some of this equipment is electrically operated, many precautions must be taken. All electrical outlets should be placed four to five feet above the floor and should have spring-locked covers and water spray deflectors. All cords and wires must be kept clear of the floor to eliminate any possibility of electrical shock. To prevent water from entering the other areas, a slightly raised, rounded curb should be built at the entrance to the area. When an athletic training room is planned, ample outlets must be provided; under no circumstances should two or more devices be operated from the same outlet. All outlets must be properly grounded using ground fault interrupters (GFI).[25]

Exercise Rehabilitation Area

Ideally, an athletic training facility should accommodate injury reconditioning under the strict supervision of the athletic trainer. Selected pieces of resistance equipment should be made available. Depending on the existing space, dumbbells and free weights; exercise machines for knee, ankle, shoulder, hip, and so forth; isokinetic equipment; devices for balance and proprioception; and space for using exercise tubing may all be available for use.

Taping, Bandaging, and Orthotics Area

Each athletic training room should provide a place in which taping, bandaging, and applying orthotic devices can be executed. This area should have three or four taping tables adjacent to a sink and a storage cabinet.

Physician's Examination Room

In colleges and universities, the team physician has a special room in which examinations and treatments may be given. This room contains an examining table, sink, locking storage cabinets, refrigerator, and small desk with a telephone. At all times, this facility must be kept locked to outsiders.

Records Area

Some space, either in the office or at the entrance to the training room, should be devoted to record keeping. Record-keeping facilities may range from a filing system to a more sophisticated computer-based system. Records should be accessible to sports medicine personnel only.

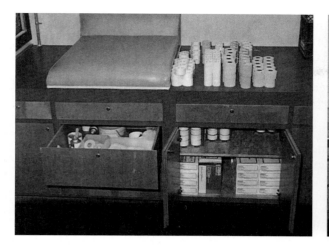

Figure 2-2

An effective athletic training program must have appropriate storage facilities that are highly organized.

Storage Facilities

Many athletic training facilities lack ample storage space. Often, storage facilities are located a considerable distance away, which is extremely inconvenient. In addition to the storage cabinets and shelves provided in each of the three special service areas, a small storage closet should be placed in the athletic trainer's office. All these cabinets should be used for the storage of general supplies as well as for the small, specialized equipment used in the respective areas. A large walk-in closet, 80 to 100 square feet in area, is a necessity for the storage of bulky equipment, medical supplies, adhesive tape, bandages, and protective devices (Figure 2-2). A refrigerator for the storage of frozen water in styrofoam cups for ice massage and other necessities is also an important piece of equipment. Many athletic trainers prefer to place the refrigerator in their office, where it is readily accessible but still under close supervision. In small sports programs, a large refrigerator will probably be sufficient for all ice needs. If at all possible, an ice-making machine should be installed in an auxiliary area to provide an ample and continuous supply of ice for treatment purposes.

> It is essential to have adequate storage space available for supplies and equipment.

Athletic Trainer's Office

A space at least ten feet by twelve feet is ample for the athletic trainer's office. The office should be located so that all areas of the training room can be well supervised without the athletic trainer's having to leave the office. Glass partitions on two sides permit the athletic trainer, even while seated at the desk, to observe all activities. A desk, chair, tackboard for clippings and other information, telephones, and record file are the basic equipment. In some cases a computer is also housed in this office. The office should have an independent lock-and-key system so that it is accessible only to authorized personnel.

Additional Areas

If space is available, several other areas could potentially be included as part of a training room facility.

Pharmacy Area

A separate room that can be secured for storing and administering medications is helpful. All medications, including over-the-counter drugs, should be kept under lock and key. If prescription medications are kept in the training room, only the team physician or pharmacist from a campus health center should have access to the storage cabinet. Records for administering medications to athletes should be kept in this area. It is essential to adhere to individual state regulations regarding the storage and administration of medications.

2-4

Critical Thinking Exercise

A high school athletic trainer is approached by the community recreation department with a request to use the athletic training facility to treat its football and basketball league participants who are injured.

? How should the athletic trainer deal with this request?

Rehabilitation Pool

It is rare that a pool is located in the training room; however, if the facility has the space and can afford one, a pool can be an extremely useful rehabilitation tool. The pool should be accessible to individuals with various types of injuries. It should have a graduated depth to at least seven feet, the deck should have a nonslip surface, and the filter system should be in a separate room.[34]

X-Ray Room

A separate room for X-ray equipment must have lead shielding in the walls. The X-ray room must be large enough to house all the necessary equipment (X-ray unit, processing unit, etc.).

RECORD KEEPING

Keeping adequate records is of major importance in the athletic training program.

Record keeping is a major responsibility of the athletic training program. Some athletic trainers object to keeping records and filling out forms, stating that they have neither the time nor the inclination to be bookkeepers. Nevertheless, because lawsuits are currently the rule rather than the exception, accurate and up-to-date records are an absolute necessity. Medical records, injury reports, treatment logs, personal information cards, injury evaluations and progress notes, supply and equipment inventories, and annual reports are essential records that should be maintained by the athletic trainer.

Maintaining Confidentiality in Record Keeping

HIPAA Regulations

The Health Insurance Portability and Accountability Act (HIPAA) regulates how coaches, athletic trainers, physicians, or any other member of the sports medicine team who has private health information (PHI) about an athlete can share that information with others.[16] The regulation guarantees that athletes have access to their medical records, gives them more control over how their protected health information is used and disclosed, and provides a clear avenue of recourse if their medical privacy is compromised. Authorization by an athlete to release medical information is not necessary on a per-injury basis. A written blanket authorization signed by the athlete at the beginning of the year will suffice for all injuries and treatments done during the course of participation for that year. These one-time, blanket authorizations must indicate what information may be released, to whom, and for what length of time. *Focus Box:* "HIPAA authorization" is a list of core elements that must be present for the authorization to be valid.

Focus

HIPAA authorization

Below is a list of core elements that must be present for a disclosure authorization to be valid:
- A description of the information to be used or disclosed
- Identification of the persons or class of persons authorized to make use of or disclosure the protected health information
- Identification of the persons or class of persons to whom the covered entity is authorized to provide or disclose to
- A description of each purpose of the use or disclosure
- An expiration date or event
- The individual's signature and date
- If signed by a personal representative, a description of his or her authority to act for the individual

FERPA Regulations

The Family Educational Rights and Privacy Act (FERPA) is a law that protects the privacy of student educational records. It has been suggested that in some instances medical records should be kept along with a student's educational records and thus the right to privacy of medical records would be protected under FERPA instead of HIPAA. FERPA gives parents certain rights with respect to their children's educational records. These rights transfer to the student when he or she reaches the age of 18 or attends a school beyond the high school level. Students to whom the rights have been transferred are "eligible students." Parents or eligible students have the right to inspect and review the student's educational records maintained by the school. Parents or eligible students have the right to request that a school correct records that they believe to be inaccurate or misleading. Schools must have written permission from the parent or eligible student to release any information from a student's educational records.

Administering Preparticipation Examinations

The first piece of information that the athletic trainer should collect on each athlete is obtained from an initial preparticipation examination done prior to the start of practice. The primary purpose of the preparticipation exam is to identify an athlete who may be at risk before he or she participates in a specific sport.[14] The preparticipation examination should consist of a medical history, a physical examination, a brief orthopedic screening, and in some situations, a wellness screening.[30] Information obtained during this examination will establish a baseline to which comparisons may be made after injury. It may also reveal conditions that could warrant disqualification from certain sports.[22] The examination will also satisfy insurance and liability issues. The preparticipation exam may be administered on an individual basis by a personal physician, or it may be done using a station examination system with a team of examiners.[15]

Examination by a Personal Physician

Examination by a personal physician has the advantage of yielding an in-depth history and an ideal physician-patient relationship. A disadvantage of this type of examination is that it may not be directed to the detection of factors that predispose the athlete to a sports injury.[40]

Station Examination

The most thorough and sport-specific type of preparticipation examination is the station examination.[40] This method can provide the athlete with a detailed examination in a short period of time. A team of nine people is needed to examine thirty or more athletes. The team should include two physicians, two medically trained nonphysicians (nurse, athletic trainer, physical therapist, or physician's assistant), and five managers, athletic training students, or assistant coaches (Table 2-1).[40]

Medical History

A medical history form should be completed before the physical examination and orthopedic screening; its purpose is to identify any past or existing medical problems.[1] This form should be updated for each athlete every year. Medical histories should be closely reviewed by both the physician and the athletic trainer so that personnel may be prepared should some medical emergency arise. Necessary participation release forms and insurance information should be collected along with the medical history (Figure 2-3).[18]

Physical Examination

The physical examination should include the assessment of height, weight, body composition, blood pressure, pulse, vision, skin, dental, ear, nose, throat, heart and lung

Preparticipation health examination:
- Medical history
- Physical examination
- Maturity assessment
- Orthopedic screening
- Wellness screening

2-5

Critical Thinking E x e r c i s e

All-American High School offers eighteen sports, six in the fall, six in the winter, and six in the spring. There are a total of approximately 500 athletes, and approximately 200 of them are involved in the fall sports. The athletic trainer is charged with the responsibility of arranging and administering preparticipation examinations so that each athlete can be cleared for competition.

? How can the athletic trainer most efficiently set up the preparticipation exams to clear 200 athletes for competition in the fall sports?

TABLE 2-1   Suggested Components of Preparticipation Physical Examination

Station	Points Noted	Personnel
1. Individual history (reviewed); height, weight, body composition, body mass index (BMI)	"Yes" answers are probed in depth; height and weight relationships	Physician, nurse, or athletic trainer
2. Snellen test, vision	Upper limits of visual acuity—20/40	Student athletic trainer or manager
3. Oral (mouth), ears, nose, throat	Dental prosthesis or caries, abnormalities of the ears, nose, throat	Physician, nurse, or athletic trainer
4. Chest, heart, lungs	Heart abnormalities, blood pressure, pulse, murmurs, clarity of lungs	Physician
5. Abdomen	Masses, tenderness, organomegaly	Physician or physician's assistant
6. Genitalia (male only)	Abnormalities of genitalia, hernia	Physician or physician's assistant
7. Skin	Suspicious rashes or lesions	Physician or physician's assistant
8. Musculoskeletal	Postural asymmetry, decreased range of motion or strength, abnormal joint laxity	Physician, athletic trainer, physical therapist, or nurse practitioner
9. Urinalysis	After its collection in a plastic cup, urine is tested in a lab for sugar and protein	Athletic training student or manager
10. Blood work	Lab test to determine hematocrit	Nurse or physician
Review	History and physical examination reports are evaluated and the following decisions are made: (a) No sports participation (b) Limited participation (no participation in specific sports such as football or ice hockey) (c) Clearance withheld until certain conditions are met (e.g., additional tests are taken, rehabilitation is completed) (d) Full, unlimited participation is allowed	Physician and athletic trainer

function, abdomen, lymphatics, genitalia, maturation index, urinalysis, and blood work (Figure 2-4).[19]

Cardiovascular Screening

In 1996 the American Heart Association (AHA) published recommendations concerning the cardiovascular component of the preparticipation exam in competitive athletes.[23] The critical task of the preparticipation cardiac examination is identifying life-threatening conditions. Although the cardiac examination needn't involve complex tests, it must permit the recognition of abnormal heart sounds and other signs of pathology.

MEDICAL HISTORY FORM

DATE OF EXAM_____

Name_____ Sex_____ Age_____ Date of birth _____

Grade____ School_____ Sport(s) _____

Address_____ Phone _____

Personal physician _____

In case of emergency, contact

Name_____ Relationship_____ Phone (H) _____ (W) _____

Explain "Yes" answers below.
Circle questions you don't know the answers to.

	Yes	No
1. Has a doctor ever denied or restricted your participation in sports for any reason?	☐	☐
2. Do you have an ongoing medical condition (like diabetes or asthma)?	☐	☐
3. Are you currently taking any prescription or nonprescription (over-the-counter) medicine or pills?	☐	☐
4. Do you have allergies to medicines, pollens, foods, or stinging insects?	☐	☐
5. Have you ever passed out or nearly passed out DURING exercise?	☐	☐
6. Have you ever passed out or nearly passed out AFTER exercise?	☐	☐
7. Have you ever had discomfort, pain, or pressure in your chest during exercise?	☐	☐
8. Does your heart race or skip beats during exercise?	☐	☐

9. Has a doctor ever told you that you have (check all that apply):

☐ High blood pressure   ☐ A heart murmur
☐ High cholesterol   ☐ A heart infection

	Yes	No
10. Has a doctor ever ordered a test for your heart? (for example, ECG, echocardiogram)	☐	☐
11. Has anyone in your family died for no apparent reason?	☐	☐
12. Does anyone in your family have a heart problem?	☐	☐
13. Has any family member or relative died of heart problems or of sudden death before age 50?	☐	☐
14. Does anyone in your family have Marfan syndrome?	☐	☐
15. Have you ever spent the night in a hospital?	☐	☐
16. Have you ever had surgery?	☐	☐
17. Have you ever had an injury, like a sprain, muscle or ligament tear, or tendonitis, that caused you to miss a practice or game? If yes, circle affected area below:	☐	☐
18. Have you had any broken or fractured bones or dislocated joints? If yes, circle below:	☐	☐
19. Have you had a bone or joint injury that required x-rays, MRI, CT, surgery, injections, rehabilitation, physical therapy, a brace, a cast, or crutches? If yes, circle below:	☐	☐

Head	Neck	Shoulder	Upper arm	Elbow	Forearm	Hand/ fingers	Chest
Upper back	Lower back	Hip	Thigh	Knee	Calf/shin	Ankle	Foot/toes

	Yes	No
20. Have you ever had a stress fracture?	☐	☐
21. Have you been told that you have or have you had an x-ray for atlantoaxial (neck) instability?	☐	☐
22. Do you regularly use a brace or assistive device?	☐	☐
23. Has a doctor ever told you that you have asthma or allergies?	☐	☐

	Yes	No
24. Do you cough, wheeze, or have difficulty breathing during or after exercise?	☐	☐
25. Is there anyone in your family who has asthma?	☐	☐
26. Have you ever used an inhaler or taken asthma medicine?	☐	☐
27. Were you born without or are you missing a kidney, an eye, a testicle, or any other organ?	☐	☐
28. Have you had infectious mononucleosis (mono) within the last month?	☐	☐
29. Do you have any rashes, pressure sores, or other skin problems?	☐	☐
30. Have you had a herpes skin infection?	☐	☐
31. Have you ever had a head injury or concussion?	☐	☐
32. Have you been hit in the head and been confused or lost your memory?	☐	☐
33. Have you ever had a seizure?	☐	☐
34. Do you have headaches with exercise?	☐	☐
35. Have you ever had numbness, tingling, or weakness in your arms or legs after being hit or falling?	☐	☐
36. Have you ever been unable to move your arms or legs after being hit or falling?	☐	☐
37. When exercising in the heat, do you have severe muscle cramps or become ill?	☐	☐
38. Has a doctor told you that you or someone in your family has sickle cell trait or sickle cell disease?	☐	☐
39. Have you had any problems with your eyes or vision?	☐	☐
40. Do you wear glasses or contact lenses?	☐	☐
41. Do you wear protective eyewear, such as goggles or a face shield?	☐	☐
42. Are you happy with your weight?	☐	☐
43. Are you trying to gain or lose weight?	☐	☐
44. Has anyone recommended you change your weight or eating habits?	☐	☐
45. Do you limit or carefully control what you eat?	☐	☐
46. Do you have any concerns that you would like to discuss with a doctor?	☐	☐

FEMALES ONLY

	Yes	No
47. Have you ever had a menstrual period?	☐	☐

48. How old were you when you had your first menstrual period?_____
49. How many periods have you had in the last 12 months?_____

Explain "Yes" answers here:_____

_____
_____
_____
_____
_____
_____

I hereby state that, to the best of my knowledge, my answers to the above questions are complete and correct.

Signature of athlete_____ Signature of parent/guardian_____ Date_____

Used with permission from ©2004 American Academy of Family Physicians, American Academy of Pediatrics, American College of Sports Medicine, American Medical Society for Sports Medicine, American Orthopedic Society for Sports Medicine, and American Osteopathic Academy of Sports Medicine.

Figure 2-3

Sample medical history examination form.

PHYSICAL EXAMINATION FORM

Name _____ Date of birth _____

Grade _____ Weight _____ % Body fat (optional) _____ Pulse _____ BP ___/_____ (___/_____, ___/_____)

Vision R 20 /_____ L 20 /_____   Corrected: Y N   Pupils: Equal _____ Unequal _____

Follow-Up Questions on More Sensitive Issues	Yes	No
1. Do you feel stressed out or under a lot of pressure?	☐	☐
2. Do you ever feel so sad or hopeless that you stop doing some of your usual activities for more than a few days?	☐	☐
3. Do you feel safe?	☐	☐
4. have you ever tried cigarette smoking, even 1 or 2 puffs? Do you currently smoke?	☐	☐
5. During the past 30 days, did you use chewing tobacco, snuff, or dip?	☐	☐
6. During the past 30 days, have you had at least 1 drink of alcohol?	☐	☐
7. Have you ever taken steroid pills or shots without a doctor's prescription?	☐	☐
8. Have you ever taken any supplements to help you gain or lose weight or improve your performance?	☐	☐
9. Questions from the Youth Risk Behavior Survey (http://www.cdc.gov/HealthyYouth/yrbs/index.htm) on guns, seatbelts, unprotected sex, domestic violence, drugs, etc.	☐	☐

Notes: _____
_____
_____

	NORMAL	ABNORMAL FINDINGS	INITIALS*
MEDICAL			
Appearance			
Eyes/ears/nose/throat			
Hearing			
Lymph nodes			
Heart			
Murmurs			
Pulses			
Lungs			
Abdomen			
Genitourinary (males only)†			
Skin			
MUSCULOSKELETAL			
Neck			
Back			
Shoulder/arm			
Elbow/forearm			
Wrist/hand/fingers			
Hip/thigh			
Knee			
Leg/ankle			
Foot/toes			

*Multiple-examiner set-up only.
†Having a third party present is recommended for the genitourinary examination.

Notes: _____
_____

Name of physician (print/type) _____ Date _____

Address _____ Phone _____

Signature of physician _____ , MD or DO

Used with permission from ©2004 American Academy of Family Physicians, American Academy of Pediatrics, American College of Sports Medicine, American Medical Society for Sports Medicine, American Orthopedic Society for Sports Medicine, and American Osteopathic Academy of Sports Medicine.

Figure 2-4
_____

Sample physical examination form.

Figure 2-5

Tanner Stages of Maturity.[32]

Males

Stage 1. **No evidence of pubic hair.**
Stage 2. **Slightly pigmented hair laterally at the base of the penis. Usually straight.**
Stage 3. **Hair becomes darker and coarser, begins to curl, and spreads over the pubic region.**
Stage 4. **Hair is adult in type but does not extend onto thighs.**
Stage 5. **Hair extends onto the thighs and frequently up the linea alba.**

Females

Stage 1. **No evidence of pubic hair.**
Stage 2. **Long, slightly pigmented, downy hair along the edges of the labia.**
Stage 3. **Darker, coarser, slightly curled hair spread sparsely over the mons pubis.**
Stage 4. **Adult type of hair but it does not extend onto thighs.**
Stage 5. **Adult distribution including spread along the medial aspects of the thighs.**

The vast majority of exams will be negative, but the physician should be alert to such potentially lethal conditions as hypertrophic cardiomyopathy, aortic stenosis, and Marfan syndrome. A history of symptoms during exertion, certain features of physical appearance, and clinical findings require referral to a cardiologist.[42]

Maturity Assessment

Maturity assessment should be part of the physical examination as a means of protecting the young, physically developing athlete.[7] The most commonly used methods are the circumpubertal (sexual maturity), skeletal, and dental assessments. Of the three, Tanner's five stages of assessment, indicating maturity of secondary sexual characteristics, is the most expedient for use in the station method of examination.[41] The Tanner approach evaluates pubic hair and genitalia development in boys and pubic hair and breast development in girls (Figure 2-5). Other indicators that may be noted are facial and axillary hair. Stage one indicates that puberty is not evident, and stage five indicates full development. The crucial stage in terms of collision and high-intensity noncontact sports is stage three, in which there is the fastest bone growth. In this stage, the growth plates are two to five times weaker than the joint capsule and tendon attachments.[7] Young athletes in grades seven to twelve must be matched by maturity, not age.[24]

Orthopedic Screening

Orthopedic screening may be done as part of the physical examination or separately by the athletic trainer. An example of a quick orthopedic screening examination appears in Figure 2-6 and usually will take about ninety seconds.[3] A more detailed orthopedic examination may be conducted to assess strength, range of motion, and stability at various joints (Figure 2-7).

Wellness Screening

Some preparticipation exams include a screening for wellness. The purpose is to determine whether the athlete is engaging in healthy lifestyle behaviors. A number of wellness screening tools are available. Figure 2-8 on page 64 provides an example of a wellness screening questionnaire.

Sport Disqualification

As discussed previously, sports participation involves risks. Certain injuries or conditions warrant concern on the part of both the athlete and sports medicine personnel about continued participation in sport activities.[10] Table 2-2 on page 65 lists those conditions.[2,4] Sports medicine physicians can only recommend that an athlete voluntarily retire from participation. The Americans with Disabilities Act of 1990 dictates that the individual athlete is the only person who can make the final decision. Most conditions

Figure 2-6

The orthopedic screening examination. Equipment that may be needed includes reflex hammer, tape measure, pin, and examining table.

Orthopedic Screening Examination	
Activity and Instruction	**To Determine**
Stand facing examiner	Acromioclavicular joints; general habitus
Look at ceiling, floor, over both shoulders; touch ears to shoulders	Cervical spine motion
Shrug shoulders (examiner resists)	Trapezius strength
Abduct shoulders 90° (examiner resists at 90°)	Deltoid strength
Full external rotation of arms	Shoulder motion
Flex and extend elbows	Elbow motion
Arms at sides, elbows 90° flexed; pronate and supinate wrists	Elbow and wrist motion
Spread fingers; make fist	Hand or finger motion and deformities
Tighten (contract) quadriceps; relax quadriceps	Symmetry and knee effusion; ankle effusion
"Duck walk" four steps (away from examiner with buttocks on heels)	Hip, knee, and ankle motion
Stand with back to examiner	Shoulder symmetry; scoliosis
Knees straight, touch toes	Scoliosis, hip motion, hamstring tightness
Raise up on toes, raise heels	Calf symmetry, leg strength

that potentially warrant disqualification should be identified by a preparticipation examination and noted in the medical history.[28]

Injury Reports and Injury Disposition

An injury report serves as a record for future reference (Figure 2-9, page 66). If the emergency procedures followed are questioned at a later date, an athletic trainer's memory of the details may be somewhat hazy, but a report completed on the spot provides specific information. In a litigation situation, an athletic trainer may be asked questions about an injury that occurred three years in the past. All injury reports should be filed in the athletic trainer's office. One is well advised to make the reports out in triplicate so that one copy may be sent to the school health office, one to the physician, and one retained.

The Treatment Log

Each athletic training facility should have a sign-in log available for the athlete who receives any service. Emphasis is placed on recording the treatments for the athlete who is receiving daily therapy for an injury. Like accident records and injury dispositions, these records often have the status of legal documents and are used to establish certain facts in a civil litigation, an insurance action, or a criminal action after injury.

Personal Information Card

Always on file in the athletic trainer's office is the athlete's personal information card. This card is completed by the athlete at the time of the health examination and serves as a means of contacting the family, personal physician, and insurance company in case of emergency.

Injury Evaluation and Progress Notes

Injuries should be evaluated by the athletic trainer, who must record information obtained in some consistent format. The SOAP format (*S*ubjective, *O*bjective, *A*ssessment, *P*lan for treatment) is a concise method of recording the initial evaluation and progress notes for the injured athlete. The subjective portion of the SOAP note refers to what the athlete tells the athletic trainer about the injury relative to the

Figure 2-7

Sample of a detailed orthopedic screening examination form.

Orthopedic Screening Form

Name: _____ SS#: _____

FLEXIBILITY	Check if Normal
Shoulder:	___ Abduction
	___ Adduction
	___ Flexion
	___ Extension
	___ Internal rot.
	___ External rot.
Hip:	___ Ext. (flex knee)
	___ Flex. (flex knee)
	___ Ext. (str. leg)
	___ Flex. (str. leg)
	___ Abduction
	___ Adduction
Knee:	___ Flexion
	___ Extension
Ankle:	___ Dorsiflexion
	___ Plantar flexion
Trunk:	___ Flexion
	___ Extension
	___ Rotation
	___ Lat. Flexion

Joint Stability

Knee:	___ Lachman
	___ Pivot shift
	___ Anterior drawer
	___ Posterior drawer
	___ Valgus
	___ Varus
	___ McMurray
	___ Apley's grind
Ankle:	___ Anterior drawer
	___ Talor tilt

Leg Length

Posture:	___ Pelvis height
	___ Shoulder height
	___ Spine

Previous Injury:

Comments:

1. Circle the appropriate response for each question.
2. Add the total number of points for each section.

Behavior	Almost Always	Sometimes	Almost Never
Tobacco Use			
If you never smoke or use tobacco products, enter a score of 10 for this section and go to the next section on Alcohol and Drugs.			
1. I avoid smoking cigarettes and chewing tobacco.	2	1	0
2. I smoke only low-tar and low-nicotine cigarettes, or I smoke a pipe or cigars.	2	1	0
		Tobacco Use Score: _____	
Alcohol and Drugs			
1. I avoid drinking alcoholic beverages or I drink no more than one or two a day.	4	1	0
2. I avoid using alcohol or other drugs (especially illegal drugs) as a way of handling stressful situations or problems in my life.	2	1	0
3. I am careful not to drink alcohol when taking certain medicines (e.g., medicine for sleeping, pain, colds, and allergies) or when pregnant.	2	1	0
4. I read and follow the label directions when using prescribed and over-the-counter drugs.	2	1	0
		Alcohol and Drug Score: _____	
Eating Habits			
1. I eat a variety of foods each day, such as fruits and vegetables, whole grain breads and cereals, lean meats, dairy products, dry peas and beans, and nuts and seeds.	4	1	0
2. I limit my intake of fat, saturated fat, and cholesterol (including fat in meats, eggs, butter, and other dairy products, shortenings, and organ meats such as liver).	2	1	0
3. I limit the amount of salt I eat by cooking with only small amounts, not adding salt at the table, and avoiding salty snacks.	2	1	0
4. I avoid eating too much sugar (especially frequent snacks of sticky candy or soft drinks).	2	1	0
		Eating Habits Score: _____	
Exercise/Fitness Habits			
1. I maintain a desired weight, avoiding overweight and underweight.	3	1	0
2. I do vigorous exercises for 15–30 minutes at least three times a week (examples include running, swimming, and brisk walking).	3	1	0
3. I do exercises that enhance my muscle tone for 15–30 minutes at least three times a week (examples include yoga and calisthenics).	2	1	0
4. I use part of my leisure time participating in individual, family, or team activities that increase my level of fitness (such as gardening, bowling, golf, and baseball).	2	1	0
		Exercise/Fitness Score: _____	

	Almost Always	Sometimes	Almost Never
Stress Control			
1. I have a job or do other work that I enjoy.	2	1	0
2. I find it easy to relax and to express my feelings freely.	2	1	0
3. I anticipate and prepare for events or situations likely to be stressful for me.	2	1	0
4. I have close friends, relatives, or others with whom I can discuss personal matters and call on for help when needed.	2	1	0
5. I participate in group activities (such as church and community organizations) or hobbies that I enjoy.	2	1	0
		Stress Control Score: _____	
Safety			
1. I wear a seat belt when riding in a car.	2	1	0
2. I avoid driving while under the influence of alcohol and other drugs.	2	1	0
3. I obey traffic rules and the speed limit when driving.	2	1	0
4. I am careful when using potentially harmful products or substances (such as household cleaners, poisons, and electrical devices).	2	1	0
5. I avoid smoking in bed.	2	1	0
6. I am not sexually active or I have sex with only one mutually faithful, uninfected partner, or I always engage in safe sex (using condoms), and I do not share needles to inject drugs.	2	1	0
		Safety Score: _____	

What your Scores Mean

Scores of 9 and 10: Excellent. Your answers show that you are aware of the importance of this area to your health.

Scores of 6 to 8: Good. Your health practices in this area are good, but there is room for improvement.

Scores of 3 to 5: Fair. Your health risks are showing.

Scores of 0 to 2: Poor. Your answers show that you may be taking serious and unnecessary risks with your health. Perhaps you are not aware of the risks and what to do about them. You can easily get the information and help you need to improve, if you wish.

If you have questions or concerns you should consult your athletic trainers for advice.

Figure 2-8

Wellness screening questionnaire.

history or what he or she felt. The objective portion documents information that the athletic trainer gathers during the evaluation, such as range of motion, strength levels, patterns of pain, and so forth. The assessment records the athletic trainer's professional opinion about the injury based on information obtained during the subjective and objective portions. The plan for treatment indicates how the injury will be managed and includes short- and long-term goals for rehabilitation.

TABLE 2-2   Recommendations for Participation in Competitive Sports

	Contact		Noncontact		
	Contact/ Collision	Limited Contact/ Collision	Strenuous	Moderately Strenuous	Nonstrenuous
Atlantoaxial instability	No	No	Yes*	Yes	Yes

*Swimming: no butterfly, breast stroke, or diving starts

Acute illnesses	*	*	*	*	*

*Needs individual assessment (e.g., contagiousness to others, risk of worsening illness)

	Contact/ Collision	Limited Contact/ Collision	Strenuous	Moderately Strenuous	Nonstrenuous
Cardiovascular					
Carditis	No	No	No	No	No
Hypertension					
Mild	Yes	Yes	Yes	Yes	Yes
Moderate	*	*	*	*	*
Severe	*	*	*	*	*
Congenital heart disease	†	†	†	†	†

*Needs individual assessment
†Patients with mild forms can be allowed a full range of physical activities; patients with moderate or severe forms or who are postoperative should be evaluated by a cardiologist before athletic participation.

	Contact/ Collision	Limited Contact/ Collision	Strenuous	Moderately Strenuous	Nonstrenuous
Eyes					
Absence or loss of function of eye	*	*	*	*	*
Detached retina	†	†	†	†	†

*Availability of American Society for Testing and Materials (ASTM)-approved eye guards may allow competitor to participate in most sports, but this must be judged on an individual basis.
†Consult ophthalmologist

	Contact/ Collision	Limited Contact/ Collision	Strenuous	Moderately Strenuous	Nonstrenuous
Inguinal hernia	Yes	Yes	Yes	Yes	Yes
Kidney: Absence of one	No	Yes	Yes	Yes	Yes
Liver: Enlarged	No	No	Yes	Yes	Yes
Musculoskeletal disorders	*	*	*	*	*

*Needs individual assessment

	Contact/ Collision	Limited Contact/ Collision	Strenuous	Moderately Strenuous	Nonstrenuous
Neurologic status					
History of serious head or spine trauma, repeated concussions, or craniotomy	*	*	Yes	Yes	Yes
Convulsive disorder					
Well controlled	Yes	Yes	Yes	Yes	Yes
Poorly controlled	No	No	Yes†	Yes	Yes††

*Needs individual assessment
†No swimming or weight lifting
††No archery or riflery

	Contact/ Collision	Limited Contact/ Collision	Strenuous	Moderately Strenuous	Nonstrenuous
Ovary: Absence of one	Yes	Yes	Yes	Yes	Yes
Respiratory status					
Pulmonary insufficiency	*	*	*	*	Yes
Asthma	Yes	Yes	Yes	Yes	Yes

*May be allowed to compete if oxygenation remains satisfactory during a graded stress test

	Contact/ Collision	Limited Contact/ Collision	Strenuous	Moderately Strenuous	Nonstrenuous
Sickle cell trait	Yes	Yes	Yes	Yes	Yes
Skin: Boils, herpes, impetigo, scabies	*	*	Yes	Yes	Yes

*No gymnastics with mats, martial arts, wrestling, or contact sports until not contagious

	Contact/ Collision	Limited Contact/ Collision	Strenuous	Moderately Strenuous	Nonstrenuous
Spleen: Enlarged	No	No	No	Yes	Yes
Testicle: Absent or undescended	Yes*	Yes*	Yes	Yes	Yes

*Certain sports may require protective cup

Name _____ Sport _____ Date: __/__/__ Time: _____ Injury number: _____

Player I.D. _____ Age: _____ Location: _____ Intercollegiate—nonintercollegiate

Initial injury   Recheck   Reinjury   Preseason—Practice—Game   Incurred while participating in sport: yes ___ no ___

Description: How did it happen? _____

Initial impression: _____

Site of injury	Body part	Structure	Treatment _____
1 Right	1 Head	25 MP joint	1 Skin	_____
2 Left	2 Face	26 PIP joint	2 Muscle
3 Proximal	3 Eye	27 Abdomen	3 Fascia
4 Distal	4 Nose	28 Hip	4 Bone
5 Anterior	5 Ear	29 Thigh	5 Nerve
6 Posterior	6 Mouth	30 Knee	6 Fat pad
7 Medial	7 Neck	31 Patella	7 Tendon
8 Lateral	8 Thorax	32 Lower leg	8 Ligament
9 Other	9 Ribs	33 Ankle	9 Cartilage
	10 Sternum	34 Achilles tendon	10 Capsule
	11 Upper back	35 Foot	11 Compartment
Site of evaluation	12 Lower back	36 Toes	12 Dental
1 SHS	13 Shoulder	37 Other	13 _____
2 Athletic Trn Rm.	14 Rotator cuff		
3 Site-Competition	15 AC joint		Medication _____
4 _____	16 Glenohumeral		
	17 Sternoclavicular	Nontraumatic	Nature of injury
Procedures	18 Upper arm	1 Dermatological	1 Contusion
1 Physical exam	19 Elbow	2 Allergy	2 Strain
2 X-ray	20 Forearm	3 Influenza	3 Sprain
3 Splint	21 Wrist	4 URI	4 Fracture
4 Wrap	22 Hand	5 GU	5 Rupture
5 Cast	23 Thumb	6 Systemic infect.	6 Tendonitis
6 Aspiration	24 Finger	7 Local infect.	7 Bursitis
7 Other		8 Other	8 Myositis
			9 Laceration
			10 Concussion	Prescription dispensed
			11 Avulsion	1 Antibiotics 5 Muscle relaxant
			12 Abrasion	2 Antiinflammatory 6 Enzyme
Disposition	Referral	Disposition of injury	13 _____	3 Decongestant 7 _____
1 SHS	1 Arthrogram	1 No part.		4 Analgesic
2 Trainer	2 Neurological	2 Part part.		Injections
3 Hospital	3 Int. Med.	3 Full part.		
4 H.D.	4 Orthropedic		Degree	1 Steroids
5 Other	5 EENT		1° 2° 3°	2 Antibiotics
	6 Dentist			3 Steriods-xylo
	7 Other			4 _____

Previous injury _____

Figure 2-9

Athletic injury record form.

Supply and Equipment Inventory

A major responsibility of the athletic trainer is to manage a budget, most of which is spent on equipment and supplies. Every year an inventory must be conducted and recorded on such items as new equipment needed, equipment that needs to be replaced or repaired, and the expendable supplies that need replenishing.

Figure 2-10
Computers are an essential tool in athletic training.

Annual Reports

Most athletic departments require an annual report on the functions of the athletic training program. This report serves as a means for making program changes and improvements. It commonly includes the number of athletes served, a survey of the number and types of injuries, an analysis of the program, and recommendations for future improvements.

Release of Medical Records

The athletic trainer may not release an athlete's medical records to anyone without written consent. If the athlete wishes to have medical records released to professional sports organizations, insurance companies, the news media, or any other group or individual, the athlete must sign a waiver that specifies which information is to be released.

THE COMPUTER AS A TOOL FOR THE ATHLETIC TRAINER

As is the case in all of our society, computers have become an indispensable tool for the athletic trainer and have completely revolutionized the way information is managed (Figure 2-10). It is becoming rare to find an athletic trainer working in any setting who does not have access to a computer. A great deal of information can be efficiently located and stored for immediate and future use because of constant improvement in storage and retrieval capacities. Software packages are available to help store and retrieve any type of relevant records or information.[21]

The first step in integrating computers into an athletic training program is to decide exactly how and for what purposes the computer will be used. Most athletic trainers do not have an extensive background or understanding of computer hardware. It is essential to seek advice from expert professionals or consultants prior to purchasing a system to ensure that the hardware and corresponding operating system is capable of supporting the software that will make the computer a useful information management and communication tool. Athletic trainers who work in secondary schools, universities, or in industry may have access to a mainframe computer that can be accessed from a network of connecting terminals. It is more likely that most athletic trainers will use either a desktop or personal computer (PC) or a portable laptop or notebook computer. Many athletic trainers are also using PDAs (personal digital assistants) which are fully functional computers that can be held in one hand. These devices receive, process, and store information and communicate with other computers and PDAs. Their small size and portability makes them always accessible, which is very useful for athletic trainers who don't spend a lot of time in an office.

There are thousands of software programs available that will allow the user to store, manipulate, and retrieve information; create written documents through word

2-6
Critical Thinking E x e r c i s e

The athletic trainer has requested that the school purchase a new computer to be housed in the athletic training room. The administrator indicates that funds are tight; however, the athletic trainer is asked to develop a written proposal to justify the purchase.

? What information can the athletic trainer include in the request that could justify purchasing a new computer for the athletic training room?

Computers facilitate the record-keeping process.

processing; analyze data statistically; and communicate with many individuals in a variety of forms.

Record keeping is a time-consuming but essential chore for all athletic trainers regardless of whether they work at a college or university, at a high school, in the clinical setting, or in industry. Several software packages are available specifically for managing injury records in the athletic training setting. A problem that athletic trainers must address is ensuring security and protecting the confidentiality of medical records stored on a computer. Databases that contain such information must only be accessible to the athletic trainer or team physician and must be protected by some type of password required for entry into the database.

Besides record keeping, computer software can also be used for word processing; budgeting; managing a personal schedule or calendar; or creating a database or a spreadsheet from which injury data can be organized, retrieved, or related to specific injury situations or other injury records for statistical analysis. Other software can analyze and provide information about nutrition, body composition, and injury risk profiles based on other anthropometric measures and can be used to record isokinetic evaluation and exercise.[25]

The use of educational software to assist in teaching and the academic preparation of athletic training students has become an integral component in the majority of athletic training educational programs. New instructional and educational software continues to become available, and the use of CD-R and DVD technologies with their interactive capabilities, has made the multimedia presentation of instructional material, and thus learning, more interesting and memorable for the student.

The Internet and the World Wide Web have impacted and changed all of our lives. We live in a world where virtually any kind of information is immediately accessible to anyone who knows how to use the system. The sports medicine community in general and the athletic trainer specifically can access websites that have direct application to our clinical practice, to the education of athletic training students, and to the general base of knowledge that is relevant to our field. The use of e-mail to share information and to communicate immediately with colleagues has created an indispensable tool that has revolutionized our daily lives.

COLLECTING INJURY DATA

Because of the vast number of physically active individuals involved with organized and recreational sports, some knowledge relative to the number and types of injuries sustained during participation in these activities is essential. Although methods are much improved over the past, many weaknesses exist in systematic data collection and analysis of sports injuries.[27]

The Incidence of Injuries

An **accident** is defined as an unplanned event capable of resulting in loss of time, property damage, injury, disablement, or even death.[31] An **injury** may be defined as damage to the body that restricts activity or causes disability to such an extent that the athlete is not able to practice or compete the next day.[31] There is little doubt that a *case study* approach, which looks at one single incidence of an injury, can yield some critical information about the cause and subsequent efficacy of treatment for that particular injury. However, an approach that analyzes a large number of similar injuries can provide the greatest amount of information. In general, the incidence of sports injuries can be studied epidemiologically from many points of view—in terms of age at occurrence, gender, body regions that sustain injuries, or the occurrence in different sports. Sports are usually classified according to the risk, or chances, of injuries occurring under similar circumstances and are broadly divided into contact or collision, limited contact, or noncontact[4] (Table 2-3).

Athletes in all sports, recreational and organized, who participate in sports in the span of one year face a 50 percent chance of sustaining some injury. Of the 50 million estimated sports injuries per year, 50 percent require only minor care and no restriction

2-7

Critical Thinking E x e r c i s e

A basketball coach at All-American High School is concerned about what seems to be an abnormally high frequency of ankle sprains on her varsity team. Her philosophy is to require all her players to wear high-top shoes, yet the budget will not permit all players' ankles to be taped by the athletic trainer for practices and games. Together the coach and athletic trainer decide to purchase a number of lace-up ankle braces in an attempt to reduce the number of ankle sprains.

? How can the athletic trainer determine if the braces are helping decrease the frequency of ankle sprains in these basketball players?

accident
An act that occurs by chance or without intention.

injury
An act that damages or hurts.

The epidemiological approach toward injury data collection provides the most information.

Risk of injury is determined by the type of sport—collision, contact, or noncontact.

TABLE 2-3 Classification of Sports*

Contact or Collision	Limited Contact	Noncontact
Basketball	Baseball	Archery
Boxing	Bicycling	Badminton
Diving	Cheerleading	Body building
Field hockey	Canoeing or kayaking	Bowling
Football (tackle)	(white water)	Canoeing or kayaking
Ice hockey	Fencing	(flat water)
Lacrosse	Field events	Crew or rowing
Martial arts	High jump	Curling
Rodeo	Pole vault	Dancing (ballet,
Rugby	Floor hockey	modern, Jazz)
Ski jumping	Football (flag)	Field events
Soccer	Gymnastics	Discus
Team handball	Handball	Javelin
Water polo	Horseback riding	Shot put
Wrestling	Racquetball	Golf
	Skating (ice, in-line, roller)	Orienteering
	Skiing (cross-country,	Power lifting
	downhill, water)	Race walking
	Skateboarding	Riflery
	Snowboarding	Rope jumping
	Softball	Running
	Squash	Sailing
	Ultimate frisbee	Scuba diving
	Volleyball	Swimming
	Windsurfing or surfing	Table tennis
		Tennis
		Track
		Weight lifting

*From the American Academy of Pediatrics Committee on Sports Medicine and Fitness: Medical conditions affecting sports participation, *Pediatrics* 107(5):1205, 2001.

of activity.[9] Approximately 90 percent of injuries are muscle contusions, ligament sprains, and muscle strains; however, 10 percent of these injuries lead to microtrauma complications and eventually to a severe, chronic condition in later life.

Of the sports injuries that must be medically treated, sprains or strains, fractures, dislocations, and contusions are the most common.[8] In terms of the body regions most often injured, the knee has the highest incidence, with the ankle second and the upper limb third. For both males and females the most commonly injured body part is the knee, followed by the ankle; however, males have a much higher incidence of shoulder and upper-arm injuries than do females.

Catastrophic Injuries

Although millions of individuals participate in organized and recreational sports, there is a relatively low incidence of fatalities or catastrophic injuries. Ninety-eight percent of individuals with injuries requiring hospital emergency room medical attention are treated and released.[30] Deaths have been attributed to chest or trunk impact with thrown objects, other players, or nonyielding objects (e.g., goalposts). Deaths have occurred when players were struck in the head by sports implements (bats, golf clubs, hockey sticks) or by missiles (baseballs, soccer balls, golf balls, hockey pucks). Death has also resulted when an individual received a direct blow to the head from another player or the ground. On record are a number of sports deaths in which a playing structure, such as a goalpost or backstop, fell on a participant.

The highest incidence of indirect sports death stems from heatstroke. Less common indirect causes include cardiovascular and respiratory problems or congenital conditions not previously known. Catastrophic injuries leading to cervical injury and quadriplegia are seen mainly in American football. Although the incidence is low for the number of players involved, it could be lowered even further if more precautions were taken.

In most popular organized and recreational sports activities, the legs and arms have the highest risk factor for injury, with the head and face next. Muscle strains, joint sprains, contusions, and abrasions are the most frequent injuries sustained by the active sports participant. The major goal of this text is to provide the reader with the fundamental principles necessary for preventing and managing illnesses and injuries common to the athlete.

Current National Injury Data-Gathering Systems

The state of the art of sports injury surveillance is at this time unsatisfactory.[6] Currently, most local, state, and federal systems are concerned with the accident or injury only after it has happened, and they focus on injuries requiring medical assistance or those that cause time loss or restricted activity.

The ideal system takes an epidemiological approach that studies the relationship of various factors that influence the frequency and distribution of sports injuries.[23] When considering the risks inherent in a particular sport, both extrinsic and intrinsic factors must be studied.[34] Thus information is gleaned from both epidemiological data and the individual measurements of the athlete. The term *extrinsic factor* refers to the type of activity that is performed, the amount of exposure to injury, factors in the environment, and the equipment. The term *intrinsic factor* refers directly to the athlete and includes age, gender, neuromuscular aspects, structural aspects, performance aspects, and mental and psychological aspects.

Over the years, a number of athletic injury surveillance systems have been implemented; most have collected data for a few years and then ceased to exist. The currently active systems that are most often mentioned are the National Safety Council, the Annual Survey of Football Injury Research, the NCAA Injury Surveillance System, the National Center for Catastrophic Sports Injury Research, the National Electronic Injury Surveillance System (NEISS).

National Safety Council

The National Safety Council* is a nongovernmental, nonprofit public service organization. It draws sports injury data from a variety of sources, including educational institutions.

Annual Survey of Football Injury Research

In 1931 the American Football Coaches Association (AFCA) conducted its first Annual Survey of Football Fatalities. Since 1965 this research has been conducted at the University of North Carolina. In 1980 the survey's title was changed to Annual Survey of Football Injury Research. Every year, with the exception of 1942, data have been collected about public school, college, professional, and sandlot football. Information is gathered through personal contact interviews and questionnaires.[20] The sponsoring organizations of this survey are the AFCA, the NCAA, and the National Federation of State High School Athletic Associations (NFSHSAA).

This survey classifies football fatalities as direct or indirect. Direct fatalities are those resulting directly from participation in football. Indirect fatalities are produced by systemic failure caused by the exertion of playing football or by a complication that arose from a nonfatal football injury.

*National Safety Council, 1121 Spring Lake Drive, Itasca, IL 60143-1121.

National Center for Catastrophic Sports Injury Research

In 1977 the NCAA initiated the National Survey of Catastrophic Football Injuries. As a result of the injury data collected from this organization, several significant rule changes have been incorporated into collegiate football. Because of the success of this football project, the research was expanded to all sports for both men and women, and a National Center for Catastrophic Sports Injury Research was established at the University of North Carolina under the direction of Dr. Fred Mueller. With support from the NCAA, the NFSHSAA, the AFCA, and the Section on Sports Medicine of the American Association of Neurological Sciences, this center compiles data on catastrophic injuries at all levels of sport.[27]

NCAA Injury Surveillance System

The NCAA Injury Surveillance System (ISS) was established in 1982 primarily for the purpose of studying the incidence of football injuries so that rule change recommendations could be made to reduce the injury rate. Since that time this system has been greatly expanded and now collects data on most major sports. For the most part, athletic trainers are primarily involved in the collection and transmission of injury data.

The ISS has relied on the willingness of athletic trainers to submit paper forms reporting injuries in various NCAA-sponsored sports. In fall of 2004 the ISS will fully convert to a Web-based data-collection system that can compile far more data than ever before, providing member institutions with a low-cost means of tracking medical information and analyzing injury trends.

National Electronic Injury Surveillance System

In 1972 the federal government established the Consumer Product Safety Act (CPSA), which created and granted broad authority to the Consumer Product Safety Commission to enforce the safety standards for more than 10,000 products that may be risky to the consumer.[8] To perform this mission, the National Electronic Injury Surveillance System (NEISS)** was established. Data on injuries related to consumer products are monitored twenty-four hours a day from a selected sample of 5,000 hospital emergency rooms nationwide. Sports injuries represent 25 percent of all injuries reported by NEISS. It should be noted that a product may be related to an injury but not be the direct cause of that injury.

Once a product is considered hazardous, the commission can seize the product or create standards to decrease the risk.[8] Also, manufacturers and distributors of sports recreational equipment must report to the commission any product that is potentially hazardous or defective.[8] The commission can also research the reasons that a sports or recreational product is hazardous.

Using Injury Data

Valid, reliable sports injury data can materially help decrease injuries. If properly interpreted, the data can be used to modify rules, assist coaches and players in understanding risks, and help manufacturers evaluate their products against the overall market.[31] The public, especially parents, should understand the risks inherent in a particular sport, and insurance companies that insure athletes must know risks in order to set reasonable costs.

SUMMARY

■ The administration of a program of health care for the athlete demands a significant portion of the athletic trainer's time and effort. The efficiency and success of the athletic training program depend in large part on the administrative abilities of the athletic trainer in addition to the clinical skills required to treat the injured athlete.

**National Electronic Injury Surveillance System, U.S. Consumer Product Safety Commission, Directorate for Epidemiology, National Injury Information Clearinghouse, Washington, DC.

2-8

Critical Thinking E x e r c i s e

A collegiate athletic trainer is approached by the school administration to determine the potential risk of injury to their football team.

? What approach is best suited to gather this information?

- The athletic training program may best serve the athlete, the institution, and the community by establishing specific policies and regulations governing the use of available services.
- Budgets should allow for the purchase of equipment and supplies essential for providing appropriate preventive and rehabilitative care for the athlete.
- The athletic training program can certainly be enhanced by designing or renovating a facility to maximize the potential use of the space available. Space designed for injury treatment, rehabilitation, modality use, office space, physician examination, record keeping, and storage of supplies should be designated within each facility.
- Preparticipation exams must be given to athletes and should include a medical history, a general physical examination, and orthopedic screenings.
- The athletic trainer must maintain accurate and up-to-date medical records in addition to the other paperwork that is necessary for the operation of the athletic training program.
- Computers are extremely useful tools that enable athletic trainers to retrieve and store a variety of records.
- A number of data collection systems tabulate the incidence of sports injuries. The systems mentioned most often are the National Safety Council, the Annual Survey of Football Injury Research, the National Electronic Injury Surveillance System, the NCAA Injury Surveillance System, and the National Center for Catastrophic Sports Injury Research.

Solutions to Critical Thinking EXERCISES

2-1 The athletic trainer should work in conjunction with the appropriate administrative personnel to develop a risk management plan that includes security issues, fire safety, electrical and equipment safety, and emergency injury management.

2-2 Federal law mandates specific policies for recruitment, hiring, and firing. All qualified applicants should receive equal consideration regardless of their race, gender, religion, or nationality. The head athletic trainer must strictly adhere to these mandates.

2-3 The athletic training room should have specific areas designated for taping and preparation, treatment and rehabilitation, and hydrotherapy. It should have an office for the athletic trainer and adequate storage facilities positioned within the space to allow for an efficient traffic flow. Equipment purchases might include four or five treatment tables and two or three taping tables (these could be made in-house, if possible), a large-capacity ice machine, a combination ultrasound/electrical stimulating unit, a whirlpool, and various free weights and exercise tubing.

2-4 It is important that the school principal, the athletic director, and the athletic trainer set policy regarding who may and who may not use the athletic training facility. It would seem that an additional demand created by such a request would be too much for the school to absorb, both in terms of the physical facility and the personnel. It is likely that accommodating this request would interfere with the day-to-day operation of the athletic training program.

2-5 The preparticipation examination should consist of a medical history, a physical examination, and a brief orthopedic screening. The preparticipation physical may be effectively administered using a station examination system with a team of examiners. A station examination can provide the athlete with a detailed examination in a short period of time. A team of people is needed to examine this many athletes. The team should include several physicians, medically trained nonphysicians (nurses, athletic trainers, physical therapists, or physician's assistants), and managers, athletic training students, or assistant coaches.

2-6 The athletic trainer should explain that the computer can be used for maintaining medical records, doing word processing, planning a budget, managing a personal schedule or calendar, and creating a database containing injury data that can be organized, retrieved, or related to specific injury situations or to other injury records for analysis. Additional software can provide the athletic trainer with analysis and information about nutrition, body composition, and injury risk profiles. The computer could also be used for e-mail and for accessing information from the Internet.

2-7 The athletic trainer should do a simple study in which one-half of the players are randomly placed in the ankle braces while the other half continue to play in their high-top shoes. By comparing the number of ankle injuries in the group wearing the braces with those in the group without the braces, the athletic trainer can make some decision as to the effectiveness of the braces in preventing ankle injuries. Collecting and analyzing injury data is helpful in determining the efficacy of many of the techniques used by the athletic trainer.

2-8 The NCAA Injury surveillance system would best suit this purpose. This system of information can also be used to prevent injuries by presenting information to coaches, referees, and administrators to enforce necessary changes to the football program.

REVIEW QUESTIONS AND CLASS ACTIVITIES

1. What are the major administrative functions that an athletic trainer must perform?
2. Design two athletic training facilities—one for a high school and one for a large university.
3. Observe the activities in the athletic training facility. Pick both a slow time and a busy time to observe.
4. Why do hygiene and sanitation play an important role in athletic training? How should the athletic training facility be maintained?
5. Fully equip a new medium-size high school, college, or clinical athletic training facility. Pick equipment from current catalogs.
6. Establish a reasonable budget for a small high school, a large high school, and a large college or university.
7. Identify the groups or individuals to be served in the athletic training facility.
8. Organize a preparticipation health examination for ninety football players.
9. Record keeping is a major function in athletic training. What records are necessary to keep? How can a computer help?
10. Debate what conditions constitute good grounds for medical disqualification from a sport.
11. Discuss the epidemiological approach to recording sports injury data.

REFERENCES

1. Abdenour TE, Weir NJ: Medical assessment of the prospective student athlete, *Ath Train* 21:122, 1986.
2. American Academy of Pediatrics Committee on Sports Medicine and Fitness: Medical conditions affecting sports participation, *Pediatrics* 107(5):1205, 2001.
3. American Academy of Pediatrics Policy Statement: Recommendations for participation in competitive sports, *Physician Sportsmed* 16(5):51, 1988.
4. American Academy of Pediatrics: *Sports medicine: health care for young athletes,* Elk Grove Village, Ill, 1991, American Academy of Pediatrics.
5. Anderson J, Courson R, Kleiner D, McLoda T: National Athletic Trainers Association Position Statement: Emergency planning in athletics. *J Ath Train* 37(1):99, 2002.
6. Bagnall D: Budget planning key in secondary schools, *NATA News.* January, 15, 2001.
7. Caine DJ, Broekhoff J: Maturity assessment: a viable preventive measure against physical and psychological insult to the young athlete? *Physician Sportsmed* 15(3):67, 1987.
8. Damron CF: Injury surveillance systems for sports. In Vinger PF, Hoerner EF, editors: *Sports injuries,* Boston, 1986, Year Book Medical Publishers.
9. Dean CH, Hoerner EF: Injury rates in team sports and individual recreation. In Vinger PF, Hoerner EF, editors: *Sports injuries,* Boston, 1986, Year Book Medical Publishers.
10. Dorsen PJ: Should athletes with one eye, kidney, or testicle play contact sports? *Physician Sportsmed* 14(7):130, 1986.
11. Doyle M: A new dimension for the athletic training room: the spirit of the room. *Athletic Therapy Today* 7(1):34, 2002.
12. Equal Opportunity Commission: *Uniform guidelines on employee selection procedures,* Washington, DC, 1979, Bureau of National Affairs.
13. Forseth EA: Consideration in planning small college athletic training facilities, *Ath Train* 21(1):22, 1986.
14. Herbert D: Professional considerations related to conduct of preparticipation exams, *Sports Med Stand Malpract Report* 6(4):49, 1994.
15. Hunt V: A general look at the preparticipation exam, *NATA News,* May, 15, 2002.
16. Hunt V: Meeting clarifies HIPAA restrictions, *NATA News,* February, 10, 2003.
17. Jones D: HIPAA: friend or foe to athletic trainers? *Athletic Therapy Today* 8(2):17, 2003.
18. Jones R: The preparticipation, sport-specific athletic profile examination, *Semin Adolesc Med* 3:169, 1987.
19. Kibler W: *The sports participation fitness examination,* Champaign, Ill, 1990, Human Kinetics.
20. Knells S: Leadership and management techniques and principles for athletic training, *J Ath Train* 29(4):328, 1994.
21. Koester M, Amundson C: Preparticipation screening of high school athletes: are recommendations enough? *Physician Sportsmed* 31(8): 330, 2003
22. Konin J, Donley P: The athletic trainer as a personnel manager. In Konin J: *The clinical athletic trainer,* Gaithersburg, Md, 1997, Slack.
23. McGrew CA: Insights into the AHA scientific statement concerning cardiovascular preparticipation screening of competitive athletes, *Medicine and science in sports and exercise* 30(10 Suppl.):S351, 1998.
24. McKeag DB: Preseason physical examination for the prevention of sports injuries, *Sports Med* 2:413, 1985.
25. Moss RI: Facilities and foibles. *Athletic Therapy Today* 7(1):22, 2002.
26. Moyer-Knowles J: Planning a new athletic facility. In Konin J: *The clinical athletic trainer,* Gaithersburg, Md, 1997, Slack.
27. Mueller F: Catastrophic sports injuries. In Mueller F, Ryan A: *Prevention of athletic injuries: the role of the sports medicine team,* Philadelphia, 1991, Davis.
28. Myers GC, Garrick JG: The preseason examination of school and college athletes. In Strauss RH, editor: *Sports medicine,* Philadelphia, 1984, Saunders.
29. Peterson E: Insult to injury: feeling understaffed, underequipped and undervalued, athletic trainers say minimum of space and equipment will yield extensive benefits, *Athletic Business* 23(1):57, 1999.
30. Physician and Sportsmedicine: preparticipation physical evaluation monograph, ed 3, New York, 2004, McGraw-Hill.
31. Powell J: Epidemiologic research for injury prevention programs in sports. In Mueller F, Ryan A: *Prevention of athletic injuries: the role of the sports medicine team,* Philadelphia, 1991, Davis.
32. Rankin J: Technology and sports health care administration, *Athletic Therapy Today* 2(5):14, 1997.
33. Rankin J: Financial resources for conducting athletic training programs in the collegiate and high school settings, *J Ath Train* 27(4):344, 1992.
34. Rankin J, Ingersoll C: *Athletic training management: concepts and applications,* St Louis, 2000, Mosby.
35. Ray R: *Management strategies in athletic training,* Champaign, Ill, 2000, Human Kinetics.
36. Sabo J: Athletic training room design and layout, in Proceedings, National Athletic Trainers' Association 50th Annual Meeting and Clinical Symposium, June 16–19, 1999, Kansas City, Mo, Human Kinetics, 1999.
37. Sabo J: Design and construction of an athletic training facility, *NATA News,* May, 10, 2001.
38. Steiner G: *Strategic planning,* New York, 1979, Free Press.
39. Streator S: Risk management in athletic training. *Athletic Therapy Today* 6(2):55, 2001.
40. Swander H: *Preparticipation physical examination,* Kansas City, 1992, American Academy of Family Physicians, American Academy of Pediatrics, American Orthopedic Society for Sports Medicine, American Osteopathic Academy for Sports Medicine.
41. Tanner M: *Growth of adolescence,* ed 2, Oxford, England, 1962, Blackwell Scientific Publications.
42. Thompson PD, Sherman C: Cardiovascular screening: tailoring the preparticipation exam, *Physician Sportsmed* 24(6):47, 1996.
43. Wikston DL et al: The effectiveness of an interactive computer program versus traditional lecture in athletic training education, *J Ath Train* 33(3):238, 1998.

ANNOTATED BIBLIOGRAPHY

Konin J: *The clinical athletic trainer,* Gaithersburg, Md, 1997, Slack.

A unique, practical book that specifically addresses the administration of a health care program for athletic trainers working in a clinical setting.

Konin J, Frederick M: Documentation for Athletic Training, Thorough-fare, NJ, 2005, Slack Incorporated.

This text presents the basic principles of medical documentation, various styles of writing, legal considerations, documentation for reimbursement and many types of written documentation including evaluations, injury reports, medical releases, etc.

Rankin J, Ingersoll C: *Athletic training management: concepts and applications,* St Louis, 2000, Mosby.

Designed for upper-division undergraduate or graduate students interested in all aspects of organization and administration of an athletic training program.

Ray R: *Management strategies in athletic training,* Champaign, Ill, 2000, Human Kinetics.

The first text that covered the principles of organization and administration as they apply to many different employment settings in athletic training; contains many examples and case studies based on principles of administration presented in the text.

Legal Concerns and Insurance Issues

Chapter 3

When you finish this chapter you should be able to

- Analyze the legal considerations for the athletic trainer acting as a health care provider.
- Define the legal concepts of torts, negligence, and assumption of risk.
- Identify measures that can be taken by both the coach and the athletic trainer to minimize the chances of litigation.
- Explain product liability.
- Categorize the essential insurance requirements for the protection of the athlete.
- Classify the types of insurance necessary to protect the athletic trainer who is acting as a health care provider.

LEGAL CONCERNS OF THE COACH AND ATHLETIC TRAINER

In recent years negligence suits against teachers, coaches, athletic trainers, school officials, and physicians arising out of sports injuries have increased both in frequency and in the amount of damages awarded.[10,32] An increasing awareness of the many risk factors present in physical activities has had a major effect on the athletic trainer in particular.[14] **Liability** means being legally responsible for the harm one causes another person.[20] A great deal of care must be taken in following athletic training procedures to reduce the risk of being sued by an athlete and being found liable for negligence.[2,25,26]

liability
The state of being legally responsible for the harm one causes another person.

The Standard of Reasonable Care

Negligence is the failure to use ordinary or reasonable care—care that persons would normally exercise to avoid injury to themselves or to others under similar circumstances.[15] The *standard of reasonable care* assumes that an individual is neither exceptionally skillful nor extraordinarily cautious, but is a person of reasonable and ordinary prudence. Put another way, it is expected that an individual will bring a commonsense approach to the situation at hand and will exercise due care in its handling. In most cases in which someone has been sued for negligence, the actions of a hypothetical, reasonably prudent person are compared with the actions of the defendant to ascertain whether the course of action followed by the defendant was in conformity with the judgment exercised by such a reasonably prudent person.[24]

negligence
The failure to use ordinary or reasonable care.

The standard of reasonable care requires that an athletic trainer will act according to the standard of care of an individual with similar educational background or training.[12] An athletic trainer who has many years of experience, who is well educated in his or her field, and who is certified or licensed must act in accordance with those qualifications.

To establish negligence, an individual making the complaint must establish three things: (a) a **duty of care** existed between the person injured and the person responsible for that injury, (b) conduct of the defendant fell short of that duty of care, and (c) resultant damages.[22]

duty of care
Part of official job description

Torts

torts
Legal wrongs committed against a person.

Torts are legal wrongs committed against the person or property of another.[20] Every person is expected to conduct themselves without injuring others. When they do so, either intentionally or by negligence, they can be required by a court to pay money to the injured party ("damages") so that, ultimately, they will suffer the pain caused by their action. A tort also serves as a deterrent by sending a message to the community as to what is unacceptable conduct.

Such wrongs may emanate from **nonfeasance** (also referred to as an *act of omission*), wherein the individual fails to perform a legal duty; from **malfeasance** (also referred to as an *act of commission*), wherein an individual commits an act that is not legally his or hers to perform; or from **misfeasance,** wherein an individual improperly does something that he or she has the legal right to do. In any instance, if injury results, the person can be held liable. In the case of nonfeasance, a coach or athletic trainer may fail to refer a seriously injured athlete for the proper medical attention. In the case of malfeasance, the coach or athletic trainer may perform a medical treatment that is not within his or her legal province and from which serious medical complications develop. In a case of misfeasance, the coach or athletic trainer may incorrectly administer a first aid procedure he or she has been trained to perform.

nonfeasance (or an act of omission)
When an individual fails to perform a legal duty.

malfeasance (or an act of commission)
When an individual commits an act that is not legally his to perform.

misfeasance
When an individual improperly does something they have the legal right to do.

Negligence

When an athletic trainer is sued by an athlete, the complaint typically is for the tort of negligence. Negligence is alleged when an individual (1) does something that a reasonably prudent person would not do or (2) fails to do something that a reasonably prudent person would do under circumstances similar to those shown by the evidence.[3] To be successful in a suit for negligence, an athlete must prove that the athletic trainer had a *duty* to exercise reasonable care, that the athletic trainer *breached* that duty by failing to use reasonable care, and that there is a reasonable connection between the failure to use reasonable care and the injury suffered by the athlete or that the athletic trainer's action made the injury worse. If the athletic trainer breaches a duty to exercise reasonable care, but there is no reasonable connection between the failure to use reasonable care and the injury suffered by the athlete, the athlete's suit for negligence will not succeed.

An example of negligence is when an athletic trainer, through improper or careless handling of a therapeutic agent, seriously burns an athlete. Another illustration, occurring all too often in sports, is one in which a coach or an athletic trainer moves a possibly seriously injured athlete from the field of play to permit competition or practice to continue and does so either in an improper manner or before consulting those qualified to know the proper course of action. Should a serious or disabling injury result, the coach or the athletic trainer may be found liable. Liability is the state of being legally responsible for the harm one causes another person.[20]

Athletic trainers employed by an institution have a duty to provide athletic training care to athletes at that institution. An athletic trainer who is employed by the public schools or by a state-funded college or university may be protected by the legal doctrine of **sovereign immunity,** which essentially states that neither the government nor any individual who is employed by the government can be held liable for negligence. However, it should be made clear that the level of protection afforded by sovereign immunity may vary significantly from state to state. Clinical athletic trainers have a greater choice than institutional trainers of whom they may choose to treat as a patient. Once the athletic trainer assumes the duty of caring for an athlete, the athletic trainer has made an obligation to make sure that appropriate care is given. It should be made clear that the athletic trainer, or any other person, is not obligated to provide first aid care for an injured person outside their scope of employment. However, if they choose to become involved as a caregiver for an injured person, they are expected to provide reasonable care consistent with their level of training. The **Good Samaritan law** has been enacted in most states to provide limited protection against

3-1

Critical Thinking Exercise

A baseball batter was struck with a pitched ball directly in the orbit of the right eye and fell immediately to the ground. The athletic trainer ran to the player to examine the eye. There was some immediate swelling and discoloration around the orbit, but the eye appeared to be normal. The player insisted that he was fine and told the trainer he could continue to bat. After the game the athletic trainer told the athlete to go back to his room, put ice on his eye, and check in tomorrow. That night the baseball player began to hemorrhage into the anterior chamber of the eye and suffered irreparable damage to his eye. An ophthalmologist stated that if the athlete's eye had been examined immediately after the injury, the bleeding could have been controlled and there would not have been any damage to his vision.

? If the athlete brings a lawsuit against the athletic trainer, what must the athlete prove if he is to win a judgment?

legal liability to any individual who voluntarily chooses to provide first aid, should something go wrong. As long as the first aid provider does not overstep the limits of his or her professional training, and exercises what would be considered reasonable care in the situation, the provider will not be held liable.

A person possessing more training in a given field or area is expected to possess a correspondingly higher level of competence than, for example, a student is.[16] An individual will therefore be judged in terms of his or her performance in any situation in which legal liability may be assessed. It must be recognized that liability per se in all its various aspects is not assessed at the same level nationally but varies in interpretation from state to state and from area to area. Athletic trainers therefore should know and acquire the level of competence expected in their particular area. In essence, negligence is conduct that results in the creation of an unreasonable risk of harm to others.[31]

Statutes of Limitation

A *statute of limitation* sets a specific length of time that individuals may sue for damages from negligence. The length of time to bring suit varies from state to state, but in general plaintiffs have between one and three years to file suit for negligence. The statute of limitations begins to run on a plaintiff's time to file a lawsuit for negligence either from the time of the negligent act or omission that gives rise to the suit or from the time of the discovery of an injury caused by the negligent act or omission. Some states permit an injured minor to file suit up to three years after the minor reaches the age of eighteen. Therefore, an injured minor athlete's cause of action for negligence against an athletic trainer remains valid for many years after the negligent act or omission occurred or after the discovery of an injury caused by the negligent act or omission.

Assumption of Risk

An athlete assumes the risk of participating in an activity when he or she knows of and understands the dangers of that activity and voluntarily chooses to be exposed to those dangers. An assumption of risk can be expressed in the form of a waiver signed by an athlete or his or her parents or guardian or can be implied from the conduct of an athlete under the circumstances of his or her participation in an activity.

Assumption of risk may be asserted as a defense to a negligence suit brought by an injured athlete. The athletic trainer bears the burden of proving that an athlete assumed the risk by producing the document signed by the athlete or his or her parents or guardian or by proving that the athlete knew the risk of the activity and understood and voluntarily accepted that risk.

Assumption of risk, however, is subject to many and varied interpretations by courts, especially when a minor is involved, because he or she is not considered able to render a mature judgment about the risks inherent in the situation. Although athletes participating in a sports program are considered to assume a normal risk, this assumption in no way excuses those in charge from exercising reasonable care and prudence in the conduct of such activities or from foreseeing and taking precautionary measures against accident-provoking circumstances. In general, courts have been fairly consistent in upholding waivers and releases of liability for adults unless there is evidence of fraud, misrepresentation, or duress.[20]

Reducing the Risk of Litigation

The coach or athletic trainer can significantly decrease the risk of litigation by paying attention to several key points.[18] The coach should follow these guidelines:
1. Warn athletes of the potential dangers inherent in their sports.[6]
2. Supervise regularly and attentively.
3. Properly prepare and condition athletes.
4. Properly instruct athletes in the skills of their sports.
5. Ensure that proper and safe equipment and facilities are used by athletes at all times.[7]

Sovereign immunity
States that neither the government nor any individual who is employed by the government can be held liable for negligence.

Good Samaritan law
Provides limited protection against legal liability to any person who voluntarily chooses to provide first aid.

3-2
Critical Thinking E x e r c i s e

? How should the first-aid care provided by a certified athletic trainer differ from the care that may be provided by a lay person?

assumption of risk
The individual, through express or implied agreement, assumes that some risk or danger will be involved in the particular undertaking. In other words, a person takes his or her own chances.

3-3
Critical Thinking E x e r c i s e

A college athletic trainer is cleaning out a filing cabinet and decides to throw some older medical files away. Concern is expressed, however, about how long these files should be maintained for legal purposes.

? What is the statute of limitations for a college-age athlete to file suit?

The athletic trainer should do as follows:

1. Work to establish good personal relationships with athletes, parents, and coworkers.
2. Establish specific policies and guidelines for the operation of an athletic training facility, and maintain qualified and adequate supervision of the training room, its environs, facilities, and equipment at all times.
3. Develop and carefully follow an emergency plan.
4. Become familiar with the health status and medical history of the athletes under his or her care so as to be aware of problems that could present a need for additional care or caution.
5. Keep factually accurate and timely records that document all injuries and rehabilitation steps, and set up a record retention policy that allows records to be kept and used in defense of litigation that may be brought by athletes. A record retention system needs to keep records for long enough to defend against suits brought by athletes after they reach the age of eighteen.
6. Document efforts to create a safe playing environment.
7. Have a detailed job description in writing.
8. Obtain, from athletes and from parents or guardians when minors are involved, written consent for providing health care.
9. Maintain the confidentiality of medical records.
10. Exercise extreme caution in the administration, if allowed by law, of nonprescription medications; athletic trainers may not dispense prescription drugs.
11. Use only those therapeutic methods that he or she is qualified to use and that the law states may be used.
12. Not use or permit the presence of faulty or hazardous equipment.
13. Work cooperatively with the coach and the team physician in the selection and use of sports protective equipment, and insist that the best equipment be obtained, properly fitted, and properly maintained.
14. Not permit injured players to participate unless cleared by the team physician. Players suffering a head injury should not be permitted to reenter the game. In some states a player who has suffered a concussion may not continue in the sport for the balance of the season.
15. Develop an understanding with the coaches that an injured athlete will not be allowed to reenter competition until, in the opinion of the team physician or the athletic trainer, he or she is psychologically and physically able. Athletic trainers should not allow themselves to be pressured to clear an athlete until he or she is fully cleared by the physician.
16. Follow the express orders of the team physician at all times.
17. Purchase professional liability insurance that provides adequate financial coverage and be aware of the limitations of the policy.
18. Know the limitations of his or her expertise as well as the applicable state regulations and restrictions that limit the athletic trainer's scope of practice.
19. Use common sense in making decisions about an athlete's health and safety.

In the case of an injury, the athletic trainer must use reasonable care to prevent additional injury until further medical care is obtained.[19] (See Chapter 10 for additional comments.)

Product Liability

Product liability refers to the liability of any or all parties along the chain of manufacture of any product for damage caused by that product.[17] This includes the manufacturer of component parts, an assembling manufacturer, the wholesaler, and the retail store owner. Products containing inherent defects that cause harm to a consumer of the product, or someone to whom the product was loaned, given, etc., are the subjects of product liability suits. Product liability claims can be based on negligence, strict liability, or breach of warranty of fitness, depending on the jurisdiction within which the claim is based. Many states have enacted comprehensive product liability statutes and these statutory provisions can be very diverse. There is no federal product liability law.

Manufacturers of athletic equipment have a duty to design and produce equipment that will not cause injury as long as it is used as intended. Manufacturers are strictly liable for defects in the design and production of equipment that produces injury. This does not excuse the athletic trainer who misuses the equipment, only equipment that is faulty. An athletic trainer must not alter the equipment in any way. To do so invalidates the manufacturer's warranty and places liability solely on the athletic trainer. An express warranty is the manufacturer's written statement that a product is safe. For example warning labels on football helmets inform the player of possible dangers inherent in using the product. Athletes must read and sign a form indicating that they have read and understand the warning. The National Operating Committee on Standards for Athletic Equipment (NOCSAE) establishes minimum standards for football helmets that must be met to ensure its safety.

INSURANCE CONSIDERATIONS

During the past forty years the insurance industry has undergone a significant evolutionary process. Health care reform initiated in the 1990s has focused on the concept of *managed care,* in which the costs of a health care provider's medical care are closely monitored and scrutinized by insurance carriers. Often preapproval is required prior to health care delivery.

Since 1971 there has been a significant increase in the number of lawsuits filed, caused in part by the steady increase in the number of individuals who have become active in sports. The costs of insurance have also significantly increased during this period. More lawsuits and much higher medical costs are causing a crisis in the insurance industry.[9] Medical insurance is a contract between an insurance company and a policyholder in which the insurance company agrees to reimburse a portion of the total medical bill after some deductible has been paid by the policyholder. The major types of insurance about which individuals concerned with athletic training and sports medicine should have some understanding are general health insurance, accident insurance, professional liability insurance, and catastrophic insurance as well as insurance for errors and omissions. There is a need to protect adequately all who are concerned with sports health and safety. *Focus Box:* "Common insurance terminology" lists some of the more common insurance terms.

Focus

Common insurance terminology

Allowable Charge: The maximum amount, according to the individual policy, that insurance will pay for each procedure or service performed.

Beneficiary: A person eligible to receive the benefits of a specific policy or program.

Benefits: Services that an insurer, government agency, or health care plan offers to pay for an insured individual.

Case Management Services: The process in which the attending physician or agent coordinates the care given to a patient by other health care providers and/or community organizations.

Claim: A form sent to an insurance company requesting payment for covered medical expenses. Information includes the insured's name and address, procedure codes, diagnostic codes, charges, and date of service.

Continued

Focus

Common insurance terminology—continued

Clean Claim: A filed claim with all the necessary information that may be immediately processed.

Contract: A legally binding agreement between an insurance company and a physician describing the duties of both parties.

Copayment: A provision in an insurance policy requiring the policyholder to pay a specified percentage of each medical claim.

Customary Fees: The average fee charged for a specified service or procedure in a defined geographic area.

Deductible: The amount owed by the insured on a yearly basis before the insurance company will begin to pay for services rendered.

Dependent: A person legally eligible for benefits based on his or her relationship with the policyholder.

Exclusions: Specified medical services, disorders, treatments, diseases, and durable medical equipment that is listed as uncovered or not reimbursable in an insurance policy.

Explanation of Benefits (EOB): An insurance report accompanying all claim payments that explains how the insurance company processed a claim.

Fee Schedule: A comprehensive listing of the maximum payment amount that an insurance company will allow for specified medical procedures performed on a beneficiary of the plan.

Gatekeeper: The primary care physician assigned by the insurer that oversees the medical care rendered to a patient and initiates all specialty and ancillary services.

Participating Provider: A health care provider who has entered into a contract with an insurance company to provide medical services to the beneficiaries of a plan. The provider agrees to accept the insurance company's approved fee and will only bill the patient for the deductible, copayment, and uncovered services.

Policyholder: The person who takes out the medical insurance policy.

Premium: A periodic payment made to an insurance company by an individual policy.

Third Party Administrator: An independent organization that collects premiums, pays claims, and provides administrative services within a health care plan.

UCR Allowable Charge: Usual, customary, and reasonable charge that represents the maximum amount an insurance company will pay for a given service based on geographical averages.

General Health Insurance

Every athlete should have a *general health insurance* policy that covers illness, hospitalization, and emergency care. Some institutions offer primary insurance coverage in which all medical expenses are paid for by the athletic department. The institutions pay an extremely high premium for this type of coverage. Most institutions offer *secondary insurance* coverage, which pays the athlete's remaining medical bills once the athlete's personal insurance company has made its payment. Secondary insurance always includes a deductible that will not be covered by the plan.

Many athletes are covered under some type of *family health insurance* policy. However, the school or university must make certain that personal health insurance is arranged for or purchased by athletes not covered under family policies.[28] A form letter directed to the parents of all athletes should be completed and returned to the institution to make certain that appropriate coverage is provided (Figure 3-1). Some so-called comprehensive plans do not cover every health need. For example, they may cover physicians' care but not hospital charges. Many of these plans require large prepayments before the insurance takes effect. Supplemental policies such as accident insurance and catastrophic insurance are designed to take over where general health insurance stops.

Every athlete should have a general health insurance policy that covers illness, hospitalization, and emergency care.

Emergency and Insurance Information on Student Athletes

Student's Name _____ Date of Birth _____ Sport _____

Home Address _____

Home Phone _____

Social Security or Student ID Number _____ Sex: M ___ F ___

Family Doctor _____ Phone _____

Address _____

Policy Holder _____ Relation to Student _____

Employer _____

Address _____

Home Phone _____ Work Phone _____

Names of Insurance Companies _____

Address of Insurance Company _____

Certificate Number _____ Group _____ Type _____

Should my son/daughter require services beyond those covered by the Sports Medicine

Program, I give permission to the Division of Sports Medicine to file a claim for such

services with the above health insurer.

I understand that any insurance payments I receive must be returned to be placed on

my child's account.

Parent's Signature _____ Date _____

Figure 3-1

Sample emergency and insurance information form

Accident Insurance

Besides general health insurance, low-cost *accident insurance* is available to the student. It often covers accidents on school grounds while the student is in attendance. The purpose of this insurance is to protect against financial loss from medical and hospital bills, encourage an injured student to receive prompt medical care, encourage prompt reporting of injuries, and relieve a school of financial responsibility.

The school's general insurance may be limited; thus accident insurance for a specific activity such as sports may be needed to provide additional protection.[9] This type of coverage is limited and does not require knowledge of fault, and the amount it pays is limited. For serious sport injuries requiring surgery and lengthy rehabilitation, accident insurance is usually not adequate. This inadequacy can put families with limited budgets into a real financial bind. Of particular concern is insurance that does not adequately cover catastrophic injuries.

Professional Liability Insurance

Most individual schools and school districts have general liability insurance to protect against damages that may arise from injuries occurring on school property. Liability insurance covers claims of negligence on the part of individuals.[11] Its major concern is whether supervision was reasonable and if unreasonable risk of harm was perceived by the sports participant.[28]

Because of the amount of litigation based on alleged negligence, premiums have become almost prohibitive for some schools. Typically, a victim's lawsuit has taken a shotgun approach, suing the coach, athletic trainer, physician, school administrator, and school district. If a protective piece of equipment is involved, the product manufacturer is also sued.

3-4

Critical Thinking Exercise

An athletic trainer who recently became certified is planning on working summer camps for an area high school before he starts his full-time employment in the fall.

? What should the athletic trainer do to protect himself from liability?

Because of the amount of litigation for alleged negligence, all professionals involved with the sports program must be fully protected by professional liability insurance.

All athletic trainers should carry *professional liability insurance* and must clearly understand the limits of its coverage. Liability insurance typically covers negligence in a civil case. If a criminal complaint is filed, however, liability insurance will not cover the athletic trainer.

Catastrophic Insurance

Although catastrophic injuries in sports participation are relatively uncommon, when they do occur the consequences to the athlete, family, and institution, as well as to society, can be staggering.[27] In the past when available funds have been completely diminished, the family was forced to seek funding elsewhere, usually through a lawsuit. Organizations such as the National Collegiate Athletic Association (NCAA) and National Association of Intercollegiate Athletics (NAIA) provide plans that deal with the problem of a lifetime that requires extensive medical and rehabilitative care because of a permanent disability.[5]

Benefits begin when expenses have reached $25,000 and are then extended for a lifetime. A program at the secondary-school level is offered to districts by the National Federation of State High School Associations (NFSHSA). This plan provides medical, rehabilitation, and transportation costs in excess of $10,000 not covered by other insurance benefits.[28] Costs for catastrophic insurance are based on the number of sports and the number of hazardous sports offered by the institution.

To offset the shotgun approach of lawsuits and to cover what is not covered by a general liability policy, *errors and omissions liability insurance* has evolved. It is designed to cover school employees, officers, and the district against suits claiming malpractice, wrongful actions, errors and omissions, and acts of negligence.[28] Even when working in a program that has good liability coverage, each person within that program who works directly with students must have his or her own personal liability insurance.

Insurance that covers the athlete's health and safety can be complex. The athletic trainer must ensure that every athlete is adequately covered by a reliable insurance company. In some athletic programs the filing of claims becomes the responsibility of the athletic trainer. This task can be highly time consuming, taking the athletic trainer away from his or her major role of working directly with the athlete. Because of the intricacies and time involved with claim filing and follow-up communications with parents, doctors, and vendors, a staff person other than the athletic trainer should be assigned this responsibility.

THIRD-PARTY REIMBURSEMENT

Third-party reimbursement is the primary mechanism of payment for medical services in the United States.[29] The policyholder's insurance company reimburses health care professionals for services performed. Medical insurance companies may provide group and individual coverage for employees and dependents. Managed care involves a prearranged system for delivering health care that is designed to control costs while continuing to provide quality care. To cut payout costs, many insurance companies pay for preventive care (to reduce the need for hospitalization) and limit where the individual can go for care. A number of different health care systems have been developed to contain costs.[21]

Health Maintenance Organizations

Health maintenance organizations (HMOs) provide preventive measures and limit where the individual can receive care. Except in emergencies, permission must be obtained before the individual can go to another provider. HMOs generally pay 100 percent of the medical costs as long as care is rendered at an HMO facility. Many supplemental policies do not cover the medical costs that would normally be paid by the general policy. Therefore an athlete treated outside the HMO may be ineligible for any insurance benefits. Many HMOs determine fees using a capitation system, which limits the amount that will be reimbursed for a specific service. It is essential for the athletic trainer to understand the limits of and restrictions on coverage at his or her institution.

3-5

Critical Thinking E x e r c i s e

During a high school gymnastics meet, a gymnast fell off the uneven parallel bars and landed on her forearm. The athletic trainer suspected a fracture and decided an X ray was needed. The gymnast's parents had general health insurance through a PPO, but because the gymnast was in severe pain, she was sent to the nearest emergency room to be treated. Unfortunately, the emergency facility was not on the list of preferred providers, and the insurance company denied the claim. The athletic trainer assured the parents that the school would take care of whatever medical costs were not covered by their insurance policy.

? Because the PPO denied the claim, what type of insurance policy should the school carry to cover the medical costs?

Third-party reimbursement involves reimbursement by the policyholder's insurance company for services performed by health care professionals.

Third-party payers:
- HMOs
- PPOs
- POS
- EPOs
- PHOs
- TPA
- Medicare
- Medicaid
- Worker Compensation
- Indemnity Plans
- Capitation

Preferred Provider Organizations

Preferred provider organizations (PPOs) provide discount health care but also limit where a person can go for treatment of an illness. The athletic trainer must be apprised in advance as to where the ill athlete should be sent. Athletes sent to a facility that is not on the approved list may be required to pay for care, whereas if they are sent to a preferred facility, all costs are paid.[9] PPOs may provide added services, such as physical therapy, more easily and at no cost or at a much lower cost than would another insurance policy. PPOs pay on a fee-for-service basis.

Point of Service Plan

The point of service (POS) plan is a combination of the HMO and PPO plans. It is based on an HMO structure, yet it allows members to go outside the HMO to obtain services. This flexibility is allowed only with certain conditions and under special circumstances.

Exclusive Provider Organizations

Exclusive provider organizations (EPOs) are also a combination of the HMO and PPO plans. They are restrictive in the number and types of providers they have and consequently are more like an HMO. Most will not pay anything if you use out-of-network providers.

Physician Hospital Organization

Physician hospital organizations (PHOs) involve a major hospital or hospital chain and its physicians. A PHO organization contracts directly with employers to provide services and/or contracts with a managed care organization.

Third Party Administrators

Third party administrators (TPAs) are frequently used to administer services and to pay claims for self-insured group plans thus function as pseudo insurance companies. They perform member services such as enrollment and billing and assist with controlling utilization without the financial risk.

Medicare

Medicare is the federal health insurance program for the aged and disabled. Most people at retirement age qualify for Medicare benefits. There are two parts or sections to Medicare. Part A, the hospital portion, is normally premium-free at retirement to the beneficiary. Part B, the physician portion, has a monthly premium charge to the beneficiary.

Medicaid

Medicaid is a health insurance program for people with low incomes and limited resources. Medicaid is funded by both the federal government and individual states, with the state responsible for handling the administration of the program. Individual states administer Medicaid and thus benefits vary by state.

Workers Compensation

Workers compensation laws and benefits for injured workers are mandated by the states. Employers pay the premiums and the claims are settled by workers compensation insurance carriers whose goal is to return injured workers to the work force as soon as possible.

Indemnity Plans

An indemnity plan is the most traditional form of billing for health care. It is a fee-for-service plan that allows the insured party to seek medical care without restrictions on utilization or cost. The provider charges the patient or a third-party payer for services provided. Charges are based on a set fee schedule.

Capitation

Capitation is a form of reimbursement used by managed care providers in which members make a standard payment each month regardless of how much service is rendered to the member by the provider.

Third-Party Reimbursement for Athletic Trainers

3-6

Critical Thinking Exercise

An athletic trainer working in a clinic is seeking third-party reimbursement for athletic training services performed. The trainer is experiencing difficulty obtaining reimbursement from certain payers because of uncertainty about the effectiveness of the treatment program.

? What can the athletic trainer do to address the concerns of the third-party payers?

Athletic trainers have always been able to bill third-party payers for services rendered. Unfortunately in the past, most insurers refused to reimburse the athletic trainer. However over the last few years there has been a significant increase in reimbursement from third-party payers for athletic trainers working in a variety of settings, including hospitals, physicians' offices, sports rehabilitation clinics, and college and university settings.[24] Reimbursement for as much as 85 percent of billings has been reported by some athletic trainers. Some have fared less favorably. There is no question that licensure is key to successful reimbursement from third-party payers. In the case of insurance/managed care contracts, the state ultimately decides who the company will reimburse for services. Most third-party payers view "licensed health care professionals" as the only reimbursable entities. Fortunately in most states this includes certified athletic trainers. Certainly, securing third-party reimbursement for athletic training services must continue to be a priority, especially for the clinical athletic trainer.[29]

In 1995 NATA established the Reimbursement Advisory Group to monitor managed care changes and to help the athletic trainer secure a place as a health care provider. Specifically this group was charged with the responsibility of developing a model for approaching third-party payers for the reimbursement of athletic training services, of educating athletic trainers on issues related to reimbursement, and perhaps most important, of designing and implementing a data-based clinical outcomes study.[8] In 1996 NATA initiated the Athletic Training Outcomes Assessment project designed to present supporting data that measures the results of interventions involving athletic training procedures. This three-year study was designed to provide data that focused on functional outcomes, including assessing the patients' perceptions of their functional capabilities and their overall satisfaction with their treatment program; assessing the physical, emotional, and social well-being of patients; assessing health care cost effectiveness relative to time lost from activity due to injury; and assessing the number of treatments.[12] The results of this study were critical in securing reimbursement for athletic training services, because the majority of third-party payers currently require outcomes research when evaluating a contract.[4,19]

Insurance Billing

The athletic trainer must file insurance claims immediately and correctly.[29] Athletic trainers working in educational settings can facilitate this process by collecting insurance information on every athlete at the beginning of the year. Letters should be drafted to the parents of all athletes explaining the limits of the school insurance policy and what the parents must do to process a claim if injury does occur. Schools with secondary policies should stress that the parents must submit all bills to their insurance company before they submit the remainder to the school. In educational institutions, most claims will be filed with a single insurance company, which will pay for medical services provided by individual health care providers.

Filing an Insurance Claim

When filing an insurance claim to submit for reimbursement, athletic trainers will find that a standard form labeled HCFA-1500/HCFA-1450. is accepted by most carriers (Blue Cross/Blue Shield uses Form UB-92). These forms must be completed in detail with as much information as possible. Experience dictates that the more accurately and thoroughly these forms are completed, the quicker and higher the rate of reimbursement.

TABLE 3-1   Description of Billing Codes Used by Athletic Trainers

The following is a guide to procedure billing codes that may be used by athletic trainers when billing for athletic training services:

Code	Description
97005/97006	Athletic trainer evaluation and reevaluation (per visit)
97750	Physical performance test (each 15 minutes) treatment charges:
97116	Gait training (each 15 minutes)
97110	Therapeutic exercise (each 15 minutes)
97112	Neuromuscular reeducation (each 15 minutes)
97530	Therapeutic activities (each 15 minutes)
97113	Aquatic therapeutic exercise (each 15 minutes)
97124	Massage (each 15 minutes)
97530	Body mechanics training (each 15 minutes)
97140	Manual therapy (each 15 minutes)
97504	Orthotics fitting and training (each 15 minutes)
97150	Therapeutic procedures—group (each visit)
97150	Supervised exercise (each visit)
11040	Debridement (each visit)
97139	Wound care (each 15 minutes)
97139	Taping (each visit)
95831	Manual muscle testing—extremity/trunk
95851	Range of Motion (ROM) measurements
95852	ROM measurements of hand, with or without comparison with normal side
97545	Work hardening/conditioning (initial 2 hours)
97035	Ultrasound (each 15 minutes)
97035	Phonophoresis (each 15 minutes) (Must bill for ultrasound if billing for this service.)
97032	Electrical stimulation (each 15 minutes)
97033	Iontophoresis (each 15 minutes)
97032	Constant electrical stimulation (each 15 minutes)
97034	Contrast baths (each 15 minutes)
97014	Electric stimulation (application to one or more areas)
97022	Whirlpool (application to one or more areas)
97010	Hot packs (application to one or more areas)
97010	Cold packs/ice massage (application to one or more areas)
97012	Traction, mechanical (not time-based)
97016	Compression pump (application to one or more areas)

Athletic trainers working in the clinical setting should understand that the clinic must be able to collect reimbursement from third-party payers for services provided. The athletic trainer should request approval from insurance companies before treating patients.

There are two types of billing codes which must be filed when submitting a claim on standard HFCA-1500 or UB-92 forms to third-party payers, one is a *diagnostic code,* and the other is a *procedural code.*[30] A diagnostic code is required for all procedural billing, and can be found in a book called the *International Classification of Diseases* (ICD-9-CM). This is a five-digit code that specifies the condition or injury that the athletic trainer or any other health care provider is treating. For example code 845.02 indicates that the patient has a sprain of the calcaneofibular ligament in the ankle.

The *Current Procedure Terminology Code* (CPT) was first developed by the American Medical Association in 1966. Each year, an annual publication is prepared, that makes changes corresponding to significant updates in medical technology and practice. The CPT code is used to identify specific medical procedures used in treating a patient. Table 3-1 lists the current CPT codes most often used by the athletic trainer.

Focus

Guidelines for documentation*

When billing for and receiving reimbursement the following points should be documented:

- Initial evaluation, including plan of treatment and goals (SOAP notes)
- Appropriate patient medical history
- Patient examination results
- Functional assessment
- Type of treatment and body parts to be treated
- Expected frequency and number of treatments
- Prognosis
- Functional, measurable, and time-based goals
- Precautions and contraindications
- A statement that the treatment plan and goals were discussed and understood by the patient and possibly by the guardian
- Daily treatment records
- A record of any changes in physical status, physician orders or treatment plan, or goals
- Weekly progress notes, especially on goals (SOAP or function-based)
- Copies of notes to or from the referring physician's office, whether by fax, e-mail, U.S. mail, or phone
- A prescription or other state-mandated documentation from a physician

*From the NATA Committee on Reimbursement

3-7

Critical Thinking E x e r c i s e

? When filing an insurance claim for an athlete following injury, what can an athletic trainer do to improve the reimbursement rate as well as to speed up the process?

Athletic trainers should never release medical records to third-party payers unless written authorization has been obtained from the patient according to HIPAA guidelines. It is also essential when billing for and receiving reimbursement that the athletic trainer keeps meticulous, accurate, and detailed documentation of all procedures, charges submitted, and payments received for services. *Focus Box:* "Guidelines for documentation" identifies criteria that should be routinely followed when billing for charges.

SUMMARY

- A great deal of care must be taken in following coaching and athletic training procedures that conform to the legal guidelines governing liability for negligence.
- Liability is the state of being legally responsible for the harm one causes another person. It assumes that an athletic trainer would act according to the standard of care of any individual with similar educational background and training.
- An athletic trainer who fails to use reasonable care—care that persons would normally exercise to avoid injury to themselves or to others under similar circumstances—may be found liable for negligence.
- Although athletes participating in a sports program are considered to assume a normal risk, this assumption in no way exempts those in charge from exercising reasonable care.
- Athletic trainers can significantly decrease the risk of litigation by making certain that they have done everything possible to provide a reasonable degree of care to the injured athlete.
- The major types of insurance about which athletic trainers should have some understanding are general health insurance, accident insurance, professional liability insurance, catastrophic insurance, and insurance for errors and omissions.
- Third-party reimbursement is the primary mechanism of payment for medical services in the United States. A number of different health care systems have been developed to contain costs.
- It is essential that the athletic trainer file insurance claims immediately and correctly using appropriate forms and billing codes.

3-8

Critical Thinking E x e r c i s e

A sports medicine clinic is considering hiring an athletic trainer. However, the clinic administrator is concerned that the athletic trainer cannot bill third-party payers for services provided.

? What does the administrator need to be told about third-party reimbursement for athletic training services?

Websites

Legal Information Institute at Cornell: http://www.law.cornell.edu/topics/sports.html

This website is part of a series of legal information and specifically addresses law in sport; the information is rather technical in nature. The area relevant to sports medicine is addressed in the section titled "Torts."

Cramer First Aider:

http://www.cramersportsmed.com/firstaider.jsp

The Cramer First Aider is a newsletter published by Cramer that provides information about current topics in sports medicine. For information relevant to this chapter, go to the section titled "Legal Issues."

Sports Lawyers Journal: http://www.law.tulane.edu

Specialized academic and professional publication on legal aspects of sports.

The Center for Sports Law & Policy:

http://www.law.duke.edu/sportscenter/

Duke University School of Law.

Health Insurance Association of America: http://www.hiaa.org

The nation's most prominent trade association representing the private health care system. It is the nation's premier provider of self-study courses on health insurance and managed care.

Duhaime & Co. Legal Dictionary: http://www.duhaime.org/dictionary

This is a site that has put together an extensive list of legal terms with clear definitions and explanations.

National Athletic Trainers Association Committee on Reimbursement: http://www.nata.org/members1/committees/cor/rag.cfm

Designed to enhance the reimbursement interests and efforts of NATABOC certified athletic trainers.

Solutions to Critical Thinking EXERCISES

3-1 An athletic trainer who assumes the duty of caring for an athlete has an obligation to make sure that appropriate care is given. If the athletic trainer fails to provide an acceptable standard of care, there is a breach of duty on the part of the athletic trainer, and the athlete must then prove that this breach caused the injury or made the injury worse.

3-2 A person possessing more training in a given field or area is expected to possess a correspondingly higher level of competence than a lay person is. A certified athletic trainer will therefore be judged in terms of his or her performance in any situation in which legal liability may be assessed.

3-3 The athlete would typically have between one and three years to file suit for negligence. The statute of limitations begins to run on a plaintiff's time to file a lawsuit for negligence either from the time of the negligent act or omission that gives rise to the suit or from the time of the discovery of an injury caused by the negligent act or omission.

3-4 The athletic trainer should purchase private professional liability insurance. In addition, the athletic trainer should keep proper records of injuries and keep those records in his possession.

3-5 Besides general health insurance, low-cost accident insurance often covers accidents on school grounds while the athlete is competing. The purpose of this insurance is to protect against financial loss from medical and hospital bills, encourage an injured athlete to receive prompt medical care, encourage prompt reporting of injuries, and relieve a school of financial responsibility.

3-6 The athletic trainer could initiate an outcomes research project designed to present supporting data that measures the results of interventions involving athletic training procedures. This research project would assess the athletes' perceptions of their functional capabilities and overall satisfaction with their treatment program, the cost-effectiveness of the health care relative to time lost from activity due to injury, and the number of treatments. The majority of third-party payers currently require outcomes research when evaluating a contract.

3-7 The athletic trainer should file an insurance claim for reimbursement using the standard form labeled HCFA-1500. The form should be completed in detail with as much information as possible. The athletic trainer who completes these forms accurately and thoroughly probably experiences a quicker and higher rate of reimbursement.

3-8 It should be pointed out that athletic trainers can bill third-party payers for services rendered to a patient. Whether the insurance company will reimburse the athletic trainer for services is up to the individual third-party payer. With the approval of the uniform billing code for athletic training services, it is more likely that the athletic trainer will be successfully reimbursed for treating patients.

REVIEW QUESTIONS AND CLASS ACTIVITIES

1. What are the athletic trainer's major legal concerns for negligence and for assumption of risk?
2. What measures can an athletic trainer take to minimize the chances of litigation should an athlete be injured?
3. Invite an attorney who is familiar with sports litigation to class to discuss how athletic trainers can protect themselves from lawsuits.
4. Discuss what the athletic trainer must do to provide reasonable and prudent care in dealing with an injured athlete.
5. Why is it necessary for an athlete to have both general health insurance and accident insurance?
6. Briefly discuss the various methods of third-party reimbursement.
7. Why should an athletic trainer carry individual liability insurance?
8. What are the critical considerations for filing insurance claims?

REFERENCES

1. Albohm M, Campbell D, Konin J: *Reimbursement for athletic trainers,* Thoroughfare, NJ, 2001, Slack.
2. Appenzeller H: *Safe at first: a guide to help sports administrators reduce their liability,* Chapel Hill, NC, 1999, Carolina Academic Press.
3. Appenzeller H: *Sports and the law: contemporary issues,* Charlottesville, Va, 1985, Michie.
4. Benjamin K: Outcomes research and the allied health professional, *J Allied Health* 24:3, 1995.
5. Berg R: Catastrophic injury insurance, an end to costly litigation, *Ath J* 8:10, 1987.
6. Borkowski RP: Coaches and the courts, *First Aider* 54:1, 1985.
7. Borkowski RP: Lawsuit less likely if safety comes first, *First Aider* 55:11, 1985.
8. Campbell D: Workshop on third party reimbursement, *NATA News* 3:34, 1996.
9. Chambers RL: Insurance types and coverage: knowledge to plan for the future (with a focus on motor skill activities and athletics), *Phys Educ* 44:233, 1986.

10. Clement A: Patterns of litigation in physical education instruction. Paper presented at the American Association of Health, Physical Education, and Dance, National Convention and Exposition, Cincinnati, April 1986.

11. Cotton DJ: What is covered by your liability insurance policy? A risk management essential, *Exercise Standard and Malpractice Reporter* 15(4):54, 2001.

12. De Carlo M: Reimbursement for health care services. In Konin J: *Clinical athletic training*, Thoroughfare, NJ, 1997, Slack.

13. Drowatzky JN: Legal duties and liability in athletic training, *Ath Train* 20:11, 1985.

14. Eickhoff-Shemek JAM, Evans JA: An investigation of law and legal liability content in masters academic programs in sports medicine and exercise science. *Journal of Legal Aspects of Sport* 10(3):172, 2000.

15. Frenkel DA: Medico-legal aspects in sport (abstract), *Exercise & Society Journal of Sport Science* (28):90, 2001.

16. Gallup E: *Law and the team physician*, Champaign, 1995, Human Kinetics.

17. Gorman L: Product liability in sports medicine. *Athletic Therapy Today* 4(4):36, 1999.

18. Graham L: Ten ways to dodge the malpractice bullet, *Ath Train* 20(2):117, 1985.

19. Harada N, Sofaer S, Kominski G: Functional status outcomes in rehabilitation: implications for prospective payment, *Medical Care* 31:345, 1993.

20. Hawkins J, Appenzeller H: Legal aspects of sports medicine. In Mueller F, Ryan A: *Prevention of athletic injuries: the role of the sports medicine team*, Philadelphia, 1991, FA Davis.

21. Health Insurance Association of America: *Fundamentals of health insurance*, Washington DC, 1997, HIAA.

22. Herbert DL, Herbert WG: Legal aspects of preventive, rehabilitative and recreational exercise programs. ed 4, Canton, Ohio, 2002, PRC Publishing.

23. Herbert D: *Legal aspects of sports medicine*, Canton, Ohio, 1995, Professional Reports Corporation.

24. Hunt V: Reimbursement efforts continue steady progress, *NATA News*, October:10–12, 2002.

25. Leverenz L, Helms L: Suing athletic trainers, parts I and II, *Ath Train* 25(3):212, 1990.

26. Mitten M, Mitten R: Legal considerations in treating the injured athlete, *J Orthop Sports Phys Ther* 21(1):38, 1995.

27. Mueller F: Catastrophic sports injuries. In Mueller F, Ryan A: *Prevention of athletic injuries: the role of the sports medicine team*, Philadelphia, 1991, FA Davis.

28. Rankin J, Ingersoll C: *Athletic training management: concepts and applications*, New York, 2000, McGraw-Hill.

29. Ray R: *Management strategies in athletic training*, Champaign, Ill, 2000, Human Kinetics.

30. Ray R: *Uniform billing code takes effect for ATCs, NATA News*, Winter: 20–12, 2000.

31. Yasser R: Calculating risk, *Sports Med Digest* 9(2):5, 1987.

32. Wong G: *Essentials of amateur sports law*, Westport, Conn, 1994, Praeger.

ANNOTATED BIBLIOGRAPHY

Albolm M, Campbell D, Konin J: *Reimbursement for athletic trainers*, Thoroughfare, NJ, 2001, Slack.

Presents a "how to" approach for filing claims, appealing denials, and approaching payers. Covers all current trends in health care reimbursement as well as future directions for reimbursement.

Appenzeller H: *Youth sports and the law: a guide to legal issues*, Chapel Hill, NC, 2000, Carolina Academic Press.

Studies various court cases to understand the legal principles involved in sport participation. The objective of the book is to provide better and safer sporting experiences for today's children.

Gayson E: *Ethics injury and the law in sports medicine*, New York, 1999, Heinemann-Butterworth.

Provides an up-to-date review of the status of sports medicine and the law. Addresses the key legal and ethical issues in sports and exercise medicine. For practitioners and students preparing for sport and exercise medicine exams.

Herbert D: *Legal aspects of sports medicine*, Canton, OH, 1995, Professional Reports Corporation.

A discussion of sports medicine, policies, procedures, responsibilities of the sports medicine team, informed consent, negligence, insurance and risk management, medication, drug testing, and other topics.

Rowell JC: *Understanding medical insurance: a step-by-step guide*, Albany, NY, 1994, Delmar Publishers.

Provides a comprehensive resource for dealing with issues related to insurance.

Training and Conditioning Techniques

Chapter 4

When you finish this chapter you should be able to

- Examine the roles of the athletic trainer and the strength and conditioning coach in getting an athlete fit.
- Identify the principles of conditioning.
- Defend the importance of the warm-up and cooldown periods.
- Evaluate the importance of flexibility, strength, and cardiorespiratory endurance for both athletic performance and injury prevention.
- Analyze specific techniques and principles for improving flexibility, muscular strength, and cardiorespiratory endurance.
- Discuss fitness testing and identify specific tests to assess various fitness parameters.
- Apply the concept of periodization and identify the various training periods in each phase.

P reventing injury to the athlete is one of the primary functions of the athletic trainer. To compete successfully at a high level, the athlete must be fit. An athlete who is not fit is more likely to sustain an injury. Both coaches and athletic trainers recognize that improper conditioning is one of the major causes of sports injuries (Figure 4-1). Thus coaches and athletic trainers should work cooperatively to supervise training and conditioning programs that minimize the possibility of injury and maximize performance.[49]

It takes time and careful preparation to bring an athlete into competition at a level of fitness that will preclude early-season injury. The athletic trainer must possess sound understanding of the principles of training and conditioning relative to flexibility, strength, and cardiorespiratory endurance.

Lack of physical fitness is one of the primary causes of sports injury.

THE RELATIONSHIP BETWEEN ATHLETIC TRAINERS AND STRENGTH AND CONDITIONING COACHES

The responsibility for making certain that an athlete is fit for competition depends on the personnel who are available to oversee this aspect of the athletic program. At the professional level and at most colleges and universities, a full-time strength and conditioning coach is employed to conduct both team and individual training sessions. Many, but not all, strength coaches are certified by the National Strength and Conditioning Association. If a strength coach is involved, it is essential that both the athletic trainers and the team coaches communicate freely and work in close cooperation with the strength coach to ensure that the athletes achieve an optimal level of fitness.

The specific role of the athletic trainer is to critically review the training and conditioning program designed by the strength and conditioning coach and to be extremely familiar with what is expected of the athletes on a daily basis. The athletic trainer should feel free to offer suggestions and make recommendations that are in the best interest of the athletes' health and well-being. If it becomes apparent that a particular exercise or a specific training session seems to be causing an inordinate number of

Figure 4-1

Athletic programs often provide elaborate strength and conditioning facilities.

A professional football player sustained a grade 2 hamstring strain during the sixth week of the season. Just before the playoffs he reinjured the muscle while doing some slow-speed cutting drills. Unfortunately, he was forced to remain on the injured reserve list for the duration of the season despite his best efforts to return. He has lost a great deal of cardiorespiratory fitness because he has been unable to run, and he exhibits weakness in lower extremity muscular strength because lifting has been difficult.

? Given that he will be required to attend two mini-camps during the spring and early summer and that preseason practice officially begins in July, what should his conditioning plan be during the postseason and the off-season?

The SAID principle indicates that the body will gradually adapt to the specific demands imposed on it.

injuries, the athletic trainer should inform the strength and conditioning coach of the problem so that some alternative exercise can be substituted.

If an athlete is injured and is undergoing a rehabilitation program, it should be the athletic trainer's responsibility to communicate to the strength and conditioning coach how the conditioning program should be limited and/or modified. The athletic trainer must respect the role of the strength and conditioning coach in getting the athlete fit. However, the responsibility for rehabilitating an injured athlete clearly belongs to the athletic trainer.

In the majority of high school settings, a strength and conditioning coach is not available; the responsibility for ensuring that the athlete gets fit lies with the athletic trainer and the team coaches. In this situation the athletic trainer very often assumes the role of a strength and conditioning coach in addition to his or her athletic training responsibilities. The athletic trainer frequently finds it necessary not only to design training and conditioning programs but also to oversee the weight room and to educate young, inexperienced athletes about getting themselves fit to compete. The athletic trainer must demand the cooperation of the team coaches in supervising the training and conditioning program.

PRINCIPLES OF CONDITIONING

The following principles should be applied in all programs of training and conditioning to minimize the likelihood of injury:

1. *Warm-up/cooldown.* Take time to do an appropriate warm-up before engaging in any activity. Do not neglect the cooldown period after a training bout.
2. *Motivation.* Athletes are generally highly motivated to work hard because they want to be successful in their sport. Varying the training program and incorporating techniques of periodization can keep the program enjoyable rather than routine and boring. (See the discussion of periodization at the end of this chapter.)
3. *Overload.* To improve in any physiological component, the athlete must work harder than he or she is accustomed to working. Logan and Wallis identified the **SAID principle,** which directly relates to the principle of overload.[48] SAID is an acronym for specific adaptation to imposed demands. The SAID principle states that *when the body is subjected to stresses and overloads of varying intensities, it will gradually*

adapt over time to overcome whatever demands are placed on it. Although overload is a critical factor in training and conditioning, the stress must not be great enough to produce damage or injury before the body has had a chance to adjust specifically to the increased demands.

4. *Consistency.* The athlete must engage in a training and conditioning program on a consistent, regularly scheduled basis if it is to be effective.

5. *Progression.* Increase the intensity of the conditioning program gradually and within the individual athlete's ability to adapt to increasing workloads.

6. *Intensity.* Stress the intensity of the work rather than the quantity. Coaches and athletic trainers too often confuse working hard with working for long periods of time. They make the mistake of prolonging the workout rather than increasing tempo or workload. The tired athlete is prone to injury.

7. *Specificity.* Identifying specific goals for the training program. The program must be designed to address specific components of fitness (i.e., strength, flexibility, cardiorespiratory endurance) relative to the sport in which the athlete is competing.

8. *Individuality.* The needs of individual athletes vary considerably. The successful coach is one who recognizes these individual differences and adjusts or alters the training and conditioning program accordingly to best accommodate the athlete.

9. *Minimize stress.* Expect that athletes will train as close to their physiological limits as they can. Push the athletes as far as possible but consider other stressful aspects of their lives and allow them time to be away from the conditioning demands of their sport.

10. *Safety.* Make the training environment safe. Take time to educate athletes regarding proper techniques, how they should feel during the workout, and when they should push harder or back off.[38]

WARM-UP AND COOLDOWN
Warm-Up

It is generally accepted that a period of warm-up exercises should take place before a training session begins, although a review of the literature reveals little data-based research to support the efficacy of a warm-up. Nevertheless, most athletic trainers would agree empirically that a warm-up period is a precaution against unnecessary musculoskeletal injuries and possible muscle soreness.[22] A good warm-up may also improve certain aspects of performance.[3,68]

The function of the warm-up is to prepare the body physiologically for some upcoming physical work. The purpose is to gradually stimulate the cardiorespiratory system to a moderate degree to increase the blood flow to working skeletal muscles and increase muscle temperature.

Moderate activity speeds up the metabolic processes that produce an increase in core body temperature. An increase in the temperature of skeletal muscle alters the mechanical properties of the muscle. The elasticity of the muscle (the length to which the muscle can be stretched) is increased, and the viscosity (the rate at which the muscle can change shape) is decreased.

The warm-up should begin with two to three minutes of whole body activities that use large muscle groups (e.g., light jogging, riding an exercise bike) to elevate the metabolic rate and raise core temperature.[68] Once the athlete breaks into a light sweat, which indicates that core temperature has been increased, a period of stretching exercises should follow. Stretching exercises should be sport-specific and related to the activity to be performed. For example, a soccer player uses the upper extremity considerably less than the lower extremity, so his or her stretching exercises should be directed more toward the lower extremity.

After stretching, the intensity of the warm-up should be increased gradually by performing sport-specific skills related to the activity in which the athlete is going to participate. For example, a basketball player should warm up by shooting layups and jump shots and by dribbling; a tennis player should hit forehand and backhand shots and serves.

SAID principle
Specific adaptation to imposed demands.

A track athlete constantly complains of feeling tightness in her lower extremity during workouts. She states that she has a difficult time during her warm-up and cannot seem to "get loose" until her workout is almost complete. She feels that she is always on the verge of pulling a muscle.

? What should the athletic trainer recommend as a specific warm-up routine that this athlete should consistently do before beginning her workout?

Warming up involves general body warming and warming specific body areas for the demands of the sport.

The warm-up should last approximately ten to fifteen minutes. The athlete should not wait longer than fifteen minutes to begin the main sports activity after the warm-up, although the effects will generally last up to about forty-five minutes. Thus the third-string football player who warms up before the game and then does nothing more than stand around until he gets into the game during the fourth quarter is running a much higher risk of injury. This player should be encouraged to stay warmed up and ready to play throughout the course of a game. In general, continued sweating is a good indication that the body has been sufficiently warmed up and is ready for more strenuous activity.[59]

Cooldown

Proper cooling down decreases blood and muscle lactic acid levels more rapidly.

Following a workout or training session, a cooldown period is essential. The cooldown period enables the body to cool and return to a resting state. Such a period should last about five to ten minutes.

Although the value of warm-up and workout periods is well accepted, the importance of a cooldown period afterward is often ignored. Again, experience and observation indicate that persons who stretch during the cooldown period tend to have fewer problems with muscle soreness after strenuous activity.[54]

IMPROVING AND MAINTAINING FLEXIBILITY

Conditioning should be performed gradually, with work added in small increments.

Flexibility is the ability to move a joint or series of joints smoothly and easily throughout a full range of motion.[4] Flexibility can be discussed in relation to movement involving only one joint, such as the knees, or movement involving a whole series of joints, such as the spinal vertebral joints, which must all move together to allow smooth bending or rotation of the trunk.

An athlete who has a restricted range of motion will have decreased performance capabilities. For example, a sprinter with tight, inelastic hamstring muscles loses some speed because the hamstring muscles restrict the ability to flex the hip joint, thus shortening stride length.

The "tight," or inflexible, athlete performs with a considerable handicap in terms of movement.

Lack of flexibility results in uncoordinated or awkward movements and predisposes the athlete to muscle strain.[13] Low back pain is frequently associated with tightness of the musculature in the lower spine and also of the hamstring muscles. Most activities require relatively normal amounts of flexibility.[4] However, some activities, such as gymnastics, ballet, diving, karate, and yoga, require increased flexibility for superior performance (Figure 4-2).

Good flexibility is essential to successful physical performance.[6] Most athletic trainers feel that maintaining good flexibility is important in prevention of injury to the musculotendinous unit, and they will generally insist that stretching exercises be included as part of the warm-up before the athlete engages in strenuous activity.

Factors That Limit Flexibility

A number of factors may limit the ability of a joint to move through a full, unrestricted range of motion. The *bony structure* may restrict the endpoint in the range. An elbow that has been fractured through the joint may deposit excess calcium in the joint space, causing the joint to lose its ability to fully extend. However, in many instances bony prominences stop movements at normal endpoints in the range.

Excessive *fat* may also limit the ability to move through a full range of motion. An athlete who has a large amount of fat on the abdomen may have severely restricted trunk flexion when asked to bend forward and touch the toes. The fat may act as a wedge between two lever arms, restricting movement wherever it is found. *Skin* might also be responsible for limiting movement. For example, an athlete who has had some type of injury or surgery involving a tearing incision or laceration of the skin, particularly over a joint, will have inelastic scar tissue formed at that site. This scar tissue is incapable of stretching with joint movement. *Muscles and their tendons,* along with their surrounding fascial sheaths, are most often responsible for limiting

Figure 4-2

Flexibility can be an important factor in decreasing sports injuries.

range of motion. An athlete who performs stretching exercises to improving flexibility about a particular joint is attempting to take advantage of the highly elastic properties of a muscle. Over time it is possible to increase the elasticity, or the length that a given muscle can be stretched.[62] Athletes who have a good deal of movement at a particular joint tend to have highly elastic and flexible muscles. *Connective tissue* surrounding the joint, such as ligaments on the joint capsule, may be subject to contractures. Ligaments and joint capsules do have some elasticity; however, if a joint is immobilized for a period of time, these structures tend to lose some elasticity and shorten. This condition is most commonly seen after surgical repair of an unstable joint, but it can also result from long periods of inactivity.

Neural tissue tightness resulting from acute compression, chronic repetitive microtrauma, muscle imbalances, joint dysfunction, or poor posture can create morphological changes in neural tissues that may result in irritation, inflammation, and pain. Pain causes muscle guarding to protect inflamed and irritated neural structures, and this alters normal movement patterns. Over time neural fibrosis results which decreases the elasticity of neural tissue and prevents normal movement of surrounding tissues.

It is also possible for an athlete to have relatively slack ligaments and joint capsules. These individuals are generally referred to as being loose-jointed. Examples of loose-jointedness would be an elbow or knee that hyperextends beyond 180 degrees (Figure 4-3). Frequently the instability associated with loose-jointedness may present as great a problem in movement as ligamentous or capsular contractures.

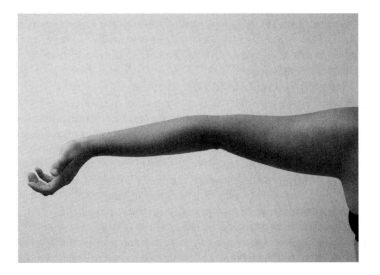

Figure 4-3

Excessive joint motion can predispose to injury.

Figure 4-4

Good flexibility is essential to successful performance in many sport activities.

The elasticity of skin contractures caused by scarring, ligaments, joint capsules, and musculotendinous units can be improved to varying degrees over time through stretching. With the exception of bony structure, age, and gender, all the other factors that limit flexibility also may be altered to increase range of joint motion.

Active and Passive Range of Motion

Active range of motion, also called *dynamic flexibility,* refers to the degree to which a joint can be moved by a muscle contraction, usually through the midrange of movement. Dynamic flexibility is not necessarily a good indicator of the stiffness or looseness of a joint because it applies to the ability to move a joint efficiently, with little resistance to motion.[59]

Passive range of motion, sometimes called *static flexibility,* refers to the degree to which a joint may be passively moved to the endpoints in the range of motion. No muscle contraction is involved to move a joint through a passive range.

When a muscle actively contracts, it produces a joint movement through a specific range of motion. However, if passive pressure is applied to an extremity, it is capable of moving farther in the range of motion. It is essential in sport activities that an extremity be capable of moving through a nonrestricted range of motion. For example, a hurdler who cannot fully extend the knee joint in a normal stride is at considerable disadvantage because stride length and thus speed will be reduced significantly (Figure 4-4).

Passive range of motion is important for injury prevention. In many sports situations, a muscle is forced to stretch beyond its normal active limits. If the muscle does not have enough elasticity to compensate for this additional stretch, the musculotendinous unit will likely be injured.

Stretching Techniques

The maintenance of a full, nonrestricted range of motion has long been recognized as critical to injury prevention and as an essential component of a conditioning program.[6] See *Focus Box:* "Guidelines and precautions for stretching." The goal of any effective flexibility program should be to improve the range of motion at a given articulation by altering the extensibility of the musculotendinous units that produce movement at that joint.[31] Exercises that stretch these musculotendinous units over a period of time increase the range of movement possible at a given joint.[64]

Stretching techniques for improving flexibility have evolved over the years. The oldest technique for stretching is called ballistic stretching, which makes use of repetitive bouncing motions. A second technique, known as static stretching, involves stretching a muscle to the point of discomfort and then holding it at the point for an extended time. This technique has been used for many years. A third technique involves a group of stretching techniques known collectively as proprioceptive neuromuscular facilitation (PNF) and uses alternating contractions and stretches.[60] Researchers have had considerable discussion about which of these techniques is most effective for improving range of motion.

Agonist versus antagonist muscles   Prior to a discussion of the three different stretching techniques, it is essential to define the terms *agonist* and *antagonist.* Most joints in the body are capable of more than one movement. The knee joint, for example, is capable of flexion and extension. Contraction of the quadriceps group of muscles on the front of the thigh causes knee extension, whereas contraction of the hamstring muscles on the back of the thigh produces knee flexion.

To achieve knee extension, the quadriceps group contracts while the hamstring muscles relax and stretch. The muscle that contracts to produce a movement, in this case the quadriceps, is referred to as the agonist muscle. The muscle being stretched in response to contraction of the agonist muscle is called the antagonist muscle. In knee extension, the antagonist muscle would be the hamstring group. Some degree of balance in strength between agonist and antagonist muscle groups is necessary to produce

Focus

Guidelines and precautions for stretching

The following guidelines and precautions should be incorporated into a sound stretching program:

- Warm up using a slow jog or fast walk before stretching vigorously.
- To increase flexibility, the muscle must be overloaded or stretched beyond its normal range but not to the point of pain.
- Stretch only to the point where you feel tightness or resistance to stretch or perhaps some discomfort. Stretching should not be painful.
- Increases in range of motion will be specific to whatever joint is being stretched.
- Exercise caution when stretching muscles that surround painful joints. Pain is an indication that something is wrong and should not be ignored.
- Avoid overstretching the ligaments and capsules that surround joints.
- Exercise caution when stretching the lower back and neck. Exercises that compress the vertebrae and their disks may cause damage.
- Stretching from a seated position rather than a standing position takes stress off the low back and decreases the chances of back injury.
- Stretch those muscles that are tight and inflexible.
- Strengthen those muscles that are weak and loose.
- Always stretch slowly and with control.
- Be sure to continue normal breathing during a stretch. Do not hold your breath.
- Static and PNF techniques are most often recommended for individuals who want to improve their range of motion.
- Ballistic stretching should be done only by those who are already flexible or are accustomed to stretching and should be done only after static stretching.
- Stretching should be done at least three times per week to see minimal improvement. It is recommended that you stretch five or six times per week to see maximum results.

4-3

Critical Thinking Exercise

A freshman collegiate football player has had a history of multiple hamstring strains throughout his high school career. He is very concerned that because of the intensity of preseason workouts, he is likely to reinjure his hamstring. He asks the athletic trainer if there is anything that he should be doing to minimize the chances of reinjury.

? What recommendations should the athletic trainer make?

normal smooth, coordinated movement and to reduce the likelihood of muscle strain caused by muscular imbalance.[59]

Dynamic (Ballistic) Stretching

Ballistic stretching involves a bouncing movement in which repetitive contractions of the agonist muscle are used to produce quick stretches of the antagonist muscle. The ballistic stretching technique, although apparently effective in improving range of motion, has been criticized in the past because increased range of motion is achieved through a series of jerks or pulls on the resistant muscle tissue. The concern was that if the forces generated by the jerks are greater than the tissues' extensibility, muscle injury may result.

Certainly successive forceful contractions of the agonist muscle that result in stretching of the antagonist muscle may cause muscle soreness. For example, forcefully kicking a soccer ball fifty times may result in muscular soreness of the hamstrings (antagonist muscle) as a result of eccentric contraction of the hamstrings to control the dynamic movement of the quadriceps (agonist muscle). Ballistic stretching that is controlled usually does not cause muscle soreness.[65] In fact, in the athletic population, ballistic stretching is now referred to as *dynamic stretching* and has seen a resurgence in popularity. The argument has been that dynamic stretching exercises are more closely related to the types of activities that athletes engage in and should be considered more functional.[50] So dynamic stretching exercises are routinely recommended for athletes prior to beginning an activity (Figure 4-5A).

ballistic stretching
Older stretching technique that uses repetitive bouncing motions.

Dynamic stretching exercises are recommended prior to beginning an activity.

Figure 4-5

Stretching techniques.
A, Dynamic (ballistic) stretch for hip flexors. **B,** Static stretch for knee extensors. **C,** Slow-reversal-hold-relax PNF techniques for hamstrings. **D,** Slump-stretch for sciatic nerve. **E,** Myofascial stretching for piriformis.

A

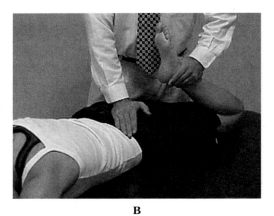

B

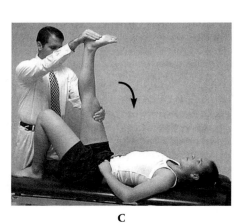

C

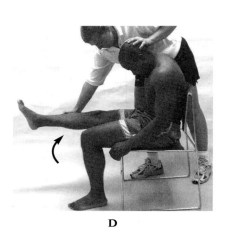

D

E

Static Stretching

The **static stretching** technique is a widely used and effective technique of stretching. This technique involves passively stretching a given antagonist muscle by placing it in a maximal position of stretch and holding it there for an extended time (Figure 4-5B). Recommendations for the optimal time for holding this stretched position vary from as short as three seconds to as long as sixty seconds.[36] Recent data indicate that thirty seconds may be an optimal time to hold the stretch. The static stretch of each muscle should be repeated three or four times.[8]

Much research has been done comparing ballistic and static stretching techniques for the improvement of flexibility. It has been shown that both static and ballistic stretching are effective in increasing flexibility and that there is no significant difference between the two. However, static stretching offers less danger of exceeding the extensibility limits of the involved joints because the stretch is more controlled. Ballistic stretching is apt to cause muscular soreness, whereas static stretching generally does not and is commonly used in injury rehabilitation of sore or strained muscles.[59]

Static stretching is certainly a much safer stretching technique, especially for sedentary or untrained individuals. However, many physical activities involve dynamic movement. Thus, stretching as a warm-up for these types of activities should begin with static stretching followed by ballistic stretching, which more closely resembles the dynamic activity.

PNF Stretching Techniques

Proprioceptive neuromuscular facilitation (PNF techniques) were first used by physical therapists for treating patients who had various types of neuromuscular paralysis.[60] More recently PNF exercises have been used as a stretching technique for increasing flexibility.

A number of different PNF techniques are currently being used for stretching, including slow-reversal-hold-relax, contract-relax, and hold-relax techniques. All involve some combination of alternating contraction and relaxation of both agonist and antagonist muscles. All three techniques use a ten-second push phase followed by a ten-second relax phase.

Using a hamstring stretching technique as an example (Figure 4-5C), the slow-reversal-hold-relax technique would be done as follows:[60]

- With the athlete lying supine with the knee extended and the ankle flexed to 90 degrees, the athletic trainer passively flexes the hip joint to the point at which there is slight discomfort in the muscle.
- At this point the athlete begins pushing against the athletic trainer's resistance by contracting the hamstring muscle.
- After pushing for ten seconds, the hamstring muscles are relaxed and the agonist quadriceps muscle is contracted while the athletic trainer applies passive pressure to further stretch the antagonist hamstrings. This action should move the leg so that there is increased hip joint flexion.
- The relaxing phase lasts for ten seconds, after which the athlete again pushes against the athletic trainer's resistance, beginning at this new position of increased hip/joint flexion.
- This push-relax sequence is repeated at least three times.

The contract-relax and hold-relax techniques are variations on the slow-reversal-hold-relax method. In the contract-relax method, the hamstrings are isotonically contracted so that the leg actually moves toward the floor during the push phase. The hold-relax method involves an isometric hamstring contraction against immovable resistance during the push phase. During the relax phase, both techniques involve the relaxation of hamstrings and quadriceps while the hamstrings are passively stretched. This same basic PNF technique can be used to stretch any muscle in the body. The PNF stretching techniques are perhaps best performed with a partner, although they may also be done using a wall as resistance.[60]

static stretching
Passively stretching an antagonist muscle by placing it in a maximal stretch and holding it there.

proprioceptive neuromuscular facilitation (PNF)
Stretching techniques that involve combinations of alternating contractions and stretches.

Figure 4-6

Stretch reflex. The muscle spindle produces a reflex resistance to stretch, and the Golgi tendon organ causes a reflex relaxation of the muscle in response to stretch.

CROSS SECTION OF SPINAL CORD

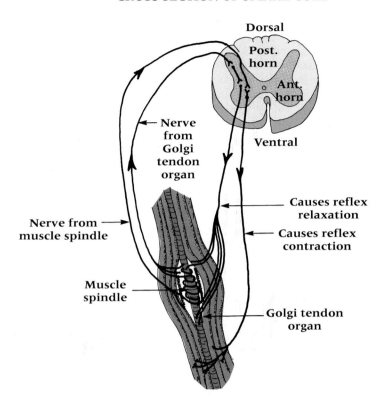

Stretching Neural Structures

The athletic trainer should be able to differentiate between tightness in the musculotendinous unit and abnormal neural tension. When the athlete performs both active and passive multiplanar movements, tension is created in the neural structures that exacerbates pain, limits range of motion, and increases neural symptoms including numbness and tingling. For example, the slump stretch position is used to detect an increase in nerve/root tension in the sciatic nerve and stretching should be done to assist in relieving tension (Figure 4-5D).

Stretching Fascia

Tight fascia can significantly limit motion. If there is damage to the fascia due to injury, disease, or inflammation, it will create pain and motion restriction. Thus it may be necessary to release tightness in the area of injury. Stretching of tight fascia can either be done manually or using a firm foam roller (Figure 4-5E).

Neurophysiologic Basis of Stretching

All three stretching techniques are based on a neurophysiologic phenomenon involving the *stretch reflex* (Figure 4-6).[60] Every muscle in the body contains mechanoreceptors that, when stimulated, inform the central nervous system of what is happening with that muscle. Two of these receptors are important in the stretch reflex: the *muscle spindles* and the *Golgi tendon organs*. Both types of receptors are sensitive to changes in muscle length. The Golgi tendon organs are also affected by changes in muscle tension.

When a muscle is stretched, the muscle spindles are also stretched, sending a volley of sensory impulses to the spinal cord that informs the central nervous system that the muscle is being stretched. Impulses return to the muscle from the spinal cord, which causes the muscle to reflexively contract, thus resisting the stretch.[48] If the stretch of

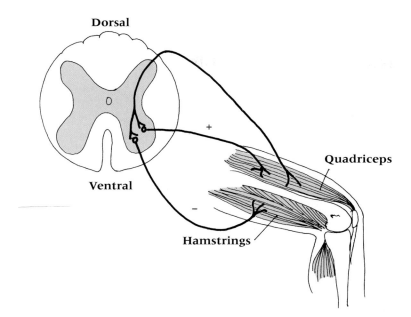

Figure 4-7

A contraction of the agonist will produce relaxation in the antagonist. Reciprocal inhibition.

the muscle continues for an extended period of time (at least six seconds), the Golgi tendon organs respond to the change in length and the increase in tension by firing off sensory impulses of their own to the spinal cord. The impulses from the Golgi tendon organs, unlike the signals from the muscle spindle, cause a reflex relaxation of the antagonist muscle. This reflex relaxation serves as a protective mechanism that will allow the muscle to stretch through relaxation before the extensibility limits are exceeded, causing damage to the muscle fibers.[60]

With the jerking, bouncing motion of ballistic stretching, the muscle spindles are being repetitively stretched; thus there is continuous resistance by the muscle to further stretch. The ballistic stretch is not continued long enough to allow the Golgi tendon organs to have any relaxing effect.

The static stretch involves a continuous sustained stretch lasting anywhere from six to sixty seconds, which is sufficient time for the Golgi tendon organs to begin responding to the increase in tension. The impulses from the Golgi tendon organs have the ability to override the impulses coming from the muscle spindles, allowing the muscle to reflexively relax after the initial reflex resistance to the change in length. Thus lengthening the muscle and allowing it to remain in a stretched position for an extended period of time is unlikely to produce any injury to the muscle.

The effectiveness of the PNF techniques may be attributed in part to these same neurophysiologic principles. The slow-reversal-hold-relax technique discussed previously takes advantage of two additional neurophysiologic phenomena.[60] The maximal isometric contraction of the muscle that will be stretched during the ten-second push phase again causes an increase in tension, which stimulates the Golgi tendon organs to effect a reflex relaxation of the antagonist muscle even before the muscle is placed in a position of stretch. This relaxation of the antagonist muscle during contractions is referred to as **autogenic inhibition**.

During the relaxing phase the antagonist is relaxed and passively stretched while a maximal isotonic contraction of the agonist muscle pulls the extremity further into the agonist pattern. In any synergistic muscle group, a contraction of the agonist muscle causes a reflex relaxation in the antagonist muscle, allowing it to stretch and protecting it from injury. This phenomenon is referred to as *reciprocal inhibition* (Figure 4-7). Thus with the PNF techniques the additive effects of autogenic inhibition and reciprocal inhibition should theoretically allow the muscle to be stretched to a greater degree than is possible with static stretching or the ballistic technique.[60]

autogenic inhibition
The relaxation of the antagonist muscle during contractions.

Figure 4-8

Pilates exercises are designed to improve muscle control, flexibility, coordination, and strength. (Photo courtesy Balanced Body, Inc., Sacramento, CA)

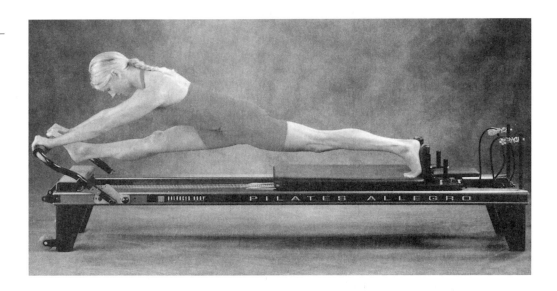

4-4

Critical Thinking Exercise

A college swimmer has been engaged in an off-season weight-training program to increase her muscular strength and endurance. Although she has seen some improvement in her strength, she is concerned that she also seems to be losing flexibility in her shoulders, which she feels is critical to her performance as a swimmer. She has also noticed that her muscles are hypertrophying to some degree and is worried that this may be causing her to lose flexibility. She has just about decided to abandon her weight-training program altogether.

? What can the athletic trainer recommend to her that will allow her to continue to improve her muscular strength and endurance while simultaneously maintaining or perhaps even improving her flexibility?

Practical Application Although all three stretching techniques have been demonstrated to effectively improve flexibility, there is still considerable debate as to which technique produces the greatest increases in range of movement. In the past, the dynamic technique has not been recommended because of the potential for causing muscle soreness. However, most sport activities are ballistic in nature (e.g., kicking, running), and those activities use the stretch reflex to enhance performance. In highly trained individuals, it is unlikely that dynamic stretching will result in muscle soreness. Static stretching is perhaps the most widely used technique. It is a simple technique and does not require a partner. A fully nonrestricted range of motion can be attained through static stretching over time.[24,67]

The PNF stretching techniques can produce dramatic increases in range of motion during one stretching session. Studies comparing static and PNF stretching suggest that PNF stretching can produce greater improvement in flexibility over an extended training period.[60,66] The major disadvantage of PNF stretching is that it requires a partner for stretching, although stretching with a partner may have some motivational advantages. An increasing number of athletic teams are adopting the PNF technique as the method of choice for improving flexibility.

The Pilates Method

The Pilates method is a somewhat different approach to stretching for improving flexibility. This method has become extremely popular and widely used among personal fitness trainers and physical therapists. Pilates is an exercise technique devised by German-born Joseph Pilates, who established the first Pilates studio in the United States before World War II. The Pilates method is a conditioning program that improves muscle control, flexibility, coordination, strength, and tone. The basic principles of Pilates exercise are to make people more aware of their bodies as single integrated units, to improve body alignment and breathing, and to increase efficiency of movement. Unlike other exercise programs, the Pilates method does not require the repetition of exercises but instead consists of a sequence of carefully performed movements, some of which are carried out on specially designed equipment (Figure 4-8). Each exercise is designed to stretch and strengthen the muscles involved. There is a specific breathing pattern for each exercise to help direct energy to the areas being worked, while relaxing the rest of the body. The Pilates method works many of the deeper muscles together, improving

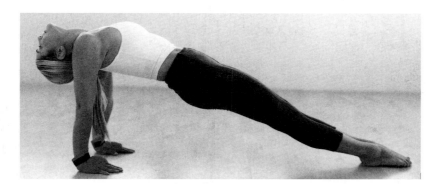

Figure 4-9

Yoga uses a variety of positions to increase flexibility in the body. (Photo courtesy International Dance Exercise Association, San Diego, CA)

coordination and balance, to achieve efficient and graceful movement. Instead of seeking an ideal or perfect body, the goal is for the practitioner to develop a healthy self-image through the attainment of better posture, proper coordination, and improved flexibility. This method concentrates on body alignment, lengthening all of the muscles of the body into a balanced whole, and building endurance and strength without putting undue stress on the lungs and heart. Pilates instructors believe that problems such as soft-tissue injuries can cause bad posture, which can lead to pain and discomfort. Pilates exercises aim to correct this.

Normally a beginner sees a Pilates instructor on a one-to-one basis for the first session. The instructor assesses the client's physical condition and asks the client about any problems and about the client's lifestyle. The client is then shown a series of exercises that work joints and muscles through a range of movement appropriate for the client's needs. A class in a studio might involve working on specially designed equipment that primarily uses resistance against tensioned springs to isolate and develop specific muscle groups. Mat work classes involve a repertoire of exercises on a floor mat only. This type of class has become very popular in health clubs and gyms and is often compared to other forms of body conditioning. In fact, the Pilates mat exercises are generally less strenuous that mat exercises in most other conditioning classes.

Yoga

Yoga originated in India approximately 6,000 years ago. Its basic philosophy is that most illness is related to poor mental attitudes, posture, and diet. Practitioners of yoga maintain that stress can be reduced through combined mental and physical approaches. Yoga can help an individual cope with stress-induced behaviors like overeating, hypertension, and smoking. Yoga's meditative aspects are believed to help alleviate psychosomatic illnesses. Yoga aims to unite the body and mind to reduce stress. For example, Dr. Chandra Patel, a yoga expert, has found that persons who practice yoga can reduce their blood pressure indefinitely as long as they continue to practice yoga. Yoga involves various body postures and breathing exercises. Hatha yoga uses a number of positions through which the practitioner may progress, beginning with the simplest and moving to the more complex (Figure 4-9). The various positions are intended to increase mobility and flexibility. However, practitioners must use caution when performing yoga positions. Some positions can be dangerous, particularly for someone who is inexperienced in yoga technique.

Slow, deep, diaphragmatic breathing is an important part of yoga. Many people take shallow breaths, however, breathing deeply, fully expanding the chest when inhaling helps lower blood pressure and heart rate. Deep breathing has a calming effect on the body. It also increases production of endorphins.

Figure 4-10

A goniometer can be used to measure joint angles and range of motion.

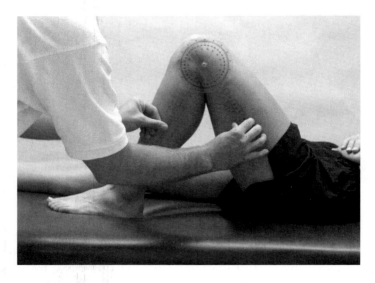

The Relationship between Strength and Flexibility

It is often said that strength training has a negative effect on flexibility.[64] For example, we tend to think of athletes who have highly developed muscles as having lost much of their ability to move freely through a full range of motion. Occasionally an athlete develops so much bulk that the physical size of the muscle prevents a normal range of motion. It is certainly true that strength training that is not properly done can impair movement; however, weight training, if done properly through a full range of motion, will not impair flexibility. Proper strength training probably improves dynamic flexibility and, if combined with a rigorous stretching program, can greatly enhance powerful and coordinated movements that are essential for success in many athletic activities. In all cases a heavy weight-training program should be accompanied by a strong flexibility program.

Measuring Range of Motion

Accurate measurement of the range of joint motion is difficult. Various devices have been designed to accommodate variations in the size of the joints and the complexity of movements in articulations that involve more than one joint. Of these devices, the simplest and most widely used is the goniometer (Figure 4-10). A goniometer is a large protractor with measurements in degrees. By aligning the two arms parallel to the longitudinal axis of the two segments involved in motion about a specific joint, it is possible to obtain relatively accurate measures of range of movement. The goniometer has its place in a rehabilitation setting, where it is essential to assess improvement in joint flexibility for the purpose of modifying injury rehabilitation programs.[30,57]

THE IMPORTANCE OF MUSCULAR STRENGTH, ENDURANCE, AND POWER

muscular strength
The maximum force that can be applied by a muscle during a single maximum contraction.

The development of **muscular strength** is an essential component of a training program for every athlete. By definition, strength is the ability of a muscle to generate force against some resistance. Most movements in sports are explosive and must include elements of both strength and speed if they are to be effective. If a large amount of force is generated quickly, the movement can be referred to as a *power* movement. Without the ability to generate power, an athlete will be limited in his or her performance capabilities.[59]

muscular endurance
The ability to perform repetitive muscular contractions against some resistance.

Muscular strength is closely associated with muscular endurance. **Muscular endurance** is the ability to perform repetitive muscular contractions against some resistance for an extended period of time. As muscular strength increases, there tends to be a corresponding increase in endurance.[44,69] For example, an athlete can lift a weight twenty-five times. If muscular strength is increased by 10 percent through weight training, it is likely that the maximum number of repetitions would be increased because it is easier for the athlete to lift the weight.

Skeletal Muscle Contractions

Skeletal muscle is capable of three different types of contraction: *isometric contraction, concentric contraction,* and *eccentric contraction.*[63] An isometric contraction occurs when the muscle contracts to increase tension but there is no change in the length of the muscle. Considerable force can be generated against some immovable resistance even though no movement occurs. In concentric contraction, the muscle shortens in length as a contraction is developed to overcome or move some resistance. In eccentric contraction the resistance is greater than the muscular force being produced, and the muscle lengthens while continuing to contract. Concentric and eccentric contractions are both considered to be dynamic movements.[63]

It is critical to understand that functional movements involve acceleration, deceleration, and stabilization in all three planes of motion simultaneously. Functional movements are controlled by neuromuscular mechanoreceptors located within the muscle.[20]

Fast-Twitch versus Slow-Twitch Fibers

All fibers in a particular motor unit are either *slow-twitch* or *fast-twitch* fibers, each of which has distinctive metabolic and contractile capabilities. Slow-twitch fibers are also referred to as type I fibers. They are more resistant to fatigue than are fast-twitch fibers; however, the time required to generate force is much greater in slow-twitch fibers.[43] Because they are relatively fatigue resistant, slow-twitch fibers are associated primarily with long-duration, aerobic-type activities.[34]

Fast-twitch fibers (also referred to as type II fibers) are capable of producing quick, forceful contractions but have a tendency to fatigue more rapidly than do slow-twitch fibers. Fast-twitch fibers are useful in short-term, high-intensity activities, which mainly involve the anaerobic system. Fast-twitch fibers are capable of producing powerful contractions, whereas slow-twitch fibers produce a long-endurance type of force. There are two subdivisions of fast-twitch fibers. Although both types of fast-twitch fibers are capable of rapid contraction, type IIa fibers are moderately resistant to fatigue, whereas type IIb fibers fatigue rapidly and are considered the "true" fast-twitch fibers.[34]

Any given muscle contains both types of fibers, and the ratio in an individual muscle varies with each person.[43] Those muscles whose primary function is to maintain posture against gravity require more endurance and have a higher percentage of slow-twitch fibers. Muscles that produce powerful, rapid, explosive strength movements tend to have a much greater percentage of fast-twitch fibers. Because this ratio is genetically determined, it may play a large role in determining ability for a given sport activity. Sprinters and weight lifters, for example, have a large percentage of fast-twitch fibers in relation to slow-twitch fibers.[15] Conversely, marathon runners generally have a higher percentage of slow-twitch fibers.

The metabolic capabilities of both fast-twitch and slow-twitch fibers may be improved through specific strength and endurance training. It now appears that there can be an almost complete change from slow-twitch to fast-twitch and from fast-twitch to slow-twitch fiber types in response to training.[51]

Physiological and Biomechanical Factors That Determine Levels of Muscular Strength

Muscular strength is proportional to the cross-sectional diameter of the muscle fibers. The greater the cross-sectional diameter or the bigger a particular muscle, the stronger it is, and thus the more force it is capable of generating. The size of a muscle tends to increase in cross-sectional diameter with weight training. This increase in muscle size is referred to as **hypertrophy**.[42] Conversely, a decrease in the size of a muscle is referred to as **atrophy**.

Skeletal muscle is capable of three types of contractions:
- Isometric
- Concentric
- Eccentric

There are three basic types of muscle fibers:
- Slow-twitch type I
- Fast-twitch type IIa
- Fast-twitch type IIb

hypertrophy
Enlargement of a muscle caused by an increase in the size of its cells in response to training.

atrophy
Decrease of a muscle caused by a decrease in the size of its cells because of inactivity.

Size of the Muscle

Strength is a function of the number and diameter of muscle fibers composing a given muscle. The number of fibers is an inherited characteristic; thus an athlete with a large number of muscle fibers to begin with has the potential to hypertrophy to a much greater degree than does someone with relatively fewer fibers.[25]

Explanations for Muscle Hypertrophy

A number of theories have been proposed to explain why a muscle hypertrophies in response to strength training.[38] Some evidence exists that the number of muscle fibers increase because fibers split in response to training.[58] However, this research has been conducted in animals and should not be generalized to humans. It is generally accepted that the number of fibers is genetically determined and does not seem to increase with training.

Another hypothesis is that because the muscle is working harder in weight training, more blood is required to supply that muscle with oxygen and other nutrients. Thus the number of capillaries is increased. This hypothesis is only partially correct; few new capillaries are formed during strength training, but a number of dormant capillaries may become filled with blood to meet the increased demand for blood supply.

A third theory to explain this increase in muscle size seems the most credible. Muscle fibers are composed primarily of small protein filaments, called myofilaments, which are the contractile elements in muscle. These myofilaments increase in both size and number as a result of strength training, causing the individual muscle fibers themselves to increase in cross-sectional diameter.[51] This increase is particularly true in men, although women also see some increase in muscle size.[1] More research is needed to further clarify and determine the specific causes of muscle hypertrophy.

Improved Neuromuscular Efficiency

Typically with weight training, an athlete sees some remarkable gains in strength initially, even though muscle bulk does not necessarily increase. This gain in strength must be attributed to something other than muscle hypertrophy. For a muscle to contract, an impulse must be transmitted from the nervous system to the muscle. Each muscle fiber is innervated by a specific motor unit. By overloading a particular muscle, as in weight training, the muscle is forced to work efficiently. Efficiency is achieved by getting more motor units to fire, causing a stronger contraction of the muscle.[71] Consequently, it is not uncommon to see extremely rapid gains in strength when a weight-training program is first begun due to an improvement in neuromuscular function.[52]

Other Physiological Adaptations to Resistance Exercise

In addition to muscle hypertrophy there are a number of other physiological adaptations to resistance training.[9] The strength of noncontractile structures, including tendons and ligaments, is increased. The mineral content of bone is increased, making the bone stronger and more resistant to fracture. Maximal oxygen uptake is improved when resistance training is of sufficient intensity to elicit heart rates at or above training levels. Several enzymes important in aerobic and anaerobic metabolism also increase.[15,51]

Biomechanical Factors

Strength in a given muscle is determined not only by the physical properties of the muscle itself but also by biomechanical factors that dictate how much force can be generated through a system of levers to an external object. If we think of the elbow joint as one of these lever systems, we would have the biceps muscle producing flexion of this joint (Figure 4-11). The position of attachment of the biceps muscle on the lever arm, in this case the forearm, will largely determine how much force this muscle is capable of generating.[29] If there are two persons, A and B, and person B has a biceps

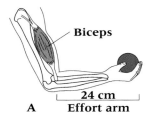

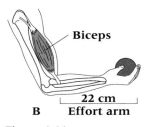

Figure 4-11

The position of attachment of the muscle tendon on the arm can affect the ability of that muscle to generate force. Person B should be able to generate greater force than person A because the tendon attachment is closer to the resistance.

attachment that is farther from the center of the joint than is person A's, then person B should be able to lift heavier weights because the muscle force acts through a longer lever (moment) arm and thus can produce greater torque around the joint.

The length of a muscle determines the tension that can be generated.[32] By varying the length of a muscle, different tensions may be produced. This length-tension relationship is illustrated in Figure 4-12. At position B in the curve, the interaction of the crossbridges between the actin and myosin myofilaments within the sarcomere is at a maximum. Setting a muscle at this length will produce the greatest amount of tension. At position A the muscle is shortened, and at position C the muscle is lengthened. In either case the interaction between the actin and myosin myofilaments through the crossbridges is greatly reduced, and the muscle is not capable of generating significant tension.

Overtraining

Overtraining can have a negative effect on the development of muscular strength. The statement "if you abuse it you will lose it" is applicable. Overtraining can result in psychological breakdown (staleness) or physiological breakdown, which may involve musculoskeletal injury, fatigue, or sickness. Engaging in proper and efficient resistance training, eating a proper diet, and getting appropriate rest can minimize the potential negative effects of overtraining.

Reversibility

If strength training is discontinued or interrupted, the muscle will atrophy, decreasing in both strength and mass. Adaptations in skeletal muscle that occur in response to resistance training may begin to reverse in as little as forty-eight hours. It does appear that consistent exercise of a muscle is essential to prevent reversal of the hypertrophy that occurs due to strength training.

Techniques of Resistance Training

There are a number of different techniques of resistance training for strength improvement, including isometric exercise, progressive resistance exercise, isokinetic exercise, circuit training, and plyometric exercise. Regardless of which of these techniques is used, one basic principle of training is extremely important. For a muscle to improve in strength, it must be forced to work at a higher level than it is accustomed to working at. In other words, the muscle must be *overloaded.* Without overload the muscle will be able to maintain strength as long as training is continued against a resistance the muscle is accustomed to. To most effectively build muscular strength, weight training requires a consistent, increasing effort against progressively increasing resistance.[23] Progressive resistance exercise is based primarily on the principles of overload and progression. If this principle of overload is applied, all five training techniques will produce improvement of muscular strength over a period of time.

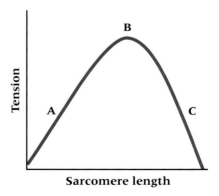

Figure 4-12

Because of the length-tension relation in muscle, the greatest tension is developed at point B, with less tension developed at points A and C.

Figure 4-13

A, Barbells and dumbbells are free weights that assist the athlete in developing isotonic strength. **B,** Many machine exercise systems provide a variety of exercise possibilities for the athlete.

A

B

Isometric Exercise

isometric exercise
Contracts the muscle statically without changing its length.

An **isometric exercise** involves a muscle contraction in which the length of the muscle remains constant while tension develops toward a maximal force against an immovable resistance.[7] The muscle should generate a maximal force for ten seconds at a time, and this contraction should be repeated five to ten times per day. Isometric exercises are capable of increasing muscular strength; unfortunately, strength gains are specific to the joint angle at which training is performed. At other angles, the strength curve drops off dramatically because of a lack of motor activity at that angle.

Another major disadvantage of isometric exercises is that they tend to produce a spike in systolic blood pressure that can result in potentially life-threatening cardiovascular accidents.[59] This sharp increase in blood pressure results from an individual holding his or her breath and increasing intrathoracic pressure. Consequently, the blood pressure experienced by the heart is increased significantly. This phenomenon has been referred to as the Valsalva effect. To avoid or minimize this increase in pressure, it is recommended that breathing be continued during the maximal contraction.

Isometric exercises are useful in the rehabilitation of certain injuries.

Progressive Resistance Exercise

A second technique of resistance training is perhaps the most commonly used and the most popular technique for improving muscular strength. *Progressive resistance exercise* training uses exercises that strengthen muscles through a contraction that overcomes some fixed resistance produced by equipment such as dumbbells, barbells, or various weight machines (Figure 4-13). Progressive resistance exercise uses isotonic contractions which generate force while the muscle is changing in length.[23]

concentric (positive) contraction
The muscle shortens while contracting against resistance.

Isotonic contractions   Isotonic contractions may be either concentric or eccentric. An athlete who is performing a biceps curl offers a good example of an isotonic contraction. To lift the weight from the starting position, the biceps muscle must contract and shorten in length. This shortening contraction is referred to as a **concentric**, or **positive, contraction**. If the biceps muscle does not remain contracted when the weight is being lowered, gravity will cause the weight to simply fall back to the starting position. Thus, to control the weight as it is being lowered, the biceps muscle must continue to contract while at the same time gradually lengthening. A contraction in which the muscle is lengthening while still applying force is called an **eccentric**, or **negative, contraction**.[39]

eccentric (negative) contraction
The muscle lengthens while contracting against resistance.

Eccentric contractions versus concentric contractions   It is possible to generate greater amounts of force against resistance with an eccentric contraction than with a concentric contraction. This greater force occurs because eccentric contractions require a much lower level of motor unit activity to achieve a certain force than do concentric contractions. Because fewer motor units are firing to produce a specific force, additional motor units may be recruited to generate increased force. In addition, oxygen utilization is much lower during eccentric exercise than during comparable concentric exercise. Thus eccentric contractions are more resistant to fatigue than are concentric contractions. The mechanical efficiency of eccentric exercise may be several times higher than that of concentric exercise.[63]

Concentric contractions accelerate movement, whereas eccentric contractions decelerate motion. For example, the hamstrings must contract eccentrically to decelerate the angular velocity of the lower leg during running. Likewise, the external rotators in the rotator cuff muscles surrounding the shoulder contract eccentrically to decelerate the internally rotating humerus during throwing. Because of the excessive forces involved with these eccentric contractions, injury to the muscles is quite common. Thus, eccentric exercise must be routinely incorporated into the strength training program to prevent injury to those muscles that act to decelerate movement.

Free weights versus machine weights   Various types of exercise equipment can be used with progressive resistance exercise, including free weights (barbells and dumbbells) or exercise machines such as those made by Universal, Nautilus, Cybex, Eagle, and Body Master. Dumbbells and barbells require the use of iron plates of varying weights that can be changed easily by adding or subtracting equal amounts of weight to both sides of the bar. The exercise machines have a stack of weights that are lifted through a series of levers or pulleys. The stack of weights slides up and down on a pair of bars that restrict the movement to only one plane. Weight can be increased or decreased simply by changing the position of a weight key.

There are advantages and disadvantages to both free weights and exercise machines. The exercise machines are relatively safe to use compared to free weights. It is also a simple process to increase or decrease the weight on exercise machines by moving a single weight key, although changes can generally be made only in increments of ten or fifteen pounds. The iron plates used with free weights must be added or removed from each side of the barbell or dumbbell.

Figure 4-14 shows examples of different isotonic strengthening exercises.

Spotting for free weight exercises   When training with free weights, it is essential that the lifter have a partner who can assist in performing a particular exercise. This assistance is particularly critical when the weights to be lifted are extremely heavy. A *spotter* has three functions: to protect the lifter from injury, to make recommendations on proper lifting technique, and to help motivate the lifter. *Focus Box:* "Proper spotting techniques" provides some guidelines for correct spotting techniques.

Focus

Proper spotting techniques
- Make sure the lifter uses the proper grip.
- Check to see that the lifter is in a safe, stable position.
- Make sure the lifter moves through a complete range of motion at the appropriate speed.
- Make sure the lifter inhales and exhales during the lift.
- When spotting dumbbell exercises, spot as close to the dumbbells as possible above the elbow joint.
- Make sure the lifter understands how to get out of the way of missed attempts, particularly with overhead techniques.
- Stand behind the lifter.
- If heavy weights exceed the limits of your ability to control the weight, use a second spotter.
- Communicate with the lifter to know how many reps are to be done, whether a liftoff is needed, and how much help the lifter wants in completing a rep.
- Always be in a position to protect both the lifter and yourself from injury.

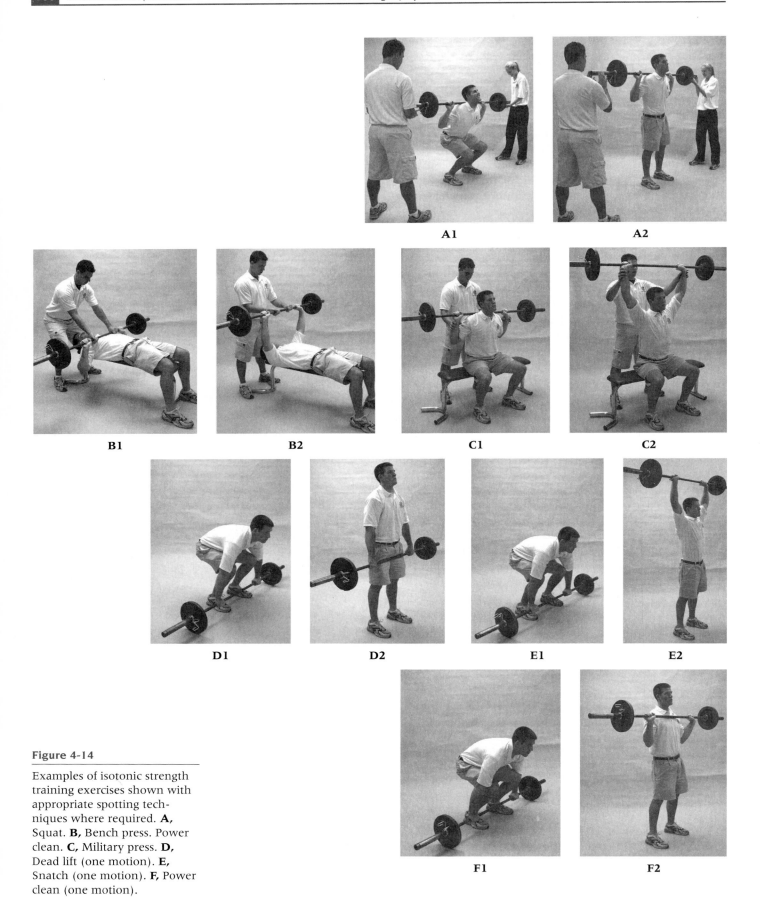

Figure 4-14

Examples of isotonic strength training exercises shown with appropriate spotting techniques where required. **A,** Squat. **B,** Bench press. Power clean. **C,** Military press. **D,** Dead lift (one motion). **E,** Snatch (one motion). **F,** Power clean (one motion).

Figure 4-14—continued
G, Leg press.

Isotonic training   Regardless of which type of equipment is used, the same principles of **isotonic exercise** may be applied. In progressive resistance exercise, it is essential to incorporate both concentric and eccentric contractions. Research has clearly demonstrated that the muscle should be overloaded and fatigued both concentrically and eccentrically for the greatest strength improvement to occur.[43,51]

When an athlete is training specifically to develop muscular strength, the concentric, or positive, portion of the exercise should require one to two seconds and the eccentric, or negative, portion of the lift should require two to four seconds. The ratio of negative to positive should be approximately one to two. Physiologically, the muscle will fatigue much more rapidly concentrically than eccentrically.

Athletes who have trained with both free weights and machines realize the difference in the amount of weight that can be lifted. Unlike the machines, free weights have no restricted motion and can thus move in many different directions, depending on the forces applied. With free weights, an element of muscular control on the part of the lifter to prevent the weight from moving in any direction other than vertical will usually decrease the amount of weight that can be lifted.[35]

One problem often mentioned in relation to isotonic training is that the amount of force necessary to move a weight through a range of motion changes according to the angle of pull of the contracting muscle. The amount of force is greatest when the angle of pull is approximately 90 degrees. In addition, once the inertia of the weight has been overcome and momentum has been established, the force required to move the resistance varies according to the force that the muscle can produce through the range of motion. Thus, it has been argued that a disadvantage of any type of isotonic exercise is that the force required to move the resistance is constantly changing throughout the range of movement.

Certain exercise machines are designed to minimize this change in resistance by using a cam system (Figure 4-15). The cam has been individually designed for each piece of equipment so that the resistance is variable throughout the movement. The cam system attempts to alter resistance so that the muscle can handle a greater load—at

isotonic exercise
Shortens and lengthens the muscle through a complete range of motion.

Figure 4-15

The cam system on the Nautilus equipment is designed to equalize the resistance throughout the full range of motion.

the points at which the joint angle or muscle length is at a mechanical disadvantage, the cam reduces the resistance to muscle movement. Whether this design does what it claims is debatable. This change in resistance at different points in the range is called accommodating resistance, or variable resistance.

Progressive resistance exercise techniques   Perhaps the single most confusing aspect of progressive resistance exercise is the terminology used to describe specific programs. The following list of terms and their operational definitions may help clarify the confusion:

- Repetitions—The number of times a specific movement is repeated.
- Repetitions maximum (RM)—The maximum number of repetitions at a given weight.
- One repetition maximum (1RM)—The maximum amount of weight that can be lifted one time.
- Set—A particular number of repetitions.
- Intensity—The amount of weight or resistance lifted.
- Recovery period—The rest interval between sets.
- Frequency—The number of times an exercise is done in one week.

A considerable amount of research has been done in the area of resistance training to determine optimal techniques in terms of the intensity or the amount of weight to be used, the number of repetitions, the number of sets, the recovery period, and the frequency of training. It is important to realize that there are many different effective techniques and training regimens. Regardless of specific techniques used, it is certain that to improve strength the muscle must be overloaded in a progressive manner.[57] This overload is the basis of progressive resistance exercise. The amount of weight used and the number of repetitions must be enough to make the muscle work at a higher intensity than it is used to working at. This overload is the single most critical factor in any strength-training program. The strength-training program must also be designed to meet the specific needs of the athlete.

There is no such thing as an optimal strength-training program. Achieving total agreement on a program of resistance training—with specific recommendations about repetitions, sets, intensity, recovery time, and frequency—among researchers or other experts in resistance training is impossible. However, the following general recommendations will provide an effective resistance-training program.

For any given exercise, the amount of weight selected should be sufficient to allow six to eight repetitions maximum (RM) in each of three sets with a recovery period of sixty to ninety seconds between sets. Initial selection of a starting weight may require some trial and error to achieve this 6 to 8 RM range. If at least three sets of six repetitions cannot be completed, the weight is too heavy and should be reduced. If it is possible to do more than three sets of eight repetitions, the weight is too light and should be increased.[10] Progression to heavier weights is determined by the ability to perform at least 8 RM in each of three sets. An increase of about 10 percent of the current weight being lifted should still allow at least 6 RM in each of three sets.

Occasionally, athletes may be tested at 1RM to determine the greatest amount of weight that can be lifted one time. Extreme caution should be exercised when trying to determine 1RM. Attention should be directed toward making sure the athlete has had ample opportunity to warm up and that the lifting technique is correct before attempting a maximum lift. Determining 1RM should be done very gradually to minimize the chances of injuring the muscle.

A particular muscle or muscle group should be exercised consistently every other day. Thus the frequency of weight training should be at least three times per week but no more than four times per week. It is common for serious weight trainers to lift every day; however, they exercise different muscle groups on successive days. For example, Monday, Wednesday, and Friday may be used for upper body muscles, whereas Tuesday, Thursday, and Saturday are used for lower body muscles.

Training for muscular strength versus endurance   Muscular endurance is the ability to perform repeated muscle contractions against resistance for an extended period

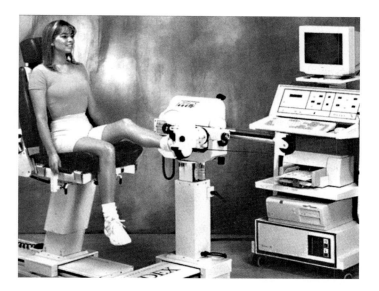

Figure 4-16

During isokinetic exercise the speed of movement is constant regardless of the force applied by the athlete.

of time. Most weight-training experts believe that muscular strength and muscular endurance are closely related.[59] As one improves, the other tends to improve also.

When weight training for strength, use heavier weights with a lower number of repetitions. Conversely, endurance training uses relatively lighter weights with a greater number of repetitions.

Endurance training should consist of three sets of ten to fifteen repetitions using the same criteria for weight selection, progression, and frequency as recommended for progressive resistance exercise.[7] Thus, suggested training regimens for muscular strength and endurance are similar in terms of sets and numbers of repetitions. Persons who possess great levels of strength also tend to exhibit greater muscular endurance when asked to perform repeated contractions against resistance.

Isokinetic Exercise

An **isokinetic exercise** involves a muscle contraction in which the length of the muscle is changing while the contraction is performed at a constant velocity.[58] In theory, maximal resistance is provided throughout the range of motion by the machine. The resistance provided by the machine will move only at some preset speed regardless of the force applied to it by the individual. Thus the key to isokinetic exercise is not the resistance but the speed at which the resistance can be moved.[16]

Currently, only one isokinetic device is available commercially—Biodex (Figure 4-16). Isokinetic devices rely on hydraulic, pneumatic, or mechanical pressure systems to produce constant velocity of motion. Isokinetic devices are capable of resisting both concentric and eccentric contractions at a fixed speed to exercise a muscle.

A major disadvantage of an isokinetic unit is its cost. The unit comes with a computer and printing device and is used primarily as a diagnostic and rehabilitative tool in the treatment of various injuries.

Isokinetic devices are designed so that regardless of the amount of force applied, the resistance can be moved only at a certain speed. That speed will be the same whether maximal force or only half the maximal force is applied. Consequently, when training isokinetically, it is absolutely necessary to exert as much force against the resistance as possible (maximal effort) for maximal strength gains to occur. This need for maximal effort is one of the major problems with an isokinetic strength-training program.

Anyone who has been involved in a weight-training program knows that on some days it is difficult to find the motivation to work out. Because isokinetic training does not require a maximal effort, it is easy to "cheat" and not go through the workout at a high level of intensity. In a progressive resistance exercise program, the individual

isokinetic exercise
Resistance is given at a fixed velocity of movement with accommodating resistance.

knows how much weight has to be lifted with how many repetitions. Thus, isokinetic training is often more effective if a partner system is used as a means of motivation toward a maximal effort.

When isokinetic training is done properly with a maximal effort, it is theoretically possible that maximal strength gains are best achieved through the isokinetic training method in which the velocity and force of the resistance are equal throughout the range of motion. However, there is no conclusive research to support this theory. Whether changing force capability is in fact a deterrent to improving the ability to generate force against some resistance is debatable.

In the athletic training setting, isokinetics are perhaps best used as a rehabilitative and diagnostic tool rather than as a training device.[58]

Circuit Training

circuit training
Exercise stations that consist of various combinations of weight training, flexibility, calisthenics, and aerobic exercises.

Circuit training employs a series of exercise stations that consist of various combinations of weight training, flexibility, calisthenics, and brief aerobic exercises. Circuits may be designed to accomplish many different training goals. With circuit training the individual moves rapidly from one station to the next and performs whatever exercise is to be done at that station within a specified time period. A typical circuit would consist of eight to twelve stations, and the entire circuit would be repeated three times.

Circuit training is most definitely an effective technique for improving strength and flexibility. Certainly, if the pace or the time interval between stations is rapid and if workload is maintained at a high level of intensity with heart rate at or above target training levels, the cardiorespiratory system may benefit from this circuit. However, little research evidence exists to show that circuit training is effective in improving cardiorespiratory endurance. It should be, and is most often, used as a technique for developing and improving muscular strength and endurance.

Calisthenic Strengthening Exercises

Calisthenics, or free exercise, is one of the more easily available means of developing strength. Isotonic movement exercises can be graded according to intensity by using gravity as an aid, by ruling gravity out, by moving against gravity, or by using the body or body part as a resistance against gravity. Most calisthenics require the athlete to support the body or move the total body against the force of gravity. Push-ups are a good example of a vigorous antigravity free exercise. To be considered maximally effective, the isotonic calisthenic exercise, like all types of exercise, must be performed in an exacting manner and in full range of motion. In most cases, ten or more repetitions are performed for each exercise and are repeated in sets of two or three.

Some free exercises use an isometric, or holding, phase instead of a full range of motion. Examples of these exercises are back extensions and sit-ups. When the exercise produces maximum muscle tension, it is held between six and ten seconds and then repeated one to three times.

Plyometric Exercise

plyometric exercise
This type of exercise maximizes the myotatic, or stretch, reflex.

Plyometric exercise is a technique that includes specific exercises that encompass a rapid stretch of a muscle eccentrically, followed immediately by a rapid concentric contraction of that muscle for the purpose of facilitating and developing a forceful explosive movement over a short period of time.[2,19] The greater the stretch put on the muscle from its resting length immediately before the concentric contraction, the greater the resistance the muscle can overcome. Plyometric exercises emphasize the speed of the eccentric phase.[18] The rate of the stretch is more critical than the magnitude of the stretch. An advantage to plyometric exercises is that they can help develop eccentric control in dynamic movements.[61]

Plyometric exercises involve hops, bounds, and depth jumping for the lower extremity and use medicine balls and other types of weighted equipment for the upper extremity. Depth jumping is an example of a plyometric exercise in which an individual jumps to the ground from a specified height and then quickly jumps again as soon as ground contact is made.[19]

Plyometrics place a great deal of stress on the musculoskeletal system. The learning and perfection of specific jumping skills and other plyometric exercises must be technically correct and specific to the athlete's age, activity, physical development, and skill development.[56]

Strength Training for the Female Athlete

Strength training is critical for the female athlete. Significant muscle hypertrophy in the female athlete is dependent on the presence of the hormone testosterone. Testosterone is considered a male hormone, although all females possess some testosterone in their systems. Females with higher testosterone levels tend to have more masculine characteristics, such as increased facial and body hair, a deeper voice, and the potential to develop a little more muscle bulk.[49]

Both males and females experience initial rapid gains in strength due to an increase in neuromuscular efficiency as discussed previously.[71] However, in the female, these rapid initial strength gains tend to plateau after three to four weeks. Minimal improvement in muscular strength will be realized during a continuing strength-training program because the muscle will not continue to hypertrophy to any significant degree.

Perhaps the most critical difference between males and females regarding physical performance is the ratio of strength to body weight. The reduced *strength-to-body-weight ratio* in females is the result of their higher percentage of body fat. The strength-to-body-weight ratio may be significantly improved through weight training by decreasing the percentage of body fat while increasing lean weight.

Strength Training in Adolescents

The principles of resistance training discussed previously may be applied to the young athlete. There are certainly a number of sociological questions regarding the advantages and disadvantages of younger, in particular prepubescent, athletes engaging in rigorous strength-training programs, From a physiological perspective, experts have for years debated the value of strength training in young athletes. Recently, a number of studies have indicated that if properly supervised, young athletes can improve strength, power, endurance, balance, and proprioception; develop a positive body image; improve sport performance; and prevent injuries. A prepubescent child can experience gains in levels of muscle strength without significant muscle hypertrophy.[27]

An athletic trainer supervising a conditioning program for a young athlete should certainly incorporate resistive exercise into the program. However, close supervision, proper instruction, and appropriate modification of progression and intensity based on the extent of physical maturation of the individual is critical to the effectiveness of the resistive exercises.[55] A strengthening program that uses calisthenic strengthening exercises with body weight as resistance should be encouraged.

CARDIORESPIRATORY ENDURANCE

By definition, **cardiorespiratory endurance** is the ability to perform whole-body, large muscle activities for extended periods of time. The cardiorespiratory system provides a means by which oxygen is supplied to the various tissues of the body.[33] Athletes find cardiorespiratory endurance critical both for performance and for preventing undue fatigue that may predispose them to injury.

Transport and Utilization of Oxygen

Basically, transport of oxygen throughout the body involves the coordinated function of four components: the heart, the lungs, the blood vessels, and the blood. The improvement of cardiorespiratory endurance through training occurs because of the increased capability of each of these four elements to provide necessary oxygen to the

4-6

Critical Thinking Exercise

A high school shot-putter has been working intensely on weight training to improve his muscular power. In particular he has been concentrating on lifting extremely heavy free weights using a low number of repetitions (three sets of six to eight repetitions). Although his strength has improved significantly over the last several months, he is not seeing the same degree of improvement in his throws, even though his coach says that his technique is very good.

? The athlete is frustrated with his performance and wants to know if there is anything else he can do in his training program that might enhance his performance.

cardiorespiratory endurance
Ability to perform activities for extended periods of time.

Figure 4-17

The greater the percentage of maximum aerobic capacity required during an activity, the less time the activity may be performed.

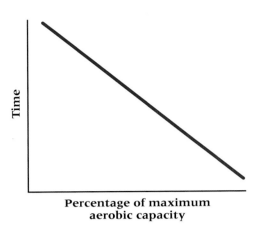

working tissues. The greatest rate at which oxygen can be taken in and used during exercise is referred to as *maximum aerobic capacity* ($\dot{V}O_2$max).[47] The performance of any activity requires a certain rate of oxygen consumption that is about the same for all persons, depending on the level of fitness. Generally, the greater the rate or intensity of the performance of an activity, the greater the oxygen consumption. Each person has his or her own maximal rate of oxygen consumption. That person's ability to perform an activity (or to fatigue) is closely related to the amount of oxygen required by that activity and is limited by the person's maximal rate of oxygen consumption. Apparently, the greater the percentage of maximum oxygen consumption required during an activity, the less time the activity may be sustained (Figure 4-17).

The maximal rate at which oxygen can be used is a genetically determined characteristic; a person inherits a certain range of maximum aerobic capacity, and the more active that person is, the higher the existing maximum aerobic capacity will be in that range.[33] A training program allows an athlete to increase maximum aerobic capacity to its highest limit within that athlete's range. Maximum aerobic capacity is most often presented in terms of the volume of oxygen used relative to body weight per unit of time (ml/kg/min). A normal maximum aerobic capacity for most college-age athletes would fall somewhere in the range of 45 to 60 ml/kg/min.[14] A world-class male marathon runner may have a maximum aerobic capacity in the 70 to 80 ml/kg/min range.

Three factors determine the maximal rate at which oxygen can be used: external respiration involving the ventilatory process or pulmonary function; gas transport, which is accomplished by the cardiovascular system (i.e., the heart, blood vessels, and blood); and internal respiration, which involves the use of oxygen by the cells to produce energy. Of these three factors the most limiting is generally the ability to transport oxygen through the system; thus the cardiovascular system limits the overall rate of oxygen consumption. A high maximum aerobic capacity within an athlete's inherited range indicates that all three systems are working well.

Effects on the Heart

The heart is the main pumping mechanism, circulating oxygenated blood throughout the body to the working tissues. As the body begins to exercise, the muscles use oxygen at a much higher rate, and the heart must pump more oxygenated blood to meet this increased demand. The heart is capable of adapting to this increased demand through several mechanisms. Heart rate shows a gradual adaptation to an increased workload by increasing proportionally to the intensity of the exercise and will plateau at a given level after about two to three minutes (Figure 4-18).

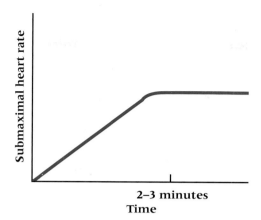

Figure 4-18

Two to three minutes are required for heart rate to plateau at a given workload.

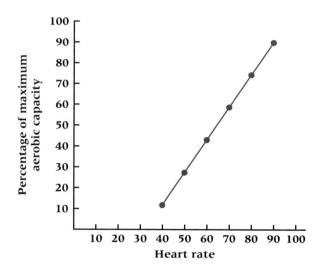

Figure 4-19

Maximal heart rate is achieved at about the same time as maximum aerobic capacity.

Monitoring heart rate is an indirect method of estimating oxygen consumption. In general, heart rate and oxygen consumption have a linear relationship, although at very low intensities and at high intensities this linear relationship breaks down (Figure 4-19).[11] During higher-intensity activities, maximal heart rate may be achieved before maximal oxygen consumption, which will continue to rise.[43] The greater the intensity of the exercise, the higher the heart rate. Because of these existing relationships it should become apparent that the rate of oxygen consumption can be estimated by taking heart rate.[15]

A second mechanism by which the heart is able to adapt to increased demands during exercise is to increase the stroke volume—the volume of blood being pumped out with each beat.[14] The heart pumps out approximately 70 ml of blood per beat. Stroke volume can continue to increase only to the point at which there is simply not enough time between beats for the heart to fill up. This point occurs at about 40 percent of maximal heart rate, and above this level increases in the volume of blood being pumped out per unit of time must be caused entirely by increases in heart rate (Figure 4-20).[51]

Stroke volume and heart rate together determine the volume of blood being pumped through the heart in a given unit of time. Approximately 5 L of blood are pumped through the heart during each minute at rest. This figure is referred to as the

Figure 4-20 (left)

Stroke volume plateaus at 40 percent of maximal heart rate.

Figure 4-21 (right)

Cardiac output limits maximum aerobic capacity.

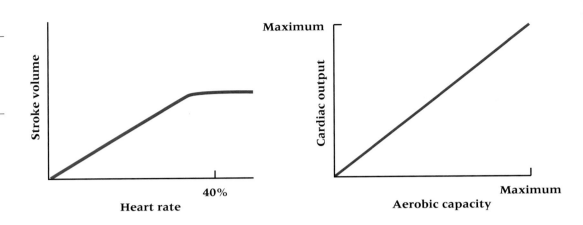

cardiac output, which indicates how much blood the heart is capable of pumping in exactly one minute. Thus, cardiac output is the primary determinant of the maximal rate of oxygen consumption possible (Figure 4-21). During exercise, cardiac output increases to approximately four times that experienced during rest in the normal individual and may increase as much as six times in the elite endurance athlete.

training effect

Stroke volume increases while heart rate is reduced at a given exercise load.

A **training effect** that occurs with regard to cardiac output of the heart is that the stroke volume increases while exercise heart rate is reduced at a given standard exercise load. The heart becomes more efficient because it is capable of pumping more blood with each stroke. Because the heart is a muscle, it will hypertrophy to some extent, but this hypertrophy is in no way a negative effect of training.

Training Effect

$$\text{Cardiac output} = \text{Increased stroke volume} \times \text{Decreased heart rate}$$

Effects on Work Ability

Cardiorespiratory endurance plays a critical role in the athlete's ability to resist fatigue. Fatigue is closely related to the percentage of maximum aerobic capacity that a particular workload demands.[59] For example, Figure 4-22 presents two athletes, A and B. Athlete A has a maximum aerobic capacity of 50 ml/kg/min, whereas athlete B has a maximum aerobic capacity of only 40 ml/kg/min. If athletes A and B are both exercising at the same intensity, athlete A will be working at a much lower percentage of maximum aerobic capacity than athlete B is. Consequently, athlete A should be able to sustain his or her activity over a much longer period of time. Athletic performance may be impaired if the ability to use oxygen efficiently is impaired. Thus, improvement of cardiorespiratory endurance should be an essential component of any training program.

The Energy Systems

Various sports activities involve specific demands for energy. For example, sprinting and jumping are high-energy activities, requiring a relatively large production of energy for a short time. Long-distance running and swimming, on the other hand, are mostly low-energy activities per unit of time, requiring energy production for a prolonged time. Other physical activities demand a blend of both high- and low-energy output. These various energy demands can be met by the different processes in which energy can be supplied to the skeletal muscles.

ATP: The Immediate Energy Source

Energy is produced from the breakdown of nutrient foodstuffs.[51] This energy is used to produce adenosine triphosphate (ATP), which is the ultimate usable form of energy for muscular activity. ATP is produced in the muscle tissue from blood glucose

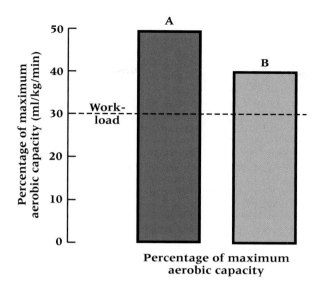

Figure 4-22

Athlete A should be able to work longer than Athlete B as a result of lower utilization of maximum aerobic capacity.

or glycogen. Glucose is derived from the breakdown of dietary carbohydrates. Glucose not needed immediately is stored as glycogen in the resting muscle and liver. Stored glycogen in the liver can later be converted back to glucose and transferred to the blood to meet the body's energy needs. Fats and proteins can also be metabolized to generate ATP.

Once much of the muscle and liver glycogen is depleted, the body relies more heavily on fats stored in adipose tissue to meet its energy needs. The longer the duration of an activity, the greater the amount of fat that is used, especially during the later stages of endurance events. During rest and submaximal exertion, both fat and carbohydrates are used as energy substrate in approximately a 60 percent to 40 percent ratio.[51]

Regardless of the nutrient source that produces ATP, it is always available in the cell as an immediate energy source. When all available sources of ATP are depleted, more must be regenerated for muscular contraction to continue.

Aerobic versus Anaerobic Metabolism

Two major energy systems function in muscle tissue: anaerobic and aerobic metabolism. Each of these systems generates ATP. During sudden outbursts of activity in intensive, short-term exercise, ATP can be rapidly metabolized to meet energy needs. After a few seconds of intensive exercise, however, the small stores of ATP are used up. The body then turns to glycogen as an energy source. Glycogen can be metabolized within the muscle cells to generate ATP for muscle contractions.[51]

Both ATP and muscle glycogen can be metabolized without the need for oxygen. Thus this energy system involves anaerobic metabolism (occurring in the absence of oxygen). As exercise continues, the body has to rely on the metabolism of carbohydrates (more specifically, glucose) and fats to generate ATP. This second energy system requires oxygen and is therefore referred to as aerobic metabolism (occurring in the presence of oxygen).[51]

In most activities both aerobic and anaerobic systems function simultaneously. The degree to which the two major energy systems are involved is determined by the intensity and duration of the activity. If the intensity of the activity is such that sufficient oxygen can be supplied to meet the demands of working tissues, the activity is considered to be *aerobic.* Conversely, if the activity is of high enough intensity or the duration is such that there is insufficient oxygen available to meet energy demands, the activity becomes *anaerobic.* Consequently, an oxygen debt is incurred that must be paid back during the recovery period. For example, short bursts of muscle contraction,

TABLE 4-1 Comparison of Aerobic versus Anaerobic Activities

	Mode	Relative Intensity	Performance	Frequency	Duration	Miscellaneous
Aerobic activities	Continuous, long-duration, sustained activities	Less intense	60% to 90% of maximum range	At least three but not more than six times per week	20 to 60 min	Less risk to sedentary or older individuals
Anaerobic activities	Explosive, short-duration, burst-type activities	More intense	90% to 100% of maximum range	Three to four times per week	10 sec to 2 min	Used in sport and team activities

as in running or swimming sprints, use predominantly the anaerobic system. However, endurance events depend a great deal on the aerobic system. Most sports use a combination of both anaerobic and aerobic metabolism (Table 4-1).

Training Techniques for Improving Cardiorespiratory Endurance

Cardiorespiratory endurance may be improved through a number of different methods. Largely, the amount of improvement possible will be determined by an individual's initial levels of cardiorespiratory endurance.

Continuous Training

Continuous training involves four considerations:

- *Mode* or type of activity
- *Frequency* of the activity
- *Duration* of the activity
- *Intensity* of the activity

Mode The type of activity used in continuous training must be aerobic.[15] Aerobic activities are those that elevate the heart rate and maintain it at that level for an extended time. Aerobic activities generally involve repetitive, whole-body, large-muscle movements performed over an extended time. Examples of aerobic activities are running, jogging, walking, cycling, swimming, rope skipping, stair climbing, and cross-country skiing. The advantage of these aerobic activities as opposed to more intermittent activities such as racquetball, squash, basketball, or tennis is that aerobic activities are easy to regulate by either speeding up or slowing down the pace. Because the given intensity of the workload elicits a given heart rate, these aerobic activities allow athletes to maintain heart rate at a specified or target level. Intermittent activities involve variable speeds and intensities that cause the heart rate to fluctuate considerably. Although these intermittent activities improve cardiorespiratory endurance, their intensity is much more difficult to monitor.

Frequency To see at least minimal improvement in cardiorespiratory endurance, it is necessary for the average person to engage in no fewer than three sessions per week.[5] If possible, an individual should aim for four or five sessions per week. A competitive athlete should be prepared to train as often as six times per week. Everyone should take at least one day per week off to allow for both psychological and physiological rest.

Duration For minimal improvement to occur, an individual must participate in at least twenty minutes of continuous activity with the heart rate elevated to its working level.[5] Recent evidence suggests that even shorter exercise bouts of as little as twelve minutes may be sufficient to show improvement. Generally, the greater the duration of the workout, the greater the improvement in cardiorespiratory endurance. The

4-7

Critical Thinking E x e r c i s e

A female soccer player has a grade I ankle sprain that is likely to keep her out of practice for about a week. She has worked extremely hard on her fitness levels and is concerned that not being able to run for an entire week will hurt her cardiorespiratory fitness.

? What types of activity should the athletic trainer recommend during her rehabilitation period that can help her maintain her existing level of cardiorespiratory endurance?

competitive athlete should train for at least forty-five minutes with the heart rate elevated to training levels.

Intensity   Of the four factors being considered, the most critical factor is the intensity of training, even though recommendations regarding training intensities vary. Intensity is particularly critical in the early stages of training, when the body is forced to make a lot of adjustments to increase workload demands.

Because heart rate is linearly related to the intensity of the exercise and to the rate of oxygen consumption, it becomes a relatively simple process to identify a specific workload (pace) that will make the heart rate plateau at the desired level. By monitoring heart rate, we know whether the pace is too fast or too slow to get the heart rate into a target range.[5]

Several formulas identify a target training heart rate.[5] Exact determination of maximal heart rate involves exercising an individual at a maximal level and monitoring the heart rate using an electrocardiogram. This process is difficult outside a laboratory. However, an approximate estimate of maximal heart rate for both males and females is 220 beats per minute. Maximal heart rate is related to age. As age increases, maximal heart rate decreases. Thus, a relatively simple estimation of maximal heart rate (HR) would be Maximal HR = 220 − Age. If an athlete is working at 70 percent of maximal rate, the target heart rate can be calculated by multiplying 0.7 × (220 − Age).

Another commonly used formula that takes into account the current level of fitness is the Karvonen equation.[40]

$$\text{Target training HR} = \text{Resting HR} + (0.6 \times [\text{Maximal HR} - \text{Resting HR}])$$

Regardless of the formula used, to see minimal improvement in cardiorespiratory endurance, the heart rate should be elevated to at least 70 percent of its maximal rate.[15] A trained individual ought to be able to sustain a heart rate at the 85 percent level.

Interval Training

Unlike continuous training, interval training involves more intermittent activities. **Interval training** consists of alternating periods of relatively intense work and active recovery. It allows for performance of much more work at a more intense workload over a longer period of time than does working continuously.[49]

It is most desirable in continuous training to work at an intensity of about 60 percent to 80 percent of maximal heart rate. Obviously, sustaining activity at a relatively high intensity over a twenty-minute period would be extremely difficult. The advantage of interval training is that it allows work at this 80 percent or higher level for a short period of time followed by an active period of recovery during which an individual may be working at only 30 percent to 45 percent of maximum heart rate.[12] Thus, the intensity of the workout and its duration can be greater than with continuous training.

Most sports are anaerobic, involving short bursts of intense activity followed by some type of active recovery period (for example, football, basketball, soccer, or tennis). Training with the interval technique allows the athlete to be more sport-specific during the workout. With interval training the overload principle is applied by making the training period much more intense.

There are several important considerations in interval training. The training period is the amount of time that continuous activity is actually being performed, and the recovery period is the time between training periods. A set is a group of combined training and recovery periods, and repetitions are the number of training and recovery periods per set. Training time or distance refers to the rate or distance of the training period. The training-recovery ratio indicates a time ratio for training versus recovery.

An example of interval training would be a soccer player running sprints. An interval workout would involve running ten 120-yard sprints with a 45-second walking recovery period between sprints. During this training session the soccer player's heart

interval training
Alternating periods of work with active recovery.

rate would probably increase to 85 percent to 90 percent of maximal level during the dash and should probably fall to the 30 percent to 45 percent level during the recovery period.

Fartlek Training

Fartlek, a training technique that is a type of cross-country running, originated in Sweden. *Fartlek* literally means "speed play." It is similar to interval training in that the athlete must run for a specified period of time; however, specific pace and speed are not identified. The course for a fartlek workout should be some type of varied terrain with some level running, some uphill and downhill running, and some running through obstacles such as trees or rocks. The object is to put surges into a running workout, varying the length of the surges according to individual purposes. One advantage of fartlek training is that because the terrain is always changing, the course may prevent boredom and may actually be relaxing.

To improve cardiorespiratory endurance, fartlek training must elevate the heart rate to at least minimal training levels. Fartlek may be utilized best as an off-season conditioning activity or as a change-of-pace activity to counteract the boredom of training using the same activity day after day.

Equipment for Improving Cardiorespiratory Endurance

The extent and variety of fitness and exercise equipment available to the consumer is at times mind boggling (Figure 4-23). Prices of equipment can range from $2 for a jump rope to $60,000 for certain computer-driven isokinetic devices. It is certainly not necessary to purchase expensive exercise equipment to see good results. Many of the same physiological benefits can be achieved from using a $2 jump rope as from running on a $10,000 treadmill. *Focus Box:* "Guidelines for choosing aerobic exercise equipment" identifies and discusses some of the more widely used pieces of exercise equipment.

FITNESS ASSESSMENT

Fitness testing provides the coach, athletic trainer, or strength and conditioning coach with information about the effectiveness of the conditioning program for an individual athlete. Testing may be done in a pretest/posttest format to determine significant improvement from some baseline measure. Tests may be used to assess flexibility, muscular strength, endurance, power, cardiorespiratory endurance, speed, balance, or agility, depending on the stated goals of the training and conditioning program. A variety of established tests can be used to assess these parameters. *Focus Box:* "Fitness testing" lists various tests that can be administered along with recommended references to consult for specific testing procedures and for in-depth testing directions.

PERIODIZATION IN TRAINING AND CONDITIONING

Serious athletes no longer engage only in preseason conditioning and in-season competition. Sports conditioning is a year-round endeavor. *Periodization* is an approach to conditioning that brings about peak performance while reducing injuries and overtraining in the athlete through a training and conditioning program that is followed throughout the various seasons.[13] Periodization takes into account that athletes have different training and conditioning needs during different seasons and modifies the program according to individual needs (Table 4-2, page 124).[21]

> Sports conditioning often falls into three seasons: off-season, preseason, and in-season.

Macrocycle

Periodization organizes a training and conditioning program into cycles. The complete training period, which could be a year in the case of seasonal sports or perhaps four years for an Olympic athlete, is referred to as a *macrocycle*. With seasonal sports the

Figure 4-23

Types of fitness equipment for improving cardiorespiratory endurance. **A,** Exercise bicycle. **B,** Treadmill. **C,** Stair climber. **D,** Cross-country ski machine. **E,** Elliptical trainer. **F,** Rowing machine. **G,** Upper body ergometer.

macrocycle can be divided into a preseason, an in-season, and an off-season. Throughout the course of the macrocycle, intensity, volume, and specificity of training are altered so that an athlete can achieve peak levels of fitness for competition. As competition approaches, training sessions change gradually and progressively from high-volume, low-intensity, non–sport-specific activity to low-volume, high-intensity, sport-specific training.[70]

Focus

Guidelines for choosing aerobic exercise equipment

Exercise bicycle (Figure 4-23A)

Most models work only the lower body, but some have pumping handlebars for arms and shoulders. Some can be programmed for various workouts, such as climbing hills. Some models let you pedal backward, which enhances the work on your hamstring muscles. Look for

- smooth pedaling motion
- a comfortable seat
- handlebars that adjust to your height
- pedal straps to keep your feet from slipping and to make your legs work on the upstroke, too
- easy-to-adjust workload
- solid construction

Treadmill (Figure 4-23B)

Some machines have adjustable inclines to simulate hills and make workouts more strenuous. Some can be programmed for various preset workouts. Look for

- easily adjustable speed and incline
- a running surface that is wide and long enough for your stride and that absorbs shock well
- a strong motor that can handle high speeds and a heavy load

Stair climber (Figure 4-23C)

Some larger models simulate real stair climbing. But most home models have pedals that work against your weight as you pump your legs; this feature puts less strain on your knees since you don't take real steps. Some people prefer pedals that remain parallel to the floor; others like pivoting pedals. Models with independent pedals provide a more natural stepping motion. Look for

- smooth stepping action
- large, comfortable pedals with no wobble
- easily adjustable resistance
- comfortable handlebars or rails for balance

Cross-country ski machine (Figure 4-23D)

These machines work most muscle groups. They simulate the outdoor sport: your feet slide in the tracks, and your hands pull on cords or poles, either independently or in synchronized movements. Machines with cords rather than poles may provide an es-

pecially strenuous upper-body workout. Look for

- a base that is long enough to accommodate your stride
- adjustable leg and arm resistance
- smooth action

Elliptical trainer (Figure 4-23E)

An elliptical exercise machine allows for a no-impact cardiovascular workout that mimics a combination of walking, stair climbing and cross-country skiing using an elliptical-shaped stride while standing upright using a forward or reverse motion. Look for

- an electronically adjustable ramp that allows the incline to be raised or lowered
- resistance that can be adjusted

Rowing machine (Figure 4-23F)

A rowing machine provides a fuller workout than does running or cycling because it tones muscles in the upper body. Most machines have hydraulic pistons to provide variable resistance; many larger models use a flywheel. Piston models have hydraulic arms and are cheaper and more compact than are flywheel models, which have a smoother action that is usually more like real rowing. One new model actually has a flywheel in a water tank to mimic real rowing. Look for

- seats and oars that move smoothly
- footrests that pivot

Upper body ergometer (UBE) (Figure 4-23G)

An upper body ergometer is essentially a stationary bicycle that you pedal with the arms rather than the legs. These machines are most often used to help maintain cardiorespiratory endurance in rehabilitation programs for individuals with injuries to the lower extremities who, for whatever reason, cannot use weight bearing activities. A UBE may also be used as a training and conditioning tool to help increase muscular endurance for the upper extremities. Look for

- easily adjustable speed and resistance
- a comfortable seat that provides some support and stabilization for the lower back
- smooth, quiet action

Focus

Fitness testing

Muscle strength, power, endurance
One repetition maximum tests
Timed push-ups
Timed sit-ups
Chin-ups
Bar dips
Flexed arm hang
Vertical jump

Flexibility
Sit-and-reach test
Trunk extension test
Shoulder lift test

Cardiorespiratory endurance
Cooper's 12-minute walk/run
1.5 mile run
Harvard step test

Speed
6-second dash
10- to 60-yard dash

Agility
T-test
Edgren side step
SEMO agility test

Balance
Stork test

Fitness testing references

Baumgartner T, Jackson A: *Measurement for evaluation in physical education and exercise science,* Dubuque, Iowa, 1999, WCB/McGraw-Hill.

Prentice W: *Fitness and wellness for life,* ed 6, Dubuque, Iowa, 1999, WCB/McGraw-Hill.

Semenick D: Testing procedures and protocols. In Baechle T, editor: *Essentials of strength training and conditioning,* Champaign, Ill, 1994, Human Kinetics.

Mesocycles

Within the macrocycle are a series of *mesocycles,* each of which may last for several weeks or even months. A mesocycle is further divided into *transition, preparatory,* and *competition* periods.[70]

Transition period   The transition period begins after the last competition and comprises the early part of the off-season. The transition period is generally unstructured, and the athlete is encouraged to participate in sport activities on a recreational basis. The idea is to allow the athlete to escape both physically and psychologically from the rigor of a highly organized training regimen.

Preparatory period   The preparatory period occurs primarily during the off-season when there are no upcoming competitions. The preparatory period has three phases: the hypertrophy/endurance phase, the strength phase, and the power phase.

TABLE 4-2 Periodization Training

Season	Period/Phase	Type of Training Activity
Off-season	Transition period	Unstructured Recreational
	Preparatory period Hypertrophy/endurance phase	Cross-training Low intensity High volume Non–sport-specific
	Strength phase	Moderate intensity Moderate volume More sport-specific
Preseason	Power phase	High intensity Decreased volume Sport-specific
In-season	Competition period	High intensity Low volume Skill-training Strategy Maintenance of strength and power gained during the off-season

4-8

Critical Thinking Exercise

Following the end of the competitive season, a college football player took the months of December and January off from intense training. He played only basketball and occasionally rode an exercise bike, thus completing the transitional period of the macrocycle. It is now time for him to begin the preparatory phase of training.

? What activities should he begin with, and how should these activities progress over the next several months?

During the hypertrophy/endurance phase, which occurs in the early part of the off-season, training is at a low intensity with a high volume of repetitions, using activities that may or may not be directly related to a specific sport. The goal is to develop a base of endurance on which more intense training can occur. This phase may last from several weeks to two months.

During the strength phase, which also occurs during the off-season, the intensity and volume progress to moderate levels. Weight-training activities should become more specific to the sport or event.

The third phase, or power phase, occurs in the preseason. The athlete trains at a high intensity at or near the level of competition. The volume of training is decreased so that full recovery is allowed between sessions.

Competition period   In certain cases the competition period may last for only a week or less. With seasonal sports, however, the competition period may last for several months. In general this period involves high-intensity training at a low volume. As training volume decreases, an increased amount of time is spent on skill training or strategy sessions. During the competition period, it may be necessary to establish microcycles, which are periods lasting from one to seven days. During a weekly microcycle, training should be intense early in the week and should progress to moderate and finally to light training the day before a competition. The goal is to make sure that the athlete will be at peak levels of fitness and performance on days of competition.[14]

Cross Training

The concept of cross training is an approach to training and conditioning for a specific sport that involves substituting alternative activities that have some carryover value to that sport. For example, a swimmer could engage in jogging, running, or aerobic exercise to maintain levels of cardiorespiratory conditioning. Cross training is particularly useful in both the transition and early preparatory periods. It adds variety to the training regimen, thus keeping training during the off-season more interesting and exciting. However, while cross training can be effective in maintaining levels of cardiorespiratory endurance, it is not sport-specific and thus should not be used during the preseason.

SUMMARY

- Proper physical conditioning for sports participation should prepare the athlete for a high-level performance while helping to prevent injuries inherent to that sport.

- Year-round conditioning is essential in most sports to assist in preventing injuries. Periodization is an approach to conditioning that attempts to bring about peak performance while reducing injuries and overtraining in the athlete by developing a training and conditioning program to be followed throughout the various seasons.

- Physical conditioning must follow the SAID principle, which is an acronym for specific adaptation to imposed demands. Conditioning must work toward making the body as lean as possible, commensurate with the athlete's sport.

- A proper warm-up should precede conditioning, and a proper cooldown should follow. It takes at least fifteen to thirty minutes of gradual warm-up to bring the body to a state of readiness for vigorous sports training and participation. Warming up consists of a general, unrelated activity followed by a specific, related activity.

- Optimum flexibility is necessary for success in most sports. Too much flexibility can allow joint trauma to occur, and too little flexibility can result in muscle tears or strains. Ballistic stretching exercises should be avoided. The safest means of increasing flexibility are static stretching and the proprioceptive neuromuscular facilitation (PNF) technique, consisting of slow-reversal-hold-relax, contract-relax, and hold-relax methods.

- Strength is the capacity to exert a force or the ability to perform work against a resistance. There are many ways to develop strength, including isometric, isotonic, and isokinetic muscle contraction. Isometric exercise generates heat energy by forcefully contracting the muscle in a stable position that produces no change in the length of the muscle. Isotonic exercise involves shortening and lengthening a muscle through a complete range of motion. Isokinetic exercise allows resisted movement through a full range at a specific velocity. Circuit training uses a series of exercise stations to improve strength and flexibility. Plyometric training uses a quick, eccentric contraction to facilitate a more explosive concentric contraction.

- Cardiorespiratory endurance is the ability to perform whole-body, large-muscle activities repeatedly for long periods of time. Maximal oxygen consumption is the greatest determinant of the level of cardiorespiratory endurance. Most sport activities involve some combination of both aerobic and anaerobic metabolism. Improvement of cardiorespiratory endurance may be accomplished through continuous, interval, or fartlek training.

Websites

Health and Fitness Worldguide Forum:
http://www.worldguide.com/main/hf.html

Includes coverage of anatomy, strength, cardiovascular exercise, eating well, and sports medicine.

Stretching and Flexibility: Everything you ever wanted to know:
http://www.cmcrossroads.com/bradapp/docs/rec/ stretching/

Prepared by Brad Appleton, website presents detailed information on stretching and stretching techniques, including normal ranges of motion, flexibility, how to stretch, the physiology of stretching, and types of stretching (including PNF).

National Strength and Conditioning Association (NSCA):
http://www.nsca-lift.org

Website for an organization that focuses on strength and conditioning to support and disseminate research-based knowledge and its practical application and to improve athletic performance and fitness.

Fitness World: http://www.fitnessworld.com

Presents information about fitness in general and includes access to Fitness Management magazine.

Kaiser Permanente Health Reference:
http://www.kaisersantaclara.org

Click on Cardiovascular Exercise and find several topics including how to start, target heart rate, and injuries.

Solutions to Critical Thinking EXERCISES

4-1 Although athletes should make every effort to maintain existing levels of fitness during the rehabilitation period, to improve their fitness to competitive levels, athletes in any sport must practice or engage in that specific activity. The football player must begin a heavy strength-training program for the upper body immediately in the postseason and must continue to progressively return to heavy lifting with the lower extremities as soon as the healing process will allow. It is essential for this player to progressively increase the intensity and variety of conditioning drills that specifically relate to performance at his particular position.

4-2 The warm-up should begin with a five- to seven-minute slow jog during which the athlete should break into a light sweat. At that point, she should engage in stretching (using either static or PNF techniques), concentrating on quadriceps, hamstrings, groin, and hip abductor muscles. Each specific stretch should be repeated four times, and the stretch should be held for fifteen to twenty seconds. Once the workout begins, the athlete should gradually and moderately increase the intensity of her activity. She may also find it effective to stretch during the cooldown period after the workout.

4-3 The athletic trainer should recommend that the athlete engage in a regular, consistent flexibility program using either static or PNF stretching techniques. Stretching should be done several times a day if possible. The athlete should also be instructed to engage in full range of motion strength training for the hamstrings. The athletic trainer should also explain that when the athlete feels tightness or discomfort during a training session, he should stop the activity immediately to avoid making a hamstring strain more severe.

4-4 Weight training will not have a negative effect on flexibility as long as the lifting technique is done properly. Lifting the weight through a full range of motion will serve to improve strength and simultaneously maintain range of motion. A female swimmer is not likely to bulk up to the point that muscle size will affect range of motion. It is also important to recommend that this athlete continue to incorporate active stretching into her training regimen.

4-5 The athletic trainer can discuss the rationale for strength and conditioning with the athlete. Helping the athlete understand why it is important to increase strength and endurance can increase her motivation. In addition to improving performance and efficiency, muscular endurance and strength is also critical in preventing athletic injuries. The athletic trainer should work with the coaches to provide a periodization program that will keep the athlete's interest and prevent atrophy from occurring.

4-6 The shot put, like many other dynamic movements in sports, requires not only great strength but also the ability to generate that strength rapidly. To develop muscular power, this athlete must engage in dynamic, explosive training techniques that will help him develop his ability. Power lifting techniques should be helpful. Plyometric exercises using weights for added resistance will help him improve his speed of muscular contraction against some resistive force.

4-7 Because this athlete suffers from a lower extremity injury in which weight bearing is limited, alternative activities such as swimming or riding a stationary exercise bike should be incorporated into her rehabilitation program immediately. If the pressure on her ankle when riding an exercise bike is too painful, she may find it helpful initially to use a bike that incorporates upper extremity exercise. The athletic trainer should recommend that this soccer player engage in a minimum of thirty minutes of continuous training as well as some higher-intensity interval training to maintain both aerobic and anaerobic fitness.

4-8 During the early part of the preparatory period, training should be at a low intensity with a high volume of repetitions, using activities that may or may not be directly related to football. This phase may last from several weeks to two months. The intensity and volume of these activities should progress to moderate levels. Weight-training activities should eventually become more specific to football. Just before the preseason, the athlete should train at a high intensity, and the volume of training should decrease to allow full recovery between sessions.

REVIEW QUESTIONS AND CLASS ACTIVITIES

1. Why is year-round conditioning so important for injury prevention?
2. In terms of injury prevention, list as many advantages as you can for conditioning.
3. How does the SAID principle relate to sports conditioning and injury prevention?
4. What is the value of proper warm-up and cooldown to sports injury prevention?
5. Critically observe how a variety of sports use warm-up and cooldown procedures.
6. Compare ways to increase flexibility and how they may decrease or increase the athlete's susceptibility to injury.
7. How may increasing strength decrease susceptibility to injury?
8. Compare different techniques of increasing strength. How may each technique be an advantage or a disadvantage to the athlete in terms of injury prevention?
9. Discuss the relationships among maximal oxygen consumption, heart rate, stroke volume, and cardiac output.
10. Differentiate between aerobic and anaerobic training methods.
11. How is continuous training different from interval training?

REFERENCES

1. Akima H, Takahashi H, Kuno SY: Early phase adaptations of muscle use and strength to isokinetic training, *Med Sci Sports Exer* 31(4): 588, 1999.
2. Allerheiligen W: Speed development and plyometric training. In Baechle T, editor: *Essentials of strength training and conditioning,* Champaign, Ill, 2000, Human Kinetics.
3. Allerheiligen W: Stretching and warm-up. In Baechle T, editor: *Essentials of strength training and conditioning,* Champaign, Ill, 2000, Human Kinetics.
4. Alter M: *The science of flexibility,* Champaign, Ill, 2004, Human Kinetics.
5. American College of Sports Medicine: *Guidelines for exercise testing and prescription,* Philadelphia, 2000, William and Wilkens.
6. Armiger P: Preventing musculotendinous injuries: a focus on flexibility, *Athletic Therapy Today* 5(4):20, 2000.
7. Baker D, Wilson G, Carlyon B: Generality vs. specificity: a comparison of dynamic and isometric measures of strength and speed-strength, *Eur J Appl Physiol* 68:350,1994.
8. Bandy WD, Irion JM, Briggler M: The effect of static stretch and dynamic range of motion training on the flexibility of the hamstring muscles, *J Orthop Sports Phys Ther* 27(4):295, 1998.
9. Bassett DR, Howley ET: Limiting factors for maximum oxygen uptake and determinants of endurance performance, *Med Sci Sports Exer* 32(1):70, 2000.
10. Berger R: *Conditioning for men,* Boston, 1973, Allyn & Bacon.

11. Bergh U, Ekblom B, Astrand PO: Maximal oxygen uptake "classical" versus "contemporary" viewpoints, *Med Sci Sports Exer* 32(1): 85, 2000.

12. Billat LV: Interval training for performance: a scientific and empirical practice. Special Recommendations for middle- and long distance running. Part I: aerobic interval training. *Sports Med* 31(1):13, 2001.

13. Blanke D: Flexibility. In Mellion M, editor: *Sports medicine secrets,* Philadelphia, 1999, Hanley & Belfus.

14. Bompa TO: *Periodization training for sports,* Champaign, Ill, 1999, Human Kinetics.

15. Brooks G, Fahey T, White T: *Exercise physiology: human bioenergetics and its applications,* Mountain View, Calif, 2000, Mayfield.

16. Brown LE: *Isokinetics in human performance,* Champaign, Ill, 2000, Human Kinetics.

17. Burke DG, Culligan CJ, Holt LE: The theoretical basis of proprioceptive neuromuscular facilitation, *Strength Cond Res* 14(4):496, 2000.

18. Chimera N, Swanik K, Swanik C: Effects of plyometric training on muscle activation strategies and performance in female athletes, *J Ath Train* 39(1):24, 2004.

19. Chu DA: Plyometics in sports injury rehabilitation and training, *Athletic Therapy Today* 4(3):7, 1999.

20. Clark M: *Integrated training for the new millennium,* Calabasas, Calif, 2001, National Academy of Sports Medicine.

21. Conroy M: The use of periodization in the high school setting, *Strength Cond J* 21(1):52, 1999.

22. Cross KM, Worrell TW: Effects of a static stretching program on the incidence of lower extremity musculotendinous strains, *J Ath Train* 34(1):11, 1999.

23. DeLorme TL, Watkins AL: *Progressive resistance exercise,* New York, 1951, Appleton-Century-Crofts.

24. DePino GM, Webright WG, Arnold BL: Duration of maintained hamstring flexibility after cessation of an acute static stretching protocol, *J Ath Train* 35(1):56, 2000.

25. Faulkner J, Green H, White T. Response and adaptation of skeletal muscle to changes in physical activity. In Bouchard C, Shepard R, Stephens J, editors: *Physical activity, fitness, and health,* Champaign, Ill, 1994, Human Kinetics.

26. Fleck S, Kraemer W: *Designing resistance training programs,* Champaign, Ill, 1997, Human Kinetics.

27. Gardner PJ: Youth strength training. *Athletic Therapy Today* 8(1):42, 2003.

28. Gravelle BL, Blessing DL: Physiological adaptation in women concurrently training for strength and endurance, *J Strength Cond* 14(1): 5, 2000.

29. Goldberg L: *Strength ball training,* Champaign, Ill, 2002, Human Kinetics.

30. Green W: *The clinical measurement of joint motion,* Rosemont, Ill, 1994, American Academy of Orthopedic Surgeons.

31. Gribble P, Prentice W: Effects of static and hold-relax stretching on hamstring range of motion using the FlexAbility LE1000, *J Sport Rehabil* 8(3):195, 1999.

32. Harman E: The biomechanics of resistance exercise. In Baechle T, editor: *Essentials of strength training and conditioning,* Champaign, Ill, 2000, Human Kinetics.

33. Hawley J, Myburgh K, Noakes T: Maximal oxygen consumption: a contemporary perspective. In Fahey T, editor: *Encyclopedia of sports medicine and exercise physiology,* New York, 1995, Mayfield.

34. Hickson R, Hidaka C, Foster C: Skeletal muscle fiber type, resistance training, and strength-related performance, *Med Sci Sports Exerc* 26:593, 1994.

35. Hilbert S, Plisk SS: Free weights versus machines, *Strength Cond J* 21(6):66, 1999.

36. Holcomb WR: Improved stretching with proprioceptive neuromuscular facilitation, *Strength Cond J* 22(1):59, 2000.

37. Holt LE, Pelham TW, Burke DG: Modifications to the standard sit-and-reach flexibility protocol, *J Ath Train* 34(1):43, 1999.

38. Jones M, Trowbridge C: Four ways to a safe, effective strength training program, *Athletic Therapy Today* 3(2):4, 1998.

39. Kaminski TW, Wabbersen CV, Murphy RM: Concentric versus enhanced eccentric hamstring strength training: clinical implications, *J Ath Train* 33(3):216, 1998.

40. Karvonen MJ, Kentala E, Mustala O: The effects of training on heart rate: a longitudinal study, *Ann Med Exp Biol* 35:305, 1957.

41. Knight K, Ingersoll C, Bartholomew J: Isotonic Contractions Might Be More Effective Than Isokinetic Contractions in Developing Muscle Strength, *J Sport Rehab* 10(2):124, 2001.

42. Kraemer W: General adaptation to resistance and endurance training programs. In Baechle T, editor: *Essentials of strength training and conditioning,* Champaign, Ill, 2000, Human Kinetics.

43. Kraemer W, Fleck S: *Strength training for young athletes,* Champaign, Ill, 2004, Human Kinetics.

44. Kraemer W, Hakkinen K, Kraemer W: *Strength training for sport.* Cambridge, Mass, Blackwell Science, 2001.

45. Kraemer W, Patton J, Gordon S: Compatibility of high-intensity strength and endurance training on hormonal and skeletal muscle adaptations, *J App Physiol* 78:976, 1995.

46. Kubukeli ZN, Noakes TD, Dennis SC: Training techniques to improve endurance exercise performances. *Sports Med* 32(8):489, 2002.

47. Laursen PB, Jenkins DG: The scientific basis for high-intensity interval training: optimizing training programmes and maximising performance in highly trained endurance athletes. *Sports Med* 32(1): 53, 2002.

48. Logan GA, Wallis EL: Recent findings in learning and performance. Paper presented at the Southern Section Meeting, California Association for Health, Physical Education, and Recreation, Pasadena, Calif, 1960.

49. MacDougall D, Sale D: Continuous vs. interval training: a review for the athlete and coach, *Can J Appl Sport Sci* 6:93, 1981.

50. Mann D, Whedon C: Functional stretching: implementing a dynamic stretching program. *Athletic Therapy Today* 6(3):10, 2001.

51. McArdle W, Katch F, Katch V: *Exercise physiology, energy, nutrition, and human performance,* Philadelphia, 2001, Lea & Febiger.

52. McComas A: Human neuromuscular adaptations that accompany changes in activity, *Med Sci Sports Exerc* 26(12):1498, 1994.

53. Merce J, Dufek J, Bates B: Analysis of peak oxygen consumption and heart rate during elliptical and treadmill exercise, *J Sport Rehab* 10(1):48, 2001.

54. Middlesworth M: More than ergonomics: warm-up and stretching key to injury prevention. *Athletic Therapy Today* 7(2):32, 2002.

55. Moreno, A: The practicalities of adolescent resistance training. *Athletic Therapy Today* 8(3):26, 2003.

56. Moss RI: Physics, plyometrics, and injury prevention. *Athletic Therapy Today* 7(2):44, 2002.

57. Norkin C, White D: *Measurement of joint motion: a guide to goniometry,* Philadelphia, 1995, F. A. Davis.

58. Perrin DH: *Isokinetic exercise and assessment,* Champaign, Ill, 1993, Human Kinetics.

59. Prentice W: *Fitness and wellness for life,* ed 7, Dubuque, Iowa, 1999, WCB/McGraw-Hill.

60. Prentice W: Proprioceptive neuromuscular facilitation techniques. In Prentice W: *Rehabilitation techniques in sports medicine,* and athletic training, St. Louis, 2004, McGraw-Hill.

61. Radcliffe JC, Farentinos RC: *High-powered plyometrics,* Champaign, Ill, 1999, Human Kinetics.

62. Rubley M, Brucker J, Knight K: Flexibility retention 3 weeks after a 5-day training regime, *J Sport Rehab* 10(2):105, 2001.

63. Sanders M: Weight training and conditioning. In Sanders B: *Sports physical therapy,* Norwalk, Conn, 1997, Appleton & Lange.

64. Schilling BK, Stone MH: Stretching: acute effects on strength and power performance, *Strength Cond J* 22(1):44, 2000.

65. Sharkey J: Is ballistic stretching back? *Ultra Fit Australia* 22:22,1995.

66. Spernoga S, Uhl T, Arnold B: Duration of maintained hamstring flexibility after a 1-time modified hold-relax stretching protocol, *J Ath Train* 36(1): 44, 2001.

67. Surburg P: Flexibility/range of motion. In Winnick JP, editor, *The Brockport physical fitness training guide*, Champaign, Ill, 1999, Human Kinetics.

68. Thomas M: The functional warm-up, *Strength Cond* 22(2): 51, 2000.

69. Walker M, Sussman D, Tamburello M: Relationship between maximum strength and relative endurance for the empty-can exercise, *J Sport Rehab* 12(1):31, 2003.

70. Wathen D: Periodization: concepts and applications. In Baechle T, editor: *Essentials of strength training and conditioning*, Champaign, Ill, 2000, Human Kinetics.

71. Wilkerson G, Colson M, Short N: Neuromuscular changes in female collegiate athletes resulting from a plyometric jump-training program, *J Ath Train* 39(1):17, 2004.

72. Zentz C: Warm up to perform up, *Athletic Therapy Today* 5(2): 59, 2000.

ANNOTATED BIBLIOGRAPHY

Alter M: *The science of flexibility*, Champaign, Ill, 2004, Human Kinetics.

This text explains the principles and techniques of stretching and details the anatomy and physiology of muscle and connective tissue. It includes guidelines for developing a flexibility program, illustrated stretching exercises, and warm-up drills.

Anderson B: *Stretching*, Bolinas, Calif, 2000, Shelter.

An extremely comprehensive best-selling text on stretching exercises for the entire body.

Baechle T, editor: *Essentials of strength training and conditioning*, Champaign, Ill, 2000, Human Kinetics.

A book from the National Strength Coaches Association that explains the science, theory, and practical application of various aspects of conditioning in a very concise, easily understood text.

Brooks G, Fahey T, White T: *Exercise physiology: human bioenergetics and its applications*, Mountain View, Calif, 2000, Mayfield.

An up-to-date, advanced text in exercise physiology that contains a comprehensive listing of the most current journal articles relative to exercise physiology.

Chu D: *Jumping into plyometrics*, Champaign, Ill, 1998, Human Kinetics.

This text helps the athlete develop a safe plyometric training program with exercises designed to improve quickness, speed, upper body strength, jumping ability, balance, and coordination. It is well illustrated.

Foss M, Keteyian S: *Fox's physiological basis for exercise and sport*, Dubuque, Iowa, 1998, McGraw-Hill.

A complete text that discusses the rationale and physiological principles underlying various aspects of an exercise program. Cardiorespiratory endurance is among several facets of fitness emphasized in this text.

Moran G, McGlynn G: *Dynamics of strength training*, St. Louis, 2000, McGraw-Hill

Provides a comprehensive resource using an individualized approach to strength training, including conditioning and cardiorespiratory fitness. Emphasizes the physiological basis of muscle strength and endurance. Illustrates the most efficient and effective training techniques.

Prentice W: *Fitness and wellness for life*, ed 7, Dubuque, Iowa, 1999, WCB/McGraw-Hill.

A comprehensive fitness text that covers all aspects of a training and conditioning program.

Wiksten D, Peters C: *The athletic trainer's guide to strength and endurance training*, Thoroghfare, NJ, 2000, Slack.

Layout offers ease of reference, sport-specific programs, information on nutritional supplements, and illustrations on weight training and supplemental routines.

Nutritional Considerations

Chapter 5

When you finish this chapter you should be able to

- Distinguish the six classes of nutrients and describe their major functions.
- Explain the importance of good nutrition in enhancing performance and preventing injuries.
- Assess the advantages or disadvantages of supplementing nutrients in the athlete's diet.
- Discuss the advantages and disadvantages of consuming a preevent meal.
- Differentiate between body weight and body composition.
- Explain the principle of caloric balance and how to assess it.
- Assess body composition using skinfold calipers.
- Evaluate methods for losing and gaining weight.
- Recognize the signs of bulimia nervosa and anorexia nervosa.

The relation of nutrition, diet, and weight control to overall health and fitness is an issue of critical importance to an athlete. Athletes who practice sound nutritional habits reduce the likelihood of injury by maintaining a higher standard of healthful living.[53] We know that eating a well-balanced diet can positively contribute to the development of strength, flexibility, and cardiorespiratory endurance.[65] Unfortunately, misconceptions, fads, and in many cases, superstitions regarding nutrition affect dietary habits, particularly in the athletic population.[42]

Many athletes associate successful performance with the consumption of special foods or supplements.[38] An athlete who is performing well may be reluctant to change dietary habits regardless of whether the diet is physiologically beneficial to overall health.[69] There is no question that the psychological aspect of allowing the athlete to eat whatever he or she is most comfortable with can greatly affect performance. The problem is that these eating habits tend to become accepted as beneficial and may become traditional when in fact they may be physiologically detrimental to athletic performance. Thus, many nutrition "experts" tend to disseminate nutritional information based on traditional rather than experimental information.[69] The athletic trainer must possess a strong knowledge of nutrition so that he or she may serve as an informational resource for the athlete.[25,43]

NUTRITION BASICS

Nutrition is the science of the substances that are found in food that are essential to life. A substance is essential if it must be supplied by the diet.[69] There are six classes of nutrients: carbohydrates (CHO), fats, proteins, vitamins, minerals, and water. Nutrients are necessary for three major roles: growth, repair, and maintenance of all tissues; the regulation of body processes; and the production of energy.[67]

Nutrient density describes foods that supply adequate amounts of vitamins and minerals in relation to their caloric value. The so-called junk foods provide excessive amounts of calories from fat and sugar in relation to vitamins and minerals and therefore are not nutrient dense. However, many people live on junk foods that displace more nutrient-dense foods from their diet.[58] This behavior is not healthful in the long run.[67]

The six classes of nutrients are carbohydrates, fats, proteins, vitamins, minerals, and water.

Nutrient-dense foods supply adequate amounts of vitamins and minerals in relation to caloric value.

ENERGY SOURCES
Carbohydrates

Athletes have increased energy needs. Carbohydrates are the body's most efficient source of energy and should be relied on to fill that need.[55] For the athlete, carbohydrate intake should account for 55 percent to 70 percent of total caloric intake. The following sections describe different forms of carbohydrates and their role in the production of energy and the maintenance of health.[67]

Sugars

Carbohydrates are sugar, starches, or fiber.

Carbohydrates are classified as simple (sugars) or complex (starch and most forms of fiber). Sugars are further divided into monosaccharides and disaccharides. Monosaccharides, or single sugars, are found mostly in fruits, syrups, and honey. Glucose (blood sugar) is a monosaccharide. Milk sugar (lactose) and table sugar (sucrose) are combinations of two monosaccharides and are called disaccharides. Because sugar contributes little in the way of other nutrients, the amount of sugar eaten should account for less than 15 percent of the total caloric intake.

Starches

Starches are complex carbohydrates. A starch is made up of long chains of glucose units. During the digestion process, the starch chain is broken down and the glucose units are free to be absorbed. Food sources of starch, such as rice, potatoes, and breads, often provide vitamins and minerals in addition to serving as the body's principal source of glucose. Many people believe that starchy foods contribute to obesity. However, most of these foods are eaten with fats from butter, margarine, sauces, and gravies that make the food more enjoyable but contribute an excess of calories.

Glycolysis is the process that breaks down glucose to produce energy.

The body cannot use starches and many sugars directly from food for energy. It must obtain the simple sugar glucose (blood sugar). During digestion and metabolism, starches and disaccharide sugars are broken down and converted to glucose. The glucose that is not needed for immediate energy is stored as glycogen in the liver and muscle cells. Glucose can be released from glycogen later if needed. The body, however, can store only a limited amount of glucose as glycogen. Any extra amount of glucose is converted to body fat. When the body experiences an inadequate intake of dietary carbohydrate, it uses protein to make glucose, but the protein is then diverted from its own important functions. Therefore, a supply of glucose must be kept available to prevent the use of protein for energy. This is called the protein-sparing action of glucose.

Fiber

In recent years, researchers have given considerable attention to the importance of fiber in the diet. Fiber forms the structural parts of plants and is not digested by humans. Fiber is not found in animal sources of food. There are two kinds of dietary fiber: soluble and insoluble. Soluble fiber includes gums and pectins; cellulose is the primary insoluble form. Sources of soluble fiber are oatmeal, legumes, and some fruits. Food sources of insoluble fiber include whole grain breads and bran cereals.

Because it is not digested, fiber passes through the intestinal tract and adds bulk. Fiber aids normal elimination by reducing the amount of time required for wastes to move through the digestive tract, which is believed to reduce the risk of colon cancer. Also, increased fiber intake is thought to reduce the risk of coronary artery disease. Soluble forms of fiber bind to cholesterol passing through the digestive tract and prevent its absorption, which can reduce blood cholesterol levels. Foods rich in saturated fats (meats, in particular) often take the place of fiber-rich foods in the diet, thus increasing cholesterol absorption and formation. Consumption of adequate amounts of fiber has been associated with lowered incidences of obesity, constipation, colitis, appendicitis, and diabetes.

The recommended amount of fiber in the diet is approximately twenty-five grams per day.[61] Unfortunately, the average person consumes only ten to fifteen grams per day. Fiber intake should be increased by increasing the amount of whole grain cereal products and fruits and vegetables in the diet rather than by using fiber supplements. Excessive consumption of fiber may cause intestinal discomfort as well as increased losses of calcium and iron.

Fats

Fats are another essential component of the diet. They are the most concentrated source of energy, providing more than twice the calories per gram when compared with carbohydrates or proteins. Fat is used as a primary source of energy. Some dietary fat is needed to make food more flavorful and for sources of the fat-soluble vitamins. Also, a minimal amount of fat is essential for normal growth and development.

Dietary fat represents approximately 40 percent to 50 percent of the total caloric intake. A substantial amount of the fat is from saturated fatty acids. This intake is believed to be too high and may contribute to the prevalence of obesity, certain cancers, and coronary artery disease. The recommended intake should be limited to less than 30 percent of total calories, with saturated fat reduced to less than 10 percent of total calories.[61]

Saturated versus Unsaturated Fat

Both plant and animal foods provide sources of dietary fat. About 95 percent of the fat consumed is in the form of triglycerides. Depending on their chemical nature, fatty acids may be saturated or unsaturated. The unsaturated fatty acids can be subdivided into monounsaturates or polyunsaturates. Therefore the terms *saturated, monounsaturated,* and *polyunsaturated* are used to describe the chemical nature of the fat in foods. The triglycerides that make up food fats are usually mixtures of saturated and unsaturated fatty acids but are classified according to the type that predominates. In general, fats containing more unsaturated fatty acids are from plants and are liquid at room temperature. Saturated fatty acids are derived mainly from animal sources.

Trans fatty acids have physical properties generally resembling saturated fatty acids, and their presence tends to harden oils. Often found in cookies, crackers, dairy products, meats, and fast foods, trans fatty acids increase the risk of heart disease by boosting levels of bad cholesterol. Because they are not essential and provide no known health benefit, there is no safe level of trans fatty acids and people should eat as little of them as possible while consuming a nutritionally adequate diet.

Other Fats

Phospholipids and sterols represent the remaining 5 percent of fats. Phospholipids include lecithin; cholesterol is the best known sterol. Cholesterol is consumed in the diet from animal foods; it is not supplied by plant sources of food. Generally, it is wise to avoid eating foods high in cholesterol. Although cholesterol is essential to many body functions, the body can manufacture cholesterol from CHO, proteins, and especially saturated fat. Thus there is little if any need to consume additional amounts of cholesterol in the diet. The American Heart Association recommends consuming less than 300 mg per day.

One type of unsaturated fatty acid seems to serve as a protective mechanism against certain disease processes. The omega-3 fatty acids apparently have the capability of reducing the likelihood of diseases such as heart disease, stroke, and hypertension. These fatty acids are found in cold-water fish. However, experts do not recommend the use of fish oil supplements as a source of omega-3 fatty acids.

Fat Substitutes

Fat-free products containing artificial fat substitutes, such as Simplese and Olean, are now available to the consumer. These products contain no cholesterol and 80 percent

5-1

Critical Thinking Exercise

A female softball player has been told by her coach that she is slightly overweight and needs to lose a few pounds. The athlete has been watching television and reading about how important it is to limit the dietary intake of fat for losing weight. She has decided to go on a diet that is essentially fat free and is totally convinced that this will help her lose weight.

? What should the athletic trainer tell her about avoiding the excessive intake of fat as a means of losing weight?

Fats may be saturated or unsaturated.

fewer calories than similar products made with fat. Despite FDA approval of these fat substitutes, some individuals have reported abdominal cramping and diarrhea when using them.[10]

Proteins

Dietary recommendations: CHO, 60 percent; fats, 25 percent; proteins, 15 percent.

Proteins make up the major structural components of the body. They are needed for growth, maintenance, and repair of all body tissues. In addition, proteins are needed to make enzymes, many hormones, and antibodies that help fight infection. In general, the body prefers not to use much protein for energy; instead it relies on fats and carbohydrates. Protein intake should be around 12 percent to 15 percent of total calories.

Amino Acids

Proteins are made up of amino acids.

The basic units that make up proteins are smaller compounds called amino acids. Most of the body's proteins are made up of about twenty amino acids. Amino acids can be linked together in a wide variety of combinations, which is why there are so many different forms and uses of proteins. Most of the amino acids can be produced as needed in the body. The others cannot be made to any significant degree and therefore must be supplied by the diet. The amino acids obtained through food are referred to as the essential amino acids. The amount of protein as well as the levels of the individual essential amino acids is important for determining the quality of diet. A diet that contains large amounts of protein will not support growth, repair, and maintenance of tissues if the essential amino acids are not available in the proper proportions.[37]

Most of the proteins from animal foods contain all the essential amino acids that humans require and are called complete, or high-quality, proteins. Incomplete proteins, that is, those sources of protein that do not contain all the essential amino acids, usually are from plant sources of food.

Protein Sources and Need

Critical Thinking Exercise

A volleyball player complains that she constantly feels tired and lethargic even though she thinks that she is eating well and getting a sufficient amount of sleep. A teammate has suggested that the player begin taking vitamin supplements, which the teammate claims gives her more energy and makes her more resistant to fatigue. The athlete comes to the athletic trainer to ask advice about what kind of vitamins she needs to take.

? What facts should the athletic trainer explain to the athlete about vitamin supplementation, and what recommendations should he or she make?

Most athletes do not have difficulty meeting protein needs because the typical diet is rich in protein, and many athletes consume more than twice the recommended levels of protein. There is no advantage to consuming more protein, particularly in the form of protein supplements. If more protein is supplied than needed, the body must convert the excess to fat for storage. This conversion can create a situation in which excess water is removed from cells, leading to dehydration and possible damage to the kidneys or liver. Protein supplements may also create imbalances of the chemicals that make up proteins, the amino acids, which is not desirable. A condition of the bones, osteoporosis, has been linked to a diet that contains too much protein.[7]

Increased physical activity increases a person's need for energy, not necessarily for protein.[37] The increases in muscle mass that result from conditioning and training are associated with only a small increase in protein requirements that can easily be met with the usual diet. Therefore an athlete does not need protein supplements.

REGULATOR NUTRIENTS
Vitamins

Although vitamins are required in extremely small amounts when compared with water, proteins, carbohydrates, and fats, they perform essential functions, primarily as regulators of body processes.[7] Thirteen vitamins have specific roles in the body, many of which are still being explored. In the past, letters were assigned as names for vitamins. Today, most are known by their scientific names. Vitamins are classified into two groups: fat-soluble vitamins, which are dissolved in fats and stored in the body, and water-soluble vitamins, which are dissolved in watery solutions and are not stored. Table 5-1 lists the vitamins and indicates their primary functions.

TABLE 5-1 Vitamins

Vitamin	Major Function	Most Reliable Sources	Deficiency	Excess (Toxicity)
A	Maintains skin and other cells that line the inside of the body; bone and tooth development; growth; vision in dim light	Liver, milk, egg yolk, deep green and yellow fruits and vegetables	Night blindness; dry skin; growth failure	Headaches, nausea, loss of hair, dry skin, diarrhea
D	Normal bone growth and development	Exposure to sunlight; fortified dairy products; eggs and fish liver oils	Rickets in children—defective bone formation leading to deformed bones	Appetite loss, weight loss, failure to grow
E	Prevents destruction of polyunsaturated fats caused by exposure to oxidizing agents; protects cell membranes from destruction	Vegetable oils, some in fruits and vegetables, whole grains	Breakage of red blood cells leading to anemia	Nausea and diarrhea; interferes with vitamin K absorption if vitamin D is also deficient; not as toxic as other fat-soluble vitamins
K	Production of blood-clotting substances	Green leafy vegetables; normal bacteria that live in intestines produce K that is absorbed	Increased bleeding time	
Thiamin	Needed for release of energy from carbohydrates, fats, and proteins	Cereal products, pork, peas, and dried beans	Lack of energy, nerve problems	
Riboflavin	Energy from carbohydrates, fats, and proteins	Milk, liver, fruits and vegetables, enriched breads and cereals	Dry skin, cracked lips	
Niacin	Energy from carbohydrates, fats, and proteins	Liver, meat, poultry, peanut butter, legumes, enriched breads and cereals	Skin problems, diarrhea, mental depression, and eventually death (rarely occurs in U.S.)	Skin flushing, intestinal upset, nervousness, intestinal ulcers
B_6	Metabolism of protein; production of hemoglobin	White meats, whole grains, liver, egg yolk, bananas	Poor growth, anemia	Severe loss of coordination from nerve damage
B_{12}	Production of genetic material; maintains central nervous system	Foods of animal origin	Neurological problems, anemia	
Folate (Folic acid)	Production of genetic material	Wheat germ, liver, yeast, mushrooms, green leafy vegetables, fruits	Anemia	
C (Ascorbic acid)	Formation and maintenance of connective tissue; tooth and bone formation; immune function	Fruits and vegetables	Scurvy (rare); swollen joints, bleeding gums, fatigue, bruising	Kidney stones, diarrhea
Pantothenic acid	Energy from carbohydrates, fats, proteins	Widely found in foods	Not observed in humans under normal conditions	
Biotin	Use of fats	Widely found in foods	Rare under normal conditions	

Fat-Soluble Vitamins

Fat-soluble vitamins: A, D, E, and K.

Vitamins A, D, E, and K are fat soluble. They are found in the fatty portions of foods and in oils. Because they are stored in the body's fat, it is possible to consume excess amounts and show the effects of vitamin poisoning.

Water-Soluble Vitamins

Water-soluble vitamins: C, thiamin, riboflavin, niacin, B_6, B_{12}, folate, biotin, and panothenic acid.

The water-soluble vitamins consist of vitamin C, known as ascorbic acid, and the B-complex vitamins, most now referred to by their scientific names. B-complex vitamins include thiamin, riboflavin, niacin, B_6, folate, B_{12}, biotin, and pantothenic acid. Although vitamins are not metabolized for energy, thiamin, riboflavin, niacin, biotin, and pantothenic acid are used to regulate the metabolism of CHO, proteins, and fats to obtain energy. Vitamin B_6 regulates the body's use of amino acids. Folate and vitamin B_{12} are important in normal blood formation. Vitamin C is used for building bones and teeth, maintaining connective tissues, and strengthening the immune system. Unlike fat-soluble vitamins, water-soluble vitamins cannot be stored to any significant extent in the body and should be supplied in the diet each day.[7]

Antioxidants

Antioxidants: vitamin C, vitamin E, and beta-carotene.

Certain nutrients, called antioxidants, may prevent premature aging, certain cancers, heart disease, and other health problems.[30] An antioxidant protects vital cell components from the destructive effects of certain agents, including oxygen. Vitamin C, vitamin E, and beta-carotene are antioxidants. Beta-carotene is a plant pigment that is found in dark green, deep yellow, or orange fruits and vegetables. The body can convert beta-carotene to vitamin A. In the early 1980s, researchers reported that smokers who ate large quantities of fruits and vegetables rich in beta-carotene were less likely to develop lung cancer than were other smokers.[45] Since that time, more evidence is accumulating about the benefits of a diet rich in the antioxidant nutrients.[45]

Some experts believe that athletes should increase their intake of antioxidants, even if it means taking supplements. Others are more cautious.[45] Excess beta-carotene pigments circulate throughout the body and may turn the skin yellow. However, the pigment is not believed to be toxic like its nutrient cousin, vitamin A is. On the other hand, increasing intake of vitamins C and E is not without some risk. Excess vitamin C is not well absorbed; the excess is irritating to the intestines and creates diarrhea. Although less toxic than vitamins A or D, too much vitamin E causes health problems.

Vitamin Deficiencies

The illness that results from a lack of any nutrient, especially those nutrients, such as vitamins, that are needed only in small amounts, is referred to as a deficiency disease.[46] Vitamin deficiency diseases are rare. Adequate amounts of the different vitamins, as with other nutrients, can be obtained if a wide variety of foods is eaten. For most people, vitamin supplements are a waste of money and can cause toxic effects if too many are taken. Many individuals think that vitamins are "foods" and are safe. However, in large doses, vitamins have druglike effects on the body. Table 5-1 describes some of vitamins' toxicity problems.

Minerals

More than twenty mineral elements have an essential role in the body and therefore must be supplied in the diet. These essential minerals are listed in Table 5-2. Most minerals are stored in the body, especially in the liver and bones. Magnesium is needed in energy-supplying reactions; sodium and potassium are important for the transmission of nerve impulses. Iron plays a role in energy metabolism but is also combined with a protein to form hemoglobin, the compound that transports oxygen in red blood cells. Calcium has many important functions: it is necessary for proper bone and teeth formation, blood clotting, and muscle contraction. In general, minerals have roles that are

TABLE 5-2 Minerals

Mineral	Major Role	Most Reliable Sources	Deficiency	Excess
Calcium	Bone and tooth formation; blood clotting; muscle contraction; nerve function	Dairy products	May lead to osteoporosis	Calcium deposits in soft tissues
Phosphorus	Skeletal development; tooth formation	Meats, dairy products, and other protein-rich foods	Rarely seen	
Sodium	Maintenance of fluid balance	Salt (sodium chloride) added to foods and sodium-containing preservatives		May contribute to the development of hypertension
Iron	Formation of hemoglobin; energy from carbohydrates, fats, and proteins	Liver and red meats, enriched breads and cereals	Iron-deficiency anemia	Can cause death in children from supplement overdose
Copper	Formation of hemoglobin	Liver, nuts, shellfish, cherries, mushrooms, whole grain breads and cereals	Anemia	Nausea and vomiting
Zinc	Normal growth and development	Seafood and meats	Skin problems, delayed development, growth problems	Interferes with copper use; may decrease high-density lipoprotein levels
Iodine	Production of the hormone thyroxin	Iodized salt, seafood	Mental and growth retardation; lack of energy	
Fluorine	Strengthens bones and teeth	Fluoridated water	Teeth are less resistant to decay	Damage to tooth enamel

too numerous to detail within the scope of this book. Eating a wide variety of foods is the best way to obtain the minerals needed in the proper concentrations.[7]

Water

Water is the most essential of all the nutrients and should be the nutrient of greatest concern to the athlete.[67] It is the most abundant nutrient in the body, accounting for approximately 60 percent of the body weight, although this varies considerably (+/−10%) among different individuals due to age and percent of body fat. Water is essential for all the chemical processes that occur in the body, and an adequate supply of water is necessary for energy production and normal digestion of other nutrients. Although water does not supply any energy (calories), an adequate supply of water is needed for energy production in all cells. Water also takes part in digestion and maintaining the proper environment inside and outside of cells. Water is also necessary for temperature control and for the elimination of waste products of nutrient and body metabolism. Too little water leads to dehydration, and severe dehydration frequently leads to death. The average adult requires a minimum of 2.5 liters or about 10 glasses of water per day.

The body has a number of mechanisms designed specifically to maintain body water at near-normal level. Too little water leads to accumulation of solutes in the blood. These solutes signal the brain that the body is thirsty while signaling the kidney to conserve water. Excessive water dilutes these solutes, which signals the brain to stop drinking and the kidneys to get rid of the excess water.

Replacing fluid after heavy sweating is far more important than replacing electrolytes.

Water is the only nutrient that is of greater importance to the athlete than to those people who are more sedentary, especially when the athlete is engaging in prolonged exercise carried out in a hot, humid environment. Such a situation may cause excessive sweating and subsequent losses of large amounts of water. When the body burns carbohydrate and fat for energy, it produces a great deal of heat. During exercise, that heat is lost from the body primarily by sweating. Sweating is how the body uses water to keep itself from overheating. Restriction of water during this time will result in dehydration. Symptoms of dehydration include fatigue, vomiting, nausea, exhaustion, fainting, and possibly death.

Electrolyte Requirements

Electrolytes: sodium, chloride, potassium, magnesium, and calcium.

Electrolytes, including sodium, chloride, potassium, magnesium, and calcium, are electrically charged ions dissolved in body water. Among many other roles, electrolytes maintain the balance of water inside and outside the cell. In other words, electrolytes especially sodium, are essential in helping the body rehydrate quickly.[3,12] Electrolyte replenishment may be needed when a person is not fit, suffers from extreme water loss, participates in a marathon, or has just completed an exercise period and is expected to perform at near-maximum effort within the next few hours. In most cases, electrolytes can be sufficiently replaced with a balanced diet, which can, if necessary, be salted slightly more than usual. Free access to water and sports drinks (ad libitum) before, during, and after activity should be the rule (see Chapter 6). In some people, electrolyte losses can produce muscle cramping and intolerance to heat. Sweating results not only in body water loss but in some electrolyte loss as well.[56]

During cold weather, water is not as critical as it is in hot weather. Therefore a stronger electrolyte solution that allows a slower, more steady release of fluid from the stomach should be used. In hot weather or in cold weather, thirst is not an indicator of hydration.

NUTRIENT REQUIREMENTS AND RECOMMENDATIONS

A nutrient requirement is that amount of the nutrient that is needed to prevent the nutrient's deficiency disease. Nutrient needs vary among individuals within a population. A recommendation for a nutrient is different from the requirement for a nutrient. Scientists establish recommendations for nutrients and calories based on extensive scientific research and assessment of present dietary intakes.[20]

In the past, the *U.S. Recommended Dietary Allowances (US RDA)* have served as the benchmarks of nutritional adequacy in the United States. Over the past several years new information has emerged about nutrient requirements that necessitated updating of the RDAs.[22] RDAs have been changed to *Dietary Reference Intakes (DRIs),* which are established using an expanded concept that includes indicators of good health and the prevention of chronic disease, as well as possible adverse effects of overconsumption.[20] The DRIs include not only recommended intakes (RDA) intended to help individuals meet their daily nutritional requirements, but also tolerable upper intake levels (ULs), which help individuals avoid harm from consuming too much of a nutrient; estimated average requirements (EAR), which are the average daily nutrient intake level estimated to meet the requirement of half the healthy individuals in a particular age group; and Adequate Intake (AI), which is the recommended average daily intake level based on experimentally developed estimates of nutrient intake that are used when the RDA cannot be determined.[20] Table 5-3 shows the latest DRIs. (Appendix B shows nutrient recommendations for Canadians.)

Food Labels

Food labels on packages help consumers to make more informed food selections (Figure 5-1). Concern over the amount of fat, cholesterol, sodium, and fiber in the typical American diet led the drive for a more health-conscious label. For more than a decade, the US RDA appeared on nutrient labels. In the early 1990s, the old food

TABLE 5-3 Dietary Reference Intakes: Recommended Levels for Individual Intake from the Food and Nutrition Board, Institute of Medicine–National Academy of Sciences[20]

Life-Stage Group	Vitamin D (µg/d)[a,b]	Thiamin B$_1$ (mg/d)	Riboflavin B$_1$ (mg/d)	Niacin (mg/d)[c]	B$_6$ (µg/d)	Folate (µg/d)[d]	B$_{12}$ (mg/d)	Pantothenic Acid (mg/d)	Biotin (µg/d)	Choline[e] (mg/d)	Vitamin A (µg/d)	Vitamin C (mg/d)	Vitamin E (mg/d)	Vitamin K (µg/d)
Males 14–18 yr	5*	1.2	1.3	16	1.3	400	2.4	5*	25*	550*	900	75	15	75*
19–30 yr	5*	1.2	1.3	16	1.3	400	2.4	5*	25*	550*	900	90	15	120*
31–50 yr	5*	1.2	1.3	16	1.3	400	2.4	5*	30*	550*	900	90	15	120*
51–70 yr	10*	1.2	1.3	16	1.7	400	2.4	5*	30*	550*	900	90	15	120*
>70 yr	15*	1.2	1.3	16	1.7	400	2.4[f]	5*	30*	550*	900	90	15	120*
Females 14–18 yr	5*	1.0	1.0	14	1.2	400[g]	2.4[f]	5*	25*	400*	700	65	15	75*
19–30 yr	5*	1.1	1.1	14	1.3	400[g]	2.4	5*	30*	425*	700	75	15	90*
31–50 yr	5*	1.1	1.1	14	1.3	400[g]	2.4	5*	30*	425*	700	75	15	90*
51–70 yr	10*	1.1	1.1	14	1.5	400[g]	2.4[f]	5*	30*	425*	700	75	15	90*
<70 yr	15*	1.1	1.1	14	1.5	400	2.4[f]	5*	30*	425*	700	75	15	90*
Pregnancy >18 yr	5*	1.4	1.4	18	1.9	600[h]	2.6	6*	30*	450*	750	80	15	75*
19–30 yr	5*	1.4	1.4	18	1.9	600[h]	2.6	6*	30*	450*	770	85	15	90*
31–50 yr	5*	1.4	1.4	18	1.9	600[h]	2.6	6*	30*	450*	770	85	15	90*
Lactation ≦18 yr	5*	1.5	1.6	17	2.0	500	2.8	7*	35*	550*	1,200	115	19	75*
19–30 yr	5*	1.5	1.6	17	2.0	500	2.8	7*	35*	550*	1,300	120	19	90*
31–50 yr	5*	1.5	1.6	17	2.0	500	2.8	7*	35*	550*	1,300	120	19	90*

Continued

TABLE 5-3 Dietary Reference Intakes: Recommended Levels for Individual Intake from the Food and Nutrition Board, Institute of Medicine–National Academy of Sciences—continued

Calcium (mg/d)	Phosphorus (mg/d)	Magnesium (mg/d)	Chromium (µg/d)	Copper (µg/d)	Iron (mg/d)	Iodine (µg/d)	Manganese (mg/d)	Molybenum (µg/d)	Selenium (µg/d)	Zinc (mg/d)	Fluoride (mg/d)
1,300*	1,250	410	35*	890	11	150	2.2*	43	55	11	3*
1,000*	700	400	35*	900	8	150	2.3*	45	55	11	7*
1,000*	700	420	35*	900	8	150	2.3*	45	55	11	4*
1,200*	700	420	30*	900	8	150	2.3*	45	55	11	4*
1,200*	700	420	30*	900	8	150	2.3*	45	55	11	4*
1,300*	1,250	360	24*	890	15	150	1.5*	43	55	9	3*
1,000*	700	310	25*	900	18	150	1.8*	45	55	8	3*
1,000*	700	320	25*	900	18	150	1.8*	45	55	8	3*
1,200*	700	320	20*	900	8	150	1.8*	45	55	8	3*
1,200*	700	320	20*	900	8	150	1.8*	45	55	8	3*
1,300*	1,250	400	29*	1,000	27	220	2.0*	50	60	12	3*
1,000*	700	350	30*	1,000	27	220	2.0*	50	60	11	3*
1,000*	700	360	30*	1,000	27	220	2.0*	50	60	11	3*
1,300	1,250	360	44*	1,300	10	290	2.6*	50	70	13	3*
1,000*	700	310	45*	1,300	9	290	2.6*	50	70	12	3*
1,000*	700	320	45*	1,300	9	290	2.5*	50	70	12	3*

Note: This table presents Recommended Dietary Allowances (RDAs) in bold type and Adequate Intakes (AIs) in ordinary type followed by an asterisk (*). RDAs and AIs may both be used as goals for individual intake. RDAs are set to meet the needs of almost all (97 to 98 percent) individuals in a group. For healthy breastfed infants, the AI is the mean intake. The AI for other life-stage groups is believed to cover their needs, but lack of data or uncertainty in the data prevent clear specification of this coverage.

[a] As cholecalciferol. 1 µg cholecalciferol = 40 IU vitamin D.

[b] In the absence of adequate exposure to sunlight.

[c] As niacin equivalents. 1 mg of niacin = 60 mg of tryptohan.

[d] As dietary folate equivalents (DFE). 1 DFE = 1 µg food folate = 0.6 µg of folic acid (from fortified food or supplement) consumed with food = 0.5 µg of synthetic (supplemental) folic acid taken on an empty stomach.

[e] Although AIs have been set for chlorine, there are few data to assess whether a dietary supply of choline is needed at all stages of the life cycle, and it may be that the choline requirement can be met by endogenous synthesis at some of these stages.

[f] Since 10 to 30 percent of older people may malabsorb food-bound B₁₂, it is advisable for those older than 50 years to meet their RDA mainly by consuming foods fortified with B₁₂ or a B₁₂-containing supplement.

[g] In view of evidence linking folate intake with neural tube defects in the fetus, it is recommended that all women capable of becoming pregnant consume 400 µg of synthetic folic acid from fortified foods and/or supplements in addition to intake of food folate from a varied diet.

[h] It is assumed that women will continue consuming 400 µg of folic acid until their pregnancy is confirmed and they enter prenatal care, which ordinarily occurs after the end of the periconceptional period—the critical time for formation of the neural tube.

Nutrition Facts Serving Size 1/2 cup (114g) Servings Per Container 4		
Amount Per Serving		
Calories 260		Calories from Fat 120
		% Daily Value*
Total Fat 13g		20%
Saturated Fat 5g		25%
Trans Fat 0g		
Cholesterol 30mg		10%
Sodium 660mg		28%
Total Carbohydrate 31g		11%
Dietary Fiber 0g		0%
Sugars 5g		
Protein 5g		
Vitamin A 4%		Vitamin C 2%
Calcium 15%		Iron 4%

*Percent Daily Values are based on a 2000 Calorie diet. Your daily values may be higher or lower depending on your calorie needs.

	Calories: 2000	2500
Total Fat	Less than 65g	80g
Sat. Fat	Less than 20g	25g
Cholesterol	Less than 300mg	300mg
Sodium	Less than 2,400mg	2,400mg
Total Carbohydrate	300g	375g
Dietary Fiber	25g	30g

Calories per gram
Fat 9 • Carbohydrate 4 • Protein 4

Figure 5-1

A food label provides nutritional information.

labels were replaced by a new format that presents the information in the form of percentages of daily values based on a standard 2,000-calorie diet.[19]

The Food Pyramid

The Basic Four Food Groups Plan, first introduced in the mid-1950s, has been redesigned into a food pyramid concept that is believed to do a better job of educating Americans about the relationship of food choices to health. Figure 5-2 illustrates the food groupings, the minimum number of servings that should be eaten daily, and examples of foods from each group. Carbohydrate-rich foods (the breads and cereals group) form the foundation of the diet, which reflects the recommendations in the Dietary Guidelines for Americans that suggest a need for people to consume a greater percentage of total calories from this group.[67] The other food groups are shown according to their relative importance in a healthy diet. One major change from the Basic Four plan is that the fruits and vegetables are separated into two distinct groups, each with a specified number of servings. Note that fats and sugars form the small apex of the pyramid. This placement indicates that foods rich in fat and sugar should provide the smallest proportion of total calories; no minimum number of servings is suggested because many Americans consume far too much fat and sugar.[69]

Figure 5-2

The food pyramid offers examples of appropriate food selections important to an athlete's diet.

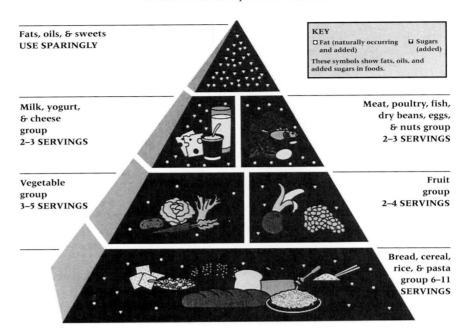

Figure 5-2

The food pyramid offers examples of appropriate food selections important to an athlete's diet.

NUTRITION AND PHYSICAL ACTIVITY

Vitamin requirements do not increase during exercise.

Athletes often believe that exercise increases requirements for nutrients such as proteins, vitamins, and minerals and that it is possible and desirable to saturate the body with these nutrients.[15] There is no scientific basis for ingesting levels of these nutrients above DRI levels.[69] Exercise increases the need for energy, not for proteins, vitamins, and minerals.[67] Additionally, many athletes use nutritional practices as an ergogenic aid to improve various aspects of performance.[63,70] Thus it is necessary to explore some of the more common myths that surround the subject of nutrition's role in physical performance.

Vitamin Supplementation

Many athletes believe that taking large amounts of vitamin supplements can lead to superior health and performance.[69] A megadose of a nutrient supplement is essentially an overdose; the amount ingested far exceeds the DRI levels.[67] The rationale used for such excessive intakes is that if taking a pill that contains the DRI for each vitamin and mineral makes an athlete healthy, taking a pill that has ten times the DRI should make the athlete ten times healthier.[8]

An example of a popular practice among athletes is to take megadoses of vitamin C. Such doses do not prevent the common cold or slow aging. They do cause diarrhea and possibly the development of painful kidney stones. An athlete has no increased need for vitamin C. Fruits, juices, and vegetables are reliable sources of vitamin C that also supply other vitamins and minerals.[8]

Taking megadoses of vitamin E has become popular among people of all ages. The vitamin functions to protect certain fatty acids in cell membranes from being damaged.[8] There is not much evidence to support the notion that this vitamin can extend life expectancy or enhance physical performance. Vitamin E does not enhance sexual ability, prevent graying hair, or cure muscular dystrophy. A person can obtain adequate amounts of vitamin E by consuming whole-grain products, vegetable oils, and nuts.

The B-complex vitamins that are involved in obtaining energy from CHO, fats, and proteins are often abused by athletes who believe that vitamins provide energy. Any increased need for these nutrients is easily fulfilled when the athlete eats more nutritious foods while training.[63] If athletes do not increase their food consumption, they will lose weight because of their high level of caloric expenditure.

If an athlete is not eating a well balanced diet, taking a multiple vitamin once each day would be helpful and in fact is recommended by many physicians to make certain that minimum DRIs are met.

Mineral Supplementation

Obtaining adequate levels of certain minerals can be a problem for some athletes.[8] Calcium and iron intakes may be low for those athletes who do not include dairy products, red meats, or enriched breads and cereals in their diet. To prevent wasting their money and overdosing, however, athletes must be careful to first determine whether they need extra minerals. The following sections explore some minerals that can be low in the diet and some suggestions for improving the quality of the diet so that supplements may not be necessary.

Calcium Deficiency

Calcium is the most abundant mineral in the body. It is essential for bones and teeth as well as for muscle contraction and the conduction of nerve impulses. However, the importance of obtaining adequate calcium supplies throughout life has become more recognized. If calcium intake is too low to meet needs, the body can remove calcium from the bones. Over time, the bones become weakened and appear porous on X-ray films. These bones are brittle and often break spontaneously. This condition is called **osteoporosis** and is estimated to be eight times more common among women than men. It becomes a serious problem for women after menopause.[7]

The AI for young adults is 1,000 mg (an eight-ounce glass of milk contains about 300 mg of calcium). Unfortunately about 25 percent of all females in the United States consume less than 300 mg of calcium per day, well below the RDA. High-protein diets and alcohol consumption also increase calcium excretion from the body. Exercise causes calcium to be retained in bones, so physical activity is beneficial. However, younger females who exercise to extremes so that their normal hormonal balance is upset are prone to develop premature osteoporosis.[34] Calcium supplementation, preferably as calcium carbonate or citrate rather than phosphate, may be advisable for females who have a family history of osteoporosis.

Milk products are the most reliable sources of calcium. Many athletes complain that milk and other dairy products upset their stomach. They may lack an enzyme called lactase that is needed to digest milk sugar lactose. This condition is referred to as lactose intolerance, or **lactase deficiency**.[67] The undigested lactose enters the large intestine, where the bacteria that normally reside there use it for energy. The bacteria produce large quantities of intestinal gas, which causes discomfort and cramps. Many lactose-intolerant people also suffer from diarrhea. Fortunately, scientists have produced the missing enzyme, lactase. Lactase is available without prescription in forms that can be added to foods before eating or taken along with meals.

Iron Deficiency

Iron deficiency is also a common problem, especially for young females. Lack of iron can result in iron-deficiency **anemia**.[47] Iron is needed to properly form hemoglobin. With anemia, the oxygen-carrying ability of the red blood cells is reduced so that muscles cannot obtain enough oxygen to generate energy. Anemia leaves a person feeling tired and weak. Obviously, an athlete cannot compete at peak level while suffering from an iron deficiency.

osteoporosis
A decrease in bone density.

lactase deficiency
Difficulty digesting dairy products.

anemia
Lack of iron.

5-4

Critical Thinking Exercise

A high-school football player has become interested in body building. He is most interested in seeing an increase in muscle mass. He is religious about his weight training but has heard that increasing protein intake will cause the muscles to hypertrophy more quickly.

? What advice can the athletic trainer give him about taking commercially produced protein supplements?

Protein Supplementation

Athletes often believe that more protein is needed to build bigger muscles.[39] It is true that a relatively small amount of extra protein is needed by athletes who are developing muscles in a training program. Many athletes, particularly those who are training with heavy weights or who are bodybuilders, routinely take protein supplements that are commercially produced and marketed.[37,39] To build muscle, athletes should consume 1 to 1.5 grams of extra protein per kilogram (0.5 to 0.7 grams per pound) of body weight every day. This range goes from slightly above to about double the protein RDA (0.8 grams per kilogram of desirable body weight). Anyone eating a variety of foods, but especially protein-rich foods, can easily meet the higher amounts. Thus, athletes do not need protein supplements, because their diets typically exceed even the most generous protein recommendations. An active adult will most likely require 0.6 grams per pound, or 66 percent more than the RDA.[20]

Creatine Supplementation

Creatine is a naturally occurring organic compound synthesized by the kidneys, liver, and pancreas. Creatine also can be obtained from ingesting meat and fish that contain approximately five grams per kilogram. Creatine has an integral role in energy metabolism.[5]

There are two main types of creatine: free creatine and phosphocreatine. Phosphocreatine is stored in skeletal muscle and is used during anaerobic activity to produce ATP with the assistance of the enzyme creatine kinase. With creatine supplementation, phosphocreatine depletion is delayed and performance is enhanced through the maintenance of the normal metabolic pathways.[41]

The positive physiological effects of creatine include increasing the resynthesis of ATP, thus allowing for increased intensity in a workout; functioning as a lactic acid buffer, thus prolonging maximal effort and improving exercise recovery time during maximal intensity activities; stimulating protein synthesis; decreasing total cholesterol while improving the HDL-to-LDL ratio; decreasing total triglycerides; and increasing fat-free mass.[5] It has been suggested that creatine supplementation may reduce the incidence of muscle cramps.[27] Side effects of creatine supplementation include weight gain, due primarily to an increase in total body water;[48] gastrointestinal disturbances, and renal dysfunction. These are apparently no other known long-term side effects.

It has been suggested that an initial loading phase should consist of twenty grams of creatine and 120 ounces of water each day for six days. The recommended amount for improving performance after the loading phase is five to ten grams per day for four weeks.[5,68] Oral supplementation with creatine may enhance muscular performance during high-intensity resistance exercise.[41,66]

In August 2000 the NCAA Committee on Competitive Safeguards and Medical Aspects of Sports banned the distribution to student athletes of all muscle-building substances, including creatine, by NCAA member institutions. The use of creatine itself is not banned.

Sugar and Performance

Ingesting large quantities of glucose in the form of honey, candy bars, or pure sugar immediately before physical activity may have a significant impact on performance.[50] As carbohydrates are digested, large quantities of glucose enter the blood. This increase in blood sugar (glucose) levels stimulates the release of the hormone insulin. Insulin allows the cells to use the circulating glucose so that blood glucose levels soon return to normal.[55] It was hypothesized that a decline in blood sugar levels was detrimental to performance and endurance. However, recent evidence indicates that the effect of eating large quantities of carbohydrates is beneficial rather than negative.

Nevertheless, some athletes are sensitive to high-carbohydrate feedings and experience problems with increased levels of insulin. Also, some athletes cannot tolerate large amounts of the simple sugar fructose. For these individuals, too much fructose leads to intestinal upset and diarrhea. Athletes should test themselves with various high-carbohydrate foods to see if they are affected (but not before a competitive event).[42]

Caffeine and Performance

Caffeine is a central nervous system stimulant. Most people who consume caffeine in coffee, tea, or carbonated beverages are aware of its effect of increasing alertness and decreasing fatigue. Chocolate contains compounds that are related to caffeine and have the same stimulating effects. However, large amounts of caffeine cause nervousness, irritability, increased heart rate, and headaches.[22] Also, headaches are a withdrawal symptom experienced when a person tries to stop consuming caffeinated products.[46]

Although small amounts of caffeine do not appear to harm physical performance, cases of nausea and light-headedness have been reported. Caffeine enhances the use of fat during endurance exercise, thus delaying the depletion of glycogen stores.[18] This delay would help endurance performance. Caffeine also helps make calcium more available to the muscle during contraction, allowing the muscle to work more efficiently. However, Olympic officials rightfully consider caffeine to be a drug. It should not be present in an Olympic competitor's blood in levels greater than that resulting from drinking five or six cups of coffee.

Alcohol and Performance

Alcohol provides energy for the body; each gram of pure alcohol (ethanol) supplies seven calories. However, sources of alcohol provide little other nutritional value with regard to vitamins, minerals, and proteins. The depressant effects of alcohol on the central nervous system include decreased physical coordination, slowed reaction times, and decreased mental alertness. Also, this drug increases the production of urine, resulting in body water losses (diuretic effect). Therefore, the use of alcoholic beverages by the athlete is not recommended before, during, or after physical activity.[32]

Eating Organic, Natural, or Health Foods

Many athletes are concerned about the quality of the foods they eat—not just the nutritional value of the food but also its safety. Organic foods are grown without the use of synthetic fertilizers and pesticides. Those who advocate the use of organic farming methods claim that these foods are nutritionally superior and safer than the same products grown using chemicals such as pesticides and synthetic fertilizers.[16]

Technically, the description of organic food is meaningless. All foods (except water) are organic; that is, they contain the element carbon. Organically produced foods are often more expensive than the same foods that have been produced by conventional means. There is no advantage to consuming organic food products. They are not more nutritious than foods produced by conventional methods. Nevertheless, for some athletes, the psychological benefit of believing that they are doing something good for their bodies justifies the extra cost.

Natural foods have been subjected to little processing and contain no additives such as preservatives or artificial flavors.[64] Processing can protect nutritional value. Preservatives save food that would otherwise spoil and have to be destroyed. Furthermore, many foods in their natural form are poisonous. The green layer often found under the skin of potatoes is poisonous if eaten in large amounts. Poisonous mushrooms and molds in peanuts cause liver cancer.

Both organic and natural foods could be described as health foods. However, there is no benefit derived from eating a diet consisting of health foods, even for the athlete.

Using Herbal Supplements

The use of herbs as natural alternatives to drugs and medicines has clearly become a trend among American consumers. Most herbs, as edible plants, are safe to ingest as foods; as natural medicines, they are claimed to have few side effects, although occasionally a mild, allergic reaction may occur.[21,46]

Herbs can offer the body nutrients that are reported to nourish the brain, glands, and hormones. Unlike vitamins, which work best when taken with food, herbs do not need to be taken with other foods, since they provide their own digestive enzymes.[23]

Herbs in their whole form are not drugs. As medicine, herbs are essentially body balancers that work with the body's functions so that it can heal and regulate itself. Herbal formulas can be general for overall strength and nutrient support or specific to a particular ailment or condition.

Hundreds of herbs are widely available today at all quality levels. They are readily available at health food stores. However, unlike both food and medicine, no federal or governmental controls regulate the sale of herbs to ensure the quality of the products being sold.[23] The consumer of herbal products must exercise extreme caution.

The *Focus Box:* "Most widely used herbs and purposes for use" lists the most popular and widely used herbal products sold in health food stores. Some additional potent and complex herbs, such as capsicum, lobelia, sassafras, mandrake tansy, canada snake root, wormwood, woodruff, poke root, and rue may be useful in small amounts and as catalysts, but should not be used alone.

≋ *Focus*

Most widely used herbs and purposes for use

cayenne—used for weight loss

cascara—used as a laxative, can cause dehydration

dong quai—to treat menstrual symptoms

echinacea—to promote wound healing and strengthen the immune system

fever few—to prevent and relieve migraine headaches, arthritis, and PMS

garlic—used as an antibiotic, antibacterial, antifungal agent to prevent and relieve coronary artery disease by reducing total blood cholesterol and triglyceride levels and raising HDL levels

garcina cambagia—used to promote loss of fat

ginkgo biloba—used to improve blood circulation, especially in the brain

ginseng—used to reduce impotence, weakness, lethargy, and fatigue

*guarana—used as a stimulant, contains large amounts of caffeine, often in weight loss products

kava—used to reduce anxiety, relax muscle tension, produce analgesic effects, act as a local anesthetic, provide antibacterial benefit

*ma huang (ephedrine)—derived from the ephedra plant, it has been used in China for medicinal purposes including increased energy, appetite suppression, increased fat burning, and preservation of muscle tissue from breaking down. It is a central nervous system stimulant drug which was used in many diet pills. In 1995, the FDA revealed adverse reactions to ephedrine such as heart attacks, strokes, paranoid psychosis, vomiting, fever, palpitations, convulsions, and comas. In 2003, it was banned by the FDA.

mate—CNS stimulant

saw palmetto—used to treat inflamed prostate; also used as a diuretic and as a sexual enhancement agent

senna—used as a laxative, can cause water and electrolyte loss

St. John's wort—used as an antidepressant; also used to treat nervous disorders, depression, neuralgia, kidney problems, wounds, and burns

valerian—used to treat insomnia, anxiety, stress

yohimbe—used to increase libido and blood flow to sexual organs in the male

*Banned by some athletic organizations and/or the FDA

Ephedrine

Ephedrine is a stimulant that has been used as an ingredient in diet pills, illegal recreational drugs, and legitimate over-the-counter medications to treat congestion and asthma.[49] Ephedrine is similar to an amphetamine. In December 2003, the FDA banned the use of ephedrine as a dietary supplement. For several years the FDA has warned consumers about the potential dangers of using ephedrine.[33] In recent years both the NCAA and minor league baseball have banned the use of ephedrine by their athletes. However some companies continue to sell dietary products that contain ephedrine or other stimulants despite the fact that these supplements have caused numerous problems. Ephedrine is know to produce the following adverse reactions: heart attack, stroke, tachycardia, paranoid psychosis, depressions, convulsions, fever, coma, vomiting, palpitations, hypertension, and respiratory depression.[49,71]

Practicing Vegetarianism

Vegetarianism has emerged as an alternative to the usual American diet. All vegetarians use plant foods to form the foundation of their diet; animal foods are either totally excluded or included in a variety of eating patterns.[15] Athletes who choose to become vegetarians do so for economic, philosophical, religious, cultural, or health reasons. Vegetarianism is no longer considered to be a fad if it is practiced intelligently. However, the vegetarian diet may create deficiencies if nutrient needs are not carefully considered. Athletes who follow this eating pattern must plan their diet carefully so that their calorie needs are met.[15] Types of vegetarian dietary patterns are categorized as follows:

- *Total vegetarians, or vegans:* People who consume plant but no animal foods; meat, fish, poultry, eggs, and dairy products are excluded from their diet. This diet is adequate for most adults if they give careful consideration to obtaining enough calories, vitamin B12, and the minerals calcium, zinc, and iron.
- *Lactovegetarians:* Individuals who consume milk products along with plant foods; meat, fish, poultry, and eggs are excluded from their diet. Iron and zinc levels can be low in this form of vegetarianism.
- *Ovolactovegetarians:* People who consume dairy products and eggs in their diet along with plant foods; meat, fish, and poultry are excluded. Again, obtaining sufficient iron could be a problem.
- *Semivegetarians:* People who consume animal products but exclude red meats. Plant products still form an important part of the diet. This diet is usually adequate.

> Vegetarians: total vegetarians, lactovegetarians, ovolactovegetarians, and semivegetarians.

PREEVENT NUTRITION

The importance and content of the preevent meal has been heatedly debated among coaches, athletic trainers, and athletes.[29] The trend has been to ignore logical thinking about what should be eaten before competition and to upholding the tradition of "rewarding" the athlete for hard work by serving foods that may hamper performance. For example, the traditional steak-and-eggs meal before football games is great for coaches and athletic trainers; however, the athlete gains nothing from this meal. The important point is that too often people are concerned primarily with the preevent meal and fail to realize that those nutrients consumed over several days before competition are much more important than what is eaten three hours before an event. The purpose of the preevent meal should be to provide the competitor with sufficient nutrient energy and fluids for competition while taking into consideration the digestibility of the food and, most important, the eating preferences of the individual athlete. (See *Focus Box:* "The pregame meal.") Figure 5-3 gives examples of preevent meals.

Athletes should be encouraged to become conscious of their diets. However, no experimental evidence exists to indicate that performance may be enhanced by altering a diet that is basically sound. There are a number of ways that a nutritious diet may be achieved, and the diet that is optimal for one athlete may not be the best for another. In many instances, the individual will be the best judge of what he or she should or

Focus

The pregame meal

- Try to achieve the largest possible storage of carbohydrates (glycogen) in both resting muscle and the liver. This storage is particularly important for endurance activities but may also be beneficial for intense, short-duration exercise.
- A stomach that is full of food during contact sports is subject to injury. Therefore, the type of food eaten should allow the stomach to empty quickly. Carbohydrates are easier to digest than are fats or proteins. A meal that contains plenty of carbohydrates will leave the stomach and be digested faster than a fatty meal. It would be wise to replace the traditional steak-and-eggs preevent meal with a low-fat one containing a small amount of pasta, tomato sauce, and bread.
- Foods should not cause irritation or upset to the gastrointestinal tract. Foods high in cellulose and other forms of fiber, such as whole grain products, fruits, and vegetables, increase the need for defecation. Highly spiced foods or gas-forming foods (such as onions, baked beans, or peppers) must also be avoided because any type of disturbance in the gastrointestinal tract may be detrimental to performance. Carbonated beverages and chewing gum also contribute to the formation of gas.
- Liquids consumed should be easily absorbed and low in fat content and should not act as a laxative. Whole milk, coffee, and tea should be avoided. Water intake should be increased, particularly if the temperature is high.
- A meal should be eaten approximately three to four hours before the event or before exercising. This timing allows for adequate stomach emptying, but the individual will not feel hungry during activity.
- The athlete should not eat any food that he or she dislikes. Most important, the individual must feel psychologically satisfied by any preevent meal. If not, performance may be impaired more by psychological factors than by physiological factors.
- Prolonged fasting and diet programs that severely restrict caloric intake are scientifically undesirable and can be medically dangerous.
- Fasting and diet programs that severely restrict caloric intake result in the loss of large amounts of water, electrolytes, minerals, glycogen stores, and other fat-free tissue (including proteins within fat-free tissues), with minimal amounts of fat loss.
- Mild calorie restriction (500 to 1,000 calories less than the usual daily intake) results in a smaller loss of water, electrolytes, minerals, and other fat-free tissue and is less likely to cause malnutrition.
- Dynamic exercise of large muscles helps maintain fat-free tissue, including muscle mass and bone density, and results in losses of body weight. Weight loss resulting from an increase in energy expenditure is primarily in the form of fat weight.
- A nutritionally sound diet resulting in mild calorie restriction coupled with an endurance exercise program, along with behavioral modification of existing eating habits, is recommended for weight reduction. The rate of sustained weight loss should not exceed 1 kg (2 lb) per week.
- To maintain proper weight control and optimal body fat levels, a lifetime commitment to proper eating habits and regular physical activity is required.

should not eat in the preevent meal or before exercising. It seems that a person's best guide is to eat whatever he or she is most comfortable with.

Liquid Food Supplements

Recently, liquid food supplements (Gatorade Nutrition Shake, Exceed) have been recommended as extremely effective preevent meals and are being used by high school, college, university, and professional teams with some indications of success.[51] These supplements supply from 225 to 400 calories per average serving. Athletes who have used these supplements report elimination of the usual pregame symptoms of dry mouth, abdominal cramps, leg cramps, nervous defecation, and nausea.

MEAL 1

³/₄ c Orange juice	³/₄ c Orange juice
¹/₂ c Cereal with 1 tsp sugar	1–2 Pancakes with:
1 Slice whole wheat toast with:	1 tsp Margarine
1 tsp Margarine	2 tbsp Syrup
1 tsp Honey or jelly	8 oz Skim or lowfat milk
8 oz Skim or lowfat milk	Water
Water	(Approximately 450–500 kcal)
(Approximately 450–500 kcal)	

MEAL 2

1 c Vegetable soup	1 c Spaghetti with tomato sauce and cheese
1 Turkey sandwich with:	¹/₂ c Sliced pears (canned) on ¹/₄ c cottage cheese
2 Slices bread	1–2 Slices (Italian) bread with 1–2 tsp margarine
2 oz Turkey (white or dark)	(avoid garlic)
1 oz Cheese slice	¹/₂ c Sherbet
2 tsp Mayonnaise	1–2 Sugar cookies
8 oz Skim or lowfat milk	4 oz Skim or lowfat milk
Water	Water
(Approximately 550–600 kcal)	(Approximately 700 kcal)

Figure 5-3

Sample preevent meals.

Under ordinary conditions, it usually takes approximately four hours for a full meal to pass through the stomach and the small intestine. Pregame emotional tension often delays the emptying of the stomach; therefore the undigested food mass remains in the stomach and upper bowel for a prolonged time, even up to or through the actual period of competition, and frequently results in nausea, vomiting, and cramps. This unabsorbed food mass is of no value to the athlete. Team physicians who have experimented with the liquid food supplements say that a major advantage to the supplements is that they clear both the stomach and the upper bowel before game time, thus making available the caloric energy that would otherwise still be in an unassimilated state. There is merit in the use of such food supplements for pregame meals.[51]

Eating Fast Foods

Eating fast food is a way of life in American society.[57] Athletes, especially young athletes, have for the most part grown up as fast-food junkies. Furthermore, travel budgets and tight schedules dictate that fast food is a frequent choice for coaches on road trips.[57] Aside from occasional problems with food flavor, the biggest concern in consuming fast foods, as can be seen in Table 5-4, is that 40 percent to 50 percent of the calories consumed are from fats. To compound this problem, these already sizable meals are now being "supersized" at a more affordable price for those who want maximum fat, salt, and calories in a single sitting.[46]

On the positive side, fast-food restaurants have broadened their menus to include whole wheat breads and rolls, salad bars, and low-fat milk products. Many of the larger fast-food restaurants provide nutritional information for consumers upon request or from well-stocked racks.[46] *Focus Box:* "Tips for selecting fast foods" provides suggestions for eating more healthfully at fast-food restaurants.

Glycogen Supercompensation

For endurance events, maximizing the amount of glycogen that can be stored, especially in muscles, may make the difference between finishing first or at the end of the pack. Athletes can increase glycogen supplies in muscle and liver by reducing the training program a few days before competing and by significantly increasing carbohydrate intake during the week before the event.[50] By reducing training for at least forty-eight hours before the competition, the athlete can eliminate any metabolic waste products that may hinder performance. The high-carbohydrate diet restores glycogen levels in

5-5

Critical Thinking E x e r c i s e

A recreational runner has been training to run his first marathon. He feels good about his level of conditioning but wants to make certain that he does everything that he can do to maximize his performance. He is concerned about eating the right type of foods both before and during the marathon to help ensure that he does not become excessively fatigued.

? What recommendations should the athletic trainer make regarding glycogen supercompensation, the preevent meal, and food consumption during the event?

TABLE 5-4 Fast-Food Choices and Nutritional Value

Food	Calories	Protein (g)	CHO (g)	Fat (g)	Calories from Fat (%)	Cholesterol (mg)	Sodium (mg)
Hamburgers							
McDonald's hamburger	263	12.4	28.3	11	38.6	29.1	506
Dairy Queen single hamburger w/cheese	410	24	33	20	43.9	50	790
Hardee's 1/4 pound cheeseburger	506	28	41	26	46.2	61	1,950
Wendy's double hamburger, white bun	560	4.1	24	34	54.6	125	575
McDonald's Big Mac	570	24.6	39.2	35	55.2	83	45
Burger King Whopper sandwich	640	27	42	41	57.6	94	842
Jack in the Box Jumbo Jack	485	26	38	26	48.2	64	905
Chicken							
Arby's chicken breast sandwich	592	28	56	27	41.0	57	1,340
Burger King chicken sandwich	688	26	56	40	52.3	82	1,423
Dairy Queen chicken sandwich	670	29	46	41	55.0	75	870
Church's Crispy Nuggets (one; regular)	55	3	4	3	49.0	—	125
Kentucky Fried Chicken Nuggets (one)	46	2.82	2.2	2.9	56.7	11.9	140
Fish							
Church's Southern fried catfish	67	4	4	4	53.7	—	151
Long John Silver's Fish & More	978	34	82	58	53.3	88	2,124
McDonald's Filet-O-Fish	435	14.7	35.9	25.7	53.1	45.2	799
Others							
Hardee's hot dog	346	11	26	22	57.2	42	744
Jack in the Box taco	191	8	1.6	11	51.8	21	406
Arby's roast beef sandwich (regular)	350	22	32	15	38.5	39	590
Hardee's roast beef sandwich	377	21	36	17	40.5	57	1,030
French fries							
Arby's french fries	211	2	33	8	34.1	6	30
McDonald's french fries (regular)	220	3	26.1	11.5	47.0	8.6	109
Wendy's french fries (regular)	280	40	35	14	45.0	15	95
Shakes							
Dairy Queen	710	14	120	19	24.0	50	260
McDonald's							
Vanilla	352	9.3	59.6	8.4	21.4	30.6	201
Chocolate	383	9.9	65.5	9	21.1	29.7	300
Strawberry	362	9	62.1	8.7	22.3	32.2	207
Soft drinks							
Coca-Cola	154	—	40	—	—	—	6
Diet Coke	0.9	—	0.3	—	—	—	16
Sprite	142	—	36	—	—	—	45
Tab	1	—	1	—	—	—	30
Diet Sprite	3	—	0	—	—	—	9

Focus

Tips for selecting fast foods

- Limit deep-fried foods such as fish and chicken sandwiches and chicken nuggets, which are often higher in fat than plain burgers are. If you are having fried chicken, remove some of the breading before eating.
- Order roast beef, turkey, or grilled chicken, where available, for a lower fat alternative to most burgers.
- Choose a small order of fries with your meal rather than a large one, and request no salt. Add a small amount of salt yourself if desired. If you are ordering a deep-fat-fried sandwich or one that is made with cheese and sauce, skip the fries altogether and try a plain baked potato (add butter and salt sparingly) or a dinner roll instead of a biscuit; or, try a side salad to accompany your meal instead.
- Choose regular sandwiches instead of "double," "jumbo," "deluxe," or "ultimate" sandwiches. And order plain types rather than those with the works, such as cheese, bacon, mayonnaise, and special sauce. Pickles, mustard, ketchup, and other condiments are high in sodium. Choose lettuce, tomatoes, and onions.
- At the salad bar, load up on fresh greens, fruits, and vegetables. Be careful of salad dressings, added toppings, and creamy salads (potato salad, macaroni salad, coleslaw). These can quickly push calories and fat to the level of other menu items or higher.
- Many fast-food items contain large amounts of sodium from salt and other ingredients. Try to balance the rest of your day's sodium choices after a fast-food meal.
- Alternate water, low-fat milk, or skim milk with a soda or a shake.
- For dessert, or a sweet-on-the-run, choose low-fat frozen yogurt where available.
- Remember to balance your fast-food choices with your food selections for the whole day.

---

muscle and the liver. This practice is called **glycogen supercompensation**. The basis for the practice is that the quantity of glycogen stored in muscle directly affects the endurance of that muscle.[50]

Glycogen supercompensation is accomplished over a six-day period divided into three phases. In phase 1 (days 1 and 2), training should be hard and dietary intake of carbohydrates restricted. During phase 2 (days 3 through 5), training is cut back and the individual eats plenty of carbohydrates. Studies have indicated that glycogen stores may be increased from 50 percent to 100 percent, theoretically enhancing endurance during a long-term event. Phase 3 (day 6) is the day of the event, during which a normal diet must be consumed.

The effect of glycogen supercompensation in improving performance during endurance activities has not as yet been clearly demonstrated. It has been recommended that glycogen supercompensation not be done more than two to three times during the course of a year. Glycogen supercompensation is only of value in long-duration events that produce glycogen depletion, such as a marathon.[46]

Recommendations for Restoring Muscle Glycogen After Exercise

When the time period between exercise sessions is relatively short (less than 8 hours), the athlete should begin consuming carbohydrates to restore supplies of muscle glycogen as soon as possible after the workout to maximize recovery between sessions.[16] Given that complete muscle glycogen restoration takes at least 20 to 24 hours, athletes should not waste time. They should ingest approximately 0.45 to 0.55 grams of carbohydrate per pound of body weight for each of the first four hours after exercise or

glycogen supercompensation
High-carbohydrate diet.

until they eat their next large meal. During this period nutrient-rich carbohydrate foods like fruits and vegetables or a high carbohydrate drink are recommended.[36] Over a 24-hour period, carbohydrate intake should range from 2.3 grams to as much as 5.5 grams per pound of body weight, depending on the intensity of the activity.[6] Pasta, potatoes, oatmeal, or a sports drink are recommended.[36]

Fat Loading

Some endurance athletes tried fat loading in place of carbohydrate loading. Their intent was to have a better source of energy at their disposal. The deleterious effects of this procedure outweigh any benefits that may be derived. Associated with fat loading is cardiac protein and potassium depletion, causing arrhythmias and increased levels of serum cholesterol as a result of the ingestion of butter, cheese, cream, and marbled beef.

WEIGHT CONTROL AND BODY COMPOSITION

Gain or loss of weight in an athlete often poses a problem because the individual's ingrained eating habits are difficult to change.[26] The athletic trainer's inability to adequately supervise the athlete's meal program in terms of balance and quantity further complicates the problem. An intelligent and conscientious approach to weight control requires that the athletic trainer, the coach, and the athlete have some knowledge of what is involved.[60] Such understanding allows athletes to better discipline themselves as to the quantity and kinds of foods they should eat.[28]

Body Composition

Ideal body weight is most often determined by consulting age-related height and weight charts such as those published by life insurance companies. Unfortunately, these charts are inaccurate because they involve broad ranges and often fail to take individual body types into account. Health and performance, rather than body weight, may best be related to body composition.[31]

Body composition refers to both the fat and nonfat components of the body. That portion of total body weight that is composed of fat tissue is referred to as the percentage of body fat. The total body weight that is composed of nonfat or lean tissue, which includes muscles, tendons, bones, and connective tissue, is referred to as lean body weight. Body composition measurements provide an accurate determination of precisely how much weight an athlete may gain or lose.[14]

The average college-age female has between 20 percent and 25 percent of her total body weight made up of fat. The average college-age male has between 12 percent and 15 percent body fat. Male endurance athletes may get their fat percentage as low as 8 percent to 12 percent, and female endurance athletes may reach 10 percent to 18 percent. Body fat percentage should not go below 3 percent in males and 12 percent in females, because below these percentages the internal organs tend to lose their protective padding of essential fat, potentially subjecting them to injury.[11]

Being overweight and being obese are different conditions. Being overweight implies having excess body weight relative to physical size and stature. Being overweight may not be a problem unless a person is also overfat, which means that the percentage of total body weight that is made up of fat is excessive. **Obesity** implies an extreme amount of excessive fat, much greater than what would be considered normal. Females with body fat above 30 percent and males with body fat above 20 percent are considered to be obese.[11]

Two factors determine the amount of fat in the body: the number of fat, or adipose, cells and the size of the adipose cell. Proliferation, or hyperplagia, of adipose cells begins at birth and continues to puberty. It is thought that after early adulthood the number of fat cells remains fixed, although some evidence suggests that the number of cells is not necessarily fixed.[17] Adipose cell size also increases gradually, or hypertrophies, to early adulthood and can increase or decrease as a function of caloric bal-

---

5–6

Critical Thinking E x e r c i s e

A female softball player has a problem controlling her weight. Her body fat percentage has been measured at 25 percent and she asks the athletic trainer what she needs to do to be able to lose some weight quickly and then to maintain her body weight thereafter.

? How should the athletic trainer respond?

obesity
Excessive amount of body fat.

ance. In adults, weight loss or gain is primarily a function of the change in cell size, not cell number. Obese adults tend to exhibit a great deal of adipose cell hypertrophy.

The **adipose cell** stores triglyceride (a form of liquid fat). This liquid fat moves in and out of the cell according to the energy needs of the body, which are determined to some extent by activity type. The greatest amount of fat is used in activities of moderate intensity and long duration. The greater the amount of triglyceride contained in the adipose cell, the greater the amount of total body weight composed of fat. One pound of body fat is made up of approximately 3,500 calories stored as triglyceride within the adipose cell.

Assessing Body Composition

Among the several methods of assessing **body composition** are measurement of skinfold thickness;[2] hydrostatic, or underwater, weighing; and measurement of electrical impedance.

Skinfold Measurements

The method of measuring the thickness of skinfolds is based on the fact that about 50 percent of the fat in the body is contained in the subcutaneous fat layers and is closely related to total fat. The remainder of the fat in the body is found around organs and vessels and serves a shock-absorptive function. The skinfold technique measures the thickness of the subcutaneous fat layer with a skinfold caliper (Figure 5-4). Its accuracy is relatively low; however, expertise in measurement is easily developed and the time required for this technique is considerably less than for the others. It has been estimated that error in skinfold measurement is plus or minus 3 percent to 5 percent.[17]

Researchers have offered several different techniques for measuring body composition via skinfolds. A technique proposed by Jackson and Pollack,[31] which measures the thigh, triceps, suprailiac, abdomen, and chest skinfolds is widely used.[44]

Hydrostatic weighing Hydrostatic (underwater) weighing involves placing a subject in a specially designed underwater tank to determine body density.[17] Fat tissue is less dense than lean tissue. Therefore the more body fat present, the more the body floats (buoyancy) and the less it weighs in water. Body composition is calculated by comparing the weight of the submerged individual with the weight before entering the tank. If done properly, this technique is very accurate. Unfortunately, the tank and equipment are expensive and generally not available to most coaches and physical educators. In addition, there are other drawbacks with this technique. It is time consuming (especially for large groups), and subjects must exhale completely and hold their breath while underwater. Many students have real problems and fears with this aspect of the technique.

Bioelectrical impedance The second technique involves the measurement of resistance to the flow of electrical current through the body between selected points.[2] This technique is based on the principle that electricity will choose to flow through the tissue that offers the least resistance or impedance. Fat is generally a poor conductor of electrical energy, whereas lean tissue is a fairly good conductor. Thus the higher the percentage of body fat, the greater the resistance to the passage of electrical energy. Very simply, this method predicts the percentage body fat by measuring bioelectrical impedance.[2] It should be mentioned that bioelectrical impedance measures can be affected by levels of hydration. If the body is dehydrated, the measurement will tend to overestimate percentage of body fat relative to measurements taken when there is normal hydration. The equipment available for taking these measurements is, again, fairly expensive and generally includes the use of computer software.

Determining Body Mass Index

A relatively easy way to determine the extent of overweight or obesity is to use a person's body weight and height measurements to calculate body mass index (BMI). BMI is a ratio of body weight to height. This technique represents a method for measuring

adipose cell
Stores triglyceride.

body composition
Percent body fat plus lean body weight.

Figure 5-4

Measuring body composition.
A, Thigh. **B,** Triceps.
C, Suprailiac. **D,** Abdomen.
E, Chest.

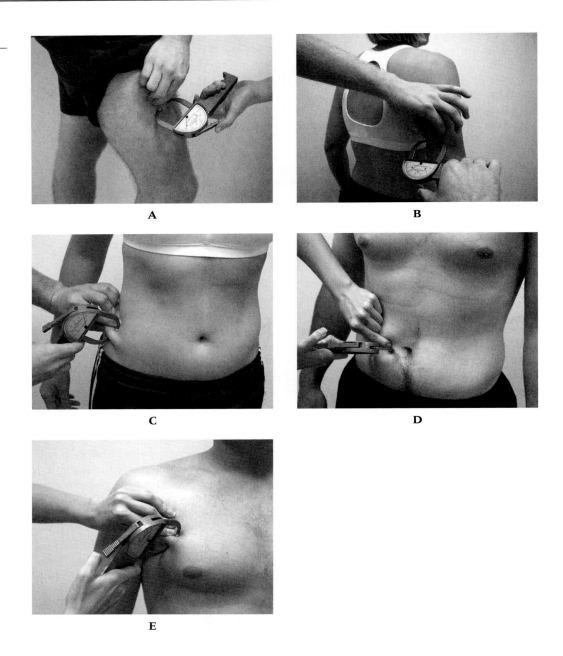

A

B

C

D

E

health risks from obesity using height/weight measurements. Health problems associated with excess body fat tend to be associated with a BMI of more than 25. A BMI of 25 to 30 indicates that a person is overweight. A BMI of 30 or more indicates a state of obesity.[46] *Focus Box:* "Determining body mass index (BMI)" will help you calculate BMI.

Assessing Caloric Balance

Changes in body weight are almost entirely the result of changes in caloric balance.[40]

Caloric balance = Number of calories consumed − Number of calories expended

If more calories are consumed than expended, this positive caloric balance results in weight gain. Conversely, weight loss results from a negative caloric balance in which more calories are expended than are consumed. Caloric balance may be calculated by maintaining accurate records of both the number of calories consumed in the

Focus

Determining body mass index (BMI) as a means of examining overweight and obesity
1. Weigh yourself to determine body weight in pounds.
2. Divide your weight in pounds by 2.2 to determine kilograms.
3. Measure your height in inches.
4. Multiply your height in inches by 2.54 and divide by 100 to convert your height to meters.
5. Multiply your height in meters by your height in meters to get your height in meters squared.
6. Divide your weight in kilograms by your height in meters squared to determine your BMI.

1. _____   Divided by 2.2 = _____
   Weight (lbs)   Weight (kg)
2. _____   Times 2.54 divided by 100 = _____
   Height (in)   Height (m)
3. _____   Times _____ = _____
   Height (m)   Height (m)   Height (m²)
4. _____   Divided by _____ = _____
   Weight (kg)   Height (m²)   Body Mass Index

diet and the number of calories expended for metabolic needs and in activities performed during the course of a day.

Caloric Consumption or Intake

Caloric balance is determined by the number of calories consumed regardless of whether the calories are contained in fat, carbohydrate, or protein. There are differences in the caloric content of these foodstuffs:

> Carbohydrate = 4 calories per gram
> Protein = 4 calories per gram
> Fat = 9 calories per gram
> Alcohol = 7 calories per gram

Estimations of caloric intake for college athletes range between 2,000 and 5,000 calories per day. Estimations of caloric expenditure range between 2,200 and 4,400 calories on average. Energy demands will be considerably higher in endurance-type athletes, who may require as many as 7,000 calories per day.[43]

Low carbohydrate diets and weight loss   For many years it was recommended that fat intake be limited as a means of controlling weight. Recently the recommendation has been to severely limit the intake of carbohydrate in the diet. There are many different versions of a low-carbohydrate diet, all of which recommend a strict reduction in the consumption of carbohydrates. Most low-carb diets replace carbohydrates with a high-fat and moderate protein diet. The low-calorie and low-fat diets that have been recommended for years have failed to realize that dietary fat is not necessarily converted into body fat. However carbohydrates are readily converted into fat. When eating a high-carbohydrate meal, the increased blood glucose stimulates insulin production by the pancreas. Insulin allows blood glucose to be used by the cells, but it also causes fat to be deposited, and it stimulates the brain to produce hunger signals. So there is a tendency to eat more carbohydrates, and the cycle repeats. It has been shown that most overweight people became overweight due to a condition called *hyperinsulinemia*—elevated insulin levels in the blood. Restricting carbohydrate intake halts this cycle by decreasing insulin levels. Carbohydrate restriction also increases the levels of glucagon which is a hormone that causes body fat to be burned and aids in removing

Positive caloric balance leads to weight gain; negative caloric balance leads to weight loss.

cholesterol deposits in the arteries. Severely restricting carbohydrate intake puts the body into a state of ketosis in which blood glucose levels stabilize, insulin level drops, and because the body is burning fat, fairly rapid weight loss occurs.

Caloric Expenditure

Calories may be expended by three different processes: basal metabolism, work (work is defined as any activity that requires more energy than sleeping), and excretion. When estimating caloric expenditure, it is first necessary to determine the amount of calories (energy) needed to support basal metabolism. This is the minimal amount of energy required to sustain the body's vital functions such as respiration, heartbeat, circulation, and maintenance of body temperature during a twenty-four-hour period. The basal metabolic rate (BMR) is the rate at which calories are spent for these maintenance activities. BMR is most accurately determined in a laboratory through a measurement process known as indirect calorimetry, which measures a person's oxygen uptake to predict BMR. Measurement of BMR using this procedure is generally done as soon as the subject awakes, in a quiet, warm environment, and after a twelve-hour fast.

Once BMR has been determined, it is necessary to calculate the energy requirements of all physical activities done in a twenty-four-hour period. This is the second component of energy needs, referred to as work. There is a wide variation in energy output for work. It is determined by the type, intensity, and duration of a physical activity. Body size is also a factor; heavier people expend more energy in an activity than do lighter people. Specific energy expenditures may be determined by consulting charts that predict energy used in an activity based on (1) the time spent in each activity in minutes and (2) the metabolic costs of each activity in kilocalories per minute per pound (kcal/min/lb) of body weight.

Methods of Weight Loss

An individual has several ways to go about losing weight: dieting, increasing the amount of physical exercise, or a combination of diet and exercise.

Weight loss through dieting alone is difficult, and in most cases dieting alone is an ineffective means of weight control. Long-term weight control through dieting alone is successful only 2 percent of the time.[67] About 35 percent to 45 percent of weight decrease due to dieting results from a loss of lean tissue. The minimum caloric intake should not go below 1,000 to 1,200 calories per day for a female and not below 1,200 to 1,400 calories per day for a male.[54]

Weight loss through exercise involves an 80 percent to 90 percent loss of fat tissue with almost no loss of lean tissue. Weight loss through exercise alone is almost as difficult as losing weight through dieting. However, exercise will not only result in weight reduction but may also enhance cardiorespiratory endurance, improve strength, and increase flexibility.[11] For these reasons, exercise has some distinct advantages over dieting in any weight-loss program.

The most efficient method of decreasing the percentage of body weight that is fat is through some combination of diet and exercise. A moderate caloric restriction combined with a moderate increase in caloric expenditure will result in a negative caloric balance. This method is relatively fast and easy compared with either of the other methods because habits are being moderately changed.

In any weight-loss program, the goal should be to lose 1.5 to 2 pounds per week. Weight loss of more than 4 to 5 pounds per week may be attributed to dehydration as opposed to a loss of body fat.[11] A weight-loss program must emphasize the long-haul approach. It generally takes a long time to put on extra weight, and there is no reason to expect that true loss of excess body fat can be accomplished in a relatively short time. The American College of Sports Medicine has made specific recommendations for weight loss.[4]

Methods of Weight Gain

The aim of a weight-gaining program should be to increase lean body mass, that is, muscle as opposed to body fat. Muscle mass should be increased only by muscle work combined with an appropriate increase in dietary intake. Muscle mass cannot be increased by the intake of any special food or vitamin.

The recommended rate of weight gain is approximately one to two pounds per week. Each pound of lean body mass gained represents a positive caloric balance. This positive balance is an intake in excess of an expenditure of approximately 2,500 calories. One pound of fat represents the equivalent of 3,500 calories; lean body tissue contains less fat, more protein, and more water and represents approximately 2,500 calories. To gain one pound of muscle, an excess of approximately 2,500 calories is needed; to lose one pound of fat, approximately 3,500 calories in excess of intake must be expended in activities. Adding 500 to 1,000 calories daily to the usual diet will provide the energy needs of gaining one to two pounds per week and fuel the increased energy expenditure of the weight-training program. Weight training must be part of the weight-gaining program. Otherwise, the excess intake of energy will be converted to fat.[15]

Disordered Eating

Disordered eating can be defined as a spectrum of abnormal eating behaviors, ranging from mild food restriction and occasional binging and purging, to severe conditions of bulimia nervosa and anorexia nervosa. Disordered eating is a multifactorial disorder that includes social, familial, physiological, and psychological components. In the athletic population, the incidence of disordered eating behaviors and pathologic eating disorders is significantly higher than in the general population.[72] This relatively high incidence in athletes has been attributed to the athlete's attempt to control body weight or body composition in an effort to improve his or her performance. In addition to the emotional stress and social pressures characteristic of eating disorders, there are also serious physiological effects that can compound one another and ultimately affect the athlete's overall health and performance. Recently a brief (four measurements and a fourteen-item questionnaire) physiologic screening test has been developed to detect eating disorders in collegiate female athletes.[9] Athletic trainers working with young athletes, particularly active females, should be educated about these disorders and work within their resources to develop strategies for prevention and management.[62]

Bulimia Nervosa

The bulimic person is commonly female, ranging in age from adolescence to middle age. It is estimated that 1 out of every 200 American girls, ages twelve to eighteen years (1 percent to 2 percent of the population), will develop patterns of bulimia nervosa, anorexia nervosa, or both.[52] The bulimic individual typically gorges herself with thousands of calories after a period of starvation and then purges herself through induced vomiting and further fasting or through the use of laxatives or diuretics. This secretive binge-eating–purging cycle may go on for years.

Typically the bulimic athlete is white and belongs to a middle-class or upper-middle-class family. She is perfectionistic, obedient, overcompliant, highly motivated, successful academically, well liked by her peers, and a good athlete.[60] She most commonly participates in gymnastics, track, and dance. Male wrestlers and gymnasts may also develop bulimia nervosa. (See *Focus Box:* "Identifying the athlete with an eating disorder.")

Binge-purge patterns of eating can cause stomach rupture, disruption of heart rhythm, and liver damage. Stomach acids brought up by vomiting cause tooth decay and chronically inflame the mucous lining of the mouth and throat.

5-7

Critical Thinking E x e r c i s e

An ice hockey attackman has an excellent level of fitness and has superb skating ability and stick work. He is convinced that the only thing keeping him from moving to the next level is his low body weight. In recent years he has engaged more in weight-training activities to improve his muscular endurance and, to a lesser extent, to increase his strength.

? What recommendations should the athletic trainer make for him to be successful in his weight-gaining efforts?

5-8

Critical Thinking E x e r c i s e

A tennis coach observes that one of her players has lost a significant amount of weight. Along with this loss of weight, this athlete's level of play has begun to decrease. The coach becomes seriously concerned when another player tells the coach that she thinks her roommate was purposely throwing up after a team meal on a recent road trip. After briefly questioning the athlete about her eating habits, the coach asks the athletic trainer to become involved in dealing with this situation.

? How should the athletic trainer respond to this request?

Focus

Identifying the athlete with an eating disorder

The athlete with an eating disorder may display the following signs:
- Social isolation and withdrawal from friends and family
- A lack of confidence in athletic abilities
- Ritualistic eating behavior (e.g., organizing food on plate)
- An obsession with counting calories
- An obsession with constantly exercising, especially just before a meal
- An obsession with weighing self
- A constant overestimation of body size
- Patterns of leaving the table directly after eating to go into the restroom
- Problems related to eating disorders (e.g., malnutrition, menstrual irregularities, or chronic fatigue)
- Family history of eating disorders

Anorexia Nervosa

It has been estimated that 30 percent to 50 percent of all individuals diagnosed as having anorexia nervosa also develop some symptoms of bulimia nervosa. Anorexia nervosa is characterized by a distorted body image and a major concern about weight gain. As with bulimia nervosa, anorexia nervosa affects mostly females. It usually begins in adolescence and can be mild without major consequences or can become life threatening. As many as 15 percent to 21 percent of individuals diagnosed as anorexic ultimately die from this disorder. Despite being extremely thin, the athlete sees herself as too fat. These individuals deny hunger and are hyperactive, engaging in abnormal amounts of exercise such as aerobics or distance running.[59] In general, the anorexic individual is highly secretive, and the coach and athletic trainer must be sensitive to eating problems. Early intervention is essential. Any athlete with signs of bulimia nervosa or anorexia nervosa must be confronted in a kind, empathetic manner by the coach or athletic trainer. When detected, individuals with eating disorders must be referred for psychological or psychiatric treatment. Unfortunately, simply referring an anorexic person to a health education clinic is not usually effective. The key to the treatment of anorexia nervosa seems to be getting the patient to realize that a problem exists and that he or she could benefit from professional help. The individual must voluntarily accept such help if treatment is to be successful.[46]

Anorexia Athletica

Anorexia athletica is a condition specific to athletes that is characterized by several of the features common to anorexia nervosa, but without the self-starvation practices. Athletes with anorexia athletica may exhibit a variety of signs including disturbance of body image, a weight loss greater than 5 percent of body weight, gastrointestinal complaints, primary amenorrhea, menstrual dysfunction, absence of medical illness explaining the weight reduction, excessive fear of becoming obese, binging or purging, compulsive eating, and/or restriction of caloric intake.

Female Athlete Triad Syndrome

Female athlete triad syndrome is a potentially fatal problem that involves a combination of an eating disorder (either bulimia or anorexia), amenorrhea, and osteoporosis (diminished bone density). The incidence of this syndrome is uncertain; however, some studies have suggested that eating disorders in female athletes may be as high as 62 percent in certain sports, with amenorrhea being common in at least 60 percent of female athletes. However, the major risk of this syndrome is that the bone lost in osteoporosis may not be regained.[44]

SUMMARY

- The classes of nutrients are carbohydrates, fats, proteins, vitamins, minerals, and water. Carbohydrates, fats, and proteins provide the energy required for muscular work during activity and also play a role in the function and maintenance of body tissues. Vitamins are substances found in food that have no caloric value but are necessary to regulate body processes. Vitamins may be either fat soluble (vitamins A, D, E, and K) or water soluble (B-complex vitamins and vitamin C). Minerals are necessary in most physiological functions of the body. Water is the most essential of all the nutrients and should be of great concern to anyone involved in physical activity.

- A nutritious diet consists of eating a variety of foods in amounts recommended in the food pyramid. A diet that meets those recommended amounts does not need nutrient supplementation.

- Protein supplementation during weight training is not necessary if a nutritious diet is maintained. Many males and especially females may require calcium supplementation to prevent osteoporosis. It may be necessary to supplement the diet with extra iron to prevent iron-deficiency anemia.

- Organic or natural foods have no beneficial effect on performance. Vegetarian diets can provide all the essential nutrients if care is taken and the diet is well thought out and properly prepared.

- The preevent meal should be higher in carbohydrates, easily digested, eaten three to four hours before an event, and psychologically pleasing.

- Glycogen supercompensation involves maximizing resting stores of glucose in the muscles, blood, and liver before a competitive event.

- Body composition indicates the percentage of total body weight composed of fat tissue versus the percentage composed of lean tissue. The size and number of adipose cells determine percentage of body fat. Percentage of body fat can be assessed by measuring the thickness of the subcutaneous fat at specific areas of the body with a skinfold caliper.

- Changes in body weight are caused almost entirely by a change in caloric balance, which is a function of the number of calories taken in and the number of calories expended. Weight can be lost either by increasing caloric expenditure through exercise or by decreasing caloric intake through dieting. Diets generally do not work. The recommended technique for losing weight involves a combination of moderate calorie restriction and a moderate increase in physical exercise during the course of each day. Weight gain should be accomplished by increasing caloric intake and engaging in a weight-training program. It is possible to gain weight and lose fat, thus changing body composition. Equal volumes of muscle weigh more than fat.

- Anorexia is a disease in which a person suffers a pathological weight loss because of a psychological aversion to food and eating. Bulimia is an eating disorder that involves binging and subsequent purging.

Websites

Gatorade Sports Science Institute: http://www.gssiweb.com/
This website provides information for coaches, athletic trainers, physicians, nutritionists, and others in the field of sports medicine, sports nutrition, and exercise science.

Healthy Biz 2000: http://www.healthybiz2000.com/
This site provides information about sports nutrition and nutritional supplements for fitness and weight loss.

Food and Nutrition Information Center:
http://www.nalusda.gov/fnic
This site is part of the information centers at the National Agricultural Library and offers access to information on healthy eating habits, food composition, and many additional resources.

Yahoo Health and Nutrition Information:
  http://www.yahoo.com/Health/Nutrition
  This site includes diet analysis information, nutritional facts, and links to many other informative sites.

Eating Disorders: http://www.eating_disorder.com/
  Eating disorder information can be found here, including information about anorexia, bulimia, and overeating as well as information about how to access support groups.

Athletes and Eating Disorders: http://www.uq.net.au/eda/documents/start/html
  This site is part of the Eating Disorders Resources website; it gives some statistics from a recent NCAA study and has a section on the coaches' responsibility. The site also includes information about warning signs and the female athlete triad.

The American Dietetic Association: http://www.eatright.org
  This site includes access to the journal published by the American Dietetic Association and provides informative nutritional tips as well as gateways to nutrition and related sites.

Solutions to Critical Thinking EXERCISES

5-1 The important consideration for weight control is the total number of calories that are consumed relative to the total number of calories expended. It makes no difference whether the calories consumed are CHO, fat, or protein. Fat contains more than twice the number of calories that either CHO or protein contains, so an athlete can eat significantly more food and still have about the same caloric intake if the diet is high in CHO. This athlete should be told that it is also essential to consume at least some fat, which is necessary for the production of several enzymes and hormones.

5-2 For an athlete who is truly consuming anything close to a well-balanced diet, vitamin supplementation is generally not necessary. However, if taking a one-a-day type of vitamin supplement makes the athlete feel better, there is no harm. Her tiredness could be related to a number of medical conditions (e.g., mononucleosis). An iron-deficiency anemia may be detected through a laboratory blood test. The athletic trainer should refer the athlete to a physician for blood work.

5-3 This athlete should be referred to the team physician and nutritionist. From her history, the athletic trainer can assume she is not consuming enough iron by not eating meats or other nutritious foods. Iron is essential for hemoglobin formation and energy formation. In addition, since she is not eating vegetables, she is not receiving an adequate amount of Vitamin K. Vitamin K is important in blood coagulation. By not eating a well balanced diet, she lacks Vitamin K, which is found in green leafy vegetables.

5-4 A small amount of protein (slightly above to about double the protein RDA) is needed for developing muscles in a training program. However, an athlete can easily meet these necessary higher amounts by eating a variety of foods, especially protein-rich foods. Thus, athletes do not need protein supplements, because their diets typically exceed protein recommendations.

5-5 The amount of glycogen that can be stored in the muscle and liver can be increased by reducing the training program a few days before competing and by significantly increasing carbohydrate intake during the week before the event. Nutrients consumed over several days before competition are much more important than what is eaten three hours before an event. The purpose of the preevent meal should be to provide the competitor with sufficient nutrient energy and fluids for competition while taking into consideration the digestibility of the food. Glucose-rich drinks taken at regular intervals are beneficial for highly intense and prolonged events that severely deplete glycogen stores.

5-6 The athletic trainer should recommend that this athlete set a goal of 18 to 20 percent body fat. If the softball player needs to lose weight, she must consume fewer calories than she is burning off, and this is not something that can be achieved in a short period of time. It also must be explained that weight control is simply a matter of achieving caloric balance and making lifestyle changes in terms of eating and exercise habits to achieve caloric balance.

5-7 This athlete must understand the importance of adding lean tissue muscle mass rather than increasing his percentage of body fat. His caloric intake must be increased so that he is in a positive caloric balance of about 500 calories per day. Additional calorie intake should consist primarily of CHO. Additional supplementation with protein is not necessary. It is absolutely essential that this athlete incorporate a weight-training program using heavy weights that will overload the muscle, forcing it to hypertrophy over a period of time.

5-8 Treating eating disorders is difficult even for health care professionals specifically trained to counsel these individuals. The athletic trainer should approach the athlete, not with accusation, but with support, showing concern about her weight loss and expressing a desire to help her secure appropriate counseling. Remember that the athlete must first be willing to admit that she has an eating disorder before treatment and counseling will be effective. Eliciting the support of close friends and family can help with treatment.

REVIEW QUESTIONS AND CLASS ACTIVITIES

1. What is the value of good nutrition in terms of an athlete's performance and injury prevention?
2. Ask coaches of different sports about the type of diet they recommend for their athletes and their rationale behind the diet.
3. Have a nutritionist talk to the class about food myths and fallacies.
4. Have each member of the class prepare a week's food diary; then compare it with other class members' diaries.
5. What are the daily dietary requirements according to the food pyramid? Should the requirements of the typical athlete's diet differ from those requirements? If so, in what ways?
6. Have the class debate the value of vitamin and mineral supplements.
7. Describe the advantages and disadvantages of supplementing iron and calcium.
8. Is there some advantage to preevent nutrition?
9. Are there advantages or disadvantages in a vegetarian diet for the athlete?
10. What is the current thinking on the value of creatine as a nutritional supplement?
11. What is the primary concern of using herbs?
12. Discuss the importance of athletes monitoring their body composition.
13. Explain the most effective technique for losing weight.
14. Contrast the signs and symptoms of bulimia nervosa and anorexia nervosa. If an athletic trainer is aware of an athlete who may have an eating disorder, what should he or she do?

REFERENCES

1. Allred J: Too much of a good thing? An overemphasis on eating low-fat foods may be contributing to the alarming increase in overweight among U.S. adults, *J Am Diet Assoc* 95:417, 1995.

2. Amato H, Wenos D: Bioelectrical impedance of hydration effects on muscular strength and endurance in college wrestlers, *J Ath Train* 28(2):170, 1993.

3. American College of Sports Medicine: Position stand on exercise and fluid replacement, *Med Sci Sports Exerc* 28:1, 1996.

4. American College of Sports Medicine: Proper and improper weight loss programs, *Med Sci Sports Exerc* 15:ix, 1983.

5. American College of Sports Medicine: The physiological and health effects of oral creatine supplementation, *Med Sci Sports Exerc* 32(3):706, 2000.

6. American Dietetic Association and Canadian Dietetic Association: Position of the American Dietetic Association and Canadian Dietetic Association: nutrition for physical fitness and athletic performance of adults, *J Am Diet Assoc* 93:691, 1993.

7. Anderson J, Stender M, Rodando P: Nutrition and bone in physical activity and sport. In Wolinsky I, Hickson J: *Nutrition in exercise and sport*, Boca Raton, 1998, CRC Press.

8. Antonio J: *Sports supplements*, Philadelphia, 2001, Lippincott, Williams and Wilkins.

9. Black D, Larkin L, Coster D: Physiologic screening test for eating disorders/disordered eating among female collegiate athletes, *J Ath Train* 38(4):286, 2003.

10. Blackburn H: Olestra and the FDA, *N Engl J Med* 334(15):984, 1996.

11. Brownell K, Fairbum C: *Eating disorders and obesity: a comprehensive handbook*, New York, 2002, Guilford Press.

12. Casa D, Armstrong L, Hillman S: National Athletic Trainers Association position statement: fluid replacement for athletes, *J Ath Train* 35(2):212, 2000.

13. Clarkson P et al: Methods and strategies for weight loss in athletics, roundtable, *Sports Science Exchange* 9(1):1998.

14. Clarkson PM: Nutritional supplements for weight gain, *Sports Science Exchange* 11(1):1, 1998.

15. Coleman E: Nutritional concerns of vegetarian athletes, *Sports Med Digest* 17(2):1, 1995.

16. Coyle E: Highs and lows of carbohydrate diets, *Sports Science Exchange* 17(2):1, 2004.

17. DeLorenzo A et al: Comparison of different techniques to measure body composition in moderately active adolescents, *British Journal of Sports Medicine* 32(3):215, 1998.

18. Dodd S, Herb R, Powers S: Caffeine and exercise performance: an update, *Sports Med* 15:14, 1993.

19. Food and Drug Administration: Food labeling: reference daily intakes, *Federal Register* 59(2):427, 1994.

20. Food and Nutrition Board, National Academy of Sciences—National Research Council: Recommended dietary allowances, ed 12, Washington, DC, 1998, U.S. Government Printing Office.

21. Foster S: *101 medicinal herbs*. Loveland, Colo, 1998, Interweave Press.

22. Friedman-Kester K: Do food triggers give you a headache? *Athletic Therapy Today* 6(6):42, 2001.

23. Friedman-Kester K: Herbal remedies are drugs, too! *Athletic Therapy Today* 7(4):40, 2002.

24. Friedman-Kester K: RDAs, RDIs—R U confused? *Athletic Therapy Today* 6(3):56, 2001.

25. Friedman-Kester K: The function of functional foods. *Athletic Therapy Today* 7(3):46, 2002.

26. Gorinski R: In pursuit of the perfect body composition: do dietary strategies make a difference? *Athletic Therapy Today* 6(6):54, 2001.

27. Greenwood M, Kreider R, Greenwood L: Cramping and injury incidence in collegiate football players are reduced by creatine supplementation, *J Ath Train* 38(3), 2003.

28. Gutgesell M, Moreau K, Thompson D: Weight concerns, problem eating behaviors, and problem drinking behaviors in female college athletes, *J Ath Train* 38(1):62, 2003.

29. Hale CW: The precompetition meal. *Athletic Therapy Today* 6(3):21, 2001.

30. Hoffman R, Garewal H: Antioxidants and the prevention of coronary heart disease, *Arch Int Med* 155:241, 1995.

31. Jackson AS, Pollack M: Generalized equations for predicting body density of women, *Med Sci Sports Exer* 12:175, 1980.

32. Jackson C: *Nutrition for recreational athletes*, Boca Raton, 1995, CRC Press.

33. Johnson, KD: Ephedra and ma huang consumption: do the benefits outweigh the risks? *Strength Cond* 23(5):32, 2001.

34. Kirshner E, Lewis R, O'Connor P: Bone mineral density and dietary intake of college gymnasts, *Med Sci Sports Exerc* 24(4):543, 1995.

35. Kleiner S: Fluids for performance, *Athletic Therapy Today* 5(1):51, 2000.

36. Kleiner SM: Postexercise-recovery nutrition. *Athletic Therapy Today* 6(2):40, 2001.

37. Kleiner SM: Protein power. *Athletic Therapy Today* 7(1):24, 2002.

38. Kleiner SM: *Power eating*, Champaign, Ill, 2001, Human Kinetics.

39. Kleiner SM: The scoop on protein supplements. *Athletic Therapy Today* 6(1):52, 2001.

40. Kleiner SM: Top-ten rules for healthy weight control. *Athletic Therapy* 7(2):38,

41. Krieder R, Ferreira M, Wilson M: Effects of creatine supplementation on body composition, strength, and sprint performance, *Med Sci Sports Exerc* 30(1):73, 1998.

42. Larson-Duyff R: *The American Dietetic Association's complete food and nutrition guide*, New York, 1998, Wiley.

43. Massad S, Headley S: Nutrition assessment: considerations for athletes, *Athletic Therapy Today* 4(6):6, 1999.

44. Merrick MA: Osteoporosis and the female athlete. *Athletic Therapy Today* 6(3):42, 2001.

45. Papas A, Quillen J: *Antioxidant status: diet, nutrition, and health*, Boca Raton, 1998, CRC Press.

46. Payne W, Hahn D: *Focus on health*, ed 8, St. Louis, 2004, McGraw-Hill.

47. Peterson D: Athletes and iron deficiency: is it true anemia or "sport anemia"? *Physician Sports Med* 26(2):24, 1998.

48. Powers M, Arnold B, Weltman A: Creatine supplementation increases total body water without altering fluid distribution, *J Ath Train* 38(1):44, 2003.

49. Powers M: Ephedra and its application to sport performance: another concern for the athletic trainer?, *J Ath Train* 36(4):420, 2001.

50. Rauch L, Rodger I, Wilson J: The effects of carbohydrate loading on muscle glycogen content and cycling performance, *Int J Sports Med* 5(l):25, 1995.

51. Reimers K: The role of liquid supplements in weight gain, *Strength Cond* 17(l):64, 1995.

52. Rhea DJ, Jambor EA, Wiginton K: Preventing eating disorders in female athletes. *JOHPER* 67(4):66, 1996.

53. Rodriguez N: The role of nutrition in injury prevention and healing, *Athletic Therapy Today* 4(6):27, 1999.

54. Sanborn CF, Horea M, Siemers BJ, Dieringer KI: Disordered eating and the female athlete triad. *Clin Sports Med* 19(2):199, 2000.

55. Schlabach G: Carbohydrate strategies for injury prevention, *J Ath Train* 29(3):244, 1994.

56. Shi X, Gisolfi CV: Fluid and carbohydrate replacement during intermittent exercise, *Sports Med* 25(3):157, 1998.

57. Skolnik H: Sport nutrition in a fast-food society: eating on the road, *Athletic Therapy Today* 4(6):22, 1999.

58. Steen S: Sports nutrition for children, *Athletic Therapy Today* 4(6):48, 1999.

59. Sundgot-Borgen J: Eating disorders in athletes. In Sundgot-Borgen J, editor: *Nutrition in sport*, Oxford, 2000, Blackwell.

60. Turk JC, Prentice WE: Collegiate coaches' knowledge of eating disorders, *J Ath Train* 34(1):19, 1999.

61. U.S. Department of Agriculture and U.S. Department of Health and Human Services: *Nutrition and your health: dietary guidelines for Americans*, ed 5, Washington, DC, 2000.

62. Vaughn J, King K, Cottrell R: Collegiate athletic trainers confidence in helping female athletes with eating disorders, *J Ath Train* 39(1): 71, 2004.

63. Vinci D: Negotiating the maze of nutritional ergogenic aids. *Athletic Therapy Today* 8(2):28, 2003.

64. Vinci DM: What's for lunch? *Athletic Therapy Today* 8(1):50, 2003.

65. Vinci, DM: The training room: developing a sports-nutrition game plan. *Athletic Therapy Today* 7(5):52, 2002.

66. Volek J, et al: Creatine supplementation enhances muscular performance during high-intensity resistance exercise, *J Am Diet Assoc* 97:765, 1997.

67. Wardlaw GM, Insel PM: *Perspectives in nutrition,* ed 6, St Louis, 2003, Mosby.

68. Wilder N, Deivert R, Hagerman F: The effects of low-dose creatine supplementation versus creatine loading in collegiate football players, *J Ath Train* 36(2):124, 2001.

69. Williams M: *Nutrition for fitness and sports,* Boston, 2004, McGraw-Hill.

70. Williams M: The use of nutritional ergogenic aids in sports: is it an ethical issue? *Int J Sport Nutr* 4:120, 1994.

71. Winterstein A, Storrs C: Herbal Supplements: Considerations for the athletic trainer, *J Ath Train* 36(4):425, 2001.

72. Zawila L, Steib C, Hoogenboom B: The female, collegiate, cross-country runner: nutritional knowledge and attitudes, *J Ath Train* 38(1):67, 2003.

ANNOTATED BIBLIOGRAPHY

American Dietetic Association, Dyrugff R: *Complete food and nutrition guide,* Minnetonka, Minn, 2002, Chronimed Publishing.

This extensive text is packed with information concerning every aspect of eating and food safety. This book is highly recommended for individuals who aspire to the highest understanding of healthful eating.

Clark N: *Sport nutrition guidebook: eating to fuel your active lifestyle,* Champaign, Ill, 2003, Human Kinetics.

Provides real-life case studies of nutritional advice given to athletes; the book also provides recommendations for pregame meals.

Sheldan M: *Wellness encyclopedia for food and nutrition.* New York, 2000, Rebus.

The encyclopedia covers every type of whole, fresh food found in supermarkets, specialty shops, and health-food stores. It also presents the latest information on what makes up a healthy diet and on the connection between diet and disease protection.

Wardlaw GM, Insel PM: *Perspectives in nutrition,* ed 6, St Louis, 2003, McGraw-Hill.

This comprehensive text deals with all aspects of nutrition.

Weil A: *Eating well for optimum health: the essential guide to food, diet, and nutrition,* New York, 2000, Knopf.

This text offers a thorough rundown of nutritional basics and a primer on micronutrients such as vitamins, minerals, and fiber.

Williams M: *Nutrition for fitness and sport,* Boston, 2004, McGraw-Hill.

This textbook provides thorough coverage of the role nutrition plays in enhancing health, fitness, and sport performance. Current research and practical activities are incorporated throughout.

Hendler S, Rorvik, D: *PDR for nutritional supplements,* Montvale, NJ, 2001, Medical Economics Company.

From the Publishers of the Physicians' Desk Reference, this new resource gathers solid clinical evidence about the use of dietary supplements from the available medical literature and presents it in a unique and authoritative manner.

Environmental Considerations

When you finish this chapter you should be able to

- Describe the physiology of hyperthermia.
- Recognize the clinical signs of heat stress and how they can be prevented.
- Identify the causes of hypothermia and the major cold disorders and how they can be prevented.
- Examine the problems that high altitude might present to the athlete and explain how they can be managed.
- Review how an athlete should be protected from exposure to the sun.
- Describe precautions that should be taken in a lightning storm.
- List the problems that air pollution presents to the athlete and how they can be avoided.
- Discuss what effect circadian dysrhythmia can have on athletes and the best procedures for handling this problem.
- Compare the effect of synthetic versus natural turf on the incidence of injury.

Environmental stress can adversely affect an athlete's performance and in some instances can pose a serious health threat. The environmental categories that are of major concern to athletic trainers, particularly those involved in outdoor sports, include hyperthermia, hypothermia, altitude, exposure to the sun, lightning storms, air pollution, and circadian dysrhythmia (jet lag).

HYPERTHERMIA

A major concern in sports is the problem of **hyperthermia**. Over the years, hyperthermia has caused a number of athlete deaths in high school, college, and at the professional level.[66]

It is vitally important that the athletic trainer and the coaching staff have knowledge about temperature and humidity factors to assist them in planning practice. The athletic trainer must clearly understand when environmental heat and humidity are at a dangerous level and must make recommendations to the coaches accordingly. In addition, the athletic trainer must recognize and properly manage the clinical symptoms and signs of heat stress.

Heat Stress

Regardless of the level of physical conditioning, athletes must take extreme caution when exercising in hot, humid weather. Prolonged exposure to extreme heat can result in heat illness.[52] Heat stress is preventable, but each year many athletes suffer illness and even death from some heat-related cause.[9] Athletes who exercise in hot, humid environments are particularly vulnerable to heat stress.[16]

The physiological processes in the body will continue to function only as long as body temperature is maintained within a normal range.[44] The maintenance of normal temperature in a hot environment depends on the body's ability to dissipate heat. Body temperature can be affected by five factors, described in the following sections.

hyperthermia
Elevated body temperature.

Heat can be gained or lost through:
- Metabolic heat production
- Conductive heat exchange
- Convective heat exchange
- Radiant heat exchange
- Evaporative heat loss

Metabolic Heat Production

Normal metabolic function in the body results in the production and radiation of heat. Consequently, metabolism will always cause an increase in body heat that depends on the intensity of the physical activity. The higher the metabolic rate, the more heat produced.

Conductive Heat Exchange

Physical contact with other objects can result in either a heat loss or a heat gain. A football player competing on artificial turf on a sunny August afternoon will experience an increase in body temperature simply by standing on synthetic turf.

Convective Heat Exchange

Body heat can be either lost or gained, depending on the temperature of the circulating medium. A cool breeze will always tend to cool the body by removing heat from the body surface. Conversely, if the temperature of the circulating air is higher than the temperature of the skin, body heat increases.

Radiant Heat Exchange

Radiant heat from sunshine causes an increase in body temperature. Obviously, the effects of this radiation are much greater in the sunshine than in the shade.[24] On a cloudy day, the body also emits radiant heat energy; thus, radiation may result in either heat loss or heat gain. During exercise the body attempts to dissipate heat produced by metabolism by dilating superficial arterial and venous vessels, thus channeling blood to the superficial capillaries in the skin.

Evaporative Heat Loss

Sweat glands in the skin allow water to be transported to the surface, where it evaporates, taking large quantities of heat with it. When the temperature and radiant heat of the environment become higher than body temperature, the loss of body heat becomes highly dependent on the process of sweat evaporation.

The rate of sweating is critical for an athlete to dissipate heat. A normal person can sweat off about one quart of water per hour for about two hours. However, certain individuals can lose as much as 2 quarts of water (4 pounds) per hour.[55] *Focus Box:* "Variations in Sweat Rates" identifies factors that influence sweat rates. Sweating does not cause heat loss. The sweat must evaporate for heat to be dissipated. But the air must be relatively free of water for evaporation to occur. Heat loss through evaporation is severely impaired when the relative humidity reaches 65 percent and virtually stops when the humidity reaches 75 percent.

Focus

Variations in sweat rates

Sweat rates can vary considerably from one athlete to another and are determined by a number of factors:

- Athlete's height and weight (heavier athletes sweat more)
- Degree of acclimatization (well acclimated athletes sweat earlier and more)
- Fitness level (fit athletes sweat more)
- Hydration status
- Environmental conditions
- Clothing
- Intensity and duration of activity
- Heredity

It should be obvious that heat-related problems have the greatest chance of occurring on days when the sun is bright and the temperature and relative humidity are high. However, cramps, heat exhaustion, and heatstroke can occur whenever the body's ability to dissipate heat is impaired.

Monitoring the Heat Index

The athletic trainer must exercise common sense when overseeing the health care of athletes who are training or competing in the heat. Obviously, when the combination of heat, humidity, and bright sunshine is present, extra caution is warranted. The universal wet bulb globe temperature (WBGT) index provides the athletic trainer with an objective means for determining necessary precautions for practice and competition in hot weather.[51] The index incorporates readings from several different thermometers. The dry bulb temperature (DBT) is recorded from a standard mercury thermometer. The wet bulb temperature (WBT) uses a wet wick or piece of gauze wrapped around the end of a thermometer that is swung around in the air. Globe temperature (GT) measures the sun's radiation and has a black metal casing around the end of the thermometer. Once the three readings have been taken, the following formula is used to calculate the WBGT index:

$$WBGT = 0.1 \times DBT + 0.7 \times WBT + GT \times 0.2$$

If only a web bulb and dry bulb temperature is taken the WBGT index is calculated using the following modified formula:

$$WBGT = 0.3 \times DBT + 0.7 \times WBT$$

Using this formula yields a universally accepted WBGT index (Table 6-1) on which recommendations relative to outdoor activity are based. Table 6-2 is a modification of the WBGT index that indicates activity restrictions for outdoor physical conditioning in hot weather.

The DBT and WBT can be measured easily using a *psychrometer.* It consists of two identical thermometers—the wet bulb thermometer, so called because its bulb is covered with a jacket of tight-fitting muslin cloth that can be saturated with distilled water, and the dry bulb thermometer. When the cloth is soaked and the thermometers are properly ventilated, the wet bulb temperature will be lower than the dry bulb temperature (actual air temperature) because of cooling due to the evaporation of water from the cloth. The drier the air is, the greater the evaporation, and thus the more wet bulb temperature is depressed. In some units such as the Physio-Dyne, ventilation is provided by a suction fan (aspiration psychrometer) (Figure 6-1A) or by whirling the thermometers at the end of a chain (sling psychrometer) (Figure 6-1B). Newer psychrometers use special digital sensors (Figure 6-1C). Recording the temperature requires about ninety seconds. Either instrument is relatively inexpensive and easy to use, although it appears that the old sling psychrometer may have the greatest accuracy.[17]

TABLE 6-I   Universal WBGT Index

Heat Category	WBGT °F	Easy Work Work/Rest*	Easy Work Water per Hour	Moderate Work Work/Rest*	Moderate Work Water per Hour	Hard Work Work/Rest*	Hard Work Water per Hour
1	78–81.9	No limit	1/2 qt	No limit	3/4 qt	40/20 min	3/4 qt
2	82–84.9	No limit	1/2 qt	50/10 min	3/4 qt	30/30 min	1 qt
3	85–87.9	No limit	3/4 qt	40/20 min	3/4 qt	30/30 min	1 qt
4	88–89.9	No limit	3/4 qt	30/30 min	3/4 qt	20/40 min	1 qt
5	>90	50/10 min	1 qt	20/40 min	1 qt	10/50 min	1 qt

*Rest means minimal physical activity (sitting or standing) and should be accomplished in the shade if possible.

TABLE 6-2 Activity Restrictions for Outdoor Physical Conditioning in Hot Weather

WBGT[a] (°F)	Flag Color[c]	Guidance[b] for nonacclimatized personnel in boldface *Guidance for fully acclimatized personnel in italics*
<78.0°F	**No flag**	**Extreme exertion may precipitate heat illness.** *Normal activity*
78.0°F–82.0°F	Green	**Use discretion in planning intense exercise.** *Normal activity* Pay special attention to at-risk individuals in both cases.
82.1°F–86.0°F	Yellow	**Limit intense exercise to 1 hour; limit total outdoor exercise to 2.5 hours.** *Use discretion in planning intense physical activity.* Pay special attention to at-risk individuals in both cases. Be on high alert; watch for early signs and symptoms in both cases.
86.1°F–89.9°F	Red	**Stop outdoor practice sessions and outdoor physical conditioning.** *Limit intense exercise to 1 hour; limit total outdoor exercise to 4 hours.* Be on high alert; watch for early signs and symptoms throughout.
≥90°F	**Black**	**Cancel all outdoor exercise requiring physical exertion.** *Cancel all outdoor exercise involving physical exertion.*

[a]WGBT is wet bulb globe temperature.
Calculation of WBGT: $0.7\,T_{wb} + 0.2\,T_{bg} + 0.1\,T_{db}$, where T_{wb} is wet bulb temperature; T_{bg} is black globe temperature; T_{db} is dry bulb temperature
[b]Guidelines assume that athletes are wearing summer-weight clothing and that all activities are constantly supervised by an athletic trainer to assure early detection of problems. When equipment must be worn, as in football, please use guidelines one step below. For example, if WBGT is 86°F (yellow) then use the guidelines for red.
[c]Flag color indicates a warning flag, which is placed in a location visible from a practice field, that is used to notify everyone using that facility what the conditions are and the restrictions that should be applied.
Modified from Nunnelly SA, Reardon MJ: Prevention of heat illness. In *Medical aspects of harsh environments: Volume I.*. Pandolf KB, Burr RE, editors: Washington, DC, 2002, TMM Publications.

Figure 6-1

A, A Physio-Dyne, **B,** a sling psychrometer, or **C,** a digital psychrometer may be used to determine the WBGT heat index.

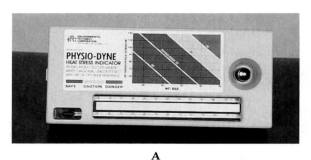

A

C

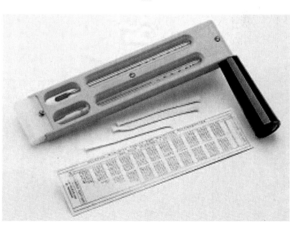

B

Exertional Heat Illnesses

In 2003, a consensus statement on exertional heat illnesses was prepared by an interassociation task force that included input from experts representing eighteen professional sports medicine organizations.[39] Exercising in a hot, humid environment can cause various forms of heat illness, including heat rash, heat syncope, heat cramps, heat exhaustion, exertional heatstroke, and exertional hyponatremia.[43]

Heat Rash

Heat rash, also called prickly heat, is a benign condition associated with a red, raised rash accompanied by sensations of prickling and tingling during sweating. It usually occurs when the skin is continuously wet with unevaporated sweat. The rash is generally localized to areas of the body that are covered with clothing. Continually toweling the body can help prevent the rash from developing.[61]

Heat Syncope

Heat syncope, or heat collapse, is associated with rapid physical fatigue during overexposure to heat. It is usually caused by standing in heat for long periods or by not being accustomed to exercising in the heat. It is caused by peripheral vasodilation of superficial vessels, hypotension, or a pooling of blood in the extremities, which results in dizziness, fainting, and nausea. Heat syncope is quickly relieved by laying the athlete down in a cool environment and replacing fluids.[61]

Heat Cramps

Heat cramps are extremely painful muscle spasms that occur most commonly in the calf and abdomen, although any muscle can be involved (Table 6-3). The occurrence of heat cramps is related to excessive loss of water and several electrolytes or ions (sodium, chloride, potassium, magnesium, and calcium), but especially sodium, that are each essential elements in muscle contraction.

> Heat cramps occur because of some imbalance between water and electrolytes.

Profuse sweating involves losses of large amounts of water and small quantities of sodium, potassium, magnesium, and calcium, thus destroying the balance in the concentration of these elements within the body. This imbalance will ultimately result in painful muscle contractions and cramps. The person most likely to get heat cramps is one who is in fairly good condition but who is not acclimatized to the heat.

Heat cramps may be prevented by adequate replacement of sodium, chloride, potassium, magnesium, calcium, and most important, fluids.[8] Ingestion of salt tablets may help prevent cramps. Simply salting food a bit more heavily can replace sodium; bananas are particularly high in potassium; and calcium is present in milk, cheese, and dairy products. The immediate treatment for heat cramps is ingestion of large quantities of fluids, preferably a sports drink, and mild prolonged stretching with ice massage of the muscle in spasm. An athlete who experiences heat cramps will generally not be able to return to practice or competition for the remainder of the day, because cramping is likely to reoccur.

Exertional Heat Exhaustion

Exertional heat exhaustion is a more moderate form of heat illness that occurs from environmental heat stress and strenuous physical exercise. In exertional heat exhaustion an athlete becomes dehydrated to the point that he or she is unable to sustain adequate cardiac output and thus cannot continue intense exercise. Mild hyperthermia is characteristic of heat exhaustion, with a rectal temperature of less than 104 degrees and no evidence of central nervous system (CNS) dysfunction. Obtaining an accurate rectal temperature measurement is essential for the athletic trainer to differentiate between heat exhaustion and heat stroke. See *Focus Box:* "Measuring rectal temperature" for a description of the procedure. An athlete who is experiencing heat exhaustion

> Exertional heat exhaustion results from dehydration.

> Measuring rectal temperature is critical to differentiate heat stroke and heat exhaustion.

TABLE 6-3 **Heat Disorders: Treatment and Prevention**

Disorder	Cause	Clinical Features and Diagnosis	Treatment	Prevention
Heat syncope	Rapid physical fatigue during overexposure to heat	Pooling of blood in extremities leading to dizziness, fainting, and nausea	Lay athlete down in a cool environment and replenish fluids	Gradually acclimatize to exercising in a hot humid environment
Exertional heat cramps	Hard work in heat; sweating heavily; imbalance between water and electrolytes (sodium)	Muscle twitching and cramps, usually after midday; spasms in arms, legs, abdomen	Ingesting large amounts of fluid, mild stretching, and ice massage of affected muscle	Acclimatize athlete properly; provide large quantities of fluids; increase intake of calcium, sodium, and potassium slightly
Exertional heat exhaustion	Prolonged sweating leading to dehydration and an inability to sustain adequate cardiac output	Excessive thirst, dry tongue and mouth; weight loss; fatigue; weakness; incoordination; mental dullness; low urine volume; slightly elevated body temperature; high serum protein and sodium; reduced swelling	Bed rest in cool room, IV fluids if drinking is impaired; increase fluid intake to 6 to 8 L/day; sponge with cool water; keep records of body weight and fluid balance; provide semiliquid food until salination is normal	Supply adequate fluids Provide adequate rest and opportunity for cooling
Exertional heatstroke	Thermoregulatory failure of sudden onset	Abrupt onset, CNS abnormalities including headache, vertigo, and fatigue; flushed skin; relatively less sweating than seen with heat exhaustion; rapidly increasing pulse rate that may reach 160 to 180; increased respiration; blood pressure seldom rises; rapid rise in temperature to 104°F (40°C); athlete feels as if he or she is burning up; diarrhea, vomiting; could lead to permanent brain damage; circulatory collapse may produce death	Take immediate emergency measures to reduce temperature (e.g., immersion in ice water bath or sponge cool water and air fan over body, massage limbs); remove to hospital as soon as possible	Ensure proper acclimatization, proper hydration Educate those supervising activities conducted in the heat Adapt activities to the environment Screen participants with past history of heat illness for malignant hyperthermia
Exertional hyponatremia	Fluid/electrolyte disorder resulting in low concentration of sodium in the blood	Progressively worsening headache, nausea and vomiting, swelling in hands and feet, lethargy or apathy, low blood sodium, compromised CNS	Do not try to rehydrate; transport to medical facility; sodium levels must be increased and fluid levels decreased	Hydrate with sports drinks; increase sodium intake; make sure fluid intake equals fluid loss

≋ *Focus* ▬

Measuring rectal temperature

Monitoring temperature with a thermometer inserted into the rectum is the most exact way of determining core temperature. Normal rectal temperature is 99.6°F (37.5°C).

- Shake the thermometer down to below the 97°F mark (36.1°C).
- Cover the tip of the thermometer with lubricating or petroleum jelly.
- Place the athlete on his or her stomach.
- Spread the buttocks and gently insert the thermometer about an inch into the rectum. Never force it. Hold the buttocks together to keep the thermometer from falling out.
- Do not release your grip on the thermometer.
- Leave the thermometer in place for three minutes.
- To read the temperature, slowly turn the thermometer until you can see the line of mercury.
- Wash the thermometer carefully in soap and warm water after each use. Store in a safe place.

will show signs and symptoms of dehydration and/or electrolyte depletion that include pale skin; profuse sweating; stomach cramps with nausea, vomiting, or diarrhea; headache; persistent muscle cramps; and dizziness with loss of coordination.

An athlete who has exertional heat exhaustion must be immediately removed from play and taken to a shaded or air-conditioned area. Excess clothing or equipment should be removed and the athlete should lie down with his or her legs elevated. Cooling efforts should continue until rectal temperature has lowered to 101 degrees. Rehydration should begin immediately with water or a sports drink as long as the athlete is not nauseated or vomiting. If the athlete cannot take fluids orally, intravenous fluid replacement should be initiated by a physician. The athletic trainer should continually monitor heart rate, blood pressure, and core temperature. If rapid improvement is not observed the athlete must be transported to an emergency facility. Before returning to play, the athlete must be completely rehydrated and should be cleared by a physician.

Exertional Heatstroke

Unlike heat cramps and exertional heat exhaustion, exertional heatstroke is a serious, life-threatening emergency (Table 6-3). It is the most severe form of heat illness and is induced by strenuous physical exercise and increased environmental heat stress. It is characterized by CNS abnormalities and potential tissue damage resulting from a significantly elevated body temperature. As body temperature rises, extreme circulatory and metabolic stresses can produce damage and severe physiological dysfunction that can ultimately result in death.

Heatstroke can occur suddenly and without warning.[27] The specific cause of heatstroke is unknown. It is clinically characterized by sudden collapse with CNS dysfunction, such as altered consciousness, seizures, confusion, emotional instability, irrational behavior, or decreased mental acuity. Measured rectal temperature is at 104°F or higher. Additionally the victim will be flushed and will have hot skin with sweating about 75 percent of the time, although about 25 percent of the cases will have less sweating than would be seen with heat exhaustion. Other symptoms include shallow, fast breathing; a rapid, strong pulse; nausea, vomiting, or diarrhea; headache, dizziness, or weakness; decreased blood pressure; and dehydration. The heatstroke victim experiences a breakdown of the thermoregulatory mechanism due to excessively high body temperature, and the body loses the ability to dissipate heat through sweating.[54]

6-1

Critical Thinking E x e r c i s e

A wrestler collapses during a match and exhibits signs of profuse sweating, pale skin, mildly elevated temperature (102°F), dizziness, hyperventilation, and rapid pulse. When questioned by the athletic trainer, the wrestler indicates that earlier in the day he took diuretic medication to facilitate water loss in an effort to help him make weight.

? What type of heat illness is the athlete experiencing, and what does the athletic trainer need to do to manage this situation appropriately?

6-2

Critical Thinking E x e r c i s e

A high school football team is doing conditioning outside. The temperature is 80 degrees with 85 percent humidity. The players have their helmets on and are running 100-yard sprints. One player looks like he is becoming fatigued and slightly disoriented. Thirty yards into the sprint, the athlete collapses.

? What is the immediate course of action to treat this athlete? What is wrong with the athlete?

Heatstroke is a life-threatening emergency.

The possibility of death from heatstroke can be significantly reduced if the victim's body temperature is lowered to normal as soon as possible. The longer that the body temperature is elevated to 104°F or higher, the higher the mortality rate. Thus the key to managing this condition is aggressive and immediate whole-body cooling.[63] Get the athlete into a cool environment, strip off all clothing, and immerse the athlete in a cold water bath (35° to 58°F).[18] If it is not possible to immerse the athlete in cold water, sponge him or her down with cool water and fan with a towel. Try to lower rectal temperature to 101°F. Call the rescue squad. It is imperative that the victim be transported to a hospital as quickly as possible, however it is recommended that the victim be cooled down first and transported second if onsite rapid cooling and adequate medical supervision are available. If rescue squad transport is delayed, it may be necessary to transport the victim in whatever vehicle happens to be available. Following an exertional heat stroke the athlete should avoid exercise for a minimum of one week and gradually return to full practice after being completely asymptomatic and cleared by a physician.

Malignant hyperthermia Malignant hyperthermia is a rare, genetically inherited muscle disorder that causes hypersensitivity to anesthesia and extreme exercise in hot environments. It is characterized by muscle breakdown.[45] This disorder causes muscle temperatures to increase faster than core temperatures, and its symptoms are similar to those of heatstroke. The athlete complains of muscle pain after exercise, and rectal temperature remains elevated for ten to fifteen minutes after exercise. During this period, muscle tissue is destroyed and breakdown products of muscle may damage the kidneys and cause acute renal failure.[25] The condition may be fatal if not treated immediately. Muscle biopsy is necessary for diagnosis. Athletes with malignant hyperthermia should be disqualified from competing in hot, humid environments.[28]

Acute exertional rhabdomyolysis Acute exertional rhabdomyolysis is a syndrome that is characterized by sudden catabolic destruction and degeneration of skeletal muscle accompanied by leakage of myoglobin (muscle protein) and muscle enzymes into the vascular system.[5] It can occur in healthy individuals during intense exercise in extremely hot and humid environmental conditions. It can result in either the gradual onset of muscle weakness, swelling, and pain; the presence of darkened urine and renal dysfunction; or, in severe cases, sudden collapse, renal failure, and death. Rhabdomyolysis has been associated with individuals with sickle-cell trait. If rhabdomyolysis is suspected, the athlete should be referred to a physician immediately.

Exertional Hyponatremia

Hyponatremia is a condition involving a fluid/electrolyte disorder that results in an abnormally low concentration of sodium in the blood.[10] It is most often caused by ingesting so much fluid before, during, and after exercise that the concentration of sodium is decreased. It also can occur due to too little sodium in the diet or in ingested fluids over a period of prolonged exercise. An individual with a high rate of sweating and a significant loss of sodium, who continues to ingest large quantities of fluid over a several hour period of exercise (as in a marathon or triathlon), is particularly vulnerable to developing hyponatremia. Hyponatremia can be avoided completely by making certain that fluid intake during exercise does not exceed fluid loss and that sodium intake is adequate.

The signs and symptoms of exertional hyponatremia may include a progressively worsening headache; nausea and vomiting; swelling of the hands and feet; lethargy, apathy, or agitation; and low blood sodium (<130 mmol/L). Ultimately, a very low concentration of sodium can compromise the central nervous system creating a life-threatening situation.[39]

If the athletic trainer suspects exertional hyponatremia and blood sodium levels cannot be determined onsite, measures to rehydrate the athlete should be delayed and the athlete should be transported immediately to a medical facility.[39] At the medical facility the delivery of sodium, certain diuretics, or intravenous solutions may be necessary. A physician should clear the athlete before he or she is allowed to return to play.

Focus

NATA recommendations for preventing heat illness[10]

- Ensure that appropriate medical care is available.
- Conduct a thorough physician-supervised preparticipation exam to identify susceptible individuals.
- Acclimatize athletes over ten to fourteen days.
- Educate athletes and coaches regarding prevention, recognition, and treatment of heat illnesses.
- Educate athletes to balance fluid intake with sweat and urine losses to maintain adequate hydration.
- Encourage athletes to sleep six to eight hours per night in a cool environment.
- Monitor environmental conditions and develop guidelines for altering practice sessions based on those conditions.
- Provide an adequate supply of water or sports drinks to maintain hydration.
- Weigh high-risk athletes before and after practice to make certain they are not dehydrated.
- Minimize the amount of equipment and clothing worn in hot humid conditions.
- Minimize warm-up time in hot humid conditions.
- Allow athletes to practice in shaded areas and use cooling fans when possible.
- Have appropriate emergency equipment available (e.g., fluids, ice, immersion tank, rectal thermometer, telephone or radio).

Preventing Heat Illness

The athletic trainer should understand that heat illness is preventable if he or she exercises some common sense and caution. An athlete can only perform at an optimal level when dehydration and hyperthermia are minimized by the ingestion of ample volumes of fluid during exercise and when commonsense precautions are used to keep cool.[56] *Focus Box:* "NATA recommendations for preventing heat illness" summarizes NATA-recommended guidelines for preventing heat illness.[59] The following factors should be considered when planning a training or competitive program that is likely to take place during hot weather.

Dehydration

An athlete who does not replenish fluids is likely to become dehydrated. Whenever an individual is exercising, some dehydration will occur, since it is difficult to balance fluid loss through sweating with fluid intake. An individual is said to have mild dehydration when fluids lost are less than 2 percent of normal body weight.[39] Even mild dehydration can impair cardiovascular and thermoregulatory response and can reduce the capacity for exercise and have a negative effect on performance.[42,56] Individuals who are becoming dehydrated may exhibit any or all of the following symptoms and signs: thirst, dry mouth, headache, dizziness, irritability, lethargy, excessive fatigue, and possibly cramps. Obviously, an athlete who is dehydrated needs to replace fluids and should be moved to a cool environment. The athlete should rehydrate with a sports drink that contains carbohydrates and electrolytes (particularly sodium and potassium) and should not return to full activity until he or she is symptom free and has returned to normal body weight. It is important to note that fluid replacement should not exceed fluid loss.

Fluid and Electrolyte Replacement

During hot weather it is essential that athletes continually replace fluids lost through evaporation by drinking large quantities of water or other beverages.[21]

The prevention of hyperthermia involves:
- Gradual acclimatization
- Identification of susceptible individuals
- Lightweight uniforms
- Routine weight record keeping
- Unrestricted fluid replacement
- Well-balanced diet
- Routine temperature and humidity readings

Mild dehydration is the loss of less than 2% of body weight.

Fluid intake should equal fluid loss.

The average adult doing minimal physical activity requires a minimum of 2.5 liters of water or about ten glasses of water a day. A normal sweat-loss rate for a person during an hour of exercise ranges between 0.8 and 3 liters with an average of 1.5 liters per hour. Because water is so vital, the healthy body carefully manages its internal water levels. When body weight drops by 1 to 2 percent (1.5 to 3 pounds in a 150-pound individual), he or she begins to feel thirsty. Drinking water and other beverages eventually returns the internal water levels to normal. However, if thirst signals are ignored and body water continues to decrease, dehydration results. People who are dehydrated cannot generate enough energy, and they feel weak. Dehydration is more likely to occur when an individual is outdoors and is sweating heavily while engaging in some strenuous activity. To prevent dehydration, an athlete should make sure to replace the lost water by drinking plenty of fluids and not relying on thirst as a signal that it's time to have a drink. By the time thirst develops, the body is already slightly dehydrated. Many people ignore their thirst, or if they do heed it, they don't drink enough, especially during physical activity. Most people replace only about 50 percent of the water they lose through sweating. For this reason, athletes should consume fluids before, during, and after practice and competition.

Athletes must have unlimited access to water. There is no acceptable reason for allowing or causing an athlete to become hypohydrated.[59] Failure to permit ad libitum access to fluids will not only undermine an athlete's performance, but may also predispose the athlete to unnecessary heat-related illnesses (Figure 6-2).

A number of adverse physiological and potentially pathological effects can be caused by hypohydration, including reduced muscular strength and endurance, decreased blood and plasma volume, altered cardiac function, impaired thermoregulation, decreased kidney function, reduced glycogen stores, and loss of electrolytes.[59]

Using sports drinks   During physical activity, it is essential to replace fluids lost through sweating.[56] It has been shown that replacing lost fluids with a sports drink is more effective than using water alone.[50] Research has shown that because of the flavor, an athlete is likely to drink more sports drinks than plain water. In addition, sports drinks replace both fluids and electrolytes that are lost in sweat, and they also provide energy to the working muscles. Water is a good thirst quencher, but it is not a good rehydrator because it actually "turns off" thirst before the body is completely rehydrated. Water also "turns on" the kidneys prematurely, so an individual loses fluid in the form of urine more quickly than when he or she is drinking a sports drink. The small amount of sodium in sports drinks allows the body to hold onto the fluid consumed rather than losing it through urine.[57]

Sports drinks are more effective than water for fluid replacement.

Figure 6-2

Athletes must have unlimited access to fluids, especially in hot weather.

Focus

Recommendations for fluid replacement*

- Athletes should begin all exercise sessions well hydrated.
- Establish a hydration protocol for fluid replacement.
- To ensure proper hydration, the athlete should consume seventeen to twenty ounces of water or a sports drink two to three hours before exercise and then seven to ten ounces twenty minutes before exercise.
- Fluid replacement beverages should be easily accessible during activity and should be consumed at a minimal rate of seven to ten ounces every ten to twenty minutes.
- During activity, the athlete should consume the maximal amount of fluid that can be tolerated, but it is important that fluid intake does not exceed fluid loss.
- A cool, flavored beverage at refrigerator temperature is recommended.
- The addition of proper amounts of carbohydrates and electrolytes to a fluid replacement solution is recommended for exercise events that last longer than forty-five to fifty minutes or are intense.
- For vigorous exercise lasting less than one hour, the addition of carbohydrates and electrolytes does enhance physical performance.
- A 6 percent carbohydrate solution appears to be optimal (fourteen grams of carbohydrate per eight-ounce serving). A concentration greater than 8 percent slows gastric emptying.
- Adding a modest amount of sodium (0.3 to 0.7 grams per liter) is acceptable to stimulate thirst and increase fluid intake.

*Based on recommendations from the National Athletic Trainers' Association,[15] American College of Sports Medicine,[2] and Gatorade Sport Science Institute.[56]

Not all sports drinks are the same. How a sports drink is formulated dictates how well it works to provide rapid rehydration and energy. The optimal level of carbohydrate is 14 grams per 8 ounces of water for the quickest fluid absorption. Thus, sports drinks should be used without diluting. Sports drinks with too much carbohydrate are absorbed more slowly. Most sports drinks contain no carbonation or artificial preservatives, so they are satisfying during exercise and cause no stomach bloating. Also, most sports drinks contain a minimal number of calories. It has been shown that sports drinks are effective not only for endurance exercise but also for improving performance during both endurance activities and short-term, high-intensity activities such as soccer, basketball, and tennis that last from thirty minutes to an hour.[39] (See *Focus Box:* "Recommendations for fluid replacement.").

Gradual Acclimatization

Gradual acclimatization is a critical consideration in avoiding heat stress. Acclimatization should involve not only becoming accustomed to heat but also becoming acclimatized to exercising in hot temperatures.[52] A good preseason conditioning program, started well before the advent of the competitive season and carefully graded as to intensity, is recommended.[59] Progressive exposure should occur over a seven- to ten-day period.[59] During the first five or six days, an 80 percent acclimatization can be achieved on the basis of a two-hour practice period in the morning and a two-hour practice period in the afternoon. Each practice period should be broken down into twenty minutes of work alternated with twenty minutes of rest in the shade.

Identifying Susceptible Individuals

Athletes with a large muscle mass are particularly prone to heat illness.[17] Body build must be considered when determining individual susceptibility to heat stress. Overweight individuals may have as much as 18 percent greater heat production than underweight individuals, because metabolic heat is produced proportionately to surface area. It has been found that heat illness victims tend to be overweight. Death from heatstroke increases at a ratio of approximately four to one as body weight increases.[17]

Women are apparently more physiologically efficient in body temperature regulation than men are. Although women possess as many heat-activated sweat glands as men do, they sweat less and manifest a higher heart rate when working in heat.[50] Although slight differences exist, the same precautionary measures apply to both genders.

Other individuals who are susceptible to heat stress include those with relatively poor fitness levels, those with a history of heat illness, and anyone with a febrile condition.[59]

Selecting Appropriate Uniforms

Uniforms should be selected on the basis of temperature and humidity. Initial practices should be conducted in short-sleeved T-shirts, shorts, and socks, and athletes should be moved gradually into short-sleeved net jerseys, lightweight pants, and socks as acclimatization proceeds. All early-season practices and games should be conducted in lightweight uniforms with short-sleeved net jerseys and socks. Rubberized suits should never be used.[59]

Maintaining Weight Records

Careful weight records of all players must be kept. Weights should be measured both before and after practice for at least the first two weeks of practice. If a sudden increase in temperature or humidity occurs during the season, weight should be recorded again for a period of time. A loss of 3 percent to 5 percent of body weight will reduce blood volume and could lead to a health threat.[67]

Monitoring Temperature and Humidity Readings

Dry bulb and wet bulb temperature readings should be taken on the field before practice to monitor the heat index.[51] Modifications to the practice schedule should be made according to the severity of existing environmental conditions. The purchase of a physiodyne or sling psychrometer for this purpose is recommended (see Figure 6-1).

Clinical Indications and Treatment

Focus Box: "Environmental conduct of sports, particularly football" and Table 6-3 (page 166) list the clinical symptoms of the various hyperthermia conditions and the indications for treatment. Although the Focus Box calls particular attention to some of the procedures for football, the precautions in general apply to all sports. Because of the specialized equipment worn by the players, football requires special consideration. Many football uniforms are heat traps and serve to compound the environmental heat problem, which is not true of lighter uniforms.

Guidelines for Athletes Who Intentionally Lose Weight

Wrestlers or other athletes who purposely dehydrate themselves as a means of making weight are predisposing themselves to heat-related illness and may in fact be creating a potentially life-threatening situation. Weight loss to make some predetermined weight limit should absolutely not be accomplished through dehydration. The process must be gradual over a period of several weeks, or even months, and should result from a reduction in the percentage of body fat relative to lean body mass. The NCAA and many state high school federations have recently established guidelines for weight loss and set policies for how and when a wrestler can weigh in officially.

HYPOTHERMIA

Cold weather is a frequent adjunct to many outdoor sports in which the sport itself does not require heavy protective clothing; consequently, the weather becomes a pertinent factor in injury susceptibility.[69] In most instances, the activity itself enables the athlete to increase the metabolic rate sufficiently to function physically in a normal

---

6-3

Critical Thinking E x e r c i s e

A high school football coach in southern Louisiana is concerned about the likelihood that several of his players will suffer heat-related illness during preseason football practice in the first two weeks of August. The school has recently hired an athletic trainer, and the coach has come to the athletic trainer to ask what can be done to minimize the risk of heat-related illnesses.

? What recommendations or intervention strategies can the athletic trainer implement to help the athletes avoid heat-related illnesses?

Many sports played in cold weather do not require heavy protective clothing; thus, weather becomes a factor in injury susceptibility.

Focus

Environmental conduct of sports, particularly football

I. General warning
- A. Most adverse reactions to environmental heat and humidity occur during the first few days of training.
- B. It is necessary to become thoroughly acclimatized to heat to successfully compete in hot or humid environments.
- C. Occurrence of a heat injury indicates poor supervision of the sports program.

II. Athletes who are most susceptible to heat injury
- A. Individuals unaccustomed to working in the heat.
- B. Overweight individuals, particularly large linemen.
- C. Eager athletes who constantly compete at capacity.
- D. Ill athletes who have an infection, fever, or gastrointestinal disturbance.
- E. Athletes who receive immunization injections and subsequently develop temperature elevations.

III. Prevention of heat injury
- A. Take complete medical history and provide physical examination.
  - 1. Include history of previous heat illnesses or fainting in the heat.
  - 2. Include inquiry about sweating and peripheral vascular defects.
- B. Evaluate general physical condition and type and duration of training activities for previous month.
  - 1. Extent of work in the heat.
  - 2. General training activities.
- C. Measure temperature and humidity on the practice or playing fields. (WBGT index)
  - 1. Make measurements before and during training or competitive sessions.
  - 2. Adjust activity level to environmental conditions.
    - a. Decrease activity if hot or humid.
    - b. Eliminate unnecessary clothing when hot or humid.
- D. Acclimatize athletes to heat gradually.
  - 1. Acclimatization to heat requires work in the heat.
    - a. Use recommended type and variety of warm weather workouts for preseason training.
    - b. Provide graduated training program for first seven to ten days and on other abnormally hot or humid days.
  - 2. Adequate rest intervals and fluid replacement should be provided during the acclimatization period.
- E. Monitor body weight loss during activity in the heat.
  - 1. Body fluid should be replaced as it is lost.
    - a. Allow additional fluid as desired by players.
    - b. Provide salt on training tables (no salt tablets should be taken).
    - c. Weigh athletes each day before and after training or competition.
      - (1) Treat athlete who loses excessive weight each day.
      - (2) Treat well-conditioned athlete who continues to lose weight for several days.
- F. Monitor clothing and uniforms.
  - 1. Provide lightweight clothing that is loose fitting at the neck, waist, and sleeves; use shorts and T-shirt at beginning of training.
  - 2. Avoid excessive padding and taping.
  - 3. Avoid the use of long stockings, long sleeves, double jerseys, and other excess clothing.
  - 4. Avoid the use of rubberized clothing or sweatsuits.
  - 5. Provide clean clothing daily—all items.
- G. Provide rest periods to dissipate accumulated body heat.
  - 1. Rest athletes in cool, shaded area with some air movement.
  - 2. Avoid hot brick walls or hot benches.
  - 3. Instruct athletes to loosen or remove jerseys or other garments.
  - 4. Provide fluids during the rest period.

IV. Trouble signs: stop activity!

Headache	Visual	Unsteadiness	Diarrhea	Weak, rapid	Faintness
Nausea	disturbance	Collapse	Cramps	pulse	Chill
Mental slowness	Fatigue	Unconsciousness	Seizures	Pallor	Cyanotic
Incoherence	Weakness	Vomiting	Rigidity	Flush	appearance

Figure 6-3

Low temperatures can pose serious problems for the athlete, but wind chill could be a critical factor.

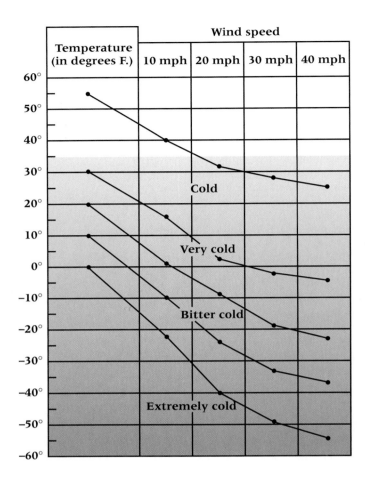

Low temperatures accentuated by wind and dampness can pose major problems for athletes.

manner and dissipate the resulting heat and perspiration through the usual physiological mechanisms.[13] An athlete may fail to warm up sufficiently or may become chilled because of relative inactivity for varying periods of time demanded by the particular sport, either during competition or training; consequently, the athlete is exceedingly prone to injury. Low temperatures alone can pose some problems, but when such temperatures are further accentuated by wind, the chill factor becomes critical (Figure 6-3).[11] For example, a runner proceeding at a pace of 10 mph directly into a wind of 5 mph creates a chill factor equivalent to a 15-mph headwind.

A third factor, dampness or wetness, further increases the risk of hypothermia. Air at a temperature of 50°F is relatively comfortable, but water at the same temperature is intolerable. The combination of cold, wind, and dampness creates an environment that easily predisposes the athlete to hypothermia.

Sixty-five percent of the heat produced by the body is lost through radiation. This loss occurs most often from the warm, vascular areas of the head and neck, which may account for as much as 50 percent of total heat loss.[59] Twenty percent of heat loss is through evaporation, of which two-thirds is through the skin and one-third is through the respiratory tract.[68]

As an athlete's muscular fatigue builds up during strenuous physical activity in cold weather, the rate of exercise begins to drop and may reach a level where the body heat loss to the environment exceeds the metabolic heat protection, resulting in definite impairment of neuromuscular responses and exhaustion.[13] A relatively small drop in body core temperature can induce shivering sufficient to materially affect an athlete's neuromuscular coordination. Shivering ceases below a body temperature of 85° to 90°F (29.4° to 32.2°C). Death is imminent if the core temperature rises to 107°F (41.6°C) or drops to between 77° and 85°F (25° and 29°C).

Prevention

Apparel for competitors must be geared to the weather.[30] The function of such apparel is to provide a semitropical microclimate for the body and to prevent chilling. Several fabrics available on the market are waterproof and windproof but permit the passage of heat and allow sweat to evaporate. The clothing should not restrict movement, should be as lightweight as possible, and should consist of material that will permit the free passage of sweat and body heat that would otherwise accumulate on the skin or the clothing and provide a chilling factor when activity ceases. The athlete should routinely dress in thin layers of clothing that can easily be added or removed as the temperature decreases or increases. Continuous adjustment of these layers will reduce sweating and the likelihood that clothing will become damp or wet. Again, wetness or dampness plays a critical role in the development of hypothermia. To prevent chilling, athletes should wear warm-up suits before exercising, during activity breaks or rest periods, and at the termination of exercise. Activity in cold, wet, and windy weather poses some problems because such weather reduces the insulating value of clothing; consequently, the individual may be unable to achieve energy levels equal to the subsequent body heat losses. Runners who wish to continue outdoor work in cold weather should use lightweight insulating clothing and, if breathing cold air seems distressful, should use ski goggles and a ski face mask or should cover the mouth and nose with a free-hanging cloth.[3]

Inadequate clothing, improper warm-up, and a high chill factor form a triad that can lead to musculoskeletal injury, chilblains, frostbite, or the minor respiratory disorders associated with lower tissue temperatures. For work or sports in temperatures below 32°F (0°C), it is advisable to add a layer of protective clothing for every 5 mph of wind.

As is true in a hot environment, athletes exercising in a cold environment need to replace fluids. Dehydration causes reduced blood volume, which means less fluid is available for warming the tissues.[58,59] Athletes performing in a cold environment should be weighed before and after practice, especially in the first two weeks of the season.[43] Severe overexposure to a cold climate occurs less often than hyperthermia does in a warm climate; however, it is still a major risk of winter sports, long-distance running in cold weather, and swimming in cold water.[30]

Dress in thin layers of clothing that can be added and removed.

Common Cold Injuries

Local cooling of the body can result in tissue damage ranging from superficial to deep. Exposure to a damp, freezing cold can cause frost nip. In contrast, exposure to dry temperatures well below freezing more commonly produces a deep, freezing type of frostbite.

Below-freezing temperatures may cause ice crystals to form between or within the cells and may eventually destroy the cell. Local capillaries can be injured, blood clots may form, and blood may be shunted away from the injury site to ensure the survival of the nonaffected tissue.

Cold injuries in sports include:
- *Frost nip*
- *Frostbite*

Frost Nip

Frost nip involves ears, nose, cheeks, chin, fingers, and toes. It commonly occurs when there is a high wind, severe cold, or both. The skin initially appears very firm, with cold, painless areas that may peel or blister in twenty-four to seventy-two hours. Affected areas can be treated early by firm, sustained pressure of the hand (without rubbing), by blowing hot breath on the spot, or if the injury is to the fingertips, by placing them in the armpits.

Frostbite

Chilblains result from prolonged and constant exposure to cold for many hours. In time, there is skin redness, swelling, tingling, and pain in the toes and fingers. This adverse response is caused by problems of peripheral circulation and can be avoided by preventing further cold exposure.

Superficial frostbite involves only the skin and subcutaneous tissue. The skin appears pale, hard, cold, and waxy. Palpating the injured area will reveal a sense of hardness but with yielding of the underlying deeper tissue structures. When rewarming, the superficial frostbite will at first feel numb, then will sting and burn. Later the area may produce blisters and be painful for a number of weeks.[41]

Deep frostbite is a serious injury indicating tissues that are frozen. This medical emergency requires immediate hospitalization. As with frost nip and superficial frostbite, the tissue is initially cold, hard, pale or white, and numb. Rapid rewarming is required, including hot drinks, heating pads, or hot water bottles that are 100° to 110°F (38° to 43°C). During rewarming, the tissue will become blotchy red, swollen, and extremely painful. Later the injury may become gangrenous, causing a loss of tissue.

ALTITUDE

Most athletic events are not conducted at high altitudes.

Most athletic events are not conducted at extreme altitudes. For example, Mexico City's elevation, which is 7,600 feet high, is considered moderate, yet at this height there is a 7 percent to 8 percent decrease in maximum oxygen uptake.[65] This loss in maximum oxygen uptake represents a 4 percent to 8 percent deterioration in an athlete's performance in endurance events, depending on the duration of effort and lack of wind resistance.[37] Often, the athlete's body compensates for this decrease in maximum oxygen uptake with corresponding tachycardia.[65] When the body is suddenly without its usual oxygen supply, hyperventilation can occur. Many of these responses result from the athlete having fewer red blood cells than necessary to adequately capture the available oxygen in the air.[20,37]

Adaptation to Altitude

A major factor in altitude adaptation is the problem of oxygen deficiency. With a reduction in barometric pressure, the partial pressure of oxygen in inspired air is also low. Under these circumstances, the existing circulating red blood cells become less saturated, depriving tissue of needed oxygen.[48]

An individual's adaptation to high altitude depends on whether he or she is a native, resident, or visitor to the area. Natives of areas with high altitudes (e.g., the Andes and Nepal) have a larger chest capacity, more alveoli, more capillaries that transport blood to tissue, and a higher red blood cell level.[20] In contrast, the resident or the individual who stays at a high altitude for months or years makes a partial adaptation. His or her later adaptation includes the conservation of glucose, an increased number of mitochondria (the sources of energy in a cell), and increased formation of hemoglobin. In the visitor or the person who is in an early stage of adaptation to high altitude, a number of responses represent a physiological struggle. The responses include increased breathing, increased heart action, increased hemoglobin in circulating blood, increased blood alkalinity, and increased myoglobin as well as changes in the distribution of blood flow and cell enzyme activity. Dehydration has also been linked to altitude sickness.[1]

There are many uncertainties about when to have an athlete go to an area of high altitude to train and compete.[12] Experts believe that having the athlete arrive two to three weeks before competition provides the best adjustment period, whereas others believe that, for psychological as well as physiological reasons, bringing in the athlete three days before competition is enough time.[65] This shorter adjustment period allows for the recovery of the acid-base balance in the blood but does not provide enough time for the athlete to achieve a significant adjustment in blood volume and maximum cardiac output.[65]

Altitude Illnesses

Coaches and athletic trainers must understand that some of their athletes may become ill when suddenly subjected to high altitudes.[74] These illnesses include acute

6-4

Critical Thinking Exercise

A track athlete from Florida is traveling to Colorado to compete in a week-long track meet. She is concerned because she will be competing at a much higher altitude than she has been training at in Florida. She wants to make certain that she has a chance to adapt to the higher altitude.

? What should the athletic trainer recommend to maximize her ability to compete at the higher altitude?

mountain sickness, pulmonary edema, and when present in some athletes, an adverse reaction to the sickle cell trait.

Acute Mountain Sickness

One out of three individuals who go from a low to a moderate altitude of 7,000 to 8,000 feet will experience mild to moderate symptoms of acute mountain sickness.[6] Symptoms include headache, nausea, vomiting, sleep disturbance, and dyspnea, which may last up to three days.[65] These symptoms have been attributed to a tissue disruption in the brain that affects the sodium and potassium balance. This imbalance can cause excess fluid retention within the cells and the subsequent occurrence of abnormal pressure.[65]

Pulmonary Edema

At an altitude of 9,000 to 10,000 feet, high-altitude pulmonary edema may occur. Characteristically, lungs at this altitude will accumulate a small amount of fluid within the alveolar walls.[65] In most individuals this fluid is absorbed in a few days, but in some it continues to collect and forms pulmonary edema. Symptoms of high-altitude pulmonary edema are dyspnea, cough, headache, weakness, and in some cases, unconsciousness.[65] The treatment of choice is to move the athlete to a lower altitude as soon as possible and give oxygen. The condition rapidly resolves once the athlete is at a lower altitude.[64]

Sickle-Cell Trait Reaction

Approximately 8 percent to 10 percent of African Americans (approximately 2 million persons) have the sickle cell trait. In most, the trait is benign. The sickle cell trait relates to an abnormality of the structure of the red blood cell and its hemoglobin content.[26] When the abnormal hemoglobin molecules become deoxygenated as a result of exercise at a high altitude, the cells tend to clump together. This process causes an abnormal sickle shape to the red blood cell, which can be destroyed easily. This condition can cause an enlarged spleen, which in some cases has been known to rupture at high altitudes.[65]

OVEREXPOSURE TO SUN

Athletes, along with coaches, athletic trainers, and other support staff, frequently spend a great deal of time outdoors in direct sunlight. Precautions to protect these individuals from overexposure to ultraviolet light by applying sunscreens are often totally ignored.

Long-Term Effects on Skin

The most serious effects of long-term exposure to ultraviolet light are premature aging of the skin and skin cancer.[24] Lightly pigmented individuals are more susceptible to these maladies. Premature aging of the skin is characterized by dryness, cracking, and a decrease in the elasticity of the skin. Skin cancer is the most common malignant tumor found in humans and has been epidemiologically and clinically associated with exposure to ultraviolet radiation. Damage to DNA is suspected as the cause of skin cancer, but the exact cause is unknown. The major types of skin cancer are basal cell carcinoma, squamous cell carcinoma, and malignant melanoma. Fortunately, the rate of cure exceeds 95 percent with early detection and treatment.[24]

Using Sunscreens

Sunscreens applied to the skin can help prevent many of the damaging effects of ultraviolet radiation. A sunscreen's effectiveness in absorbing the sunburn-inducing radiation is expressed as the sun protection factor **(SPF).** An SPF of 6 indicates that an athlete can be exposed to ultraviolet light six times longer than without a sunscreen before the skin will begin to turn red. Higher numbers provide greater protection. However, athletes who have a family or personal history of skin cancer may experience

---

6-5

Critical Thinking Exercise

A track athlete is competing in a day-long outdoor track meet. She is extremely concerned about getting sunburned and has liberally applied sunscreen with an SPF of 30 during the early morning. It is a hot, sunny day, and she is sweating heavily. She is worried that her sunscreen has worn off and asks the athletic trainer for more sunscreen. The athletic trainer hands her sunscreen with an SPF of 15 and she complains that it is not strong enough to protect her.

? What can the athletic trainer tell the athlete to assure her that she will be well protected by the sunscreen she has been given?

SPF
Sun protection factor.

significant damage to the skin even when wearing an SPF-15 sunscreen. Therefore, these individuals should wear an SPF-30 sunscreen.

Sunscreen should be worn regularly by athletes, coaches, and athletic trainers who spend time outside, particularly if the individual has a fair complexion, light hair, blue eyes, or skin that burns easily.[22] People with dark complexions should also wear sunscreens to prevent sun damage.[24]

Sun exposure causes a premature aging of skin (wrinkling, freckling, prominent blood vessels, coarsening of skin texture), induces the formation of precancerous growths, and increases the risk of developing basal and squamous cell skin cancers. Because 60 percent to 80 percent of our lifetime sun exposure is often obtained by age twenty, everyone over six months of age should use sunscreens.

Sunscreens are needed most between the months of March and November but should be used year-round. They are needed most between the hours of 10 A.M. and 4 P.M. and should be applied fifteen to thirty minutes before sun exposure. Although clothing and hats provide some protection from the sun, they are not a substitute for sunscreens (a typical white cotton T-shirt provides an SPF of only 5). Reflected sunlight from water, sand, and snow may effectively increase sun exposure and the risk of burning.

LIGHTNING SAFETY

Research indicates that lightning is the number two cause of death by weather phenomena, accounting for 110 deaths per year.[49,72] As a result of the inherent danger associated with electrical storms to athletes and staff who practice and compete outdoors, the NATA has established a position statement with specific guidelines for athletic trainers.[70] Each institution should develop a specific emergency action plan to be implemented in case of a lightning storm that includes establishing a chain of command to determine who should monitor both the weather forecast and changing weather of a threatening nature, and to determine who makes the decision both to remove from, and ultimately to return a team to, the practice field based on specific preestablished criteria.[71] If you hear thunder or see lightning, you are in immediate danger and should seek a protective shelter in an indoor facility at once. An indoor facility is recommended as the safest protective shelter. However, if an indoor facility is not available, an automobile is a relatively safe alternative. If neither of these is available, the following guidelines are recommended. Avoid standing near large trees, flagpoles, or light poles. Choose an area that is not on a hill. As a last alternative, find a ditch, ravine, or valley. At times, the only natural forewarning that might precede a strike is feeling your hair stand on end and your skin tingle. At this point, you are in imminent danger of being struck by lightning and should drop to the ground, assuming a crouched position immediately. Do not lie flat. Should a ground strike occur near you, lying flat increases the body's surface area that is exposed to the current traveling through the ground.[72] Avoid standing water (pools), showers, telephones, and metal objects at all times (metal bleachers, umbrellas, etc.).[7]

The most dangerous storms give little or no warning; thunder and lightning are not heard or seen. Lightning is always accompanied by thunder, although 20 percent to 40 percent of thunder cannot be heard because of atmospheric disturbances. The **flash-to-bang** method provides an estimation of how far away lightning is occurring.[7] From the time lightning is sighted, count the number of seconds until the bang occurs and divide by 5 to calculate the number of miles away the lightning is occurring.[60] When the flash-to-bang count is at 30 there is inherent danger, and conditions should be closely monitored. When the count is 15, everyone should leave the field immediately and seek safe shelter.[60]

Both the NATA and the National Severe Storms Service recommend that 30 minutes should pass after the last sound of thunder is heard or lightning strike is seen before resuming play.[60] This is enough time to allow the storm to pass and move out of lightning strike range. The perilous misconception that it is possible to see lightning coming and

6-6

Critical Thinking E x e r c i s e

A lacrosse team is practicing on a remote field with no indoor facility in close proximity. The weather is rapidly worsening with the sky becoming dark and the wind blowing harder. Twenty minutes are left in the practice session, and the coach is hoping to finish practice before it begins to rain. Suddenly, there is a bolt of lightning and an immediate burst of thunder.

? How should the athletic trainer manage this extremely dangerous situation?

The most dangerous storms give little or no warning.

flash-to-bang
Number of seconds from lightning flash until the sound of thunder divided by five.

Focus

have time to act before it strikes could prove to be fatal. In reality, the lightning that we see flashing is actually the return stroke flashing upward from the ground to the cloud, not downward. When you see the lightning strike, it already has hit.[72]

Focus Box: "Lightning safety" identifies guidelines that should be followed during an electrical storm.

Lightning Detectors

A lightning detector is a hand-held instrument with an electronic system to detect the presence and the distance of lightning/thunderstorm activity occurring within a 40 mile distance (Figure 6-4). It allows you to know the level of activity of the storm, and it determines whether the storm is moving towards, away, or parallel to your position. When the lightning detector detects a lightning stroke, it emits an audible warning tone and lights the range indicator allowing you to see the distance to the last, closest, detected lightning strike. Lightning detectors are under $200 and are thus an inexpensive alternative to contracting with a weather service to provide information on potentially dangerous weather conditions over a pager system.

Figure 6-4

Portable hand-held lightning detector. (Courtesy Novalynx Corp., Grass Valley, CA)

AIR POLLUTION

Air pollution is a major problem in urban areas with large industries and heavy automobile traffic. Because athletes are outside for long periods of time during training or competition, they may be more susceptible to the effects of air pollution than is a sedentary individual who remains indoors.[4] There are two types of pollution: photochemical haze and smog. Photochemical haze consists of nitrogen dioxide and stagnant air that are acted on by sunlight to produce ozone.[4] Smog is produced by the combination of carbon monoxide and sulphur dioxide, which emanates from the combustion of a fossil fuel such as coal.

Air pollution is a major problem in urban areas with large industries and heavy automobile traffic.

Ozone

Ozone is a form of oxygen in which three atoms of the element combine to form the molecule O_3. It is produced by a reaction of oxygen (O_2), nitrogen oxides, and hydrocarbon plus sunlight.[31]

When individuals are engaged in physical tasks requiring minimum effort, an increase in ozone in the air does not usually reduce functional capacity in normal work output. However, when individuals increase their work output (e.g., during exercise), their work capacity is decreased. The athlete may experience shortness of breath, coughing, chest tightness, pain during deep breathing, nausea, eye irritation, fatigue, lung irritation, and a lowered resistance to lung infections. Over a period of time, individuals may to some degree become desensitized to ozone. Asthmatics are at greater risk when ozone levels increase.

Sulfur Dioxide

Sulfur dioxide (SO_2) is a colorless gas that is a component of burning coal or petroleum. As an air contaminant it causes an increased resistance to air movement in and out of the lungs, a decreased ability of the lungs to rid themselves of foreign matter, shortness of breath, coughing, fatigue, and increased susceptibility to lung diseases. Sulfur dioxide causes an adverse effect mostly on asthmatics and other sensitive individuals. Nose breathing lessens the effects of sulfur dioxide because the nasal mucosa acts as a sulfur dioxide scrubber.[31]

Carbon Monoxide

Carbon monoxide (CO) reduces hemoglobin's ability to transport and release oxygen in the body.

Carbon monoxide (CO) is a colorless, odorless gas. In general, it reduces hemoglobin's ability to transport oxygen and restricts the release of oxygen to the tissue. Besides interfering in performance during exercise, carbon monoxide exposure interferes with various psychomotor, behavioral, and attention-related activities.[31]

Prevention

To avoid problems created by air pollution, the athlete must stop or significantly decrease physical activity during periods of high pollution. If activity is conducted, it should be performed when commuter traffic has lessened and when ambient temperature has lowered. Ozone levels rise during dawn, peak at midday, and are much reduced after the late-afternoon rush hour. Running should be avoided on roads containing a concentration of auto emissions and carbon monoxide.[31]

CIRCADIAN DYSRHYTHMIA (JET LAG)

Jet power has made it possible to travel thousands of miles in just a few hours. Athletes and athletic teams are now quickly transported from one end of the country to the other and to foreign lands. For some athletes, such travel induces a particular physiological stress, resulting in a syndrome that is identified as *circadian dysrhythmia* and that reflects a desynchronization of the athlete's biological and biophysical time clock.[29]

The term *circadian* (from the Latin *circa dies,* "about a day") implies a period of time of approximately twenty-four hours. The body maintains many cyclical mechanisms (circadian rhythms) that follow a pattern (e.g., the daily rise and fall of body temperature or the tidal ebb and flow of the cortical steroid secretion, which produces other effects on the metabolic system that are in themselves cyclical in nature). Body mechanisms adapt at varying rates to time changes. Some adjust immediately (e.g., protein metabolism), whereas others take time (e.g., the rise and fall of body temperature, which takes approximately eight days to adjust). Other body mechanisms, such as the adrenal hormones, which regulate metabolism and other body functions, may take as long as three weeks to adjust. Even intellectual proficiency, or the ability to think, clearly is cyclical.

The term *jet lag* refers to the physical and mental effects caused by traveling rapidly across several time zones.[62] It results from the disruption of both circadian rhythms and the sleep-wake cycle. As the length of travel increases over several time zones, the effects of jet lag become more profound.

Disruption of circadian rhythms has been shown to cause fatigue, headache, problems with the digestive system, and changes in blood pressure, heart rate, hormonal

6-7

Critical Thinking E x e r c i s e

A college tennis team from the West Coast must travel to the East Coast to play a scheduled match. The coach has done a lot of traveling and knows that traveling from west to east seems to be more difficult than traveling east to west. This match is important, and the tennis coach asks the athletic trainer for advice to help the athletes minimize the effects of jet lag.

? What can the athletic trainer recommend to help the athletes adjust to the new time zone in as short a time as possible?

Focus

Minimizing the effects of jet lag

- Depart for a trip well rested.
- Preadjust circadian rhythms by getting up and going to bed one hour later for each time zone crossed when traveling west and one hour earlier for each time zone crossed when traveling east.
- When traveling west, eat light meals early and heavy meals late in the day. When traveling east, eat a heavy meal earlier in the day.
- Drink plenty of fluids to avoid dehydration, which occurs because of dry, high-altitude, low-humidity cabin air.
- Consume caffeine in coffee, tea, or soda when traveling west. Caffeine should be avoided when traveling east.
- Exercise or training should be done later in the day if traveling west and earlier in the day if traveling east.
- Reset watches according to the new time zone after boarding the plane.
- If traveling west, get as much sunlight as possible on arrival.
- On arrival, immediately adopt the local time schedule for training, eating, and sleeping. Forget about what time it is where you came from.
- Avoid using alcohol before, during, and after travel.

release, endocrine secretions, and bowel habits.[73] Any of these changes may have a negative effect on athletic performance and may predispose the athlete to injury.[23,77]

Younger individuals adjust more rapidly to time zone changes than do older people, although the differences are not great. The stress induced in jet travel occurs only when flying either east or west at high speed. There is 30 percent to 50 percent faster adaptation in individuals flying westward than in individuals flying eastward.[36] In fact, flying from the west to the east has been demonstrated to decrease performance.[75] Travel north or south has no effect on the body unless several time zones are crossed in an east or west progression. The changes in time zones, illumination, and environment prove somewhat disruptive to the human physiological mechanisms, particularly when a person flies through five or more time zones, as occurs in some international travel.[36] Some people are more susceptible to the syndrome than are others, but the symptoms can be sufficiently disruptive to interfere with an athlete's ability to perform maximally in a competitive event.[40] In some cases, an athlete will become ill for a short period of time with anorexia, severe headache, blurred vision, dizziness, insomnia, or extreme fatigue. The negative effects of jet lag can be reduced by paying attention to the guidelines in *Focus Box:* "Minimizing the effects of jet lag."

SYNTHETIC TURF

Synthetic turf was first used in the Houston Astrodome in 1966 and was first marketed under the trade name AstroTurf. The artificial surface was said to be more durable, offer greater consistency, require less maintenance, be more "playable" during inclement weather, and offer greater performance characteristics such as increased speed and resiliency. Since the late 1960s, a number of companies have manufactured synthetic surfaces that are variations of AstroTurf. Today synthetic surfaces have a relatively new option in "resilient infill turf," which claims to be more similar to natural grass and is considerably less expensive than other types of synthetic turf.[13] It is made of polyethylene and polypropylene yarns that sit on a base of either sand or crumbled rubber pellets or a combination of both. The consumer can choose from a number of artificial turf products, including AstroTurf, Nexturf, FirstTurf, FieldTurf, AstroPlay, Sof-Step 200, HomeField, SpinTurf, and Avery SportsTurf.[1]

6-8

Critical Thinking Exercise

A collegiate athletic director says that he is trying to make a decision about replacing a natural grass playing field with a new synthetic playing surface. He asks the athletic trainer to provide him with recommendations relative to the incidence of injury on natural grass versus synthetic turf.

? What can the athletic trainer tell him?

There has been an ongoing debate over the advantages and disadvantages of synthetic surfaces compared to natural surfaces.[46] From an injury perspective, there is not enough conclusive evidence in the literature to indicate that a synthetic surface is more likely to cause injury than a natural surface.[19,47,48,60] Empirically, it seems that most athletes, coaches, and athletic trainers agree that injuries are more likely to occur on synthetic surfaces than on natural grass, and most of these individuals would rather practice and play on natural grass. In recent years the trend in many colleges, universities, and professional arenas has been to move away from synthetic surfaces, replacing them with natural grass. New hybrid grasses are now available that are more durable.

It has been argued that synthetic surfaces lose their inherent shock absorption capability as they age.[46] It has been demonstrated that training injuries are more likely to occur if training always occurs on artificial turf.[23] Higher speeds are said to be possible on artificial surfaces; thus, injuries involving collision can potentially be more severe because of increased force on impact.[8] A shoe that does not "stick" to the artificial surface but still provides solid footing will significantly reduce the likelihood of injury.[35]

Two injuries that seem to occur more frequently in athletes competing on an artificial surface are abrasions and turf toe (a hyperextension of the great toe). The incidence of abrasions can be greatly reduced by wearing pads on the elbows and knees. Turf toe is less likely to occur if the shoe has a stiff, firm sole.

SUMMARY

- Environmental stress can adversely affect an athlete's performance and pose a serious health problem.
- Hyperthermia is one of sport's major concerns. In times of high temperatures and humidity, athletes should always exercise caution. The key to preventing heat-related illness is rehydration, acclimatization, and common sense. Losing 2 percent or more of body weight due to fluid loss could pose a potential health problem.
- Cold weather requires athletes to wear the correct apparel and to warm up properly before engaging in sports activities. The wind chill factor must always be considered when performing. As is true in a hot environment, athletes in cold conditions must ingest adequate fluids. Extreme cold exposure can cause conditions such as frost nip, chilblains, and frostbite.
- An athlete going from a low to a high altitude in a short time may encounter problems with performance and may perhaps experience some health problems. Researchers are unsure about how much time it takes for adaptation to occur and about when to bring the athlete to the higher altitude, especially for an endurance event. Many athletic trainers believe that three days at the higher altitude will provide enough time for adaptation to occur. Others believe that a much longer time period is needed. An athlete who experiences a serious illness because of his or her presence at a particular altitude must be returned to a lower altitude as soon as possible.
- Air pollution can produce a major decrement to performance and, in some cases, can cause illness. Increased ozone levels can cause respiratory distress, nausea, eye irritation, and fatigue. Sulfur dioxide, a colorless gas, can also cause physical reactions in some athletes and can be a serious problem for asthmatics. Carbon monoxide, a colorless and odorless gas, reduces hemoglobin's ability to use oxygen and, as a result, adversely affects performance.
- Travel through different time zones can place a serious physiological stress on the athlete. This stress is called circadian dysrhythmia, or jet lag. This disruption of biological rhythm can adversely affect performance and may even produce health problems. The athletic trainer must pay careful attention to helping the athlete acclimatize to time-zone shifting.
- There is inconclusive evidence that the incidence of injury on artificial surfaces is higher than on natural surfaces, although most coaches, athletes, and athletic trainers seem to prefer practicing and playing on natural grass. Two frequently seen injuries that occur on artificial turf are turf toe and abrasions.

Websites

National Lightning Safety Institute (NLSI): http://www.lightningsafety.com/

The National Lightning Safety Institute provides consulting, education, training, and expert witnesses relating to lightning hazard mitigation.

FEMA: Extreme Heat Fact Sheet: http://www.fema.gov/library/hazards/extremeheat/heatf.shtm

Doing too much on a hot day, spending too much time in the sun, or staying too long in an overheated place can cause heat-related illnesses.

OnHealth: Heat Illness (Heat Exhaustion, Heatstroke, Heat Cramps): http://my.webmd.com/medical_information/condition_centers/default.htm

Prolonged or intense exposure to hot temperatures can cause heat-related illnesses, such as heat exhaustion, heat cramps, and heatstroke (also known as sunstroke).

A Hypothermia Treatment Technology Website: http://www.hypothermia-ca.com/

OA Guide to Hypothermia & Cold Weather Injuries: http://www.princeton.edu/~oa/safety/hypocold.shtml

National Athletic Trainers Association: http://www.nata.org

This site contains detailed position papers on heat illness, fluid replacement, and lightning safety.

Sports Turf Managers Association: www.sportsturfmanager.com

Gatorade Sport Science Institute: http://www.gssiweb.com

This site provides the most up-to-date recommendations for fluid replacement and preventing heat illnesses.

Solutions to Critical Thinking EXERCISES

6-1 The wrestler is experiencing heat exhaustion, which results from inadequate fluid replacement or dehydration. If conscious, the athlete should be forced to drink large quantities of water. By far the most rapid method of fluid replacement is for a physician to use an IV (fluids administered intravenously). It is desirable but not necessary to move the athlete to a cooler environment. The athlete should be counseled about the dangers of using diuretic medication.

6-2 The athletic trainer may suspect that the athlete is experiencing a heat stroke. The course of action includes checking the athlete's vitals (airway, breathing, circulation) and activating the emergency action plan. Remove his helmet and as much excess clothing as is appropriate. The first priority is to cool the individual down as quickly as possible by immersing him in a cold water tub. Continuously monitor his vital signs until the rescue squad arrives. The athlete's core temperature should be around 100°F before he is removed from the cold tub. If a cold tub is not available, use cold packs or cold water spray. Move the athlete into the shade or to a cooler environment, if possible.

6-3 The athletic trainer should explain to the coach that heat-related illnesses are, for the most part, preventable. The athletes should

come into preseason practice at least partially acclimatized to working in a hot, humid environment and during the first week of practice should become fully acclimatized. Temperature and humidity readings should be monitored, and practice should be modified according to conditions. Practice uniforms should maximize evaporation and minimize heat absorption to the greatest extent possible. Weight records should be maintained to identify individuals who are becoming dehydrated. Most important, the athletes must keep themselves hydrated by constantly drinking large quantities of water both during and between practice sessions.

6-4 The safest recommendation would be for the athlete to travel to Colorado two to three weeks before the event. If this arrival time is not practical, she should be in Colorado for at least three days before her first event.

6-5 The sun protection factor (SPF) indicates the sunscreen's effectiveness in absorbing the sunburn-inducing radiation. An SPF of 15 indicates that an athlete can be exposed to ultraviolet light 15 times longer than without a sunscreen before the skin will begin to turn red. Therefore the athlete needs to understand that a higher SPF does not indicate a greater degree of protection. She must simply apply the sunscreen with an SPF of 15 twice as often as would be necessary with a sunscreen with an SPF of 30.

6-6 As soon as lightning is observed, the athletic trainer should immediately end practice and get the athletes under cover. If an indoor facility is not available, automobiles are a relatively safe alternative. The athletes should avoid standing under large trees or telephone poles. As a last alternative, athletes should assume a crouched position in a ditch or ravine. If possible, athletes should avoid any standing water or metal objects around the fields.

6-7 Most important, the athletes should leave for the trip well rested. The day before leaving, the athletes should go to bed and get up three hours earlier than normal. Athletes should reset their watches according to the new time zone once they board the plane. During the trip they should drink plenty of fluids to prevent dehydration, but they should avoid caffeine. Their largest meal should be eaten earlier in the day. On arrival, athletes should immediately adopt the local time schedule for training, eating, and sleeping, and they should get as much sunlight as possible. Training sessions should be done earlier in the day.

6-8 The athletic trainer should inform the athletic director that the trend seems to be moving toward natural grass fields. The research data collected over the years has not clearly indicated that there is a difference in injury rates between natural grass and synthetic turf. However, it does seem that most athletes, coaches, and athletic trainers would prefer natural turf. It should also be stressed that the newer synthetic surfaces are more like natural grass and may perhaps warrant additional investigation.

REVIEW QUESTIONS AND CLASS ACTIVITIES

1. How do temperature and humidity cause heat disorders?
2. What steps should be taken to avoid heat disorders?
3. Describe the symptoms and signs of the most common heat disorders.
4. How is heat lost from the body to produce hypothermia?
5. What should an athlete do to prevent heat loss?
6. Identify the physiological basis for the body's susceptibility to a cold disorder.

7. Describe the symptoms and signs of the major cold disorders affecting athletes.

8. How should athletes protect themselves from the effects of ultraviolet radiation from the sun?

9. What precautions can be taken to minimize the possibility of injury during an electrical storm?

10. What concerns should an athletic trainer have when athletes are to perform an endurance sport at high altitudes?

11. What altitude illnesses might be expected among some athletes, and how should those illnesses be managed?

12. What adverse effects could high air concentrations of ozone, sulfur dioxide, and carbon monoxide have on the athlete? How should they be dealt with?

13. How can the adverse effects of circadian dysrhythmia be avoided or lessened?

14. What are two common injuries in athletes who compete on artificial turf?

REFERENCES

1. A dehydration link to altitude sickness?; *Physician Sportsmed* 30(10):13, 2002.

2. American College of Sports Medicine: position stand on exercise and fluid replacement, *Med and Sci Sports Exerc* 28(17), 1996.

3. Armstrong LE, Epstein Y, Greenleaf JE: Heat and cold illnesses during distance running, *Med Sci Sports Exerc* 28(12), 1996.

4. Atkinson G: Air pollution and exercise, *Sports Exercise and Injury* 3(1):2, 1997.

5. Baxter R, Moore J: Diagnosis and Treatment of Acute Exertional Rhabdomyolysis, *J Ortho Sports Phys Ther* 33(3):124, 2003.

6. Bellis F: Acute mountain sickness: an unexpected management problem, *British Journal of Sports Medicine* 36(2):147, 2002.

7. Bennett B: A model lightning safety policy for athletics, *J Ath Train* 32(3):251, 1997.

8. Bergeron MF: Averting heat cramps, *Physician Sportsmed* 30(11):14, 2002.

9. Bernard TE: Risk management for preventing heat illness in athletes, *Athletic Therapy Today* 1(4):19, 1996.

10. Binkley H, Beckett J, Casa D: National Athletic Trainers' Association position statement: exertional heat illnesses, *J Ath Train* 37(3):329, 2002.

11. Bodine KL: Avoiding hypothermia: caution, forethought and preparation, *Sports Medicine Alert* 6(1):6, 2000.

12. Bovard R, Schoene RB, Wappes JR: Don't let altitude sickness bring you down, *Physician Sportsmed* 23(2):87, 1995.

13. Brukner P: Exercise in the cold. In Brukner P, editor: *Clinical sports medicine*, ed 2, Sydney, McGraw-Hill, 2002.

14. Brzozowski-Gardner C: New options under foot. *Athletic Management* 13(3):47, 2001.

15. Casa DJ, Armstrong LE, Hillman S: National Athletic Trainers' Association position statement: fluid replacement for athletes, *J Ath Train* 35(2):212, 2000.

16. Casa DJ: Exercise in the heat. I. Fundamentals of thermal physiology, performance implications, and dehydration, *J Ath Train* 34(3):246, 1999.

17. Casa DJ: Exercise in the heat. II. Critical concepts in rehydration, exertional heat illnesses, and maximizing athletic performance, *J Ath Train* 34(3):253, 1999.

18. Clements J, Casa DJ, Knight C: Ice-water immersion and cold-water immersion provide similar cooling rates in runners with exercise-induced hyperthermia, *J Ath Train* 37(2):146, 2002.

19. Conklin AR: Grass gets greener: Division 1-A football programs are gradually switching from synthetic turf to grass—and the reasons behind the shift may surprise you, *Sports Med Update* 15(1):11, 2000.

20. Coote JH: Medicine and mechanisms in altitude sickness: recommendations, *Sports Med* 20(3):148, 1995.

21. Coyle E: Fluid and carbohydrate replacement during exercise: how much and why? *Sports Science Exchange* 7(50):1, 1994.

22. Davis JL: Sun and active patients: preventing cumulative skin damage, *Physician Sportsmed* 28(7):79, 2000.

23. Davis JO et al: *Jet lag and athletic performance*, Colorado Springs, 1986, United States Olympic Committee Sports Medicine Council.

24. Davis M: Ultraviolet therapy. In Prentice W, editor: *Therapeutic modalities in sports medicine*, St. Louis, 2003, McGraw-Hill.

25. Ehlers G, Ball T, Liston L: Creatine kinase levels are elevated during 2-a-day practices in collegiate football players, *J Ath Train* 37(2):151, 2002.

26. Eichner ER: Sickle cell trait, exercise, and altitude, *Physician Sportsmed* 14(11):144, 1986.

27. Epstein Y, Moran D, Shapiro Y: Exertional heat stroke: a case series, *Med Sci Sports Exerc* 31(2):224, 1999.

28. Folinsbee LJ: Air pollution and exercise. In Welsh RP, Shephard RJ, editors: *Current therapy in sports medicine 1985–1986*, Philadelphia, 1985, Decker.

29. French J: Circadian rhythms, jet lag, and the athlete. In Torg J, Shephard R, editors: *Current therapy in sports medicine*, St Louis, 1995, Mosby.

30. Fritz R, Perrin D: Cold exposure injuries: prevention and treatment. In Ray R, editor: *Clinics in sports medicine*, Philadelphia, 1989, Saunders.

31. Gong H: How pollution and airborne allergens affect exercise, *Physician Sportsmed* 23(7):35, 1995.

32. Grose K, Mickey C, Bierhals A: Conditioning injuries associated with artificial turf in two preseason football training programs, *J Ath Train* 32(4):304, 1997.

33. Gutierrez G: Solar injury and heat illness, *Physician Sportsmed* 23(7):43, 1995.

34. Harrelson GL, Fincher L, Robinson J: Acute exertional rhabdomyolysis and its relationship to sickle cell trait, *J Ath Train* 30(4):309, 1995.

35. Heidt RS, Dormer SG, Crawley PW: Differences in friction and torsional resistance in athletic shoe–turf surface interfaces, *Am J Sports Med* 24(6):834, 1996.

36. Herbert DL: Does "jet lag" for teams traveling west-to-east adversely affect performance? *Sports Med Stand Malpract Report* 8(3):43, 1996.

37. Hoffman J: Exercise at altitude. In Hoffman J, editor: *Physiological aspects of sport training and performance*, Champaign, Ill., Human Kinetics, 2002.

38. Hunter SL et al: Malignant hyperthermia in a college football player, *Physician Sportsmed* 15(12):77, 1987.

39. Inter-Association Task Force on Exertional Heat Illnesses Consensus Statement, *NATA News* 6:24, 2003.

40. Johnson R, Tulin B: *Travel fitness*, Champaign, Ill, 1995, Human Kinetics.

41. Kanzanbach TL, Dexter WW: Cold injuries: protecting your patients from the dangers of hypothermia and frostbite, *Post Graduate Medicine* 105(1):72, 1999.

42. Kay D, Marino FE: Fluid ingestion and exercise hyperthermia: implications for performance, thermoregulation, metabolism, and development of fatigue, *Journal of Sports Sciences* 18(2):71, 2000.

43. Kleiner, DM: A new exertional heat illness scale. *Athletic Therapy Today* 7(6):65, 2002.

44. Knochel JP: Management of heat conditions, *Athletic Therapy Today* 1(4):30, 1996.

45. Kozack JK, MacIntyre DL: Malignant hyperthermia, *Phys Ther* 81:945, 2001.

46. Kraeger DR: Playing surfaces in sports. In Baker CL et al, editors: *The Hughston Clinic sports medicine book*, Baltimore, 1995, Williams & Wilkins.

47. Lemack L: The artificial turf debate. *Sports Med Update* 15(1):14, 2000.

48. Levine B, Stray-Gundersen J: Exercise at high altitudes. In Torg J, Shephard R, editors: *Current therapy in sports medicine*, St Louis, 1995, Mosby.

49. Lightning casualties on the rise in recreational and sports settings, *Athletic therapy* 6(5):33, 2001.

50. McArdle WD, Katch FI, Katch VL: *Exercise physiology,* Philadelphia, 2001, Lea & Febiger.

51. McCann DJ, Adams WC: Wet bulb globe temperature index and performance in competitive distance runners, *Med Sci Sports Exerc* 29(7):955, 1997.

52. Mellion MB, Shelton GL: Thermoregulation, heat illness, and safe exercise in the heat. In Mellion MB, editor: *Office sports medicine,* ed 2, Philadelphia, 1996, Hanley & Belfus.

53. Montain SJ, Maughan RJ, Sawka MN: Fluid replacement strategies for exercise in hot weather, *Athletic Therapy Today* 1(4):24, 1996.

54. Moss RI: Another look at sudden death and exertional hyperthermia. *Athletic Therapy Today* 7(3):44, 2002.

55. Murray B: Fluid replacement: the American College of Sports Medicine position stand. *Sports Science Exchange* 9(4):1, 1996.

56. Murray R: Dehydration, hyperthermia, and athletes: science and practice, *J Ath Train* 31(3):248, 1996.

57. Murray R: Guidelines for fluid replacement during exercise. *Australian Journal of Nutrition and Dietetics* 53(4 suppl):S17, 1996.

58. Murray R: Practical advice for exercising in cold weather. In Murray R: *Endurance training for performance,* Barrington, Ill, 1995, Gatorade Sports Science Institute.

59. *NCAA sports medicine handbook, 2004–2005,* Indianapolis, 2004, National Collegiate Athletic Association.

60. Noncontact knee injuries in the NFL: the role of field surface and footwear. *Sports Med Digest* 19(4):37, 1997.

61. Pandolf K: Avoiding heat illness during exercise. In Torg J, Shephard R, editors: *Current therapy in sports medicine,* St Louis, 1995, Mosby.

62. Reilly T, Atkinson G, Waterhouse J: Travel fatigue and jet lag, *Journal of Sports Sciences* 15(3):365, 1997.

63. Sandor RP: Heat illness: on-site diagnosis and cooling. *Physician Sportsmed* 25(6):35, 1997.

64. Schoene RB, Bracker MD: High-altitude pulmonary edema: the disguised killer, *Physician Sportsmed* 16(8):103, 1988.

65. Shephard RJ: Adjustment to high altitude. In Welsh RP, Shephard RJ, editors: *Current therapy in sports medicine 1985–1986,* Philadelphia, 1985, Decker.

66. Sparling PB, Milford-Stafford M: Keeping sports participants safe in hot weather, *Physician Sportsmed* 27(7):27, 1999.

67. Thein L: Environmental conditions affecting the athlete, *J Orthop Sports Phys Ther* 21(3):158, 1995.

68. Thompson RL, Hayward JS: Wet-cold exposure and hypothermia: thermal and metabolic responses to prolonged exercise in rain, *J App Physiol* 81(3):1128, 1996.

69. Vellerand A: Exercise in the cold. In Torg J, Shephard R, editors: *Current therapy in sports medicine,* St Louis, 1995, Mosby.

70. Walsh K, Bennett B, Cooper M: National Athletic Trainers' Association position statement: lightning safety for athletics and recreation, *J Ath Train* 35(4):471, 2000.

71. Walsh K, Hanley M, Graner S: A survey of lightning policy in selected division I colleges, *J Ath Train* 32(3):206, 1997.

72. Walters F: Position stand on lightning and thunder: the Athletic Health Care Services of the District of Columbia Public Schools, *J Ath Train* 28(3):201, 1993.

73. Waterhouse J: Identifying some determinants of "jet lag" and its symptoms: a study of athletes and other travellers. *British Journal of Sports Medicine* 36(1):54, 2002.

74. White-Clergerie AM: Mountaineering without oxygen: courting death? *Physician Sportsmed* 15(3):38, 1987.

75. Worthen JB, Wasde CE: Direction of travel and visiting team athletic performance: support for a circadian dysrhythmia hypothesis, *Journal of Sport Behavior* 22(2):279, 1999.

76. www.lycos.com

77. Youngstedt SD, O'Connor PJ: The influence of air travel on athletic performance, *Sports Med* 28(3):197, 1999.

ANNOTATED BIBLIOGRAPHY

Haymes EM, Wells CL: *Environment and human performance,* Champaign, Ill, 1986, Human Kinetics.

This text examines sports performance during a variety of environmental conditions. Two hundred and fifty references are reported.

Strauss RH, editor: *Sports medicine,* Philadelphia, 1996, Saunders.

This book provides four pertinent chapters on the subject of environmental disorders that could affect the athlete.

Johnson R, Tulin B: *Travel fitness.* Champaign, Ill, 1995, Human Kinetics.

Chapters include health and fitness in transit; coping with jet lag; getting to sleep; taking your workout on the road; avoiding excess baggage; how to eat right on your next trip; managing your travel stress; and coming home strong.

NCAA sports medicine handbook, 2004–2005, Indianapolis, 2005. National Collegiate Athletic Association.

This handbook contains guidelines and recommendations for preventing heat illness and hypohydration, for cold, for stress, and for lightning safety.

Maughan R, Murray R: *Sports drinks: basic science and practical aspects,* Boca Raton, Fla, 2001, CRC Press.

Provides a review of current knowledge on issues relating to the formulation of sports drinks and the physiological responses to their ingestion during physical activity.

Graver D, Armstrong, L: *Exertional heat illness,* Champaign, Ill, 2003, Human Kinetics.

This text focuses on all aspects of heat illness and is a good resource for the athletic trainer.

Chapter 7

Protective Gear and Sports Equipment

When you finish this chapter you should be able to

- Fit selected protective equipment properly (e.g., football helmets, shoulder pads, and running shoes).
- Differentiate between good and bad features of selected protective devices.
- Contrast the advantages and disadvantages of customized versus off-the-shelf foot and ankle protective devices.
- Rate the protective value of various materials used in sports to make pads and orthotic devices.
- List the steps in making a customized foam pad with a thermomoldable shell.

Because of the nature of sports activity, injuries often occur. One of the main responsibilities of the athletic trainer is to try to minimize the likelihood of injury. A number of factors either singly or collectively can contribute to the incidence of injury. Certainly the selection, fitting, and maintenance of protective equipment are critical in injury prevention. Thus it is essential that the athletic trainer have some knowledge about the types of protective equipment available for a particular sport and how that equipment should best be fitted and maintained to reduce the possibility of athletic injury.[44]

This protection is particularly important in direct contact and collision sports such as football, hockey, and lacrosse, but it can also be important in indirect contact sports such as basketball and soccer. When protective sports equipment is selected and purchased, a major commitment is made to safeguard athletes' health and welfare.

SAFETY STANDARDS FOR SPORTS EQUIPMENT AND FACILITIES

There is serious concern about the standards for protective sports equipment, particularly material durability standards. These concerns include who should set the standards, the mass production of equipment, equipment testing methods, and requirements for wearing protective equipment. Standards are also needed for protective equipment maintenance, repair, and replacement. Too often, old, worn-out, and ill-fitting equipment is passed down from the varsity players to the younger and often less-experienced players, compounding their risk of injury.[47] It is critical for those responsible for purchasing athletic equipment to be less concerned with the color, look, and style of a piece of equipment and more concerned with its ability to prevent injury.[51] Many national organizations are addressing these issues. Engineering, chemistry, biomechanics, anatomy, physiology, physics, computer science, and other related disciplines are applied to solve problems inherent in safety standardization of sports equipment and facilities. *Focus Box:* "Equipment regulatory agencies" lists agencies that regulate protective sports equipment.

LEGAL CONCERNS IN USING PROTECTIVE EQUIPMENT

As with other aspects of sports participation, there is increasing litigation related to the use of protective equipment. Both manufacturers and those who purchase sports

Old, worn-out, poorly-fitted equipment should never be passed down to younger, less-experienced players because it compounds their chances for injury.

Focus

Equipment regulatory agencies

American National Standards Institute
1819 L Street NW
Washington, DC 20036
(202) 293-8020
http://www.ansi.org

American Society for Testing Materials
100 Barr Harbor Drive
West Conshohocken, PA 19428-2959
(610) 832-9585
http://www.astm.org

Athletic Equipment Manufacturers Association
Dorothy Cutting
Cornell University Athletic Department
P.O. Box 729
Ithaca, NY 14851
(607) 255-4115
http://www.wisc.edu/ath/aema/

Hockey Equipment Certification Council
18103 Trans Canada Highway
Kirkland, QC H9J324
Canada
(514) 697-9900
http://www.hecc.net

National Athletic Trainers' Association
2952 Stemmons Freeway
Dallas, TX 75247-6196
(214) 637-6282
http://www.nata.org

National Collegiate Athletic Association
700 W. Washington Street
P.O. Box 6222
Indianapolis, IN 46206-6222
http://www.ncaa.org

National Association of Intercollegiate Athletics
6120 S. Yale Avenue
Suite 1450
Tulsa, OK 74136
(918) 494-8828
http://www.naia.org

National Federation of State High School
   Athletic Associations
P.O. Box 690
Indianapolis, IN 46200
(317) 972-6900
http://www.nfhs.org

National Operating Committee on Standards
   for Athletic Equipment
P.O. Box 12290
Overland, KS 66282-2290
http://www.nocsae.org

Sporting Goods Manufacturers Association
200 Castlewood Drive
North Palm Beach, FL 33418
(561) 842-4100
http://sgma@ix.netcom.com

U.S. Consumer Product Safety Commission
4330 East-West Highway
Bethesda, MD 20814-4408
(301) 504-0990
http://www.cpsc.gov

equipment must foresee all possible uses and misuses of the equipment and must warn the user of any potential risks inherent in using or misusing that equipment.

If an injury occurs as the result of an athlete using a piece of equipment that is determined to be defective or inadequate for its intended purpose, the manufacturer is considered liable. If a piece of protective equipment is modified in any way by an athlete, coach, or athletic trainer (e.g., removing some pads from inside a football helmet), the liability on the part of the manufacturer is voided, and the individual who modified the equipment becomes liable. *The best way for an athletic trainer to avoid litigation is to follow exactly the manufacturer's instructions for using and maintaining protective equipment.*

If an athletic trainer modifies a piece of equipment and an athlete wearing that equipment is injured, it is likely that any lawsuit would involve both the athletic trainer individually and the employing institution. This becomes a case of tort (described in Chapter 3) in which the injured athlete must show that the athletic trainer

Focus

Guidelines for selecting, purchasing, and fitting protective gear and sports equipment to help minimize liability

- Buy sports equipment from reputable manufacturers.
- Buy the safest equipment that resources will permit.
- Make sure that all equipment is assembled correctly.
- Ensure that the person who assembles equipment is competent to do so and follows the manufacturer's instructions to the letter.
- Maintain all equipment properly, according to the manufacturer's guidelines.
- Use equipment only for the purpose for which it was designed.
- If an athlete is wearing some type of immobilization device (i.e., cast, brace), make certain that this does not violate the rules of that sport.[15]
- Warn athletes who use the equipment about all possible risks that using the equipment could entail.
- Use great caution in constructing or customizing of any piece of equipment.
- Do not use defective equipment.
- Routinely inspect all equipment for defects and render all defective equipment unusable.

was negligent in his or her decision to alter a piece of equipment and that the negligence resulted in injury. The athletic trainer would then be legally liable for that action. (See *Focus Box:* "Guidelines for selecting, purchasing, and fitting protective gear and sports equipment to help minimize liability.")

EQUIPMENT RECONDITIONING AND RECERTIFICATION

The National Operating Committee on Standards for Athletic Equipment (NOCSAE) is an organization that has established voluntary test standards to reduce head injuries by establishing minimum safety requirements for football helmets/face masks, baseball/softball batting helmets, baseballs and softballs, and lacrosse helmets/face masks. These standards are adopted by various regulatory bodies for sports, including the NCAA and the National Federation of State High School Associations (NFSHSA). Factors such as the type of helmet and the amount and intensity of usage will determine the condition of each helmet over a period of time. The NOCSAE helmet standard is not a warranty, but simply a statement that a particular helmet model met the requirements of performance tests when it was manufactured or reconditioned. NOCSAE does recommend that the consumer adhere to a program of periodically having used helmets reconditioned and recertified. Because of the difference in the amount and intensity of usage on each helmet, the consumer should use discretion regarding the frequency with which certain helmets are to be reconditioned and recertified. Helmets which regularly undergo the reconditioning and recertification process can meet standard performance requirements for many seasons, depending on the model and usage. *Focus Box:* "Purchasing and reconditioning helmets" provides some guidelines.

USING OFF-THE-SHELF VERSUS CUSTOM PROTECTIVE EQUIPMENT

"Off-the-shelf" equipment is premade and packaged by the manufacturer and when taken out of the package may be used immediately without modification. Examples of off-the-shelf equipment would be neoprene sleeves, sorbethane shoe inserts, and protective ankle braces. Customized equipment is constructed according to the individual characteristics of the athlete. Using off-the-shelf items may cause problems with sizing and exact fit. In contrast, a custom-made piece of equipment can be specifically sized and made to fit the protective and support needs of the individual.

7-1

An athletic training student must acquire a basic understanding of protective sports equipment.

? What competencies in protective sports equipment must student athletic trainers have?

Focus

Guidelines for purchasing and reconditioning helmets

- Purchase only NOCSAE-approved helmets.
- Purchase helmets for the appropriate skill level. For example, do not purchase youth helmets for high school football.
- Assign a code number to each helmet purchased and record the date of purchase.
- Fit helmets according to manufacturer's recommendations.
- Recheck helmets for proper fit during the season.
- Review written warranty information and comply with manufacturer's requirement(s) for cleaning/reconditioning/recertification.
- Replace or repair broken or damaged helmets before returning to service.
- Develop a written accounting of player use, inspections, reconditioning, recertification and disposal of each helmet.
- Clean helmets according to manufacturer's recommendations on a regular schedule during the season and at the end of the season prior to off-season storage.
- Recertify/recondition each football helmet according to manufacturer's warranty.
- Recertify/recondition helmets every two years using a certified NOCSAE-approved vendor if no warranty exists or after the warranty expires.

HEAD PROTECTION

Direct collision sports such as football and hockey require special protective equipment, especially for the head. Football provides more frequent opportunities for body contact than does hockey, but hockey players generally move faster and therefore create greater impact forces. Besides direct head contact, hockey has the added injury elements of swinging sticks and fast-moving pucks. Other sports using fast-moving projectiles are baseball, with its pitched ball and swinging bat, lacrosse, and track and field, with the javelin, discus, and shot, which can also produce serious head injuries.[12]

Football Helmets

NOCSAE has developed standards for football helmet certification. An approved helmet must protect against concussive forces that may injure the brain. Collisions that cause concussions are usually with another player or the turf.[35]

Schools must provide the athlete with quality equipment, especially football helmets. All helmets must have NOCSAE certification. However, a helmet that is certified is not necessarily completely fail-safe. Athletes as well as their parents must be apprised of the dangers that are inherent in any sport, particularly football.[35]

To make this danger especially clear, NOCSAE has adopted the following recommended warning to be placed on all football helmets:

> WARNING: Do not strike an opponent with any part of this helmet or face mask. This is a violation of football rules and may cause you to suffer severe brain or neck injury, including paralysis or death. Severe brain or neck injury may also occur accidentally while playing football. NO HELMET CAN PREVENT ALL SUCH INJURIES. USE THIS HELMET AT YOUR OWN RISK.

Each player's helmet must have this visible, exterior warning label or a similar one ensuring that players have been made aware of the risks involved in the game of American football. The warning label must be attached to each helmet by both the manufacturer and the reconditioner.[25] It is important to have each player read this warning, after which it is read aloud by the equipment manager. The athlete then should sign a statement agreeing that he or she understands this warning.

There are a variety of different football helmets available on the market (Figure 7-1), although the number of companies producing these helmets has decreased significantly

Football helmets must withstand repeated blows that are of high mass and low velocity.

7-2

Critical Thinking E x e r c i s e

Freshman or junior varsity high school football players are issued their equipment. These athletes and their parents know very little about the equipment's potential for preventing injury. The athletic trainer is given the responsibility to reduce legal liability by educating the players and their parents about the equipment safety limits.

? What steps should the athletic trainer take?

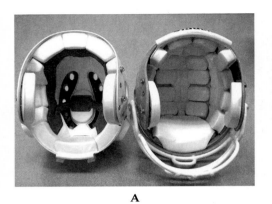

A

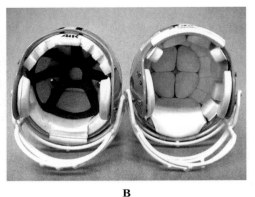

B

C

Figure 7-1

A, B, The air- and fluid-filled padded football helmets.
C, Helmet air pump.

over the years. This decrease in the number of helmet manufacturers can be attributed primarily to the number of lawsuits and liability cases that have forced many companies out of business.

The lightweight Revolution helmet from Riddell marks the first significant structural change in football helmet design in nearly 25 years (Figure 7-2).[40] The protective shell has been computer designed and extends to the jaw area to provide protection to the side of the head and the jaw as well as improved front-to-back fit and stability. The distance between the helmet shell and the head has been increased. The padding inflates to provide a custom fit to every player's head shape. The face guard system is designed to isolate the attachment points of the face guard from the shell, thus reducing jarring to the player from low-level impacts to the face guard.

Fitting a Football Helmet

When fitting a football helmet, always wet the player's hair to simulate playing conditions; this makes the initial fitting easier. Closely follow the manufacturer's directions for a proper fit. (See *Focus Box:* "Properly fitting the helmet.") The football helmet must be routinely checked for proper fit, especially in the first few days that it is worn. A check for snugness should be made by inserting a credit card between the head and the liner. Fit is proper when the credit card is resisted firmly when moved back and forth. If air bladder helmets are used by a team that travels to a different altitude and air pressure, the helmet fit must be routinely rechecked.

Chin straps are also important in maintaining the proper head and helmet relationship. Three basic types of chin straps are in use today: a two-snap, a four-snap, and a six-snap strap. Many coaches prefer the four-snap chin strap because it keeps

Figure 7-2

The Revolution helmet features a new design and different shape for football helmets. (Courtesy Riddell Inc.)

Focus

Properly fitting the helmet

In general, the helmet should adhere to the following fit standards:

- The helmet should fit snugly around all parts of the player's head (front, sides, and crown), and there should be no gaps between the pads and the head or face.
- It should cover the base of the skull. The pads placed at the back of the neck should be snug but not to the extent of discomfort.
- It should not come down over the eyes. It should set (front edge) ¾ inch (1.91 cm) above the player's eyebrows (approximately two finger widths).
- The ear holes should match.
- It should not shift when manual pressure is applied.
- It should not recoil on impact.
- The chin strap should be an equal distance from the center of the helmet. Straps must keep the helmet from moving up and down or side to side.
- The cheek pads should fit snugly against the sides of the face.
- The face mask should be attached securely to the helmet, allowing a complete field of vision, and should be positioned three finger widths from the nose.

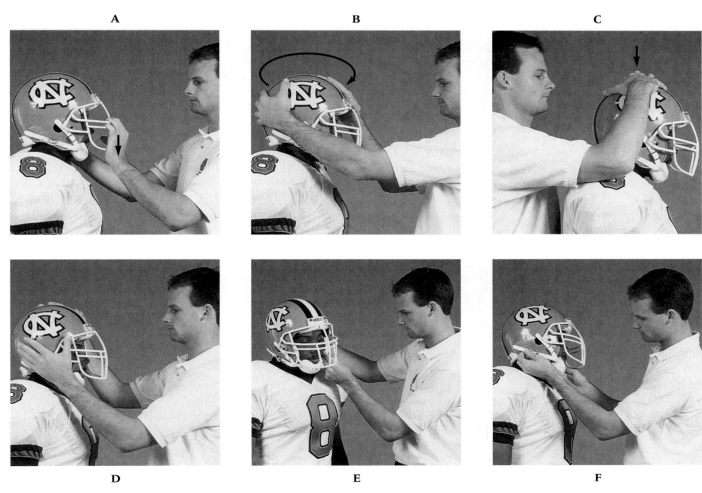

Figure 7-3

Fitting a football helmet. **A,** Pull down on face mask; helmet must not move. **B,** Turn helmet to position on the athlete's head. **C,** Push down on helmet; there must be no movement. **D,** Try to rock helmet back and forth; there must be no movement. **E,** Check for a snug jaw pad fit. **F,** Proper adjustment of the chin strap is necessary to ensure proper helmet fit.

Figure 7-4

Ice hockey helmets.

the helmet from tilting forward and backward. The chin strap should always be locked so that it cannot be released by a hard external force to the helmet (Figure 7-3).

Jaw pads are also essential to keep the helmet from rocking laterally. They should fit snugly against the player's cheekbones. Certification of a helmet's ability to withstand the forces of the game is of no avail if the helmet is not properly fitted or maintained.

Ice Hockey Helmets

Like football helmets, ice hockey helmets have been upgraded and standardized.[35] Blows to the head in ice hockey, in contrast to football, are usually singular rather than multiple. An ice hockey helmet must withstand not only high-velocity impacts (e.g., being hit with a stick or a puck, which produces low mass and high velocity) but also the high-mass–low-velocity forces produced by running into the boards or falling on the ice. In each instance, the hockey helmet, like the football helmet, must be able to disperse the impact over a large surface area through a firm exterior shell and, at the same time, be able to decelerate forces that act on the head through a proper energy-absorbing liner. It is essential for all hockey players to wear protective helmets that carry the stamp (Figure 7-4) of approval from the Canadian Standards Association (CSA).

Baseball/Softball Batting Helmets

Like ice hockey helmets, the baseball/softball batting helmet must withstand high-velocity impacts.[35] Unlike football and ice hockey, baseball and softball have not produced a great deal of data on batting helmets. It has been suggested, however, that baseball and softball helmets do little to adequately dissipate the energy of the ball during impact (Figure 7-5). A possible solution is to add external padding or to improve the helmet's suspension. The use of a helmet with an ear flap can afford some additional protection to the batter. Each runner and on-deck batter is required to wear a baseball or softball helmet that carries the NOCSAE stamp, which is similar to the warning on football helmets.

Figure 7-5

There is some question about how well baseball batting helmets protect against high-velocity impacts. **A,** Batters helmet. **B,** Catcher's helmet and mask.

A B

Cycling Helmets

Unlike other helmets discussed, cycling helmets are designed to protect the head during one single impact. Football, hockey, and baseball helmets are more durable and can survive repeated impacts. Many states require the use of cycling helmets, especially by adolescents (Figure 7-6).

Soccer Headgear

Recently several companies have been actively marketing headgear to be worn by soccer players for the purpose of reducing concussions and other head injuries that occur from heading a soccer ball.[9] The headgear is essentially a headband with a piece of foam in the front that is about 1½ to 2 inches wide. To date there are no studies that demonstrate that this headgear is effective in reducing the incidence of concussions or other head injuries. It is far more likely that a soccer player will get a concussion from hitting his or her head on another player, the goalpost, or the ground rather than from heading a soccer ball.

FACE PROTECTION

Devices that provide face protection fall into five categories: full face guards, throat protection, mouth guards, ear guards, and eye protection devices.

Face Guards

Face guards are used in a variety of sports to protect against flying or carried objects during a collision with another player (Figure 7-7). Since the adoption of face guards and mouth guards for use in football, the incidence of facial injuries (i.e. lacerations, nose fractures, eye injuries, etc.) has dramatically decreased. However, the number of concussions and, to some extent, neck injuries has increased, because the head is more often used to make initial contact. The catcher in baseball, the goalie in hockey, and the lacrosse player should all be adequately protected against facial injuries, particularly lacerations and fractures (Figure 7-8).

A variety of face masks and bars is available to the player, depending on the position played and the degree of protection needed.[20] In football, no face guard should have less than two bars. Proper mounting of the face mask and bars is imperative for maximum safety. All mountings should be made in such a way that the bar attachments are flush with the helmet. A 3-inch (7.62 cm) space should exist between the top of the face guard and the lower edge of the helmet. No helmet should be drilled more than one time on each side, and this drilling must be done by a factory-authorized

Figure 7-6

Cycling helmet.

In sports, the face may be protected by:
- Face guards
- Mouth guards
- Ear guards
- Eye protection devices
- Throat protection devices

Figure 7-7

Sports such as fencing require complete face protection.

Figure 7-8

A, Football face mask.
B, Baseball catcher's face mask.
C, Ice hockey face mask.
D, Lacrosse face mask.

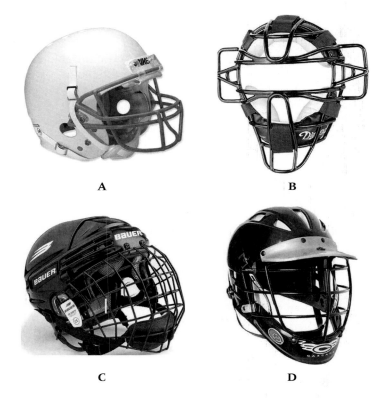

reconditioner. Attachment of a bar or face mask not specifically designed for the helmet can invalidate the manufacturer's warranty.

Ice hockey face masks have been shown to reduce the incidence of facial injuries. In high school, face masks are required not just for the goalie but for all players. Helmets should be equipped with commercial plastic-coated wire mask guards, which must meet standards set by the Hockey Equipment Certification Council (HECC) and the American Society for Testing Materials (ASTM).[25] The openings in the guard must be small enough to prevent a hockey stick from entering. Plastic guards such as polycarbonate face shields have been approved by the HECC, ASTM, and the CSA Committee on Hockey Protective Equipment. The rule also requires that goalkeepers wear commercial throat protectors in addition to face protectors. The National Federation of High School Associations (NFHSA) rule is similar to the NCAA rule that requires players to wear face guards.

Throat (Laryngotracheal) Protection

A laryngotracheal injury, though relatively uncommon, can be fatal.[35] Baseball catchers, lacrosse goalies, and ice hockey goalies are most at risk. Throat protection should be mandatory for these sports (Figure 7-9).

Mouth Guards

A properly fitted mouth guard protects the teeth, absorbs blows to the chin, and can prevent concussion.

The majority of dental traumas can be prevented if the athlete wears a correctly fitted, customized, intraoral mouth guard (Figure 7-10).[31,36] In addition to protecting the teeth, the intraoral mouth guard absorbs the shock of chin blows and helps prevent a possible cerebral concussion.[2] Mouth guards also serve to minimize lacerations to lips and cheeks and fractures to the mandible. The mouth protector should give the athlete proper and tight fit, comfort, unrestricted breathing, and unimpeded speech during competition. A loose mouthpiece will soon be ejected onto the ground or left unused in the locker room.[2] The athlete's air passages should not be obstructed in any way by the mouthpiece. It is best when the mouthpiece is retained on the upper jaw and projects backward only as far as the last molar, thus permitting speech. Maximum

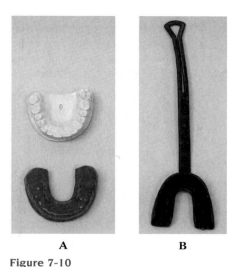

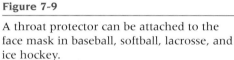

A   B

Figure 7-9

A throat protector can be attached to the face mask in baseball, softball, lacrosse, and ice hockey.

Figure 7-10

Mouthpieces. **A,** Custom fit from a mold and **B,** heat moldable.

protection is afforded when the mouth guard is composed of a flexible, resilient material and is formed to fit to the teeth and upper jaw.[30]

Cutting down mouth guards to cover only the front teeth should never be permitted. This invalidates the manufacturer's warranty against dental injuries, and a cut-down mouth guard can potentially become dislodged and lead to an obstructed airway.

The three types of mouth guards generally used in sports are the stock variety, the commercial mouth guard formed after submersion in boiling water, and the custom fabricated type, which is formed over a mold made from an impression of the athlete's maxillary arch.[35]

Many high schools and colleges now require that mouth guards be worn at all times during participation. For example, the NCAA football rules mandate that all players wear a properly manufactured mouth guard. A time-out is charged to a team if a player fails to wear the mouth guard.[23] To assist enforcement, official mouth guards are increasingly made in a highly visible color.

Ear Guards

With the exception of wrestling, water polo, and boxing, most contact sports do not make a special practice of protecting the ears. All these sports can cause irritation of the ears to the point that permanent deformity can ensue. To avoid this problem, special ear guards should be worn routinely (Figure 7-11).

Eye Protection Devices

The National Society to Prevent Blindness estimates that the highest percentage of eye injuries are sports or play related. Most injuries are from blunt trauma. Protective devices must be sport-specific.

Glasses

For the athlete who must wear corrective lenses, glasses can be both a blessing and a nuisance. They may slip on sweat, get bent when hit, fog from perspiration, detract from peripheral vision, and be difficult to wear with protective headgear. Even with all these disadvantages, properly fitted and designed glasses can provide adequate protection and withstand the rigors of the sport. Athletes should wear polycarbonate lenses, which are virtually unbreakable.[55] These are the newest type of lenses available, and they are certainly the safest. If the athlete has glass lenses, they must be

7-4

Critical Thinking E x e r c i s e

The ice hockey team has traditionally been responsible for obtaining their own mouth guards. Lately, however, several players have complained about their mouth guards and do not want to wear them. The athletic trainer would like to purchase the supplies necessary to make custom fabricated mouth guards.

? How can the athletic trainer justify this request to the athletic department?

Figure 7-11

Ear protection. **A,** Wrestler's ear guard. **B,** Water polo player's ear protection.

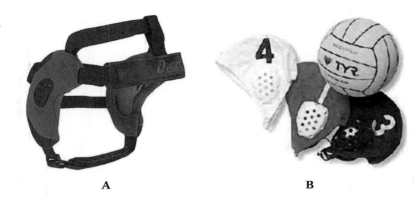

A   B

case-hardened to prevent them from splintering on impact. When a case-hardened lens breaks, it crumbles, eliminating the sharp edges that may penetrate the eye. The cost of this process is relatively low. The only disadvantages are that the glasses are heavier than average and may be scratched more easily than regular glasses.[26]

Another possible sports advantage of glass-lensed glasses is that they can be created so the lenses will become color tinted when exposed to ultraviolet rays from the sun and then return to a clear state when removed from the sun's rays. These lenses are known as photochromic lenses. Plastic lenses for glasses are popular with athletes. They are much lighter weight than glass lenses and they can be made scratch resistant with a special coating.

Contact Lenses

The athlete who can wear contact lenses without discomfort can avoid many of the inconveniences of glasses. The greatest advantage to contact lenses is probably the fact that they "become a part of the eye" and move with it.

Contact lenses come mainly in two types: the corneal type, which covers just the iris of the eye, and the scleral type, which covers the entire front of the eye, including the white. Peripheral vision as well as astigmatism and corneal waviness is improved through the use of contact lenses. Unlike regular glasses, contact lenses do not normally cloud during temperature changes. They also can be tinted to reduce glare. For example, yellow lenses can be used against ice glare and blue ones against glare from snow. One of the main difficulties with contact lenses is their high cost compared with regular glasses. Some other serious disadvantages of wearing contact lenses are the possibility of corneal irritation caused by dust getting under the lens and the possibility of a lens becoming dislodged during body contact. In addition, only certain individuals can wear contacts with comfort, and some individuals are unable to ever wear them because of certain eye idiosyncrasies. Athletes currently prefer the soft, hydrophilic lenses to the hard type. Adjustment time for the soft lenses is shorter than for the hard, they can be more easily replaced, and they are more adaptable to the sports environment. There are also disposable lenses and lenses that can be worn for an extended period. In the last few years, the cost of contact lenses has dropped significantly.

The advent of two eye surgery procedures, radial kerotectomy (RK) and laser in-situ keratomileusis (LASIK), has potentially reduced the need for individuals to wear vision-correcting glasses or contact lenses. Although relatively expensive, the LASIK procedure has proven to be a safe and effective technique for correcting faulty vision.

Eye and Glasses Guards

Eye protection must be worn by all athletes who play sports that use fast-moving projectiles.

It is essential that athletes take special precautions to protect their eyes, especially in sports that use fast-moving projectiles and implements, such as handball or racquetball (Figure 7-12).[26] Besides the more obvious sports of ice hockey, lacrosse, and baseball, the racquet sports can also cause serious eye injury. Athletes not wearing glasses should wear closed eye guards to protect the orbital cavity. Athletes who normally

Figure 7-12

A & B, Athletes playing sports that involve small, fast projectiles should wear closed eye guards. **C,** Polycarbonate shield for a football helmet. **D,** Shield for an ice hockey face mask. **E,** Lacrosse/field hockey goggle.

wear glasses with plastic or case-hardened lenses are to some degree already protected against eye injury from an implement or projectile; however, greater safety is afforded by the polycarbonate frame that surrounds and fits over the athlete's glasses. The protection that the guard affords is excellent, but it hinders vision in some planes. Polycarbonate eye shields can be attached to football face masks, hockey helmets, and baseball and softball helmets.

Neck Protection

Experts in cervical injuries consider the major value of commercial and customized cervical collars to be mostly a reminder to the athlete to be cautious rather than to provide a definitive restriction (see Figure 7-16B on page 200).

TRUNK AND THORAX PROTECTION

Trunk and thorax protection is essential in many contact and collision sports. Sports such as football, ice hockey, baseball, and lacrosse use extensive body protection. Areas that are most exposed to impact forces must be properly covered with some material that offers protection against soft-tissue compression. Of particular concern are the external genitalia and the exposed bony protuberances of the body that have insufficient soft tissue for protection, such as shoulders, ribs, and spine (Figure 7-13).

As discussed earlier, the problem that arises in wearing protective equipment is that, although it is armor against injury to the athlete wearing it, it can also serve as a weapon against all opponents. Standards must become more stringent in determining

Figure 7-13

Chest and thorax protectors. **A,** Baseball catcher's chest protector. **B,** Lacrosse goalie chest protector. **C,** Ice hockey thorax protector and shoulder pads.

Figure 7-14

Shoulder pads protect both the shoulder and thorax. **A,** Non-cantilever. **B,** Cantilever pads.

A

B

what equipment is absolutely necessary for body protection and at the same time is not itself a source of trauma. Proper fit and proper maintenance of equipment are essential.

Football Shoulder Pads

There are two general types of shoulder pads: cantilevered and noncantilevered (Figure 7-14). The player who uses the shoulder a great deal in blocking and tackling requires the bulkier cantilevered type, whereas the quarterback or a receiver might prefer to use the noncantilever pads that don't restrict shoulder motion as much as the cantilevered pads. Over the years, the shoulder pad's front and rear panels have been extended along with the cantilever. The following are rules for fitting the football shoulder pad (Figure 7-15):

- The width of the shoulder is measured to determine the proper size of pad.
- The inside shoulder pad should cover the tip of the shoulder in a direct line with the lateral aspect of the shoulder.
- The epaulets and cups should cover the deltoid muscle and allow movements required by the athlete's specific position.
- The neck opening must allow the athlete to raise the arm overhead but not allow the pad to slide back and forth.
- If a split-clavicle shoulder pad is used, the channel for the top of the shoulder must be in the proper position.
- Straps underneath the arm must hold the pads firmly in place, but not so they constrict soft tissue. A collar and drop-down pads may be added to provide more protection.

Some athletic trainers use a combination of football and ice hockey shoulder pads to prevent injuries high on the upper arm and shoulder. A pair of supplemental shoulder pads are placed under the football pads (Figure 7-16 on page 200). The deltoid cap of the hockey pad is connected to the main body of the hockey pad by an adjustable lace. The distal end of the deltoid cap is held in place by a Velcro strap. The chest pad is adjustable to ensure proper fit for any size athlete. The football shoulder pads are placed over the hockey pads. The athletic trainer should observe for a proper fit. Larger football pads may be needed. A neck collar can be attached to the shoulder pads and has been shown to be effective in minimizing neck movement (Figure 7-16B).[19]

Sports Bras

To be effective, a bra should hold the breasts tightly to the chest.

Manufacturers have made significant efforts to develop athletic support bras for women who participate in all types of physical activity. In the past, the primary concern was for breast protection against external forces that could cause bruising. Most sports bras are now designed to minimize excessive vertical and horizontal movements of the breasts that occurs with running and jumping.[42]

To be effective, a bra should hold the breasts to the chest and prevent stretching of the Cooper's ligament, which causes premature sagging (see Figure 7-17 on page 200). Metal parts (snaps, fasteners, underwire support) rub and abrade the skin.

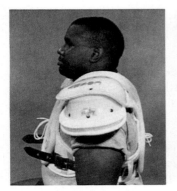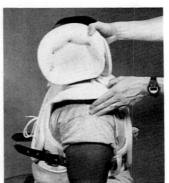

Breastplate

Figure 7-15

Football shoulder pads should be made to protect the player against direct force to the entire shoulder complex.

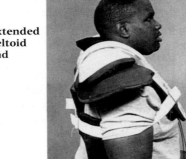

Extended deltoid pad

Pectoral pad

Belt strap

Nonsupport bras lack sufficient padding, and seams over nipples compound the rubbing of the bra on the nipple, which can lead to irritation.[8]

Several styles of sports bras are now available:

1. For women with smaller breasts it is not as critical to provide compression or support and thus a less elastic, lightweight bra is sufficient (Figure 7-18A on page 201).

2. A compressive pullover bra is perhaps the most common and is recommended for women with medium-size breasts. Compressive bras function like wide elastic bandages, binding the breasts to the chest wall (Figure 7-18B on page 201).

3. Support bras are a bit more heavy duty and provide good upward support with elastic material and an underwire. They tend to have wide bands under the breasts with elastic shoulder straps in the back. They are designed for women with larger breasts (Figure 7-18C on page 201).

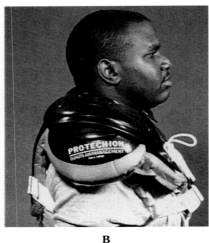

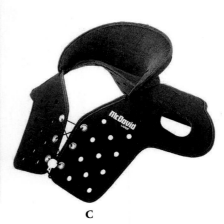

A   B   C

Figure 7-16

A, B, Customized foam is placed on the underside of the shoulder pad to provide additional protection. **C,** A cowboy collar can be attached to the shoulder pad.

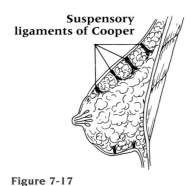

Suspensory ligaments of Cooper

Figure 7-17

Stretching of Cooper's ligament causes premature sagging.

All athletic socks should be clean and dry and without holes. Socks of the wrong size can irritate the skin.

In contact sports, additional padding may be placed inside the cup if needed. Women competing in ice hockey, for example, wear protective plastic chest pieces that attach to their shoulder pads to protect the breast tissue from contusions (Figure 7-18D).

Thorax and Rib Protection

Several manufacturers provide equipment for thorax protection. Many of the thorax protectors and rib belts can be modified by replacing stock pads with customized thermomoldable plastic protective devices.[35] Recently, many lightweight pads have been developed to protect the athlete against external forces. A jacket for the protection of a rib injury incorporates a pad composed of air-inflated, interconnected cylinders that protect against severe external forces (Figure 7-19). This same principle has been used in the development of other protective pads.

Hips and Buttocks

Pads in the region of the hips and buttocks are often needed in collision and high-velocity sports such as hockey and football. Other athletes needing protection in this region are amateur boxers, snow skiers, equestrians, jockeys, and water skiers. Two popular commercial pads are the girdle and belt types (Figure 7-20).

Groin and Genitalia

Sports involving high-velocity projectiles (e.g., hockey, lacrosse, and baseball) require cup protection for male participants. It comes as an off-the-shelf item that fits into place in a jockstrap, or athletic supporter (Figure 7-21 on page 202).

LOWER EXTREMITY PROTECTIVE EQUIPMENT
Footwear

It is essential that the athletic trainer and equipment personnel make every effort to fit their athletes with proper shoes and socks.

Socks

Poorly fitted socks can cause abnormal stresses on the foot. For example, socks that are too short crowd the toes, especially the fourth and fifth ones. Socks that are too long can wrinkle and cause skin irritation. All athletic socks should be clean, dry, and without holes to avoid irritations. Manufacturers are now providing different types of socks for various sports. The composition of the sock's material also should be noted. Cotton socks can be too bulky, whereas a combination of materials such as cotton and polyester is less bulky and dries faster.

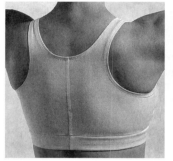
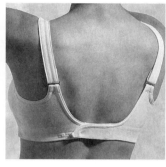
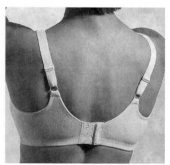

A   **B**   **C**   **D**

Figure 7-18

Sports bras. **A,** Lightweight pullover bra. **B,** Compressive bra. **C,** Support bra with underwire. **D,** Protective sports bra with cup inserts.

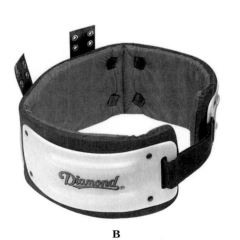

A   **B**

Figure 7-19

Protective rib belts.

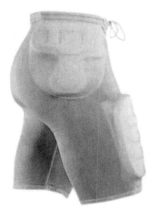

A   **B**

Figure 7-20

Girdle-style hip and coccygeal pads.

Figure 7-21

A cup, held in place by an athletic supporter, used for protecting the genitals against high-velocity projectiles.

Shoe Selection

The athletic and fitness shoe manufacturing industry has become extremely sophisticated and offers a number of options when it comes to purchasing shoes for different activities.[46] Figure 7-22 shows the major parts of a shoe. The following guidelines can help in selecting the most appropriate shoe:[13]

- *Toe Box.* There should be plenty of room for the toes in the fitness shoe. Most experts recommend a ½- to ¾-inch distance between the longest toe and the front of the shoe. A few fitness shoes are made in varying widths. If an athlete has a very wide or narrow foot, most shoe salespersons can recommend a specific shoe for that foot. The best way to make sure there is adequate room in the toe box is to have the foot measured and then try on the shoe.

- *Sole.* The sole should possess two qualities. First, it must provide a shock absorptive function; second, it must be durable. Most shoes have three layers on the sole: a thick, spongy layer, which absorbs the force of the foot strike under the heel; a midsole, which cushions the midfoot and toes; and a hard rubber layer, which comes in contact with the ground. The average runner's feet strike the ground between 1,500 and 1,700 times per mile. Thus it is essential that the force of the heel strike be absorbed by the spongy layer to prevent overuse injuries from occurring in the ankles and knees. Heel wedges are sometimes inserted either on the inside or outside surface of the sole underneath the heel counter to accommodate and correct for various structural deformities of the foot that may alter normal biomechanics of the running gait. A flared heel may be appropriate for running shoes but is not recommended in aerobic or court shoes. The sole must provide good traction and must be made of tough material that is resistant to wear. Most of the better-known brands of shoes have well-designed, long-lasting soles.

- *Heel counters.* The heel counter is the portion of the shoe that prevents the foot from rolling from side to side at heel strike. The heel counter should be firm but well fitted to minimize movement of the heel up and down or side to side. A good heel counter may prevent ankle sprains and painful blisters.

- *Shoe uppers.* The upper part of the shoe is made of some combination of nylon and leather. The uppers should be lightweight, quick drying, and well ventilated. The uppers should have some type of extra support in the saddle area, and there should be some extra padding in the area of the Achilles tendon just above the heel counter.

Figure 7-22

Parts of a well-designed sport shoe.

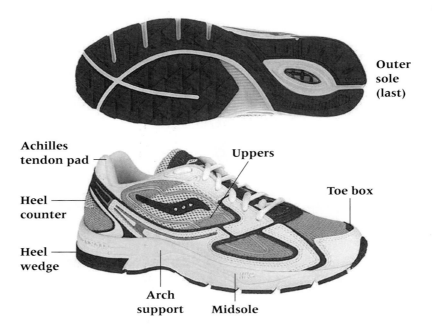

Focus

> **Proper running shoe design and construction**
>
> To avoid injury to the athlete, the running shoe should meet the following requirements:[21]
>
> - Have a strong heel counter that fits well around the foot and locks the shoe around the foot.
> - Always have good flexibility in the forefoot where toes bend.
> - Preferably have a fairly high heel for the athlete with a tight Achilles tendon.
> - Have a midsole that is moderately soft but does not flatten easily.
> - Have a heel counter that is high enough to surround the foot but still allows room for an orthotic insert, if needed.
> - Have a counter that is attached to the sole to avoid the possibility of it coming loose from its attachment.
> - Always be of quality construction. A properly fitted shoe will bend where the foot bends.

- *Arch support.* The arch support should be made of some durable yet soft supportive material and should smoothly join with the insole. The support should not have any rough seams or ridges inside the shoe, which may cause blisters.
- *Price.* Unfortunately, in many instances price is the primary consideration in buying athletic shoes. When buying athletic shoes, remember that in many activities shoes are important for performance and prevention of injury. Thus it is worth a little extra investment to buy a quality pair of shoes.

Shoe fitting   Fitting athletic shoes can be difficult.[6] Frequently the athlete's left foot varies in size and shape from the right foot. Therefore measuring both feet is imperative. To fit the sports shoe properly, the athlete should approximate the conditions under which he or she will perform, such as wearing athletic socks, jumping up and down, or running. It is also desirable to fit the athlete's shoes at the end of the day to accommodate the gradual increase in foot volume that occurs during weight-bearing. The athlete must carefully consider this shoe choice because he or she will be spending countless hours in those shoes (see *Focus Box:* "Proper running shoe design and construction" for suggestions about shoe fitting).[16]

During performance conditions the new shoe should feel snug but not too tight. The sports shoe should be long enough that all toes can be fully extended without being cramped. Its width should permit full movement of the toes, including flexion, extension, and some spreading. A good point to remember is that the wide part of the shoe should match the wide part of the foot to allow the shoe to crease evenly when the athlete is on the balls of the feet. The shoe should bend (or "break") at its widest part; when the break of the shoe and the ball joint coincide, the fit is correct. However, if the break of the shoe is in back of or in front of the normal bend of the foot (metatarsophalangeal joint), the shoe and the foot will oppose one another, causing abnormal skin and structural stresses to occur. Two measurements must be considered when fitting shoes: (1) the distance from the heel to the metatarsophalangeal joint and (2) the distance from the heel to the end of the longest toe. An individual's feet may be equal in length from the heels to the balls of the feet but different between the heels and the toes. One type of shoe is not appropriate for all athletes in a particular sport. Shoes therefore should be selected for the longer of the two measurements. Other factors to consider when buying the sports shoe are the stiffness of the sole and the width of the shank, or narrowest part of the sole. A shoe with a sole that is too rigid and nonyielding places a great deal of extra strain on the foot tendons. A shoe with a shank that is too narrow also causes extra strain because it fails to adequately support the athlete's inner, longitudinal arches.[46] Lacing techniques can help adjust the width of the shoe to the foot. *Focus Box:* "Shoe lacing techniques" provides some

7-5

Critical Thinking E x e r c i s e

A high school basketball player asks the athletic trainer for advice on purchasing a pair of basketball shoes.

? What fitting factors must be taken into consideration when purchasing basketball shoes?

A properly fitted shoe will bend where the foot bends

Figure 7-23

Variations in cleated shoes: the longer the cleat, the higher the incidence of injury.

A

B

C

D

suggestions for alternative lacing techniques. Two other shoe features to consider are insoles to reduce friction and arch supports.

The cleated shoe   The cleated shoe presents some additional fitting problems. For example, American football uses the multi–short-cleated, soccer-type polyurethane sole with cleats no longer than ½ inch (1.27 cm) (Figure 7-23). Specially soled shoes are also worn when playing on a synthetic surface. Whenever cleated shoes are used, the cleats must be properly positioned under the two major weight-bearing joints and must not be felt through the soles of the shoes (see Table 7-1 for shoe comparisons).[46]

TABLE 7-1 Shoe Comparisons

	Tennis	Aerobic	Running
Flexibility	Firm sole, more rigid than running shoe	Sole between running and tennis shoe	Flexible ball of foot
Uppers	Leather or leather with nylon	Leather or leather with nylon	Nylon or nylon mesh
Heel flare	None	Very little	Flared for stability
Cushioning	Less than a running shoe	Between running and tennis shoe	Heel and sole well padded
Soles	Polyurethane	Rubber or polyurethane	Carbon-based material for greater durability
Tread	Flattened	Flat or pivot dot	Deep grooves for grip

Foot Orthotics

An orthotic is a device for correcting biomechanical problems that exist in the foot that can potentially cause an injury.[19,53] The orthotic is a plastic, thermoplastic, rubber, sorbethane, or leather support that is placed in the shoe as a replacement for the existing insole.[41] Ready-made orthotics can be purchased in sporting goods or shoe stores. Some athletes need orthotics that are custom made by a physician, podiatrist, athletic trainer, or physical therapist. These are more expensive but can be well worth the expense if the athlete's feet cause pain and discomfort, especially when exercising (Figure 7-24).

**Focus**

Shoe lacing techniques

A shoe that doesn't fit just right may be adjusted to provide a more secure, comfortable, and supportive fit by using specific lacing techniques to accommodate a narrow heel, a high/low arch, or a wider foot. Athletic shoes with a large number of eyelets make it easier to adjust the laces for a custom fit.

Narrow foot or heel (Technique A)

If the shoe has two rows of eyelets that appear to zig-zag use the row furthest from the tongue tightening from the outer eyelets and pulling the body of the shoe towards the center. If there is only one row of eyelets, follow a normal lacing pattern up to the last pair of holes. At the last hole, tighten the laces and thread into the last hole leaving a loop on each side. Cross the laces and thread them each through the loop on the other side before tightening and tying.

Wide Foot (Technique B)

If the shoe has two rows of eyelets that appear to zig-zag use the row closest to the tongue. If there is only a single row, thread laces through the first set of eyelets and then straight up each side without criss-crossing at all. Continue this way for two or three holes until the laces are above the forefoot and can tighten without squeezing. Then begin criss-crossing and finish lacing as normal.

Low Arch (pes planus) (Technique C)

Beginning at the bottom, criss-cross lace shoes as normal halfway up the eyelets. Use the loop lacing technique used for a narrow heel the rest of the way.

High arches (pes cavus) (Technique D)

Begin lacing as normal, criss-crossing and stopping after the first set of holes. Thread laces straight up each side, criss-crossing only before threading the last hole.

| A | B | C | D |

Figure 7-24

Commercially manufactured orthotic devices.

Figure 7-25

Heel cups and pads, including lifts of orthotic felt.

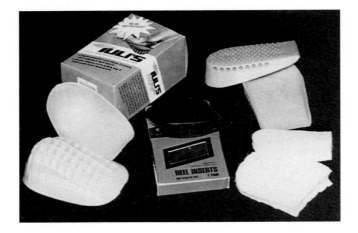

Heel Cups

Heel cups should be used for a variety of conditions including plantar fasciitis, a heel spur, Achilles tendonitis, and heel bursitis (Figure 7-25). Heel cups may be either hard plastic or spongy rubber. The heel cup helps to compress the fat pad under the heel, providing more heel cushioning during weight-bearing activities.

Off-the-Shelf Foot Pads

Off-the-shelf foot pads are intended for use by the general public and are not usually designed to withstand the rigors of sports activities. Off-the-shelf pads that are suited for sports are generally not durable enough for hard, extended use. If money is no object, the ready-made off-the-shelf pad, which is replaced more often, has the advantage of saving time. Off-the-shelf pads are manufactured for almost every type of common structural foot condition, ranging from corns and bunions to fallen arches and pronated feet. Off-the-shelf foot pads are commonly used before more customized orthotic devices are made. These products offer a compromise to the custom-made foot orthotics by providing some biomechanical control.[16] Indiscriminate use of these

Indiscriminate use of commercial foot orthotics may give the athlete a false sense of security.

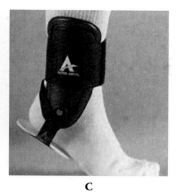

A   B   C

Figure 7-26

Commercial ankle supports for an injured ankle. **A,** Lace up brace. **B,** Lace up with straps brace. **C,** Rigid support brace.

Figure 7-27

Soccer shin guards.

aids, however, may intensify the pathological condition or cause the athlete to delay seeing the team physician or team podiatrist for evaluation.[24]

For the most part, foot devices are fabricated and customized from a variety of materials such as foam, felt, plaster, aluminum, and spring steel (see the section titled "Construction of Protective and Supportive Devices," later in this chapter).

Ankle Supports

Ankle stabilizers, either alone or in combination with ankle taping, are becoming increasingly popular in sports (Figure 7-26).[14,58] There has been significant debate regarding the efficacy of ankle supports in the prevention of ankle sprains.[15,27] Most studies indicate that bracing is effective in reducing ankle injury,[33,43,50] while other studies have shown no effects[7,21] or even negative effects.[34,37] Bracing probably has little or no effect on performance; any change in performance is due to the athlete's perception of support and comfort.[3] When compared with ankle taping, these devices do not loosen significantly during exercise.[14,54] Recent studies have focused on the proprioceptive effects and how ankle braces influence balance, postural sway, and joint position sense.[22,29,56]

Shin and Lower Leg

The shin is an area of the body that is commonly neglected in contact and collision sports. Commercially marketed hard-shelled, molded shin guards are used in field hockey and soccer (Figure 7-27).

Thigh and Upper Leg

Thigh and upper leg protection is necessary in collision sports such as hockey, football, and soccer. Generally, pads slip into ready-made pockets in the uniform (Figure 7-28A). In some instances, customized pads should be constructed and held in place with tape or an elastic wrap. Neoprene sleeves can be used for support following strain to the hamstring, groin, or quadriceps muscles (Figure 7-28B).

7-6

Critical Thinking Exercise

A basketball player with a history of ankle sprains needs support during practice.

? Which type of ankle support is cost-efficient and most reliable: tape or commercial supports?

Figure 7-28

A, Protective thigh pads.
B, Neoprene thigh sleeve.

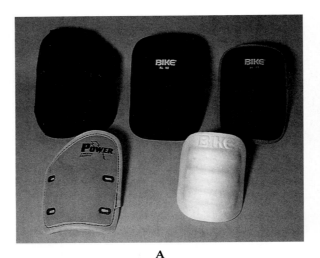
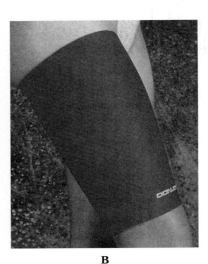

A   B

Knee Supports and Protective Devices

Knee Pads

Elastic knee pads or guards are extremely valuable in sports in which the athlete falls or receives a direct blow to the anterior aspect of the knee. An elastic sleeve containing a resilient pad may help dissipate an anterior striking force but fails to protect the knee against lateral, medial, or twisting forces.

Knee Braces

Because of the high incidence of injury to the knee joint, manufacturers have designed a host of different knee braces for a variety of purposes.[49] *Protective knee braces* are used prophylactically to prevent injuries to the medial collateral ligament in contact sports such as football (Figure 7-29A).[39,48] Although these protective braces have been widely used in the past, the American Orthopedic Society for Sports Medicine has expressed concern about their efficacy in reducing injuries to the collateral ligaments. Several studies have actually shown an increase in the incidence of injuries to the medial collateral ligament in athletes wearing these braces.[48] Others have shown a positive influence on joint position sense[28] but little or no effect on performance.[21]

Rehabilitative braces are widely used following surgical repair or reconstruction of the knee joint to allow for controlled progressive immobilization (Figure 7-29B).[4] These braces have hinges that can be easily adjusted to allow range of motion to be progressively increased over time.

Functional knee braces may be worn both during and following the rehabilitative period to provide support during functional activities (Figure 7-29C).[1,11] Functional braces can be purchased ready made or can be custom made.[52] Some physicians strongly recommend that their patients consistently[38] wear these braces during physical activity, whereas others do not feel that they are necessary.[10,57]

Neoprene braces with medial and lateral supports may be used by individuals who have sustained injury to the collateral ligaments and feel that they need extra support medially and laterally (Figure 7-29D).

A variety of *neoprene sleeves* may also be used to provide some support for patellofemoral conditions (Figure 7-29E).[5]

ELBOW, WRIST, AND HAND PROTECTION

As with the lower extremity, the upper extremity requires protection from injury and prevention of further injury after trauma. Although the elbow joint is less commonly injured than the ankle, knee, or shoulder, it is still vulnerable to instability, contusion, and muscle strain. A variety of off-the-shelf protective neoprene sleeves and pads and hinged adjustable rehabilitative braces can offer protection to the elbow (Figure 7-30).[45]

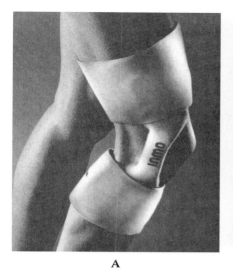

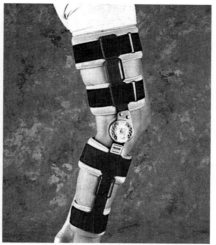

A

B

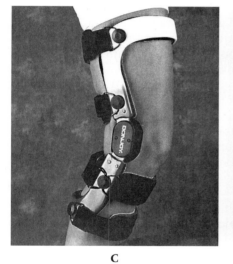

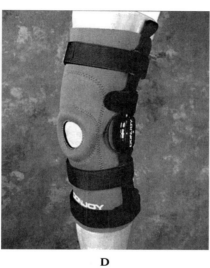

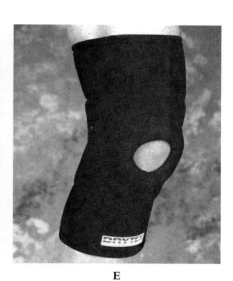

C

D

E

Figure 7-29

Knee braces. **A,** Prophylactic knee brace. **B,** Rehabilitative brace. **C,** Functional brace. **D,** Neoprene with medial support-brace. **E,** Neoprene brace.

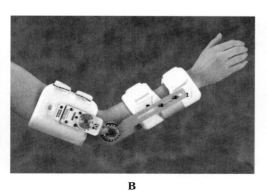

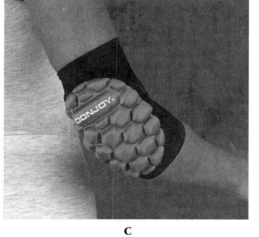

A

B

C

Figure 7-30

A, Neoprene elbow sleeve. **B,** Hinged rehabilitative elbow brace. **C,** Elbow pad.

Figure 7-31

The hand is an often neglected area of the body in sports.

In sports medicine, injuries to the wrist, hand, and fingers are often trivialized and considered insignificant. But injuries to the distal aspect of the upper extremity can be functionally disabling, especially in those sports that involve throwing and catching.[1] In both contact and noncontact sport activities the wrist, hand, and particularly the fingers are susceptible to fracture, dislocation, ligament sprains, and muscle strains. Protective gloves are essential in preventing injuries in sports like lacrosse and ice hockey (Figure 7-31). It is also common to use both off-the-shelf and custom-molded splints both for support and to immobilize an injury.

CONSTRUCTION OF PROTECTIVE AND SUPPORTIVE DEVICES

The athletic trainer should be able to design and construct protective and supportive devices when necessary. Certainly the athletic trainer must understand the theoretical basis for constructing protective pads and supports. However, the ability to construct an effective and appropriate protective device is more of an art than a science.

Custom Pad and Orthotic Materials

Many different materials are available to the athletic trainer attempting to protect or support an injured area. In general, these materials can be divided into soft and hard materials (Figure 7-32).

Soft Materials

The primary soft-material media found in athletic training rooms are cotton, gauze pads, adhesive felt or adhesive foam rubber felt, and an assortment of foam rubber.

Gauze padding is less versatile than other pad materials. It is assembled in varying thicknesses and can be used as an absorbent or protective pad.

Cotton is probably the cheapest and most widely used material in sports. It has the ability to absorb, to hold emollients, and to offer a mild padding effect.

Adhesive felt (moleskin) or *sponge rubber* material contains an adhesive mass on one side, thus combining a cushioning effect with the ability to be held in a specific spot by the adhesive mass. It is a versatile material that is useful on all body parts.

Figure 7-32

Types of sports orthoses. **A,** Orthoplast with a foam rubber doughnut. **B,** Orthoplast splint. **C,** Orthoplast rib protector with a foam rubber pad. **D,** Fiberglass material for splint construction. **E,** Plaster of paris material for cast construction. **F,** Foam rubber pad. **G,** Aloplast foam moldable material for protective pad construction.

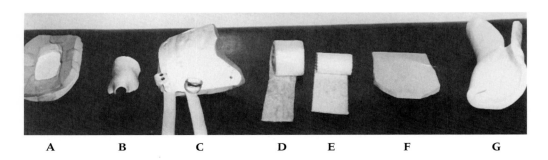

A   B   C   D   E   F   G

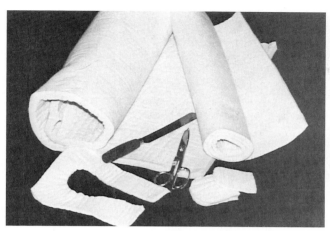

Figure 7-33

Orthopedic felt, both ½- and ¼-inch wide, with broad-blade knife and large scissors for contouring.

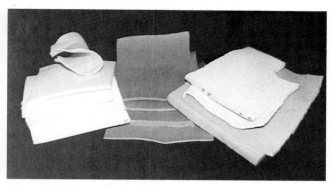

Figure 7-34

Foam assortment: *left,* thermomoldable; *center,* closed celled; *right,* open celled.

Felt is a material composed of matted wool fibers pressed into varying thicknesses that range from ¼ to 1 inch (0.6 to 2.5 cm). Its benefit lies in its comfortable, semiresilient surface, which gives a firmer pressure than most sponge rubbers. Because felt absorbs perspiration, it clings to the skin, and it has less tendency to move than sponge rubber does (Figure 7-33). Because of its absorbent qualities, felt should be replaced daily. Currently, it is most often used as support and protection for a variety of foot conditions.

Foams are currently the materials most often used for providing injury protection in sports. They come in many different thicknesses and densities (Figure 7-34). They are usually resilient, nonabsorbent, and able to protect the body against compressive forces. Some foams are open celled, whereas others are closed. The closed-cell type is preferable in sports because it rebounds and returns to its original shape quickly. Foams can be easily worked through cutting, shaping, and faceting. Some foams are thermomoldable and, when heated, become highly pliant and easy to shape. When cooled, they retain the shape in which they were formed. A new class of foams are composed of viscoelastic polymers. Sorbothane is one example. This foam has a high energy-absorbing quality, but it also has a high density, making it heavy. Used in inner soles in sports shoes, foam helps prevent blisters and also effectively absorbs anterior/posterior and medial/lateral ground reaction forces. Foams generally range from ⅛ to ½ inch (0.3 to 1.25 cm) in thickness.

Nonyielding Materials

A number of hard, nonyielding materials are used in athletic training for making protective shells and splints.

Thermomoldable plastics   Plastic materials are widely used in sports medicine for customized orthotics. They can brace, splint, and shield a body area. They can provide casting for a fracture; support for a foot defect; or a firm, nonyielding surface to protect a severe contusion.

Plastics used for these purposes differ in their chemical composition and reaction to heat. The three major categories are heat-forming plastics, heat-setting plastics, and heat-plastic foams.

Heat-forming plastics are of the low-temperature variety and are the most popular in athletic training. When heated to 140° to 180°F (60° to 82.2°C), depending on the material, the plastic can be accurately molded to a body part. Aquaplast (polyester sheets) and Orthoplast (synthetic rubber thermoplast) are popular types.

Heat-setting plastics require relatively higher temperatures for shaping. They are rigid and difficult to form, usually requiring a mold rather than being formed directly

Heat-forming plastics of the low-temperature variety are the most popular in athletic training.

Figure 7-35

Casting material: *left*, fiberglass; *right*, plaster including cast saw used to trim pictured shin guard.

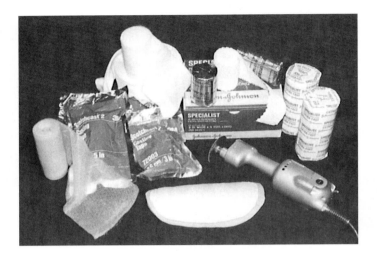

to the body part. High-impact vinyl (polyvinyl chloride), Kydex (polyvinyl chloride acrylic), and Nyloplex (heat-plastic acrylic) are examples of the more commonly used thermoforming plastics.

Heat-plastic foams are plastics that have differences in density as a result of the addition of liquids, gas, or crystals. They are commonly used as shoe inserts and other body padding. Aloplast and Plastazote (polyethylene foams) are two commonly used products.

Usually the plastic is heated until soft and malleable. It is then molded into the desired shape and allowed to cool, thereby retaining its shape. Various pads and other materials can also be fastened in place. The rules and regulations of various sport activities may place limitations on the use of rigid thermomoldable plastics.

Casting materials   Applying casts to injured body areas has long been a practice in sports medicine. The material of choice is fiberglass, which uses resin and a catalytic converter, plus water, to produce hardening. Besides casts, this material makes effective shells for splints and protective pads. Once hardened, the fiberglass is trimmed to shape with a cast saw (Figure 7-35).

Tools Used for Customizing

Many different tools are needed to work with the various materials used to customize protective equipment. These tools include adhesives, adhesive tapes, heat sources, and shaping tools.

Adhesives   A number of adhesives are used in constructing custom protective equipment. Many cements and glues join plastic to plastic or join other combinations of materials.

Adhesive tape   Adhesive tape is a major tool in holding various materials in place. Linen and elastic tape can hold pads to a rigid backing or to adhesive felt (moleskin) and can be used to protect against sharp edges (see Chapter 8).

Heat sources   To form thermomoldable plastics, a heat source must be available. Three sources are commonly found in training rooms: the commercial moist heat unit, a hot air gun or hair dryer, and a convection oven with a temperature control. The usual desired temperature is 160° F (71° C) or higher.

Shaping tools   Commonly, the tools required to shape custom devices are heavy-duty scissors, sharp-blade knives, and cast saws.

Fastening material   Once formed, customized protective equipment often must be secured in place. Fastening this equipment requires the availability of a great variety of different materials. For example, if something is to be held securely, Velcro can be used when a device must be continually put on and removed. Leather can be cut and riveted in place to form hinge straps with buckles attached. Various types of laces can

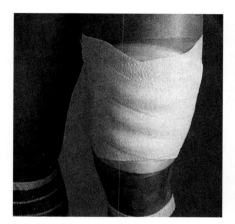

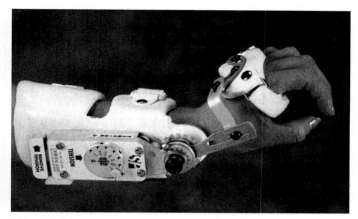

Figure 7-36

Hard shell pad wrapped on the thigh.

Figure 7-37

A dynamic splint for the hand and fingers.

be laced through eyelets to hold something in place. Tools that allow for this type of construction include a portable drill, a hole punch, and an ice pick.

Customized Hard-Shell Pads

A hard-shell pad is often required for an athlete who has acquired an injury, such as a painful contusion (bruise), that must be completely protected from further injury. *Focus Box:* "How to construct a hard-shell pad" provides the procedures needed to customize such a pad (Figure 7-36).

Dynamic Splints

Occasionally it is necessary to fabricate and apply a dynamic splint in treating injuries to the hand and fingers (Figure 7-37). Most often, an occupational therapist would make a dynamic splint; however, the athletic trainer is certainly capable of designing such a splint. A dynamic splint is used to provide long-duration tension on a healing structure (usually a tendon) so that it can return to normal function. Dynamic splints use a combination of thermoplastic material, Velcro, and pieces of rubber band or elastic to provide dynamic assistance.

7-7

Critical Thinking Exercise

A soccer player has incurred a number of contusions to the right quadriceps muscle.

? How does the athletic trainer customize a hard-shell protective thigh pad for the soccer player?

Focus

How to construct a hard-shell pad

1. Select proper material and tools, which might include
   a. Thermomoldable plastic sheet (Orthoplast, Hexalite)
   b. Scissors
   c. Felt material
2. Palpate and mark the margins of the tender area that needs protection.
3. Cut a felt piece to fit in the area of tenderness.
4. Heat plastic until malleable.
5. Place heated plastic over felt and wrap in place with an elastic wrap.
6. When cooled, remove elastic wrap and felt pad.
7. Trim shell to desired shape; a protective shell has now been made to provide a "bubble" relief.
8. If needed, add a softer inner layer of foam to distribute and lessen force further.
   a. Cut a doughnut-type hole in softer foam material the same size as the injury site.
   b. Cut foam the same shape as the hard shell.
   c. Use tape or an adhesive to affix the foam to the shell.

SUMMARY

- The proper selection and proper fitting of sports equipment are essential in the prevention of many sports injuries. Because of the number of current litigations, sports equipment standards regarding the durability of the material and the fit and wear requirements of the equipment are of serious concern. Manufacturers must foresee all possible uses and misuses of their equipment and warn the user of any potential risks.

- Sports professionals must be concerned about head protection in many collision and contact sports. The football helmet must be used only for its intended purpose and not as a weapon. To avoid unwarranted litigation, a warning label must be placed on the outside of the helmet indicating that the helmet is not fail-safe and must be used as intended. Properly fitting the helmet is of critical importance.

- Face protection is of major importance in sports that have fast-moving projectiles, use implements that are in close proximity to other athletes, and facilitate body collisions. Protecting teeth and eyes is of particular significance. The customized mouth guard, fitted to individual requirements, provides the best protection for the teeth and also protects against concussions. Eyes must be protected against projectiles and sports implements. The safest eye guard for the athlete wearing contact lenses or glasses is the closed type that completely protects the orbital cavity.

- Many sports require protection of various parts of the athlete's body. American football players, ice hockey players, and baseball catchers are examples of players who require body protection. Commonly, the protection is for the shoulders, chest, thighs, ribs, hips, buttocks, groin, genitalia (male athletes), and breasts (female athletes).

- Footwear is essential to prevent injuries. Socks must be clean, without holes, and made of appropriate materials. Shoes must be suited to the sport and must be properly fitted. The wide part of the foot must match the wide part of the shoe. If the shoe has cleats, they must be positioned at the metatarsophalangeal joints.

- Currently, there are many off-the-shelf pieces of specialized, protective equipment on the market. They may be designed to support ankles, knees, or other body parts. In addition to stock equipment, athletic trainers often construct customized equipment out of a variety of materials to pad injuries or support feet. Professionals such as orthopedists and podiatrists may devise orthopedic footwear and orthotic devices to improve the biomechanics of the athlete's foot.

Websites

Riddell: http://riddell.com/

Riddell is an equipment manufacturing company, and this site gives information about the safety of the products they sell and the necessary standards for safety equipment.

Healthyway Sporting Protective Eyewear: http://www.hb. sympatico.ca/contentshealth/HEALTHYWAY/ archive/feature_vis3c.html

This site emphasizes the importance of protective eyewear for young athletes and provides links to related informative sites.

National Operating Committee on Standards for Athletic Equipment: http://www.nocsae.org

National Institute for Sports Science and Safety (NISSS): http://www.nisss.org/

Provides information on research, design, and testing of sports equipment and sports protective equipment.

The Training Room: http://www.thetrainingroom.com

Provides information on sports orthopedic braces, orthotics, protective sports equipment, and athletic injury treatment.

Athletic Protective Equipment: http://www.rapidwear.com/

Provides information on a variety of protective equipment.

Douglas Protective Equipment: http://www.douglaspads.com/

Manufacturer and distributor of football, hockey, and baseball protective padding. Custom fitting players at all levels for over twelve years.

The Sports Authority: http://www.thesportsauthority.com

Provides a wide selection of protective equipment for virtually all sports.

Solutions to Critical Thinking EXERCISES

7-1 The athletic training student must acquire the following protective equipment competencies:
- Identify good-quality and poor-quality commercial protective equipment
- Properly fit commercial protective equipment
- Construct protective and supportive devices

7-2 The athletic trainer should initiate the following steps:
1. Call a team meeting in which he or she fully explains the risks entailed in the use and fitting of the equipment.
2. Report and repair any defective pieces of equipment are immediately.
3. Send out a letter to each parent or guardian explaining equipment limitations. This letter must be signed and returned to the athletic trainer.
4. Call a meeting of parents, team members, and coaches in which he or she further explains equipment limitations.

7-3 The athletic trainer explains that the helmet cannot prevent serious neck injuries. Striking an opponent with any part of the helmet or face mask can place abnormal stress on cervical structures. Most severe neck injuries occur from striking an opponent with the top of the helmet; this action is known as axial loading.

7-4 Mouth guards serve several important purposes in preventing injury in athletics, especially contact sports such as ice hockey. Mouth guards help to prevent or minimize lacerations, fractures, and possibly reduce the incidence of cerebral concussions. For a mouth guard to work effectively, proper fit is essential and needs to not interfere with breathing or speech. A custom fabricated mouth guard is produced from a mold of each individual athlete causing the fit to be more precise. If the fit is improved, athletes are more likely to wear their mouth guards.

7-5 The athletic trainer provides the following advice:
- Shoes should be purchased to fit the larger foot.
- Athlete should wear athletic socks when fitting shoes.
- Shoes should be purchased at the end of the day.
- Shoes should feel snug but comfortable when the athlete jumps up and down and performs cutting motions.
- Shoe length and width should allow full toe function.
- Wide part of foot should match wide part of shoe.
- Shoe should bend at its widest part.
- Each foot should be measured from the heel to the end of the largest toe.

7-6 A verified commercial ankle support provides more consistent support for a longer period of time and is more cost-efficient.

7-7 To construct a hard-shell protective thigh pad, the athletic trainer follows these steps:
1. Mark the area on the athlete to be protected.
2. Cut a foam piece to temporarily cover the injury.
3. Heat thermomoldable plastic and place over the foam piece to form a bubble.
4. Cut a plastic sheet to form to the athlete's thigh.
5. Create a doughnut-shaped foam lining to surround the injury.
6. Secure the foam doughnut to the plastic piece.
7. Secure the pad in place with elastic wrap.

REVIEW QUESTIONS AND CLASS ACTIVITIES

1. What are the legal responsibilities of the equipment manager, athletic trainer, and coach in terms of protective equipment?

2. Invite an attorney to class to discuss product liability and its impact on the athletic trainer.
3. What are the various sports with high risk factors that require protective equipment?
4. How can the athletic trainer select and use safety equipment to decrease the possibility of sports injuries and litigation?
5. Why is continual inspection and/or replacement of used equipment important?
6. What are the standards for fitting football helmets? Are there standards for any other helmets?
7. Invite your school equipment manager to class to demonstrate all the protective equipment and how to fit it to the athlete.
8. Why are mouth guards important, and what are the advantages of custom-made mouth guards over the stock type?
9. What are the advantages and disadvantages of glasses and contact lenses in athletic competition?
10. How do you fit shoulder pads for the different-sized players and their positions?
11. Why is breast protection necessary? Which types of sports bras are available and what should the athlete look for when purchasing one?
12. How do you properly fit shoes? What type of shoes should you use for the various sports and the different floor and field surfaces?

REFERENCES

1. Alexy C, De Carlo M: Rehabilitation and use of protective devices in hand and wrist injuries. In Rettig AC, editor: *Hand and wrist injuries. Clinic in sports medicine*, vol 17, no 3, July 1998.
2. Amis T, Di Somma E, Bacha F, Wheatley J: Influence of intra-oral maxillary sports mouthguards on the airflow dynamics of oral breathing, *Med Sci Sports Exerc* 32(2):284, 2000.
3. Beriau M, Cox W, Manning J: Effects of ankle braces upon agility course performance in high school athletes, *J Ath Train* 29(3):224, 1994.
4. Beynnon B, Good L, Risberg M: The effect of bracing on proprioception of knees with anterior cruciate ligament injury, *J Ortho Sports Phys Ther* 32(1):32, 2002.
5. Birmingham TB, Inglis JT, Kramer JF: Effect of a neoprene sleeve on knee joint kinesthesis: influence of different testing procedures, *Med Sci Sports Exerc* 32(2):304, 2000.
6. Bone S: If the shoe fits …, *Athletic Therapy Today* 6(6):52, 2001.
7. Bot SDM, van Mechelen W: The effect of ankle bracing on athletic performance, *Sports Med* 27(3):171, 1999.
8. *Breast support for female athletes, Sport research review/Nike sport research review* 1:1, 2002.
9. Broglio S, Yan-Ying J, Broglio M: The efficacy of soccer headgear, *J Ath Train* 38(3), 2003.
10. Brownstein B. Migration and design characteristics of functional knee braces, *J Sport Rehabil* 7(1):33, 1998.
11. Carlson L: Use of functional knee braces after ACL reconstruction, *Athletic Therapy Today* 7(3):48, 2002.
12. Caswell S, Deivert R: Lacrosse helmet designs and the effects of impact forces, *J Ath Train* 37(2):164, 2002.
13. Cuddy S: The right running shoe: the first step in avoiding running injuries. *Sports Med Update* 13(3):8, 1998.
14. Davis PF, Trevino SG: Ankle injuries. In Baxter DE, editor: *The foot and ankle in sport*, St Louis, 1995, Mosby.
15. Fiolkowski P: Considerations in the use of ankle braces, *Athletic Therapy Today* 3(4):38, 1998.
16. Frey C: The shoe in sports. In Baxter DE, editor: *The foot and ankle in sport*, St Louis, 1995, Mosby.
17. Garth W, Flowers K: Efficacy of knee sleeves in the management of patellofemoral dysfunction, *Athletic Therapy Today* 3(4):23, 1998.
18. Gorden J, Straub S, Swanik C: Effects of football collars on cervical hyperextension and lateral flexion, *J Ath Train* 38(3), 2003.

19. Gross MT: The impact of custom semirigid foot orthotics on pain and disability for individuals with plantar fasciitis, *Journal of Ortho Sports Phys Ther* 32(4):149, 2002.

20. Halstead PD: Performance testing updates in head, face, and eye protection, *J Ath Train* 36(3):322, 2001.

21. Hartsell H: Effects of bracing on isokinetic torque for the chronically unstable ankle, *J Sport Rehabil* 8(2):83, 1999.

22. Hartsell H: The effects of external bracing on joint position sense awareness for the chronically unstable ankle, *J Sport Rehabil* 9(4):279, 2000.

23. Hawn K, Visser M, Sexton P: Enforcement of mouthguard use and athlete compliance in National Collegiate Athletic Association men's collegiate ice hockey competition, *J Ath Train* 37(2):204, 2002.

24. Hermann TJ: Taping and padding of the foot and ankle. In Sammarco GI, editor: *Rehabilitation of the foot and ankle*, St Louis, 1995, Mosby.

25. Hodgson VR, Thomas LM: *Biomechanical study of football head impacts using a head model—condensed version.* Final report prepared for National Operating Committee on Standards for Athletic Equipment (NOCSAE), 1975.

26. International Federation of Medicine: Position statement: eye injuries and eye protection in sports, *Athletic Therapy Today* 4(5):6, 1999.

27. Kaminski T: The history and current use of ankle brace technology, *Athletic Therapy Today* 3(4):32, 1998.

28. Kaminski TW, Perrin D: Effect of prophylactic knee bracing on balance and joint position sense, *J Ath Train* 31(2):131, 1996.

29. Kinzey SJ, Ingersoll CD, Knight KL: The effects of selected ankle appliances on postural control, *J Ath Train* 32(4):300, 1997.

30. Labella CR, Smith RW, Sigurdsson A: Effect of mouth guards on dental injuries and concussions in college basketball, *Med Sci Sports Exerc* 34(1)41, 2002.

31. Lahti H: Dental injuries in ice hockey games and training, *Med Sci Sports Exerc* 34(3):400, 2002.

32. Liggett C, Tandy R, Young J: The effects of prophylactic knee bracing on running gait, *J Ath Train* 30(2):159, 1995.

33. Lindley T: Taping and semirigid bracing may not affect ankle functional range of motion, *J Ath Train* 30(2):109, 1995.

34. Locke A et al: Long-term use of a soft-shell prophylactic ankle stabilizer on speed, agility, and vertical jump performance, *J Sport Rehabil* 6(3):235, 1997.

35. Lord JL: Protective equipment in high-risk sports. In Birrer RB, editor: *Sports medicine for the primary care physician,* ed 3, Boca Raton, Fla, 2004, CRC Press.

36. McCrory P: Do mouthguards prevent concussion?, *British Journal of Sports Medicine* 35(2):81, 2001.

37. Metcalfe RC, Schlabach GA, Looney MA et al: A comparison of moleskin tape, linen tape, and lace-up brace on joint restriction and movement performance, *J Ath Train* 32(2):136, 1997.

38. Miller J et al: Dynamic analysis of custom-fitted functional knee braces: EMG and brace migration during physical activity, *J Sport Rehabil* 8(2):109, 1999.

39. Montgomery DL: Prophylactic knee braces. In Torg JS, Shephard RJ, editors: *Current therapy in sports medicine,* St Louis, 1995, Mosby.

40. New Revolution helmet being put to the test for improved safety on the field, *Sports Medicine Alert* 8(7):55, 2002.

41. Nigg BM, Nurse MA, Stefanyshyn DJ: Shoe inserts and orthotics for sport and physical activities, *Med Sci Sports Exerc* 31(7 Suppl.): S421,1999.

42. Page KA, Steele JR: Breast motion and sports brassiere design: implications for future research, *Sports Med* 27(4):205, 1999.

43. Paris D, Vardaxis V, Kokkaliaris J: Ankle ranges of motion during extended activity periods while taped and braced, *J Ath Train* 30(3):223, 1995.

44. Peterson L, Renstrom P: Sports and protective equipment. In Peterson, L, editor: *Sports injuries: their prevention and treatment,* ed 3, Champaign, Ill, 2001, Human Kinetics.

45. Pincivero D, Rijke A, Heinrichs K et al: The effects of a functional elbow brace on medial joint stability: a case study, *J Ath Train* 29(3):232, 1994.

46. Prentice W: *Fitness and wellness for life,* ed 7, Winston-Salem, NC, 2004, Kendall-Hunt.

47. Rules and equipment. In *Coaching youth football,* ed 3, Champaign, Ill, 2001, Human Kinetics, 63–90.

48. Sauers E, Harter R: Efficacy of prophylactic knee braces: current research perspectives, *Athletic Therapy Today* 3(4):14, 1998.

49. Scriber K: The history and current use of knee brace technology, *Athletic Therapy Today* 3(4):7, 1998.

50. Sharpe SR, Knapik J, Jones B: Ankle braces effectively reduce recurrence of ankle sprains in female soccer players, *J Ath Train* 32(1):21, 1997.

51. Steinbach P. Armor for all. With player safety paramount, the purchasing of football equipment must ensure adequate supply and proper fit of helmets, shoes and everything in between, *Athletic Business* 26(8):96, 2002.

52. Styf J: The effects of functional knee bracing on muscle function and performance, *Sports Med* 28(2):77, 1999.

53. Swanik CB: Orthotics in sports medicine, *Athletic Therapy Today* 5(1):5, 2000.

54. Vaes P et al: Influence of ankle strapping, taping, and nine braces on talar tilt: a stress roentgenologic comparison, *J Sport Rehabil* 7(3):157, 1998.

55. Vinger PF: A practical guide for sports eye protection. *Physician Sportsmed* 28(6):49, 2000.

56. Wilkerson GB: Biomechanical and neuromuscular effects of ankle taping and bracing, *J Ath Train* 37(4):436, 2002.

57. Wojtys EM, Huston LJ: Functional knee braces—the 25-year controversy. In Chan KM, editor: *Controversies in orthopedic sports medicine.* Champaign, Ill, 2002, Human Kinetics.

58. Yaggie J, Kinzey S: A comparative analysis of selected ankle orthoses during functional tasks, *Journal Sport Rehabil* 10(3):174, 2001.

ANNOTATED BIBLIOGRAPHY

Hunter S, Dolan M, Davis M: *Foot orthotics in therapy and sport,* Champaign, Ill, 1995, Human Kinetics.

This text takes a detailed look at the fabrication of orthotic devices.

Nicholas JA, Hirshman EB, editors: *The upper extremity in sports medicine,* St Louis, 1995, Mosby.

This book includes a special chapter on protective equipment for the shoulder, elbow, wrist, and hand.

Street S, Runkle D: *Athletic protective equipment: care, selection and fitting,* Boston, 2000, McGraw-Hill.

This reference book provides an overview of available athletic equipment and its usage. The text is a resource for athletic trainers, coaches, and physical education teachers.

Bandaging and Taping

When you finish this chapter you should be able to

- Explain the need for and demonstrate the application of a cloth ankle wrap.
- Explain the need for and demonstrate the application of triangular and cravat bandages.
- Demonstrate site preparation for taping.
- Demonstrate basic skill in the use of taping in sports.
- Demonstrate the skillful application of tape for a variety of musculoskeletal problems.

Bandaging and taping techniques are used routinely by athletic trainers. They may be used to accomplish a variety of specific objectives, including:

- providing compression to minimize swelling in the initial management of injury.
- reducing the chances of injury by applying tape prophylactically before an injury occurs.
- providing additional support to an injured structure.

Correctly and effectively applying a bandage or a "tape job" to a specific body part is a skill usually left to the athletic trainer. It is true that athletic trainers have been instructed in and generally become highly proficient in applying a variety of bandaging and taping techniques to accomplish the objectives listed. Certainly bandaging and taping skills are not difficult. They can be mastered by anyone willing to spend time practicing and learning what works best in a given situation. Of course certain taping and bandaging techniques are more advanced and should be used only by those with some advanced experience. However, there are some very basic techniques that can be easily applied with only a little training.

BANDAGING

A **bandage**, when properly applied, may contribute to recovery from sports injuries. Bandages carelessly or improperly applied may cause discomfort, allow wound contamination, and/or hamper repair and healing. In all cases bandages must be firmly applied—neither so tightly that circulation is impaired nor so loosely that the **dressing** is allowed to slip.

Bandages used on sports injuries consist of gauze, cotton cloth, and elastic wrapping.

Gauze comes in three forms: (1) a roller bandage for holding dressings and compresses in place, (2) padding in the prevention of blisters on a taped ankle, and (3) sterile pads for wounds.

Cotton cloth is used primarily for cloth ankle wraps and for triangular and cravat bandages.

Elastic Bandages

The *elastic bandage* is extremely popular with athletic trainers because of its extensibility, which allows it to conform to most parts of the body. Elastic wraps are active bandages; they let the athlete move without restriction. They act as controlled compression bandages where hemorrhage or swelling must be prevented, and they can also help support soft tissue.

bandage
Strip of cloth or other material used to cover a wound or hold a dressing in place.

dressing
Covering, protective or supportive, that is applied to an injury or wound.

A *cohesive elastic bandage* exerts constant, even pressure. It is lightweight and contours easily to the body part. The bandage is composed of two layers of nonwoven rayon, which are separated by strands of spandex material. The cohesive elastic bandage is coated with a substance that makes the material adhere to itself, eliminating the need for metal clips or adhesive tape to hold it in place.

Elastic bandages are commonly used in the athletic training room. The width and length vary according to the body part to be bandaged. The sizes most frequently used are the 2-inch (5 cm) width by 6-yard (5.5 m) length for hand, finger, toe, and head bandages; the 3-inch (7.5 cm) width by 10-yard (9 m) length for the extremities; and the 4-inch (10 cm) or 6-inch (15 cm) width by 10-yard (9 m) length for thigh, groin, and trunk. For ease and convenience in the application of the elastic bandage, the strips of material are first rolled into a cylinder. When a bandage is selected, it should be a single piece that is free from wrinkles, seams, and any other imperfections that may cause skin irritation.[15]

> Wrinkles or seams in roller bandages may irritate skin.

Application

Application of the elastic bandage must be executed in a specific manner to maximize its effectiveness. When an elastic bandage is about to be placed on a body part, the roll should be held in the preferred hand with the loose end extending from the bottom of the roll. The back surface of the loose end is placed on the injured area and held in position by the other hand. The bandage cylinder is then unrolled and passed around the injured area. As the hand pulls the material from the roll, it also standardizes the bandage pressure and guides the bandage in the proper direction. To anchor and stabilize the bandage, a number of turns, one on top of the other, are made. Circling a body part requires the athletic trainer to alternate the bandage roll from one hand to the other and back again.

> To apply a roller bandage, hold it in the preferred hand with the loose end extending from the bottom of the roll.

To provide maximum benefit, an elastic bandage should be applied uniformly and firmly but not too tightly (Figure 8-1). Excessive or unequal pressure can hinder the normal blood flow within the part. The following points should be considered when using the elastic bandage:

1. A body part should be wrapped in the position of maximum muscle contraction to ensure unhampered movement or circulation.
2. It is better to use a large number of turns with moderate tension than a limited number of turns applied too tightly.
3. Each turn of the bandage should be overlapped by at least one half of the overlying wrap to prevent the separation of the material while the athlete is engaged in activity. Separation of the bandage turns tends to pinch and irritate the skin and also leaves a space where swelling/edema can collect.

8-1
Critical Thinking E x e r c i s e

A freshman football player has a chronically weak ankle that he has sprained several times before. He wants to have the ankle taped before games and practices but has never had it taped before.

? What can the athletic trainer do to minimize the occurrence of blisters and ensure that the tape provides support?

Figure 8-1

Elastic bandages should be applied with firm, even pressure.

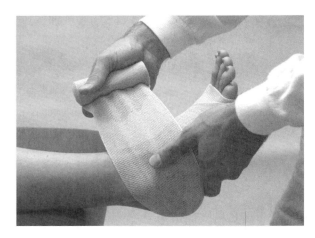

4. When limbs are wrapped, fingers and toes should be checked often for signs of circulation impairment. Abnormally cold or cyanotic phalanges are signs of excessive bandage pressure.

The usual anchoring of elastic bandages consists of several circular wraps directly overlying each other. Whenever possible, anchoring is commenced at the smallest circumference of a limb and is then moved upward. Wrists and ankles are the usual sites for anchoring bandages of the limbs. Bandages are applied to these areas in the following manner:

1. The loose end of the elastic bandage is laid obliquely on the anterior aspects of the wrist or ankle and held in this position. The roll is then carried posteriorly under and completely around the limb and back to the starting point.
2. The triangular portion of the uncovered oblique end is folded over the second turn.
3. The folded triangle is covered by a third turn, which finishes a secure anchor.

After an elastic bandage has been applied, it is held in place by a locking technique. The method most often used to finish a wrap is to firmly tie or pin the bandage or place adhesive tape over several overlying turns.

Once a bandage has been put on and has served its purpose, it can be removed either by unwrapping or by carefully cutting with bandage scissors. Whatever method of bandage removal is used, the athletic trainer must take extreme caution to avoid additional injury.

Elastic Bandage Techniques

Any time an athletic trainer applies an elastic bandage to the athlete, the trainer must always check for decreased circulation and blueness of the extremity as well as for a blood capillary refill.

Ankle and foot spica   The ankle and foot **spica** bandage (Figure 8-2) is primarily used in sports for the compression of new injuries and for holding wound dressings in place.

Materials needed   Depending on the size of the ankle and foot, a 2-inch (5 cm) or 3-inch (7.5 cm) wrap is used.

Position of the athlete   The athlete sits with his or her ankle and foot extended over the edge of a table.

Procedure

1. Place an anchor around the foot near the metatarsal arch.
2. Bring the elastic bandage across the instep and around the heel, and return to the starting point.
3. Repeat the procedure several times, with each succeeding revolution progressing upward on the foot and the ankle.
4. Overlap each spica over the preceding layer by approximately three fourths.

Spiral bandage

The spiral bandage (Figure 8-3) is widely used in sports for covering a large area of a cylindrical part.

Materials needed   Depending on the size of the area, a 3-inch (7.5 cm) or 4-inch (10 cm) wrap is required.

Position of the athlete   If the wrap is for the lower limb, the athlete bears weight on the opposite leg.

Procedure

1. Anchor the elastic spiral bandage at the smallest circumference of the limb and wrap upward in a spiral against gravity.
2. To prevent the bandage from slipping down on a moving extremity, fold two pieces of tape lengthwise and place them on the bandage at either side of the limb, or spray tape adherent on the injured area.
3. After the bandage is anchored, carry it upward in consecutive spiral turns, each overlapping the other by at least ½ inch.

Begin anchoring bandages at the smallest part of the limb.

Check circulation after applying an elastic wrap.

spica
A figure-eight bandage with one of the two loops larger than the other.

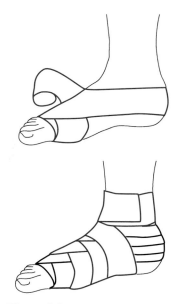

Figure 8-2

Ankle and foot spica.

Figure 8-3

Spiral bandage.

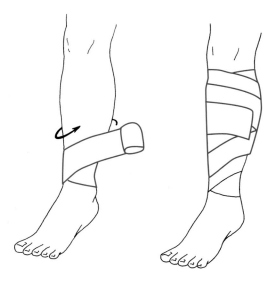

4. Terminate the bandage by locking it with circular turns, and then firmly secured the bandage with tape.

Groin support   The following procedure is used to support a groin strain and hip adductor strains (Figure 8-4).

Materials needed   One roll of extra-long 6-inch (15 cm) elastic bandage, a roll of 1½-inch (3.8 cm) adhesive tape, and nonsterile cotton.

Position of the athlete   The athlete stands on a table and places his or her weight on the uninjured leg. The affected limb is relaxed and internally rotated. This procedure is different from that described in Figure 8-4, in which the wrap was used for pressure only.

Procedure

1. Place a piece of nonsterile cotton or a felt pad, if needed, over the injured site to provide additional compression and support.
2. Start the end of the elastic bandage at the upper part of the inner aspect of the thigh and carry it posteriorly around the thigh. Then bring it across the lower abdomen and over the crest of the ilium on the opposite side of the body.
3. Continue the wrap around the back, repeating the same pattern and securing the wrap end with a 1½-inch (3.8 cm) adhesive tape.

8-2

Critical Thinking Exercise

A baseball player strains his right groin while running the bases.

? Which elastic wrap should the athletic trainer apply when the athlete returns to his sport? Why?

Figure 8-4

Elastic groin support.

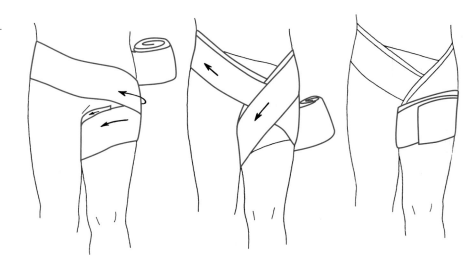

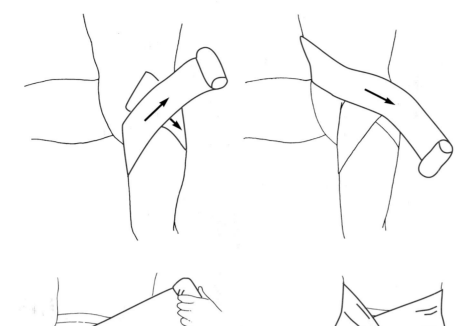

Figure 8-5

Hip spica for hip flexors.

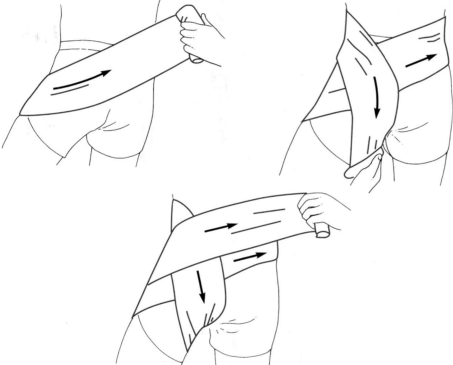

Figure 8-6

Method used to limit movement of buttocks.

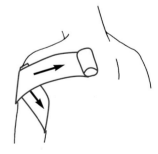

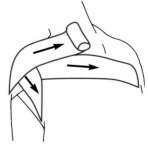

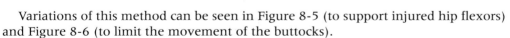

Variations of this method can be seen in Figure 8-5 (to support injured hip flexors) and Figure 8-6 (to limit the movement of the buttocks).

Shoulder spica   The shoulder spica (Figure 8-7) is used mainly for the retention of wound dressings and for moderate muscular support.

Materials needed   One roll of extra-long 4-inch (10 cm) to 6-inch (15 cm) elastic wrap, 1½-inch (3.8 cm) adhesive tape, and padding for axilla.

Position of the athlete   The athlete stands with his or her side toward the athletic trainer.

Procedure
1. Pad the axilla well to prevent skin irritation and constriction of blood vessels.
2. Anchor the bandage by one turn around the affected upper arm.

Figure 8-7

Elastic shoulder spica.

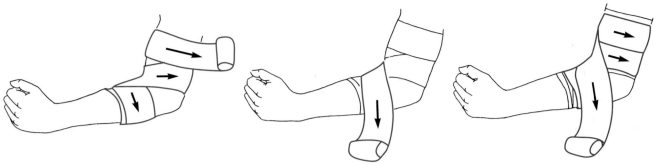

Figure 8-8

Elastic elbow figure-eight bandage.

3. After anchoring the bandage around the arm on the injured side, carry the wrap around the back under the unaffected arm and across the chest to the injured shoulder.
4. Encircle the affected arm again by the bandage, which continues around the back. Every figure-eight pattern moves progressively upward with an overlap of at least half of the previous underlying wrap.

Elbow figure-eight bandage   The elbow figure-eight bandage (Figure 8-8) can be used to secure a dressing in the antecubital fossa or to restrain full extension in hyperextension injuries. When it is reversed, it can be used on the posterior aspect of the elbow.

Materials needed   One 3-inch (7.5 cm) elastic roll and 1½-inch (3.8 cm) adhesive tape.

Position of the athlete   The athlete flexes his or her elbow between 45 degrees and 90 degrees, depending on the restriction of movement required.

Procedure
1. Anchor the bandage by encircling the lower arm.
2. Bring the roll obliquely upward over the posterior aspect of the elbow.
3. Carry the roll obliquely upward, crossing the antecubital fossa; then pass once again completely around the upper arm and return to the beginning position by again crossing the antecubital fossa.
4. Continue the procedure as described, but for every new sequence move upward toward the elbow one half the width of the underlying wrap.

Gauze hand and wrist figure eight   A figure-eight bandage (Figure 8-9) can be used for mild wrist and hand support and for holding dressings in place.

8-3

Critical Thinking E x e r c i s e

A wrestler sustains a left shoulder point injury. The athletic trainer cuts a sponge rubber doughnut to protect the shoulder point from further injury.

? How is the doughnut held in place?

Figure 8-9

Hand and wrist figure-eight bandage.

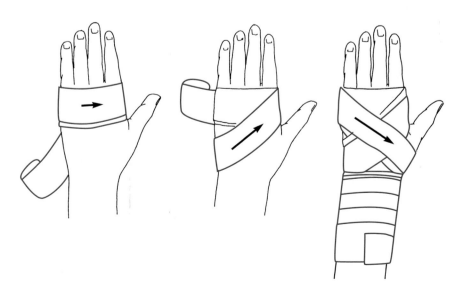

Materials needed   One roll of ½-inch (1.25 cm) gauze, ½-inch (1.25 cm) tape, and scissors.

Position of the athlete   The athlete positions his or her elbow at a 45-degree angle.

Procedure

1. The anchor is executed with one or two turns of the bandage around the palm of the hand.
2. The roll is then carried obliquely across the anterior or posterior portion of the hand, depending on the position of the wound, to the wrist, which it circles once; then it is returned to the primary anchor.
3. As many figure eights as needed are applied.

Cloth Ankle Wrap

Because tape is so expensive, the ankle wrap is an inexpensive and expedient means of mildly protecting ankles (Figure 8-10). Due to an increase in the use of ankle braces and supports, the cloth ankle wrap is used infrequently in an athletic training setting.

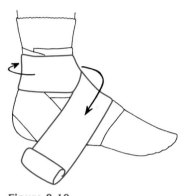

Figure 8-10
Ankle wrap.

Materials needed   Each wrap should be 1½ to 2 inches (3.8 to 5 cm) wide and 72 to 96 inches (180 to 240 cm) long to ensure complete coverage and protection. The purpose of this wrap is to give mild support against lateral and medial motion of the ankle. It is applied over a sock.

Position of the athlete   The athlete sits on a table, extending the leg and positioning the foot at a 90-degree angle. To avoid any distortion, it is important that the ankle be neither overflexed nor overextended.

Procedure

1. Start the wrap above the instep around the ankle, circle the ankle, and move it at an acute angle to the inside of the foot.
2. From the inside of the foot, move the wrap under the arch, coming up on the outside and crossing at the beginning point, and continue around the ankle, hooking the heel.
3. Move the wrap up, inside, over the instep, and around the ankle, hooking the opposite side of the heel. This completes one series of the ankle wrap.
4. Complete a second series with the remaining material.
5. For additional support, apply two heel locks with adhesive tape over the ankle wrap.

Triangular and Cravat Bandages

Triangular and cravat bandages, usually made of cotton cloth, may be used if roller types are not applicable or available. The triangular and cravat bandages are primarily used as first aid devices.[15] They are valuable in emergency bandaging because they are easy and quick to apply. In sports the more diversified roller bandages are usually available and lend themselves more to the needs of the athlete. The principal use of the triangular bandage in athletic training is for arm slings. There are two basic kinds of slings, the cervical arm sling and the shoulder arm sling, and each has a specific purpose.

Triangular and cravat bandages can be applied easily and quickly.

Cervical arm sling   The cervical arm sling (Figure 8-11) is designed to support the forearm, wrist, and hand. A triangular bandage is placed around the neck and under the bent arm that is to be supported.

Materials needed   One triangular bandage.

Position of the athlete   The athlete stands with the affected arm bent at approximately a 70-degree angle.

Procedure

1. Position the triangular bandage under the injured arm with the apex facing the elbow.
2. Carry the end of the triangle nearest the body over the shoulder of the uninjured arm. Allow the other end to hang down loosely.
3. Pull the loose end over the shoulder of the injured side.

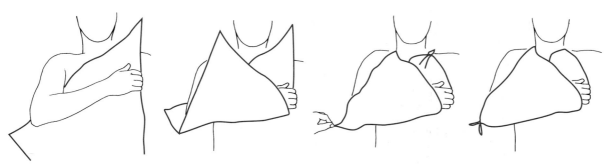

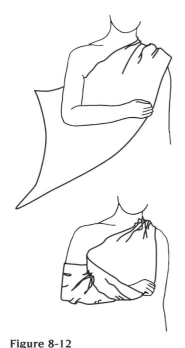

Figure 8-11

Cervical arm sling.

Figure 8-12

Shoulder arm sling.

Figure 8-13

Sling and swathe.

4. Tie the two ends of the bandage in a square knot behind the neck. For the sake of comfort, the knot should be on either side of the neck, not directly in the middle.
5. Bring the apex of the triangle around to the front of the elbow and fasten by twisting the end, then tying in a knot.

If greater arm stabilization is required than that afforded by a sling, an additional bandage can be swathed about the upper arm and body.

Shoulder arm sling   The shoulder arm sling (Figure 8-12) is suggested for forearm support when there is an injury to the shoulder girdle or when the cervical arm sling is irritating to the athlete.

Materials needed   One triangular bandage and one safety pin.

Position of the athlete   The athlete stands with his or her injured arm bent at approximately a 70-degree angle.

Procedure

1. Place the upper end of the shoulder sling over the uninjured shoulder side.
2. Bring the lower end of the triangle over the forearm and draw it between the upper arm and the body, swinging it around the athlete's back and then upward to meet the other end, where a square knot is tied.
3. Bring the apex end of the triangle around to the front of the elbow and fasten with a safety pin.

Sling and swathe   The sling and swathe combination is designed to stabilize the arm securely in cases of shoulder dislocation or fracture (Figure 8-13).

NONELASTIC AND ELASTIC ADHESIVE TAPING

Historically, taping has been an important part of athletic training. In recent years athletic taping has become decreasingly important as an adjunct to sports medicine because current research questions long-held ideas about the effectiveness of taping.[17,22,28] The psychological effect of taping on the athlete is currently unknown.

Tape Usage

Injury Care

When used for sports injuries, adhesive tape offers a number of possibilities:

- Retention of wound dressings.[16]
- Stabilization of compression bandages that control external and internal hemorrhaging.[16]
- Support of recent injuries to prevent additional insult that might result from the activities of the athlete.[5]
- Stabilization of an injury while the athlete is undergoing an exercise rehabilitation procedure.[5]

Injury Protection

Protecting against acute injuries is another major use of tape support. This protection can be achieved by limiting the motion of a body part or by securing some special device.

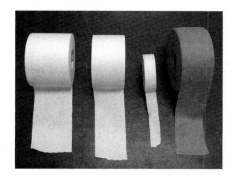

Figure 8-14

Nonelastic adhesive tape 2″, 1½″, ½″, and Leukotape.

Nonelastic Adhesive Tape

Nonelastic adhesive tape has great adaptability for use in sports because of its uniform adhesive mass, adhering qualities, and lightness and because of the relative strength of the backing materials.[21] All these qualities are of value in holding wound dressings in place and in supporting and protecting injured areas. This tape comes in a variety of sizes; widths of ½, 1, 1½, and 2 inches (1.25, 2.5, 3.75, and 5 cm) are commonly used in sports medicine (Figure 8-14). When linen tape is purchased, factors such as cost, grade of backing, quality of adhesive mass, and properties of unwinding should be considered.

Tape Grade

White adhesive tape is most often graded according to the number of longitudinal and vertical fibers per inch of backing material.[4] The heavier and more costly backing contains 85 or more longitudinal fibers and 65 vertical fibers per square inch. The lighter, less expensive grade has 65 or fewer longitudinal fibers and 45 vertical fibers.

Adhesive Mass

As a result of improvements in adhesive mass, certain essentials should be expected from tape. It should adhere readily when applied and should maintain this adherence in the presence of profuse perspiration and activity. Besides sticking well, the mass must contain as few skin irritants as possible and must be able to be removed easily without leaving a mass residue or pulling away the superficial skin.

Winding Tension

The winding tension of a tape roll is important to the athletic trainer. The demands of sport activity place a unique demand on the unwinding quality of tape; if tape is to be applied for protection and support, there must be even and constant unwinding tension. In most cases, a proper wind needs little additional tension to provide sufficient tightness.

Elastic Adhesive Tape

Elastic adhesive tape is commonly used in sports medicine, often in combination with nonelastic adhesive tape. Because of its conforming qualities, elastic tape is used for small, angular body parts, such as the feet, wrist, hands, and fingers. As with nonelastic adhesive tape, elastic tape comes in a variety of widths (1, 2, 3, and 4 inch) (Figure 8-15).

Tape Storage

When storing tape, take the following steps:
1. Store in a cool place such as in a low cupboard.
2. Stack so that the tape rests on its flat top or bottom to avoid distortion.

8-4

Critical Thinking Exercise

An athlete falls and sustains a dislocated right shoulder.

? How should the athlete be transported safely to the hospital?

When purchasing linen tape, consider:
- Grade of backing
- Quality of adhesive mass
- Winding tension

Increasingly, tape with varying elasticity is being used in sports medicine.

Store tape in a cool place, and stack it flat.

Figure 8-15

Elastic adhesive tape.
A, 2″ and 1″ light wrap tape.
B, 3″, 2″, and 1″ elastic tape.

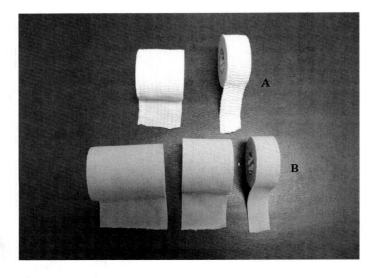

Using Adhesive Tape in Sports

Preparation for Taping

Skin should be cleansed and hair should be shaved before tape is applied.

The athletic trainer must pay special attention when applying tape directly to the skin.[23] A list of supplies needed for proper taping appears later in this chapter. Perspiration, oil, and dirt prevent tape from adhering to the skin. Whenever tape is used, the skin surface should be cleaned with soap and water to remove all dirt and oil. Also, hair should be shaved to prevent additional irritation when the tape is removed (Figure 8-16A). A quick-drying tape adherent spray can be used to help the tape adhere to the skin, although it is not absolutely necessary (Figure 8-16B). Also, at certain points such as over bony prominences, the tape can produce friction blisters. Extra foam or gauze pads (heel and lace pads) with a small amount of lubricant can help to minimize the occurrence of blisters (Figure 8-16C). Taping directly on skin provides maximum sup-

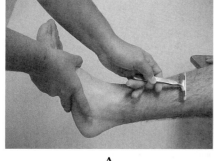

A

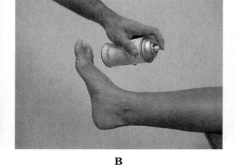

B

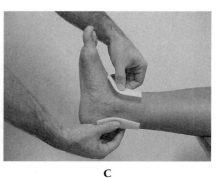

C

D

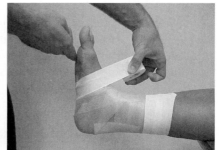

E

Figure 8-16

Taping preparation. **A,** Shaving. **B,** Applying tape adherent. **C,** Placing heel and lace pads. **D,** Applying one layer of under wrap. **E,** Applying anchor strips.

port. However, applying tape day after day can lead to skin irritation. A roll of foam that is thin, porous, extremely lightweight, and resilient, called underwrap or prewrap, easily conforms to the contours of the part to be taped and protects the skin to some degree. Underwrap material should be applied only one layer thick (Figure 8-16D). The underwrap should be anchored both proximally and distally (Figure 8-16E).

Proper Taping Technique

The correct tape width depends on the area to be covered. The more acute the angles, the narrower the tape must be to fit the many contours. For example, the fingers and toes usually require $\frac{1}{2}$- or 1-inch (1.25 or 2.5 cm) tape; the ankles require $1\frac{1}{2}$-inch (3.75 cm) tape; and the larger skin areas such as thighs and back can accommodate 2- to 3-inch (5 to 7.5 cm) tape with ease.

NOTE: Supportive tape improperly applied can aggravate an existing injury or can disrupt the mechanics of a body part, causing an initial injury to occur.

Tearing Tape

Athletic trainers use various techniques to tear tape (Figure 8-17). The tearing method should permit the operator to keep the tape roll in hand most of the time.[30] The following is a suggested procedure:

1. Hold the tape roll in the preferred hand with the middle finger hooked through the center of the tape roll and the thumb pressing its outer edge.
2. With the other hand, grasp the loose end between the thumb and index finger.
3. With both hands in place, pull both ends of the tape so that it is tight. Next, make a quick, scissorslike move to tear the tape. In tearing tape, one hand moves away from the body and the other hand moves toward the body. Remember, do not try to bend or twist the tape to tear it.

> To tear tape, move hands quickly in opposite directions.

When tearing is properly executed, the torn edges of the nonelastic adhesive tape are relatively straight, without curves, twists, or loose threads sticking out. Once the first thread is torn, the rest of the tape tears easily. Learning to tear tape effectively from many different positions is essential for speed and efficiency. Many tapes other than the linen-backed type cannot be torn manually but require a knife, scissors, or razor blade.

Rules for Tape Application

The following are a few of the important rules to be observed in the use of adhesive tape. In practice the athletic trainer will identify others.

1. *If the part to be taped is a joint, place it in the position in which it is to be stabilized.* If the part is musculature, make the necessary allowance for contraction and expansion.
2. *Overlap the tape at least half the width of the tape below.* Unless tape is overlapped sufficiently, the active athlete will separate it, exposing the underlying skin to irritation and allowing a space in which swelling/edema can occur.

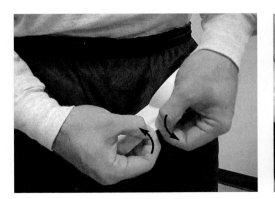 

Figure 8-17

Technique for tearing adhesive tape.

3. *Avoid continuous taping.* Tape continuously wrapped around a part may cause constriction. Make one turn at a time and tear each encirclement to overlap the starting end by approximately 1 inch. This rule is particularly true of the nonyielding linen-backed tape.

4. *Keep the tape roll in the hand whenever possible.* By learning to keep the tape roll in the hand, seldom putting it down, and by learning to tear the tape, an athletic trainer can develop taping speed and accuracy.

5. *Smooth and mold the tape as it is laid on the skin.* To save additional time, smooth and mold tape strips to the body part as they are put in place; this is done by stroking the top with the fingers, palms, and heels of both hands.

6. *Allow tape to fit the natural contour of the skin.* Each strip of tape must be placed with a particular purpose in mind. Linen-backed tape is not sufficiently elastic to bend around acute angles but must be allowed to fall as it may, fitting naturally to the body contours. Failing to allow this fit creates wrinkles and gaps that can result in skin irritations.

7. *Start taping with an anchor piece and finish by applying a lock strip.* Commence taping, if possible, by sticking the tape to an anchor piece that encircles the part. This placement affords a good medium for the stabilization of succeeding tape strips so that they will not be affected by the movement of the part.

8. *Where maximum support is desired, tape directly over skin.* In cases of sensitive skin, prewrap may be used as tape bases. With prewrap, some movement can be expected between the skin and the base.[3]

9. *Do not apply tape if skin is hot or cold from a therapeutic treatment.*

Removing Adhesive Tape

Tape usually can be removed from the skin by hand, by tape scissors or tape cutters, or by chemical solvents.[30]

> Peel the skin from the tape, not the tape from the skin.

Manual removal   When pulling tape from the body, be careful not to tear or irritate the skin. Tape must not be wrenched in an outward direction from the skin but should be pulled in a direct line with the body (Figure 8-18). Remember to remove the skin carefully from the tape and not to peel the tape from the skin. Use one hand to gently pull the tape in one direction, and the opposite hand to gently press the skin away from the tape.

Figure 8-18

Removing tape by pulling in a direct line with the body.

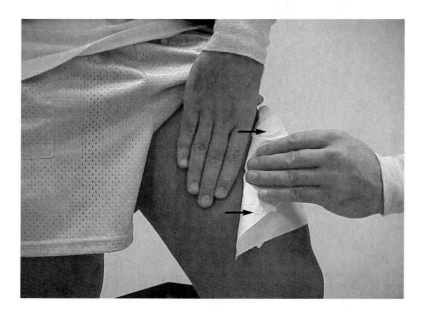

Use of tape scissors or cutters   The characteristic tape scissors have a blunt nose that slips underneath the tape smoothly without gouging the skin. Take care to avoid cutting the tape too near the site of the injury, so the scissors do not aggravate the condition. Cut on the uninjured side.

Taping Supplies

Effective taping requires the availability of numerous supplies:

1. Razor—hair removal
2. Soap—cleaning skin
3. Alcohol—oil removal from skin
4. Adhesive spray—tape adherent
5. Prewrap material—skin protection
6. Heel and lace pads
7. White nonelastic adhesive tape (½ inch, 1 inch, 1½-inch, and 2 inch [1.25 cm, 2.5 cm, 3.8 cm, and 5 cm])
8. Elastic adhesive tape (1 inch, 2 inch, and 3 inch [2.5 cm, 5 cm, and 7.5 cm])
9. Felt and foam padding material
10. Tape scissors
11. Tape cutters
12. Elastic bandages (2 inch, 3 inch, 4 inch, and 6 inch [5 cm, 7.5 cm, 10 cm, and 15 cm])

Common Taping Procedures

The Arch

Arch technique no. 1: with pad support   Arch taping with pad support strengthens weakened arches (Figure 8-19). NOTE: The longitudinal arch should be lifted. CAUTION: When applying tape around the forefoot, be aware that the metatarsals must have room to spread when bearing weight.

Materials needed   One roll of 1½-inch (3.8 cm) tape, tape adherent, and a ⅛- or ¼-inch (0.3 or 0.6 cm) adhesive foam rubber pad or wool felt pad, cut to fit the longitudinal arch.

Site preparation   Clean foot of dirt and oil; if hairy, shave dorsum of foot. Spray area with tape adherent.

Position of the athlete   The athlete lies face down on the table with the foot that is to be taped extending approximately 6 inches (15 cm) over the edge of the table. To ensure proper position, allow the foot to hang in a relaxed position.

Procedure

1. Place a series of strips of tape directly around the arch or, if added support is required, around an arch pad and the arch. The first strip should go just above the metatarsal arch (1).
2. Each successive strip overlaps the preceding piece about half the width of the tape (2 through 4).

CAUTION: Avoid putting on so many strips of tape that the action of the ankle is hampered.

Arch technique no. 2: the X for the longitudinal arch   Use the figure-eight method for taping the longitudinal arch (Figure 8-20).

Materials needed   One roll of 1-inch (2.5 cm) tape and tape adherent.

Site preparation   Same as for arch technique no. 1.

Position of the athlete   The athlete lies face down on the table with the affected foot extending approximately 6 inches (15 cm) over the edge of the table. To ensure proper position, allow the foot to hang in a relaxed position.

Procedure

1. Lightly place an anchor strip around the ball of the foot, making certain not to constrict the action of the toes (1).

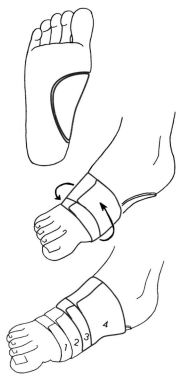

Figure 8-19

Arch taping technique no. 1, including an arch pad and circular tape strips.

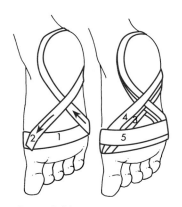

Figure 8-20

Arch taping technique no. 2 (X taping).

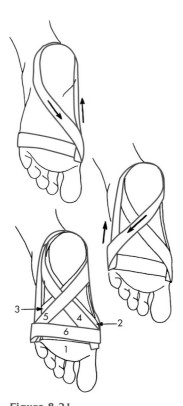

Figure 8-21

Teardrop arch taping technique no. 3 with double X and forefoot support.

Figure 8-22

Fan arch taping technique.

2. Start tape strip 2 from the lateral edge of the anchor. Move it upward at an acute angle, cross the center of the longitudinal arch, encircle the heel, and descend. Then cross the arch again and end at the medial aspect of the anchor (2). Repeat three or four times (3 and 4).

3. Lock the taped Xs with a single piece of tape placed around the ball of foot (5).

After all the X strips are applied, cover the entire arch with 1½-inch (3.8 cm) circular tape strips.

Arch technique no. 3: the X teardrop arch and forefoot support   As its name implies, this taping both supports the longitudinal arch and stabilizes the forefoot into good alignment (Figure 8-21).

Materials needed   One roll of 1-inch (2.5 cm) tape and tape adherent.

Position of the athlete   The athlete lies face down on the table with the foot to be taped extending approximately 6 inches (15 cm) over the edge of the table.

Procedure

1. Place an anchor strip around the ball of the foot (1).

2. Start tape strip 2 on the side of the foot, beginning at the base of the great toe. Take the tape around the heel, crossing the arch and returning to the starting point (2).

3. The pattern of the third strip of tape is the same as the second strip except that it is started on the little toe side of the foot (3). Repeat two or three times (4 and 5).

4. Lock each series of strips by placing tape around the ball joint (6). A completed procedure usually consists of a series of three strips.

Arch technique no. 4: fan arch support   The fan arch technique supports the entire plantar aspect of the foot (Figure 8-22).

Materials needed   One roll of 1-inch (2.5 cm) tape, one roll of 1½-inch (3.8 cm) tape, and tape adherent.

Position of athlete   The athlete lies face down on the table with the foot to be taped extending approximately 6 inches (15 cm) over the edge of the table.

Procedure

1. Using the 1-inch (2.5 cm) tape, place an anchor strip around the ball of the foot (1).

2. Starting at the third metatarsal head, take the tape around the heel from the lateral side and meet the strip where it began (2 and 3).

3. Start the next strip near the second metatarsal head and finish it on the fourth metatarsal head (4).

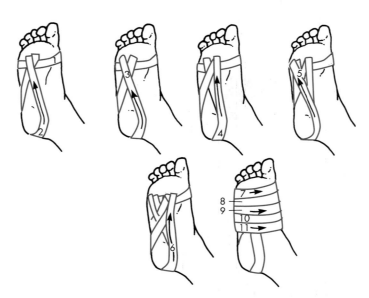

Figure 8-23

LowDye taping technique.

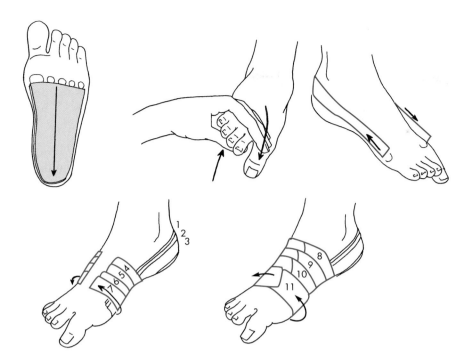

4. Begin the last strip on the fourth metatarsal head and finish it on the fifth metatarsal head (5). The technique, when completed, forms a fan-shaped pattern covering the metatarsal region (6).

5. Lock strips using 1½-inch (3.8 cm) tape and encircling the complete arch (7 through 11).

LowDye technique   The LowDye technique is an excellent method for managing the fallen medial longitudinal arch, foot pronation, arch strains, and plantar fascitis.[13,27] Moleskin is cut in 3-inch (7.5 cm) strips to the shape of the sole of the foot. It should cover the head of the metatarsal bones and the calcaneus bone (Figure 8-23).

Materials needed   One roll of 1-inch (2.5 cm) tape, one roll of 2-inch (5 cm) tape, and moleskin.

Position of the athlete   The athlete sits with the foot in a neutral position with the great toe and medial aspect of the foot in plantar flexion.

Procedure

1. Apply the moleskin to the sole of the foot, pulling it slightly downward before attaching it to the calcaneus.

2. Grasp the forefoot with the thumb under the distal 2 to 5 metatarsal heads, pushing slightly upward, with the tips of the second and third fingers pushing downward on the first metatarsal head. Apply two or three 1-inch (2.5 cm) tape strips laterally, starting from the distal head of the first metatarsal bone (1 through 3). Keep these lateral strips below the outer malleolus.

3. Secure the moleskin and lateral tape strip by circling the forefoot with four 2-inch (5 cm) strips (4 through 7). Start at the lateral dorsum of the foot, circle under the plantar aspect, and finish at the medial dorsum of the foot. Apply four strips of 2-inch stretch tape that encircle the arch (8 through 11).

A variation of this method is to use two 2-inch (5 cm) moleskin strips, one at the ball of the foot and the other at the base of the fifth metatarsal. Cross the strips and extend them along the plantar surface of the foot. For anchors, apply 2-inch (5 cm) elastic tape around the forefoot, lateral to medial, giving additional support.[13,27]

8-5

Critical Thinking Exercise

A football lineman has a severe right foot pronation with a fallen medial longitudinal arch. He is subject to arch strains.

? What taping technique is designed for this situation?

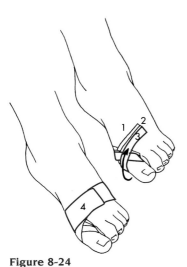

Figure 8-24

Taping for a sprained great toe.

The Toes

The sprained great toe   This procedure is used for taping a sprained great toe (Figure 8-24).

Materials needed   One roll of 1-inch (2.5 cm) tape and tape adherent and one roll of 1½-inch (3.8 cm) tape.

Site preparation   Clean foot of dirt and oil, shave hair from toes, and spray area with tape adherent.

Position of the athlete   The athlete assumes a sitting position.

Procedure

1. The greatest support is given to the joint by a half-figure-eight taping (1 through 3). Start the series at an acute angle on the top of the foot and swing down between the great and first toes, first encircling the great toe and then coming up, over, and across the starting point. Repeat this process, starting each series separately.
2. After the required number of half-figure-eight strips are in position, place 1½-inch lock piece around the ball of the foot (4).

Bunions

Materials needed   One roll of 1-inch (2.5 cm) tape, tape adherent, and ¼-inch (0.6 cm) sponge rubber or felt (Figure 8-25).

Position of the athlete   The athlete assumes a sitting position.

Procedure

1. Cut the ¼-inch sponge rubber to form a wedge between the great and second toes.
2. Place anchor strips to encircle the midfoot and distal aspect of the great toe (1 and 2).
3. Place two or three strips on the medial aspect of the great toe to hold the toe in proper alignment (3 through 5).
4. Lock the ends of the strips with tape (6 and 7).

Turf toe   Turf toe taping is designed to prevent excessive hyperextension of the metatarsophalangeal joint (Figure 8-26).

Materials needed   One roll of 1½-inch (3.8 cm) adhesive tape, one roll of 1-inch (2.5 cm) adhesive tape, and tape adherent.

Site preparation   Shave hair off the top of the forefoot and great toe. Spray the area with tape adherent.

Position of the athlete   The great toe is in a neutral position.

Procedure

1. Apply a one 1-inch (2.5 cm) tape strip around the great toe. Using 1½-inch (3.8 cm) tape, apply two arch anchors to the midarch area.
2. On the middle of the great toe, attach three 1-inch (2.5 cm) tape strips to create a checkrein.
3. Attach the checkrein to the arch anchor tapes, strip-crossing the metatarsophalangeal joint line.
4. Lock both ends of the checkrein in place.

Figure 8-25

Bunion taping.

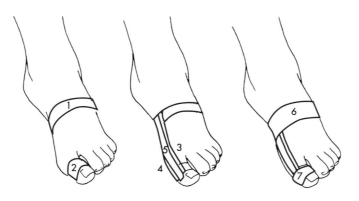

Hammer, or clawed, toes   This technique is designed to reduce the pressure of the bent toes against the shoe (Figure 8-27).[26]

Materials needed   One roll of ½- or 1-inch (1.25 or 2.5 cm) adhesive tape and tape adherent.

Position of the athlete   The athlete sits on the table with the affected leg extended over the edge.

Procedure

1. Tape one affected toe; then lace under the adjacent toe and over the next toe.
2. Tape can be attached to the next toe or can be continued and attached to the fifth toe.

Fractured toes   This technique splints the fractured toe with a nonfractured one (Figure 8-28).

Materials needed   One roll of ½- or 1-inch (1.25 or 2.5 cm) tape, ⅛-inch (0.3 cm) sponge rubber, and tape adherent.

Position of the athlete   The athlete assumes a sitting position.

Procedure

1. Cut a ⅛-inch (0.3 cm) sponge rubber wedge and place it between the affected toe and a healthy one.
2. Wrap two or three strips of tape around both toes.

The Ankle Joint

The combination of foam prewrap plus tape provides significantly better ankle support during exercise than does taping directly on the skin. Both procedures diminish over time, but prewrap appears to decline more slowly. It is most effective immediately after initial application because it provides some minor resistance to ankle inversion movements.[10,18,32]

Ankle joint taping is most appropriate for sports with short bursts of at-risk activity, such as high jumping, and for endurance sports, such as soccer or basketball. Whether ankle braces are as effective as ankle taping has been debated and remains controversial.[1,6,12,20,24,25]

Routine prophylactic (preventative) taping

Materials needed   One roll of 1½-inch (3.8 cm) tape, tape adherent, and underwrap (Figure 8-29).

Site preparation   Ankle taping applied directly to the athlete's skin affords the greatest support; however, when it is applied and removed daily, skin irritation will occur. To avoid this problem, apply an underwrap material. Before taping, follow these procedures:

1. Clean foot and ankle thoroughly.
2. Shave all the hair off the foot and ankle.
3. Apply a coating of tape adherent to protect the skin and offer an adhering base.
4. Apply a gauze pad coated with friction-reducing material such as grease over the instep and to the back of the heel.
5. If underwrap is used, apply a single layer. The tape anchors extend beyond the underwrap and adhere directly to the skin.
6. Do not apply tape if skin is cold or hot from a therapeutic treatment.

Position of the athlete   The athlete sits on the table with the leg extended and the foot held at a 90-degree angle.

Procedure

1. Place an anchor around the ankle approximately 5 or 6 inches (12.5 or 15 cm) above the malleolus.
2. Apply two strips in consecutive order, starting behind the outer malleolus, taking care that the second strip overlaps the first by half the width of the tape (2 and 3).
3. After applying the strips, wrap seven or eight circular strips around the ankle, from the point of the anchor downward, until the malleolus is completely covered (4 through 12).

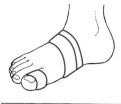
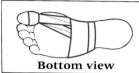

Figure 8-26

Turf toe taping.

Figure 8-27

Hammer, or clawed, toe taping.

Figure 8-28

Fractured toe taping.

Figure 8-29

Routine noninjury ankle taping.

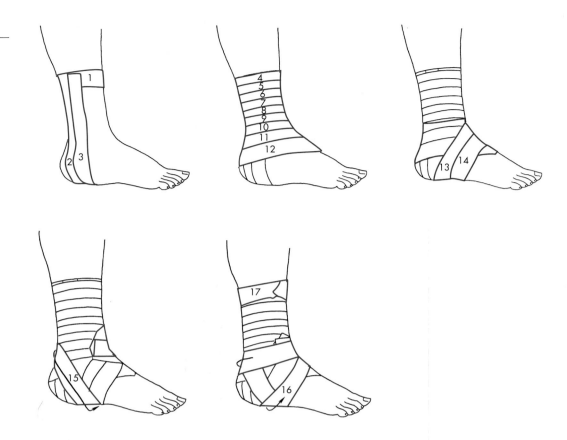

4. Apply two or three arch strips from lateral to medial, giving additional support to the arch (13 and 14).
5. Additional support is given by a heel lock. Starting high on the instep, bring the tape along the ankle at a slight angle, hooking the heel, leading under the arch, then coming up on the opposite side, and finishing at the starting point. Tear the tape to complete half of the heel lock (15). Repeat on the opposite side of the ankle (16). Finish with a band of tape around the ankle (17).

Closed basket weave (Gibney) technique   The closed basket weave, or Gibney, technique offers strong tape support and is primarily used in athletic training for newly sprained or chronically weak ankles (Figure 8-30). A U-shaped felt pad can be used with this taping technique to provide focal compression and thus assist in controlling swelling. The technique for controlling swelling initially following injury is discussed in detail in Chapter 12.

Materials needed   One roll of 1½-inch (3.8 cm) tape, underwrap, and tape adherent.

Position of the athlete   The athlete sits on the table with the leg extended and the foot at a 90-degree angle.

Procedure

1. Place one anchor piece around the ankle approximately 5 or 6 inches (12.5 or 15 cm) above the malleolus just below the belly of the gastrocnemius muscle. Place a second anchor around the instep directly over the styloid process of the fifth metatarsal (1 and 2).
2. Apply the first strip posteriorly to the malleolus and attach it to the ankle anchor (3). NOTE: When applying strips, pull the foot into eversion for an inversion strain and into a neutral position for an eversion strain.
3. Start the first Gibney directly under the malleolus and attach it to the foot anchor (4).
4. In an alternating series, place three strips and three Gibneys on the ankle with each piece of tape overlapping at least half of the preceding strip (5 through 8).

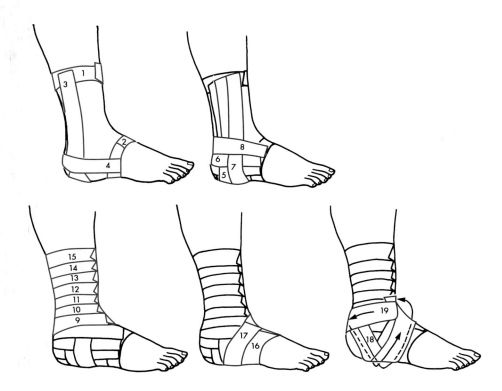

Figure 8-30

Closed basket weave ankle taping.

5. After applying the basket weave series, continue the Gibney strips up the ankle, thus giving circular support (9 through 15).

6. For arch support, apply two or three circular strips laterally to medially (16 and 17).

7. After completing the conventional basket weave, apply two or three heel locks to ensure maximum stability (18 and 19).

Open basket weave   This modification of the closed basket weave, or Gibney, technique is designed to give freedom of movement in dorsiflexion and plantar flexion while providing lateral and medial support and allowing swelling room. Taping in this pattern may be used immediately after an acute sprain in conjunction with a pressure bandage and cold applications because it allows for swelling (Figure 8-31).

Materials needed   One roll of 1½-inch (3.8 cm) tape and tape adherent.

Position of the athlete   The athlete sits on the table with the leg extended and the foot held at a 90-degree angle.

Procedure

1. The procedures are the same as for the closed basket weave (Figure 8-30) with the exception of incomplete closures of the Gibney strips (11 through 17).

2. Lock the gap between the Gibney ends with two pieces of tape running on either side of the instep (18 through 21). NOTE: Application of a 1½-inch (3.8 cm) elastic bandage over the open basket weave affords added control of swelling; however, the athlete should remove it before going to bed. Apply the elastic bandage distal to proximal to prevent swelling from moving into the toes.

Of the many ankle taping techniques in use today, those using combinations of strips, basket weaves, and heel locks offer the best support.

Continuous-stretch tape technique   This technique provides a fast alternative to other taping methods for the ankle (Figure 8-32).[23]

Materials needed   One roll of 1½-inch (3.8 cm) linen tape, one roll of 2-inch (5 cm) stretch tape, tape adherent, and underwrap.

Position of the athlete   The athlete sits on the table with the leg extended and the foot at a 90-degree angle.

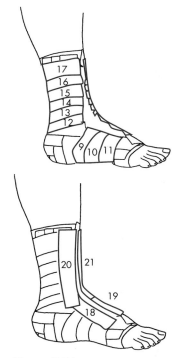

Figure 8-31

Open basket weave ankle taping.

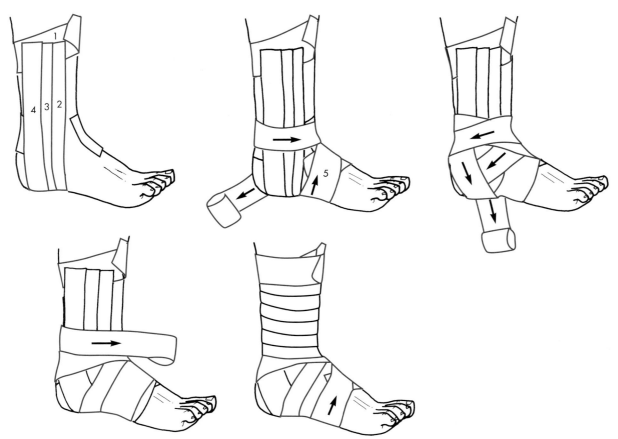

Figure 8-32

Continuous-stretch tape technique for the ankle.

A cross-country runner steps in a hole and suffers a lateral sprain to the right ankle.

? What taping technique should be selected to provide ankle joint support while still allowing for swelling?

Procedure

1. Place one anchor strip around the ankle approximately 5 to 6 inches (12.5 cm to 15 cm) above the malleolus (1).
2. Apply three strips, covering the malleolli (2 through 4).
3. Start the stretch tape in a medial-to-lateral direction around the midfoot and continue it in a figure-eight pattern to above the lateral malleolus (5).
4. Continue to stretch tape across the midfoot, then across the heel.
5. Apply two heel locks, one in each direction.
6. Next, repeat a figure-eight pattern followed by a spiral pattern, filling the space up to the anchor.
7. Use the lock technique at the top with a linen tape strip.

The Lower Leg

Achilles tendon   Achilles tendon taping is designed to prevent the Achilles tendon from overstretching (Figure 8-33).

Materials needed   One roll of 3-inch (7.5 cm) elastic tape, one roll of 1½-inch (3.8 cm) linen tape, and tape adherent.

Site preparation   Clean and shave the area, spray with tape adherent, and apply underwrap to the lower one-third of the calf.

Position of the athlete   The athlete kneels or lies face down with the affected foot hanging relaxed over the edge of the table.

Procedure

1. Apply two anchors with 1½-inch (3.8 cm) tape, one circling the leg loosely approximately 7 to 9 inches (17.5 to 22.5 cm) above the malleoli, and the other encircling the ball of the foot (1 and 2).

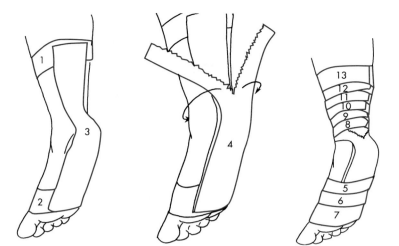

Figure 8-33

Achilles tendon taping.

2. Cut two strips of 3-inch (7.5 cm) elastic tape approximately 8 to 10 inches (20 to 25 cm) long. Moderately stretch the first strip from the ball of the athlete's foot along its plantar aspect up to the leg anchor (3). The second elastic strip (4) follows the course of the first, but cut it and split it down the middle lengthwise. Wrap the cut ends around the lower leg to form a lock. CAUTION: Keep the wrapped ends above the level of the strain.

3. Complete the series by placing two or three lock strips of elastic tape (5 through 7) loosely around the arch and five or six strips (8 through 13) around the athlete's lower leg.

Note that locking too tightly around the lower leg and foot will tend to restrict the normal action of the Achilles tendon and create more tissue irritation.

A variation on this method is to use three 2-inch (5 cm) elastic strips in place of strips 3 and 4. Apply the first strip at the plantar surface of the first metatarsal head and end it on the lateral side of the leg anchor. Apply the second strip at the plantar surface of the fifth metatarsal head and end it on the medial side of the leg anchor. Center the third strip between the other two strips and end it at the posterior aspect of the calf. Lock the strips with anchors of 3-inch (7.5 cm) elastic tape around the forefoot and lower calf.[2]

The Knee

Medial collateral ligament   Like athletes with ankle instabilities, athletes with unstable knees should never use tape and bracing as a replacement for proper exercise rehabilitation.[14] If properly applied, taping can help protect the knee and aid in the rehabilitation process (Figure 8-34).[8]

Materials needed   One roll of 2-inch (5 cm) linen tape, one roll of 3-inch (7.5 cm) elastic tape, a 1-inch (2.5 cm) heel lift, lubricant, gauze pad, tape adherent, and underwrap.

Site preparation   Clean, shave, and dry skin to be taped. Cover skin wounds. Lubricate the hamstring and popliteal areas and apply tape adherent.

Position of the athlete   The athlete stands on a 3-foot (90 cm) table with the injured knee held in a moderately relaxed position by a 1-inch (2.5 cm) heel lift. Completely remove the hair from an area 6 inches (15 cm) above to 6 inches (15 cm) below the patella.

Procedure

1. Lightly encircle the thigh and leg at the hairline with a 3-inch (7.5 cm) elastic anchor strip (1 and 2).

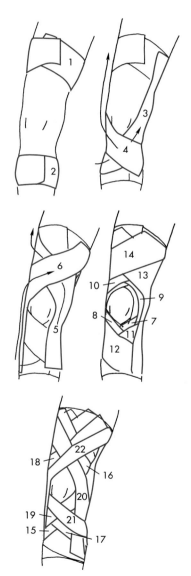

Figure 8-34

Collateral ligament knee taping.

Figure 8-35

Rotary taping.

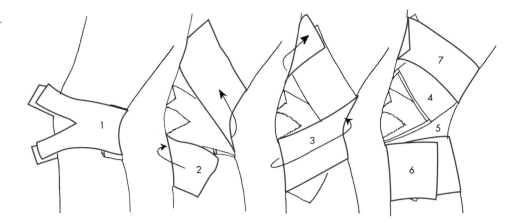

2. Precut twelve elastic tape strips, each approximately 9 inches (22.5 cm) long. Stretching them to their utmost, apply them to the knee as indicated in Figure 8-34 (3 through 14).

3. Apply a series of three strips of 2-inch (5 cm) linen tape (15 through 22). Some individuals find it advantageous to complete a knee taping by wrapping with an elastic wrap, thus providing an added precaution against the tape coming loose due to perspiration.

NOTE: Tape must not constrict the patella.

Rotary taping for instability of an injured knee   The rotary taping method is designed to provide the knee with support when it is unstable from injury to the medial collateral and anterior cruciate ligaments (Figure 8-35).

Materials needed   One roll of 3-inch (7.5 cm) elastic tape, tape adherent, 4-inch (10 cm) gauze pad, lubricant, scissors, and underwrap.

Position of the athlete   The athlete sits on the table with the affected knee flexed 15 degrees.

Procedure

1. Cut a 10-inch (25 cm) piece of elastic tape with both the ends snipped. Place the gauze pad in the center of the 10-inch (25 cm) piece of elastic tape to limit skin irritation and protect the popliteal nerves and blood vessels.

2. Put the gauze with the elastic tape backing on the popliteal fossa of the athlete's knee. Stretch both ends of the tape to the fullest extent and tear them. Place the divided ends firmly around the patella and interlock them (1).

3. Starting at a midpoint on the gastrocnemius muscle, spiral a 3-inch (7.5 cm) elastic tape strip to the front of the leg, then behind, crossing the popliteal fossa, and around the thigh, finishing anteriorly (2).

4. Repeat procedure 3 on the opposite side (3).

5. Apply three or four spiral strips for added strength (4 and 5).

6. Once they are in place, lock the spiral strips with two strips around the thigh and two around the calf (6 and 7).

NOTE: Tracing the spiral pattern with linen tape yields more rigidity.

Hyperextension   Hyperextension taping is designed to prevent the knee from hyperextending and also may be used for a strained hamstring muscle or for slackened cruciate ligaments (Figure 8-36).

Materials needed   One roll of 2½-inch (6.25 cm) tape or 2-inch (5 cm) elastic tape, cotton or a 4-inch (10 cm) gauze pad, tape adherent, underwrap, and a 2-inch (5 cm) heel lift.

Position of the athlete   Completely shave the athlete's leg, including the area above midthigh and below midcalf. The athlete stands on a 3-foot (90 cm) table with the injured knee flexed by a 2-inch (5 cm) heel lift.

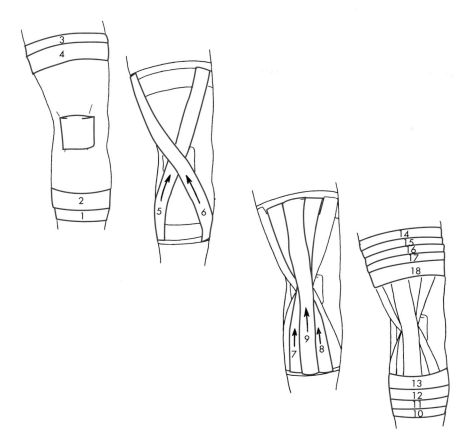

Figure 8-36

Hyperextension taping.

Procedure

1. Place four anchor strips at the hairlines, two around the thigh and two around the leg (1 through 4). The strips should be loose enough to allow for muscle expansion during exercise.
2. Place a gauze pad at the popliteal space to protect the popliteal nerves and blood vessels from constriction by the tape.
3. Start the supporting tape strips by forming an X over the popliteal space (5 and 6).
4. Cross the tape with two more strips, and place one up the middle of the leg (7 through 9).
5. Complete the technique by applying four or five locking strips around the thigh and calf (10 through 18).
6. Apply an additional series of cross strips if the athlete is heavily muscled. Lock the additional supporting strips in place with two or three strips around the thigh and leg.

Patellofemoral taping (McConnell technique)   Patellofemoral orientation may be corrected to some degree by using tape.[34] The McConnell technique evaluates four components of patellar orientation: glide, tilt, rotation, and anteroposterior (AP) orientation.[19]

The glide component looks at side-to-side movement of the patella in the groove. The tilt component assesses the height of the lateral patellar border relative to the medial border. Patellar rotation is determined by looking for deviation of the long axis of the patella from the long axis of the femur. Anteroposterior alignment evaluates whether the inferior pole of the patella is tilted either anteriorly or posteriorly relative to the superior pole. Correction of patellar position and tracking is accomplished by passive taping of the patella in a more biomechanically correct position.[29,33] In addition to correcting the orientation of the patella, the tape provides a prolonged gentle stretch to soft-tissue structure that affects patellar movement.[11,19]

8-7

Critical Thinking E x e r c i s e

A female basketball player complains of a chronic dull ache in her right patella.

? What taping technique can be used to correct this problem?

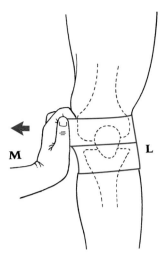

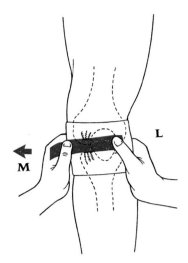

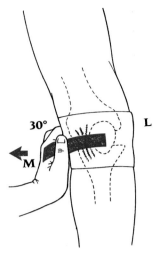

Figure 8-37

The McConnell patellar technique uses a base to which additional tape is adhered.

Figure 8-38

McConnell patellar technique to correct a lateral glide.

Figure 8-39

McConnell patellar technique to correct a lateral tilt.

Materials needed   Two special types of extremely sticky tape are required. Fixomull and Leuko Sportape are manufactured by Biersdorf Australia, Ltd.

Site preparation   Clean and shave, and apply tape adherent.

Position of the athlete   The athlete is seated with the knee fully extended.

Procedure

1. Extend two strips of Fixomull from the lateral femoral condyle just posterior to the medial femoral condyle around the front of the knee. This tape is used as a base to which the other tape may be adhered. Leuko Sportape is used from this point on to correct patellar alignment (Figure 8-37).
2. To correct a lateral glide, attach a short strip of tape one thumb's width from the lateral patellar border, pushing the patella medially in the frontal plane. Crease the skin between the lateral patellar border and the medial femoral condyle and secure the tape on the medial side of the joint (Figure 8-38).
3. To correct a lateral tilt, flex the knee to 30 degrees, adhere a short strip of tape beginning at the middle of the patella, and pull medially to lift the lateral border. Again, crease the skin underneath and adhere it to the medial side of the knee (Figure 8-39).
4. To correct an external rotation of the inferior pole relative to the superior pole, adhere a strip of tape to the middle of the inferior pole, pulling upward and medially while internally rotating the patella with the free hand. The tape is attached to the medial side of the knee (Figure 8-40).
5. For correcting AP alignment in which there is an inferior tilt, take a 6-inch piece of tape, place the middle of the strip over the upper one-half of the patella, and attach it equally on both sides to lift the inferior pole (Figure 8-41).
6. Once patellar taping is completed, the athlete should be instructed to wear the tape all day during all activities. The athlete should periodically tighten the strips as they loosen.

NOTE: The McConnell technique for treating patellofemoral pain also stresses the importance of more symmetrical loading of the patella through reeducation and strengthening of the vastus medialis.[19] Patellar taping may also enhance proprioception in the knee joint.[7]

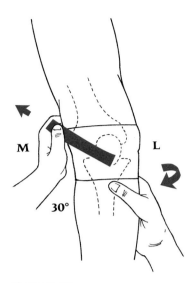

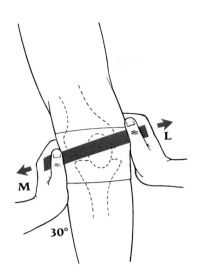

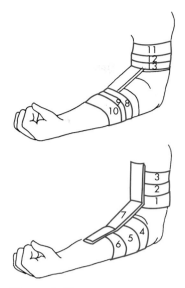

Figure 8-40

McConnell patellar technique to correct external rotation of the inferior pole.

Figure 8-41

McConnell patellar technique to correct AP alignment with an inferior tilt.

Figure 8-42

Elbow restriction taping.

The Elbow

Elbow restriction   Taping the elbow prevents hyperextension[31] (Figure 8-42).

Materials needed   One roll of 1½-inch (3.8 cm) tape, tape adherent, and 2-inch (5 cm) elastic bandage.

Site preparation   Clean and shave area and apply adherent.

Position of the athlete   The athlete stands with the affected elbow flexed at 90 degrees.

Procedure

1. Apply three anchor strips loosely around the upper arm using 2-inch (5 cm) elastic adhesive tape (1 through 3).
2. Apply three anchor strips around the upper forearm using 2-inch (5 cm) elastic adhesive tape (4, 5, and 6).
3. Construct a checkrein by cutting a 10-inch (25 cm) and a 4-inch (10 cm) strip of tape and placing the 4-inch (10 cm) strip against the center of the 10-inch (25 cm) strip, blanking out that portion. Place the checkrein so that it spans the two anchor strips with the blanked-out side facing downward. Leave the checkrein extended 1 to 2 inches past the anchor strips on both ends. This allows anchoring of the checkreins with circular strips to secure against slippage (7).
4. Place five additional 10-inch (25 cm) strips of tape over the basic checkrein.
5. Finish the procedure by securing the checkrein with three lock strips on each end (8 through 13). A figure-eight elastic wrap applied over the taping will prevent the tape from slipping because of perspiration.

NOTE : A variation of this method is to fan the checkreins, dispersing the force over a wider area (Figure 8-43).

The Wrist and Hand

Wrist technique no. 1   This wrist taping technique is designed for mild wrist strains and sprains (Figure 8-44).

Materials needed   One roll of 1-inch (2.5 cm) tape and tape adherent.

8-8

Critical Thinking Exercise

A volleyball player attempts to block a ball and reports that her elbow "bent backwards."

? What taping technique can be used to prevent this incident from reoccurring?

Figure 8-43

Fanned checkrein technique.

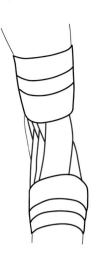

Figure 8-44

Wrist-taping technique no. 1.

Position of the athlete   The athlete stands with the affected hand flexed toward the injured direction and the fingers moderately spread to increase the breadth of the wrist for the protection of nerves and blood vessels.

Procedure

1. Starting at the base of the wrist, bring a strip of 1-inch (2.5 cm) tape from the palmar side upward and around both sides of the wrist (1).
2. In the same pattern, with each strip overlapping the preceding one by at least half its width, lay two additional strips in place (2 and 3).

Wrist technique no. 2   This wrist taping technique stabilizes and protects badly injured wrists (Figure 8-45).

Materials needed   One roll of 1-inch (2.5 cm) tape and tape adherent.

Position of the athlete   The athlete stands with the affected hand flexed toward the injured side and the fingers moderately spread to increase the breadth of the wrist for the protection of nerves and blood vessels.

Procedure

1. Apply one anchor strip around the wrist approximately 3 inches (7.5 cm) from the hand (1); wrap another anchor strip around the spread hand (2).
2. With the wrist bent toward the side of the injury, run a strip of tape from the anchor strip near the little finger obliquely across the wrist joint to the wrist anchor strip. Run another strip from the anchor strip and the index finger side across the wrist joint to the wrist anchor. This forms a crisscross over the wrist joint (3 and 4). Apply a series of four or five crisscrosses, depending on the extent of splinting needed (5 through 8).

Figure 8-45

Wrist-taping technique no. 2.

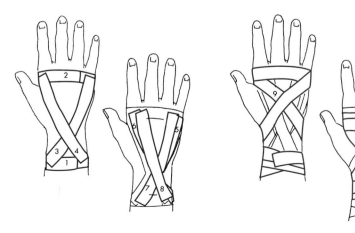

3. Apply two or three series of figure-eight tapings over the crisscross taping (9 through 11). Starting by encircling the wrist once, carry a strip over the back of the hand obliquely upward across the back of the hand to where the figure-eight started. Repeat this procedure to ensure a strong, stabilizing taping.

Bruised hand   The following method is used to tape a bruised hand (Figure 8-46).

Materials needed   One roll of 1-inch (2.5 cm) adhesive tape, one roll of ½-inch (1.25 cm) tape, ¼-inch (0.6 cm) thick sponge rubber pad, and tape adherent.

Position of the athlete   The fingers are spread moderately.

Procedure

1. Lay the protective pad over the bruise and hold it in place with three strips of ½-inch (1.25 cm) tape laced through the webbing of the fingers.
2. Apply a basic figure-eight bandage made of 1-inch (2.5 cm) tape.

Sprained thumb   Sprained thumb taping is designed to give protection to the muscle and joint as well as support to the thumb (Figure 8-47).[9]

Materials needed   One roll of 1-inch (2.5 cm) tape and tape adherent.

Position of the athlete   The athlete should hold the injured thumb in a relaxed, neutral position.

Procedure

1. Place an anchor strip loosely around the wrist and another around the distal end of the thumb (1 and 2).
2. From the anchor at the tip of the thumb to the anchor around the wrist, apply four splint strips in a series on the side of greater injury (dorsal or palmar side) (3 through 5) and hold them in place with one lock strip around the wrist and one encircling the tip of the thumb (6 and 7).
3. Add three thumb spicas. Start the first spica on the radial side at the base of the thumb; carry it under the thumb, completely encircling it; cross the strip and continue around the wrist; finish at the starting point. Each of the subsequent spica strips should overlap the preceding strip by at least ⅔ inch (1.7 cm) and move downward on the thumb (8 and 9).

The thumb spica with tape provides an excellent means of protection during recovery from an injury (Figure 8-48).

Finger and thumb checkreins   The sprained finger or thumb may require the additional protection afforded by a restraining checkrein (Figure 8-49).[9]

Materials needed   One roll of 1-inch (2.5 cm) tape.

Position of the athlete   The athlete spreads the injured fingers widely but within a range that is free of pain.

Procedure

1. Bring a strip of 1-inch (2.5 cm) tape around the middle phalanx of the injured finger over to the adjacent finger and around it also. The tape left between the two fingers, which are spread apart, is called the checkrein.
2. Add strength with a lock strip around the center of the checkrein.

SUMMARY

- Elastic bandages, when properly applied, can contribute to recovery from sport injuries.
- Elastic bandages must be applied uniformly, firmly but not so tightly as to impede circulation.
- Historically, taping has been an important aspect of athletic training. Sports tape is used in a variety of ways—as a means of holding a wound dressing in place, as support, and as protection against musculoskeletal injuries.
- For supporting and protecting musculoskeletal injuries, two types of tape are currently used—nonelastic white adhesive and elastic adhesive.
- Tape must be stored in a cool place and must be stacked on the flat side of each roll.
- The skin of the athlete must be carefully prepared before tape is applied.
- The skin should first be carefully cleaned; then all hair should be removed.

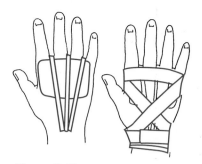

Figure 8-46

Bruised hand taping.

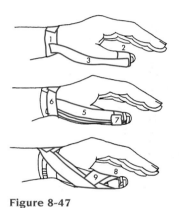

Figure 8-47

Sprained thumb taping.

Figure 8-48

Thumb spica.

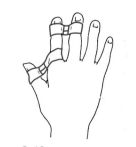

Figure 8-49

Finger and thumb checkreins.

- An adherent may be applied, followed by an underwrap material, if need be, to help avoid skin irritation.
- When tape is applied, it must be done in a manner that provides the least amount of irritation and the maximum support.
- For all tape applications, the proper materials must be used, the athlete must be in the proper position, and the proper procedures must be carefully followed.

Websites

Properties of Athletic Tape:
http://www.bloodandbones.com/tape.html

Cramer Sports Medicine: http://www.cramersportsmed.com/

Mueller Sports Medicine—Retail Tape and Wrap:
http://www.muellersportsmed.com/retailtapeandwrap.htm

Johnson & Johnson: http://www.jnj.com/

Cramer First Aider:
http://www.cramersportsmed.com/first_aider.jsp

Solutions to Critical Thinking EXERCISES

8-1 First the ankle should be shaved. Then a tape adherent spray should be applied. Heel and lace pads with a small amount of lubricant should be applied over bony prominences. One layer of underwrap can be applied. Tape should be applied with even pressure, leaving no gaps.

8-2 The athletic trainer should apply a 6-inch (15 cm) elastic wrap as a hip adductor restraint. This technique is designed to prevent the groin from being overstretched and the hip adductors reinjured.

8-3 The athletic trainer should apply tape and a 4-inch (10 cm) elastic shoulder spica to hold the doughnut in place.

8-4 The athletic trainer should apply a sling and swathe combination. This combination stabilizes the shoulder joint and upper arm.

8-5 The LowDye technique is designed to assist in the management of foot pronation and fallen medial longitudinal arch, which predisposes the athlete to arch strain.

8-6 Initially, for a sprained ankle, the athletic trainer should select the open basket weave taping technique. This technique in conjunction with a pressure bandage and cold application can also control swelling.

8-7 The McConnell taping technique can be employed to correct a lateral patellar glide.

8-8 The elbow restriction taping will help prevent elbow hyperextension.

REVIEW QUESTIONS AND CLASS ACTIVITIES

1. What are some common types of bandages used in sports medicine today?
2. Observe the athletic trainer when he or she is dressing wounds in the training room.
3. Demonstrate proper use of the elastic, triangular, and cravat bandages.
4. What types of tape are available? What is the purpose of each type? What qualities should you look for in selecting tape?
5. How should you prepare an area to be taped?
6. How should you tear tape?
7. How should you remove tape from an area? Demonstrate the various methods and cutters that can be used to remove tape.
8. Bring the different types of tape to class. Discuss their uses and the qualities to look for in purchasing tape. Have the class practice tearing tape and preparing an area for taping.
9. Take each joint or body part and demonstrate the common taping procedures used to give support to that area. Have the students pair up and practice these tapings on each other. Discuss the advantages and disadvantages of using tape as a supportive device.

REFERENCES

1. Alt W, Lohrer H, Gollhofer A: Functional properties of adhesive ankle taping: neuromuscular and mechanical effects before and after exercise, *Foot & Ankle International* 20(4):238, 1999.
2. Austin K et al: *Taping techniques*, Chicago, 1994, Mosby-Wolfe.
3. Benefit of ankle taping is short-lived with or without prewrap, *Sports Med Digest* 19(1):130, 1997.
4. Bragg RW, Macmahon JM, Overom EK: Failure and fatigue characteristics of adhesive athletic tape, *Med Sci Sports Exerc* 34(3):403, 2002.
5. Briggs J: Bandaging, strapping and taping. In Briggs J, editor: *Sports therapy: theoretical and practical thoughts and considerations*, Chichester, England, 2001, Corpus Publishing Limited.
6. Callaghan MJ: Role of ankle taping and bracing in the athlete, *British Journal of Sports Medicine* 31(2):102, 1997.
7. Callaghan M, Selfe J, Bagley P: The effects of patellar taping on knee joint proprioception, *J Ath Train* 37(1):19, 2002.
8. Cartwright LA, Pitney WA: Protective taping and wrapping. In Cartwright LA, editor: *Athletic training for student assistants*, Champaign, Ill, 2001, Human Kinetics.
9. Deivert R: Functional thumb taping procedure, *J Ath Train* 29(4):357, 1994.
10. DesRochers DM, Cox DE: Proprioceptive benefit derived from ankle support, *Athletic Therapy Today* 7(6):44, 2002.
11. Ernst GP, Kawaguchi J, Saliba E: Effect of patellar taping on knee kinetics of patients with patellofemoral pain syndrome, *J Ortho Sports Phys Ther* 29(11):661, 1999.
12. Heit EJ, Lephart SM, Rozzi SL: The effect of ankle bracing and taping on joint position sense in the stable ankle, *J Sport Rehabil* 5(3):206, 1996.
13. Holmes C, Wilcox D, Fletcher J: Effect of a modified, low-dye medial longitudinal arch taping procedure on the subtalar joint neutral position before and after, light exercise, *J Ortho Sports Phys Ther* 32(5), 2002.
14. Jones K: Athletic taping and bracing. In Sailis RE and Massamino F, editors: *Essentials of sport medicine*, St. Louis, 1996, Mosby-Year Book.

15. Karren K, Limmer D, Mistovich J, Hafen B: *First aid for colleges and universities,* San Francisco, 2003, Benjamin-Cummings.

16. Knight KL: Taping, wrapping, bracing, and padding. In Knight KL, editor: *Assessing clinical proficiencies in athletic training: a modular approach,* ed 3, Champaign, Ill, 2001, Human Kinetics.

17. Lindley T: Taping and semirigid bracing may not affect ankle functional range of motion, *J Ath Train* 30(2):109, 1995.

18. Manfroy PP, Ashton-Miller JA, Wojtys EM: The effect of exercise, prewrap, and athletic tape on the maximal active and passive ankle resistance to ankle-inversion, *Am J Sports Med* 25(2):156, 1997.

19. McConnell J: A novel approach to pain relief pre-therapeutic exercise, *Journal of Science and Medicine in Sport* 3(3):325, 2000.

20. Merrick MA: Do ankle bracing and taping work? *Athletic Therapy Today* 5(6):40, 2000.

21. Metcalfe RC, Schlabach GA, Looney MA et al: A comparison of moleskin tape, linen tape, and lace-up brace on joint restriction and movement performance, *J Ath Train* 32(2):136, 1997.

22. Paris D, Vardaxis V, Kokkaliaris J: Ankle ranges of motion during extended activity periods while taped and braced, *J Ath Train* 30(3):223, 1995.

23. Perrin DH: *Athletic taping and bracing,* Champaign, Ill, 1998, Human Kinetics.

24. Refshauge KM, Kilbreath SL, Raymond J: The effect of recurrent ankle inversion sprain and taping on proprioception at the ankle, *Med Sci Sports Exerc* 32(1):10, 2000.

25. Riemann B, Schmitz R, Gale M: Effect of ankle taping and bracing on vertical ground reaction forces during drop landings before and after treadmill jogging, *J Ortho Sports Phys Ther* 32(12), 2002.

26. Reuter B: Taping the hammer toe, *J Ath Train* 30(2):178, 1995.

27. Schulthies S, Draper D: A modified low-dye taping technique to support the medial longitudinal arch and reduce excessive pronation, *J Ath Train* 30(3):266, 1995.

28. Simoneau GG, Degner RM, Kramper CA et al: Changes in ankle joint proprioception resulting from strips of athletic tape applied over the skin, *J Ath Train* 32(2):141, 1997.

29. Somes S et al: Effects of patellar taping on patellar position in the open and closed kinetic chain: a preliminary study, *J Sport Rehabil* 6(4):299, 1997.

30. Sports Medicine Council of British Columbia: *Manual of athletic taping,* Philadelphia, 1995, FA Davis.

31. Vicenzino B, Brooksbank J, Minto J: Initial effects of elbow taping on pain-free grip strength and pressure pain threshold, *J Ortho Sports Phys Ther* 33(7), 2003.

32. Wilkerson GB: Biomechanical and neuromuscular effects of ankle taping and bracings. *Journal Ath Train* 37(4):436, 2002.

33. Wilson T, Carter N, Thomas G: A multicenter, single-masked study of medial, neutral, and lateral patellar taping in individuals with patellofemoral pain syndrome, *J Ortho Sports Phys Ther* 33(8), 2003.

34. Worrell T et al: Effect of patellar taping and bracing on patellar position as determined by MRI in patients with patellofemoral pain, *J Ath Train* 33(1):16, 1998.

ANNOTATED BIBLIOGRAPHY

Austin K et al: *Taping techniques,* Chicago, 1994, Mosby-Wolfe.
   This book is an illustrated atlas of taping.

Baxter R, Peck, K: *Sports medicine taping techniques volumes 1 and 2,* Wichita Falls, TX, 2003, Sports Medicine Publishing.
   This is a 2 volume set of CD-Rom software that presents detailed instruction on taping techniques.

Kennedy R, Berry R: *Mosby's Sports therapy guide,* St. Louis, 1995, Mosby.
   This text is a well-illustrated guide to taping for the athletic trainer.

MacDonald R: *Taping techniques: principles and practice.* Burlington, MA, 2003, Butterworth-Heinemann Medical.
   This is a concise practical text on functional taping for treatment and rehabilitation of the injured athlete.

Perrin D: *Athletic taping,* Champaign, Ill, 1998, Human Kinetics.
   This text is a complete book of athletic taping for the practitioner.

Sports Medicine Council of British Columbia: *Manual of athletic taping,* Philadelphia, 1995, FA Davis.
   Guidelines for taping and wrapping athletes' joints and limbs to both prevent and manage injuries. Chapters include: injury recognition; anatomy and taping techniques for the ankle, foot, knee, wrist, hand, elbow, and muscles and tendons; and resources.

Sports taping basics: lower body. Champaign, Ill, 1996, Human Kinetics.
   1 videocassette: sd., col.; 41 min.

Sports taping basics: upper body. Champaign, Ill, 1996, Human Kinetics.
   1 videocassette: sd., col.; 24 min.
   A videotape series demonstrating the various taping techniques for the upper and lower extremities.

Wright K, Whitehill, W: Taping Technique-Video Series, St. Louis, 1994, McGraw-Hill.
   A series of videotapes that consists of 5 volumes on athletic taping techniques.

Chapter 9

Mechanisms and Characteristics of Sports Trauma

When you finish this chapter you should be able to

- Analyze the biomechanical factors in sports injuries.
- Distinguish the major biomechanical forces occurring in sports injuries.
- Categorize the most common exposed skin injuries.
- Review the normal structures of soft tissue and identify the specific mechanical forces that cause skin, internal soft-tissue, synovial joint, and bone injuries.
- Define the terminology that describes injuries incurred during sports participation.
- Describe the various types of bone fractures and explain how they occur.
- Explain how a nerve is injured.

trauma
A physical injury or wound sustained in sport and produced by an external or internal force is called trauma.

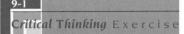

9-1

Critical Thinking Exercise

To effectively present and manage sports injuries, the athletic trainer must understand tissue susceptibility to sports trauma.

? What should the athletic trainer know about tissue properties?

Figure 9-1

A sports injury can be sustained from an external or internal force.

Many factors produce mechanical injuries or trauma in sports. **Trauma** is defined as a physical injury or wound sustained in sport and produced by an external or internal force (Figure 9-1).[6] This chapter provides a foundation for the identification, understanding, and management of sports injuries. It examines mechanical forces and tissue characteristics of sports injuries and the classification of these injuries.[16]

MECHANICAL INJURY

"Force or mechanical energy is that which changes the state of rest or uniform motion of matter. When a force applied to any part of the body results in a harmful disturbance in function and or structure, a mechanical injury is said to have been sustained."[22] Injuries related to sports participation can be caused by external forces directed on the body or can occur internally within the body.[23] Understanding sports injuries requires a knowledge of tissue susceptibility to trauma and the mechanical forces involved.

Tissue Properties

Tissues have relative abilities to resist a particular load. The stronger the tissue, the greater the magnitude of load it can withstand. Strength pressure, or power, is often used to imply a force. A force can be defined as a push or pull.[25] Tissue properties are described according to engineering terminology.[18] A **load** can be a singular force or a group of outside or internal forces acting on the body. The resistance to a load is called a mechanical **stress**, and the internal response is a deformation, or change in dimensions. Deformation is also defined as a mechanical **strain**. All human tissue is **viscoelastic**; it has both viscous and elastic properties, allowing for deformation. Tissue such as bone is brittle and has fewer viscoelastic properties than soft tissue. Tissue also is anisotropic, responding with greater or lesser strength depending on the direction of the load that is being applied. When tissue is deformed to the extent that its elasticity is almost fully exceeded, a **yield point** has been reached. When the yield point has been exceeded, **mechanical failure** occurs, resulting in tissue damage.[2]

Tissue Stresses

There are five primary tissue stresses leading to sports injuries: tension, stretching, compression, shearing, and bending.[18]

Tension is that force which pulls or stretches tissue. Muscle strains and ligament sprains both occur due to increased tension.

Stretching beyond the yield point leads to rupturing of soft tissue or fracturing of a bone. Examples of stretching injuries are sprains, strains, and avulsion fractures.

Compression is a force that, with enough energy, crushes tissue. When the force can no longer be absorbed, injury occurs. Constant submaximum compression over a period of time can cause the contacted tissue to develop abnormal wear. Compression occurs when a muscle or bone is stretched directly or when cartilage bone is directly loaded. Arthritic changes, fractures, and contusions are commonly caused by compression force.

Shearing is a force that moves across the parallel organization of the tissue. Injury occurs once shearing has exceeded the inherent strength of a tissue. Shearing stress can result in skin injuries such as blisters, rips of the hands, abrasions, or vertebral disk injuries (Figure 9-2).

Bending is a force on a horizontal beam or bone that places stresses within the structure, causing it to bend or strain.[25] This force is known as three-point bending (Figure 9-3). Compression occurs parallel to the beam's length if the force is on the concave side, and tension occurs if the force is on the convex side. Shear stress is also caused in two directions within the bending beam.[25] Bending strain can also occur perpendicular to or along the length of a beam, with compression, tension, and shearing occurring. Injuries to the hip and femur are examples of this type of bending strain. A torsion, or twisting, load causes compression and tension in a spiral pattern,

load
Outside force or forces acting on tissue.

stress
The internal reaction or resistance to an external load.

strain
Extent of deformation of tissue under loading.

viscoelastic
Any material whose mechanical properties vary depending on rate of load.
Human tissue is viscoelastic—it has both viscous and elastic properties.

yield point
Elastic limit of tissue.

mechanical failure
Elastic limit of tissue is exceeded, causing tissue to break.

Tissue stresses
- Tension
- Stretching
- Compression
- Shearing
- Bending

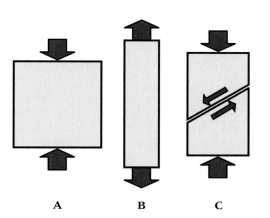

Figure 9-2

Mechanical forces that can cause injury. **A,** Compression. **B,** Tension. **C,** Shear.

A   B   C

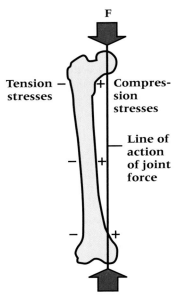

Figure 9-3

Bending strain. Compression and tension stress caused by a bending of the femur.

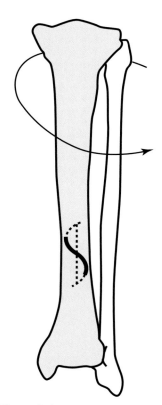

Figure 9-4

A torsion force could lead to a spiral fracture.

with shearing stresses occurring parallel to the long axes. An example of a torsion injury is the spiral fracture that occurs in snow skiing (Figure 9-4).[28]

SOFT-TISSUE TRAUMA

Soft tissue, or nonbony tissue, is categorized as inert (noncontractile) and contractile. Inert tissues are skin, joint capsules, ligaments, fascia, cartilage, dura mater, and nerve roots. Contractile tissues are those structures that are a part of the muscle, its tendon, or its bony insertion.[3]

SKIN INJURIES

Generally, trauma that happens to the skin is visually exposed and is categorized as a skin wound. It is defined as a break in the continuity of the soft parts of body structures caused by a trauma to these tissues.

Anatomical Characteristics

The skin, or integument, is the external covering of the body. It represents the body's largest organ system and consists of two layers—the epidermis and the dermis (corium). Because of the soft, pliable nature of skin, it can be easily traumatized.

Injurious Mechanical Forces

Numerous mechanical forces can adversely affect the skin's integrity. These forces are friction or rubbing, scraping, compression or pressure, tearing, cutting, and penetrating.

Wound Classification

Wounds are classified according to the mechanical force that causes them (Table 9-1).

Friction Blister

Continuous rubbing over the surface of the skin causes a collection of fluid below or within the epidermal layer called a blister.

Abrasion

Abrasions are common conditions in which the skin is scraped against a rough surface. The epidermis and dermis are scraped away, exposing numerous blood capillaries.

Incision

An incision wound is one in which the skin has been sharply cut.

TABLE 9-1 Soft-Tissue Trauma

Primary Tissue	Type	Mechanical Forces	Condition
Skin	Acute	Rubbing/friction	Blister
		Compression/contusion	Bruise
		Tearing	Laceration
		Tearing/ripping	Avulsion
		Penetrating	Puncture
Muscle/tendon	Acute	Compression	Contusion
		Tension	Strain
	Chronic	Tension/shearing	Myositis/fasciitis
		Tension	Tendinitis/tenosynovitis
		Compression/tension	Bursitis
		Compression/tension	Ectopic calcification—myositis ossificans, calcific tendinitis

Laceration

A laceration is a wound in which the flesh has been irregularly torn.

Skin Avulsion

Skin that is torn by the same mechanism as a laceration to the extent that tissue is completely ripped from its source is an avulsion injury.

Puncture Wound

Puncture wounds, as the name implies, are penetrations of the skin by a sharp object.

Skin Bruise (Contusion)

When a blow compresses or crushes the skin surface and produces bleeding under the skin, the condition is identified as a bruise, or contusion.

SKELETAL MUSCLE INJURIES
Anatomical Characteristics

Muscles are composed of contractile cells, or fibers, that produce movement. Muscle fibers possess the ability to contract as well as the properties of irritability, conductivity, and elasticity. There are three types of muscles in the body—smooth, cardiac, and striated. Of major concern in sports medicine are conditions that affect striated, or skeletal, muscles. Within the fiber cell is a semifluid substance called sarcoplasm (cytoplasm). Myofibrils are surrounded by the endomysium, fiber bundles are surrounded by the perimysium, and the entire muscle is covered by the epimysium (Figure 9-5). The epimysium, perimysium, and endomysium may be combined with

Skin Wounds
- Friction Blister
- Abrasion
- Contusion
- Incision
- Laceration
- Avulsion
- Puncture

9-2

Critical Thinking E x e r c i s e

A baseball player slides into home base, severely scraping the skin on the left side.

? What is the force and type of injury produced?

3 Types of Muscle
- Smooth
- Cardiac
- Striated

Figure 9-5

Connective tissue associated with skeletal muscle.

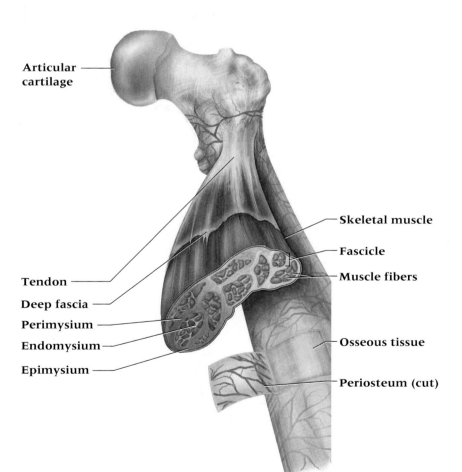

Articular cartilage

Tendon

Deep fascia

Perimysium

Endomysium

Epimysium

Skeletal muscle

Fascicle

Muscle fibers

Osseous tissue

Periosteum (cut)

the fibrous tendon. The fibrous wrapping of a muscle may become a flat sheet of connective tissue (aponeurosis) that attaches to other muscles. Tendons and aponeuroses are extremely resilient to injuries. They will pull away from a bone, a bone will break, or a muscle will tear before tendons and aponeuroses are injured. Skeletal muscles are generally well supplied with blood vessels that permeate throughout their structure. Arteries, veins, lymph vessels, and bundles of nerve fibers spread into the perimysium. A complex capillary network goes throughout the endomysium, coming into direct contact with the muscle fibers.[35]

Acute Muscle Injuries

Contusions

A bruise, or contusion, occurs from a sudden traumatic blow to the body. The intensity of a contusion can range from superficial to deep tissue compression and hemorrhage (Figure 9-6).

Interrupting the continuity of the circulatory system results in a flow of blood and lymph into the surrounding tissues. A hematoma (blood tumor) is formed by the localization of the extravasated blood into a clot, which becomes encapsulated by a connective tissue membrane. The speed of healing of a contusion, as with all soft-tissue injuries, depends on the extent of tissue damage and internal bleeding.

A contusion can penetrate to the skeletal structures, causing a bone bruise. The extent to which an athlete may be hampered by this condition depends on the location of the bruise and the force of the blow. Typical in cases of severe contusion are the following:

1. The athlete reports being struck by a hard impact.
2. The impact causes pain and a transitory paralysis caused by pressure on and shock to the motor and sensory nerves.
3. Palpation often reveals a hardened area, indurated because of internal hemorrhage.
4. Ecchymosis, or tissue discoloration, may take place.

Muscle contusions are usually rated by the extent to which the muscle is able to produce range of motion in a part (see Chapter 10). A blow to a muscle can be so great that the related fascia is ruptured, allowing muscle tissue to protrude through it.

Strains

A strain is a stretch, tear, or rip in the muscle or adjacent tissue such as the fascia or muscle tendons (Figure 9-7). The cause of muscle strain is often obscure. Most often a strain is produced by an abnormal muscular contraction. The cause of this abnormality has been attributed to many factors. One popular theory suggests that a fault in the reciprocal coordination of the agonist and antagonist muscles takes place. The cause of this fault or incoordination is a mystery. However, possible explanations are that it may be related to an electrolyte imbalance caused by profuse sweating, or to a strength imbalance between agonist and antagonist muscles.

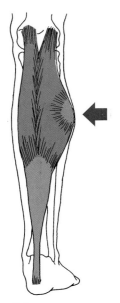

Figure 9-6

A contusion is caused by a compression force.

9-3
Critical Thinking E x e r c i s e

A shortstop is hit in the shin by a batted ball that took a bad hop.

? What is the force and type of injury sustained by this athlete?

Figure 9-7

A muscle strain results in tearing or separation of fibers.

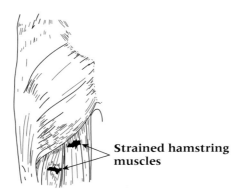

Strained hamstring muscles

A strain may range from a minute separation of connective tissue and muscle fibers to a complete tendinous avulsion or muscle rupture (grade 1, 2, or 3).[12] The resulting pathology is similar to that of the contusion or sprain, with capillary or blood vessel hemorrhage.

- *Grade 1 strain.* Some muscle fibers have been stretched or actually torn. There is some tenderness and pain on active motion. Movement is painful, but full range of motion is usually possible.
- *Grade 2 strain.* A number of muscle fibers have been torn, and active contraction of the muscle is extremely painful. Usually a depression or divot can be felt somewhere in the muscle belly at the place at which the muscle fibers have been torn. Some swelling may occur because of capillary bleeding; therefore, some discoloration is possible.
- *Grade 3 strain.* A complete rupture of a muscle has occurred in the area of the muscle belly at the point at which muscle becomes tendon or at the tendinous attachment to the bone. There is significant impairment to or perhaps total loss of movement. Initially, pain is intense but quickly diminishes because of complete nerve fiber separation.

Tendon Injuries

The tendon contains wavy parallel collagenous fibers that are organized in bundles surrounded by a gelatinous material that decreases friction. A tendon attaches a muscle to a bone and concentrates a pulling force in a limited area. Tendons can produce and maintain a pull from 8,700 to 18,000 pounds per square inch. When a tendon is loaded by tension, the wavy collagenous fibers straighten in the direction of the load; when the tension is released, the collagen returns to its original shape. In tendons, collagen fibers will break if their physiological limits have been reached. A breaking point occurs after a 6 percent to 8 percent increase in length (Figure 9-8). Because a tendon is usually double the strength of the muscle it serves, tears commonly occur at the muscle belly, musculotendinous junction, or bony attachment.[8] Clinically, however, a constant abnormal tension on tendons increases elongation by the infiltration of fibroblasts, which will cause more collagenous tissue to be produced. Repeated microtraumas can evolve into chronic muscle strain that resorbs collagen fibers and eventually weakens the tendon.[30] Collagen resorption occurs in the early period of sports conditioning and during the immobilization of a part. During resorption, collagenous tissues are weakened and susceptible to injury; therefore a gradually paced conditioning program and early mobilization in the rehabilitation process are necessary.

Muscle Spasms

A spasm is a reflex reaction caused by trauma of the musculoskeletal system. The two types of spasms are the **clonic** type, with alternating involuntary muscular contraction and relaxation in quick succession, and the **tonic** type, with rigid muscle contraction that lasts a period of time. Muscle spasms may lead to a muscle strain.

Overexertional Muscle Problems

One constant problem in conditioning and fitness training is overexertion. Even though the gradual pattern of overloading the body is the best way for ultimate success, many athletes and even coaches believe that "if there is no pain, there is no gain."

Exercise overload is reflected in muscle soreness, decreased joint flexibility, and general fatigue that occurs twenty-four hours after activity. Four specific indicators of possible overexertion are acute muscle soreness, delayed muscle soreness, muscle stiffness, and muscle cramping.

Muscle soreness   Overexertion in strenuous muscular exercise often results in muscular pain. Most people, at one time or another, have experienced muscle soreness, usually resulting from some physical activity to which they are unaccustomed. The older a person gets, the more easily muscle soreness seems to develop.

9-4

Critical Thinking E x e r c i s e

While performing an arm tackle, a football player severely injures his upper arm.

? What injury mechanism has occurred, and what is the subsequent injury produced?

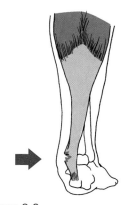

Figure 9-8

Tendon injuries occur due to excessive tension in the musculotendinous unit.

clonic

Involuntary muscle contraction characterized by alternate contraction and relaxation in rapid succession.

tonic

Muscle contraction characterized by constant contraction that lasts for a period of time.

The two major types of muscle soreness associated with severe exercise are acute and delayed-onset muscle soreness (DOMS).

There are two types of muscle soreness. The first type is *acute-onset muscle soreness,* which accompanies fatigue. This muscle pain is transient and occurs during and immediately after exercise. The second type of soreness involves delayed muscle pain that appears approximately twelve hours after injury. This *delayed-onset muscle soreness* (DOMS) becomes most intense after twenty-four to forty-eight hours and then gradually subsides so that the muscle becomes symptom-free after three or four days. This second type of pain is described as a syndrome of delayed muscle pain leading to increased muscle tension, swelling, stiffness, and resistance to stretching.[9]

Delayed-onset muscle soreness is thought to result from several possible causes. It may occur from very small tears in the muscle tissue, which seems to be more likely with eccentric or isometric contractions. It may also occur because of disruption of the connective tissue that holds muscle tendon fibers together.[10]

Muscle soreness may be prevented by beginning an exercise at a moderate level and gradually increasing the intensity of the exercise over time. Treatment of muscle soreness usually involves static or PNF stretching activities. Like other conditions discussed in this chapter, muscle soreness can be treated with ice applied within the first forty-eight to seventy-two hours.[9]

Muscle stiffness   Muscle stiffness does not produce pain. It occurs when a group of muscles have been worked hard for a long period of time. The fluids that collect in the muscles during and after exercise are absorbed into the bloodstream at a slow rate. As a result, the muscle becomes swollen, shorter, and thicker and therefore resists stretching. Light exercise, massage, and passive mobilization assist in reducing stiffness.

Muscle cramps   Cramps are painful involuntary skeletal muscle contractions.[14] Muscle cramps are different than heat cramps (discussed in Chapter 6) which occur in individuals who are performing hard muscular work in a hot environment and are sweating profusely. Muscle cramps are most likely to occur in well-developed individuals and develop when a muscle, already in a shortened position, involuntarily contracts. This most often occurs at rest, usually at night, asymmetrically in either the gastrocnemius or small foot muscles.[37]

Muscle Guarding

Following injury, the muscles that surround the injured area contract to, in effect, splint that area, thus minimizing pain by limiting movement. Quite often this splinting is incorrectly referred to as a muscle spasm. The terms *spasm* and *spasticity* are more correctly associated with increased tone or contractions of muscle that occur because of some upper motor neuron lesion in the brain. Thus, *muscle guarding* is a more appropriate term for the involuntary muscle contractions that occur in response to pain following musculoskeletal injury.[7]

Myofascial Trigger Points

A *myofascial trigger point* is a discreet, hypersensitive nodule found within a taut band of skeletal muscle and/or fascia.[11] Palpation of this nodule reveals an area of harder-than-normal consistency. Trigger points are classified as being latent or active, depending on their clinical characteristics. A *latent trigger point* does not cause spontaneous pain, but may restrict movement or cause muscle weakness. The individual presenting with muscle restrictions or weakness may become aware of pain originating from a latent trigger point only when pressure is applied directly over the point. An *active trigger point* causes pain at rest. Firm pressure applied over the point usually elicits a "jump sign," with the patient crying out, wincing, or withdrawing from the stimulus. It is tender to palpation with a referred pain pattern that is similar to the patient's pain complaint. This referred pain is not felt at the site of the trigger-point origin but rather at a remote point. The pain is often described as spreading or radiating. Referred pain is an important characteristic of a trigger point. It differentiates a trigger point from a tender point, which is associated with pain at the site of palpation only. They are palpable within

9-5

Critical Thinking E x e r c i s e

A tennis player with a pronounced topspin style of hitting a backhand stroke sustains a painful elbow.

? What are the forces and type of elbow injury sustained by the tennis player, and what are ways to prevent this problem?

muscles as cordlike bands within a sharply circumscribed area of extreme tenderness. Trigger points are found most commonly in muscles involved in postural support.[7] Acute trauma or repetitive microtrauma may lead to the development of stress on muscle fibers and the formation of trigger points.

Chronic Musculotendinous Injuries

Chronic injuries usually progress slowly over a long period of time. Often, repeated acute injuries can lead to a chronic condition. A constant irritation caused by poor performance techniques or a constant stress beyond physiological limits can eventually result in a chronic condition. These injuries are often attributed to overuse microtraumas.[31]

Chronic muscle injuries are representative of a low-grade inflammatory process with a proliferation of fibroblasts and scarring. The acute injury that is improperly managed or that allows an athlete to return to activity before healing has completely occurred can cause chronic injury. The athletic trainer should be especially knowledgeable about five chronic muscle conditions: myositis, tendinitis, tenosynovitis, ectopic calcification, and muscle atrophy and contracture.

Myositis/fasciitis   In general, the term *myositis* means inflammation of muscle tissue. More specifically, it can be considered a fibrositis, or connective tissue inflammation. Fascia that supports and separates muscle can also become chronically inflamed after injury. A typical example of this condition is plantar fasciitis.

Tendinitis   Tendinitis has a gradual onset, diffuse tenderness because of repeated microtraumas, and degenerative changes. Obvious signs of tendinitis are swelling and pain.

Tenosynovitis   Tenosynovitis is inflammation of the synovial sheath surrounding a tendon. In its acute state there is rapid onset, articular crepitus, and diffuse swelling. In chronic tenosynovitis the tendons become locally thickened, with pain and articular crepitus present during movement (Figure 9-9).

Ectopic calcification   Striated muscles can become chronically inflamed, resulting in myositis. An **ectopic** calcification known as *myositis ossificans* can occur in a muscle that directly overlies a bone. Two common sites for this condition are the quadriceps region of the thigh and the brachial muscle of the arm. In myositis ossificans, osteoid material that resembles bone rapidly accumulates. If there is no repeated injury, the growth may subside completely in nine to twelve months, or it may mature into a calcified area, at which time surgical removal can be accomplished with little fear of recurrence. Occasionally, tendinitis leads to deposits of minerals, primarily lime, and is known as *calcific tendinitis*.

ectopic
Located in a place different from normal.

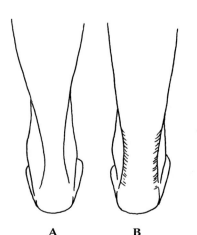

Figure 9-9

Tenosynovitis is an inflammation of the sheath covering a tendon. **A,** Normal. **B,** Inflamed.

A   B

Atrophy and contracture   Two complications of muscle and tendon conditions are atrophy and contracture. Muscle atrophy is the wasting away of muscle tissue. Its main cause in athletes is immobilization of a body part, inactivity, or loss of nerve stimulation. A second complication in sport injuries is muscle contracture, an abnormal shortening of muscle tissue in which there is a great deal of resistance to passive stretch. A contracture is associated with a joint that, because of muscle injury, has developed unyielding and resisting scar tissue.

SYNOVIAL JOINTS

A joint in the human body is defined as the point at which two bones join together. A joint must also transmit forces between articulating bones.[22]

Anatomical Characteristics

The joint consists of cartilage and fibrous connective tissue. Joints are classified as immovable (synarthrotic), slightly movable (amphiarthrotic), and freely movable (diarthrotic). Diarthrotic joints are also called synovial articulations. Anatomical characteristics of synovial articulations consist of four features: they have a capsule or ligaments, the capsule is lined with a synovial membrane, the opposing bone surfaces contain hyaline or articular cartilage, and there is a joint space (joint cavity) containing a small amount of fluid (synovial fluid) (Figure 9-10). In addition, nerves and blood are supplied to the synovial articulation, and muscles cross the joint or are intrinsic to it.[35]

Joint Capsule

Bones of the diarthrotic joint are held together by a cuff of fibrous tissue known as the capsule, or capsular ligament. It consists of bundles of collagen and functions primarily to maintain a relative joint position. It is extremely strong and can withstand cross-sectional forces of 500 kg/cm^2. Parts of the capsule become slack or taut, depending on the joint movements.

Ligaments

Ligaments are sheets or bundles of collagen fibers that form a connection between two bones. Ligaments fall into two categories: ones that are considered intrinsic and ones that are extrinsic to the joint. Intrinsic ligaments occur where the articular capsule has become thickened in some places. Extrinsic ligaments are separate from the capsular thickening.[35]

Ligaments and capsules, found in synovial joints, are similar in composition to tendons; however, ligaments and capsules contain elastic fibers and collagen fibers that

Figure 9-10

General anatomy of a synovial joint.

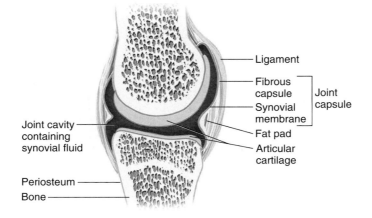

have a wavy, irregular, spiral configuration. Ligaments are strongest in their middle and weakest at their ends. When an intact ligament is traumatically stretched, the injury often produces an avulsion-type fracture or tear at the ends rather than in the middle. Tears in the middle of the ligament are referred to as *midsubstance tears.* Avulsion fractures are more common when bone tissue is comparatively weaker than ligamentous tissue—for instance, in older individuals or postmenopausal women in whom significant osteoporosis has occurred or in children in whom the epiphyseal plates are relatively wide and soft.[35]

A primary factor in ligamentous injury is the viscoelastic tissue properties of ligaments and capsules. Viscoelasticity refers to extensibility when loaded that is time dependent. Constant compression or tension causes ligaments to deteriorate, whereas intermittent compression and tension increases strength, especially at the bony attachment. Chronic inflammation of ligamentous, capsular, and fascial tissue causes a shrinkage of collagen fibers; therefore, repeated microtraumas over time make capsules and ligaments highly susceptible to major acute injuries.

Ligaments act as protective backups for the joint. Primary protection occurs from the dynamic aspect of muscles and their tendons.[1] In a fast-loading situation, ligament failure ultimately will occur; however, the capsule and ligament provide maximum protection during rapid movements. Nevertheless, capsular and ligamentous tissues are highly sensitive to movement deprivation stress through joint immobilization.[1] Capsular and ligamentous tissue respond to Roux's law of functional adaptation: An organ will adapt itself structurally to an alteration, quantitative or qualitative, of function.[22]

> Constant compression or tension will cause ligaments to deteriorate; intermittent compression and tension will increase strength and growth.

Synovial Membrane and Synovial Fluid

Lining the synovial articular capsule is a synovial membrane made of connective tissue with flattened cells and villi (small projections) on its inner aspect. Fluid is secreted and absorbed by the synovial membrane. Synovial fluid has the consistency of egg white and acts as a joint lubricant. It has the ability to vary its viscosity. During slow movement, the fluid thickens; during fast movement it thins. This variation in viscosity is produced by the presence of hyaluronic acid.[35]

Articular Cartilage

Cartilage, a connective tissue, provides firm and flexible support. It occurs throughout the body and consists of three types: hyaline (articular), fibrous, and elastic. Cartilage is a semifirm connective tissue with a predominance of ground substance in the extracellular matrix. Within the ground substance are varying amounts of collagenous and elastic fibers. Cartilage has a bluish white or gray color and is semiopaque. It has no direct blood or nerve supply. Hyaline cartilage composes part of the nasal septum, the larynx, the trachea, the bronchi, and the articular ends of bones of the synovial joints. Fibrocartilage makes up the vertebral disks, symphysis pubis, and menisci of the knee joint. Elastic cartilage is found in the external ear and the eustachian tube.

As mentioned previously, the ends of the bones in a diarthrotic joint are covered by hyaline cartilage, which cushions the bone ends. Its general appearance is smooth and pearly. Hyaline cartilage acts like a sponge in relation to synovial fluid. As movement occurs, the articular cartilage helps provide both static and dynamic stability; it also absorbs and squeezes out the fluid as pressures vary between the joint surfaces. Because of its great strength, cartilage can be deformed without damage and can still return to its original shape. However, cartilaginous degeneration, producing microtrauma, may occur during the abnormal compressional forces that take place over time. Hyaline cartilage has no direct blood supply; it receives its nourishment from the synovial fluid, or more specifically, from the synovial membrane located at its edges. Deeper aspects of the cartilage are fed by spaces (lacunae) in the adjacent bone. The articular cartilage provides three major functions: motion control, stability, and load transmission.[24]

Motion Control

The shape of the articular cartilage determines what motion will occur. An enarthrodial joint, or a ball-and-socket joint such as the hip, is considered a universal joint, allowing movement in all planes. In contrast, a hinge joint such as the interphalangeal joint allows movement in only one plane.

Stability

Bones that form a joint have articulating surfaces that are at least somewhat congruent with one another and that produce varying degrees of stability, depending on their particular shape. The less congruent the articulating surfaces, the greater the instability.

Load Transmission

The articular cartilage assists in transmitting a joint load smoothly and uniformly across the articulating surface.

Additional Synovial Joint Structures

Fat

In some joints, such as the knee and elbow, pads of fat lie between the synovial membrane and the capsule. These pads of fat tend to fill in the spaces between the bones that form joints. As movement occurs, they move in and out of these spaces.

Articular (Fibrocartilage) Disks

Some diarthrotic joints have an additional fibrocartilaginous disk. These disks vary in shape and are connected to the capsule. They are found in joints in which two planes of movement exist, and they may act to disperse the synovial fluid between the joint surfaces. In some joints, a fibrocartilaginous disk is referred to as a meniscus.

Nerve Supply

The articular capsule, ligaments, outer aspects of the synovial membrane, and fat pads of the synovial joint are well supplied with nerves. The inner aspect of the synovial membrane, cartilage, and articular disks, if present, have nerves as well. Mechanoreceptors (encapsulated nerve endings) provide information about the relative position of the joint and are found in the fibrous capsule and ligaments. Mechanoreceptors are myelinated, whereas nonmyelinated fibers are pain receptors or blood vessel suppliers.[32]

Types of Synovial Joints

Synovial joints are subdivided into six types: ball-and-socket, hinge, pivot, ellipsoidal, saddle, and gliding.[35] Ball-and-socket joints allow all possible movement (e.g., shoulder and hip joints). Hinge joints allow only flexion and extension (e.g., elbow joint). Pivot joints permit rotation around an axis (e.g., cervical atlas and axis, proximal ends of radius and ulna). Ellipsoidal joints have an elliptical convex head in an elliptical concave socket (e.g., wrist joint). Saddle-shaped joints are reciprocally concavo-convex (e.g., carpometacarpal joint of the thumb). Gliding joints allow a small amount of gliding back and forth or sideways (e.g., joints between the carpal and tarsal bones and all the joints between the articular processes of the vertebrae).[39]

Functional Synovial Joint Characteristics

Synovial joints differ in their ability to withstand trauma, depending on their skeletal, ligamentous, and muscular organization. Table 9-2 provides a general guide to the relative strength of selected articulations in terms of sports participation.

Synovial Joint Stabilization

Muscle tension is important in limiting synovial joint movement. Limitation may be the result of contacting another anatomic structure. When the joint capsule is overstretched, a reflex contraction of muscles in the area occurs to prevent overstretching.

TABLE 9-2 General Relative Strength Grades in Selected Articulations

Articulation	Skeleton	Ligaments	Muscles
Ankle	Strong	Moderate	Weak
Knee	Weak	Moderate	Strong
Hip	Strong	Strong	Strong
Lumbosacral	Weak	Strong	Moderate
Lumbar vertebrae	Strong	Strong	Moderate
Thoracic vertebrae	Strong	Strong	Moderate
Cervical vertebrae	Weak	Moderate	Strong
Sternoclavicular	Weak	Weak	Weak
Acromioclavicular	Weak	Moderate	Weak
Glenohumeral	Weak	Moderate	Moderate
Elbow	Moderate	Strong	Strong
Wrist	Weak	Moderate	Moderate
Phalanges (toes and fingers)	Weak	Moderate	Moderate

This reaction demonstrates Hilton's law, which states that the joint capsule, the muscles moving that joint, and the skin overlying the insertion of the muscles have the same nerve supply. Ligaments, for the most part, are not extensible but can be extended as a result of the collagen fibers being arranged in bundles at right angles to one another. As the angles of the bundles are changed, ligaments can be extended without lengthening the collagen fiber.

Ligaments and capsular structures are important to joint stability. Characteristically, joints that are shallow and relatively poor fitting must depend on their capsular structures or muscles for major support. The knee is an example of an articulation that lacks bony congruence and depends mainly on muscles and ligaments for its support.

Besides moving limbs, muscles also provide joint stabilization to a greater or lesser extent and absorb the forces of load transmission. Muscles help stabilize joints in the following ways: muscles that cross joints assist in maintaining proper articular alignment, and some muscles attach directly to the articular capsule (shunt muscles) and, when stretched, also tighten the capsule. By becoming taut, the shunt muscles prevent the articulations from separating and also assist in maintaining proper alignment.

Articular Capsule and Ligaments

Capsular and ligamentous tissue helps maintain anatomical integrity and structural alignment of synovial joints. Unlike tendons, however, these tissues contain elastic fibers, and their collagenous fibers, although they have many configurations, are irregular and have a spiral arrangement. Ligaments, which attach bone to bone, are generally strongest in the middle and weakest at the ends. Compared to ligaments and capsular tissues, with their fast, protective response, muscles respond much more slowly. For example, a muscle begins to develop protective tension within just a few hundredths of a second when overly stretched, but will not fully respond until approximately one-tenth of a second has elapsed.

Synovial Joint Trauma

A major factor in joint injuries is the viscoelastic tissue properties of ligaments and capsules (Table 9-3). Constant compression or tension can cause ligaments or capsular tissue to deteriorate. In contrast, intermittent compression and tension will, over time, increase overall strength, including that of the bony attachments of the connective tissue. Like tension forces, torsional or twisting forces that exceed the relative strength of collagen fibers can produce injury. Although occurring less often, a shearing action that cuts across the collagen fiber can traumatize capsular and ligamentous tissue. Tissue damage may occur when articular cartilage fails to properly transmit the

9-8

Critical Thinking Exercise

A basketball player steps on another player's foot and sustains a lateral ankle injury.

? What forces are applied, and what type of injury has been incurred?

TABLE 9-3 Synovial Joint Trauma

Primary Tissue	Type	Mechanical Forces	Condition
Capsule	Acute	Tension/compression	Sprains Dislocation/subluxation Synovial swelling
	Chronic	Tension/compression/ shearing	Capsulitis Synovitis Bursitis
Articular cartilage (hyaline)	Chronic	Compression/shearing	Osteochondrosis Traumatic arthritis

applied loads. In other words, the bones and hyaline cartilage that form a joint become out of accordance with each other's compressional forces over a period of time and predispose the joint to degenerative changes.

Synovial Joint Injury Classification

Acute Joint Injuries

The major injuries that happen to synovial joints are sprains, subluxations, and dislocations.

Joint Sprains   A sprain, one of the most common and disabling injuries seen in sports, is a traumatic joint twist that results in stretching or total tearing of the stabilizing connective tissues (Figure 9-11). When a joint is forced beyond its normal anatomical limits, microscopic and gross pathologies occur. Specifically, there is injury to ligaments and to the articular capsule and synovial membrane. According to the extent of injury, sprains are graded in three degrees. A grade 1 sprain is characterized by some pain, minimum loss of function, mild point tenderness, little or no swelling, and no abnormal motion when tested. With a grade 2 sprain there is pain, moderate loss of function, swelling, and in some cases slight to moderate instability.[11] A grade 3 (or severe) sprain is extremely painful initially, with loss of function, severe instability, tenderness, and swelling. A grade 3 sprain may also represent a subluxation that has been reduced spontaneously.

Effusion of blood and synovial fluid into the joint cavity during a sprain produces joint swelling, local temperature increase, pain or point tenderness, and skin discoloration (ecchymosis). Ligaments and capsules, like tendons, can experience forces that completely rupture or produce an avulsion fracture. Ligaments and capsules heal slowly because of a relatively poor blood supply; however, their nerves are plentiful, often producing a great deal of pain when injured.[38]

The joints that are most vulnerable to sprains in sports are the ankles, knees, and shoulders. Sprains occur less often to the wrists and elbows. Because it is often difficult to distinguish between joint sprains and tendon strains, the athletic trainer should expect the worst possible condition and manage it accordingly. Repeated joint twisting can eventually result in chronic inflammation, degeneration, and arthritis.

Acute synovitis   The synovial membrane of a joint can be acutely injured by a contusion or a sprain. Irritation of the membrane causes an increase in fluid production, and swelling occurs. The result is joint pain during motion, along with skin sensitivity from pressure at certain points. In a few days, with proper care, effusion and extravasated blood are absorbed, and swelling and pain diminish.

Subluxations, dislocations, and diastasis   Dislocations are second to fractures in terms of disabling the athlete. The highest incidence of dislocations involves the fingers, followed by the shoulder joint (Figure 9-12). Dislocations, which result primarily from forces causing the joint to go beyond its normal anatomical limits, are divided into two classes: subluxations and luxations. Subluxations are partial dislocations in which an incomplete separation between two articulating bones occurs. Luxations are

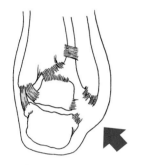

Figure 9-11

A sprain mainly involves injury to ligamentous and capsular tissue; however, muscle tendons can be secondarily strained.

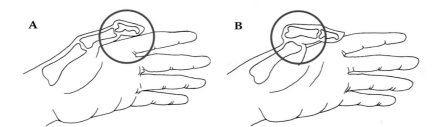

Figure 9-12

A point that is forced beyond its anatomical limits can become **A,** partially dislocated (subluxated), or **B,** completely dislocated (luxated).

complete dislocations, presenting a total disunion of bone apposition between the articulating surfaces. A diastasis is of two types: a disjointing of two bones parallel to one another, such as the radius and ulna; and the rupture of a "solid" joint, such as the symphysis pubis.[1] A diastasis commonly occurs with a fracture.

Several factors are important in recognizing and evaluating dislocations:

1. There is a loss of limb function. The athlete usually complains of having fallen or of having received a severe blow to a particular joint and then suddenly being unable to move that part.
2. Deformity is almost always apparent. Because the deformity can often be obscured by heavy musculature, it is important for the athletic trainer to palpate the injured site to determine the loss of normal body contour. Comparison of the injured side with its normal counterpart often reveals distortions.
3. Swelling and point tenderness are immediately present.

At times, X-ray examination of the dislocation, as with a fracture, is the only absolute diagnostic measure. First-time dislocations or joint separations may result in a rupture of the stabilizing ligamentous and tendinous tissues surrounding the joint and in avulsion, or pulling away from the bone. Trauma is often so violent that small chips of bone are torn away with the supporting structures, or the force may separate growth epiphyses or cause a complete fracture of the neck in long bones. These possibilities indicate the importance of administering complete and thorough medical attention to first-time dislocations. It has often been said, "Once a dislocation, always a dislocation." In most cases this statement is true because once a joint has been either subluxated or completely luxated, the connective tissues that bind and hold it in its correct alignment are stretched to such an extent that the joint will be extremely vulnerable to subsequent dislocations. Chronic, recurring dislocations may take place without severe pain because of the somewhat slack condition of the stabilizing tissues.

A first-time dislocation should always be considered and treated as a possible fracture. Once the athletic trainer has ascertained that the injury is a dislocation, a physician should be consulted for further evaluation. However, before the patient is taken to the physician, the injury should be properly splinted and supported to prevent any further damage.

> A first-time dislocation should always be considered a possible fracture.

Chronic Joint Injuries

Like other chronic physical injuries or problems occurring from sports participation, chronic synovial joint injuries stem from microtraumas and overuse. The two major categories in which they fall are osteochondrosis and osteoarthritis (traumatic arthritis), or inflammation of surrounding soft tissues such as the bursal capsule and the synovium.[17] Another general expression for the chronic synovial conditions of the child or adolescent is articular epiphyseal injury. A major cause of chronic joint injury such as osteoarthritis is failure of the muscle to control or limit deceleration. Athletes can avoid such injuries by avoiding chronic fatigue and training when tired and by wearing protective gear to enhance active absorption of impact forces.[29]

Osteochondrosis   Osteochondrosis is a category of conditions of which the causes are not well understood. In general, the term refers to degenerative changes in the

9-9

Critical Thinking Exercise

A young female gymnast has a pronounced knee malalignment. She complains of a left knee locking, pain, and swelling.

? What is the gymnast's possible condition?

ossification centers of the epiphyses of bones, especially during periods of rapid growth in children. Synonyms for this condition are, if it is located in a point such as the knee, *osteochondritis dissecans* and, if located at a tubercle or tuberosity, *apophysitis*. Apophyseal conditions are discussed in the section on bone trauma in this chapter.

One suggested cause of osteochondrosis is aseptic necrosis, in which circulation to the epiphysis has been disrupted. Another suggestion is that trauma causes particles of the articular cartilage to fracture, eventually resulting in fissures that penetrate to the subchondral bone. If trauma to a joint occurs, pieces of cartilage may be dislodged, which can cause joint locking, swelling, and pain. If the condition occurs in an apophysis, there may be an avulsion fracture and fragmentation of the epiphysis along with pain, swelling, and disability.

osteoarthritis
A wearing down of hyaline cartilage.

Osteoarthritis   Any mechanical system wears out with time. The joints in the body are mechanical systems, and wear and tear, even from normal activity, is inevitable. The most common result of this wear and tear, a degeneration of the articular or hyaline cartilage, is referred to as **osteoarthritis**.[5] The cartilage may be worn away to the point of exposing, eroding, and polishing the underlying bone.

Any process that changes the mechanics of the joint eventually leads to degeneration of that joint. Degeneration is a result of repeated trauma to the joint and to tendons, ligaments, and fasciae surrounding the joint. Such injuries may be caused by a direct blow or fall, by pressure of carrying or lifting heavy loads, or by repeated trauma to the joint as in running or cycling.[26]

Osteoarthritis most often affects the weight-bearing joints: the knees, hips, and lumbar spine. Also affected are the shoulders and cervical spine. Although many other joints may show pathological degenerative change, clinically the disease only occasionally produces symptoms in them. Any joint that is subjected to acute or chronic trauma may develop osteoarthritis.[5]

Athletes with improperly immobilized joint injuries or who are allowed to return to activity before proper healing has occurred may eventually be afflicted with arthritis.

The symptoms of osteoarthritis are relatively local in character. Osteoarthritis may be localized to one side of the joint or may be generalized about the joint. One of the most distinctive symptoms is pain, which is brought about by friction that occurs with use and which is relieved by rest. Stiffness is a common complaint that occurs with rest and is quickly loosened with activity. This symptom is prominent upon rising in the morning. Joints may also show localized tenderness, creaking, or grating that may be heard and felt.[27] Clinical studies indicate that glucosamine sulfate has been shown to be a safe and relatively effective treatment for osteoarthritis. However, no evidence to date supports or refutes a carryover effect to the athletic population and the injuries that occur in sport.[24]

bursitis
Inflammation of bursa at sites of bony prominences between muscle and tendon.

Bursitis   Bursa are pieces of synovial membrane that contain small amounts of synovial fluid. They are found in places at which friction might occur within body tissues. Bursae provide protection between tendons and bones, between tendons and ligaments, and between other structures where there is friction. Sudden irritation can cause acute **bursitis**, and overuse of muscles or tendons as well as constant external compression or trauma can result in chronic bursitis. The signs and symptoms of bursitis include swelling, pain, and some loss of function. Repeated trauma may lead to calcific deposits and degeneration of the internal lining of the bursa. Bursitis in the knee, elbow, and shoulder is common among athletes.

9-10

Critical Thinking Exercise

A wrestler complains of pain, swelling, and warmth around the knee that always seems to be worse after practice.

? What should an athletic trainer suspect is wrong with his knee and how should it be treated?

Capsulitis and synovitis   After repeated joint sprains or microtraumas, a chronic inflammatory condition called capsulitis may occur. Usually associated with capsulitis is synovitis. Synovitis also occurs acutely, but a chronic condition can arise with repeated joint injury or with joint injury that is improperly managed. Chronic synovitis involves active joint congestion with edema. As with the synovial lining of the bursa, the synovium of a joint can undergo degenerative tissue changes. The synovium becomes irregularly thickened, exudation occurs, and a fibrous underlying tissue is present. Several movements may be restricted, and there may be joint noises such as grinding or creaking.

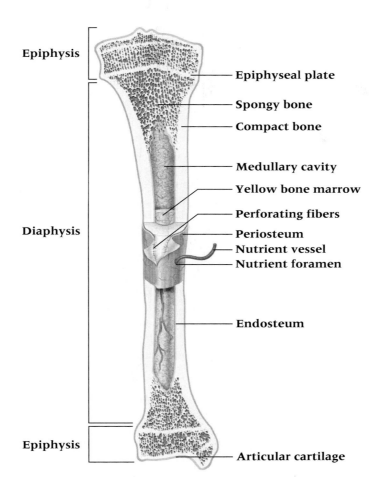

Epiphysis

Epiphyseal plate

Spongy bone

Compact bone

Medullary cavity

Yellow bone marrow

Perforating fibers

Diaphysis

Periosteum

Nutrient vessel

Nutrient foramen

Endosteum

Epiphysis

Articular cartilage

Figure 9-13

Anatomical characteristics of bone (longitudinal section).

BONE TRAUMA

Bone provides shape and support for the body. Like soft tissue, bone can be traumatized during sports participation.

Anatomical Characteristics

Bone is a specialized type of dense connective tissue consisting of bone cells (osteocytes) that are fixed in a matrix, which consists of an intercellular material. The outer surface of a bone is composed of compact tissue, and the inner aspect is composed of a more porous tissue known as cancellous bone (Figure 9-13). Compact tissue is tunneled by a marrow cavity. Throughout the bone run countless branching canals, which contain blood vessels and lymphatic vessels. These canals form the haversian system. On the outside of a bone is a tissue covering, the periosteum, which contains the blood supply to the bone.[35]

Bone Functions

Bones perform five basic functions: body support, organ protection, movement (through joints and levers), calcium storage, and formation of blood cells (hematopoiesis).

Types of Bone

Bones are classified according to their shapes. Classifications include bones that are flat, irregular, short, and long. Flat bones are in the skull, the ribs, and the scapulae; irregular bones are in the vertebral column and the skull. Short bones are primarily in the wrist and the ankle. Long bones, the most commonly injured bones in sports, consist of the humerus, ulna, femur, tibia, fibula, and phalanges.

Flat, irregular, and short bones have the same inner cancellous bone over which there is a layer of compact bone. A few irregular and flat bones (e.g., the vertebrae and the sternum) have some space in the cancellous bone that is filled with red marrow and sesamoid bones.

Gross Structures

The gross structures of bone that are visible to the naked eye include the diaphysis, epiphysis, articular cartilage, periosteum, medullary (marrow) cavity, and endosteum. The diaphysis is the main shaft of the long bone. It is hollow, cylindrical, and covered by compact bone. The epiphysis is located at the ends of long bones. It is bulbous in shape, providing space for the muscle attachments. The epiphysis is composed primarily of cancellous bone, giving it a spongelike appearance. As discussed previously, the ends of long bones have a layer of hyaline cartilage that covers the joint surfaces of the epiphysis. This cartilage provides protection during movement and cushions jars and blows to the joint. A dense, white, fibrous membrane, the periosteum, covers long bones except at joint surfaces. Many fibers, called Sharpey's fibers, emanate from the periosteum and penetrate the underlying bone. Interlacing with the periosteum are fibers from the muscle tendons. Throughout the periosteum on its inner layer exist countless blood vessels and osteoblasts (bone-forming cells). The blood vessels provide nutrition to the bone, and the osteoblasts provide bone growth and repair. The medullar cavity, a hollow tube in the long bone diaphysis, contains a yellow, fatty marrow in adults. Lining the medullar cavity is the endosteum.[35]

Microscopic Structures

Calcium salts impregnate the intercellular substance of bone, making it hard. Osteocytes are found in small, hollow spaces called lacunae. Running throughout the bone is the haversian system, consisting of a central tube (haversian canal) with alternate layers of intercellular matrix surrounding it in concentric cylinders. Haversian systems are the structural units of compact bone. Compact and cancellous bones differ in their structures. In compact bone, interspersed lamellae fill the spaces between adjacent haversian systems. In cancellous bone, numerous open spaces are located between thin processes called trabeculae. Trabeculae act like scaffolding, joining cancellous bone. They arrange themselves along the line of greatest stress, providing additional structural strength to the bone. The blood circulation connects the periosteum with the haversian canal through the Volkmann's canal. The medullary cavity and the bone marrow are supplied directly by one or more arteries.[35]

Bone Growth

Bone ossification occurs from the synthesis of bone's organic matrix by osteoblasts, followed immediately by the calcification of this matrix.

The epiphyseal growth plate is a cartilaginous disk located near the end of each long bone. The growth of the long bones depends on these plates. Ossification in long bones begins in the diaphysis and in both epiphyses. It proceeds from the diaphysis toward each epiphysis and from each epiphysis toward the diaphysis. The growth plate has layers of cartilage cells in different stages of maturity, with immature cells at one end and mature ones at the other end. As the cartilage cells mature, immature osteoblasts replace them later to produce solid bone.

Epiphyseal growth plates are often less resistant to deforming forces than are ligaments of nearby joints or the outer shaft of the long bones; therefore, severe twisting or a blow to an arm or leg can result in growth disruption. Injury can prematurely close the growth plate, causing a loss of length in the bone. Growth plate dislocation can also cause deformity of the long bone.[20]

Bone diameter may increase as a result of the combined action of osteoblasts and osteoclasts. Osteoblasts build new bone on the outside of the bone; at the same time, osteoclasts increase the medullary cavity by breaking down bony tissue. Once a bone has reached its full size, there occurs a balance of bone formation and bone destruction, or osteogenesis and resorption, respectively. This process of balance may be disrupted by factors in sports conditioning or participation. These factors may cause greater osteogenesis than resorption. Conversely, resorption may exceed osteogenesis in situations in which the athlete is out of shape but overtrains. On the other hand, women whose estrogen is decreased as a result of training may experience bone loss.[3] In general, bone loss begins to exceed bone gain by ages thirty-five to forty. Gradually, bone is lost in the endosteal surfaces and then is gained on the outer surfaces. As the thickness of long bones decreases, they are less able to resist the forces of compression. This process also leads to increased bone porosity, known as osteoporosis.

Like other structures in the human body, bones are morphologically, biochemically, and biomechanically sensitive to both stress and stress deprivation. Therefore, bone's functional adaptation follows Wolff's law;[41] that is, every change in the form and function of a bone, or in its function alone, is followed by certain definite changes in its internal architecture and equally definite secondary alterations in its mathematical laws.

Bone Injuries

Because of its viscoelastic properties, bone will bend slightly. However, bone is generally brittle and is a poor shock absorber because of its mineral content. This brittleness increases under tension forces more than under compression forces.

Many factors of bone structure affect its strength. Anatomical strength or weakness can be affected by a bone's shape and its changes in shape or direction. A hollow cylinder is one of the strongest structures for resisting both bending and twisting—stronger than a solid rod, which has much less resistance to such forces.[19] This may be why bones such as the tibia are primarily cylinders. Most spiral fractures of the tibia occur at its middle and distal third, where the bone is most solid (Figure 9-14).

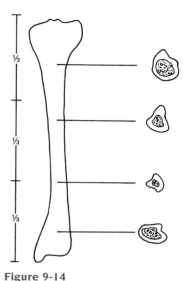

Figure 9-14

Anatomical strengths or weaknesses of a long bone can be affected by its shape, changes of direction, and hollowness.

Anatomical Weak Points

Stress forces become concentrated at points at which a long bone suddenly changes shape and direction. Long bones that change shape gradually are less prone to injury than are those that change suddenly. The clavicle, for example, is prone to fracture because it changes from round to flat at the same point at which it changes direction.

Load Characteristics

Long bones can be stressed or loaded to failure by tension, compression, bending, twisting (torsion), and shearing. These forces, either singularly or in combination, can cause a variety of fractures. For example, spiral fractures are caused by twisting, whereas oblique fractures are caused by the combined forces of axial compression, bending, and torsion. Transverse fractures occur by bending (Figure 9-15).

Another stress factor is the amount of the load. An increase in energy causes a more complex fracture. Energy is used in deforming the bone and breaking the bony tissue, and some energy becomes dissipated in adjacent soft tissue.[28] The rate at which a force is applied to a long bone can affect tissue failure. Depending on the type of bony tissue, more energy is required to cause an abrupt fracture than to cause a fracture to develop over a period of time.[9]

A bone's magnitude of stress and strain is most prevalent at its outer surface and gradually decreases to zero at its center.[29]

Long bones can be stressed by tension, compression, bending, torsion, and shearing.

Bone Trauma Classification

Bone trauma can generally be classified as either periostitis, acute fractures, stress fractures, or epiphyseal conditions.

Periostitis   An inflammation of the periosteum can result from various sports traumas, mainly contusions. Periostitis is often manifest as skin rigidity over the overlying muscles. It can occur as an acute episode or can become chronic.

Acute bone fractures   A bone fracture can be a partial or complete interruption in a bone's continuity; it can occur without external exposure or can extend through the skin, creating an external wound (open fracture). Fractures can result from direct

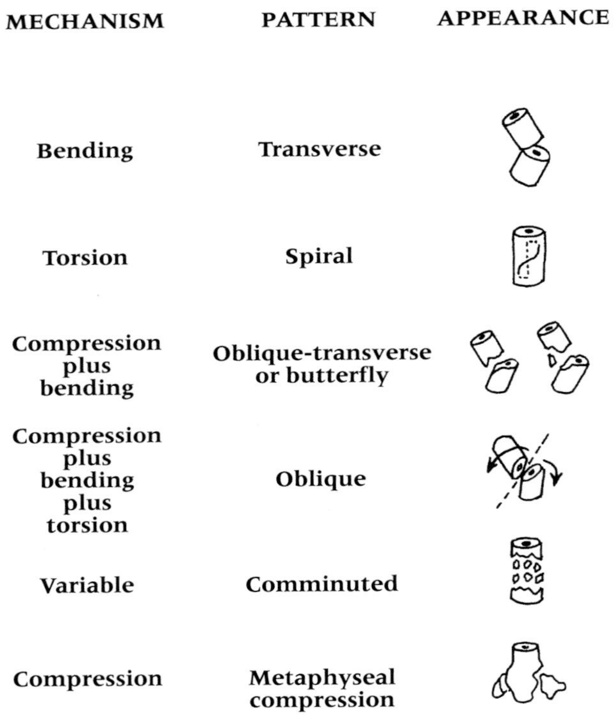

Figure 9-15

Mechanisms, patterns, and appearances of acute bone fractures.

MECHANISM	PATTERN	APPEARANCE
Bending	Transverse	
Torsion	Spiral	
Compression plus bending	Oblique-transverse or butterfly	
Compression plus bending plus torsion	Oblique	
Variable	Comminuted	
Compression	Metaphyseal compression	

Figure 9-15

Mechanisms, patterns, and appearances of acute bone fractures.

trauma; in other words, the bone breaks directly at the site where a force is applied. A fracture that occurs some distance from where force is applied is called an indirect fracture. A sudden, violent muscle contraction or repetitive abnormal stress to a bone can also cause a fracture. Fractures must be considered among the most serious hazards of sports and should be routinely suspected in musculoskeletal injuries. The next sections present more detailed descriptions of acute fractures.[21]

Depressed fracture   Depressed fractures occur most often in flat bones such as those found in the skull. They are caused by falling and striking the head on a hard, immovable surface or by being hit with a hard object. Such injuries also result in gross pathology of soft areas.

Greenstick fracture   Greenstick fractures are incomplete breaks in bones that have not completely ossified, such as the bones of adolescents. This injury occurs most frequently in the convex bone surface, while the concave surface remains intact. The name is derived from the similarity of the fracture to the break in a green twig taken from a tree.

Impacted fracture   Impacted fractures can result from a fall from a height, which causes a long bone to receive, directly on its long axis, a force of such magnitude that the osseous tissue is compressed. This stress telescopes one part of the bone on the other. Impacted fractures require immediate splinting by the athletic trainer and traction by the physician to ensure a normal length of the injured limb.

Longitudinal fracture   Longitudinal fractures are those in which the bone splits along its length. They are often the result of an athlete jumping from a height and landing in such a way as to impart force or stress to the long axis.

Spiral fracture   Spiral fractures have an S-shaped separation. They are common in football and skiing, sports in which the foot is firmly planted when the body is suddenly rotated in an opposing direction.

Oblique fracture   Oblique fractures are similar to spiral fractures. Oblique fractures occur when one end of the bone receives sudden torsion or twisting while the other end is fixed or stabilized.

Serrated fracture   Serrated fractures, in which the two bony fragments have a sawtooth, sharp-edged fracture line, are usually caused by a direct blow. Because of the

9-11

Critical Thinking E x e r c i s e

An alpine skier catches his right ski tip and severely twists the lower leg.

? What type of serious injury could be created by this mechanism?

sharp and jagged bone edges, extensive internal damage, such as the severance of vital blood vessels and nerves, often occurs.

Transverse fracture   Transverse fractures occur in a straight line, more or less at right angles to the bone shaft. A direct outside blow usually causes this injury.

Comminuted fracture   Comminuted fractures consist of three or more fragments at the fracture site. This injury could be caused by a hard blow or a fall in an awkward position. These fractures impose a difficult healing situation because of the displacement of the bone fragments. Soft tissues are often interposed between the fragments, causing incomplete healing. Such cases may need surgical intervention.

Contrecoup fracture   Contrecoup fractures occur on the side opposite to the point at which trauma was initiated. Fracture of the skull is, at times, a contrecoup fracture. An athlete may be hit on one side of the head with such force that the brain and internal structures compress against the opposite side of the skull, causing a fracture.

Blowout fracture   Blowout fractures occur to the wall of the eye orbit as the result of a blow to the eye.

Avulsion fracture   An avulsion fracture is the separation of a bone fragment from its cortex at an attachment of a ligament or tendon. This fracture usually occurs as a result of a sudden, powerful twist or stretch of a body part. A ligamentous avulsion can occur, for example, when a sudden eversion of the foot causes the deltoid ligament to avulse bone away from the medial malleolus. A tendinous avulsion can occur when an athlete falls forward while suddenly bending a knee, which causes a patellar fracture. The stretch of the patellar tendon pulls a portion of the inferior patellar pole apart. Figure 9-16 illustrates a tendinous avulsion of the sartorius muscle.

Stress fractures   Stress fractures have been variously called march, fatigue, and spontaneous fractures, although stress fracture is the most commonly used term. The exact cause of this fracture is not known, but there are a number of likely possibilities: an overload caused by muscle contraction, an altered stress distribution in the bone accompanying muscle fatigue, a change in the ground reaction force such as movement from a wood surface to a grass surface, or the performance of a rhythmically repetitive stress that leads up to a vibratory summation point, which appears to be the most likely cause.[22] Rhythmic muscle action performed over a period of time at a subthreshold level causes the stress-bearing capacity of the bone to be exceeded, hence, a stress fracture. A bone may become vulnerable to fracture during the first few weeks of intense physical activity or training. Weight-bearing bones undergo bone resorption and become weaker before they become stronger. The sequence of events results from increased muscular forces plus an increased rate of remodeling that leads to bone resorption, weakening of the out surface of the bone, and rarefaction, which progresses to produce increasingly more severe fractures.[33] The four progressively severe fractures are focal microfractures, periosteal or endosteal response (stress fractures), linear fractures (stress fractures), and displaced fractures.

Typical causes of stress fractures in sports are as follows:

1. Coming back into competition too soon after an injury or illness.
2. Going from one event to another without proper training in the second event.
3. Starting initial training too quickly.
4. Changing habits or the environment (e.g., running surfaces, the bank of a track, or shoes).

Susceptibility to fracture can also be increased by a variety of postural and foot conditions. Flatfeet, a short first metatarsal bone, or a hypermobile metatarsal region can predispose an athlete to stress fractures.

Early detection of the stress fracture may be difficult. Because of their frequency in a wide range of sports, stress fractures always must be suspected in susceptible body areas that fail to respond to usual management. Until there is an obvious reaction in the bone, which may take several weeks, X-ray examination may fail to reveal any change. Although nonspecific, a bone scan can provide early indications in a given area.

The signs of a stress fracture are swelling, focal tenderness, and pain. In the early stages of the fracture, the athlete complains of pain when active but not at rest. Later,

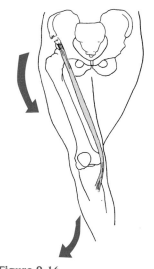

Figure 9-16

Tendinous avulsion fracture of the sartorius muscle.

Critical Thinking E x e r c i s e

A long jumper experiences a sudden sharp pain in the region of the left ischial tuberosity during a jump.

? What injuries are possible through this mechanism?

Figure 9-17

The most common stress fracture sites.

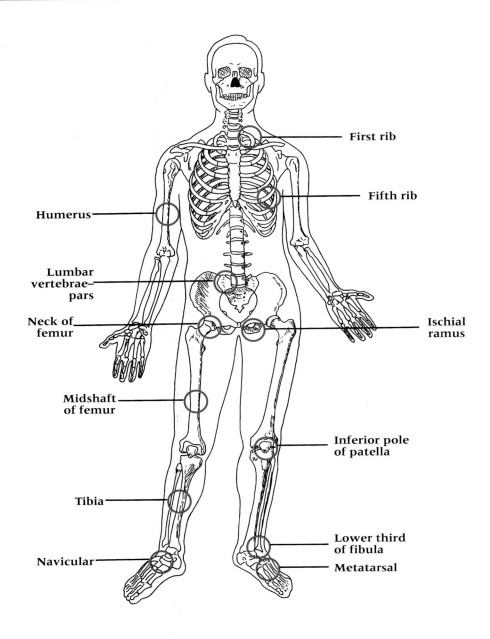

First rib

Fifth rib

Humerus

Lumbar vertebrae—pars

Neck of femur

Ischial ramus

Midshaft of femur

Inferior pole of patella

Tibia

Lower third of fibula

Navicular

Metatarsal

9-13

Critical Thinking Exercise

A track athlete training for a marathon is complaining of pain in the lower leg. She consults with her physician, who determines that she has a stress fracture. When she returns to practice, she is confused about how a stress fracture is different from a real fracture.

? How should the athletic trainer explain the difference between the two, and what is the course of management?

the pain is constant and becomes more intense at night. Percussion, by light tapping on the bone at a site other than the suspected fracture, will produce pain at the fracture site.

The most common sites of stress fracture are the tibia, fibula, metatarsal shaft, calcaneus, femur, pars interarticularis of the lumbar vertebrae, ribs, and humerus (Figure 9-17).

The management of stress fractures varies with the individual athlete, injury site, and extent of injury. Stress fractures that occur on the compression side of bone heal more rapidly and are managed more easily compared with those on the tension side. Stress fractures on the tension side can rapidly produce a complete fracture.

Epiphyseal conditions   Three types of epiphyseal growth site injuries can be sustained by children and adolescents performing sports activities. They are injury to the epiphyseal growth plate, or physis articular epiphyseal injuries, and apophyseal injuries. The most prevalent age range for these injuries is from ten to sixteen years.

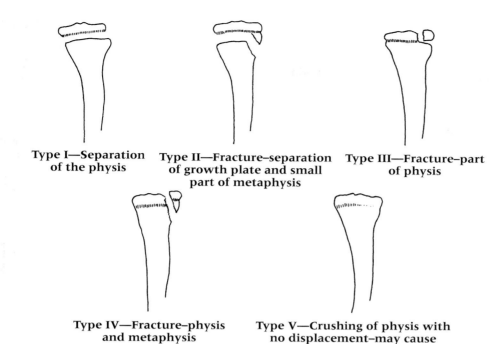

Type I—Separation of the physis

Type II—Fracture–separation of growth plate and small part of metaphysis

Type III—Fracture–part of physis

Type IV—Fracture–physis and metaphysis

Type V—Crushing of physis with no displacement–may cause premature closure

Figure 9-18

Salter-Harris classification of long bone epiphyseal injuries in children.

Epiphyseal growth plate injuries (Figure 9-18) have been classified by Salter-Harris into five types as follows:[4]

- Type I—complete separation of the physis in relation to the metaphysis without fracture to the bone.
- Type II—separation of the growth plate and a small portion of the metaphysis.
- Type III—fracture of the physis.
- Type IV—fracture of a portion of the physis and metaphysis.
- Type V—no displacement of the physis, but the crushing force can cause a growth deformity.

Apophyseal injuries   The young, physically immature athlete is particularly prone to apophyseal injuries. The apophyses are traction epiphyses in contrast to the pressure epiphyses of the long bones. These apophyses serve as origins or insertions for muscles on growing bone that provide bone shape but not length. Common apophyseal avulsion conditions found in sports are Sever's disease and Osgood-Schlatter's disease.

NERVE TRAUMA

A number of abnormal nerve responses can be attributed to athletic participation or injury. The most frequent type of nerve injury is neuropraxia produced by a direct trauma. A laceration can cut nerves, causing complications in healing of the injury. Fractures and dislocation can avulse or abnormally compress nerves.

Anatomical Characteristics

Nerve tissue provides sensitivity and communication from the central nervous system (brain and spinal cord) to the muscles, sensory organs, various systems, and the periphery. The basic nerve cell is the neuron. The neuron cell body contains a large nucleus and branched extensions called dendrites, which respond to neurotransmitter substances released from other nerve cells. From each nerve cell arises a single axon, which conducts the nerve impulses. Large axons found in peripheral nerves are

A musculoskeletal injury to a child or adolescent should always be considered a possible epiphyseal condition.

9-14

Critical Thinking E x e r c i s e

An 11-year-old soccer player fell on an outstretched hand during practice. There is obvious deformity in her right wrist.

? What is a possible complication with a fracture in this wrist?

enclosed in neurilemmal sheaths composed of Schwann cells and satellite cells, which are tightly wound around the axon. In the central nervous system, various types of neuroglial cells including astrocytes, oligodendrocytes, ependymal cells, and microglia function collectively to bind neurons together and provide a supportive framework for the nervous tissue.[35]

Nerve Injuries

The two main forces that cause major nerve injury responses are compression and tension. As with injuries to other tissues in the body, the injurious forces to nerves may be acute or chronic.

Physical trauma to nerves in general produces pain as part of the inflammatory process. Any number of traumas directly affecting nerves can also produce a variety of sensory responses, including pain. For example, a sudden nerve stretch or pinch can produce muscle weakness as well as a sharp burning pain that radiates down a limb. **Neuritis**, a chronic nerve problem, can be caused by a variety of forces that usually have been repeated or continued for a long period of time. Symptoms of neuritis can range from minor nerve problems to paralysis.

Pain that is felt at a point of the body other than its actual origin is known as **referred pain**.[15] Another potential cause of referred pain is a trigger point, which occurs in the muscular system but refers pain to some other distant body part.

BODY MECHANICS AND INJURY SUSCEPTIBILITY

If you carefully study the mechanical structure of the human body, it is amazing that humans can move so effectively in the upright posture. Not only must the body overcome constant gravitational force, but it also must be manipulated through space by a complex system of somewhat inefficient levers, fueled by a machinery that operates at an efficiency level of approximately 30 percent. The bony levers that move the body must overcome considerable resistance in the form of inertia and muscle viscosity and must work in most instances at an extremely unfavorable angle of pull. All these factors mitigate the effectiveness of lever action to the extent that most movement is achieved at an efficiency level of less than 25 percent.

When determining the mechanical reasons for sports injuries to the musculoskeletal system, many factors can be identified. Hereditary, congenital, or acquired defects may predispose an athlete to a specific type of injury. Anomalies in anatomical structure or in body build (somatotype) may make an athlete prone to injuries. The habitually incorrect application of skill is a common cause of overuse injuries.

Microtrauma and Overuse Syndrome

Injuries as a result of abnormal and repetitive stress and microtraumas fall into a class with certain identifiable syndromes.[36] Such stress injuries frequently result in either limitation or curtailment of sports performance. Most of these injuries in athletes are directly related to the dynamics of running, throwing, or jumping. The injuries may result from constant and repetitive stresses placed on bones, joints, or soft tissues; from forcing a joint into an extreme range of motion; or from prolonged strenuous activity. Some of the injuries falling into this category may be relatively minor; still, they can be disabling. Among injuries classified as repetitive stress and microtrauma are Achilles tendinitis; shin splints; stress fractures, particularly of the fibula and second and fifth metatarsal bones; Osgood-Schlatter's disease; runner's and jumper's knee; patellar chondromalacia; apophyseal avulsion, especially in the lower extremities of growing athletes; and intertarsal neuroma.

Postural Deviations

Postural deviations are often an underlying cause of sports injuries.[36] Postural malalignment may be the result of unilateral muscle and soft-tissue asymmetries or

neuritis
Inflammation of a nerve.

referred pain
Pain that is felt at a point of the body other than its origin.

bony asymmetries. As a result, the athlete engages in poor mechanics of movement (pathomechanics). Many sports activities are unilateral, thus leading to asymmetries in body development. The resulting imbalance is manifested by a postural deviation as the body seeks to reestablish itself in relation to its center of gravity. Often, such deviations are a primary cause of injury. For example, a consistent pattern of knee injury may be related to asymmetries within the pelvis and the legs (short-leg syndrome). Unfortunately, not much in the form of remedial work is usually performed. As a result, an injury often becomes chronic—sometimes to the point that participation in a sport must be halted. When possible, the athletic trainer should seek to ameliorate or eliminate faulty postural conditions through therapy. A number of postural conditions offer genuine hazards to athletes by making them exceedingly prone to specific injuries. Some of the more important are discussed in the chapters on foot and leg anomalies, spinal anomalies, and various stress syndromes.

SUMMARY

- "When a force applied to any part of the body results in a harmful disturbance in function or structure, a mechanical injury is said to have been sustained."[17] Engineering terminology is used to describe tissue properties and sport injuries. Examples of this terminology are *load, stress, deformation, viscoelastic, anisotropic, yield point,* and *tissue failure.*

- The five primary stresses leading to tissue trauma are tension, stretching, compression, shearing, and bending. Bending strain can produce a torque on a bone followed by injury. A torsion, or twisting, load can produce a spiral fracture along the long axis of a bone.

- Soft tissue (nonbony tissue) is categorized as noncontractile and contractile (muscle) tissues.

- Skin trauma can occur from a variety of forces (e.g., friction, scraping, compression, tearing, cutting, and puncturing) that produce blisters, skin bruises, lacerations, skin avulsions, incisions, and puncture wounds.

- Skeletal muscle trauma from sports participation can involve any aspect of the muscle-tension unit. Forces that injure muscles are compression, tension, and shearing. Acute muscle injuries include contusions and strains. Avulsion fractures and muscle ruptures can occur from an acute episode. Chronic muscle conditions are myositis, fasciitis, tendinitis, and tenosynovitis. Chronic muscle irritation can cause ectopic calcification; muscle disuse can cause atrophy; and immobilization can cause joint contracture.

- Sports injuries to the synovial joints are common. Anatomically, synovial joints have relative strengths or weaknesses based on their ligamentous or capsular type and their muscle arrangements. Forces that can injure synovial joints are tension, compression, torsion, and shear. Sprains involve acute injury to ligaments or the joint capsule. A grade 3 sprain may cause ligament rupture or an avulsion fracture. Acute synovial joint injuries that go beyond the third degree may result in a dislocation. Two major chronic synovial joint conditions are osteochondrosis and traumatic arthritis. Other chronic conditions are bursitis, capsulitis, and synovitis.

- Because of their shape, long bones are anatomically susceptible to fractures caused by changes in direction of the force applied to them. Mechanical forces that cause injury are compression, tension, bending, torsion, and shear. Bending and torsional forces are forms of tension. Acute fractures include avulsion, blowout, comminuted, depressed, greenstick, impacted, longitudinal, oblique, serrated, spiral, transverse, and contrecoup types. Stress fractures are commonly the result of overload to a given bone area. Stress fractures are apparently caused by an altered stress distribution or by the performance of a rhythmically repetitive action that leads to a vibratory summation and thus a fracture. Three major epiphyseal injuries in sports occur to the growth plate, the articular cartilage, and the apophysis.

- Nerve trauma can be produced by overstretching or compression. Like other injuries, nerve injuries can be acute or chronic. The sudden stretch of a nerve can cause a burning sensation. A variety of traumas to nerves can produce acute pain or a chronic pain such as neuritis.
- An athlete with faulty body mechanics has an increased potential for injury.

Websites

Biomechanics World Wide: http://www.per.ualberta.ca/
biomechanics

This site enables the reader to search the biomechanics journals for recent information regarding mechanism of injury.

Cramer First Aider: http://www.cramersportsmed.com/
first_aider.com

American Red Cross: http://www.redcross.org

National Institute of Health: http://www.nih.gov

Wheeless' Textbook of Orthopedics:
http://www.wheelessonline.com

Solutions to Critical Thinking EXERCISES

9-1   All human tissue has viscous and elastic properties. The resistance of tissue is dependent on its viscoelastic characteristics and the types of forces that are applied.

9-2   The friction force produced by sliding into home base causes a serious abrasion skin injury.

9-3   The ball created a compressive force that crushed tissue, causing a secondary contusion.

9-4   The football player has sustained a tension force to the long head of the biceps tendon that caused a rupture or severe strain.

9-5   The mechanism of this elbow injury is repeated tension to the extensor tendons attached to the lateral epicondyle, causing microtraumas. Stress to this area can be reduced by increasing the grip circumference and flattening the backhand stroke.

9-6   Repeated contusion of any muscle may lead to the development of myositis ossificans. The key to treating myositis ossificans is prevention. An initial contusion to any muscle should be immediately protected with padding to prevent reinjury.

9-7   Repeated contusions to the quadriceps could produce an ectopic calcification known as myositis ossificans.

9-8   In stepping on another player's foot, the basketball player produces an abnormal ankle torsion and lateral ankle tension, stretching and tearing ligaments.

9-9   Knee malalignment produces abnormal compression and shearing forces on the lateral menisci, which can lead to osteochondritis dissecans and osteochondritis.

9-10   The athletic trainer should suspect that the wrestler has developed bursitis from constantly kneeling on the mat. Inflammation may best be treated by rest, ice, antiinflammatory medication, and protective padding of the knee.

9-11   Catching the ski tip produces a torsional force that could cause a boot-top spiral fracture.

9-12   During the jump, a powerful stretch of the biceps femoris could cause a serious strain or an avulsion fracture in the region of the ischial tuberosity.

9-13   A stress fracture is not an actual break of the bone, it is simply an irritation of the bone. Treatment of a stress fracture requires about fourteen days of rest. However, the athletic trainer should point out that a stress fracture can become a true fracture if it is not rested; if that happens, four to six weeks of immobilization in a cast is necessary. Thus, it is critical that this athlete rest for the required amount of time.

9-14   An epiphyseal condition, such as an epiphyseal growth plate fracture, can occur in children and adolescents and needs to be considered with any musculoskeletal injury. These injuries can impair growth and further skeletal development.

REVIEW QUESTIONS AND CLASS ACTIVITIES

1. Describe the mechanics that produce inert and contractile sports injuries.
2. Describe the mechanical forces that injure skin.
3. What forces injure muscle tissue?
4. Describe all types of acute muscle injuries.
5. Describe all types of chronic muscle injuries.
6. Describe the major acute injuries occurring to joints.
7. What mechanical forces traumatize the musculotendinous unit and the synovial joint? How are the forces similar to one another, and how are they different?
8. What forces gradually weaken tendons and ligaments?
9. Contrast two chronic synovial joint injuries.
10. List the structural characteristics that make a long bone susceptible to fracture.
11. What mechanical forces cause acute fracture of a bone?
12. How do stress fractures probably occur?
13. Describe the most common epiphyseal conditions that result from sports participation.
14. What are the relationships of postural deviations to sports injuries?
15. Discuss the concept of pathomechanics as it relates to microtraumas and overuse syndromes.

REFERENCES

1. Akeson WH et al: The biology of ligaments. In Hunter LY, Funk FJ Jr, editors: *Rehabilitation of the injured knee,* St Louis, 1984, Mosby.
2. American Academy of Orthopaedic Surgeons: *Athletic training and sports medicine,* Park Ridge, Ill, 1991, American Academy of Orthopaedic Surgeons.

3. Barak T et al: Basic concepts of orthopaedic manual therapy. In Malone T, McPhail T, editors: *Orthopaedic and sports physical therapy*, ed 3, St Louis, 1996, Mosby.

4. Blavelt CT, Nelson FRT: *A manual of orthopaedic terminology*, ed 6, Philadelphia, PA, 1998, Elsevier.

5. Brinker M: *Review of orthopaedic trauma*, Philadelphia, 2001, WB Saunders.

6. Browner B: *Skeletal trauma: basic science, management, and reconstruction*, Philadelphia, 2002, WB Saunders.

7. Brukner P, Khan K: Sports injuries. In Brukner P, editor, *Clinical sports medicine*, ed 2, Sydney, 2002, McGraw-Hill.

8. Butterwick DJ: Recognition of complete muscle or tendon ruptures. *Athletic Therapy Today* 7(l):43, 2002.

9. Byrnes WB, Clarkson PM: Delayed onset muscle soreness and training. In Katch FL, Freedson PS, editors: *Clinics in sports medicine*, vol 5, Philadelphia, 1986, Saunders.

10. Cleary M, Kimura I, Sitler M: Temporal pattern of the repeated bout effect of eccentric exercise on delayed-onset muscle soreness, *J Ath Train* 37(1):32, 2002.

11. Delee J, Drez D, Miller M: *Delee & Drez's orthopaedic sports medicine: principles and practice*, Philadelphia, 2002, WB Saunders.

12. Delforge G: *Musculoskeletal trauma: implications for sports injury management*, Champaign, Ill, 2002, Human Kinetics.

13. DiFiori JP: Overuse injuries in young athletes: an overview, *Athletic Therapy Today* 7(6):25, 2002.

14. Dumke CL: Muscle cramps are not all created equal. *Athletic Therapy Today* 8(3):42, 2003.

15. Fine PG: The biology of pain. In Heil J, editor: *Psychology of sport injury*, Champaign, Ill, 1993, Human Kinetics.

16. Gallaspie J, May D: *Signs and symptoms of athletic injuries*, St. Louis, 1996, McGraw-Hill.

17. Geesink RGT et al: Stress response of articular cartilage, *Int J Sports Med* 5:100, 1984.

18. Gomez M: *Biomechanics of soft-tissue injury*, Tuscon, Ariz, 2000, Lawyers & Judges Publishing Company.

19. Gonza ER: Biomechanics of long bone injuries. In Gonza ER, Harrington IJ, editors: *Biomechanics of musculoskeletal injury*, Baltimore, 1982, Williams & Wilkins.

20. Hirsch CS, Lumwalt RE: Injuries caused by physical agents. In Kissane JM, editor: *Anderson's pathology*, ed 9, vol 1, Philadelphia, PA, 1996, Elsevier.

21. Hoppenfield S, Murthy V, Taylor K: *Treatment and rehabilitation of fractures*, Philadelphia, 2000, Lippincott Williams & Wilkins.

22. Huson A: Mechanics of joints, *Int J Sports Med* 5:83, 1984.

23. Hutson, M: Sports injuries: recognition and management, ed 3, Oxford, England, 2001, Oxford University Press.

24. James C, Uhl T: A review of articular cartilage pathology and the use of glucosamine sulfate, *J Ath Train* 36(4):413, 2001.

25. Leaveau BF: Basic biomechanics in sports and orthopaedic therapy. In Malone T, McPhail T, editors: *Orthopaedic and sports physical therapy*, ed 3, St Louis, 1996, Mosby.

26. Levine D, Prall E, Marcellin-Little D: Running and the development of osteoarthritis, Part I: Animal studies, *Athletic Therapy Today* 8(1):6, 2003.

27. Levine D: Running and the development of osteoarthritis. Part II. Human studies. *Athletic Therapy Today* 8(1):12, 2003.

28. Malone T, McPhoil T, Nitz A, editors: *Orthopaedic and sports physical therapy*, ed 2, St Louis, 1996, Mosby.

29. Markey KL: Stress fractures. In Hunter-Griffin LY, editor: *Overuse injuries. Clinics in sports medicine*, vol 6, Philadelphia, 1987, Saunders.

30. Merrick M: Secondary injury after musculoskeletal trauma: a review and update. *J Ath Train* 37(2):209, 2002.

31. Porth CM: *Pathophysiology*, ed 6, Philadelphia, 2003, Lippincott, Williams and Wilkins.

32. Riemann B, Lephart S: The sensorimotor system, Part I: The physiologic basis of functional joint stability, *J Ath Train* 37(1):71, 2002.

33. Romani W, Gieck J, Perrin D: Mechanisms and management of stress fractures in physically active persons, *J Ath Train* 37(3):306, 2002.

34. Roux W: *Die entwichlungsmechanic*, Leipzig, Germany, 1905, Englemann.

35. Saladin K: *Anatomy and physiology*, New York, 2001, McGraw-Hill.

36. Shamus E, Shamus L: *Sports injury: prevention and rehabilitation*, New York, 2001, McGraw-Hill.

37. Stone MB: Exercise-associated muscle cramps. *Athletic Therapy Today* 8(3):30, 2003.

38. Weintraub W: *Tendon and ligament healing: a new approach to sports and overuse injury*, Herndon, WV, 2003, Paradigm Publications.

39. Whiting W, Zernicke, R: *Biomechanics of musculoskeletal injury*, Champaign, Ill, 1998, Human Kinetics.

40. Wilson TC: Articular-cartilage lesions of the knee and osteoarthritis in athletes: an overview. *Athletic Therapy Today* 8 (1):20, 2003.

41. Wolff J: *Das geset der transformation der knockan*, Berlin, 1892, Hirschwald.

ANNOTATED BIBLIOGRAPHY

Blavelt CT, Nelson RRT: *A manual of orthopaedic terminology*, ed 6, Philadelphia, 1998, Elsevier.

This resource book is for all individuals who need to identify medical words or their acronyms.

Booher JM, Thibodeau GA: *Athletic injury assessment*, Boston, 2001, McGraw-Hill.

An excellent guide to the recognition, assessment, classification, and evaluation of athletic injuries.

Dandy D, Edwards D: *Essential orthopaedics and trauma*, 2003, Elsevier.

Presents essential core information for students and emphasizes common conditions and current orthopaedic practice.

Delforge G: *Musculoskeletal trauma: implications for sport injury management*, Champaign, Ill, 2003, Human Kinetics.

This text focuses on the therapeutic management of sport-related soft tissue injuries, fractures, and proprioceptive/sensorimotor impairments.

Garrick JG, Webb DR: *Sports injuries: diagnosis and management*. Philadelphia, 1999, WB Saunders.

An overview of musculoskeletal injuries that are unique to sports and exercise.

Griffith HW, Pederson M: *Complete guide to sports injuries: how to treat fractures, bruises, sprains, dislocations, and head injuries*, New York, 1997, Perigee.

Tells readers how to treat, avoid, and rehabilitate nearly 200 of the most common sports injuries, including fractures, bruises, sprains, strains, dislocations, and head injuries.

Peacinn M, Bojanic I: *Overuse injuries of musculoskeletal system*, Boca Raton, FL, 2003, CRC Press.

A comprehensive text describing overuse injuries of the tendon, tendon sheath, bursae, muscle, muscle-tendon function, cartilage, and nerve.

Williams JGP: *Color atlas of injury in sport*, Chicago, 1990, Mosby.

This excellent visual guide to the area of sports injuries covers the nature and incidence of sport injury, types of tissue damage, and regional injuries caused by a variety of sports activities.

Weintraub W: *Tendon and ligament healing: a new approach to sports and overuse injury*, Herndon, WV, 2003, Paradigm Publications.

Gives readers a clear understanding of the dynamic nature of tendons and ligaments from an excellent review of their structure, function, mechanics, injury, and healing processes.

Chapter 10

On-the-Field Acute Care and Emergency Procedures

When you finish this chapter you should be able to

- Establish a plan for handling emergency situations at your institution.
- Explain the importance of knowing cardiopulmonary resuscitation and how to manage an obstructed airway.
- Describe the types of hemorrhage and their management.
- Assess the types of shock and their management.
- Describe the emergency management of musculoskeletal injuries.
- Describe techniques for moving and transporting the injured athlete.

Time becomes critical in an emergency situation.

M ost sports injuries do not result in life-or-death emergency situations, but when such situations do arise, prompt care is essential.[5] An emergency is defined as an unexpected serious occurrence that may cause injuries that require immediate medical attention.[55] Time becomes the critical factor, and assistance to the injured person must be based on knowledge of what to do and how to do it—on how to perform effective first aid immediately.[15] There is no room for uncertainty, indecision, or error. A mistake in the initial management of an injury can prolong the length of time required for rehabilitation and can potentially create a life-threatening situation for the athlete.[6]

THE EMERGENCY ACTION PLAN

The prime concern of emergency aid is to maintain cardiovascular function and, indirectly, central nervous system function.[10] Failure of either of these systems may lead to death. The key to emergency aid in the sports setting is the initial evaluation of the injured athlete. Time is of the essence, so this evaluation must be done rapidly and accurately so that proper first aid can be rendered without delay. In some instances, these first steps not only will be lifesaving but also may determine the degree and extent of permanent disability.

As discussed in Chapters 1 and 3, the sports medicine team—the athletic trainer, the team physician, and the coach—must at all times act reasonably and prudently.[44] This behavior is especially important during emergencies.

All sports programs must have a separate emergency action plan.

All sports programs must have a prearranged emergency action plan (EAP) that can be implemented immediately when necessary.[21,22,60] The following issues must be addressed when developing the emergency action plan:

1. Develop separate emergency action plans for each sport's field, courts, or gymnasiums (see *Focus Box:* "Sample emergency action plan").
   a. Determine the personnel who will be on the field during practices and competitions. (e.g., athletic trainers, student athletic trainers, physicians, emergency medical technicians, rescue squad) Each person should understand exactly what his or her role and responsibility is if an emergency occurs. It is also recommended that the sports medicine team practice the use and operation of emergency equipment, such as stretchers and automatic external defibrillators.[25]

Focus

    b. Decide what emergency equipment should be available for each sport. The emergency equipment needs for football will likely be different from those of the cross-country team.

2. Establish specific procedures and policies regarding the removal of protective equipment, particularly the helmet and shoulder pads. These procedures will be discussed later in this chapter.[25,34]

3. Make sure phones are readily accessible. Cellular or digital phones are best because the athletic trainer can carry one at all times. However, a land line should also be readily available in case cell phone service is not available. If cellular phones are not available, the athletic training students, coaches, and athletes should know the location of the telephone; phones should be clearly marked. Use 911 if available, but realize that in some areas all service is not accessible by cellular phones and thus land lines should be used to access the emergency medical system.

4. The athletic trainer should be familiar with the community-based emergency health care delivery plan, including existing communication and transportation policies. It is also critical for the athletic trainer to be familiar with emergency care facility admission and treatment policies, particularly when rendering emergency care to a minor. The athletic trainer should specifically designate someone to make an emergency phone call. Most emergency medical systems can be accessed by dialing 911, which connects the caller to a dispatcher who has access to rescue squad, police, and fire personnel. The person making the emergency phone call must provide the following information:

   a. Type of emergency situation
   b. Type of suspected injury
   c. Present condition of the athlete
   d. Current assistance being given (e.g., cardiopulmonary resuscitation)
   e. Location of telephone being used
   f. Exact location of emergency (give names of streets and cross streets) and how to enter facility

5. Make sure keys to gates or padlocks are easily accessible. Both the athletic trainer and the coach should have the appropriate key.

6. Inform all coaches, athletic directors, school nurses, and maintenance personnel of the emergency plan at a meeting held annually before the beginning of the school year. Each individual must know his or her responsibilities should an emergency occur.

7. Assign someone to accompany the injured athlete to the hospital.

8. Carry contact information for all athletes, coaches, and other personnel at all times, particularly when traveling (see Figure 3-1). For minors, consent forms should also be available when traveling.

9. In certain situations at both high schools and colleges, the athletic trainer may be called upon to provide emergency services not only to athletes but also to coaches, referees, and in some cases parents and other spectators who may develop an emergent condition during the course of an athletic event. The emergency action plan should include plans for managing these situations with the help of emergency medical services and other local health care providers.

In 2002, the NATA released a position statement relative to an emergency action plan.[4] The objective was to provide guidelines for athletic trainers in the development of emergency plans and to advocate documentation of emerging planning.

Cooperation between Emergency Care Providers

Emergency practice sessions for athletic trainers and EMTs should be held at least once a year.

Individuals providing emergency care to injured athletes must cooperate and act professionally. The athletic trainer should make every effort to nurture the relationship with the emergency medical technicians (EMTs) and, if possible, incorporate them into the development and implementation of the emergency action plan. Occasionally, disagreement arises between rescue squad personnel, the physician, and the athletic trainer over exactly how the injured athlete should be handled and transported. The athletic trainer is usually the first to deal with the emergency situation. The athletic trainer has generally had more training and experience in moving and transporting an injured athlete than the physician has. If an athletic trainer or physician is not available, the coach should not hesitate to call 911 to let the rescue squad handle an emergency situation. If the rescue squad is called and responds, the EMTs should have the final say on how that athlete is to be transported while the athletic trainer assumes an assistive role.

To alleviate potential conflicts, the athletic trainer should establish procedures and guidelines and should arrange practice sessions at least once a year that include everyone responsible for handling an injured athlete.[10] Rescue squad personnel may not be experienced in dealing with someone who is wearing a helmet or other protective

Focus

> **Consent form for medical treatment of a minor**
>
> By this signature, I hereby consent to allow the physician(s) and other health care provider(s) selected by myself or the school to perform a preparticipation examination on my child and to provide treatment for any injury or condition resulting from participating in athletics and activities for his or her school during the school year covered by this form. I further consent to allow said physician(s) or health care provider(s) to share appropriate information concerning my child that is relevant to participation in athletics and activities with coaches and other school personnel as deemed necessary.
>
> _____   _____
>
> Parent or Guardian   Date

equipment. The athletic trainer should make sure before an incident occurs that the EMTs understand the correct management of athletes wearing various types of athletic equipment.

Parent Notification

If the injured athlete is a minor, the athletic trainer should try to obtain consent from the parent to treat the athlete during an emergency.[32] *Focus Box:* "Consent form for medical treatment of a minor" provides an example of a consent form that may be signed by the parents or guardians of a minor. Consent may be given in writing either before or during an emergency. This consent is notification that the parent has been informed about what the athletic trainer thinks is wrong and what the athletic trainer intends to do, and parental permission is granted to give treatment for a specific incident. If the athlete's parents cannot be contacted, the predetermined wishes of the parent given at the beginning of a season or school year can be enacted. The athletic trainer should have these consent forms available when traveling in case the need for medical care arises. If no informed consent exists, implied consent on the part of the athlete to save the athlete's life takes precedence.

PRINCIPLES OF ON-THE-FIELD INJURY ASSESSMENT

The athletic trainer cannot deliver appropriate acute medical care to the injured athlete until some systematic assessment of the situation has been made on the playing field or court where the injury occurs.[52] This *on-the-field assessment* helps determine the nature of the injury and provides direction in the decision-making process concerning the emergency care that must be rendered (Figure 10-1).[7] The on-the-field assessment may be subdivided into a primary survey and a secondary survey.

The **primary survey,** which is done initially, determines the existence of potentially life-threatening situations, including problems with airway, breathing, circulation, severe bleeding, and shock. The primary survey takes precedence over all other aspects of victim assessment and should be used to correct life-threatening situations.[36] Any athlete who has a life-threatening situation should be transported to an emergency care facility as soon as possible.

Once the primary survey has ruled out the existence of a life-threatening injury or illness, the **secondary survey** takes a closer look at the athlete's injury. The secondary survey gathers specific information about the injury from the athlete, systematically assesses vital signs and symptoms, and allows for a more detailed evaluation of the injury. The secondary survey is done to uncover problems that do not pose an immediate threat to life but that may do so if they remain uncorrected.[36]

An injured athlete who is conscious and stable will not require a primary survey. However, the unconscious athlete must be monitored for life-threatening problems throughout the assessment process.

primary survey
assesses life-threatening injuries.

secondary survey
performed after life-threatening injuries have been ruled out.

Figure 10-1

Flowchart showing the appropriate emergency procedures for the injured athlete.

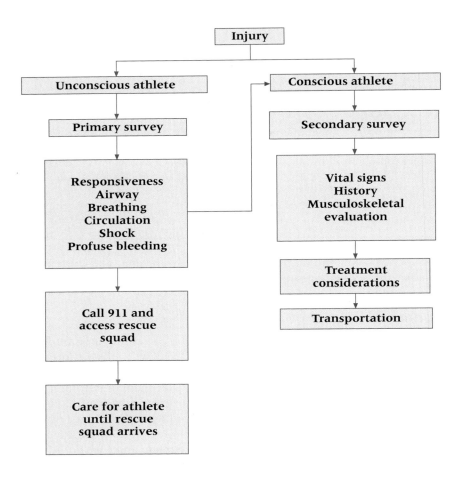

Life-threatening conditions
■ Airway obstruction
■ No breathing
■ No circulation
■ Profuse bleeding
■ Shock

10-1

Critical Thinking E x e r c i s e

A football defensive back is making a tackle and drops his head on contact with the ball-carrier. He hits the ground and does not move. When the athletic trainer gets to him, the athlete is lying prone, is unconscious, but is breathing.

? How should the athletic trainer manage this situation?

THE PRIMARY SURVEY
Treatment of Life-Threatening Injuries

Life-threatening injuries take precedence over all other injuries sustained by the athlete. Situations that are considered life-threatening include those that require cardiopulmonary resuscitation (i.e., obstruction of the airway, no breathing, no circulation), profuse bleeding, and shock.

Dealing with the Unconscious Athlete

The state of unconsciousness provides one of the greatest dilemmas for the athletic trainer. Whether to move the athlete and allow the game to resume or to await the arrival of a physician is a decision that too often is resolved hastily and without much forethought. Unconsciousness may be defined as a state of insensibility in which the athlete exhibits a lack of conscious awareness. This condition can be brought about by a blow to either the head or the solar plexus, it may result from general shock, or it may result from fainting (syncope) due to inadequate blood flow to the brain. It is often difficult to determine the exact cause of unconsciousness (Table 10-1).

The unconscious athlete always must be considered to have a life-threatening injury, which requires an immediate primary survey. The following guidelines should be used when working with the unconscious athlete:

1. The athletic trainer should immediately note the body position and determine the level of consciousness and unresponsiveness.
2. Airway, breathing, and circulation should be established immediately.
3. Injury to the neck and spine should always be considered a possibility in the unconscious athlete.[14]

TABLE 10-1 Evaluating the Unconscious Athlete

Functional Signs	Fainting	Concussion	Grand Mal Epilepsy	Brain Compression and Injury	Heatstroke	Diabetic Coma	Shock
Selected Conditions							
Onset	Usually sudden	Usually sudden	Sudden	Usually gradual	Gradual or sudden	Gradual	Gradual
Mentality	Complete unconsciousness	Confusion or unconsciousness	Unconsciousness	Unconsciousness, gradually deepening	Delirium or unconsciousness	Drowsiness, later unconsciousness	Listlessness, later unconsciousness
Pulse	Fast and feeble	Feeble and irregular	Fast	Gradually slower	Fast and feeble	Fast and feeble	Fast and feeble
Respiration	Quick and shallow	Shallow and irregular	Noisy, later deep and slow	Slow and noisy	Difficult	Deep and sighing	Rapid and shallow, with occasional deep sigh
Skin	Pale, cold, and clammy	Pale and cold	Livid, later pale	Hot and flushed	Hot and relatively dry	Livid, later pale	Pale, cold, and clammy
Pupils	Equal and dilated	Equal	Equal and dilated	Unequal	Equal	Equal	Equal and dilated
Paralysis	None	None	None	May be present in leg, arm, or both	None	None	None
Convulsions	None	None	None	Present in some cases	Present in some cases	None	None
Breath	N/A	N/A	N/A	N/A	N/A	Acetone smell	N/A
Special features	Giddiness and sway before collapse	Signs of head injury, vomiting during recovery	Bites tongue, voids urine and feces, may injure self while falling	Signs of head injury, delayed onset of symptoms	Vomiting in some cases	In early stages, headache, restlessness, and nausea	May vomit; early stages shivering, thirst, defective vision, and ear noises

4. If the athlete is wearing a helmet, it should never be removed until neck and spine injury have been unequivocally ruled out. However, the face mask must be cut away and removed to allow for cardiopulmonary resuscitation (CPR).

5. If the athlete is supine and not breathing, airway, breathing, and circulation (ABC) should be established immediately.

6. If the athlete is supine and breathing, nothing should be done until he or she regains consciousness.

7. If the athlete is prone and not breathing, he or she should be logrolled carefully to the supine position and ABC should be established immediately.

8. If the athlete is prone and breathing, nothing should be done until he or she regains consciousness, then the athlete should be carefully logrolled onto a spine board because CPR could be necessary at any time.

9. Life support for the unconscious athlete should be monitored and maintained until emergency medical personnel arrive.

10. Once the athlete is stabilized, the athletic trainer should begin a secondary survey.

Overview of Emergency Cardiopulmonary Resuscitation

A careful evaluation of the injured person must be made to determine whether CPR should be conducted. This overview of adult CPR is not intended to be used by persons who are not certified in CPR. Because of the serious nature of CPR, individuals should routinely be recertified through the American Red Cross, the American Heart Association, or the National Safety Council.

The athletic trainer should follow the emergency action steps: *check-call-care.*[2] *Check* the scene to find out what happened and to identify other individuals who might help and then check the victim for consciousness. *Call* 911 to access the rescue squad and then initiate *care* for the victim.

Equipment Considerations

Protective equipment worn by an athlete may complicate lifesaving CPR procedures. The presence of a football, ice hockey, or lacrosse helmet as well as a face mask and various types of shoulder pads will obviously make CPR more difficult if not impossible. Over the years, significant debate has raged in the sports medicine community about removing the helmet of an athlete with suspected cervical spine injury, and a number of differing opinions have been expressed.[16,20,26,27,29,34,35,37,38,39,41,42,45,47,48,51]

It has been proposed that removing the face mask should be the first step.[42] The face mask does not hinder the evaluation of the airway, but it may hinder treatment.[12] Thus the face mask should be removed immediately when a decision is made to transport the athlete to a medical care facility, regardless of the current respiratory status. It is also recommended that the face mask be removed completely by cutting all of the loop straps rather than simply cutting the bottom two loop-straps and retracting the helmet guard. Various instruments have been recommended to remove the face mask, including wire cutters, bolt cutters, trainer's scissors, and scalpels, none of which work very well. Thus using any of these tools as a primary means of removing a face mask is not recommended. Using an electric screwdriver has been shown to be faster and produce less torque on the helmet than tools that cut through the loop straps[25] as long as the screws are not rusted. Three devices—the Anvil Pruner, the Trainer's Angel, and the FM Extractor—have been recommended for their effectiveness in quickly cutting the plastic clips (Figure 10-2).[37,53] It also has been suggested that the athletic trainer should be proficient in removing the face mask within thirty seconds.[37] Studies comparing the efficacy of using these various devices suggest that the Anvil Pruner seems to be easier to use than the Trainer's Angel.[29] Other studies have shown that the Anvil Pruner and the FM Extractor were faster in removing the face mask than the Trainer's Angel.[54] Furthermore, using a Trainer's Angel seems to cause more motion in the cervical spine than either a manual or powered screwdriver.[47]

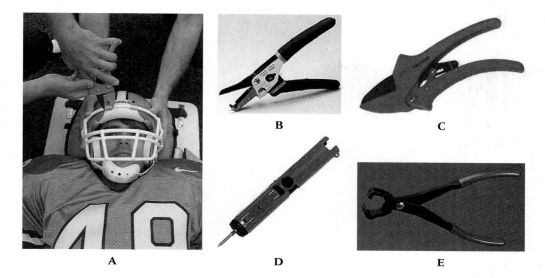

Figure 10-2

A, A number of different tools can be used to cut or remove the plastic grommets that hold the face mask. **B,** FM Extractor. **C,** Anvil Pruner. **D,** Electric cordless screwdriver. **E,** Trainers Angel.

In 1992 the Occupational Safety and Health Administration (OSHA) mandated the use of a barrier device or pocket mask to protect the athletic trainer from the transmission of bloodborne pathogens during CPR (Figure 10-7B, page 282). It is possible to slip the pocket mask under the face mask, attach the one-way mouthpiece or valve through the bars of the face mask, and begin CPR within five to ten seconds without removing the face mask.[45] Also, the use of a pocket mask appears to cause less extraneous motion in the cervical spine than does the use of either screwdrivers or the Trainer's Angel to remove the face mask.[47] It also has been shown that using a pocket mask is quicker for initiating rescue breathing than rotation of the face mask using screwdriver removal.[46]

As mentioned earlier, controversy has existed for some time as to whether the helmet and shoulder pads should be left in place or removed.[38] The current recommendation is to leave the helmet and shoulder pads in place.[34,35,56] The football helmet and chin strap should only be removed if: 1) the helmet and chin strap do not hold the head securely and immobilizing the helmet does not immobilize the head; 2) the design of the helmet and chin strap is such that, even after removal of the face mask, the airway cannot be controlled or ventilation provided; 3) the face mask cannot be removed after a reasonable period of time; or 4) the helmet prevents the athlete from being immobilized appropriately for transportation.[19] If the helmet must be removed, spinal immobilization must be maintained during removal. In most circumstances, it may be helpful to remove cheek padding and/or deflate air padding prior to removing the helmet.

The athletic trainer must either remove both the helmet and shoulder pads or leave them both in place. Removing one or the other independently will force the cervical spine into either flexion or extension. If they are left in place, the face mask should be dealt with as recommended previously, and the jersey and shoulder pad strings or straps should be cut, spreading the shoulder pads apart so that the chest may be compressed according to CPR guidelines. Although removal of the helmet and shoulder pads has been recommended by some individuals,[13] it seems that no matter how much care is taken, removal would create unnecessary movement of the cervical spine and would delay the initiation of CPR, neither of which is best for the injured athlete.[30] If cervical neck injury is suspected, yet the athlete is conscious and breathing and does not require CPR, the athlete should be transported with the helmet, chin strap, and shoulder pads in place. The face mask should be removed in case CPR becomes necessary.

Figure 10-3

Establish unresponsiveness by gently shaking the victim and asking, "Are you okay?"

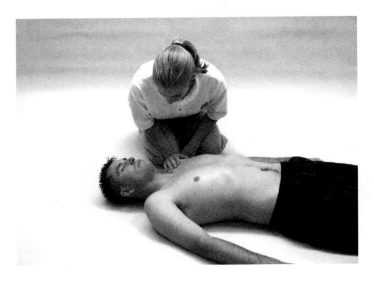

Figure 10-4

Victims who are breathing should be placed on their side in the recovery position.

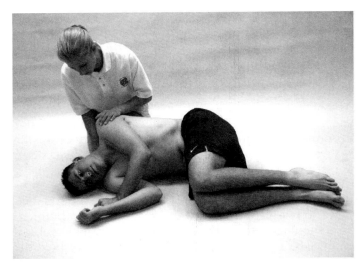

Establishing Unresponsiveness

The athletic trainer should first, establish unresponsiveness of the athlete by tapping or gently shaking his or her shoulder and shouting, "Are you okay?" (Figure 10-3). Note that shaking should be avoided if there is a possible neck injury. If the athlete is unresponsive, the emergency medical system (EMS) should be activated immediately by specifically directing someone to dial 911. An athlete who is lying prone or on his or her side and is breathing should be placed in the recovery position (Figure 10-4). This position can be maintained for as long as thirty minutes. If the athlete is not breathing, he or she should be carefully placed in the supine position. If the athlete is in a position other than supine, he or she must be carefully rolled over as a unit, avoiding any twisting of the body, because CPR can be administered only with the athlete lying flat on the back with knees straight or slightly flexed. In cases of suspected cervical spine injury, cervical movement must be minimized during logrolling. Then CPR should be performed.[36]

Opening the airway

Open the airway by using the head tilt–chin lift method (Figure 10-5A).[59] Lift under the chin with one hand while pushing down on the victim's forehead with the other,

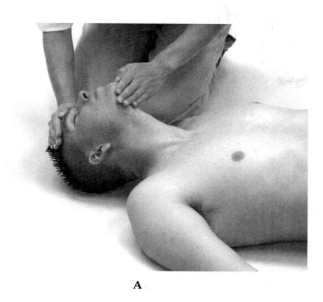

A

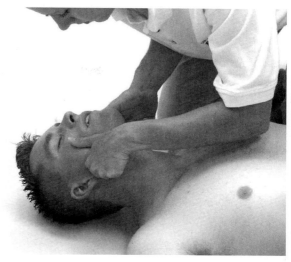

B

Figure 10-5

A, Head tilt–chin lift technique for establishing an airway.
B, Jaw thrust technique.

avoiding the use of excessive force. The tongue is the most common cause of airway obstruction; the forward lift of the jaw raises the tongue away from the back of the throat, thus clearing the airway.

NOTE: On victims with suspected head or neck injuries, perform a modified jaw thrust maneuver by grasping each side of the lower jaw at the angles, thus displacing the lower mandible forward as the head is tilted backward (Figure 10-5B).[59] In executing this maneuver, both elbows should rest on the same surface the victim is lying on. If the victim's lips close, open them by retracting the lower lip with a thumb. If the victim is not breathing, additional forward displacement of the jaw may help.

Establishing breathing

1. To determine if the victim is breathing, maintain the open airway; place your ear over the victim's mouth; observe the chest; and look, listen, and feel for breath sounds (Figure 10-6).
2. Using the hand on the athlete's forehead, pinch the nose shut, keeping the heel of the hand in place to hold the head back (if there is no neck injury). Take a deep breath, place your mouth over the athlete's mouth to provide an airtight seal, and give two slow, full breaths at a rate of $1\frac{1}{2}$ to 2 seconds per inflation. Observe the chest rise and fall. Remove your mouth, and listen for the air to escape through passive exhalation. If the airway is obstructed, reposition the victim's head and try again to ventilate. If the airway is still obstructed, give fifteen chest compressions followed by a finger sweep with the index finger to clear visible objects from the mouth.[17] Be careful not to push the object further into the throat. Continue to repeat this sequence until ventilation occurs.

If available, use a bag/valve mask for artificial respiration. Although the bag/valve mask is easy to use, some instruction and practice in its use is recommended (Figure 10-7A). NOTE: OSHA has mandated the use of barrier shields by athletic trainers to minimize the risk of transmitting bloodborne pathogens (Figure 10-7B). These shields have a plastic or silicone sheet that spreads over the face and separates the athletic trainer from the athlete. Some models have a tubelike mouthpiece, which may help in situations in which the athlete is wearing a face mask.

Establishing circulation

1. To determine whether a pulse exists, locate the Adam's apple with the index and middle fingers of the hand closest to the victim's head. Then slide your fingers down into the groove on the side of the body on which you are kneeling to locate

Figure 10-6

Once the airway is established look, listen, and feel for breathing.

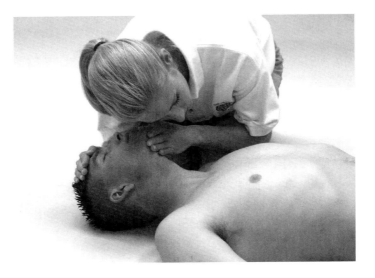

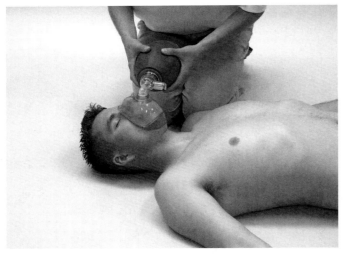

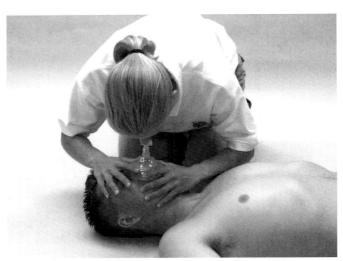

A

B

Figure 10-7

A, A bag/valve mask can be used for respiration. **B,** A barrier mask protects the athletic trainer from potential exposure to bloodborne pathogens.

the carotid artery. Palpate the carotid pulse with one hand for five to ten seconds while maintaining head tilt with the other hand (Figure 10-8).

2. Maintain an open airway. Position yourself close to the side of the athlete's chest. With the middle and index fingers of the hand closest to the victim's waist, locate the lower margin of his or her rib cage on the side next to you (Figure 10-9).

3. Run the fingers up along the rib cage to the xiphoid notch, where the ribs meet the sternum.

4. Place the middle finger on the notch and the index finger next to it on the lower end of the sternum.

5. Next, position the hand closest to the athlete's head on the lower half of the sternum next to the index finger of the first hand that located the notch; then place the heel of that hand on the long axis of the sternum.

6. Then remove the first hand from the notch and place it on top of the hand on the sternum so that the heels of both hands are parallel and the fingers are directed straight away from you (Figure 10-10).

7. Fingers can be extended or interlaced, but they must be kept off the chest wall.

8. Keep elbows in a locked position with arms straight and shoulders positioned over the hands, enabling the thrust to be straight down.

9. In a normal-sized adult, apply enough force to depress the sternum $1\frac{1}{2}$ to 2 inches (3.8 to 5 cm). After depression, completely release the sternum to allow the heart to refill. The time of release should equal the time of compression. For one rescuer, compression must be given at the rate of 80 to 100 times per minute, maintaining a rate of fifteen chest compressions to two full breaths.

10. After four cycles of fifteen compressions and two breaths (15:2), or about one minute, recheck the pulse at the carotid artery for five seconds while maintaining the head tilt. If no pulse is found, continue the 15:2 cycle, beginning with chest compressions.

Every coach and athletic trainer should be certified in CPR and should take a refresher examination at least once a year. All assistants should be certified as well.[44]

Obstructed Airway Management

Choking is a possibility in many sports activities; for example, an athlete may choke on a mouth guard, a broken piece of dental work, chewing gum, or even a chaw of tobacco. When such emergencies arise, early recognition and prompt, knowledgeable action are necessary to avert a tragedy. An unconscious athlete can have an obstructed airway when the tongue falls back in the throat, blocking the upper airway. Blood clots resulting from head, facial, or dental injuries may impede normal breathing, as may vomiting. When complete airway obstruction occurs, the individual is unable to speak, cough, or breathe. If the athlete is conscious, there is a tremendous effort made to breathe, the head is forced back, and the face initially is flushed and then becomes cyanotic as oxygen deprivation occurs. If partial airway obstruction is causing the choking, some air passage can be detected, but during a complete obstruction no air movement is discernible.

For the victim who is conscious and has an airway obstruction, the standing abdominal thrust technique should be performed until he or she is relieved. In cases of unconsciousness, fifteen chest compressions are applied, followed by a finger sweep with an attempt at ventilation.[2]

First, if the victim cannot cough, speak, or breathe, have someone call 911. Stand behind and to one side of the athlete. Place both arms around the waist just above the belt line, and permit the athlete's head, arms, and upper trunk to hang forward (Figure 10-11). Grasp one of your fists with the other, placing the thumb side of the grasped fists immediately below the xiphoid process of the sternum and clear of the rib cage. Then sharply and forcefully thrust the fists into the abdomen, inward, and upward, several times. This "hug" pushes up on the diaphragm, compressing the air in the lungs, creating forceful pressure against the blockage, and thus usually causing

All coaches and athletic trainers must have current CPR certification.

Figure 10-8

To check the carotid pulse locate the Adam's apple and then slide the index and middle fingers into the groove on the side of the body where you are kneeling.

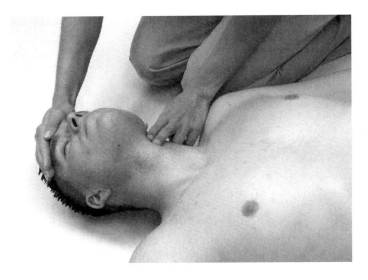

Figure 10-9

With the middle and index fingers of the hand closest to the waist, locate the lower margin of the victim's rib cage. Then run the fingers along the rib cage to the notch where the ribs meet the sternum. Place the middle finger on the notch with the index finger next to it on the lower end of the sternum.

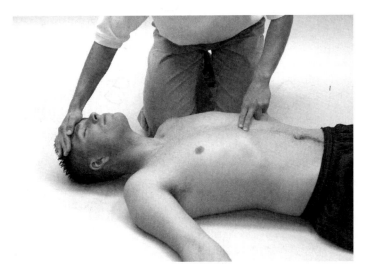

Figure 10-10

Place the heel of the hand closest to the athelete's head on the long axis of the lower half of the sternum next to the index fingers of the first hand. Remove the first hand from the notch and place it on top of the hand on the sternum with fingers extended or interlaced.

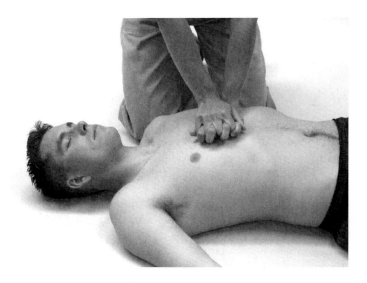

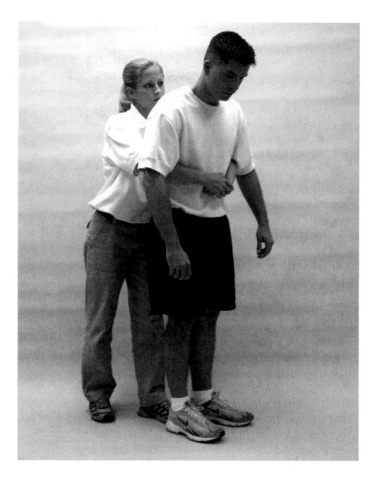

Figure 10-11

Perform standing abdominal thrusts for a conscious victim with an obstructed airway.

the obstruction to be promptly expelled. Repeat the maneuver until the athlete is relieved or becomes unconscious. If the athlete loses consciousness, by using the head tilt/chin lift or jaw thrust techniques open the airway and try to ventilate. If the airway is still obstructed, reposition the head and try again. Then give fifteen chest compressions (see Figure 10-10). Perform a finger sweep only if the object is visible. Repeat this sequence as long as necessary (Figure 10-12). Victims who begin breathing on their own should be placed on their side in the recovery position (see Figure 10-4, page 280).[2] Take care to avoid applying extreme force over the rib cage because fractures of the ribs and damage to the organs can result.

Finger sweeping   If a foreign object such as a mouth guard is lodged in the mouth or the throat and is visible, it may be possible to remove or release it with the fingers. Take care that the probing does not drive the object deeper into the throat. It is usually impossible to open the mouth of a conscious victim who is in distress, so the Heimlich maneuver should be used immediately. In the unconscious athlete, turn the head either to the side or face up, open the mouth by grasping the tongue and the lower jaw, hold them firmly between the thumb and fingers, and lift—an action that pulls the tongue away from the back of the throat and from the impediment. If this action is difficult to do, the crossed finger method is usually effective. Insert the index finger of the free hand (or if both hands are used, an assistant can probe) into one side of the mouth along the cheek and deeply into the throat; using a hooking maneuver, attempt to free the impediment by moving it into a position from which it can be removed (Figure 10-12). Attempt to ventilate after each sweep until the airway is open. Once the object is removed, if the athlete is not already breathing, attempt to ventilate.

Figure 10-12

A finger sweep of the mouth is essential in attempting to remove a foreign object from a choking victim. The finger sweep should be performed only if the object is visible.

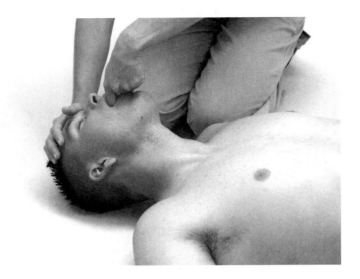

Using an Automatic External Defibrillator

An automatic external defibrillator (AED) is a device that evaluates the heart rhythm of a victim of sudden cardiac arrest.[56] It is capable of delivering an electrical charge to the heart, and does not require the expertise of a medical professional.[50] To prevent human error, all machines now have computers that evaluate heart rhythm and decide if deployment is appropriate. AEDs have become an essential tool in the treatment of out-of-hospital cardiac arrest.[11] The American Heart Association estimates that 100,000 deaths could be prevented each year with rapid defibrillation. Over the years, the devices have become safer, more reliable and more maintenance free. The new technologies used in these devices make them suitable for use by anyone who has had basic training.[50]

AEDs are extremely easy to use; anyone trained to use cardiopulmonary resuscitation (CPR) can be trained to use an AED. Most AEDs are designed to be used by people without medical backgrounds, such as police, firefighters, flight attendants, security guards, and lay rescuers, as long as the procedure is coordinated with existing EMS systems and the person administering the procedure has received proper training. Public places where AEDs might be located include police cars, theaters, sports arenas, public buildings, business offices, and airports. An increasing number of commercial airplanes are now equipped with AEDs and enhanced medical kits. Formal training programs, such as those offered by the American Heart Association's Heartsaver AED course, can be taught in as little as 4 hours. However, operating an AED is so simple that it can be done successfully even without formal training. Training is recommended for as many people as possible. Local and state regulations determine the training requirements for public access defibrillator (PAD) programs.

The legal requirements that allow the lay public to use AEDs are determined on a state-by-state basis. In some states there is true public access defibrillation, meaning that anyone with knowledge of an AED can use one any time it is available. For example, a traveler in an airport may retrieve and use an AED mounted in a public location. In other states, use of AEDs is more restricted. Some states require a formal training program, the direct involvement of an authorizing doctor, or that the AED rescuer be part of a formal in-house response team. In most states, any individual using an AED in a good faith attempt to save the life of a cardiac arrest victim will be covered by some form of a "good Samaritan" statute.

The broad deployment of a new generation of portable defibrillators for use by trained lay rescuers can help save countless lives.

Focus

Official statement—automated external defibrillators

The National Athletic Trainers' Association (NATA), as a leader in health care for the physically active, strongly believes that the treatment of sudden cardiac arrest is a priority. An AED program should be part of an athletic trainer's emergency action plan. NATA strongly encourages athletic trainers, in every work setting, to have access to an AED. Athletic trainers are encouraged to make an AED part of their standard emergency equipment. In addition, in conjunction and coordination with local EMS, athletic trainers should take a primary role in implementing a comprehensive AED program within their work setting.

Athletic trainers can be certified to use an AED in most states and can learn to use an AED in about an hour.[56] AED users also need yearly training not only on the use of the device but also on CPR. Maintenance is minimal on AEDs. The devices are equipped with long-life batteries and have features that notify the users when the battery needs replacement. To date most professional teams and many college teams have AEDs readily available.

To use an AED the athletic trainer simply applies the two electrodes to the left apex and the right base of the chest. (Figure 10-13). To operate most devices, push the "on" button and listen for a voice on the machine to direct you whether or not to push the defibrillator button. If the pulse resumes, place the victim into the recovery position (see Figure 10-4, page 280) until the rescue squad arrives. NATA's official statement on using AEDs appears in the *Focus Box:* "Official statement—automated external defibrillators."

Administering Supplemental Oxygen

Serious and life-threatening medical emergencies often cause oxygen to be depleted in the body, leaving the victim at risk for cardiac arrest or brain damage. Supplemental oxygen may prove to be a critical step in treating a severe or life-threatening illness or injury. An athletic trainer who has been specifically trained in supplemental oxygen administration should routinely give oxygen to a victim who is having trouble breathing. Administering supplemental oxygen requires using a bag-valve-mask and a pressurized cylinder or canister containing oxygen (Figure 10-14).

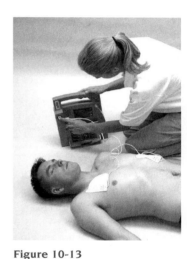

Figure 10-13

An automatic external defibrillator (AED) can be used if the victim has no heartbeat.

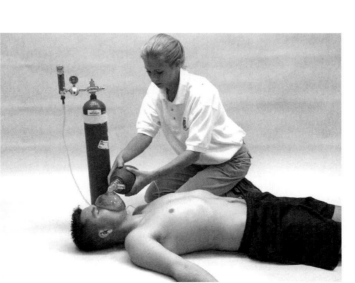

Figure 10-14

Administering supplemental oxygen to facilitate breathing.

The air that a person normally breathes contains about 21 percent oxygen. During rescue breathing the victim receives only about 16 percent oxygen, but a bag-valve-mask provides about 21 percent oxygen. Giving supplemental oxygen can provide the victim with a significantly higher oxygen concentration.

All oxygen cylinders are easily identified because they are green with a yellow diamond that clearly says oxygen. During administration, a face mask with an attached oxygen reservoir bag and a one-way valve between the mask and the bag are attached to the oxygen cylinder. As the athlete breathes, the concentrated oxygen is inhaled from the bag, and exhaled air freely escapes from the side of the mask. As much as 90 percent oxygen can be delivered to the victim. The oxygen should be delivered at a rate of ten to fifteen liters per minute as indicated by a flow rate meter.

In some states it is illegal to administer oxygen without a physician's prescription.

Control of Hemorrhage

An abnormal discharge of blood is called a hemorrhage. The hemorrhage may be venous, capillary, or arterial and may be external or internal. Venous blood is characteristically dark red with a continuous flow; capillary bleeding exudes from tissue and is a reddish color; and arterial bleeding flows in spurts and is bright red. NOTE: The athletic trainer must be concerned with exposure to bloodborne pathogens and other diseases when coming into contact with blood or other body fluids. It is essential to take universal precautions to minimize this risk. The athletic trainer should use disposable latex gloves whenever he or she comes into contact with blood or other body fluids. This topic is discussed in detail in Chapter 11.

External Bleeding

External bleeding stems from open skin wounds such as abrasions, incisions, lacerations, punctures, or avulsions. The control of external bleeding includes the use of direct pressure, elevation, and pressure points.[58]

Direct pressure Pressure is directly applied with the hand over a sterile gauze pad. The pressure is applied firmly against the resistance of a bone (Figure 10-15).

Elevation Elevation, in combination with direct pressure, provides an additional means for reducing external hemorrhaging. Elevating a hemorrhaging part against gravity reduces hydrostatic blood pressure and facilitates venous and lymphatic drainage, which slows bleeding.

Pressure points When direct pressure combined with elevation fails to slow hemorrhage, the use of pressure points may be the method of choice. Eleven points on each side of the body have been identified for controlling external bleeding; the two

10-2

Critical Thinking Exercise

A football player is injured while making a tackle. The athletic trainer quickly realizes that the athlete is not breathing and immediately begins CPR. After only a few seconds the athlete begins breathing spontaneously and regains consciousness.

? What might the athletic trainer choose to do while waiting for the rescue squad to arrive to facilitate the player's recovery from this life-threatening incident?

10-3

Critical Thinking Exercise

A soccer player jumps to win a head ball and an opponent's head smashes his right eyebrow, creating a significant laceration. The athlete is conscious but is bleeding profusely from the wound.

? What techniques may be most effectively used to control the bleeding, and what should be done to close the wound?

External bleeding can usually be managed through direct pressure, elevation, or pressure points.

Figure 10-15

Direct pressure for the control of bleeding is applied with the hand over a sterile gauze pad.

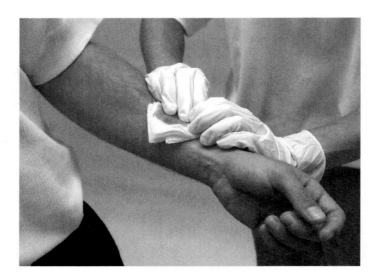

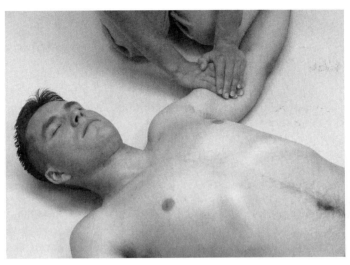

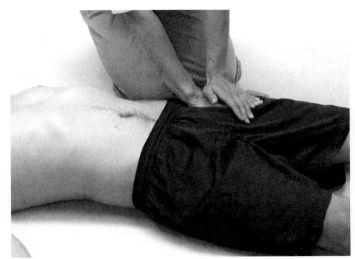

A

B

Figure 10-16

The two most common sites for direct pressure. **A,** The brachial artery. **B,** The femoral artery.

most commonly used are the brachial artery in the upper limb and the femoral artery in the lower limb. The brachial artery is compressed against the medial aspect of the humerus, and the femoral artery is compressed as it is detected within the femoral triangle (Figure 10-16).

Internal Hemorrhage

Internal hemorrhage is invisible to the eye unless manifested through some body opening or identified through X-ray studies or other diagnostic techniques. Its danger lies in the difficulty of diagnosis. When internal hemorrhaging occurs, either subcutaneously such as in a bruise or contusion, intramuscularly, or in joints, the athlete may be moved without danger in most instances. However, the detection of bleeding within a body cavity such as the skull, thorax, or abdomen is a life-and-death situation. Because the symptoms are obscure, internal hemorrhage is difficult to diagnose properly. As a result, athletes with internal injuries require hospitalization under complete and constant observation by a medical staff to determine the nature and extent of the injuries. All severe hemorrhaging will eventually result in shock and should therefore be treated on this premise. Even if the athlete shows no outward indication of shock, he or she should be kept quiet and body heat should be maintained at a constant and suitable temperature. (See the following section on shock for the preferred body position.)

Shock

With any injury, shock is a possibility.[58] But when severe bleeding, fractures, or internal injuries are present, the development of shock is more likely. Shock occurs when a diminished amount of blood is available to the circulatory system; that is, when the vascular system loses its capacity to hold the fluid portion of the blood because of dilation of the blood vessels and disruption of the osmotic fluid balance. When shock occurs, a quantity of plasma moves from the blood vessels into the tissue spaces of the body, leaving the blood cells within the vessels, causing stagnation and slowing the blood flow. As a result, not enough oxygen-carrying blood cells are available to the tissues, particularly those of the nervous system. With this general collapse of the vascular system comes widespread tissue death, which will eventually cause the death of the individual unless treatment is given.

Certain conditions, such as extreme fatigue, extreme exposure to heat or cold, extreme dehydration of fluids and mineral loss, or illness predispose an athlete to shock. In a situation in which there is a potential shock condition, there are other signs by which the athletic trainer should assess the possibility of the athlete's lapsing into a

A wrestler is thrown to the mat and suffers an open fracture of both the radius and ulna in the forearm. There is significant bleeding from the wound. The athlete begins to complain of light-headedness, his skin is pale and feels cool and clammy, and his pulse becomes rapid and weak.

? What potential problem may be developing, and how should the athletic trainer manage this situation?

Signs of shock:
- Blood pressure is low
- Systolic pressure is usually below 90 mm Hg
- Pulse is rapid and weak
- Athlete may be drowsy and appear sluggish
- Respiration is shallow and extremely rapid
- Skin is pale, cool, and clammy

state of shock as an aftermath of the injury. The most important clue to potential shock is the recognition of a severe injury. It may happen that none of the usual signs of shock is present.[58]

The main types of shock are hypovolemic, respiratory, neurogenic, psychogenic, cardiogenic, septic, anaphylactic, and metabolic.[3]

Hypovolemic shock stems from trauma in which there is blood loss. Decreased blood volume causes a decrease in blood pressure. Without enough blood in the circulatory system, organs are not properly supplied with oxygen.

Respiratory shock occurs when the lungs are unable to supply enough oxygen to the circulating blood. Trauma that produces a pneumothorax or an injury to the breathing control mechanism can produce respiratory shock.

Neurogenic shock is caused by the general dilation of blood vessels within the cardiovascular system. When it occurs, the typical six liters of blood can no longer fill the system. As a result, the cardiovascular system can no longer supply oxygen to the body.

Psychogenic shock refers to what is commonly known as fainting (syncope). It is caused by a temporary dilation of blood vessels that reduces the normal amount of blood in the brain.

Cardiogenic shock refers to the inability of the heart to pump enough blood to the body.

Septic shock occurs from a severe, usually bacterial, infection. Toxins liberated from the bacteria cause small blood vessels in the body to dilate.

Anaphylactic shock is the result of a severe allergic reaction caused by foods, insect stings, or drugs or by inhaling dusts, pollens, or other substances.

Metabolic shock happens when a severe illness such as diabetes goes untreated. Another cause is an extreme loss of body fluid (e.g., through urination, vomiting, or diarrhea).

Symptoms and Signs

The major signs of shock are moist, pale, cool, clammy skin; weak and rapid pulse; increased and shallow respiratory rate; decreased blood pressure; and in severe situations, urinary retention and fecal incontinence.[24,36] If conscious, the athlete may display a disinterest in his or her surroundings or may display irritability, restlessness, or excitement. He or she may also exhibit extreme thirst.

Management

Depending on the cause of the shock, the following emergency care should be given:
1. Maintain body temperature as close to normal as possible.
2. Elevate the feet and legs eight to twelve inches for most situations. However, shock positioning varies according to the type of injury.[24] For a neck injury, for example, the athlete should be immobilized as found; for a head injury, his or her head and shoulders should be elevated; and for a leg fracture, his or her legs should be kept level and should be raised after splinting.

Shock can also be compounded or even initially produced by the psychological reaction of the athlete to an injury situation. Fear or the sudden realization that a serious situation has occurred can result in shock. In the case of a psychological reaction to an injury, the athlete should be instructed to lie down and avoid viewing the injury. The athlete should be handled with patience and gentleness but also with firmness. Spectators should be kept away from the injured athlete. Reassurance is of vital concern to the injured individual. The person should be given immediate comfort through the loosening of clothing. Nothing should be given by mouth until a physician has determined that no surgical procedures are indicated.

THE SECONDARY SURVEY

After the primary survey has determined that no life-threatening injuries or illnesses exist, and the athlete appears to be in stable condition, the athletic trainer should conduct an on-the-field secondary survey to assess the existing injury more precisely.

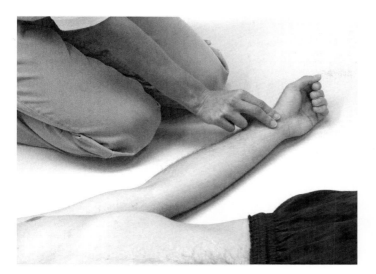

Figure 10-17
Pulse rate taken at the radial artery.

Recognizing Vital Signs

The ability to recognize physiological signs of injury is essential to the proper handling of potentially critical injuries. When evaluating the seriously ill or injured athlete, the coach, athletic trainer, or physician must be aware of nine response areas: heart rate, breathing rate, blood pressure, temperature, skin color, pupils of the eye, movement, the presence of pain, and unconsciousness. The three primary vital signs are pulse, respiration, and blood pressure.

Pulse

The pulse is the direct extension of the functioning heart. In emergency situations, the pulse is usually determined at the carotid artery in the neck or the radial artery in the wrist (Figure 10-17). A normal pulse rate per minute for adults ranges between 60 and 100 beats, and in children, between 80 and 100 beats; however, trained athletes usually have slower pulses than the typical population.

An alteration of a pulse from normal may indicate the presence of a pathological condition. For example, a rapid but weak pulse could mean shock, bleeding, diabetic coma, or heat exhaustion. A rapid and strong pulse may mean heatstroke or severe fright; a strong but slow pulse could indicate a skull fracture or stroke; and no pulse means cardiac arrest or death.[12]

Respiration

The normal breathing rate per minute is approximately 12 to 20 breaths in adults and 15 to 30 breaths in children. Breathing rate may be normal but breath may be shallow (indicating shock), labored, or noisy. Frothy blood being coughed up indicates a chest injury, such as a fractured rib, that has affected a lung. The athletic trainer should look, listen, and feel: look to ascertain whether the chest is rising or falling; listen for air passing in and out of the mouth, nose, or both; and feel where the chest is moving.

Blood Pressure

Blood pressure, as measured by the sphygmomanometer, indicates the amount of pressure exerted against the arterial walls. It is indicated at two pressure levels: systolic and diastolic. **Systolic blood pressure** occurs when the left ventricle contracts, thereby pumping blood, and **diastolic blood pressure** is the residual pressure present in the arteries when the heart is between beats. The blood pressure for fifteen- to twenty-year-old males should be less than 120 **mm Hg** (systolic) and less than 80 mm Hg (diastolic). The normal blood pressure for females is usually

Vital signs to observe:
- Pulse
- Respiration
- Blood pressure
- Temperature
- Skin color
- Pupils
- Level of consciousness
- Movement
- Abnormal nerve response

Respiratory Patterns
Apnea—temporary cessation of breathing
Tachypnea—rapid breathing
Bradypnea—slow breathing
Dyspnea—difficult breathing
Hyperventilation—labored breathing
Obstructed—blocked airway caused by either partial or complete obstruction

systolic blood pressure
The pressure caused by the heart pumping.

diastolic blood pressure
The residual pressure when the heart is between beats.

mm Hg
millimeters of mercury

Figure 10-18

Blood pressure is measured using a sphygmomanometer and a stethoscope.

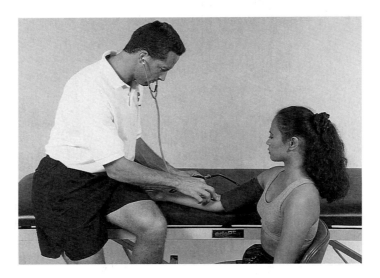

8 to 10 mm Hg lower than in males for both systolic and diastolic pressures. Between the ages of fifteen and twenty, a systolic pressure of greater than 120 mm Hg and a diastolic pressure of greater than 80 mm Hg may be excessive. A lowered blood pressure (hypotension) could indicate hemorrhage, shock, heart attack, or internal organ injury.

Blood pressure is measured by applying the cuff circumferentially around the upper arm just proximal to the elbow (Figure 10-18). The cuff should be inflated to 200 mm Hg, which occludes blood flow in the brachial artery distal to the cuff in the cubital fossa. The cuff should be slowly deflated with the stethoscope in place; the first beating sound is recorded as systolic pressure. The cuff continues to be deflated until the beating sound disappears; diastolic pressure is then recorded.

Temperature

Body temperature is maintained by water evaporation and heat radiation. It is normally 98.6° F (37° C). Temperature is measured with a thermometer, which is placed under the tongue, in the armpit, against the tympanic membrane in the ear, or, in case of unconsciousness, in the rectum. Core temperature is most accurately measured in the rectum. The tympanic membrane temperature measurement in the ear (Figure 10-19), while easily taken, is not a very accurate indication of core temperature. It is difficult to achieve the same temperature in consecutive trials due to difficulty

Figure 10-19

A, Thermometer for **B,** measuring tympanic membrane temperature.

A

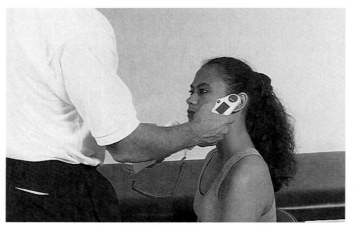

B

replicating the depth and angle of insertion. Changes in body temperature can be reflected in the skin. For example, hot, dry skin might indicate disease, infection, or overexposure to environmental heat. Cool, clammy skin could reflect trauma, shock, or heat exhaustion; cool, dry skin is possibly the result of overexposure to cold.

A rise or fall of internal temperature may be caused by a variety of circumstances such as the onset of a communicable disease, cold exposure, pain, fear, or nervousness. Characteristically, a lowered body temperature is accompanied by chills with chattering teeth, blue lips, goose bumps, and pale skin.

Skin Color

For individuals who are lightly pigmented, the skin can be a good indicator of the state of health. Normal skin tone is pink. A flushed or red skin color may indicate heatstroke, sunburn, allergic reaction, high blood pressure, or elevated temperature. A pale, ashen, or white skin can mean insufficient circulation, shock, fright, hemorrhage, heat exhaustion, or insulin shock. Skin that is bluish in color (cyanotic), primarily in the lips and fingernails, usually means an airway obstruction or respiratory insufficiency. A yellowish or jaundice color may indicate liver disease or dysfunction.

Assessing skin color in a dark-skinned athlete is more difficult. These individuals normally have pink coloration of the nail beds and inside the lips, mouth, and tongue. When a dark-skinned person goes into shock, the skin around the mouth and nose will often have a grayish cast, and the tongue, the inside of the mouth, the lips, and the nail beds will have a bluish cast. Shock resulting from hemorrhage will cause the tongue and inside of the mouth to become a pale, grayish color instead of blue. Fever in these athletes can be noted by a red flush at the tips of the ears.[24]

Pupils

The pupils of the eyes are extremely sensitive to situations affecting the nervous system. Although most persons have pupils of regular outline and equal size, some individuals normally have pupils that may be irregular and unequal. This disparity requires the athletic trainer to know which athletes deviate from the norm.

A constricted pupil may indicate that the athlete is using a central nervous system depressant drug. If one or both pupils are dilated, the athlete may have sustained a head injury; may be experiencing shock, heatstroke, or hemorrhage; or may have ingested a stimulant drug (Figure 10-20). The pupils' response to light also should be noted. If one or both pupils fail to accommodate to light, there may be brain injury or alcohol or drug poisoning. When examining an athlete's pupils, the examiner should note the presence of contact lenses. Pupil response is more critical in evaluation than pupil size.

Level of Consciousness

When recognizing vital signs, the examiner must always note the athlete's level of consciousness. Normally the athlete is alert, is aware of the environment, and responds quickly to vocal stimulation. Head injury, heatstroke, and diabetic coma can alter the athlete's level of conscious awareness.

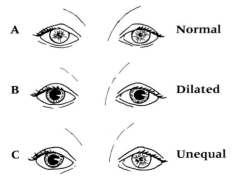

A   Normal

B   Dilated

C   Unequal

To convert Fahrenheit to centigrade (Celsius):
$$^\circ C = (^\circ F - 32) \div 1.8$$
To convert centigrade to Fahrenheit: $^\circ F = (1.8 \times {}^\circ C) + 32$

Some athletes normally have irregular and unequal pupils.

Figure 10-20

The pupils of the eyes are extremely sensitive to situations affecting the nervous system. **A,** Normal pupils. **B,** Dilated pupils. **C,** Unequal pupils.

The level of consciousness can be assessed by using several different scales: the AVPU scale, the ACDU scale, or the Glasgow Coma Scale. The AVPU scale is widely used by EMTs for assessing the neurologic status of trauma patients as originally taught in Advanced Trauma Life Support (ATLS). Both the AVPU and the ACDU scales are simpler to use than the Glasgow Coma Scale.

The AVPU scale is as follows:

- A for alert signifies that the patient is alert; awake; responsive to voice; and oriented to person, time, and place.
- V for verbal signifies that the patient responds to voice but is not fully oriented to person, time, or place.
- P for pain signifies that the patient does not respond to voice but does respond to painful stimulus such as a squeeze to the hand.
- U for unresponsive signifies that the patient does not respond to painful stimulus.

The ACDU scale is as follows:

- Alert
- Confused
- Drowsy
- Unresponsive

Movement

The inability to move a body part can indicate a serious central nervous system injury that has involved the motor system. An inability to move one side of the body (hemiplegia) could be caused by a head injury or cerebrovascular accident (stroke). Bilateral tingling and numbness or sensory or motor deficits of the upper extremity may indicate a cervical spine injury. Weakness or inability to move the lower extremities could mean an injury below the neck, and pressure on the spinal cord could lead to limited use of the limbs.[24,36]

Abnormal Nerve Response

The injured athlete's pain or other reactions to adverse stimuli can provide valuable clues to the coach or athletic trainer. Numbness or tingling in a limb with or without movement can indicate nerve or cold damage. Blocking of a main artery can produce severe pain, loss of sensation, or lack of a pulse in a limb. A complete lack of pain or of awareness of serious but obvious injury may be caused by shock, hysteria, drug usage, or a spinal cord injury. Generalized or localized pain in the injured region probably means there is no injury to the spinal cord.

Musculoskeletal Assessment

A logical process must be used to evaluate accurately the extent of a musculoskeletal injury.[52] The athletic trainer must be aware of the major signs that reveal the site, nature, and above all, severity of the injury. Detection of these signs can be facilitated by understanding the mechanism or traumatic sequence and by methodically inspecting the injury. Knowledge of the mechanism of an injury is extremely important in determining which area of the body is most affected. When the injury mechanism has been determined, the examiner proceeds to the next phase: physical inspection of the affected region. At this point, information is gathered by what is seen, heard, and felt.[31]

In an attempt to understand the mechanism of injury, a brief *history* of the complaint must be taken. The athlete is asked, if possible, about the events leading up to the injury and how it occurred and what he or she heard or felt when the injury took place. Sounds occurring at the time of injury or during manual inspection yield pertinent information about the type and extent of pathology present. Such uncommon sounds as grating or harsh rubbing may indicate fracture. Joint sounds may be detected when either arthritis or internal derangement is present. Areas of the body that have abnormal amounts of fluid may produce crepitus when palpated or moved. Such sounds as a snap, crack, or pop at the moment of injury often indicate bone fracture or injury to ligaments or tendons.

The athletic trainer should make a visual *observation* of the injured site, comparing it to the uninjured body part. The initial visual examination can disclose obvious deformity, swelling, and skin discoloration.

Finally, the region of the injury should be gently *palpated*. Feeling, or palpating, a part with trained fingers can, in conjunction with visual and audible signs, indicate the nature of the injury. Palpation is started away from the injury and gradually moves toward it. As the examiner gently feels the injury and surrounding structures with the fingertips, several factors can be revealed: the extent of point tenderness, the extent of irritation (whether it is confined to soft tissue alone or extends to the bony tissue), and deformities that may not be detected by visual examination alone.

Assessment Decisions

After a quick on-site injury inspection and evaluation, the athletic trainer should make the following decisions:

1. The seriousness of the injury.
2. The type of first aid and immobilization necessary.
3. Whether the injury warrants immediate referral to a physician for further assessment.
4. The manner of transportation from the injury site to the sidelines, training room, or hospital.

All information about the initial history, signs, and symptoms of the injury must be documented, if possible, so that they may be described in detail to the physician.

Immediate Treatment

Musculoskeletal injuries are extremely common in sports. The athletic trainer must be prepared to provide appropriate first aid immediately to control hemorrhage and associated swelling. Every first aid effort should be directed toward one primary goal—reducing the amount of swelling and inflammation resulting from the injury.[33] If swelling and inflammation can be controlled initially, the amount of time required for injury rehabilitation will be significantly reduced. Initial management of musculoskeletal injuries should include rest, ice, compression, and elevation (RICE) (see Figure 10-21).

Rest   Rest after any type of injury is an extremely important component of any treatment program. Once a body part is injured, it immediately begins the healing process.[40] If the injured part is not rested and is subjected to external stresses and strains, the healing process never takes place. Consequently, the injured part does not heal, and the time required for rehabilitation is greatly increased. The number of days necessary for resting varies with the severity of the injury. Parts of the body that have experienced minor injury should rest for approximately seventy-two hours before a rehabilitation program is begun.

Decisions that can be made from the secondary survey:
- Seriousness of injury
- Type of first aid required
- Whether injury warrants physical referral
- Type of transportation needed

Figure 10-21

RICE technique: **A,** A wet compression wrap should be applied over the horseshoe pad. **B,** Ice bags should be secured in place by a dry compression wrap. **C,** The leg should be elevated during the initial treatment period.

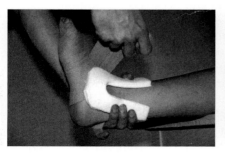

A

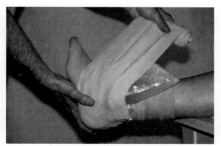

B

C

Rest, ice, compression, and elevation (RICE) are essential in the emergency care of musculoskeletal injuries.

Ice (cold application) The initial treatment of acute injuries should use cold.[20] Therefore ice is used for most conditions involving strains, sprains, and contusions. Cold is most commonly used immediately after injury to decrease pain and promote local superficial constriction of the vessels (vasoconstriction), thus controlling hemorrhage and edema.[40] Cold applied to an acute injury will lower metabolism and tissue demands for oxygen and will reduce hypoxia.[28] This benefit extends to uninjured tissue, preventing injury-related tissue death from spreading to adjacent normal cellular structures. Cold is also used in the acute phase of inflammatory conditions such as bursitis, tenosynovitis, and tendinitis conditions in which heat may cause additional pain and swelling. Cold is also used to reduce the muscle guarding that accompanies pain. Its pain-reducing (analgesic) effect is probably one of its greatest benefits. One explanation of the analgesic effect is that cold slows the speed of nerve transmission, so the pain sensation is reduced. It is also possible that cold bombards pain receptors with so many cold impulses that pain impulses are lost. With ice treatments, the athlete usually reports an uncomfortable sensation of cold, followed by burning, then an aching sensation, and finally complete numbness.

Because the subcutaneous (under the skin) fat slowly conducts the cold temperature, applications of cold for short periods of time will be ineffective in cooling deeper tissues. For this reason, longer treatments of at least twenty minutes are recommended. However, prolonged application of cold can cause tissue damage.[28]

Cold treatments seem to be more effective in reaching deep tissues than most forms of heat are. Cold applied to the skin is capable of significantly lowering the temperature of tissues at a considerable depth. The temperature to which the deeper tissues can be lowered depends on the type of cold that is applied to the skin, the duration of its application, the thickness of the subcutaneous fat, and the region of the body to which it is applied.[28] Ice packs should be applied to the area for at least seventy-two hours after an acute injury. With many injuries, regular ice treatments may be continued for several weeks.

For best results, ice packs (crushed ice and towel) should be applied over a compression wrap. Frozen gel packs should not be used directly against the skin because they reach much lower temperatures than do ice packs. A good rule of thumb is to apply a cold pack to a recent injury for a twenty-minute period and repeat every 1 to 1½ hours throughout the waking day. Depending on the severity and site of the injury, cold may be applied intermittently for one to seventy-two hours. For example, a mild strain will probably require one day of twenty-minute periods of cold application, whereas a severe knee or ankle sprain might need three to seven days of intermittent cold. If the severity of an injury is in doubt, the best approach is to extend the time that ice is applied.

Compression In most cases immediate compression of an acute injury is considered an important adjunct to cold and elevation and in some cases may be superior to them. Placing external pressure on an injury assists in decreasing hemorrhage and hematoma formation by mechanically reducing the space available for swelling to accumulate.[36] Fluid seepage into interstitial spaces is retarded by compression, and absorption is facilitated. However, applying compression to an anterior compartment syndrome or to certain injuries involving the head and neck is contraindicated.

Many types of compression are available. An elastic wrap that has been soaked in water and frozen in a refrigerator can provide both compression and cold when applied to a recent injury. Pads can be cut from felt or foam rubber to fit difficult-to-compress body areas. For example, a horseshoe-shaped pad placed around the malleolus in combination with an elastic wrap and tape provides focal compression to reduce ankle edema.[62] Although cold is applied intermittently, compression should be maintained throughout the day and if possible throughout the night. Because of the pressure buildup in the tissues, the athlete may find it painful to leave a compression wrap in place for a long time. However, it is essential to leave the wrap in place in spite of significant pain because compression is so important in the control of swelling. The

10-5

Critical Thinking E x e r c i s e

A field hockey player trips over an opponent's stick, plantar flexing and inverting her ankle, and she falls to the turf with a grade 2 ankle sprain. She has immediate effusion and significant pain. On examination, there appears to be some laxity in the ankle joint. The athletic trainer transports the athlete to the training room so that the ankle sprain can be managed properly.

? What specifically should the athletic trainer do to most effectively control the initial swelling associated with this injury?

compression wrap should be left in place for at least seventy-two hours after an acute injury. In many chronic overuse problems, such as tendinitis, tenosynovitis, and particularly bursitis, the compression wrap should be worn until all swelling is almost entirely gone.

Elevation   Along with cold and compression, elevation reduces internal bleeding. The injured part, particularly an extremity, should be elevated to eliminate the effects of gravity on blood pooling in the extremities.[40] Elevation assists the veins, which drain blood and other fluids from the injured area, returning them to the central circulatory system. The greater the degree of elevation, the more effective the reduction in swelling. In an ankle sprain, for example, the leg should be placed so that the ankle is virtually straight up in the air. The injured part should be elevated as much as possible during the first seventy-two hours.

Emergency Splinting

Any suspected fracture should always be splinted before the athlete is moved.[13] Transporting a person with a fracture without proper immobilization can result in increased tissue damage, hemorrhage, and shock.[33] Conceivably, a mishandled fracture could cause death. Therefore a thorough knowledge of splinting techniques is important. Applying splints should be a simple process using commercial emergency splints.[18,33] The athletic trainer usually does not have to improvise a splint because such devices are readily available in most sports settings.

Rapid form vacuum immobilizer   The rapid form vacuum immobilizer is widely used by both EMTs and athletic trainers.[43] It consists of styrofoam chips contained inside an airtight cloth sleeve that is pliable. This splint can be molded to the shape of any joint or angulated fracture through the use of Velcro straps. A handheld pump sucks the air out of the sleeve, giving it a cardboardlike rigidity. This splint is most useful for injuries that are angulated and must be splinted in the position in which they are found (Figure 10-22A).

Air splint   An air splint is a clear plastic splint that is inflated with air around the affected part and can be used for extremity splinting, but its use requires some special training. This splint provides support and moderate pressure to the body part and affords a clear view of the site for X-ray examination. The inflatable splint should not be used if it will alter a fracture deformity (Figure 10-22B).

Half-ring splint   For fractures of the femur, the half-ring traction splint offers the best support and immobilization but takes considerable practice to master. An open fracture must be carefully dressed to avoid additional contamination (Figure 10-22C).

Whatever the material used, the principles of good splinting remain the same. Two major concepts of splinting are to splint from one joint above the fracture to one joint below the fracture and to splint where the athlete lies. If at all possible, do not move the athlete until he or she has been splinted.

Splinting of lower-limb fractures   Fractures of the ankle or leg require immobilization of the foot and knee. Any fracture involving the knee, thigh, or hip needs splinting of all the lower-limb joints and one side of the trunk.

Splinting of upper-limb fractures   Fractures around the shoulder complex are immobilized by a sling and swathe bandage, with the upper limb securely bound to the body. Upper-arm and elbow fractures must be splinted, with immobilization effected in a straight-arm position to lessen bone override. Lower-arm and wrist fractures should be splinted in a position of forearm flexion and should be supported by a sling. Hand and finger dislocations and fractures should be splinted with tongue depressors, roller gauze, or aluminum splints.[49]

Splinting of the spine and pelvis   Injuries involving a possible spine or pelvic fracture are best splinted and the athlete moved using a spine board. Recently, a total body rapid form vacuum immobilizer has been developed for dealing with spinal injuries (Figure 10-23). The effectiveness of this piece of equipment as an immobilization device has yet to be determined.[43]

A suspected fracture must be splinted before the athlete is moved.

10-6

Critical Thinking Exercise

During practice, a lacrosse player is involved in a collision on the field. When the athletic trainer reaches the athlete, the athlete's ankle is deformed and obviously fractured.

? How should the athletic trainer immobilize this injury?

Figure 10-22

Examples of splints. **A,** Rapid form vacuum immobilizer. **B,** Air splint. **C,** Half-ring splint.

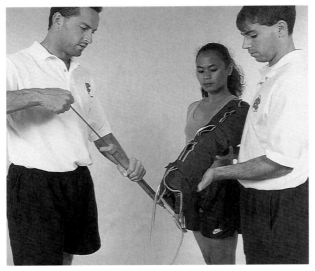

A

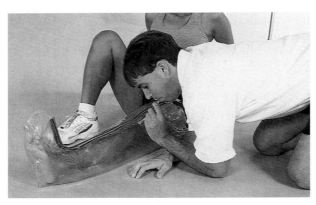

B

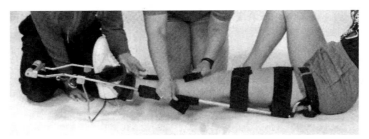

C

Figure 10-23

Full body mattress vacuum splint immobilizer (From MDI Immobile Inc.).

EMERGENCY EMOTIONAL CARE

Besides evaluating and responding to the emergency physical requirements of an injury, the athletic trainer must evaluate and respond appropriately to the emotions engendered by the situation. The American Psychiatric Association has set forth major principles for the emergency care of emotional reactions to trauma.[24] Those principles are as follows:

1. Accept everyone's right to personal feelings, because everyone comes from a unique background and has had different emotional experiences. Do not tell the injured person how he or she should feel. Show empathy, not pity.
2. Accept the injured person's limitations as real.
3. Accept your own limitations as a provider of first aid.

   In general, the athletic trainer dealing with an injured athlete's emotions should be empathetic and calm and should make it obvious that the athlete's feelings are understood and accepted.

MOVING AND TRANSPORTING THE INJURED ATHLETE

Moving, lifting, and transporting the injured athlete must be executed with the use of techniques that will prevent further injury. Moving or transporting the athlete improperly causes more additional injuries than does any other emergency procedure.[24,36] There is no excuse for poor handling of the injured athlete. Planning should take into consideration all the possible transportation methods and the necessary equipment to execute them.[8] Capable and well-trained personnel, spine boards, stretchers, and a rescue vehicle may be needed to transport the injured athlete. Special consideration must be given to extracting the injured athlete from a pool.

> Great caution must be taken when transporting the injured athlete.

Placing the Athlete on a Spine Board

In cases of suspected cervical spine injury, the athletic trainer should generally access the EMS and wait until the rescue squad arrives before attempting to move the athlete. The only exception would be if the athlete is not breathing. Then the athlete must be logrolled onto his or her back for CPR.

A suspected spinal injury requires extremely careful handling and is best left to properly trained paramedics or EMTs or to athletic trainers who are well trained and have access to the proper equipment for transport. (See the back inside cover of this text for a list of emergency equipment that should be available on the sidelines.) If such personnel are not available, the athlete should be moved under the express direction of a physician, and a spine board should be used (Figure 10-24). The most important principle in transporting an individual on a spine board is to maintain the head and neck in alignment with the long axis of the body. In such cases, it is best to have one person whose sole responsibility is to ensure and maintain proper positioning of the head and neck until the head is secured to a spine board.

Primary emergency care involves helping the athlete maintain normal breathing, treating the athlete for shock, and keeping the athlete quiet and in the position found until medical assistance arrives. Ideally, transportation should not be attempted until a physician has examined the athlete and has given permission to move him or her. Neck stabilization must be maintained throughout transportation, first to the emergency vehicle, then to the hospital, and throughout the hospital procedure.[1]

These steps should be followed when moving an athlete with a suspected neck injury:

1. The examiner must determine whether the athlete is breathing and has a pulse.
2. A spine board is retrieved for moving the athlete.
3. If the athlete is lying prone, he or she must be logrolled onto his or her back for CPR or to be secured to the spine board. An athlete with a possible cervical fracture is transported face up. An athlete with a spinal fracture in the lower trunk area may be transported face down.

a. All extremities are placed in an axial alignment (Figure 10-24A).
b. To roll the athlete over requires four or five persons, with the captain of the team protecting the athlete's head and neck. The neck must be stabilized and must not be moved from its original position, no matter how distorted it may appear.
c. The spine board is placed close to the side of the athlete (Figure 10-24B).
d. Each assistant is responsible for one of the athlete's body segments. One assistant is responsible for turning the trunk, another the hips, another the thighs, and the last the lower legs.
4. With the spine board close to the athlete's side, the captain gives the command to logroll him or her onto the board as one unit (Figure 10-24C).
5. On the board, the athlete's head and neck continue to be stabilized by the captain (Figure 10-24D).
6. If the athlete is a football player, the helmet is not removed; however, the face guard is removed or lifted away from the face for possible CPR. NOTE: To remove the face guard, the plastic fasteners holding it to the helmet should be removed.

A

C

B

D

Figure 10-24

A, When moving an unconscious athlete, first establish whether the athlete is breathing and has a pulse. An unconscious athlete must always be treated as having a serious neck injury. If lying prone, the athlete must be turned over for CPR or be secured to a spine board for possible cervical fracture. One person (the "captain") should stabilize the athlete's neck and head. **B,** The spine board is placed as close to the athlete as possible. **C,** Each assistant is responsible for one of the athlete's segments. When the coach or athletic trainer gives the command "roll," the athlete is moved as a unit onto the spine board. **D,** The face mask is cut away while the captain continues to stabilize the athlete's neck.

Continued

7. Next, the head and neck are stabilized on the spine board by a chin strap secured to metal loops.[57] Finally, the trunk and lower limbs are secured to the spine board by straps (Figure 10-24E and F).

8. The rescuers place themselves in a position to stand, and then on the command of the person stabilizing the head, they collectively lift the athlete on the spine board (Figure 10-24G and H).

If the athlete is face up, the lift and slide technique can be used to move the athlete onto a spine board. Four or five persons are needed: a captain stationed at the athlete's head and three or four assistants. One assistant is in charge of lifting the athlete's trunk, one the hips, and one the legs. At the captain's lift command, the athlete is lifted while the fourth assistant slides a spine board under the athlete between the feet of the captain and the assistants (Figure 10-25A). The lift and slide technique has been shown to be more effective in restricting motion in the head, reducing both lateral flexion and axial rotation compared to the logroll technique.[9]

A scoop stretcher may also be used for transporting an athlete with a potential injury to the spine although it is not generally considered to be as safe as using a spine board (Figure 10-25B). A scoop stretcher has detachable hinges at each end, and thus

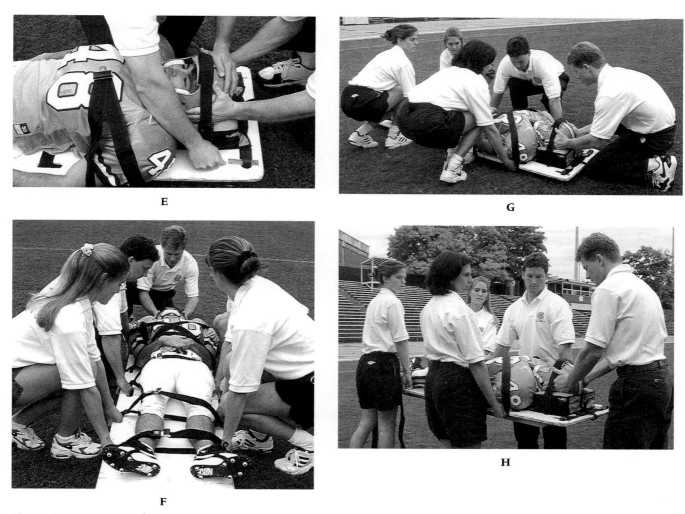

E

G

F

H

Figure 10-24—continued

E, The head and neck are stabilized onto the spine board by means of a chin strap secured to metal loops. **F,** The trunk and lower limbs are secured to the spine board by straps. **G,** All carriers assume a position to stand. **H,** Once the carriers are standing, the athlete may be transported.

A

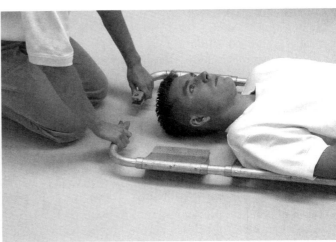

C

B

Figure 10-25

Alternative methods of placing the athlete on a spine board. **A,** The lift and slide technique. **B,** The scoop stretcher. **C,** Latching the top of the scoop stretcher.

can be split into two halves (Figure 10-25C). Each half of the stretcher is placed on either side of the prone athlete. The athletic trainer can easily slide each half of the stretcher under the athlete until the hinges are locked together, in effect "scooping" the athlete onto the stretcher. The advantage in using a scoop stretcher is that it is not necessary to roll the injured athlete onto his or her side to get the stretcher underneath.

Ambulatory Aid

Ambulatory aid is that support or assistance given to an injured athlete who is able to walk (Figure 10-26). Before the athlete is allowed to walk, he or she should be carefully scrutinized to make sure that the injuries are minor. Whenever serious injuries are suspected, walking should be prohibited. Complete support should be given on both sides of the athlete by two individuals who are approximately the same height. The athlete's arms are draped over the assistants' shoulders, and their arms encircle his or her back.

Manual Conveyance

Manual conveyance may be used to move a mildly injured individual a greater distance than could be walked with ease (Figure 10-27). Any decision to carry the athlete, like a decision to use ambulatory aid, must be made only after a complete examination to determine the existence of potentially serious conditions. The most convenient carry is performed by two assistants.

Stretcher Carrying

Whenever a serious injury is suspected, the best and safest mode of transportation for a short distance is by stretcher. With each segment of the body supported, the athlete is gently lifted and placed on the stretcher, which is carried adequately by a minimum of four assistants, two supporting either side (Figure 10-28). Any person with an injury serious enough to require the use of a stretcher must be carefully examined before being moved.

Figure 10-26

The ambulatory aid method of transporting a mildly injured athlete.

A

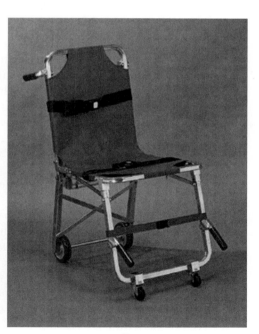

B

Figure 10-27

A, Manual conveyance method for transporting a mildly injured athlete. **B,** A stair chair can also be used if the athlete is too large for the athletic trainer to lift manually.

Figure 10-28

Whenever a serious injury is suspected, a stretcher is the safest method for transporting the athlete. A scoop stretcher makes it easy to get underneath the injured athlete.

A limb injury must be splinted properly before the athlete is transported. Athletes with shoulder injuries are more comfortably moved in a semisitting position, unless other injuries preclude such positioning. If injury to the upper extremity is such that flexion of the elbow is not possible, the individual should be transported on a stretcher with the limb properly splinted and carried at the side, with adequate padding placed between the arm and the body.

Pool Extraction

Removing an injured athlete from a swimming pool requires some special consideration on the part of the athletic trainer. Obviously an athletic trainer who is providing coverage for athletes training or competing in a pool must be able to swim and should have water safety or lifeguard training. The athletic trainer should routinely have immediate access to both a rescue tube and an aquatic spine board in case an athlete sustains an injury while in the pool. A rescue tube should always be used to extract an injured athlete from the pool.[3] The rescue tube will not only serve as a floatation device but also can help prevent an athlete who is distressed from grabbing the athletic trainer while in the water.

The following procedures are recommended for removing an injured athlete from a pool:

1. When dealing with an athlete who has sustained what appears to be a minor injury in the pool, if the athlete is close to the edge of the pool, the athletic trainer can reach out to the athlete with the rescue tube while standing on the pool deck and holding onto the shoulder strap with the other hand. Have the athlete grab the tube, then pull him or her to the edge of the pool (Figure 10-29A).[3]
2. If the athlete is too far away from the pool deck, the athletic trainer should get into the water, approach the athlete from the front, extend the rescue tube, have the athlete grab the tube and kick if possible, while the athletic trainer pulls them to the edge of the pool (Figure 10-29B).[3]

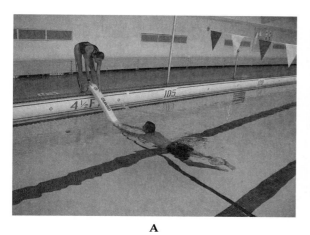

A   **B**

Figure 10-29

Techniques for pool rescue. **A,** Athlete is close to edge of pool. **B,** Athlete is in middle of pool.

3. If an athlete appears to be more severely injured, the athletic trainer should get into the water, approach the athlete from behind, reach under the armpits and grab the athlete's shoulders while putting the rescue tube between the athlete's back and the athletic trainer's chest. The athletic trainer should keep his or head to either side to avoid being hit by the athlete's head should it fall backwards. The athletic trainer should lean back pulling the athlete onto the rescue tube, which should support the athlete keeping the athlete's mouth and face out of the water; the athletic trainer should pull the athlete to the edge of the pool while attempting to keep him or her calm (Figure 10-30).[3]

4. Deciding to remove an injured athlete from the water depends on several factors including the athlete's condition, size, and the availability of help or how long until help arrives. For example, an injured athlete requiring CPR should be removed immediately from the water; rescue breathing should not be attempted in the water. A spine board should be used by two people to remove any athlete from the water who is unable to get out on his or her own, even if a spinal injury is not suspected. The primary rescuer brings the injured athlete to the side of the pool and turns him or her to face the pool deck. A second rescuer standing on the pool deck grabs the athlete's opposite wrists and pulls the athlete up, keeping the head above water and away from the edge of the pool (Figure 10-31A). The primary rescuer gets out of the water, grabs the spine board, then guides the spine board foot-end

10-7

*Critical **Thinking*** Exercise

A diver, attempting a 2½ inward dive on a 3-meter board, hits her head on the end of the board. She lands on her face in the water, is briefly submerged, but floats quickly to the surface. She is conscious but disoriented; she has a bump on her forehead but is not bleeding. A teammate nearby jumps immediately in the water and, using a cross-chest technique, tows her about 10 feet to the side of the pool.

? The athletic trainer is concerned about both a head and neck injury. What precautions should be taken when removing the injured athlete from the pool?

Figure 10-30

Technique for removing a severely injured athlete from the water.

A

B

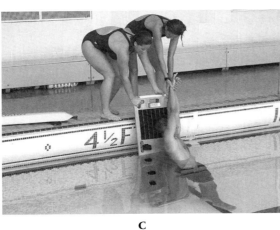

C

D

Figure 10-31

Technique for removing an athlete from the water who can't get out on their own.

first down into the water between the athlete and the edge of the pool (Figure 10-31B). The second rescuer then turns the athlete so his or her back rests against the spine board (Figure 10-31C). Each rescuer then grasps a wrist with one hand and the spine board with the other. The rescuers pull the spine board upward and backward leveraging the board onto the pool deck (Figure 10-31D).[3]

5. An athlete with a suspected head or cervical neck injury or an athlete who is unconscious requires special precaution. An athlete's cervical spine can be immobilized in the water by a single primary rescuer placing one forearm over the sternum and cupping the athlete's lower jaw while placing the other forearm over the athlete's spine and holding the back of his or her head. Squeezing the forearms together stabilizes the spine and head. The athlete may be held face-up in the water in this position until help arrives (Figure 10-32A). While the primary rescuer continues stabilizing the head and neck, a second rescuer submerges the spine board, positioning it appropriately under the athlete. The primary rescuer maintains stabilization of the athlete's chin while removing the other arm and repositioning it to support the back of the spine board (Figure 10-32B). Rescue tubes may be used to help float the spine board. The second rescuer moves to the athlete's head and, with the forearms resting against the sides of the spine board, assumes responsibility for stabilizing the athlete's head. The primary rescuer then securely straps the chest, hips, thighs, and finally immobilizes and secures the head to the spine board (Figure 10-32C). Both rescuers then remove the spine board from the pool, head first, by initially lifting the board onto the edge of the pool while still in the water. Then one rescuer gets on the pool deck while the other remains in the water to complete the pool extraction (Figure 10-32D).[3]

A

B

C

D

Figure 10-32

Technique for putting an athlete with a suspected spinal injury on a spine board and removing him or her from the pool.

PROPER FIT AND USE OF THE CRUTCH OR CANE

Weight bearing may be contraindicated for an athlete with a lower-limb injury, in which case a crutch or cane should be used for ambulation. The athletic trainer must be responsible for properly fitting the crutch or cane to the injured athlete and then for providing instruction in its use. If the crutch or cane is not properly fitted, the athlete may experience discomfort in the axilla from excessive pressure as well as pain in the low back. Faulty mechanics in the use of the crutch or cane when ambulating and particularly when ascending or descending stairs can cause the athlete to fall.

Fitting the Athlete

The adjustable wooden crutch is well suited to the athlete. For a correct fit, the athlete should wear low-heeled shoes and stand with good posture and the feet close together. The crutch length is determined first by placing the tip 6 inches (15 cm) from the outer margin of the shoe and 2 inches (5 cm) in front of the shoe. The underarm crutch brace is positioned 1 inch (2.5 cm) below the anterior fold of the axilla. Next, the hand brace is adjusted so that it is even with the athlete's hand when the elbow is flexed at approximately a 30-degree angle (Figure 10-33).

Fitting a cane to the athlete is relatively easy. Measurement is taken from the superior aspect of the greater trochanter of the femur to the floor while the athlete is wearing street shoes.

Properly fitting a crutch or cane is essential to avoid placing abnormal stresses on the body.

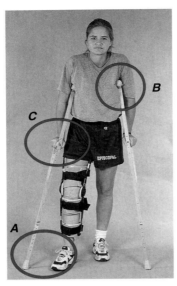

Figure 10-33

The crutch must be properly fitted to the athlete. **A,** The crutch tips are placed 6 inches (15 cm) from the outer margin of the shoe and 2 inches (5 cm) in front of the shoe. **B,** The underarm crutch brace is positioned 1 inch (2.5 cm) below the anterior fold of the axilla. **C,** The hand brace is placed even with the athlete's hand, with the elbow flexed approximately 30 degrees.

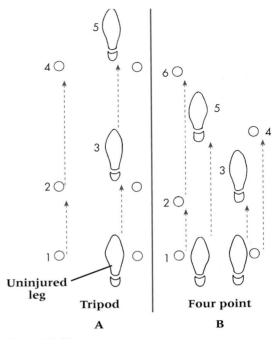

Figure 10-34

Crutch gait. **A,** Tripod method. **B,** Four-point gait.

Walking with the Crutch or Cane

Many elements of crutch walking correspond with normal walking. The technique commonly used in sports injuries is the tripod method. In this method, the athlete swings through the crutches without making any surface contact with the injured limb or by partially bearing weight with the injured limb. The following sequence is performed:

1. The athlete stands on the uninjured leg with no weight or partial weight on the injured leg.
2. Placing the crutch tips 12 to 15 inches (30 to 37.5 cm) ahead of the feet, the athlete leans forward, straightens the elbows, pulls the upper crosspiece firmly against the side of the chest, and swings or steps with the uninjured leg between the stationary crutches (Figure 10-34A). The athlete should avoid placing the major support in the axilla.
3. After moving through, the athlete recovers the crutches and again places the tips forward repeating the sequence. The crutches and the injured or non–weight-bearing leg always move together.

An alternative method is the four-point crutch gait. In this method, the athlete stands on both feet, moves one crutch forward, and steps forward with the opposite foot. The athlete moves the crutch on the same side as the foot that moved forward to just ahead of the foot, steps forward, using the opposite foot followed by the crutch on the same side, and so on (Figure 10-34B).

The tripod gait that is used for crutch walking on a level surface is also used on stairs. In going up stairs, the uninjured support leg moves up one step while the body weight is supported by the hands on the crutches. The full weight of the body is transferred to the uninjured leg, and the crutch tips and injured leg are moved to that step. In going down stairs, the crutch tips and the injured leg move down one step, followed by the uninjured leg. If a handrail is available, the athlete uses the tripod gait holding both crutches with the outside hand.

Crutch walking will generally follow a progression from non–weight-bearing (NWB) to touch down weight bearing (TDWB) to partial weight bearing (PWB) to full weight bearing (FWB). The rate of progression will be dictated by limitations of the injury as well as capabilities of the athlete.

When the injured athlete needs to be partially weight bearing, a cane or perhaps a single crutch can be used to help with balance. In this case the athlete should hold the cane or crutch in the hand on the uninjured side and move the cane forward simultaneously with the injured leg. The athlete should avoid leaning too heavily on the cane or crutch. If this is a problem then the athlete should use two crutches.

SUMMARY

- An emergency is defined as "an unforeseen combination of circumstances and the resulting state that calls for immediate action."[24] The primary concern of emergency aid is to maintain cardiovascular function and, indirectly, central nervous system function. All sports programs should have an emergency action plan that is activated whenever an athlete is seriously injured.

- The athletic trainer must make a systematic assessment of the injured athlete to determine appropriate emergency care. A primary survey assesses and deals with life-threatening situations. Once the athlete is stabilized, the secondary survey makes a more detailed assessment of the injury.

- In adult CPR, the ratio of compression to breaths is 15 to 2, with 80 to 100 compressions per minute. An obstructed airway is relieved by using chest compressions, the finger sweep of the throat, or both.

- Hemorrhage can occur externally and internally. External bleeding can be controlled by direct pressure, by applying pressure at pressure points, and by elevation. Internal hemorrhage can occur subcutaneously, intramuscularly, or within a body cavity.

- Shock can occur from a variety of situations. Shock can be hypovolemic, respiratory, neurogenic, psychogenic, cardiogenic, septic, anaphylactic, and metabolic. Symptoms include pale skin, dilated eyes, weak and rapid pulse, and rapid, shallow breathing. Management includes maintaining normal body temperature and slightly elevating the feet.

- Rest, ice, compression, and elevation (RICE) should be used for the immediate care of a musculoskeletal injury. Ice should be applied for at least twenty minutes every 1 to 1½ hours, and compression and elevation should be continuous for at least seventy-two hours after injury.

- Any suspected fracture should be splinted before the athlete is moved. Commercial rapid form vacuum immobilizers and air splints are most often used as splints in an athletic training setting.

- Great care must be taken in moving the seriously injured athlete. The unconscious athlete must be handled as though he or she has a cervical fracture. Moving an athlete with a suspected serious neck injury must be performed only by persons specifically trained to do so. A spine board should be used for transport to avoid any movement of the cervical region.

- Athletes who are injured will respond emotionally to the situation. Their feelings must be understood and fully accepted by the coach and the athletic trainer.

- The athletic trainer should be responsible for the proper fitting and instruction in the use of crutches or a cane by an athlete with an injury to the lower extremity.

- When removing an injured athlete from a swimming pool, the athletic trainer should make every effort to minimize movement of the head and cervical spine while placing the athlete on a spine board in the water.

Websites

American Red Cross: http://www.redcross.org/what.html

The American Red Cross offers many emergency services and training. This site describes those services, introduces the information provided in various training opportunities, and explains how to obtain that training,

American Heart Association: http://www.amhrt.org

Cervical Spine Stabilization:
http://www.trauma.org/spine/cspine-stab.html

This brief article describes the considerations with cervical spine stabilization.

The National Safety Council: http://www.nsc.org/

The National Safety Council is a membership organization with resources on safety, health and environmental topics, training, products, publications, news, and more.

First Aid with Parasol EMT: http://www.parasolemt.com.au

This site provides a comprehensive on-line first aid reference.

First Aid: http://www.mayohealth.org

This Website on first aid care is maintained by the Mayo Clinic.

Solutions to Critical Thinking EXERCISES

10-1 Because of the mechanism of injury, the athletic trainer should suspect that the athlete has a cervical neck injury, and the head should be stabilized throughout. Because the athlete is prone and breathing, the athletic trainer should do nothing until the athlete regains consciousness. An on-field exam should determine the athlete's neurological status. Then the player should be carefully logrolled onto a spine board because CPR could be necessary at any time. The face mask should be removed in case CPR is required. The helmet and shoulder pads should be left in place. The athlete should then be transported to an emergency facility. In this situation the worst mistake the athletic trainer can make is not exercising enough caution.

10-2 If the athletic trainer has been trained to do so and the appropriate equipment is available, supplemental oxygen can be administered using a bag-valve-mask and a pressurized oxygen cylinder to facilitate recovery.

10-3 The athletic trainer must first take precautions to protect against the transmission of bloodborne pathogens. The wound should be cleaned with soap and water. The athletic trainer should apply direct pressure using a gauze pad and should apply cold. If the athlete is not dizzy, he should remain in a sitting position. The athlete should be referred to a physician for suturing. Sterile strips or a butterfly bandage may also be applied, although sutures will generally leave a smaller scar. All blood-contaminated supplies should be disposed of in a clearly marked biohazard bag.

10-4 The athlete may be going into hypovolemic shock secondary to hemorrhage and trauma, which can be a life-threatening situation. The athletic trainer should first direct someone to dial 911 to access the emergency medical system. Next, the athletic trainer must control the bleeding by using direct pressure, elevation, and pressure points. If bleeding is controlled and the rescue squad has not arrived, the forearm should be immobilized in a rapid form

vacuum immobilizer. The athlete should be supine, and his feet should be elevated in the shock position. His body temperature should be maintained.

10-5 The ankle should be wrapped with a wet elastic compression wrap. Ice should be applied to both sides of the joint over the compression wrap and secured. The ankle should be elevated so that the leg is above 45 degrees at a minimum. The compression wrap, ice, and elevation should be maintained initially for at least thirty minutes but not longer than an hour. The athletic trainer should also make some determination as to whether a fracture is suspected and make the appropriate referral.

10-6 A rapid form vacuum immobilizer will work well for this injury because of its ability to mold the splint to the joint without causing unnecessary movement. Therefore, the ankle can be immobilized in the current position before transporting the athlete.

10-7 The athletic trainer should place the athlete on a spine board and secure her before extracting her from the pool. Several people may be required to get the athlete appropriately positioned on the spine board while still in the water. The athlete should be given a brief neurological exam to determine the extent of the injury. The athlete should then be transported to an emergency facility in a rescue vehicle.

10-8 The athletic trainer should instruct the athlete in the tripod gait, in which the athlete swings through the crutches without making any surface contact with the injured limb. The tripod gait is also used on stairs. In negotiating stairs, the rule of thumb is go up with the good leg first, followed by crutches, and to go down with the crutches first, followed by the good leg. If the stairs have a handrail, the athlete can hold both crutches with his outside hand. Crutch walking will generally follow a progression: NWB to TDWB to PWB to FWB.

REVIEW QUESTIONS AND CLASS ACTIVITIES

1. What considerations are important in a well-planned system for handling emergency situations?
2. Discuss the rules for managing and moving an unconscious athlete.
3. What are the life-threatening conditions that should be evaluated in the primary survey?
4. What are the ABCs of life support?
5. Identify the major steps in giving CPR and managing an obstructed airway. When might these procedures be used in a sports setting?
6. List the basic steps in assessing a musculoskeletal injury.
7. What techniques should be used to stop external hemorrhage?
8. Numerous types of shock can occur from a sports injury or illness; list them and their management.
9. What first-aid procedures are used to decrease hemorrhage, inflammation, muscle spasm, and pain from a musculoskeletal injury?
10. Describe the basic concepts of emergency splinting.
11. How should an athlete with a suspected spinal injury be transported?
12. What techniques can be used to transport an athlete with a suspected musculoskeletal injury?
13. Discuss the methods for extracting an injured athlete from a swimming pool.
14. Explain how to properly fit crutches.
15. Describe methods that should be used when dealing with an injured athlete's emotional response to the injury.

REFERENCES

1. Almquist J: Spine injury management: a comprehensive plan for managing the cervical spine–injured football player, *Sports Med Update* 13(1):8, 1998.

2. American Red Cross: American Red Cross first aid/CPR/AED program instructors manual, Boston, 2001, American Red Cross.

3. American Red Cross: *Lifeguarding Instructors Manual training,* San Bruno, Calif., 2001, Staywell.

4. Andersen J, Courson R, Kleiner D: National Athletic Trainers' Association position statement: emergency planning in athletics, *J Ath Train* 37(1):99, 2002.

5. Brukner P, Kahn K, Hunte G: Sporting emergencies. In Brukner P, editor: *Clinical sports medicine,* ed 2, Sydney, 2002, McGraw-Hill.

6. Cartwright LA, Pitney WA: Extrication. In Cartwright LA, editor: *Athletic training for student assistants,* Champaign, Ill, 1999, Human Kinetics.

7. Delforge G: Sports injury assessment and problem identification. In Delforge G, editor: *Musculoskeletal trauma implications for sports injury management,* Champaign, IL, 2002, Human Kinetics.

8. Del Rossi G: Management of cervical-spine injuries. *Athletic Therapy Today* 7(2):46, 2002.

9. Del Rossi G, Horodyski M, Powers M: A comparison of spine-board transfer techniques and the effect of training on performance, *J Ath Train* 38(3), 2003.

10. Dick BH, Anderson JM: Emergency care of the injured athlete. In Zachazewski JE et al, editors: *Athletic injuries and rehabilitation,* Philadelphia, 1996, WB Saunders.

11. Farrell RN: AEDs and cardiac resuscitation: is prevention part of your plan? *Athletic Therapy Today* 6(3):46, 2001.

12. Feld F: Management of the critically injured football player, *J Ath Train* 28(3):206, 1993.

13. Feld F: Technology and emergency care, *Athletic Therapy Today* 2(5):28, 1997.

14. Fessey J: First aid for head and spinal injuries in sport, *Physiotherapy in Sport* 20(3):4, 1997.

15. Fincher AL: Managing medical emergencies, Part 1, *Athletic Therapy Today* 6(3):44, 2001.

16. Fuchs E: Face mask removal time of four face mask extrication devices. Master's thesis, San Jose State University, 1994.

17. Green BN: Important changes in the 2000 CPR guidelines, *J Sports Chiropractic & Rehabilitation* 15(2):80, 2001.

18. Hay JM: Taping, splinting, and fitting of athletic equipment. In Baker CL et al, editors: *The Hughston Clinic sports medicine book,* Baltimore, Md, 1995, Williams & Wilkins.

19. Helmet removal guidelines. In Schultz S, editor: *Sports medicine handbook,* Indianapolis, 2001, National Federation of State High School Athletic Associations.

20. Helmut removal guidelines, *Sports Med Update* 15(1):4, 2000.

21. Herbert D: Plan to save lives: create and rehearse an emergency response plan, *ACSM's Health & Fitness Journal* 1(5):34, 1997.

22. Herbert DL: Developing a comprehensive sports medicine emergency care plan, *Sports Med Stand Malprac Report* 7(4):49, 1995.

23. Jenkins H, Valovich T, Arnold B: Removal tools are faster and produce less force and torque on the helmet than cutting tools during face-mask retraction, *J Ath Train* 37(3):246, 2002.

24. Karren KJ, Hafen BQ: *First aid for colleges and universities,* Boston, 2003, Benjamin Cummings.

25. Kleiner D, Almquist J, Bailes J: *Prehospital care of the spine-injured athlete: a document from the Inter-Association Task Force for Appropriate Care of the Spine-Injured Athlete,* Dallas, 2001, National Athletic Trainers' Association.

26. Kleiner DM: 10 questions about football-helmet and face-mask removal: a review of the recent literature, *Athletic Therapy Today* 6(3):29, 2001.

27. Kleiner DM: Football helmet face mask removal, *Athletic Therapy Today* 1(1):11, 1996.

28. Knight K: *Cryotherapy in sport injury management,* Champaign, Ill, 1995, Human Kinetics.

29. Knox KE, Kleiner DM: The efficiency of tools used to retract a football helmet face mask, *J Ath Train* 32(3):211, 1997.

30. LaPrade RF, Schnetzler KA, Broxterman RJ: Cervical spine alignment in the immobilized ice hockey player: a computed tomographic analysis of the effects of helmet removal, *Am J Sports Med* 28(6):800, 2000.

31. Magee DL: *Orthopedic physical assessment,* Philadelphia, 2002, WB Saunders.

32. Martin DE: Emergency medicine and the underage athlete, *J Ath Train* 29(3):200, 1994.

33. Meredith RM, Butcher JD: Field splinting of suspected fractures: preparation, assessment, and application. *Physician Sportsmed* 25(10):29, 1997.

34. National Athletic Trainers' Association: *Position stand: helmet removal guidelines,* Dallas, 1998, National Athletic Trainers' Association.

35. National Collegiate Athletic Association: Guidelines for helmet fitting and removal. In Benson M, editor: *2003–2004 NCAA sports medicine handbook,* Indianapolis, Ind, 2003. National Collegiate Athletic Association.

36. National Safety Council: *First aid and CPR,* Boston, 2001, Jones & Bartlett.

37. Ortolani A: Helmets and face masks, *J Ath Train* 27(4):294, 1992 (letter).

38. Palumbo MA, Hulstyn MJ, Fadale PD: The effect of protective football equipment on alignment of the injured cervical spine: radiographic analysis in a cadaveric model, *Am J Sports Med* 24(4):446, 1996.

39. Patel M, Rund D: Emergency removal of football helmets, *Physician Sportsmed* 22(9):57, 1994.

40. Prentice WE: Considerations in designing a rehabilitation program, In Prentice WE: *Rehabilitation techniques in sports medicine and athletic training,* St. Louis, 2004, McGraw-Hill.

41. Prinsen R, Syrotuik D, Reid D: Position of the cervical vertebrae during helmet removal and cervical collar application in football and hockey, *Cl J Sports Med* 5(3):155, 1995.

42. Putman L: Alternative methods for football helmet face mask removal, *J Ath Train* 27(2):107, 1992.

43. Ransone J, Kersey R, Walsh K: The efficacy of the rapid form cervical vacuum immobilizer in cervical spine immobilization of the equipped football player, *J Ath Train* 35(1):65, 2000.

44. Ransone J, Dunn-Bennett LR: Assessment of first-aid knowledge and decision making of high school athletic coaches, *Journal Ath Train* 34(3): 267, 1999.

45. Ray R: Helmets and face masks, *J Ath Train* 27(4):294, 1992 (letter).

46. Ray R, Luchies C, Frens M: Cervical spine motion in football players during 3 airway-exposure techniques, *J Ath Train* 37(2):172, 2002.

47. Ray R, Luchies C, Bazuin D: Airway preparation techniques for the cervical spine–injured football player, *J Ath Train* 30(3):217, 1995.

48. Roberts WO: Helmet removal in head and neck trauma, *Physician Sportsmed* 26(7): 77, 1998.

49. Sailer SM, Lewis SB: Rehabilitation and splinting of common upper-extremity injuries in athletes, *Clin Sports Med* 14(2):411, 1995.

50. Schnirring L: AEDs gain foothold in sports medicine, *Physician Sportsmed* 29(4): 2001.

51. Segan RD, Cassidy C, Bentkowski J: A discussion of the issue of football helmet removal in suspected cervical spine injuries, *J Ath Train* 28(4):294, 1993.

52. Starkey C, Ryan J: *Evaluation of orthopedic and athletic injuries,* Philadelphia, 2002, FA Davis.

53. Swartz E, Armstrong C, Rankin J: A 3-dimensional analysis of face-mask removal tools in inducing helmet movement, *J Ath Train* 37(2):178, 2002.

54. Swartz E, Norkus S, Armstrong C: Face-mask removal: movement and time associated with cutting of the loop straps, *J Ath Train* 38(2):120, 2003.

55. *Taber's cyclopedic medical dictionary*, Philadelphia, 2002, FA Davis.

56. Terry G, Kyle J, Ellis J: Sudden cardiac arrest in athletic medicine, *J Ath Train* 36(2):205, 2001.

57. Tierney R, Mattacola C, Sitler M: Head position and football equipment influence cervical spinal-cord space during immobilization, *J Ath Train* 37(2):185, 2002.

58. United States Olympic Committee/American Red Cross: *Sport safety training: injury prevention and care handbook*, St Louis, 1997, Mosby Lifeline.

59. Veenema KR, Swenson EJ: Laryngeal trauma: securing the airway on the field, *Physician Sportsmed* 23(1):71, 1995.

60. Walsh K: Thinking proactively: the emergency action plan. *Athletic Therapy Today* 6(5):57, 2001.

61. Waninger KN: On-field management of potential cervical spine injury in helmeted football players: leave the helmet on, *Cl J Sports Med* 8(2):124, 1998.

62. Wilkerson GB: External compression for controlling traumatic edema, *Physician Sportsmed* 13:96, 1985.

ANNOTATED BIBLIOGRAPHY

American Red Cross: American Red Cross *First aid: responding to emergencies*, San Brunon, CA, 2001, Staywell, Co.

Karren KJ, Hafen BQ: *First aid for colleges and universities*, Boston, 2003, Benjamin Cummings.

A well-illustrated, simple approach to the treatment of emergency illness and injury.

Kleiner D, Almquist J, Bailes J: *Prehospital care of the spine-injured athlete: a document from the Inter-Association Task Force for Appropriate Care of the Spine-Injured Athlete*, Dallas, 2001, National Athletic Trainers' Association.

A well-referenced monograph that details consensus recommendations from NATA and a variety of other sports medicine organizations relative to the emergency care of an athlete with a suspected spinal injury from the time of injury until arrival at a medical care facility.

Leikin JB, Feldman BJ: *American Medical Association handbook of first aid and emergency care*, Philadelphia, 2000, Random House.

Covering urgent emergency situations as well as the common injuries and ailments that occur in every family, this AMA guide takes the reader step-by-step through basic first-aid techniques, the medical symptoms to recognize before an emergency occurs, and what to do when one does occur.

Magee DJ: *Orthopedic physical assessment*, Philadelphia, 2002, WB Saunders.

An extremely well-illustrated book, with excellent coverage. Its strength lies in its coverage of injuries commonly found during athletic training.

National Safety Council: *First aid and CPR*, Boston, 2001, Jones & Bartlett.

All three are standard, well-written, and extremely well-illustrated texts that deal with first aid and emergency procedures. Although most of the information is directed at the general population, the principles and techniques can certainly be applied to the injured athlete. Any one of the three will provide an excellent resource for the athletic trainer.

Bloodborne Pathogens

When you finish this chapter you should be able to

- Explain what bloodborne pathogens are and how they can infect athletes and athletic trainers.
- Describe the transmission, symptoms, signs, and treatment of hepatitis B virus.
- Describe the transmission, symptoms, signs, and treatment of hepatitis C.
- Describe the transmission, symptoms, and signs of human immunodeficiency virus.
- Explain how human immunodeficiency virus is most often transmitted.
- List the pros and cons of athletes with hepatitis B virus, hepatitis C virus, or human immunodeficiency virus participating in sports.
- Evaluate universal precautions as mandated by the Occupational Safety and Health Administration and how they apply to the athletic trainer.

Bloodborne pathogens are transmitted through contact with blood or other bodily fluids. Hepatitis, especially the hepatitis B virus (HBV), the hepatitis C virus (HCV), and human immunodeficiency virus (HIV) are of special concern.[3] Despite the media attention given to bloodborne pathogens in recent years, many athletic trainers have only a moderate understanding of the magnitude of the problem.[10]

It has always been important for the athletic trainer as a health care provider to be concerned with maintaining an environment in the athletic training room that is as clean and sterile as possible.[1,18] In our society it has become critical for everyone to take measures to prevent the spread of infectious diseases.[12] Failure to do so may predispose any individual to life-threatening situations. The athletic trainer must take every precaution to minimize the potential for exposure to blood or other infectious materials (Figure 11-1).

VIRUS REPRODUCTION

A virus is a submicroscopic parasitic organism that is dependent on the nutrients within cells. A virus consists of a strand of either deoxyribonucleic acid (DNA) or ribonucleic acid (RNA). A virus contains one or the other, but not both. A virus consists

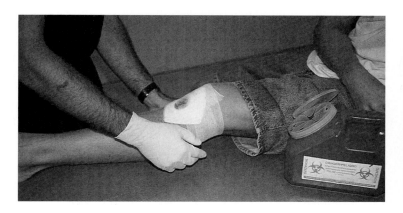

Chapter 11

Figure 11-1

The athletic trainer must take precautions to prevent exposure to and transmission of bloodborne pathogens.

Figure 11-2

The reproducing virus.

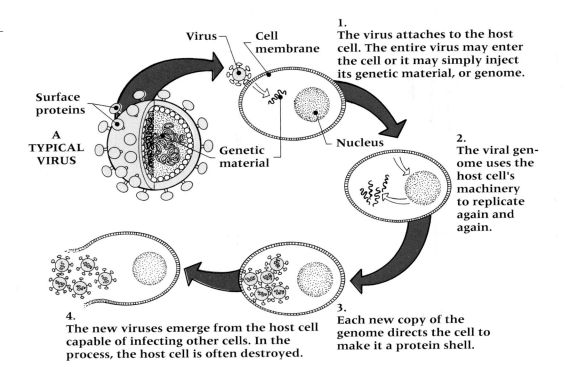

1. The virus attaches to the host cell. The entire virus may enter the cell or it may simply inject its genetic material, or genome.

2. The viral genome uses the host cell's machinery to replicate again and again.

3. Each new copy of the genome directs the cell to make it a protein shell.

4. The new viruses emerge from the host cell capable of infecting other cells. In the process, the host cell is often destroyed.

of a shell of proteins surrounding genetic material. It is a parasite that depends on a host cell for metabolic and reproductive requirements. In general, viruses make their cell hosts ill by redirecting cellular activity to create more viruses (Figure 11-2).

BLOODBORNE PATHOGENS

Bloodborne pathogens are pathogenic microorganisms that can potentially cause disease and are present in human blood and other body fluids, including semen, vaginal secretions, cerebrospinal fluid, synovial fluid, and any other fluid contaminated with blood. The three most significant bloodborne pathogens are HBV, HCV, and HIV.

Although HIV has been widely addressed in the media, HBV and HCV have a higher possibility for spread than does HIV, and thus athletic trainers should be more concerned about contracting HBV and HCV.[14] Hepatitis B virus is stronger and more durable than HIV and can be spread more easily via sharp objects, open wounds, and bodily fluids.[20]

Three additional viruses—hepatitis A, D, and E—exist, which, while related, are not generally considered to be bloodborne pathogens. Hepatitis A (HAV) is a virus that causes inflammation of the liver but does not lead to chronic disease of the liver. HAV is transmitted by the fecal or oral routes, through close personal contact, or through ingestion of contaminated food or water. For example it may be transmitted by an infected food preparer who doesn't wash his or her hands after going to the bathroom. HAV may show no outward symptoms or signs, but adults may have dark urine, light stools, fatigue, fever, and jaundice. Hepatitis D (HDV), like HAV, causes inflammation of the liver, but it will only infect those individuals who are already infected with HBV. It is transmitted through contact with infected blood or contaminated needles or through sexual contact. Hepatitis E (HEV) also causes inflammation of the liver, although it is rare in the United States. It is transmitted through the fecal or oral routes or through contaminated water supplies in foreign countries.[18]

Hepatitis B Virus

Hepatitis B virus is a major cause of viral infection; it results in swelling, soreness, and loss of normal liver function. The number of cases of HBV has risen dramatically

Mode of transmission includes:
- Human blood
- Semen
- Vaginal secretions
- Cerebrospinal fluid
- Synovial fluid

Bloodborne pathogens include:
- Hepatitis B virus (HBV)
- Hepatitis C virus (HCV)
- Human immunodeficiency virus (HIV)

during the last ten years. It has been estimated that 1.25 million people in the United States have chronic hepatitis and can potentially infect others. New cases are occurring at rates as high as 300,000 per year.[29]

Symptoms and Signs

The symptoms and signs in a person infected with HBV include flulike symptoms such as fatigue, weakness, and nausea; abdominal pain; headache; fever; and possibly jaundice. It is possible that an individual infected with HBV will exhibit no signs or symptoms, and the virus may go undetected. In these individuals, the HBV antigen will always be present. Thus the disease may be unknowingly transmitted to others through exposure to blood or other body fluids or through intimate contact. Cases of chronic active hepatitis may occur because of a problem with the immune system that prevents the complete destruction of virus-infected liver cells.

An infected person's blood may test positive for the HBV antigen within two to six weeks after the symptoms develop. Approximately 85 percent of those infected recover within six to eight weeks.

Prevention

Good personal hygiene and avoiding high-risk activities is the best way to avoid HBV.[13] Hepatitis B virus can survive for at least one week in dried blood or on contaminated surfaces and may be transmitted through contact with these surfaces. Caution must be taken to avoid contact with any blood or other fluid that potentially contains a bloodborne pathogen.[38]

Management

Vaccination against HBV must be made available by employers at no cost to any individual who may be exposed to blood or other body fluids and may thus be at risk of contracting HBV.[40] All athletic trainers and any individual working in an allied health care profession should receive immunization. An estimated 8,700 health care workers contract HBV each year, and as many as 200 of these cases end in death.[29] The vaccine is given in three doses over a six-month period. Approximately 87 percent of those receiving the vaccine will be immune after the second dose, and 96 percent develop immunity after the third dose. Postexposure vaccination is available when individuals have come into direct contact with bodily fluids of an infected person.[7]

Hepatitis C

Originally referred to as non-A, non-B hepatitis, hepatitis C is both an acute and chronic form of liver disease caused by the hepatitis C virus (HCV). HCV is the most common chronic bloodborne infection in the United States. At least 85 percent of those infected acutely with HCV become chronically infected, and 67 percent develop chronic liver disease. It is the leading indication for liver transplant. Three percent of those with chronic liver disease die from cirrhosis or liver cancer. It is estimated that 3.9 million Americans have been infected with HCV, of whom 2.7 million are chronically infected. There were 25,000 new infections in 2001.[17]

Symptoms and Signs

Eighty percent of those infected with HCV have no signs or symptoms. Those who are symptomatic may be jaundiced and/or have mild abdominal pain, particularly in the upper right quadrant; loss of appetite; nausea, fatigue; muscle or joint pain; and/or dark urine.

Prevention

HCV is not spread by sneezing, hugging, coughing, food or water, sharing eating utensils or drinking glasses, or casual contact. It is rarely spread through sexual contact. It is spread by contact with the blood of an infected person.[38] It is most commonly

11-1

Critical Thinking E x e r c i s e

The athletic trainer is responsible for taking every precaution to prevent infection by bloodborne pathogens.

? How are bloodborne pathogen infections prevented from spreading from one athlete to another?

11-2

Critical Thinking E x e r c i s e

A wrestler has been diagnosed with hepatitis B virus.

? What are the symptoms and signs of HBV infection?

transmitted by sharing needles or syringes. However it can also be transmitted by sharing personal care items that might have blood on them (razors, toothbrushes). Consider the risks of getting a tattoo or body piercing. Athletic trainers should always follow routine barrier precautions and safely handle needles and other sharp objects.

Management

Unlike for HBV, presently there is no vaccine for preventing HCV transmission. There are several blood tests that can be done to determine if a person has been infected with HCV. A physician may order just one or a combination of these tests. It is possible to find HCV within one to two weeks after being infected with the virus. A single positive test indicates infection with HCV. However a single negative test does not prove that a person is not infected. When hepatitis C is suspected, even though an initial test is negative, the test should be repeated.[17]

HCV-positive persons should be evaluated by their doctor for liver disease. Interferon and ribavirin are two drugs used in combination that appear to be the most effective for the treatment of persons with chronic hepatitis C. Drinking alcohol can make liver disease worse.

Human Immunodeficiency Virus

retrovirus
A virus that enters a host cell and changes its RNA to a proviral DNA replica.

Human immunodeficiency virus is a **retrovirus** that combines with a host cell. A number of cells in the immune system may be infected, such as T^4 blood cells, B cells, and monocytes (macrophages), which decreases their effectiveness in preventing disease. As of the end of 2003, an estimated 40 million people worldwide were living with HIV/AIDS. Worldwide, approximately 11 of every 1,000 adults ages 15 to 49 are infected with HIV. An estimated 5 million new HIV infections occurred worldwide during 2003. That is about 14,000 infections each day. In 2003 alone, HIV/AIDS-associated illnesses caused approximately 3 million deaths worldwide.[44]

Symptoms and Signs

As is the case with HBV, HIV is transmitted by exposure to infected blood or other body fluids or by intimate sexual contact.[45] Symptoms of HIV include fatigue, weight loss, muscle or joint pain, painful or swollen glands, night sweats, and fever. Antibodies to HIV can be detected in a blood test within one year after exposure. As with HBV, people with HIV may be unaware that they have contracted the virus and may go for eight to ten years before developing any signs or symptoms. Unfortunately most individuals who test positive for HIV will ultimately develop acquired immunodeficiency syndrome (AIDS). Table 11-1 summarizes information on HBV and HIV.

Acquired Immunodeficiency Syndrome A syndrome is a collection of signs and symptoms that are recognized as the effects of an infection. An individual with AIDS has no protection against even the simplest infections and thus is extremely vulnerable to developing a variety of illnesses, opportunistic infections, and cancers (such as Kaposi's sarcoma and non-Hodgkin's lymphoma) that cannot be stopped.[7,24]

According to the Centers for Disease Control (CDC), it is estimated that 850,000 to 950,000 U.S. residents are living with HIV infection, and that approximately 40,000 new HIV infections occur each year. As of the end of 2002, an estimated 384,906 people in the United States were living with AIDS, and an estimated 501,669 people with AIDS in the United States had died.[44]

A positive HIV test cannot predict when the individual will show the symptoms of AIDS.[32] About 50 percent of people develop AIDS within ten years of becoming HIV-infected. Those individuals who develop AIDS generally die within two years after the symptoms appear.

TABLE 11-1   Transmission of Hepatitis B and C Viruses and Human Immunodeficiency Virus

Disease	Symptoms and Signs	Mode of Transmission	Infectious Materials
Hepatitis B virus	Flulike symptoms, jaundice	Direct and indirect contact	Blood, saliva, semen, feces, food, water, and other products
Hepatitis C virus	Jaundice, upper right quadrant pain, loss of appetite, nausea, fatigue, dark urine	Direct and indirect contact with blood	Blood
Human immuno-deficiency virus/ acquired immuno-deficiency syndrome	Fever, night sweats, weight loss, diarrhea, severe fatigue, swollen lymph nodes, lesions	Direct and indirect contact	Blood, semen, vaginal fluid

Management

Unlike HBV, there is no vaccine for HIV. Even though some drug therapy may extend their lives, there is currently no available treatment to cure patients with AIDS. Much research is being done to find a preventive vaccine and an effective treatment. Presently, the most effective treatment seems to be a therapy consisting of a combination of three drugs. One drug blocks the action of an enzyme that the virus needs to make some of the components for new virus cells. A second drug blocks the copying of viral genes that can enter the host cell's nucleus (a process called reverse transcription) and thus disables the synthesis of new viruses. A third drug helps protect the T cells and thus slows the progression of HIV.[32]

Although new treatments have extended the healthy life span of many people with AIDS, HIV prevalence has continued to increase. As the number of AIDS cases declines because of these new treatments, the number of people with HIV will increase, which means there will be a greater need for both prevention and treatment services.

Prevention

Athletes must understand that their greatest risk for contracting HIV is through intimate sexual contact with an infected partner.[23] Practicing safe sex is of major importance. The athlete must choose nonpromiscuous sex partners and use condoms for vaginal or anal intercourse. Latex condoms provide a barrier against both HBV and HIV. Male condoms should have reservoir tips to reduce the chance of ejaculate being released from the sides of the condom. Condoms that are prelubricated are less likely to tear. Water-based, greaseless spermicides or lubricants should be avoided.[39] If the condom tears, a vaginal spermicide should be used immediately. The condom should carefully be removed and discarded.[39] Additional ways to reduce the risk of HIV infection can be found in *Focus Box:* "HIV risk reduction."

Human immunodeficiency virus is most often transmitted through intimate sexual contact.

The use of latex condoms can reduce the chances of contracting HIV.

BLOODBORNE PATHOGENS IN ATHLETICS

In general the chances of transmitting HIV among athletes is low.[11,21,34,41] There is minimal risk of on-field transmission of HIV from one player to another in sports.[15,34] One study involving professional football estimated that the risk of transmission from player to player was less than 1 per 1 million games.[16] At this time there have been no validated reports of HIV transmission in sports.[27]

Focus

HIV risk reduction
- Avoid contact with others' bodily fluids, feces, and semen.
- Avoid sharing needles (e.g., when injecting anabolic steroids or human growth hormones).
- Choose nonpromiscuous sex partners.
- Limit sex partners.
- Consistently use condoms.
- Avoid drugs that impair judgment.
- Avoid sex with known HIV carriers.
- Get regular tests for sexually transmitted diseases.
- Practice good hygiene before and after sex.

Some sports may have a potentially higher risk for transmission because of close contact and the possibility of passing blood on to the other person.[15] Sports such as the martial arts, wrestling, and boxing have more theoretical potential for transmission (see *Focus Box:* "Risk categories for HIV transmission in sports").[27]

Policy Regulation

11-3

Critical Thinking Exercise

A wrestler comes into the training room very concerned that his wrestling partner got a bloody nose and that he came in contact with a few drops of that athlete's blood.

 What should the athletic trainer tell the athlete about the transmission of HIV from this type of contact?

Athletes participating in organized sports are subject to procedures and policies about the transmission of bloodborne pathogens.[37] The National Athletic Trainers' Association, U.S. Olympic Committee, National Collegiate Athletic Association, National Federation of State High School Athletic Associations, National Basketball Association, National Hockey League, National Football League, and Major League Baseball all have established policies to help prevent the transmission of bloodborne pathogens. These organizations have also initiated programs to help educate athletes under their control. The Centers for Disease Control and Prevention is another useful resource for the athletic trainer seeking information and guidelines for medical assistance on disease control, epidemic prevention, and notification.

All institutions should take responsibility for educating their student athletes about how bloodborne pathogens are transmitted.[37] In the case of a high school athlete, efforts should also be made to educate the parents.[6] Professional, collegiate, and high school athletes should be made aware that the greatest risk of contracting HBV or HIV is through their off-the-field activities, which may include unsafe sexual practices and sharing of needles, particularly in the use of steroids. Athletes, perhaps more than

Focus

Risk categories for HIV transmission in sports[12]

Although the risk for HIV transmission in athletics is minimal, the following classifications of sports indicate risks relative to one another:
- Highest risk: boxing, martial arts, wrestling, rugby
- Moderate risk: basketball, field hockey, football, ice hockey, judo, soccer, team handball
- Lowest risk: archery, badminton, baseball, bowling, canoeing/kayaking, cycling, diving, equestrianism, fencing, figure skating, gymnastics, modern pentathlon, racquetball, rhythmic gymnastics, roller skating, rowing, shooting, softball, speed skating, skiing, swimming, synchronized swimming, table tennis, volleyball, water polo, weight lifting, yachting

other individuals in the population, think that they are immune and that infection will always happen to someone else. The athletic trainer should also assume the responsibility of educating and informing student trainers about exposure control policies.

Each institution should implement policies and procedures concerning bloodborne pathogens.[34] A recent survey of NCAA institutions found that a large number of athletic trainers and other health care providers at many colleges and universities demonstrated significant deficits in following the universal guidelines mandated by OSHA. Universal precautions in a sports medicine or other health care setting protect both the athlete and the health care provider.[25]

Human Immunodeficiency Virus and Athletic Participation

There is no definitive answer to whether asymptomatic HIV carriers should participate in sports.[42] Bodily fluid contact should be avoided, and the participant should also avoid engaging in exhaustive exercise that may lead to an increased susceptibility to infection.[42]

The Americans with Disabilities Act of 1991 says that athletes infected with HIV cannot be discriminated against and may be excluded from participation only on a medically sound basis.[27] Exclusion must be based on objective medical evidence and must take into consideration the extent of risk of infection to others, the potential harm to the athlete, and what means can be taken to reduce this risk.[19]

Testing Athletes for Human Immunodeficiency Virus

Testing for HIV should not be used as a screening tool to determine if an athlete can participate in sports.[9,34] Mandatory testing for HIV may not be allowed because of legal reasons related to the Americans with Disabilities Act.[34] In terms of importance, mandatory testing should be secondary to education to prevent the transmission of HIV.[24] Neither the NCAA nor the Centers for Disease Control and Prevention recommends mandatory HIV testing for athletes.[34]

Athletes who engage in high-risk activities should be encouraged to seek voluntary anonymous testing for HIV.[36] A blood test analyzes serum using an enzyme-linked immunosorbent assay (ELISA) or an enzyme immunoassay (EIA). These tests detect antibodies to HIV proteins. Positive EIA or ELISA tests should be repeated to rule out false-positive results. A second positive test requires the Western blot examination, which is a more sensitive test.[7] Detectable antibodies may appear from three months to one year after exposure. Testing, therefore, should occur at six weeks, three months, and one year.[39]

Home testing kits are also available in which an individual can collect a sample for testing in the privacy of his or her home and then send it to a laboratory for analysis. There are more than a dozen different HIV home test kits being advertised on the market today. Only the Home Access test system is FDA approved and legally marketed in the United States. This approved system uses a simple finger prick process for home blood collection, which results in dried blood spots on special paper. The dried blood spots are mailed to a laboratory with a confidential and anonymous personal identification number (PIN). The sample is then analyzed by trained clinicians in a certified medical laboratory using the same procedures that are used for samples taken in a doctor's office. The purchaser obtains results by calling a toll-free telephone number and using the PIN; post-test counseling is provided by telephone when results are obtained.[4]

Many states have enacted laws that protect the confidentiality of the HIV-infected person. The athletic trainer should be familiar with state law and make every effort to guard the confidentiality and anonymity of HIV testing for athletes.

UNIVERSAL PRECAUTIONS IN AN ATHLETIC ENVIRONMENT

In 1991 the Occupational Safety and Health Administration (**OSHA**) established standards for an employer to follow that govern occupational exposure to bloodborne pathogens.[31]

11-4

Critical Thinking E x e r c i s e

A female athlete has had unprotected sex with a male whom she has dated only once previously. She knows that she should be tested for HIV but is so worried and embarrassed that she has avoided going to a medical facility to have a test. Finally she goes to her athletic trainer and confides her concerns.

? What should the athletic trainer tell her about being tested for HIV?

For additional information on HIV and AIDS care, contact the CDC National AIDS Hotline: 1 (800) 342-2437.

OSHA
Occupational Safety and Health Administration.

BIOHAZARD

The guidelines instituted by OSHA were developed to protect the health care provider and the patient against bloodborne pathogens.[29] OSHA has mandated that training programs for dealing with bloodborne pathogens be repeated each year to provide the most current information. It is essential that every sports program develop and carry out a bloodborne pathogen exposure control plan.[35] NATA has established specific guidelines for athletic trainers.[22,28] This plan should include counseling, education, volunteer testing, and the management of bodily fluids.[34]

These guidelines should be followed by anyone coming into contact with blood or other bodily fluids.[4,43] Following are considerations specifically in the sports arena.

Preparing the Athlete

Before an athlete participates in practice or competition, all open skin wounds and lesions must be covered with a dressing that is fixed in place and does not allow for transmission to or from another athlete.[33] An occlusive dressing lessens the chances of cross-contamination. One example is the hydrocolloid dressing, which is considered a superior barrier. This type of dressing also reduces the chances that the wound will re-open because it keeps the wound moist and pliable.[33]

When Bleeding Occurs

As mandated by the NCAA and the USOC, open wounds or other skin lesions considered a risk for disease transmission should be given aggressive treatment. Athletes with active bleeding must be removed from participation as soon as possible and can return only when it is deemed safe by the medical staff.[16] Uniforms containing blood must be evaluated for infectivity. A uniform that is saturated with blood must be removed and changed before the athlete can return to competition. All personnel managing potential infective wound exposure must follow universal precautions.[16,29]

Personal Precautions

The health care personnel working directly with bodily fluids on the field or in the athletic training facility must make use of the appropriate protective equipment in all situations in which there is potential contact with bloodborne pathogens. Protective equipment includes disposable nonlatex gloves, nonabsorbent gowns or aprons, masks and shields, eye protection, and disposable mouthpieces for resuscitation devices.[5] Equipment for dealing with bloodborne pathogens should be included in sideline emergency kits.[30] Disposable nonlatex gloves must be used when handling any potentially infectious material. Double gloving is suggested when there is heavy bleeding or sharp instruments are used. Gloves should always be removed carefully after use. In cases of emergency, heavy toweling may be used until gloves can be obtained[1] (see *Focus Box:* "Glove use and removal") (Figure 11-3).

11-5

Critical Thinking Exercise

A sports program must initiate and carry out a bloodborne pathogen exposure control plan.

? What are the universal precautions in an athletic environment as proposed by OSHA?

Nonlatex gloves should be worn whenever the athletic trainer handles blood or bodily fluids.

Focus

Glove use and removal
1. Avoid touching personal items when wearing contaminated gloves.
2. Remove first glove, turn it inside out and, beginning at wrist, peel off second glove without touching skin.
3. Remove second glove, making sure not to touch soiled surfaces with ungloved hand.
4. Discard gloves that have been used, discolored, torn, or punctured.
5. Wash hands immediately after glove removal.

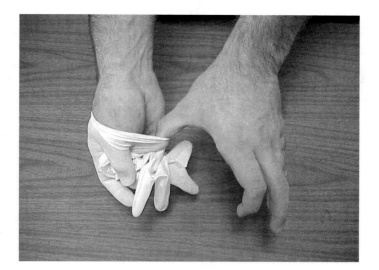

Figure 11-3

Technique for removing nonlatex gloves.

Hands and all skin surfaces that come in contact with blood or other bodily fluids should be washed immediately with soap and water or other antigermicidal agents. Hands should also be washed between each patient treatment. If there is the possibility of bodily fluids becoming splashed, spurted, or sprayed, the mouth, nose, and eyes should be protected. Aprons or nonabsorbent gowns should be worn to avoid clothing contamination.

First aid kits must contain protection for hands, face, and eyes and resuscitation mouthpieces. Kits should also contain towelettes for cleaning skin surfaces.[3]

Latex Sensitivity and Using Nonlatex Gloves

It is recommended that athletic trainers use nonlatex gloves.[8] There are a number of manufacturers who produce nonlatex gloves. Latex, a sap from the rubber tree, is composed of compounds that may cause an allergic reaction of a severity that can range from a contact dermatitis to a systemic reaction. Recognizing the signs and symptoms associated with these reactions may help to prevent a more severe reaction from occurring. Some individuals are more at risk of latex allergies due to repetitive exposure to latex through their career paths, multiple surgeries, other allergies, or respiratory conditions. Management of an acute reaction involves removing the irritant, cleansing the affected area, monitoring vital signs for changes, and seeking additional medical assistance as warranted.[8]

Availability of Supplies and Equipment

In keeping with universal precautions, the sports program must also have available chlorine bleach, antiseptics, proper receptacles for soiled equipment and uniforms, wound care bandages, and a designated container for disposal of sharp objects such as needles, syringes, and scalpels.[16]

Biohazard warning labels should be affixed to containers for regulated wastes, refrigerators containing blood, and other containers used to store or ship potentially infectious materials (Figure 11-4). The labels are fluorescent orange or red. Red bags or containers should be used for the disposal of potentially infected materials.

Disinfectants

All contaminated surfaces such as treatment tables, taping tables, work areas, and floors should be cleaned immediately with a solution consisting of one part bleach to ten parts water (1:10) or with a disinfectant approved by the Environmental Protection Agency.[6] Disinfectants should inactivate the HIV virus. Towels or other linens that have been contaminated should be bagged and separated from other laundry. Soiled

11-6

Critical Thinking E x e r c i s e

During a basketball game, one of the players sustains a nosebleed. Blood is visible on the court and on the player's jersey and skin.

? What actions need to take place before the game can resume?

Universal precautions minimize the risk of exposure and transmission.

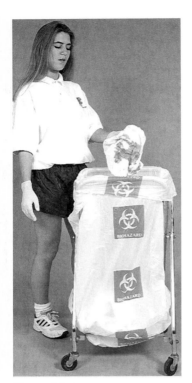

Figure 11-4

Soiled linens should be placed in a leakproof bag marked as a biohazard.

Sharps include:
■ Scalpels
■ Razor blades
■ Needles

Figure 11-5

Sharps should be disposed of in a red or orange puncture-resistant plastic container marked as a biohazard.

linen should be transported in red or orange containers or bags that prevent soaking or leaking and are labeled with biohazard warning labels (see Figure 11-4). Contaminated laundry should be washed in hot water (71° C/159.8° F for 25 minutes) using a detergent that deactivates the virus. Laundry done outside the institution should be sent to a facility that follows OSHA standards. Gloves must be worn during bagging and cleaning of contaminated laundry.

Sharps

Sharps refers to sharp objects used in athletic training, such as needles, razor blades, and scalpels. Extreme care should be taken when handling and disposing of sharps to minimize the risk of puncturing or cutting the skin. Athletic trainers rarely use needles, but it is not unusual for them to use scalpels or razor blades. Whenever needles are used, they should not be recapped, bent, or removed from a syringe. Sharps should be disposed of in a leakproof and puncture-resistant container.[6] The container should be red or orange and should be labeled as a biohazard (Figure 11-5). Scissors and tweezers are not as likely to cause injury as sharps are, but they should be sterilized with a disinfecting agent and stored in a clean place after use.

Protecting the Coach and Athletic Trainer

OSHA guidelines for bloodborne pathogens are intended to protect the coach, athletic trainer, and other employees and not the athlete.[31] Coaches do not usually come in contact with blood or other bodily fluids from an injured athlete, so their risk is considerably reduced. It is the responsibility of the high school, college, professional team, or clinic to ensure the safety of the athletic trainer as a health care provider by instituting and annually updating policies for education on the prevention of transmitting bloodborne pathogens through contact with athletes. The institution must provide the necessary supplies and equipment to carry out these recommendations.

The athletic trainer has the personal responsibility of adhering to these policies and guidelines and enforcing them in the training room. Athletic trainers may further minimize the risk of exposure in the athletic training setting by not eating, drinking, applying cosmetics or lip balm, handling contact lenses, or touching the face before washing hands. Food products should never be placed in a refrigerator containing contaminated blood.[2]

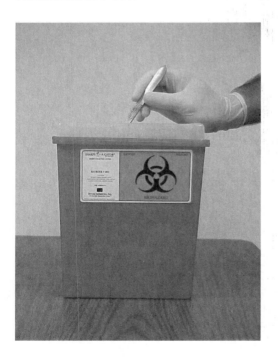

Protecting the Athlete from Exposure

Several additional recommendations may further help to protect the athlete. The USOC supports the required use of mouthpieces in high-risk sports. It is also recommended that all athletes shower immediately after practice or competition. Athletes who may be exposed to HIV, HBV, or HCV should also be evaluated for immunization against HBV.

Postexposure Procedures

After a report of an exposure incident, the athletic trainer should have a confidential medical evaluation that includes documentation of the exposure route, identification of the source individual, a blood test, counseling, and an evaluation of reported illness. Again, the laws that pertain to reporting and confidentiality of test results notification vary from state to state.[31]

SUMMARY

- Bloodborne pathogens are microorganisms that can potentially cause disease and are present in human blood and other bodily fluids, including semen, vaginal secretions, cerebrospinal fluid, synovial fluid, and any other fluid contaminated with blood. Hepatitis B virus, hepatitis C virus, and HIV are bloodborne pathogens.
- A virus is a submicroscopic parasitic organism that contains either DNA or RNA, but not both. It is dependent on the host cell to function and reproduce.
- A vaccine is available to prevent HBV. Currently no effective vaccine exists for treating HCV or HIV.
- An individual infected with HIV may develop AIDS, which is fatal.
- The risks of contracting HBV, HCV, or HIV may be minimized by avoiding exposure to blood and other bodily fluids and by practicing safe sex.
- The risk of an athlete being exposed to bloodborne pathogens on the field is minimal. Off-field activities involving risky sexual behaviors pose the greatest threat for transmission.
- Various national medical and sports organizations have established policies and procedures for dealing with bloodborne pathogens in the athletic population.
- The Occupational Safety and Health Administration has established rules and regulations that protect the health care employee.
- Universal precautions must be taken to avoid bloodborne pathogen exposure. All sports programs must carry out a plan for counseling, education, volunteer testing, and the management of exposure.

Websites

Occupational Safety and Health Administration (OSHA):
http://www.osha.gov

Department of Health and Human Services:
http://www.os.dhhs.gov

HIV/AIDS Prevention:
http://cdc.gov/nchstp/hiv_aids/dhap.htm

Centers for Disease Control and Prevention:
http://www.cdc.gov

National Institutes of Health: http://www.nih.gov

Bloodborne Pathogens Self Study Module:
http://www2.umdnj.edu/eohssweb/uhbbp/intro.htm

Solutions to Critical Thinking EXERCISES

11-1 During competition or practice the athlete should be most concerned about coming in contact with blood from another athlete. There should be little or no concern about exposure to sweat or saliva. The chances of contracting HIV during athletic participation are minimal. Certainly, the athlete is most likely to be exposed to HIV during unprotected intimate sexual contact.

11-2 The wrestler complained of flulike symptoms such as headache, fever, fatigue, weakness, nausea, and some abdominal pain. A blood test revealed the presence of the HBV antigen.

11-3 The greatest risk of contracting HIV is through intimate sexual contact with an infected partner. The athletic trainer should explain to the athlete that there is little chance of HIV transmission among athletes. There is a theoretical potential risk of transmission among athletes in close contact who pass blood from one to the other.

11-4 The athletic trainer should inform her that it is best if she waits for six weeks before being tested. The athletic trainer should strongly encourage her to seek testing and should explain to her that if she is uncomfortable with being tested in a medical care facility, there is a home test available that has been approved by the FDA and provides confidentiality. The athletic trainer should add that if the athlete were to test positive on the home test, it becomes imperative that she seek additional testing at a medical care facility.

11-5 Universal precautions should be practiced by anyone coming in contact with blood or other bodily fluids. This plan must include counseling, education, volunteer testing, and management of bodily fluids.

11-6 To prevent possible transmission of bloodborne pathogens, several precautions need to be followed. The athlete must be removed from the game until active bleeding has ceased and he or she has been cleared by the medical staff. The jersey must be removed and changed if the uniform is saturated with blood. Any blood on the skin must be cleaned off before the athlete can return to play. In addition, the basketball court needs to be properly cleaned and disinfected. The solution used to clean the court should be one part bleach to ten parts water or a solution approved by the Environmental Protective Agency. All contaminated products need to be properly disposed of according to OSHA standards.

REVIEW QUESTIONS AND CLASS ACTIVITIES

1. Define and identify the bloodborne pathogens.
2. Describe HBV and HCV transmission, symptoms, signs, prevention, and treatment.
3. Explain the pros and cons of allowing an athlete who is an HBV carrier to participate.
4. Describe HIV transmission, symptoms, signs, prevention, and treatment.
5. How is HIV transmitted, and why is it eventually fatal at this time?
6. Should an athlete who tests positive for HBV or HIV be allowed to participate in sports? Why or why not?
7. How can an athlete reduce the risk of HIV infection?
8. Define OSHA universal precautions for preventing bloodborne pathogen exposure.
9. What precautions would you, as an athletic trainer, take when caring for a bleeding wound on the field?

REFERENCES

1. American Academy of Pediatrics: Human immunodeficiency virus (acquired immunodeficiency syndrome [AIDS] virus) in athletic settings, *Pediatrics* 88:640, 1991.
2. American College Health Association: *General statement of institutional response to AIDS,* 1–6, Rockville, Md, 1988, Task Force on AIDS, American College Health Association.
3. American Medical Association Department of HIV, Division of Health Science: *Digest of HIV/AIDS policy,* 1–15, Chicago, Ill, 1993, Department of HIV, American Medical Association.
4. American Medical Society for Sports Medicine and the American Academy for Sports Medicine: Human immunodeficiency virus (HIV) and bloodborne pathogens in sport: joint position statement, *Am J Sports Med* 23:510, 1995.
5. American Red Cross: *Emergency response,* San Bruno, Calif, 2001, Staywell.
6. Arnold BL: A review of selected bloodborne pathogen position statements and federal regulations, *J Ath Train* 30(2):171, 1995.
7. Berkow R, editor: *The Merck manual diagnosis of therapy,* ed 16, Raway, NJ, 1992, Merck Sharp and Dohne Research Laboratories.
8. Binkley H, Schroyer T, Catalfano J: Latex Allergies: A review of recognition, evaluation, management, prevention, education, and alternative product use, *J Ath Train* 38(2):133, 2003.
9. Bitting LA, Trowbridge CA, Costello LE: A model for a policy on HIV/AIDS and athletics, *J Ath Train* 31(4):356, 1996.
10. Boyle M, Sitler M, Rogers K: Knowledge and attitudes of certified athletic trainers in Pennsylvania toward HIV/AIDS and treating HIV-positive athletes, *J Ath Train* 32(1):40, 1997.
11. Brown L, Dortman P: What is the risk of HIV infection in athletic competition? 19939:PO-C21-3102, International Conference on AIDS, 1993.
12. Brown LS, Phillips RY, Brown CL: HIV/AIDS policies and sports: the National Football League, *Med Sci Sports Exerc* 26(4):403, 1994.
13. Buxton BP et al: Prevention of hepatitis B virus in athletic training, *J Ath Train,* 29(2):107, 1994.
14. Coorts J, Michael T, Whitehill W: Hepatitis B immunization of athletic trainers in District IX, *J Ath Train* 32(4):315, 1997.
15. Deere R, Stopka C, Curran K, Bolger C: Universal precautions for bloodborne pathogens: a checklist for your program, *Strategies* 14(6):18, 2001.
16. Dick R: *National Collegiate Athletic Association 2002–2003 NCAA sports medicine handbook,* Indianapolis, Ind, 2002, National Collegiate Athletic Association.
17. Dolan M: *The hepatitis C handbook,* Berkeley, Calif, 1999, North Atlantic Books.
18. Hamann B: *Disease: identification, prevention, and control,* New York, 2001, McGraw-Hill.
19. Herbert DL: Mandatory testing for HIV and exclusion from athletic participation, *Sports Med Stand Malpract Report* 8(4):59, 1996.
20. Hunt BP, Pujol TJ: Athletic trainers as HIV/AIDS educators, *J Ath Train* 29(2):102, 1994.
21. Kleiner DM, Holcomb WR: Bloodborne pathogens: current information for the strength and conditioning professional, *Strength Cond* 17(4):42, 1995.
22. Knight K: Guidelines for preventing bloodborne pathogen diseases, *J Ath Train* 30:197, 1995.
23. Landry GL: HIV infection and athletes, *Sports Med Digest* 15(4):1, 1993.
24. LaPerriere A, Klimas N, Major P: Acquired immune deficiency syndrome. In American College of Sports Medicine: *ACSM's exercise management for persons with chronic disease and disabilities,* Champaign, Ill, 1997, Human Kinetics.
25. McGrew C: HIV and HBV in sports medicine. Part 2. *Sports Medicine in Primary Care* 1(4):29, 1995.
26. McGrew C, Dick R, Schneidewind K: Survey of NCAA institutions concerning HIV/AIDS policies and universal precautions, *Med Sci Sports Exerc* 25:917, 1993.
27. Mitten MJ: HIV-positive athletes, *Physician Sportsmed,* 22(10):63, 1994.
28. National Athletic Trainers' Association: Blood-borne pathogens guidelines for athletic trainers, *J Ath Train* 30(3):203, 1995.
29. National Safety Council: *Bloodborne pathogens,* Boston, 1998, Jones & Bartlett.
30. Nelson RC, Rinn TB: Sideline emergency kits and the need to include universal precautions against blood-borne pathogens, *J Sports Chiropractic & Rehabilitation* 10(1):32, 1996.
31. OSHA: The OSHA bloodborne pathogens standard, *Federal Register* 55(235):64175, 1991.
32. Payne W, Hahn D: *Understanding your health,* St. Louis, 2001, McGraw-Hill.
33. Rheinecker SB: Wound management: the occlusive dressing, *J Ath Train* 30(2):143, 1995.

34. Rogers KJ: Human immunodeficiency virus in sports. In Torg JS and Shephard RJ, editors: *Current therapy in sports medicine,* St Louis, 1995, Mosby.

35. Ross CM, Young SJ: Understanding the OSHA bloodborne pathogens standard and its impact upon recreational sports, *NIRSSA* J 19(2):12, 1999.

36. Sankaran G, Volkwein KAE, Bonsall DR: HIV infection: risk, right to know, and requirement to divulge, *Athletic Therapy Today* 1(3):49, 1996.

37. Sankaran G, editor: *HIV/AIDS in sport: impact, issues and challenges,* Champaign, Ill, 1999, Human Kinetics.

38. Schultz SJ: Preventing transmission of bloodborne pathogens. In Schultz SJ, editor, *Sports medicine handbook,* Indianapolis, Ind, 2001, National Federation of State High School Associations.

39. Seltzer DG: Educating athletes on HIV disease and AIDS, *Physician Sportsmed* 21(1):109, 1993.

40. Strikas RA: Immunizations: recommendations and resources for active patients. *Physician Sportsmed* 29(10):33, 2001.

41. Stringer WW: HIV and aerobic exercise: current recommendations, *Sports Med* 28(6):389, 1999.

42. Thomas CE: The HIV athlete: policy, obligations, and attitudes, *Sport Science Review* 5(2): 12, 1996.

43. Thygerson A: *First aid and CPR,* Boston, 2001, Jones & Bartlett.

44. United States Department of Health and Human Services: AIDS/HIV Statistics, http://www.niaid.nih.gov/factsheets/aidsstat.htm, 2004.

45. Zeigler T: *Management of bloodborne infections in sport,* Champaign, Ill, 1997, Human Kinetics.

ANNOTATED BIBLIOGRAPHY

Dick RA, editor: *National Collegiate Athletic Association 2002–2003 sports medicine handbook,* Indianapolis, Ind, 2002, National Collegiate Athletic Association.

This text offers a complete discussion of bloodborne pathogens and intercollegiate athletic policies and administration.

Berkow R, editor: *The Merck manual of diagnosis and therapy,* ed 16, Rahway, NJ, 1992, Merck Sharp and Dohne Research Laboratories.

This excellent guide discusses diagnosis, symptoms, signs, and treatment of bloodborne pathogens.

Bradley-Springer L, Fendrick RA: *AIDS/HIV instant instructor,* El Paso, Texas, 1994, Skidmore-Roth.

This excellent card system covers transmission, transmission prevention, occupational exposure prevention, testing, counseling, disease progression, and treatment of HIV and AIDS.

Dolan M: *The hepatitis C handbook,* Berkeley, Calif, 1999, North Atlantic Books.

This definitive guide outlines the course of the disease and associated symptoms. It discusses available treatments and lifestyle changes and contains an extensive section on herbs, vitamins, and nutritional supplements.

Hall K et al: *Bloodborne pathogens,* Boston, 1997, Jones & Bartlett.

This manual is dedicated to presenting OSHA regulations specific to bloodborne pathogens.

Hamann B: *Disease: identification, prevention, and control,* St Louis, 2000, McGraw-Hill.

This text is designed for health educators and covers AIDS and hepatitis in detail.

Neilson RP: *OSHA regulations and guidelines: a guide to health care providers,* Clifton Park, NY, 1998, Delmar Learning.

Presents OSHA standards with special emphasis on bloodborne pathogens and incident and injury reporting.

Zeigler T: *Management of bloodborne infections in sport,* Champaign, Ill, 1997, Human Kinetics.

Perhaps the most comprehensive single text available on dealing with bloodborne pathogens in an athletic population, this text contains procedure and policy statements from several different sport and health organizations on managing bloodborne pathogens in the athletic environment.

Glossary

A

abduction Movement of a body part away from the midline of the body.

accident An act that occurrs by chance or without intention.

active range of motion (AROM) Joint motion that occurs because of muscle contraction.

acute injury An injury with sudden onset and short duration.

adduction Movement of a body part toward the midline of the body.

adipose cell Stores triglyceride.

afferent nerves Nerves that transport messages toward the brain.

agonist muscles Muscles directly engaged in contraction as related to muscles that relax at the same time.

ambient Environmental (e.g., temperature or air that invests one's immediate environment).

ambulation Move or walk from place to place.

ameboid action Cellular action like that of an amoeba, using protoplasmic pseudopod.

amenorrhea Absence or suppression of menstruation.

ampere Volume or amount of electrical energy.

analgesia Pain inhibition.

analgesic Agent that relieves pain without causing a complete loss of sensation.

anaphylaxis Increased susceptibility or sensitivity to a foreign protein or toxin as the result of previous exposure to it.

androgen Any substance that aids the development and controls the appearance of male characteristics.

anemia Lack of iron.

anesthesia Partial or complete loss of sensation.

anomaly Deviation from the normal.

anorexia Lack or loss of appetite; aversion to food.

anorexia nervosa Eating disorder characterized by a distorted body image.

anoxia Lack of oxygen.

antagonist muscles Muscles that counteract the action of the agonist muscles.

anterior Before or in front of.

anteroposterior Refers to the position of front to back.

anteversion Tipping forward of a part as a whole, without bending.

antipyretic Agent that relieves or reduces fever.

anxiety A feeling of uncertainty or apprehension.

apnea Temporary cessation of breathing.

apophysis Bony outgrowth to which muscles attach.

apophysitis Inflammation of an apophysis.

arrhythmical movement Irregular movement.

arthrogram Radiopaque material injected into a joint to facilitate the taking of an X ray.

arthrokinematics Physiological and accessory movements of the joint.

arthroscopic examination Viewing the inside of a joint through an arthroscope, which uses a small camera lens.

assumption of risk An individual, through express or implied agreement, assumes that some risk or danger will be involved in a particular undertaking; a person takes his or her own chances.

asymmetry (body) Lack of symmetry of sides of the body.

ATC Certified Athletic Trainer.

atrophy Wasting away of tissue or of an organ; decrease in the size of a body part or muscle.

attenuation Decrease in intensity as ultrasound enters deeper into tissues.

aura Preepileptic phenomenon, involving visual sensation of fire or glow, along with other possible sensory hallucinations and dreamlike states.

autogenic inhibition The relaxation of the antagonist muscle during contractions.

automatism Automatic behavior before consciousness or full awareness has been achieved after a brain concussion.

avascular Devoid of blood circulation.

avascular necrosis Death of tissue caused by the lack of blood supply.

avulsion Forcible tearing away of a part or a structure.

axilla Armpit.

B

bacteremia Bacterial infection in the blood.

bacteria Morphologically, the simplest group of nongreen vegetable organisms, various species of which are involved in fermentation and putrefaction, the production of disease, and the fixing of atmospheric nitrogen; a schizomycete.

bacteriostatic Halting the growth of bacteria.

ballistic stretching Older stretching technique that uses repetitive bouncing motions.

bandage Strip of cloth or other material used to cover a wound or hold a dressing in place.

beam nonuniformity ratio (BNR) Amount of variability in intensity of the ultrasound beam.

bending Force on a horizontal beam or bone that places stresses within the structure, causing it to bend or strain.

beta-endorphin Chemical substance produced in the brain.

bioavailability How completely a particular drug is absorbed by the system.

bioequivalence Having a similar biological effect.

biomechanics Branch of study that applies the laws of mechanics to living organisms and biological tissues.

biotransformation Transforming a drug so it can be metabolized.

bipedal Having two feet or moving on two feet.

BMR Basal metabolic rate.

body composition Percent body fat plus lean body weight.

bradykinin Peptide chemical that causes pain in an injured area.

bradypnea Slow breathing.

buccal Pertaining to the cheek or mouth.

bulimia Binge-purge eating disorder.

bursitis Inflammation of bursa at sites of bony prominences between muscle and tendon such as those of the shoulder and knee.

C

calcific tendinitis Deposition of calcium in a chronically inflamed tendon, especially the tendons of the shoulder.

calisthenic Exercise involving free movement without the aid of equipment.

calorie (large) Amount of heat required to raise 1 kg of water 1° C; used to express the fuel or energy value of food or the heat output of the organism; the amount of heat required to heat 1 lb of water to 4° F.

cardiorespiratory endurance Ability to perform activities for extended periods of time.

catastrophic injury Relates to a permanent injury of the spinal cord that leaves the athlete quadriplegic or paraplegic.

catecholamine Active amines, epinephrine and norepinephrine, that affect the nervous and cardiovascular systems.

cellulitis An inflammation of cells and connective tissue that extends deep into the tissues.

cerebrovascular accident Stroke.

chafing Superficial inflammation that develops when skin is subjected to friction.

chemical mediator A chemical that causes or produces a specific physiological response.

chemotaxis Response to influence of chemical stimulation.

chiropractor One who practices a method for restoring normal condition by adjusting the segments of the spinal column.

Chlamydia trachomatis A microorganism that can cause a wide variety of diseases in humans, one of which is venereal and causes nonspecific urethritis.

chondromalacia Abnormal softening of cartilage.

chronic injury Injury with long onset and long duration.

cicatrix Scar or mark formed by fibrous connective tissue; left by a wound or sore.

circadian rhythm Biological time clock by which the body functions.

circuit training Exercise stations that consist of various combinations of weight training, flexibility, calisthenics, and aerobic exercises.

circumduct Act of moving a limb such as the arm or hip in a circular manner.

clonic muscle contraction Alternating involuntary muscle contraction and relaxation in quick succession.

coenzymes Enzyme activators.

collagen Main organic constituent of connective tissue.

collision sport Sport in which athletes use their bodies to deter or punish opponents.

colloid Liquid or gelatinous substance that retains particles of another substance in a state of suspension.

commission (legal liability) Person commits an act that is not legally his or hers to perform.

communicable disease Disease that may be transmitted directly or indirectly from one individual to another.

compression Force that crushes tissue.

concentric (positive) contraction The muscle shortens while contracting against resistance.

conduction Heating through direct contact with a hot medium.

conjunctiva Mucous membrane that lines the eyes.

contact sport Sport in which athletes do make physical contact but not with the intent to produce bodily injury.

contrast bath procedure Technique that uses immersion in ice slush, followed by immersion in tepid water.

contrecoup brain injury After head is struck, brain continues to move within the skull, resulting in injury to the side opposite the force.

convection Heating indirectly through another medium such as air or liquid.

conversion Heating through other forms of energy (e.g., electricity).

convulsions Paroxysms of involuntary muscular contractions and relaxations.

core temperature Internal, or deep, body temperature monitored by cells in the hypothalamus, as opposed to shell, or peripheral, temperature, which is registered by that layer of insulation provided by the skin, subcutaneous tissues, and superficial portions of the muscle masses.

corticosteroid Steroid produced by the adrenal cortex.

coryza Profuse nasal discharge.

counterirritant Agent that produces mild inflammation and acts, in turn, as an analgesic when applied locally to the skin (e.g., liniment).

coupling medium Used to facilitate the transmission of ultrasound into the tissues.

crepitation Crackling sound heard during the movement of ends of a broken bone.

cryokinetics Cold application combined with exercise.

cryotherapy Cold therapy.

cubital fossa Triangular area on the anterior aspect of the forearm directly opposite the elbow joint (the bend of the elbow).

cyanosis Slightly bluish, grayish, slatelike, or dark purple discoloration of the skin caused by a reduced amount of blood hemoglobin.

D

DAPRE Daily adjustable progressive resistance exercise.

debride Removal of dirt and dead tissue from a wound.

deconditioning State in which the athlete's body loses its competitive fitness.

degeneration Deterioration of tissue.

dermatome Segmental skin area innervated by various spinal cord segments.

diagnosis Identification of a specific condition.

diapedesis Passage of blood cells, via ameboid action, through the intact capillary wall.

diarthrodial joint Ball-and-socket joint.

diastolic blood pressure The residual pressure when the heart is between beats.

DIP Distal interphalangeal joint.

diplopia Seeing double.

distal Farthest from a center, from the midline, or from the trunk.

DNA Deoxyribonucleic acid.

doping The administration of a drug that is designed to improve the competitor's performance.

dorsiflexion Bending toward the dorsum or rear; opposite of plantar flexion.

dorsum The back of a body part.

dressing Covering, protective or supportive, that is applied to an injury or wound.

drug A chemical agent used in the prevention, treatment, or diagnosis of disease.

drug vehicle The substance in which a drug is transported.

dyspnea Difficult breathing.

dysrhythmia Irregular heartbeats.

E

eccentric (negative) contraction The muscle lengthens while contracting against resistance.

ecchymosis Black-and-blue skin discoloration caused by hemorrhage.

ectopic Located in a place different from normal.

edema Swelling as a result of the collection of fluid in connective tissue.

effective radiating area Portion of the transducer that produces sound energy.

efficacy A drug's capability of producing a specific therapeutic effect.

effleurage Stroking.

electrolyte Solution that is a conductor of electricity.

embolus A mass of undisolved matter.

emetic Agent that induces vomiting.

endurance Body's ability to engage in prolonged physical activity.

enthesitis Group of conditions characterized by inflammation, fibrosis, and calcification around tendons, ligaments, and muscle insertions.

enzyme An organic catalyst that can cause chemical changes in other substances without being changed itself.

epidemiological approach Study of sports injuries that involves the relationship of as many factors as possible.

epilepsy Recurrent paroxysmal disorder characterized by sudden attacks of altered consciousness, motor activity, sensory phenomena, or inappropriate behavior.

epiphysis Cartilaginous growth region of a bone.

epistaxis Nosebleed.

ethics Principles of morality.

etiology Science dealing with causes of disease.

eversion of the foot To turn the foot outward.

excoriation Removal of a piece or strip of skin.

exostoses Benign bony outgrowths, usually capped by cartilage, that protrude from the surface of a bone.

extraoral mouth guard Protective device that fits outside the mouth.

extracellular matrix Collagen, elastin, ground substance, proteoglycans, and glycosaminoglycans.

extravasation Escape of a fluid from its vessels into the surrounding tissues.

exudate Accumulation of fluid in an area.

F

facilitation To assist the progress of.

fascia Fibrous membrane that covers, supports, and separates muscles.

fasciitis Inflammation of fascia.

fibrinogen Blood plasma protein that is converted into a fibrin clot.

fibroblast Any cell component from which fibers are developed.

fibrocartilage Type of cartilage (e.g., intervertebral disks) in which the matrix contains thick bundles of collaginous fibers.

fibroplasia Period of scar formation.

fibrosis Development of excessive fibrous connective tissue; fibroid degeneration.

first intention Normal healing of a wound where new cells are formed to take the place of damaged cells leaving little or no scar.

flash-to-bang Number of seconds from lightning flash until the sound of thunder divided by five.

foot pronation Combined foot movements of plantar flexion, adduction, and eversion.

foot supination Combined foot movements of dorsiflexion and inversion.

force couple Depressor action by the subscapularis, infraspinatus, and teres minor muscles to stabilize the head of the humerus and to counteract the upward force exerted by the deltoid muscle during abduction of the arm.

frequency Measured in hertz (Hz), cycles per second (CPS), or pulses per second (PPS).

friction Heat producing.

FSH Follicle-stimulating hormone.

G

GAS theory General adaptation syndrome.

genitourinary Pertaining to the reproductive and urinary organs.

genu recurvatum Hyperextension at the knee joint.

genu valgum Knock-knee.

genu varum Bowleg.

GH Growth hormone.

glycogen supercompensation High-carbohydrate diet.

glycosuria Abnormally high proportion of sugar in the urine.

Good Samaritan law Provides limited protection against legal liability to any individual who voluntarily chooses to provide first aid.

granulation tissue Fibroblasts, collagen, and capillaries.

H

half-life Rate at which a drug disappears from the body through metabolism, excretion, or both.

hemarthrosis Blood in a joint cavity.

hematolytic Pertaining to the degeneration and disintegration of the blood.

hematoma Blood tumor.

hematuria Blood in the urine.

hemoglobin Coloring substance of the red blood cells.

hemoglobinuria Hemoglobin in the urine.

hemolysis Destruction of red blood cells.

hemophilia Hereditary blood disease in which coagulation is greatly prolonged.

hemopoietic Forming blood cells.

hemorrhage Discharge of blood.

hemothorax Bloody fluid in the pleural cavity.

hertz (Hz) Number of sound waves per second.

hirsutism Excessive hair growth or the presence of hair in unusual places.

homeostasis Maintenance of a steady state in the body's internal environment.

HOPS Evaluation scheme that includes history, observation, palpation, and special tests.

hunting response Causes a slight temperature increase during cooling.

hyperemia Unusual amount of blood in a body part.

hyperextension Extreme stretching of a body part.

hyperflexibility Flexibility beyond a joint's normal range.

hyperhidrosis Excessive sweating; excessive foot perspiration.

hyperkeratosis Excessive growth of the horny tissue layer.

hypermobility Extreme mobility of a joint.

hyperpnea Hyperventilation; increased minute volume of breathing; exaggerated deep breathing.

hypertension High blood pressure; abnormally high tension.

hyperthermia Elevated body temperature.

hypertonic Having a higher osmotic pressure than a compared solution.

hypertrophy Enlargement of a body part or muscle caused by an increase in the size of its cells.

hyperventilation Labored breathing.

hypoallergenic Low allergy producing.

hypoxia Lack of an adequate amount of oxygen.

I

idiopathic Cause of a condition is unknown.

iliotibial band friction syndrome Runner's knee.

injury An act that damages or hurts.

innervation Nerve stimulation of a muscle.

interosseous membrane Connective tissue membrane between bones.

intertrigo Chafing of the skin.

interval training Alternating periods of work with active recovery.

inunctions Oily or medicated substances (e.g., liniments) that are rubbed into the skin to produce a local or systemic effect.

inversion of the foot To turn the foot inward; inner border of the foot lifts.

ions Electrically charged atoms.

ipsilateral Situated on the same side.

ischemia Lack of blood supply to a body part.

isokinetic exercise Resistance is given at a fixed velocity of movement with accommodating resistance.

isokinetic muscle resistance Accommodating and variable resistance.

isometric exercise Contracts the muscle statically without changing its length.

isotonic exercise Shortens and lengthens the muscle through a complete range of motion.

J

joint capsule Saclike structure that encloses the ends of bones in a diarthrodial joint.

joint play Movement that is not voluntary but accessory.

K

keratolytic Loosening of the horny skin layer.

keratosis Excessive growth of the horny tissue layer.

kilocalorie Amount of heat required to raise 1 kg of water 1° C.

kinesthesia; kinesthesis Sensation or feeling of movement; the awareness one has of the spatial relationships of one's body and its parts.

kyphosis Exaggeration of the normal curve of the thoracic spine.

L

labile Unsteady; not fixed and easily changed.

lactase deficiency Difficulty digesting dairy products.

laser Light amplification by stimulated emission of radiation.

leukocytes Consist of two types—granulocytes (e.g., basophils and neutrophils) and agranulocytes (e.g., monocytes and lymphocytes).

LH Luteinizing hormone.

liability The state of being legally responsible for the harm one causes another person.

load Outside force or forces acting on tissue.

lordosis Abnormal lumbar vertebral convexity.

luxation Complete joint dislocation.

lymphocytes Cells that are the primary means of providing the body with immune capabilities.

lysis To break down.

M

macerated skin Skin that has been softened by exposure to wetting.

macrophage A phagocytic cell of the immune system.

macrotear Soft tissue damage generally caused by acute trauma.

malaise Discomfort and uneasiness caused by an illness.

malfeasance (or act of commission) When an individual commits an act that is not legally his or hers to perform.

margination Accumulation of leukocytes on blood vessel walls at the site of injury during early stages of inflammation.

mast cells Connective tissue cells that contain heparin and histamine.

MCP Metacarpophalangeal joint.

mechanical failure Elastic limits of tissue are exceeded, causing tissue to break.

mechanism Mechanical description of the cause.

menarche Onset of menstrual function.

metabolism Changing a drug into a water-soluble compound that can be excreted.

metatarsalgia A general term to describe pain in the ball of the foot.

microtear Minor soft tissue damage associated with overuse.

microtrauma Microscopic lesion or injury.

misfeasance When an individual improperly does something that he or she has the legal right to do.

muscle contracture Permanent contraction of a muscle as a result of spasm or paralysis.

muscular endurance The ability to perform repetitive muscular contractions against some resistance.

muscular strength The maximal force that can be applied by a muscle during a single maximum contraction.

myocarditis Inflammation of the heart muscle.

myoglobin Respiratory protein in muscle tissue that is an oxygen carrier.

myositis Inflammation of muscle.

myositis ossificans Myositis marked by ossification of muscles.

N

necrosin Chemical substance that stems from inflamed tissue, causing changes in normal tissue.

negative resistance Slow, eccentric muscle contraction against a resistance.

negligence The failure to use ordinary or reasonable care.

nerve entrapment Nerve compressed between bone or soft tissue.

neuritis Inflammation of a nerve.

neuroma A bulging that emanates from a nerve.

nociceptor Receptor of pain.

noncontact sport Sport in which athletes are not involved in any physical contact.

nonfeasance (or an act of omission) When an individual fails to perform a legal duty.

nystagmus Constant involuntary back and forth, up and down, or rotary movement of the eyeball.

O

obesity Excessive amount of body fat.

obstructed Blocked airway caused by either partial or complete obstruction.

ohm Resistance.

omission (legal) Person fails to perform a legal duty.

orthopedic surgeon One who corrects deformities of the musculoskeletal system.

orthosis Used in sports as an appliance or apparatus to support, align, prevent, or correct deformities or to improve function of a movable body part.

orthotics Field of knowledge relating to orthoses and their use.

OSHA Occupational Safety and Health Administration.

osteoarthritis Chronic disease involving joints in which there is destruction of articular or hyaline cartilage and bony overgrowth.

osteoblasts Bone-producing cells.

osteochondral Refers to relationship of bone and cartilage.

osteochondritis Inflammation of bone and cartilage.

osteochondritis dissecans Fragment of cartilage and underlying bone is detached from the articular surface.

osteochondrosis Disease state of a bone and its articular cartilage.

osteoclasts Cells that resorb bone.

osteoporosis A decrease in bone density.

P

palpation Feeling an injury with the fingers.

paraplegia Paralysis of lower portion of the body and of both legs.

paresis Slight or incomplete paralysis.

paresthesia Abnormal or morbid sensation such as itching or prickling.

passive range of motion Movement that is performed completely by the examiner.

pathogenic Disease producing.

pathology Science of the structural and functional manifestations of disease.

pathomechanics Mechanical forces that are applied to a living organism and adversely change the body's structure and function.

pediatrician Specialist in the treatment of children's diseases.

pes anserinus tendinitis Cyclist's knee.

permeable Permitting the passage of a substance through a vessel wall.

petrissage Kneading.

phagocytosis Destruction of injurious cells or particles by phagocytes (white blood cells).

phalanges Bones of the fingers and toes.

phalanx Any one of the bones of the fingers and toes.

pharmacokinetics The method by which drugs are absorbed, distributed, metabolized, and eliminated.

pharmacology The study of drugs and their origin, nature, properties, and effects on living organisms.

phonophoresis Introduction of ions of soluble salt into the body through ultrasound.

photophobia Unusual intolerance to light.

piezoelectric effect Electrical current produced by applying pressure to certain crystals.

PIP Proximal interphalangeal joint.

plyometric exercise Type of exercise that maximizes the myotatic, or stretch, reflex.

pneumothorax Collapse of a lung as a result of air in the pleural cavity.

podiatrist Practitioner who specializes in the study and care of the foot.

point tenderness Pain produced when an injury site is palpated.

posterior Toward the rear or back.

potency The dose of a drug that is required to produce a desired therapeutic effect.

primary assessment Initial first aid evaluation.

primary survey An evaluation used to determine the existence of life-threatening, emergent conditions or illnesses.

prognosis Prediction as to probable result of a disease or injury.

prophylaxis Guarding against injury or disease.

proprioception The ability to determine the position of a joint in space.

proprioceptive neuromuscular facilitation (PNF) Stretching techniques that involve combinations of alternating contractions and stretches.

proprioceptor One of several receptors, each of which responds to stimuli elicited from within the body itself (e.g., the muscle spindles that invoke the myotatic, or stretch, reflex).

prostaglandin Acidic lipid widely distributed in the body; in musculoskeletal conditions it is concerned with vasodilation, a histamine-like effect; it is inhibited by aspirin.

prosthesis Replacement of an absent body part with an artificial part; the artificial part.

prothrombin Interacts with calcium to produce thrombin.

proximal Nearest to the point of reference.

psychogenic Of psychic origin; that which originates in the mind.

purulent Consisting of or containing pus.

Q

quadriplegia Paralysis affecting all four limbs.

R

radiation Transfer of heat through space from one object to another.

Raynaud's phenomenon Condition in which cold exposure causes vasospasm of digital arteries.

referred pain Pain that is felt somewhere other than its origin.

regeneration Repair, regrowth, or restoration of a part such as tissue.

residual That which remains; often used to describe a permanent condition resulting from injury or disease (e.g., a limp or a paralysis).

resorption Act of removal by absorption.

retroversion Tilting or turning backward of a part.

retrovirus A virus that enters a host cell and changes its RNA to a proviral DNA replica.

revascularize Restoration of blood circulation to an injured area.

RICE Rest, ice, compression, and elevation.

ringworm (tinea) Common name given to many superficial fungal infections of the skin.

RNA Ribonucleic acid.

rotation Turning around an axis in an angular motion.

rubefacients Agents that redden the skin by increasing local circulation through the dilation of blood vessels.

S

SAID principle Specific adaptation to imposed demands.

scoliosis Lateral rotary curve of the spine.

sebaceous cyst A cyst filled with sebum; usually found in the scalp.

secondary assessment Follow-up; a more detailed examination.

secondary survey An evaluation of existing signs and symptoms performed after the presence of life-threatening conditions has been ruled out.

second intention Healing where granulation tissue replaces damaged cells creating increased scar tissue and delays the healing process.

seizure Sudden attack.

septic shock Shock caused by bacteria, especially gram-negative bacteria commonly seen in systemic infections.

sequela Pathological condition that occurs as a consequence of another condition or event.

serotonin Hormone and neurotransmitter.

shearing Force that moves across the parallel organization of the tissue.

sign Objective evidence of an abnormal situation within the body.

sovereign immunity States that neither the government or any individual who is employed by the government can be held liable for negligence.

SPF Sun protection factor.

spica A figure-eight bandage with one of the two loops larger than the other.

stance phase Portion of the gait cycle from initial contact to toe-off.

Staphylococcus Genus of gram-positive bacteria normally present on the skin and in the upper respiratory tract and prevalent in localized infections.

stasis Blockage or stoppage of circulation.

static stretching Passively stretching an antagonist muscle by placing it in a maximal stretch and holding it there.

steady-state When the amount of the drug taken is equal to the amount that is excreted.

strain Extent of deformation of tissue under loading.

stretching Force which pulls beyond the yield point leading to rupturing of soft tissue or fracturing of a bone.

Streptococcus Genus of gram-positive bacteria found in the throat, respiratory tract, and intestinal tract.

stress The internal reaction or resistance to an external load.

stressor Anything that affects the body's physiological or psychological condition, upsetting the homeostatic balance.

subluxation Partial or incomplete dislocation of an articulation.

swing phase Portion of the gait cycle that is a period of non–weight bearing.

symptom Subjective evidence of an abnormal situation within the body.

syndrome Group of typical symptoms or conditions that characterize a deficiency or disease.

synergy To work in cooperation with.

synovitis Inflammation of the synovium.

synthesis To build up.

systolic blood pressure The pressure caused by the heart's pumping.

T

tachypnea Rapid breathing.

tapotement Percussion.

tenosynovitis Inflammation of a tendon synovial sheath.

tension Force which pulls or stretches tissue.

tetanus (lockjaw) An acute, often fatal condition characterized by tonic muscular spasm, hyperreflexia, and lockjaw.

tetanus toxoid Tetanus toxin modified to produce active immunity against *Clostridium tetani.*

thermotherapy Heat therapy.

thrombi Plural of thrombus; blood clots that block small blood vessels or a cavity of the heart.

tinea (ringworm) Superficial fungal infections of the skin.

tonic muscle spasm Rigid muscle contraction that lasts over a period of time.

torsion Act or state of being twisted.

torts Legal wrongs committed against a person.

training effect Stroke volume increases while heart rate is reduced at a given exercise load.

transitory paralysis Temporary paralysis.

translation Refers to anterior gliding of tibial plateau.

trauma (*pl* **traumas** or **traumata**) A physical injury or wound sustained in sport and produced by an external or internal force.

traumatic Pertaining to an injury or wound.

trigger points Small hyperirritable areas within a muscle.

V

valgus Position of a body part that is bent outward.

varus Position of a body part that is bent inward.

vasoconstriction Decrease in the diameter of a blood vessel.

vasodilation Increase in the diameter of a blood vessel.

vasospasm Blood vessel spasm.

vehicle The substance in which a drug is transported.

verruca Wart caused by a virus.

vibration Rapid shaking.

viscoelastic Any material whose mechanical properties vary depending on rate of load.

viscosity Resistance to flow.

volar Referring to the palm or the sole.

voltage Force.

volume of distribution The volume of plasma in which a drug is dissolved.

W

Watt Power.

Y

yield point Elastic limit of tissue.

Credits

Chapter **1** *Focus boxes, pp. 4–8, 11, 13, 36, 37,* Courtesy, The National Athletic Trainers' Association; *Figure 1-2, p. 3,* From Prentice, WE and Arnheim, DD: *Essentials of athletic training,* ed. 6, St. Louis: McGraw-Hill Higher Education, 2005.

Chapter **2** *Figure 2-1A, p. 52,* Adapted from Myers, GC and Garrick, JG: The preseason examination of school and college athletes. In Strauss, RH (ed.): *Sports medicine,* Philadelphia: WB Saunders, 1984; *Figure 2-1B, p. 53,* From Prentice, WE and Arnheim, DD: *Essentials of athletic training,* ed. 6, St. Louis: McGraw-Hill Higher Education, 2005; *Figures 2-3, 2-4, pp. 59, 60,* Used with permission from *The Physician and Sportsmedicine; Figure 2-5, p. 61,* Adapted from Tanner, M: *Growth of adolescence,* Oxford, England: Blackwell Scientific Publications, 1962; *Figure 2-7, p. 63,* Courtesy, The University of North Carolina at Chapel Hill; *Figure 2-8, p. 64,* Modified from *Health Style: A Self Test,* U.S. Department of Health and Human Services, Public Health Service, National Clearing House, Washington, DC; *Table 2-2, pp. 65,* From Committee on Sports Medicine: *Pediatrics* 81: 738, 1988, Used with permission; *Figure 2-9, p. 66,* Courtesy, D. Bailey, California State University at Long Beach.

Chapter **3** *Focus box, pp. 79–80,* Source: DeCarlo, M: Reimbursement for health care services. In Kronin, J: *Clinical athletic training,* Thorofare, NJ: Slack, 1997.

Chapter **4** *Figure 4-12G, p. 109,* From Prentice, WE: *Get fit stay fit,* St. Louis: Mosby, 1996; *Focus box, p. 122,* From White, T: The wellness guide to lifelong fitness, *The University of California at Berkeley Wellness Letter,* New York: Random House, 1993.

Chapter **5** *Tables 5-1, 5-2, Figures 5-1, 5-4, pp. 133, 135, 139, 152,* From Prentice, WE: *Get fit stay fit,* ed. 3, St. Louis: McGraw-Hill Higher Education, 2004; *Table 5-3, pp. 127, 128,* Modified from *Recommended dietary allowances,* copyright 1998 by the National Academy of Sciences, National Academy Press, Washington, DC; *Figure 5-2, p. 140,* U.S. Department of Agriculture/U.S. Department of Health and Human Services, August, 1992; *Figure 5-3, p. 147,* From Prentice, WE: *Fitness for college and life,* ed. 6, Dubuque, IA: WCB/McGraw-Hill Higher Education, 1999; *Table 5-4, p. 148,* Source: Wardlaw, GM: *Perspectives in nutrition,* ed. 5, Dubuque, IA: McGraw-Hill Higher Education, 2002.

Chapter **6** *Table 6-3, p. 166,* Modified from Berkow, R: *The Merck manual of diagnosis and therapy,* ed. 14, Rahway, NJ: Merck & Co, 1982; *Focus box, p. 173,* Courtesy, ER Buskirk and WC Grasley, Human Performance Laboratory, The Athletic Institute, The Pennsylvania State University.

Chapter **7** *Figures 7-1 A&B, 7-25, 7-26, 7-27, pp. 190, 206, 207,* From Prentice, WE and Arnheim, DD: *Essentials of athletic training,* ed. 6, St. Louis: McGraw-Hill Higher Education, 2005; *Figures 7-1C, 7-5, 7-12, 7-13, 7-19, 7-20, 7-21, 7-22, 7-23, 7-27, pp. 190, 192, 197, 201, 202, 204,* Courtesy Sports Authority (www.thesportsauthority.com); *Figures 7-15, 7-16, pp. 199, 200,* From Nicholas, JA and Hershman, EB: *The upper extremity in sports medicine,* ed. 2, St. Louis: Mosby, 1995; *Figure 7-18 A–C, p. 201,* Courtesy Title 9 Sports (www.title9sports.com); *Figure 7-18D, p. 201,* Courtesy TKO; *Figures 7-28, 7-29A & E, pp. 208, 209,* Courtesy Mueller Sports Medicine; *Figures 7-33, 7-34, 7-35, pp. 211, 212,* From Nicholas, JA and Hershman, EB: *The lower extremity and spine in sports medicine,* ed. 2, St. Louis: Mosby, 1995.

Chapter **8** *Figures 8-2, 8-6, 8-10, 8-22, 8-25, 8-29, 8-32, 8-42, 8-43, pp. 219, 221, 223, 230, 232, 234, 236, 241, 242,* From Prentice, WE and Arnheim, DD, *Essentials of athletic training,* ed. 6, St. Louis: McGraw-Hill Higher Education, 2005; *Figures 8-26, 8-37, 8-38, 8-39, pp. 233, 240,* art by Donald O'Connor.

Chapter **9** *Figures 9-2, 9-3, 9-4, pp. 247, 248,* art by Donald O'Connor; *Figures 9-5, 9-10, 9-13, pp. 249, 254, 261,* From Saladin, KS: *Anatomy and physiology,* ed. 2, Dubuque, IA: McGraw-Hill Higher Education, 2001, *Figure 9-7,* p. 251, From Prentice, WE: *Rehabilitation techniques in sports medicine,* ed. 4, St. Louis: McGraw-Hill Higher Education, 2004.

Chapter **10** *Table 10-1, p. 277,* Modified from *International medical guide for ships,* Geneva: World Health Organization; *Figure 10-2, p. 279,* From Prentice, WE and Arnheim, DD, *Essentials of athletic training,* ed. 6, St. Louis: McGraw-Hill Higher Education, 2005.

Chapter **11** *Figure 11-2, p. 314,* art by Donald O'Connor; *Focus box, p. 318,* From Hahn, DB and Payne, WA: *Focus on health,* ed. 5, Dubuque, IA: McGraw-Hill Higher Education, 2001; *Figures 11-3, 11-5, pp. 321, 322,* From Prentice, WE and Arnheim, DD, *Essentials of athletic training,* ed. 6, St. Louis: McGraw-Hill Higher Education, 2005.

Index

A

AAFP (American Academy of Family Physicians), 8
Abrasions of skin, 248
Accident, 68
Acclimatization, 171
ACDU scale for level of consciousness, 294
Achilles tendon, taping technique for, 236–237
ACSM (American Colleges of Sports Medicine), 4, 9, 33
Active trigger point, 252–253
Acute exertional rhabdomyolysis, 168
Acute mountain sickness, 177
Acute synovitis, 258
Adolescent athletes, training of, 33, 113
AED (automatic external defibrillator), 286–287
Aerobic metabolism, 117–118
AFCA (Annual Survey of Football Injury Research), 70, 72
Aging athletes, 33
Agonist vs. antagonist muscles, 94–95
AHA (American Heart Association), 58, 278, 286
AIDS (acquired immunodeficiency syndrome), 316–323
Air pollution, effects on performance, 179–180
Air splints, 297, 298
Alcohol, effects on performance, 143
Altitude
 acute mountain sickness, 177
 adaptation to, 176
 effects on athletic performance, 176–177
 pulmonary edema, 177
 sickle-cell trait reaction to, 177
AMA (American Medical Association), 33, 39
AMCIA (Appropriate Medical Coverage for Intercollegiate Athletics), 31
American Academy of Pediatrics, Sports Committee, 9
American Association of Neurological Sciences, 71
American Journal of Sports Medicine, 9
American Psychiatric Association, 299
American Red Cross, 278
AMTA NSMT (American Massage Therapy Association National Sports Massage Team), 28–29
Anaerobic metabolism, 117–118
Anaphylactic shock, 290
Anemia, iron-deficiency, 141
Ankle
 bandaging, wrapping, taping techniques for, 219–220, 223, 233–236
 protective gear and devices for, 207
 splinting of fractures in, 297
Anorexia athletica, 156
Anorexia nervosa, 156
Antioxidants, 134

Anvil Pruner, 279
AOSSM (American Orthopaedic Society for Sports Medicine), 9
Apnea, 291
Apophysitis, 260
APTA (American Physical Therapy Association), 10, 39
Arches of the foot, taping techniques for, 229–231
Arm slings, 223–224
AROM (active range of motion), 94
ASPA (Association of Specialized Professional Accreditors), 34
Association for the Advancement of Sport Psychology, 28
Assumption of risk, 77
ASTM (American Society for Testing Materials), 194
AstroTurf, advantages/disadvantages of, 181–182
ATC (Certified Athletic Trainer), 35
Athletic trainers. *See also* NATA (National Athletic Trainers' Association)
 as accredited allied health professional, 33–40
 adaptability and personal qualities of, 20–21
 administering drugs/medications to athletes, 15
 administrative tasks of, 17–18, 44–72
 awareness of risk and liability factors, 75
 biohazard training for, 322–323
 certification and licensure requirements of, 1–3, 12–13, 33–40
 CEUs (continuing education units) requirements of, 36–37
 clinical evaluations and diagnosis skills of, 15–16
 as counselor and social support, 17, 19
 CPR training and certification of, 278–288
 determining therapies and rehabilitation programs, 16–17
 employment settings/opportunities for, 29–33
 encouraging good health habits, 48
 history and evolution of, 1–3
 knowledge of pathology of injury and illnesses, 16
 making referrals to other support services, 16, 26–29
 memberships in professional organizations, 4–8, 21
 preparticipation examination and screenings by, 57–66
 priorities of, 21–22
 professional liability coverage of, 75, 81–82
 professional responsibilities of, 18–19
 providing immediate care of injuries and illnesses, 16–17
 relationship with physical therapists, 38–39
 research opportunities for, 19

Athletic trainers—*cont.*
 risk management skills of, 13–18, 75
 state regulation of, 37–38
 teacher and educator roles of, 18–19
 working with physically active populations by, 32–33
Athletic training programs
 budget considerations in, 48–49
 collecting injury data by, 68–71
 community-based health services for, 50–51
 computer management of data/information of, 67–68
 emergency action plan and communication systems in, 48, 50
 equipment and supplies in, 66–68, 78–79, 186–214
 facilities for, 47–48, 51–56
 human resources and personnel for, 51
 hygiene and sanitary environments in, 46–48
 personnel coverage and supervision in, 46
 physical examinations and screening in, 57–66
 policies and procedures of, 45
 record keeping and documents required in, 56–67
 risk management plans for, 49–50
 safety of, 49–50
 scope and operations of, 45–46
 strategic planning for, 44–45
 WOTS UP (Weakness, Opportunities, Threats, and Strengths) analysis of, 44
ATLS (Advanced Trauma Life Support), 294
ATP (adenosine triphosphate), 116–118
Atrophy, 103–104, 254
Autogenic inhibition, 99
AVPU scale for level of consciousness, 294
Avulsion injuries
 bone fractures, 265
 of skin, 249

B

Ball-and-socket joints, 256
Ballistic stretching, 95, 96
Bandaging. *See also* Taping
 elastic bandages, 217–223
 gauze and cotton cloth in, 217, 223–224
 triangular and cravat bandages, 223–224
Baseball, protective gear/equipment for, 192, 194, 197
Bending stress of tissue, 247, 248
Bilik, S. E., 2
Bioelectrical impedance, 151
Biohazard precautions, 320–323
Biomechanics, 28
Biophysical time clock, 180–181
Bleeding, controlling hemorrhage and shock, 288–290
Blisters, 248

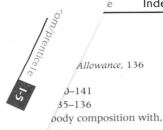